Troublemakers

For
Petra and Christoph
in friendship

The man is [. . .] a misfit from the start.
Ralph Waldo Emerson

*You want to transcend yourself
and have to knock on a strange door.*
Marieluise Fleisser

Dieter Thomä

Troublemakers

A Philosophy of *Puer Robustus*

Translated by Jessica Spengler

polity

First published in German as *Puer Robustus. Eine Philosophie des Störenfrieds*
© Suhrkamp Verlag, Berlin, 2016

This English edition © Polity Press, 2019

The translation of this work was funded by Geisteswissenschaften International –
Translation Funding for Humanities and Social Sciences from Germany, a joint initiative
of the Fritz Thyssen Foundation, the German Federal Foreign Office, the collecting society
VG WORT and the Börsenverein des Deutschen Buchhandels (German Publishers &
Booksellers Association).

Polity Press
65 Bridge Street
Cambridge CB2 1UR, UK

Polity Press
101 Station Landing
Suite 300
Medford, MA 02155, USA

ISBN-13: 978-1-5095-2558-4

A catalogue record for this book is available from the British Library.

Library of Congress Cataloging-in-Publication Data
Names: Thoma, Dieter, 1959- author.
Title: Troublemakers : a philosophy of puer robustus / Dieter Thoma.
Other titles: Puer robustus. English
Description: Cambridge, UK ; Medford, MA : Polity Press, 2019. | Includes
  bibliographical references and index.
Identifiers: LCCN 2018040003 (print) | LCCN 2018049498 (ebook) | ISBN
  9781509525614 (Epub) | ISBN 9781509525584 (hardback)
Subjects: LCSH: Political science--Philosophy. | Political
  ethics--Philosophy. | Revolutions--Philosophy. | Despotism--Philosophy. |
  Alienation (Social psychology)--Philosophy.
Classification: LCC B65 (ebook) | LCC B65 .T47613 2019 (print) | DDC
  320.01--dc23
LC record available at https://lccn.loc.gov/2018040003

Typeset in 10 on 11.5 pt Sabon by Servis Filmsetting Ltd, Stockport, Cheshire
Printed and bound in Great Britain by CPI Group (UK) Ltd, Croydon

The publisher has used its best endeavours to ensure that the URLs for external websites
referred to in this book are correct and active at the time of going to press. However, the
publisher has no responsibility for the websites and can make no guarantee that a site will
remain live or that the content is or will remain appropriate.

Every effort has been made to trace all copyright holders, but if any have been overlooked
the publisher will be pleased to include any necessary credits in any subsequent reprint or
edition.

For further information on Polity, visit our website:
politybooks.com

CONTENTS

vi

ACKNOWLEDGEMENTS

First and foremost, I want to thank the people who introduced me to my own inner troublemaker, namely, my housemates in the "Rainbow Factory" in Berlin-Kreuzberg in the 1980s. Luckily, my wife and children have kept me from retiring ever since.

The troublemaker may have a fractured relationship with institutions, but I cannot deny that my thoughts about the *puer robustus* were particularly nurtured by two institutions. Toward the end of my time at the Wissenschaftskolleg zu Berlin in 2009–10, after long months spent working doggedly on a different book, I finally began to feel the exuberance that is often blocked by everyday university life. I let my thoughts wander, stumbled across the *puer robustus* in Tocqueville, and started to follow his tracks. I was supported and encouraged in this by my esteemed co-Fellows and the kindly souls and brilliant minds of the "Wiko," especially Sonja Grund, director of the library. I am grateful to the Carl Friedrich von Siemens Foundation and its director, Heinrich Meier, for the heartening invitation to give my first presentation on the topic of this book in Munich. On other occasions I was able to present my interim findings, and I benefited from the questions and objections of countless conversational partners whom I cannot mention by name here.

The team in the Department of Philosophy at the University of St. Gallen gave me wonderful advice and support: Florian Grosser as well as Emmanuel Alloa, Maria Dätwyler, Michael Festl, Federica Gregoratto, and Christoph Paret. My secretary, Barbara Jungclaus, was a constant source of help, advice, and equanimity when it came to bibliographical research and editorial fine-tuning. The President of the University of St. Gallen generously allowed me to reduce my teaching load for research purposes; had he not done so, my work on this book would have stretched far into the future. Eva Gilmer from Suhrkamp rolled out the "red carpet" for me, as she once put it; I thank her for her critical and constructive energy, and for her love of the German language. Moreover, I am grateful to the editorial staff at Polity Press, especially to John Thompson and Paul Young, and to Jessica Spengler for her congenial translation. This translation is based on a slightly abridged version of the German original, but includes additional material in chapter XII.5 ("The little savage and the populism of Donald Trump"). This material is based on the afterword to the German paperback edition, published by Suhrkamp in 2018.

INTRODUCTION

The *puer robustus* strikes, scandalizes, rebels. He does not play along, he does not back down, he acts on his own initiative, he breaks the rules. He is unruly, unabashed, uncomfortable, undomiciled, and unconcerned. He is feared, marginalized, and punished, but also admired and celebrated. The *puer robustus* – the strong child, the sturdy boy – is a troublemaker.

The troublemaker makes trouble. He is, therefore, not a welcome sight – unless he happens to trouble waters that are only sluggishly and deceptively peaceful. Then he is thanked for breaking with the stagnant times. His alternately abhorrent and attractive face would fit well on the "tilt cards" I played with as a child. If you angled them just a bit, the ferocious countenance would turn into a friendly one – and vice versa. The *puer robustus* as we know him is either a horror or a hero, *bête noire* or *beau idéal*, feared opponent or leading figure.

The *puer robustus* as we *knew* him, I should say. Today he has been forgotten, despite having stirred emotions for over three centuries. Thomas Hobbes, Jean-Jacques Rousseau, Denis Diderot, Victor Hugo, Alexis de Tocqueville, Karl Marx, and many others devoted their attention to him and were divided by the question of what to make of him. The *puer robustus* deserves another turn on the stage of political philosophy. He has what it takes to shake up established patterns of thought and action and to transform the entire scene. Were he not so boyish, he could be considered an *éminence grise* in the history of ideas.

The debate that raged around the *puer robustus* relates not to *any old* problem in political philosophy, but rather to *the* problem – namely, the question of how a political order establishes and legitimizes itself, how it is criticized, transformed, or attacked, how people are included in this order or excluded from it, how they adapt to it or obstruct it. The subject of *order* necessarily brings up the subject of *disturbance*, and thus the

1

role of outsiders and marginal figures, obstructionists and malcontents. The political awakenings and upheavals of the modern age represent crises originating, as I see it, not in the centers of power but on the edges. Consequently, this is where we must look to learn how to cope with these crises and find solutions to them.

It was a spark in the seventeenth century that set off the intellectual fireworks surrounding the *puer robustus*. Thomas Hobbes first ushered him onto the stage of the modern era. In the second edition of his *De cive* (*On the Citizen*), published in 1647, Hobbes included a preface in which he wrote that the "vir malus" was almost the same as a "puer robustus, vel vir animo puerili." The English translation that was published in Hobbes's lifetime reads: "A wicked man is almost the same thing with a childe growne strong and sturdy, or a man of a childish disposition." This *puer robustus* represented the ultimate threat to the state order, and Hobbes considered him the very epitome of an evil troublemaker.

The *puer robustus* made what was to be his last notable appearance (for the time being) in China during a brief period of political liberalization in the spring of 1957. "Let a hundred flowers bloom," Mao had declared. The students at Peking University took him at his word, established a Hundred Flowers Society and publicly proclaimed their opinions in newspapers pasted to the walls. Tan Tianrong, one of the student spokespersons, began a message from May 20, 1957, with a quote from Heraclitus, which stated that the "governance of the city should be handed over to beardless young men"; he signed the notice with the Latin phrase "Puer robustus sed malitiosus." This *puer* – very much unlike that of Hobbes – took the guise of a democratic activist: a good troublemaker.

The *puer robustus* roamed hither and yon, making his way from seventeenth-century London to twentieth-century Beijing – and many other places as well. But as of yet, no one has taken much heed of the tangled, intriguing history of this *enfant terrible* and reaped its benefits for the theory of order and disturbance. My book is dedicated to rediscovering, envisioning, and evaluating the *puer robustus*.

This book is constructed somewhat like a revolving stage. Each act reveals a new setting and a different *puer robustus*. He changes lickety-split, appearing pigheaded or happy-go-lucky, as a barbarian or a fool, freeloader or artist, robber or redeemer, Siegfried or Oedipus. Cries of lamentation and jubilation erupt all around him. This book naturally deals with his history after Hobbes and the lengthy, productive dispute about him conducted by writers ranging from Rousseau to Leo Strauss – and beyond. But it is not for purely decorative purposes that two of the most unusual heroes in French literature – Rameau's nephew and the Hunchback of Notre Dame – also take the stage as embodiments of the *puer robustus*. They are joined by Parisian street urchins, European proletarians, the Californian pioneers of the nineteenth century, the youth movement of the early twentieth century, rebellious German teens, Italian communists, the Chinese students of the 1950s mentioned earlier, and many others. The thinkers who pay their respects to the *puer robustus* expose him to a frenzy of conflicts. They perform a dance around the subject – or, indeed, multiple subjects – of history.

There is more to this dance than simply striking up a paean to or requiem for the troublemaker. It may be tempting to focus only on the triumphal march of liberators or, conversely, to do away with spongers, malcontents, and provocateurs once and for all. But such tidy solutions and divisions are ruled out by the contradictory, recalcitrant *puer robustus*. He refuses to be forced into the confines of a bildungsroman in which "the subject" slowly but surely "sows his wild oats" (Hegel, HA 593).

If this book were a living creature, it would probably have two hearts beating in its chest. It is a philosophical treatise – but also something like an adventure story. Admittedly, I am no competition for the reporters who hang out in the hip-hop scene or the Occupy Wall Street movement, who run around with revolutionaries and rioters. But I comfort myself with the belief that intellectual adventures exist, too, and I throw myself into them wholeheartedly. One might tentatively characterize this book as tracing an arc from Hobbes to the present day – but that would be somewhat off the mark. An arc is an uninterrupted, unbroken line. If you follow its course, you know where it will lead. An "adventure novel," on the other hand, offers no such certainty. As a literary genre, it deals with a hero who occupies no fixed "place in life" and shows "how an individual becomes other than what he was."[1]

My hero – the *puer robustus* – is *on the move*. He does not know where or who he will be tomorrow. Instead of stringing his experiences like pearls on a thread until everything fits perfectly, he muddles through and hopes everything will turn out fine in the end. He admits that he does not know his way about. The adventure novel is unjustly viewed as a genre with anachronistic traits. It is *the* genre of a world – our world – in which we are called upon to "descend into the old chaos and feel at home there."[2] This goes hand in hand with a view of history in which individual situations contain an excess, an element of surprise, and resist being categorized. "The adventure is the exclave of life."[3]

Behind the affinity for the adventure novel lies a mistrust of theory. I do not think it wise for political philosophers to work through the question of order and disturbance at the drawing board. It is not enough to analyze arguments and establish rules, and it is also not enough to simulate situations or conduct thought experiments for putting such rules to the test. There is a "ridiculous immodesty" (Nietzsche, GS 239) to the assumption that one could get to grips with the subject matter in this way.

3

This immodesty is counteracted by the lack of restraint that distinguishes the character of the *puer robustus*. After all, the *puer robustus* is exactly that: a character who appears here and there, in one form or another, not an argument or a thesis that could be clearly formulated and discussed. The thinkers who make use of the *puer robustus* might like to believe he is their compliant tool, but he scoffs at their self-certainty, leads his own life and advances to become one of the leading actors of the modern age. I could never dream up the internal transformations and external disputes that buffet him (and certainly not while I was awake).

What is required here, however, is not just a mistrust of theory, but trust in equal measure. With a bit of luck, by understanding its limitations and embracing the chaos of the adventure upon which it embarks, theory can take wing instead of being weakened. It can help us look beyond the individual situation, enabling us to look at ourselves *and* at everyone else. Hence, while this book is an adventure story, it is also accompanied by a theory of the troublemaker. This theory aims to identify the tricks he uses to change shape and help us determine what we should make of each of his appearances.

To maintain the balance between adventure story and theory, most of my systematic thoughts about the troublemaker will only develop over the course of the journey. I will ask questions such as why the *puer robustus* is so *darn male* and what happens to him when he discovers his female (or simply human) side. His masculinity is striking, but his individualism is also notable – and perhaps vulnerable. He is associated with the idea of negotiating social cooperation following the schema of concluding and breaking contracts. This interests me, as does the question of whether the *puer robustus* is destined to remain a loner, or if he can gain access to communities and collectives. (The distinction between sympathetic and synergetic socialization will prove beneficial here.) But before the revolving stage starts to turn to reveal the *puer robustus*, before we examine his moves and tactics in detail, I want to introduce one basic concept behind the theory of the troublemaker and briefly outline a typology of the various forms he takes. This basic concept is the *threshold*.

As I said at the start, this book deals with the relationship between order and disturbance. For any number of different reasons, the *puer robustus* slips to the margins, throws a wrench in the works, straddles two worlds. Regardless of how the troublemaker behaves, he finds himself on the periphery, on a border or – to put it more accurately – on a threshold. This threshold is one of the most inconspicuous and yet most important structural details in the edifice of political philosophy.

I prefer the word *threshold* to *border* because thresholds have two special characteristics. First of all, a threshold is typically *low*. You can step over it, stumble over it, or come to a stop right on top of it. The permeability of the threshold is far more variable and negotiable than that of the border. Second, a threshold can be used to divide two spaces and define one as being inside and one outside. This kind of distinction is also possible with borders, but in the case of a border, the definition of inside and outside depends entirely on the position of the observer. One person's outland is the other person's inland, and vice versa. By contrast, the most prominent version of a threshold is an *entrance*, which definitively marks the boundary between inside and outside. It is not possible for someone standing outside a door to convince themselves they are actually inside. The border, with its variable classifications, is less well suited to the political problem of order and disturbance than the threshold. The threshold relates to an interior space delineated by edges where members of the political order are confronted with outsiders. This is precisely what makes the permeability of the threshold a key issue.

A border separates domains or realms, each of which has its own members. But the *puer robustus* who roams around on the threshold is not caught between two different political orders; instead, he moves along the edge of a single world that is defined by the reach of its power. This edge is not a *different place*, it is actually a *non-place*. The *puer robustus* does not belong in one place or the other; he is the very epitome of non-belonging. He finds it hard to settle down in this non-place. He cannot simply bask in the feeling of wanting *nothing to do with* the world. Instead, he inevitably relates to the political order and finds himself in a state of tension with it. He leads a life "*on the threshold*" and remains "internally *unfinalized*."[4]

Because an order cannot exist without an edge marking its ambit, it must take into account that there will be people outside of its domain, beyond its boundaries. As Hegel points out, "something is already transcended by the very fact of being determined as a restriction."[5] The political order therefore actually creates the troublemaker that it observes and opposes. It wants to be exclusive and must live with the unrest that surrounds it like a ring of fire. This inside/outside schema is tied to a centralist model of politics in which the only opponents are outsiders. Historically speaking, this means the *puer robustus* must be a child of the early modern period, a time in which the power play between different authorities (monarchy, church, nobility, etc.) was replaced by the power monopoly of the state. It is no coincidence that Hobbes was the one to introduce the *puer robustus* to the field of political philosophy. But this character survives as long as these centers of power (be they nation states, imperial forces, transnational institutions or other global players) continue to call the shots – in other words, to the present day. It is therefore clear that, by the end of this book, the *puer robustus* will have become a contemporary of ours.

When we talk about thresholds or liminality, the ethnological theory of threshold creatures or "liminal entities" inevitably comes into play.[6]

And yet the *puer robustus* is not, in an ethnological sense, a being whose existence is tied to a hiatus or interim period, such as a youth who briefly runs riot or spends a week in the wilderness in preparation for adulthood. The transitional ritual is not just a phase or episode for the troublemaker; transition is the troublemaker's purpose in life. He pauses right when his life hangs in the balance and, in doing so, spoils the closure of the political order. This order can put on a show of force and punish him for his refusal, of course, or use all of its might to make him back down. But the troublemaker is not limited to a choice between exclusion and integration. By challenging the order and testing its elasticity, he can also shake its very foundations. This raises the question of the direction of fit. Who is adapting to whom? Will the political order make short work of the troublemaker, or will the troublemaker cause an upheaval and force the order itself to change?

As a threshold creature, the *puer robustus* is pitted against the *homo sacer*, a figure whom Giorgio Agamben rescued from oblivion. Both characters represent exclusion, and just as Hobbes's *puer robustus* is said to be a *vir malus*, the *homo sacer* is referred to as a *homo malus* in Roman law.[7] But in Agamben's analysis, "exclusion" and "abandonment" are *definitive*.[8] The *homo sacer* is banished to an absolute outside, he is the complete Other against whom an order defines itself and whom (in antiquity, at least) it can kill without punishment. The distinction "between the State and the non-State"[9] is cemented here, and the threshold, which Agamben also frequently mentions, is transformed into an insurmountable barrier.[10]

Unlike Agamben and many others, however, I am interested not only in borders, but also in border crossings. When exclusion is made absolute, the outsider – and history along with him – is paralyzed. Instead of being an actor, he becomes a victim.[11] We could deploy Foucault against Agamben here: "We have to move beyond the outside-inside alternative; we have to be at the frontiers." – "To interrogate a culture about its limit-experiences is to question it at the confines of history about a tear that is something like the very birth of its history."[12] If "limit-experiences" themselves have a history, it means that limits must be continually confirmed, debated, defended, shifted, and broken. And for all of this to be possible, there must be not only victims but also actors among the included and excluded alike. The *puer robustus* is just such an actor. We can count on him to influence the course of the world – for good or for evil.

My critique of Agamben is tied to a more general point: I have the impression that political philosophy suffers from an unfortunate opposition between identity and alterity.

On the one hand, the outsider has become such a popular theoretical subject that one could, paradoxically, believe he or she were one of us.

Even back in 1990, Stuart Hall noted that many "elegant treatises on the 'other'" could be written without their authors necessarily "having encountered what 'otherness' is really like for some people."[13] A certain strain of political theory cannot get by without mentioning alterity, marginality, multitude, etc. There is, broadly speaking, both a cheerful and a melancholy version of this; namely, one that focuses on the mobilization of heterodox energies and one that refers to the fundamentally unfathomable otherness of the Other.

On the other hand, an equally prominent strain of political theory is fixated on models of collective identity, and it goes about gathering materials that could form the cement of society. The relevant buzzwords here are dominant culture, social capital, communities of memory, solidarity, public welfare, global ethics, etc. There are different versions of this strain of theory, too: one that exhibits a constructivist zeal to establish universally binding and unifying standards, and one that makes restorative gestures toward safeguarding traditions.

When (as one might hope) the validity of this formal contrast becomes apparent to representatives of both sides, the next step is to determine whether it is advisable to come down on one side or the other. In light of the threshold theory I have just outlined, this seems absurd to me. Those who celebrate the play of alterities while simultaneously mistrusting the institutionalization of communal life should note that they are not actually promoting difference but rather indifference, a state of apathy. The debate about deviation is only conceivable as a debate about commonalities. Those who cling to identity might be brought to bay most easily with a quote from Goethe's *Wilhelm Meister's Apprenticeship*:

> Whether this be a theatrical company or an empire, [. . .] a moment is usually reached when it is at its zenith, its best, its greatest unity, well-being and effectiveness. Then personalities change, new individuals arrive on the scene, and the persons no longer suit the circumstances and the circumstances the persons. Everything becomes different [. . .].[14]

The discrepancy between "circumstances" and "persons" is not limited to the possibility that the latter may not agree on what form their political framework should take. In fact, this discrepancy can radically destabilize institutions. They are on shaky ground because the "personalities," as Goethe calls them, are always changing. A sense of otherness does not come from spatial distance alone; it originates first and foremost in temporal life changes. Political orders are exposed to these changes as soon as they relate to and rely on the initiative of their members in one way or another – and this applies to every modern society since Hobbes.

When we think of strangers today, we immediately think of the migration flows in our globalized world, which inevitably appear on the horizon of this book. But what must be described first is the *inner migration* in a society – that is, the intense activity and impetus on the threshold where political subjects become what they are, where political orders are challenged to assert or renew themselves. And it is precisely because modern societies deal with inner migration on their own initiative (willingly or not) that they are prepared to deal with external migration.

How does the *puer robustus* fare as he stands on the threshold of the political order? He can be broken and defeated by it, or he can surrender and slowly but surely become reputable. But along with these more or less fatal endings, there are also scenarios of self-assertion open to him. They take extremely different forms and can be summarized in a brief typology of the troublemaker, which will be the thread that guides me through this book.

First, there is the *egocentric* troublemaker, who – figuratively speaking – stamps his foot on the threshold, bridles against the state order, and acts on his self-will. (Hobbes kick-starts the history of the *puer robustus* with this type of troublemaker.) Next there is the *eccentric* troublemaker, who flouts the rules but cannot rely entirely on his self-will because he is still searching for himself. The margin on which he stands is not a place for him to settle down but a springboard into the unknown. (Diderot will introduce this type of troublemaker to the history of the *puer robustus*, and Tocqueville will vacillate between antipathy toward the egocentric troublemaker and sympathy for the eccentric one.) Then there is the *nomocentric* troublemaker, who fights against the political order in anticipation of a different set of rules that will one day take its place. (We find this type of troublemaker in the writings of Rousseau; Schiller will bring him to the stage in the characters of Karl Moor and Wilhelm Tell; and Marx will try to drag him off the stage and into the reality of the class struggle.)

The triad of the egocentric, eccentric, and nomocentric troublemaker covers all of the characters who appear in this book – or nearly all of them. In the later years of the *puer robustus*, we will run into a type who makes mischief by unleashing a kind of disturbed disturbance. His relentless rabble-rousing requires something that actually goes against the self-image of the troublemaker: the protection of the mass, in which he disappears and in whose name he acts. There is, therefore, no better name for him than the *massive* troublemaker.

This sequence of types might suggest that I am describing a historical development in which different troublemakers appear and make their exit one after the other. But this is not my intention at all. The history of the *puer robustus* is and always will be an adventure story, meaning there is no underlying logical consequence or historical-philosophical tendency. The different types of troublemaker take to the stage, disappear, and then pop up again elsewhere. And they are in fruitful-frightful competition with one another. The *puer robustus* is in conflict with himself because the thinkers who concern themselves with him force him into a wide variety of roles. They fabricate him in order to attack or defend him.

The story I have to tell coincides temporally and factually with the establishment of democracy in the Western world. As a result, the image of the political order held up by the respective thinkers to counter the troublemaker is also subject to change. Attachment or aversion to the troublemaker goes hand in hand with the fight for or against democracy, though it is not always the same coalitions and fronts that form in this dual for-and-against. Ultimately, we will have to ask which agenda the troublemaker pursues when democracy declares itself ready to welcome him with open arms, when democracy refers to itself as "wild" (Lefort), "insurgent" (Abensour) or "creative" (Dewey). I will say this much: he will not disappear.

In this book, I will analyze the strengths and weaknesses of the roles into which the *puer robustus* slips. This role-playing can only be understood in light of the backdrop against which the *puer robustus* appears, and in contrast with the defenders of order who wrestle with him. If we want to know the troublemaker, we must get to know his enemies as well as his friends – and there will be a few false enemies and false friends among them. It remains to be seen which troublemaker deserves recognition and encouragement and how one can be properly devoted to him. I can tell you now that it is the eccentric troublemaker to whom I am most attached.

On the revolving stage that beckons the *puer robustus*, the precarious, risky positions of the outsider will be marked, the strategies of the political order to exclude or tame him will be explored, and the troublemaker's attempts to rattle or reform this order will be acted out. The curtain rises. Let the play begin.

— I. —

THE *PUER ROBUSTUS* AS
AN EVIL MAN

Thomas Hobbes

1. The threshold creature caught between power, morality, and history

The *puer robustus* has a father who disowns him. His name is Thomas Hobbes. All who subsequently turn their attention to this character hark back to Hobbes. Had Hobbes been able to witness the long career of the *puer robustus*, he would have eyed it warily. Hobbes wanted to hold him up as a negative example and banish him from history. He did not succeed. Who is this *puer robustus* who first saw the light of day in Hobbes's political philosophy?

At the very start of his long journey, the *puer robustus* burrows right into the heart of political philosophy. After all, the preface to *De cive* in which he appears is, according to Leo Strauss, Hobbes's "most purely theoretical exposition of his theory of the state."[1] In this preface, as mentioned earlier, Hobbes says "ut vir malus idem fere sit quod puer robustus, vel vir animo puerili" – "a wicked man" is like a "childe growne strong and sturdy, or a man of a childish disposition" (C[l] 81; C[e] 33).[2] These few words reveal three characteristics of the *puer robustus*.

First, there is the most striking word in Hobbes's dictum: the fellow is *robustus*. Dictionaries offer a wide range of definitions for *robustus* and *robur*, including strength, vigor, force, and power. In the metaphorical transition from nature to civilization, the hardness of oak is translated into the strength of man. He is defined as an active agent, and the issue up for discussion is "the power of a man" (L[e] 62).

The *second* characteristic of the *puer robustus*, as Hobbes puts it bluntly, is that he is *malus* – evil. The question of power is thus joined by the question of morality. This presupposes the existence of an authority who is entitled or empowered to cast judgment on him. This authority

10

therefore also has a claim to power, one that stands in opposition to the strength or power of the strong boy.

The *third* point in Hobbes's definition refers not to a fixed characteristic attributed to a person – that someone is strong or wicked, for example – but to the fact that the person can change or grow: the boy will become a man. Broadly speaking, the passing of generations is a temporal process representing nothing less than the course of history. And the *puer robustus* disrupts this history. He is a grown man, but he still has a childish spirit. His immaturity stands in contrast to the act of growing up as a process of growing into a role, a confirmation of belonging. Hobbes tries to usher people out of this stage of arbitrary childishness. His good adult slips into the role of the subject, but in doing so – to jump straight to the conclusion – he resembles a well-adapted child in whom traces of insubordination can still be found.

Power, morality, and history are the big themes that preoccupy the political philosophy of Hobbes and others. I want to start with the third aspect. The *puer robustus* belongs first and foremost to a large group of characters who are treated as outsiders in political theory. But unlike almost all of these other characters, the *puer robustus* thrives on a dynamic concept of borders and the forms of integration and exclusion that are created by them. Historical development inevitably comes into play when the issue in question is not evil as a static characteristic, but rather the making of evil. By coupling the questions of power and morality to the question of generations (boy-and-man or child-and-adult), Hobbes describes a world in motion. But within this state of motion, he seizes on only a single moment in which the individual reaches the threshold of having to choose between good and evil. Hobbes's consideration of history extends solely to the dramatization of this decision-making moment. For Hobbes, the question of adaptation or deviation, submission or insurrection, is decided in an instant. He clings to the methodological fiction that men "[spring] out of the earth, and suddainly (*like* Mushromes) come to full maturity" (C[l] 160; C[e] 117). He dreams the dream of the "old shepherd" in Shakespeare's *The Winter's Tale*, who believes it would be best for youth to "sleep out" the ages between "ten and three-and-twenty," when they would otherwise merely be "wronging the ancientry" – so that they can finally awaken as righteous adults.[3] There is truth to the claim that "Hobbes's political philosophy is 'unhistorical'" (Strauss, PPH 102). At the same time, one can give him credit for undermining the unhistorical qualities of his own thought by hinting at historical, generational "becoming" in the form of his *puer robustus*. Even Hobbes knew that "all men [. . .] are born in Infancy" (C[l] 92; C[e] 44).

The *puer robustus* is someone who made the wrong decision and has thus grown up in the wrong way. He has failed to make the transition

11

from "nature" to "society," the transformation from "a Beast to a Man" (C[l] 92, 159; C[e] 44, 116). The *puer robustus* is invited to cross this threshold, but he refuses to accede to Hobbes's demand that he submit to the Leviathan. Even though his deviation is negotiated in the unremarkable context of the generation game and the act of growing up, it harbors a sinister, serious threat: alienation from or animosity toward the political order.

Medieval theologians sent infants who had died before being baptized to *limbus puerorum*, a place on this side of salvation and damnation. Even in Hobbes's lifetime, the character of the Child in Calderón's *The Great Theater of the World* from 1655 ends up in this limbo, not in heaven or hell.[4] Hobbes himself avoids the question of salvation, and he also does not mention limbo. But, gazing across the densely populated field on the threshold of order that Hobbes and his successors have sighted, one gets the impression that this is also a type of limbo, an expansive non-place of indecision. In this case, however, the moral and social litmus test is not forestalled by death, as it is for children. Instead, the test is simply rejected on a massive scale by the living.

I am not alone in calling this a threshold; even Hobbes refers to it this way – a fact that is usually overlooked. He uses the word *limen* in an annotation[5] to the first chapter of *De cive*, which was probably written at the same time as the "Preface to the Reader":

> Since we now see actually a constituted Society among men, and none living out of it, since we discern all desirous of congresse, and mutuall correspondence, it may seeme a wonderfull kind of stupidity, to lay in the very threshold of this Doctrine, such a stumbling block before the Readers, as to deny Man to be born fit for Society. (C[l] 92; C[e] 44)

Hobbes is not talking about a simple beginning, a foundational act that would allow one to cast off all that has come before, but rather an actual "threshold" with two sides – inside and outside, before and after – that must be taken into account. Furthermore, this threshold is a characteristic not just of the *doctrine* of the state but of the state itself. In the "Preface to the Reader" of *De cive*, Hobbes notes that in order to "make a more curious search into the rights of States, and duties of Subjects," it is not necessary "to take them in sunder," only to consider them "as if they were dissolved" (C[l] 79; C[e] 32).[6] This passage is usually taken to mean that Hobbes considers a state of nature to be not a reality but part of a thought experiment. As long as it only seems "as if" the state were dissolved, then Hobbes is in the clear. And yet he is playing with fire, because the state is – fictionally or factually – being contrasted with the individuals alienated from it. Order is placed in relation to disorder and its boundaries are defined – more than Hobbes would probably like in the end. No one is automatically a part of it. The liminality or marginality of the individual plays a key role in Hobbes's political philosophy – and in this book.

Hobbes admits to the existence of this threshold, but he does so reluctantly and makes every effort to fortify the opposition between order and disorder. The fact that he lives in an "Age wherein all men's Souls are in a kind of fermentation"[7] does not suit him at all. The title page of the first edition of *De cive* makes it clear that Hobbes prefers to think in terms of conditions rather than transitions. The illustration on this page shows two figures, each standing on a pedestal: on the left, an elegantly clothed woman holding a sword and scales; on the right, an armed male (or female?) American Indian in a feathered skirt. In the background on the left we see peaceful activity, on the right a cannibalistic hunt. This worldly double image is accompanied by two scenes from the Last Judgment above it. To the left the saved are being led into heaven by angels, to the right the devil is shooing sinners into hell. Scholars who have studied this image[8] have made great strides in interpreting it, but they have failed to mention one important detail: a void. This void runs through the entire frontispiece, in the top section as well as the bottom. The two figures look past each other, the groups above turn away from one another. And between the figures and the groups, *nothing* is happening. This might be understandable, since heaven and hell are destinations very far removed from one another. And yet, Hobbes is concerned and obsessed with this void. It represents a threshold and an unanswered question: Under which circumstances could the Indian reach the other side? How does one transition from a state of nature to a state of civil society? There is surely more to say about this than *nothing*.

If, instead of driving natural and civilized life apart, we explore the threshold between them, then on the precipice of the political order we encounter not only far-flung strangers, such as savages, but also strangers very close by, those closest to us of all: children. They are outsiders who come from the inside. With his *puer robustus*, Hobbes is referencing a foreign element that is continuously generated within society itself, one which Ralph Waldo Emerson described in a superlative sentence that serves as the motto of this book: "The man is [...] a misfit from the start."[9]

From Hobbes's point of view, the socialization of the individual represents a development that starts in some disarray but ends with the creation of order. We continue to hark back to these cornerstones even if, unlike Hobbes, we do not want to turn them into bulwarks based on the antithesis between nature and society. For Hobbes, the *puer robustus* represents a case of something going wrong in the transition from a state of nature to a state of civil society. But what exactly triggers the fault?

To fully understand this, we must look to the two other major themes associated with the *puer robustus*: power and morality.

Hobbes describes the *puer robustus* as strong, and he judges him to be evil. This double blow initially gives rise to a somewhat unusual constellation of power and morality: a contrast between arbitrariness, the individual's abuse of power, and the morality of the whole. This division naturally cries out for reshuffling and reinterpretation.

First and foremost, it is important to note that power and morality are not simply in opposition to one another. Instead, they can also be in coalition. When the morality of the whole passes judgment on the *puer robustus*, its intention is to gird itself with power in order to put him in his place. The power of the whole is bolstered against the individual power-seeker. On the other hand, the *puer robustus* might have more than just malice in his repertoire. He can hold up a different morality to that claimed by the whole. The prime example of this is Antigone, who replies to her dutiful sister Ismene ("I must obey") with the wonderful, paradoxical declaration that she will commit "an outrage sacred to the gods."[10]

When individuals challenge the powers that be, the question of whether or not they are evil depends not only on how they misbehave, but also on the rules of the game they either ignore or violate. Émile Durkheim was not the first to realize that "it is not enough for rules to exist, for occasionally it is these very rules that are the cause of evil."[11] The troublemaker can make a virtue of not playing along by rejecting collaboration and complicity. And if he decides to play along after all, it does not necessarily mean that he must immediately cease his harassing fire. He can back down, but his participation can also put the political order to the test. Then the outsider who crosses the threshold can strive to renegotiate this order in a way that will transform it. Belonging and obedience are not automatically a package deal. The individual who eventually belongs might not disappear unnoticed in the crowd but actually change what the crowd looks like. So the jury is still out on the troublemaker. Sigmund Freud describes the alternatives here:

> What makes itself felt in a human community as a desire for freedom may be their revolt against some existing injustice, and so may prove favourable to a further development of civilization; it may remain compatible with civilization. But it may also spring from the remains of their original personality, which is still untamed by civilization and may thus become the basis in them of hostility to civilization. (SE 21, 96)

The fact that power and morality can be reshuffled goes a long way toward explaining the appeal of the *puer robustus* after Hobbes. The fellow is truly an ambiguous figure. He attracts controversial interpretations covering the entire spectrum of power and morality in the relationship between the individual and society. He not only allows this, he practically invites or insists on it. For Hobbes, however, the *puer robustus* is the epitome of the "bad boy" or even the *vir malus*. As stated earlier, even though Hobbes himself dragged the *puer robustus* onto the stage of history, he would have preferred to immediately chase him off again. He cares little about the ambiguities and ambitions of the troublemaker and believes the *puer robustus* forces the political order not into self-examination but self-defense. For the political order, the conflict with the *puer robustus* becomes a fight for survival.

I now want to show, first, how Hobbes envisions the integration of the man of nature – that is, how he hopes to keep him from becoming "evil" and the problems he encounters along the way (section 2). These problems are considerable, as can be seen not least in the fact that Hobbes feels he is surrounded by a motley crowd of troublemakers who threaten the political order. He runs into fools, epileptics, and madmen, and he discovers flashpoints among rich and poor alike (section 3). To counter all of them, Hobbes holds up the Leviathan as the ideal state order, though even this cannot bring innate rebels under its control (section 4). Finally, I explore the question of how Hobbes's *puer robustus* relates to one of his predecessors: the *puer robustus* of Horace (section 5).

2. Self-interest and reason

When a monstrous *outside* opens up on the margins of society, populated by all sorts of creatures of nature, then what we need first is a precise description of the evildoers. Not everyone roaming around out there is evil. Hobbes has to circumscribe the circle of evildoers because an uncomfortable question lurks in the background (cf. Strauss, PPH 13): whether man is evil by nature. Hobbes answers this theologically explosive question in the negative, thus opening up the possibility that a creature of nature could be motivated to join the good company of society.

Hobbes observes the behavior of children who do not get "all they aske for," and he tuts at how they "are peevish, and cry, and strike their Parents sometimes." He writes that "all this they have from nature," but he comforts himself by noting that they are "free from guilt" and not "wicked." They have no access to morality, he says, because they are not yet capable of the "use of reason" (C[l] 81; C[e] 33). It is in the nature of man to "desire and doe whatsoever is best pleasing." The "passions" derived from nature are necessary for self-preservation and therefore morally neutral (ibid.). Rousseau will follow Hobbes's thinking here – and Nietzsche, in *Human, All Too Human*, will outdo him:

15

What is innocent in so-called evil actions. – All "evil" actions are motivated by the drive for preservation, or more exactly, by the individual's
striving for pleasure and avoidance of pain; thus, they are motivated,
but are not evil. [. . .] The basis for all morality can be established only
when a greater individual or a collective individual (society or the state,
for example) subjugates individuals [. . .]. *Coercion* precedes morality
[. . .]. (NCW 3, 75f.)

But Nietzsche's apparently Hobbesian argument is more venomous
than the original. His first dose of venom is that he absolves not only
children of malice but also the "sovereign individual" who can "vouch
for" himself (NCW 8, 248 [*On the Genealogy of Morality*]). The second
dose is administered when he derives morality from "coercion," making
morality a dependent variable of state power. This goes against Hobbes's
assumption that the syllabus of life involves learning the "use of reason,"
which enables individuals to find their way to morality on their own.

How can Hobbes get around Nietzsche's escalation of the conflict
between the "individual" and the "state"? He concedes that people
have desires, but he also trusts that they will behave in a moral way. For
Hobbes, people invested with desires will only grow to be evil if two additional conditions have been met. First, such people must have the power
to assert their desires at the cost and to the detriment of others. The
moral assessment of an individual thus takes on consequentialist traits.
Second, and most importantly, these people must have neglected to take
advantage of learning opportunities that were available to them growing
up, which would have taught them the destructive consequences of their
actions. Hobbes counts on the fact that "a spark of reason (*ratio*)"[12] will
flash in the individual. Strictly speaking, wickedness is an omission here,
a deviation from the expected degree of reason. When adults display a
"defect of reason" (C[l] 81; C[e] 33) and are thus impervious to moral
insight, they are considered evil. According to Hobbes, the evil man does
not actually behave any differently than the not-yet-evil child, but he
acts with the full power of an adult, and he deliberately and knowingly
disregards the option of acting in any other way. "Ignorance of the Law
of Nature excuseth no man," Hobbes says, because one can assume that
"every man" had "attained to the use of Reason" (L[e] 202). The only
ones who might be excused are those who still have this learning process
ahead of them or who are incapable of learning in the first place:

The want of means to know the Law, totally Excuseth: For the Law
whereof a man has no means to enforme himself, is not obligatory. But
the want of diligence to enquire, shall not be considered as a want of
means; Nor shall any man, that pretendeth to reason enough for the
Government of his own affairs, be supposed to want means to know

16

the Lawes of Nature; because they are known by the reason he pretends to: only Children, and Madmen are Excused from offences against the Law Naturall. (L[e] 208)

The *puer robustus* sets himself against an order in which, according to Hobbes, morality and power stand shoulder to shoulder. He remains hard-headed and empty-headed and believes he can assert himself through sheer force alone. The autonomous, individual power to which he lays claim falls on the side of evil. For Hobbes, this fellow – the man-child who has grown old and strong but remains stupid – is a threat to the establishment of a peaceful society. Mind you, it is not the robustness, strength, or power of these individuals with which Hobbes takes issue, but rather the fact that they are unlearned and uncouth. Evil is a product of thoughtlessness. Where the individual's development goes wrong, according to Hobbes, is that as the child grows ever stronger, he neglects to use his sense of reason. The *first* preliminary finding here is that Hobbes's moral theory is *intellectualistic*. "It is the sum total of Hobbes's moral theory" – though I would say only the *sub*-total – "that he who 'sins' or errs is he who acts unreasonably."[13]

What happens if I tentatively put myself in the situation of the *puer robustus*? Then I stand on the threshold of order and am judged to be evil. But this does not actually *bother* me in the least because I have no idea what is meant by "evil." After all, I am a man of nature who, according to Hobbes, has the peculiarity of interpreting language as I see fit. There is no "common Rule of Good and Evill"; it emerges instead "from the Person of the man (where there is no Common-wealth;)" (L[e] 39). What I consider good is what is good for me (L[e] 93), even if it is bad for others. It does not surprise me to find that others are like my mirror image in that they consider things harmful to me to be good for themselves. If I am accused of wickedness, the accusation comes from a place I neither know nor acknowledge. The political order is *terra incognita* for me, which is why the moral exhortations and commands that go with it remain alien. What would a poor devil like me know about reason? Universally valid assertions or rules are closed off to me.

Hobbes knows all of this, and thankfully he is even sympathetic to my narrow-mindedness. But he is also confident that I am willing to employ reason. He starts with my "own reason," which helps me satisfy my needs, primarily to ensure my self-preservation. With this practical or instrumental[14] reason, I specify the "Precept" or "Rule" whereby my life "may be best preserved" (L[e] 91). We must therefore qualify the preliminary finding that Hobbes advocates an intellectualistic moral theory. Reason comes second to self-interest, which precedes it. It thus plays the subordinate role of a tool: "For the Thoughts, are to the Desires,

17

as *Scouts, and Spies*, to range abroad, and find the way to the things Desired" (L[e] 53). Even this kind of reason should be enough for me to conclude – in my individualistic assessment of the situation, with no claim to universal validity – that it would be a good idea for me to submit to the political order.

Following Hobbes's famous argument, I have an easy choice to make between a life that is "solitary, poore, nasty, brutish, and short" and a life in which I can hold onto my possessions and conduct my business free of fear, with time on the side to dedicate myself to the fine arts (cf. L[e] 89): "The Passions that encline men to Peace, are Feare of Death; Desire of such things as are necessary to commodious living; and a Hope by their Industry to obtain them. And Reason suggesteth convenient Articles of Peace [...]" (L[e] 90). Peace is the prerequisite for individuals to be able to pursue their self-interest. And securing this peace requires the "common power" or sovereign authority of the Leviathan: "The finall Cause, End, or Designe of men [...] in the introduction of that restraint upon themselves, (in which wee see them live in Commonwealths,) is the foresight of their own preservation, and of a more contented life thereby" (L[e] 120, 117).

It is now clear what the *puer robustus* does wrong and why Hobbes chalks this up to a "defect of reason." He pursues the goal of self-preservation, but he takes a path that does not even lead to this goal. He throws subordination and state allegiance to the wind, trusts in his own strength, and tries to get by on his own account and at the expense of others. With this obstinacy, he just hurts himself in the end. The Leviathan – which keeps the peace in part through the "benefit"[15] of arbitrating the war of words and establishing a universally valid vocabulary – then judges this *puer robustus* to be evil.

To put it briefly, if I vanquish the *puer robustus* within myself and submit to an order that is considered good, I require no moral backing whatsoever to do so. I become moral without having the faintest idea of what morality is. The *second* preliminary finding, therefore, is that Hobbes's moral theory is *amoral*. The troublemaker is persuaded to cease his harassing fire without anyone pestering him to set aside his self-interest. It is precisely when he indulges in this self-interest that he lands in the arms of the state.

This paradoxical image of an amoral moral theory is supported by an influential strain of Hobbes scholarship that places self-interest ahead of reason and manages to secure the political order in doing so. The thinking here is that I only obey the law because it is useful to me. Hobbes thus becomes the herald of rational choice theory.[16] He thinks he knows exactly how men of nature function. He believes they are driven by self-interest – and he latches on to this trait and drags them into a peaceful, lawful life for their own self-preservation. By means of "education" (C[l] 81; C[e] 34) if necessary, individuals come to the reasonable conclusion that it is in their best interest to follow the rules set down in the social contract, now and forever.

By turning the intellect into the servant of an amoral self-interest, Hobbes seems to stray ever further from the moral demands that ultimately underpin his judgment of the "evil" *puer robustus*. But there is a *third* and final finding to take into account here: Hobbes offers not only an intellectualist and amoral approach to morality, but also a genuinely *ethical* approach. (These three categories describe the main lines of thinking in the interpretation of Hobbes.[17])

Since Hobbes views reason as a tool to be used to reach a goal – the goal of self-preservation – he neglects to include it in any deliberation about goals themselves. And yet, the goal he presupposes is in no way self-evident. The apparently amoral approach to legal order, which starts with self-interest, is itself the outcome of an ethical decision. Universal rules arise from a value judgment that places peaceful survival ahead of everything else. This ethical premise has been the subject of debate. Samantha Frost takes the position that "peace," for Hobbes, is "the primary ethical value." Roberto Esposito, by contrast, argues that, in Hobbes's work, "life is sacrificed to the preservation of life."[18] When Hobbes declares survival to be the highest ethical value, he is certainly not voicing a truism. Plato, for example, disputes this in his dialog *Gorgias*; Kant states that "life, in and for itself, is not the highest good"[19]; Schiller says "no good supreme is life" (CWS 5, 319); and the closing line in the film *Slow West* by John Maclean is "there is more to life than survival."

Hobbes was familiar with Ficino's translations of Plato, though he did not concern himself with the Platonic distinction between life and survival. But in his immediate surroundings he encountered a type of morality that deviated from his minimal goal of survival: aristocratic morality, whose ideals he disputes, according to Leo Strauss (PPH 113). It is worth noting this, not because aristocratic honor and fearlessness would be preferable to individualistic self-interest, but because it shows that it is not necessarily a self-evident, amoral automatism that Hobbes would take self-interest as his starting point. Leo Strauss writes:

> Hobbes's political philosophy rests not on the illusion of an amoral morality, but on a new morality, or, to speak according to Hobbes's intention, on a new grounding of the one eternal morality. [...] [H]e finally denied the moral value of all virtues which do not contribute to the making of the State, to consolidating peace. (PPH 15, 18, cf. 27f.)

There is, therefore, an alternative to Hobbes's minimal morality of self-preservation. In addition to the concepts already mentioned, other moral viewpoints could be proposed, such as the moral sense that under-pins eighteenth-century Scottish philosophy. Hobbes's image of the man of nature is a stylized type that must be so simple and one-dimensional that an equally simple and one-dimensional state can be created for it: a state that must wield total power, because the goal of keeping the peace supersedes all else.

The *puer robustus* is particularly well-suited to exposing the fragility of this tidy scenario. Regardless of which of Hobbes's three versions of morality is deployed against him, they all fall short of the mark. The troublemaker does not simply suffer from a "defect of reason"; he is perfectly capable of employing a rational strategy. His individual power can induce him to pursue his own interests without the protection of an all-powerful order. Since he does not come out of nowhere but rather has *become* what he is, he can be guided by ethical stances that are at odds with Hobbes's premises.

The *puer robustus* is a living provocation for Hobbes. He is simultane-ously the most important and most unfamiliar troublemaker to appear in Hobbes's political philosophy – and he is by far not the only one. A variety of other obstructionists gather around him. Who are they, and what do they get up to?

3. Hobbes's egocentric troublemakers:
Fools, epileptics, madmen, the poor, and the rich

If people followed the rules of their own accord, there would be no need for an authority to quell their temptation to seek the first available opportunity to breach a contract after concluding it.[20] The existence of the Leviathan is further proof that people are not as streamlined as Hobbes would like. He is aware of the disturbances that plague the con-tractual world; he describes them in detail in the "Preface to the Reader" in which the *puer robustus* appears, and elsewhere as well (particularly in chapter 12 of *De cive*, chapters 8 and 29 of *Leviathan*, and chapter 8 of *De corpore politico*). According to Hobbes, the characters responsible for these disturbances are *fools*, *madmen*, and *epileptics*, though he also discovers obstructionists among the *rich* and the *poor*. I want to try to understand these characters that Hobbes brings to the stage, identify their all-too-numerous heirs and, at the end of this section, reveal a criti-cal weakness in Hobbes's theory of the troublemaker.

The fool. According to Hobbes, the troublemaker – like everyone else – is driven by self-interest. As we have seen, what Hobbes objects to here is not self-interest as such, but the fact that it is asserted in the wrong way. While "solid Reason" works as an "antidote" to rebellion among individuals loyal to the state (L[e] 225), the "authors of rebellion" are characterized by a "want of *wisdom*."[21] Hobbes describes this "want" as a defect, a sickness that seizes the mind. Seditionists are "Mad-men" (*homines insani*; L[e] 55, cf. 54–9; C[l] 189; C[e] 150). This is clearly an idiosyncratic pathology. Unlike the children and mentally ill people whom Hobbes absolves of responsibility and excludes from wickedness, these madmen are culpable. Their behavior may be mad, but there is method to it. Hobbes's rather labored[22] distinction between innocent mentally ill individuals and guilty madmen is a wonderful example (sadly not mentioned by Foucault himself) of Foucault's theory of a "continuum" between pathologization and criminalization, between "hospital" and "prison": "This continuum with its therapeutic and judicial poles, this institutional mixture, is actually a response to danger. This institutional system is aimed at the dangerous individual [. . .]."[23]

Hobbes may not believe this dangerous madman is unreasoning, but he calls him unreasonable nonetheless. He is a *homo in-sapiens* or, to put it in correct Latin, a *homo insipiens*. This is precisely the term chosen by Hobbes: he refers to the madman as *insipiens* (in the Latin version of *Leviathan*) or "the Foole" (in the English version; L[e] 101; L[l] 112).[24]

The "Foole" is not a barbarian, savage, or childish clown. He may seem imprudent or unreasonable, but he does try to employ his own kind of reason. This whispers a seductive message in his ear – namely, that it is in his interest to occasionally flout the rules. Hobbes's fool wonders "whether Injustice [. . .] may not sometimes stand with that Reason, which dictateth to every man his own good; and particularly then, when it conduceth to such a benefit" (L[e] 101; L[l] 112). The fool flirts with this solution and thus becomes the perfect foil or evil twin to the individualist who is loyal to the state. They have self-interest in common, but they differ in that the fool uses flawed reasoning which threatens to become his downfall. Because he fails to make rational calculations, he will commit a crime or break the law for the sake of an enticing increase in pleasure. He thus does himself out of his spoils, according to Hobbes, and ruins his chance of future pleasures at the same time.

Scholars of Hobbes have paid scant attention to the *puer robustus*,[25] but his doppelgänger, the fool, is very popular with them.[26] This probably has to do with the fact that the fool seems to offer a clear view of the threshold between the state of nature and the state order. On one side is the fool who goes astray, and on the other are the people who only employ reason in Hobbes's narrow, instrumental sense and thereby come to realize the necessity of the state order. The attempt to categorize the fool's lack of cooperation as irrational is therefore also at the heart of the influential strain of Hobbes scholarship based on rational choice and game theory.

In my view, it is futile to try to prove that the fool is actually irrational.[27] It is important to bear in mind that Hobbes defines this character in very broad terms. His definition does not only apply to the drastic cases in which someone in the house of the law behaves like a bull in a china shop. Even if someone only "sometimes"[28] believes that a breach of law – one that might even go unnoticed[29] – is reasonable, this is enough for Hobbes to consider him a fool. Hobbes lobs accusations of foolishness for the most minor infractions – as he must, following his own logic, because he cannot accept an order that is capable of dealing with only major infractions. But with this broad interpretation, he overstrains and overstretches the accusation of foolishness leveled against the troublemaker. This accusation cannot apply to occasional, secret breaches of the law, because these could well be rational in terms of self-interest.

When the fool breaks a law, he appears at first glance to be a common criminal, and like a criminal, he counts on not being caught. But there is an important difference between these characters, one which reveals that the fool is actually an enemy of the political order. A criminal who breaks a law for the sake of personal advantage may well feel that he is doing something bad or evil. He does not have to cast doubt on the validity of the law. Not so the so-called fool, who has general reservations about the political order and establishes a tactical distance to it. It is not his individual deed but rather this aversion that poses the ultimate challenge for the political order, because the "generall Covenant of obedience" is being "renounc[ed]" here. Therefore, according to Hobbes, he must be punished not as a common criminal but in accordance with "the Right of Warre" – as if he were a foreigner – and then "left, or cast out of Society" (C[l] 216f.; C[e] 180f.; L[e] 102). He represents *anarchy*: "The promotion of anarchy is the ultimate – or perhaps the only – crime against the state" (Hegel, PW 81).

The fool's behavior may be offensive, but it is certainly not as insane as Hobbes claims. In any case, Hobbes's criticism has not diminished the appeal of this character, who has subsequently attracted myriad followers – even into the present day. These followers are not just failures and lost souls; they include fairly successful freeloaders and spongers, along with countless people who like to seek loopholes in the political order while still remaining half-loyal to it, as it were.

Epileptics and madmen. Hobbes says troublemakers exist not only because a failure of reason causes people to miscalculate their odds of winning, but also because people allow themselves to be gripped by unreasonableness, or by "Passions contrary to peace" (C[l] 185; C[e] 146). In a typically Hobbesian manner, Norbert Elias describes how individuals can give in to the "passionate impulse urging [them] to attack

22

another physically" and endanger the "pacified social spaces" if they are unable to "suppress" their desires by means of "self-compulsion."[30]

Hobbes wonders why and how passions escalate. He says they are not wild, external forces that break into the political order, but they are instead channeled and amplified by specific life circumstances. He draws on various disorders as metaphors for political crises: Siamese twins, intestinal worms, clogged arteries, pleurisy, lethargy, pruritus, etc. (L[e] 225–30). I want to highlight just two of the diseases commonly found among Hobbes's rebels: epilepsy and rabies.[31]

Hobbes writes that "the Jewes" take epilepsy to be "one kind of possession by Spirits," which manifests itself in "violent, and irregular motions (which men call Convulsions) in the parts." He says epilepsy is triggered when hopes and fears that are directed not at real issues but at "Ghosts" or products of the imagination are stirred up among the people. Loyalty to the earthly kingdom is then shaken by the vision of a "Kingdom of Fayries." Those responsible for this development include certain representatives of a "Ghostly" or "Spirituall" power, who drive the people "into the Fire of a Civill warre" (L[e] 226ff.).

As described here, epilepsy is a kind of confusion that causes people to be torn between different "Soules." In addition to this there is rabies, which infects people with a single soul and drives them to "Rebellion." While Hobbes blames political epilepsy on the clergy, he attributes rabies to "the Reading of the books of Policy, and Histories of the ancient Greeks, and Romans." Their depictions of great exploits are said to be like a "Venime," the effect of which is comparable to "the biting of a mad Dogge [*canis rabidis*]" (L[e] 225f.; L[l] 236). Hobbes is playing not only on the urge to bite and the destructive rage of someone infected by rabies, but also – much more cleverly – on a specific symptom that occurs in the final stage of the disease. In both Hobbes's writing and modern medicine, rabies is known as "*Hydrophobia, or fear of Water*" (ibid.). This refers to the fact that, shortly before dying of the disease, someone infected with rabies will be thirsty but will recoil in panic at the prospect of quenching this thirst. Applied to the political sphere, this means that the individual needs a strong government but is so deluded that he "abhorreth" it and plans to commit regicide instead (ibid.). The fool, the epileptic, and the madman all produced many offspring in the period after Hobbes. Epileptic confusion has recurred in the form of indiscriminate aggression, rabid obsession in the form of political fanaticism.

The poor and the rich. Hobbes believes he has identified a trait shared by all of the troublemakers he tackles: the familiar deficit of reason that plays a trick on them as they pursue their self-interest. I mentioned that Hobbes carefully analyzes the external circumstances that aggravate this deficit. Looking only at the passions that drive individuals for the sake of self-preservation – namely, fear of death and desire for power – we can guess where these passions might gain the upper hand and cloud the vision. We hit pay dirt at the lower and upper ends of society, among the desperate weak and the power-hungry strong: "Needy men, and hardy, not contented with their present condition; as also, all men that are ambitious of Military command, are enclined to [. . .] stirre up trouble and sedition" (L[e] 70f.). In purely economic terms, this means Hobbes must keep a close eye on both the poor and the rich, because they are equally wanting the rational insight that would lead them to submit to the sovereign:

> They whom necessity, or covetousnesse keepeth attent on their trades, and labour; and they, on the other side, whom superfluity, or sloth car-rieth after their sensuall pleasures (which two sorts of men take up the greatest part of Mankind,) [are] diverted from [. . .] deep meditation. (L[e] 236)

Both groups pose a threat to the state order, though Hobbes believes the poor are more harmless than the rich. He envisions the people not as a collective capable of acting together but as a "Multitude" (L[e] 118). The poor are distracted from the use of reason because they are afflicted by their situation as if by an "Incubus" (C[l] 191; C[e] 152). This is also why they tend to be passive rather than active. To control the poor, Hobbes suggests incorporating breaks into their usual working hours, during which they could receive the state instruction that will teach them obedience. They would be receptive to such instruction because their minds, he says, "are like clean paper, fit to receive whatsoever by Publique Authority shall be imprinted in them" (L[e] 233).[32] These poor people are the *tabula rasa* that every pedagogue or demagogue dreams of – but it is just a dream, not reality.

Although Hobbes countenances social inequality (L[e] 238), he sets a limit on it. The state is expected to ensure that those who are impov-erished through no fault of their own are "provided for, (as far-forth as the necessities of Nature require)" (L[e] 239). This is not just a matter of charity, it also prevents disturbances in the political order. The following lines are included only in the Latin version of *Leviathan*, not the English version: "The common people is the pillar of the state! [. . .] The common people may not be antagonized even by kings, much less by other power-ful citizens; because the people, when it takes revenge on these others, will also attack the state that did not put a stop to them" (L[l] 247).

In their desperation, the poor can apparently turn into threaten-ing savages. Even at the end of the nineteenth century, they were said to resemble the people in "darkest Africa" (regarding this topos, see p. 204).[33] But Hobbes comes to the conclusion – a conclusion also reached by Moses Wall in 1659, John Locke in 1691, Jean-Jacques Rousseau in 1764, Louis Sébastien Mercier in 1784, and Theodor Mommsen in 1854[34] – that the poor are not capable of attacking the state order. Since they lack means and power, he believes they can be controlled. Having said that, it is easy to imagine how Hobbes's poor rebels could become revolutionaries – they would simply have to join forces. Marx will introduce us to this collective subject under the name of *puer robustus*, thus taking the eponymous hero of this book out of the evil corner to which Hobbes wants to banish him.

As we will soon see, even rich troublemakers have a future ahead of them, one in which they will appear as a *puer robustus* of a very different type. Hobbes – to stay with him for the moment – believes the rich are more dangerous to the state than the poor because they have more power and are not occupied with concerns about their daily bread. It is in keeping with the logic of his individualism that he thinks the dull masses are less dangerous than the "potent men" who ruthlessly seek an advantage and are hardly influenced by any "Power to bridle their affections" (L[e] 233): "Therefore it happeneth commonly, that such as value themselves by the greatnesse of their wealth, adventure on Crimes, upon hope of escaping punishment, by corrupting publique Justice, or obtaining Pardon by Mony, or other rewards" (L[e] 205).

The hostility of the rich toward the state is different than that of the poor. The rich undermine the state in a mundane, inconspicuous way. They do not openly break the rules, they skirt around them – like the fool, as we have seen. The rich, as depicted by Hobbes, would like everyone to follow the rules – except for themselves. Just as a parallel is drawn between the poor and the "savage," the same applies in a different way to the relationship between the "savage who emerges from his forests" and the "savage Homo economicus whose life is devoted to exchange and barter."[35] And just as Hobbes's poor rebel is a precursor to the proletarian of the nineteenth century, who will be characterized as a wild animal and as a *puer robustus*, we find in Hobbes's rich rebel a precursor to the Californian pioneer, who gives free rein to his self-granted authority and is given a name by Tocqueville that should be familiar by now: *puer robustus*.

In his late dialogic work *Behemoth*, Hobbes reassesses the dangers to the state order in light of growing unrest in the population. "Those great capital cities," one of the speakers in his dialog says, "must needs be of the rebel party." Responsibility for this unrest is assigned not to the poor, however, but to the "citizens," the "merchants," who are so certain of their power that they refuse to pay taxes, and whose "only glory" is to "grow excessively rich." They are nothing less than enemies of the state. The other speaker objects, saying that such citizens contribute to the common good by giving work to the poor. But the notion that this function supports the state or the common good is rejected with the remark that the poor are worse off in such jobs than they would be in a workhouse. The short-term danger of rebellion in the cities comes from the rich, according to Hobbes; but he believes the long-term danger arising from the growing discontent of the poor is greater than it was in *Leviathan*.[36]

Regarding the proliferation of rich and poor and their potential for disturbance, an important consideration was raised by a thinker we would not expect to find among the ranks of Hobbes's critics: the Marquis de Sade. In his work *Justine*, he turns on Hobbes with the following questions: "Can those individuals who isolate themselves fight everyone else? Can they truly be happy and tranquil if they do not accept the social contract [...]?" Sade replies that rejecting this contract is actually in the interest of two groups: the strong and the weak. "Those who, considering themselves to be the strongest, [need] to give nothing away in order to be happy; and those who, being the weakest, [find] themselves conceding infinitely more than they were promised" if they submit to the contractual order. Sade's clever punchline is that he claims there is absolutely no one who does not belong to one group or the other, as "society is made up only of the weak and the strong."[37] In Sade's opinion, there is no middle of society to serve as a *juste milieu* upon which Hobbes could base his contractual order, because even here the engines driving the distinction between rich and poor are revving up. Compliance crumbles wherever you look.

It is important to remember that even Hobbes – if we take *Leviathan* and *Behemoth* together – acknowledges the disturbances coming from all sides, from rich and poor alike. Regrettably, Hobbes's interpreters make little use of his findings concerning these all-around disturbances. They focus instead on his opposition to the rebellious and increasingly influential bourgeoisie, to the Levellers and the Diggers. Even Michel Foucault, who devotes the utmost attention to the underworld of the excluded, settles for portraying Hobbes as an opponent of the "Levellers and the Diggers," who, "far from agreeing with the parliamentarians that laws should be established [...], say that a war declared in response to that war must free us from all laws."[38] Foucault thus fails to see that a fascinating figure wanders through Hobbes's works, one who does not rise up in the centers of power, like the bourgeois rebel, but instead haunts their edges: the "masterlesse" man.[39] This character appears again and again in *Leviathan* when Hobbes discusses the "restiveness" of the "Subjects" and the "war, of every man against his neighbour" (L[e] 128f., 149).

Hobbes did not invent the "masterlesse" men himself; everyone was talking about them at the time. They owe their name to the fact that they literally had no master, meaning they were not subjects. They were part of a rapidly expanding group of people in the sixteenth and seventeenth centuries who dropped out of the estatist order, out of rural communities and church congregations: beggars, vagabonds, itinerant workers, actors, etc. The masterless men are a symptom of political and economic mobilization and disintegration. They stand at the edge of the centripetal order that Hobbes wants to establish in a centrifugal world. The Spanish humanist Juan Luis Vives notes in his *De subventione pauperum*, written in 1526, after a prolonged stay in England: "They wander about begging [. . .], and no one knows what law or religion they live by."[40] Unlike the powerful burghers, the masterless men do not represent the fight against legal regulations but rather the gulf between law and lawlessness. The "masterlesse" are living proof that the central political order creates its own boundaries. They are a real counterpart to Hobbes's theoretical man of nature, and they remain excluded from participation in the social contract. Many of these masterless men lived in what were known as the "Liberties of London" outside the city walls, in the "suburbs of the urban world, forming an underworld officially recognized as lawless."[41] They are therefore also precursors to the excluded groups of our day who bang on the walls of the state order, try to surmount them, or remain stuck outside in a political nowhere.

Hobbes's rich collection of troublemakers is strikingly modern. We can take any of his characters and find their descendants among us today. What is alarming, however, is that they are all driven by a characteristic with which Hobbes has absolutely no problem: the pursuit of their self-interest. Clearly none of these egocentric troublemakers are going to be impelled – as Hobbes imagines – to become socially acceptable of their own volition. Before summarizing my critique of Hobbes's image of the troublemaker, I want to address one special and particularly notable aspect of it: regardless of where we look, all we see are *men*. This naturally applies in a special way to the *puer robustus* himself, who rebels against the power of the state not as a person but as a "man" with a "childish disposition." How should we interpret Hobbes's one-sidedness? This question of gender theory cannot be ignored, either here or in later chapters.

The simplest answer to the question is that, in Hobbes's time, the political sphere was occupied solely by men, regardless of whether they held power or rebelled against it. Women could certainly be outsiders, too, but they were not taken seriously as troublemakers. Rebellion therefore appears to be a purely male – or, as Freud would later say, Oedipal – undertaking, and the political power grappling with these troublemakers is also coded as male. This is the entire premise of *De patriarcha*, a work by Hobbes's contemporary Robert Filmer (they were both born in 1588), in which the state order is defined as paternal rule.[42] Interestingly,

Hobbes himself devises a different scenario – in terms of both state power and the troublemaker.

By releasing people from all communal bonds and radically conceiving of them as individuals focused solely on their own interests, Hobbes pushes all familial and emotional relationships into the background. This is why he even interprets devotion as a "contract"[43] and applies the contractual agreement between individuals to the sphere of the family. He explains that the rule of the father or mother (both are plausible in his mind!) is based on the "Childs Consent, either expresse, or by other sufficient arguments declared" (L[e] 139).[44] Since he describes the individual as a gender-neutral contractual partner, the sovereign to whom the individual submits must also, strictly speaking, be genderless. Filmer's "father" never stands a chance in Hobbes's work.

Sticking with the clichés that dominate historical representations of gender, we can go a step further and say that Hobbes's sovereign is not just neutral but actually *bisexual*. In the sovereign's punitive role, he is paternal-male, but as the authority who keeps domestic peace, she is maternal-female. The subjects who submit to this dual rule do so based on mature, rational insight, but it causes them to fall back into the role of the child – no longer wild now, of course, but obedient. One could also say that these subjects are *asexual*. It is all the more striking, therefore, that the troublemaker who resists infantilization is depicted by Hobbes as a man. This may have something to do with the fact that his inherent robustness or strength is stereotypically considered to be the privilege of men.

As I see it, the problem with Hobbes's political philosophy is not that he tailors it to men, but that his conception of humanity – and of the troublemaker – is restricted to the *individual*. If this individual is denoted as male, then he is a rather unusual man, as he can be neither father nor son. As an alternative to this absurd consequence, we might draw a more daring conclusion. If the Leviathan is actually both male *and* female, then we can imagine the opponents of the Leviathan to be both male *and* female. The *puer robustus* will, however, have to wait a long time – until Hans Kelsen – before he discovers his female side.

The blindness to gender theory exhibited by Hobbes (and many later interpreters of the *puer robustus*) is fairly dismal. But this is not what compels me to distance myself from Hobbes's theory of the troublemaker. The main weakness of his theory lies in the individualism he attributes to his troublemakers, as already mentioned several times before. They all raise their voices and presume to decide for themselves what is good for them. They first set up their own world and then they set themselves against it. Hobbes links the discord they sow to a simple fact: "the tongue of man is a trumpet of warre, and sedition" (C[l] 133; C[e] 88). Every troublemaker, regardless of type, wreaks havoc first and foremost

28

by means of language. "The ailment of politics is first the ailment of words."[45] Hobbes says that troublemakers act idiotically (as fools), seek refuge in dreams (as epileptics and madmen), descend into their own underworld (as poor men), or create their own realm (as rich men). From the perspective of the state power that tries to control all of these troublemakers, their behavior can be summed up in one short acronym: the troublemaker is AWOL, absent without leave, just like a soldier who leaves his unit without permission.

Hobbes employs a killer argument here in the truest sense of the phrase. He claims that people are doomed unless they join a political order that can end the war of words with a command from above. Only this, according to Hobbes, can create agreement and unity. The various "trumpets of sedition" are silenced by the state, whose monopoly on violence is, first and foremost, the authority to define "the meaning of good or bad." This "Draconian solution"[46] is the real "Hobbesian howler."[47] It is the assumption that, in the absence of orders from on high, people will speak only for themselves.

Appiah's argument can be expanded with a play on words that he himself did not devise, but which appeals to him very much.[48] Appiah speaks of a "Hobbesian howler," meaning a mistake or blunder. But a puppy that has been left on its own can also be a "howler." Hobbes acts as though someone using the "trumpet" of their voice will only make sounds interpreted by others as a declaration of war. But neither a trumpeting human nor a howling puppy are on a total ego trip; they can and want to be understood – if only someone were there to hear them. Hobbes's mistake is that he does not really listen to the "howler" or his human counterpart, he simply dictates a new melody, a march from on high. A close relative[49] of the *puer robustus* – Caliban from Shakespeare's *Tempest* – seems to have poked fun at Hobbes's scenario much earlier:

Miranda: Abhorred slave,
Which any print of goodness wilt not take,
Being capable of all ill; I pitied thee,
Took pains to make thee speak, taught thee each hour
One thing or other. When thou didst not, savage,
Know thine own meaning, but wouldst gabble like
A thing most brutish, I endowed thy purposes
With words that made them known [. . .]
Caliban: You taught me language, and my profit on't
Is I know how to curse. The red plague rid you
For learning me your language.[50]

Hobbes's analysis is incorrect above all in that the problem it tackles does not even exist. The troublemaker does not confront the state as a lone speaker; he does not take on the state from a social void. He may roam the edges of the political order, but he still moves within a web of relationships, no matter how porous and hastily formed. In the war of words, no one acts alone.

Hobbes's linguistic-philosophical critique of the troublemaker has a fatal socio-philosophical implication: if everyone spoke only their own words, then their *only option* really would be to obstinately champion their self-interest. They could not conceive or be capable of doing anything else. Mind you, my objection to Hobbes does not start with the question of whether (all? some?) people (only? mainly?) champion their self-interest. As is evident in the impact of Hobbes's theory, which stretches all the way to the concept of *homo oeconomicus*, such people certainly do exist. My real complaint is that Hobbes incorrectly *claims* that people speak only a private language so that he can *demand* that the state prohibit this private language and rob people of their own voice. Hobbes tries to artificially increase the people's willingness to submit by making them believe that, if they do not, they will hopelessly talk and look past one other. The individualistic isolation he peddles fits perfectly with an authoritarian political order. Alexis de Tocqueville made this fantastically clear:

> Despotism, which, by its nature, is fearful, sees in the isolation of men the most certain guarantee of its own duration, and it ordinarily puts all its efforts into isolating them. There is no vice of the human heart that pleases it as much as egoism: a despot easily pardons the governed for not loving him, provided that they do not love each other. [...] Those who claim to unite their efforts in order to create common prosperity, he calls unruly and restless spirits [*esprits turbulents et inquiets*]; and, changing the natural meaning of words, he calls good citizens those who withdraw narrowly into themselves. (DIA 3, 887; O 2, 616)

More recent critics of Hobbes take the same line as Tocqueville but strangely ignore his groundwork. Rancière, for example, writes of Hobbes's "frivolity" in "initially breaking down the people into individuals," and Esposito criticizes the "drastic elimination of every kind of social bond."[51] Their opposition is not to Hobbes alone but to contract theory as a whole, and their objections were anticipated by a long line of prominent writers, including David Hume, Georg Wilhelm Friedrich Hegel, John Stuart Mill, Karl Marx, Friedrich Nietzsche, Émile Durkheim, Max Weber and John Dewey.[52] I agree with their criticism in principle.

Political contract theory – especially that of Hobbes – can be credited with acknowledging that people are threshold creatures instead of assuming they are members of an order from the outset. But it paints a false picture of the scope available to people on the margins and their ability to join orders and leave them again at will. Instead of tracing the transitions and upheavals on this threshold, contract theory places starting blocks there, as it were, which are reserved for individualistic decision-makers. These individuals are expected to leap into the political order, assent to it, and thus guarantee its legitimacy. But the accord demanded by this order is discordant. For one thing, a political order can never claim to have the assent of everyone affected by it, and for another, it can only invoke an assent that is granted subject to individual benefit considerations and must therefore remain halfhearted. For Hobbes, the troublemaker's pattern of behavior is limited to refusing any form of assent. Because he clings to his self-interest, he can be neither an eccentric dissenter who transcends himself nor the nomocentric pioneer of a different order.

Looking at Hobbes, I feel that *this* egocentric troublemaker holds no appeal for me, but I also do not want to belong to *this* state that declares war on him. I am compelled to move beyond Hobbes. But before giving in to this compulsion, I want to learn everything I can from him. In the next section, therefore, I will use Hobbes to argue against Hobbes, and I will change the scene. Instead of lingering on the margins where Hobbes wages his defensive battle against the troublemaker, I will make my way to the center of his system, to the heart of the Leviathan. We might expect to find only obedient subjects there who can tell us nothing about the troublemaker. We would be mistaken!

4. Author–actor–audience theory:
The eccentric troublemaker in the belly of the Leviathan

Carl Schmitt doffs his hat to the

> unprecedented achievement of having at least outwardly dammed a sea of unbridled, blinkered egoism and the basest instincts and rendered them harmless, and forcing even the influential villain at least into hypocrisy [. . .] [and] bringing these wildly divergent interests into an order that one can count on with some certainty to function regularly.[53]

Schmitt describes this "achievement" here – in his early work *The Value of the State and the Importance of the Individual* from 1914 – without attributing it to Hobbes. In later years he would develop an attitude toward Hobbes that vacillated between admiration and disappointment. Schmitt views Hobbes as someone who strove for "order" but did not know how to safeguard it with the Leviathan, "that *Mortall God*" (L[e] 120). In 1936–7 he referred to the Hobbesian state as a "machine whose 'mortality' is based on the fact that it will one day be crushed

31

by civil war or rebellion."[54] Ultimately, Schmitt wrote, Hobbes was not capable of handling the "wildly divergent interests" (see above) of his troublemakers.

Hobbes's state is indeed fragile – but not only because it is under attack by the egoists reviled by Schmitt. I am leaving them behind for now and moving into the inner world of the Leviathan, where I will mingle with the subjects who are supposed to be an intact counterimage to the rebels. A fine, barely visible crack runs through this counterimage, and I want to poke at it before Hobbes's model falls to pieces. We will see that even the loyal subject harbors an inner troublemaker, though it is one who differs drastically from the egocentric troublemaker. Aside from sedition, the venom of which is a mixture of self-interest and want of reason, Hobbes inadvertently creates the conditions for a different, political form of disturbance. I want to familiarize myself with this before I leave Hobbes behind. I want to *immerse* myself in his political order and find out how to move *beyond* it.

To this end, I will return to the threshold on the edge of the political order, the original scene of the contract's formation. The contract that brings an end to the (in)famous war of all against all must be concluded by individuals. They have to force themselves to do so through a bottom-up process. "Sovereignty is always shaped from below," Foucault writes about Hobbes.[55] If Hobbes does not want morality to degenerate into "coercion" in the Nietzschean sense, he absolutely requires a willingness from below that leads to connection and commitment.

Even if I submit to the power of the peacekeeping state, a slight feeling of restlessness may linger in the back of my mind.[56] My lurking distrust of others keeps me on guard, but I also remain "on guard against [myself]" (Nietzsche, NCW 5, 24 [*Dawn*]); I am suspicious of the *puer robustus* I carry within me, who is just waiting to lash out. And yet, as a citizen and subject, I am generally obedient – and this *does* something to me. Alongside my distrust of others and myself, there is a systemic trust that I place in the state.

This could be expressed in a somewhat unwieldy way by saying that, as a person loyal to the state, I reject the attitude of the man of nature who is captive to his own interests and completely absorbed in his own *presence*. I think of things beyond myself and place myself in a framework that gives me stability and protects me from the *puer robustus* inside myself and others. One could say that the state stands for *the best in me*; with its set of rules, it is the pure form of that which I represent only in impure form. I do not dwell in my own *presence*, I stand by the sovereign as the *representative* of an ordered life, which is also my life.

I mentioned presence and representatives as a way of stealing in to the very heart of Hobbes's political theory. It is, at its core, a *theory of representation*, of representative power. People transcend the constraints of their own presence, they pull together beyond their plurality of interests in order to relate to something greater, something that stands for what they cannot be on their own. They authorize the sovereign to act in their name and turn their desire for order and peace into a reality. According to Hobbes, the representative relationship between the individual and the state sovereign consists of the "author" or initiator granting his or her "authority" to an "actor" or representative (L[e] 112).

Hobbes's thoughts on representation, authors and actors are worthy of much attention – and they have received it. It is particularly interesting that the concept of representation is found not just in political theory but also in aesthetics. Hobbes's use of the terms "author" and "actor" moves politics into the realm of theater. F. R. Ankersmit, Michael Bristol, Victoria Kahn, Hanna F. Pitkin, Christopher Pye, Quentin Skinner, and his student Mónica Brito Vieira have all shown how fruitful it can be to compare these two forms of representation.[57] In fact, Hobbes is not just aware of the theatrical dimension of politics, he actually embraces it:

> *Persona* in latine signifies the *disguise*, or *outward appearance* of a man, counterfeited on the Stage, and sometimes more particularly [...] a Mask [...]. And from the Stage, hath been translated to any Representer of speech and action, as well in Tribunalls, as Theaters. So that a *Person*, is the same that an *Actor* is, both on the Stage and in common Conversation [...]; and he that acteth another, is said to beare his Person, or act in his name. (L[e] 112)

If we want to explain the author–actor relationship in a different context, it is helpful to look to economics and its much-discussed principal–agent theory.[58] The principal is the client (such as a shareholder) who assigns to the agent (such as a CEO) the responsibility of controlling an organization. Principal–agent theorists have dedicated a tremendous amount of attention to the dynamics behind this relationship. The principal can be disappointed or even deceived by the agent, but the agent can also surpass the principal's expectations. Many other scenarios are possible as well. The power relationship between the entities is the result of complicated negotiations. The first impression here – that there is a clear hierarchy between the principal who assigns responsibility and the agent who accepts it – is deceiving. Although the agent is formally subordinate to the principal, he is granted an authority that enables him to take the controls himself. He knows the ropes and has them in hand. (This recalls the power shift from the "lord" to the "bondsman" in Hegel's dialectic, in which the inaction of the lord and the work of the bondsman also play an important role; PS 115ff.)

Reading Hobbes's model in light of principal–agent theory, it is immediately clear that the power shift from principal to agent is especially drastic in this case. The Leviathan is granted authority not by a single principal but by "many Authors," by a "Multitude of men" who consent to the formation of the contract (L[e] 114). As an actor,[59] the Leviathan represents a multitude made up of principals in the form of individuals with fragmented voting rights. It shines in its role as the supra-individual champion of peace. The mandate it receives from the principals is of a very special type: the Leviathan is supposed to govern their own lives. Hobbes's political model resembles a scenario in which minority shareholders instruct a CEO to tell them what they may or may not do. The bottom-up approach that starts with the formation of the contract therefore ends in a top-down strategy: "The state is, in fact, nothing but the institutionalization of our readiness to look at ourselves from the top down."[60] After the individuals have each performed the act of authorization that establishes the Leviathan, the Leviathan turns the tables and transforms the individuals themselves. They cease to live their lives unconnected from one another. The "multitude" disappears once the people have projected themselves onto their representative. This is when they finally become "*One* Person" (L[e] 114). Hobbes writes: "This is more than Consent, or Concord; it is a reall Unitie of them all, in one and the same Person [. . .]. This done, the Multitude so united in one Person, is called a COMMON-WEALTH, in latine CIVITAS" (L[e] 120).[61]

Unity is created because every single author instructs the state, as their representative, to issue orders which "bindeth" them and to which they are "subjecteth" (L[e] 112). The "author" thus becomes the "subject" (L[e] 121). The subject is expected to listen to what the state says, which is why I suggest referring to Hobbes's approach as an author–actor–audience theory. The individuals are not just authors, and they do not just authorize a representative – they are also addressees, recipients, listeners.

At the start of this section, I said there was a fine crack running through Hobbes's model of the state, one that was worth exploring. As I am on the lookout for troublemakers, I am less interested in the role of the state itself, although a splendid debate could be had regarding its mandate as an actor. Instead, I want to find the fault line within individuals that reveals their internal unrest. To this end, I have set my sights on the author or principal on the one hand, and on the subject or audience on the other – in each case with the intention of contributing to the *emancipation* of these characters and positioning them against the Leviathan as political troublemakers.

I have already quoted Hobbes's definition of the "person" as an "actor" and recalled that, for Hobbes, the state functions as an "actor" for the people. In order for individuals to move beyond their own presence and allow themselves to be represented, one simple prerequisite must be fulfilled: these individuals must be familiar with the doubling of author and actor. Christopher Pye argues that the "'Feigned person' of the sovereign" invented by Hobbes is only "capable of fully embodying any individual in the state because each individual is already a self-impersonator [. . .]."[62] Samantha Frost essentially says the same thing (without mentioning Pye): "It is clear that one must be a 'Person' oneself before one can authorize another to act on one's behalf: an individual must be seen as able 'to Act, or to Represent himselfe' before another can 'beare his Person.'"[63]

Hobbes is indifferent to this two-step strategy highlighted by Pye and Frost; in the same breath, he says that a person can represent his or her own "words and actions" or those of another (L[e] 112). But this precise sequence is definitive; only when individuals are able to represent *themselves* can they understand and endorse the suggestion that they be represented by someone else. The fact that the author must be an actor himself helps us identify him as a troublemaker in the belly of the Leviathan.

Samantha Frost provides an interesting, though incomplete, explanation of how the individual puts his author–actor relationship into practice. On the one side, she notes the existence of the "dissimulating maverick" who fakes obedience but behaves seditiously. On the other side, she describes those who simply play along and act "as if" they were peaceful citizens, without having a sinister hidden agenda or any strong convictions whatsoever. The first character – who corresponds to the egocentric troublemaker in my categorization – must be opposed, according to Frost. The second character embodies what Frost defines as a positive form of "feigned self-presentation," which becomes a fundamental element of the political order.[64] In accordance with this, people stabilize their cooperation by continually asserting and affirming that they are playing the role of peaceable citizens. This is analogous to a theater performance in which the actors take each other seriously and, by doing so, convince the audience that something like an intact world is being created on the stage. Anyone who presents themselves as being peaceable can ultimately be represented by the peacekeeping Leviathan. This should make it possible for individual and political representation to fit together.

But this is where things grind to a halt. The dangerous point for Hobbes is found at the seam between author and actor, principle and agent. There is much more to this relationship than Samantha Frost can encompass with her observations about dissimulation and faking. I want to look more closely at this relationship in order to formulate a critique of Hobbes's idiosyncratic use of the theater metaphor and ultimately to *emancipate the author*.

When I represent a person as an actor, then I can be someone *other* than who I really am. I can *play* a different person. This requires the ability to understand that person's experiences, feelings, and intentions. This ability is nothing other than a powerful veto of the notion that I am constrained by self-interest. As an author, I can pursue the aim of placing myself in someone else's shoes as an actor. When I present myself as an actor, I do (or he does) *what I want*. But what I want is *not to be myself at all*. In terms of subject and social theory, this means that I am receptive to other forms of life; I am capable of appropriating what is alien to me and of alienating myself from my singularity.[65] (Diderot will make productive use of this idea of transgression; see p. 104.) Subject and social theory opens up a unique approach to politics. The affirmation of otherness that takes place in theatrical play leads to the acknowledgment of difference and diversity, but also to the creation of community. When real particularity is surmounted, the enacted role or virtual form of life becomes a projection screen, an opportunity for identification that is open to all. It functions as a kind of meeting place that brings people together. This results in attunement or coordination between everyone involved.

If we hold this scenario up to Hobbes's theatrical interpretation of politics, we can see that Hobbes drives a wedge between the author and actor, triggering a crisis of authorship. Hobbes believes the author has a single act to perform: he must give a mandate to the Leviathan. In the wake of this, the author is transformed into "the passion of another's action" and sees how the representative "becomes the actor of deeds that one owns."[66] The sovereign has power of authority to ensure peace and security, and he writes his own script for this major undertaking. He is an agent who puts the principal in the uncomfortable position of having to look on passively after delegating authority and "transfer[ing] agency."[67] What this suppresses and prohibits is the productive or creative moment in the transition from author to actor. It is in this transition that forms of life are invented, experienced and put to the test; people immerse themselves in them and expose themselves to them. In more abstract terms, this exercise applies not only to forms of life but also to rules and orders of life, or to the "social imaginary."[68] The author can only make use of this creative leeway if he or she can access and influence the actor.

Political theory takes this fact into account. In a representative democracy, there are procedures that grant leeway to representatives beyond their imperative mandate, but that also hold them accountable and expose them to the formation of political will from below. In accordance with this, the actor (as a political representative) cannot not be identical to the author, because otherwise he would only stew in his own juices and remove the thorn of self-distance from his life. And yet, the actor is not placed at an insurmountable distance from the author, as is the case in Hobbes's work. Representation involves an interplay of near and far in which the difference between author and actor is negotiable. The actor transcends the little life of the author without trampling all over him.

This interplay of near and far is *destroyed* by Hobbes – and this is one of the main complaints leveled against him by Spinoza.[69] Hobbes makes the sovereign unassailable as the "Judge" of all "Opinions and Doctrines" (L[e] 125). The fact that he places certain limits on the sovereign changes nothing about this. There is, of course, one situation in which Hobbes's actor forfeits power: if the state fails in its obligation to "protect" its subjects (L[e] 153), then resistance is allowed.[70] But this special situation certainly does not prove that Hobbes helps the author come into his own in the representation game. This is not a celebration of the productive tension between author and actor but rather its death knell. If the sovereign fails, this sets the seal on the end of representation as such; the state is then "dissolved" and the people return to a state of nature (cf. L[e] 231). The only alternatives offered by Hobbes are order or anarchy.

Hobbes keeps the author and actor separated; he wants something to be acted out for the author, but he does not let the author act himself. Behind the sovereign's monopolization of the actor role there is a battle against the individual as an actor. Hobbes invites the enemy into the house by using his theater model and (thankfully!) introducing an author–actor character whose dangers he immediately wants to mitigate. An actor can conjure up different forms of life, play through conflicts, explore potential courses of action, and link this rehearsed behavior to claims of transferability or generalizability. The individual, who is author and actor alike, can abandon the grand role play in which the sovereign appears as the sole actor. All of this is intolerable to Hobbes.

The multiplicity of actors is not just a theoretical problem for Hobbes, it is an acute practical political problem. The actor is a real opponent, and he belongs to a group of troublemakers who are a particular thorn in Hobbes's side: the "masterlesse."[71] Strictly speaking, the actor is not just a member of this group; in his pure version, he represents the form of life this group has claimed as its own. The loss of social classification among the "masterlesse" corresponds to the theatrical distance from rehearsed forms of life. Just as the "masterlesse" individual evolves from an outsider into a pioneer of a new social mobility, the actor wanders from the edge of society into the middle of it. This dynamic was apparent in England in the early modern period:

The public playhouses were born [...] at a time when traditional hierarchies were breaking down [...]. Like a plague [...], theatricality subjected the city. [...] It infected the body politic. [...] Beyond mere entertainment or diversion, the re-presentation and disguise of theatricality suggested a potential social fluidity, a recreation of the self, that extended beyond the playing space of the scaffold.[72]

One could also say that this author–actor is characterized by a "special way of being, which we have called eccentric."[73] He is nothing other than an *eccentric troublemaker*. Hobbes can cope with his egocentric counterpart; he grabs him by his self-interest and tries to bring him to his senses. But Hobbes falls apart when it comes to the eccentric troublemaker. This character transcends himself, inclines toward others, experiments with change, breaks the rules. He is capable of meddling in politics and mixing it up. Hobbes cannot ostracize him as a madman, nor can he co-opt him as a subject. This eccentric troublemaker will be depicted by Diderot as a *puer robustus* who garners a good deal of sympathy.

The rise of the eccentric troublemaker reflects the history of the emancipation of the author, who defends his creative leeway as an actor. He does not want to be represented solely by an all-powerful state player. However, it is possible to launch an attack on the sovereign from another flank as well, starting not with the author but rather with the audience, who is forced to listen to the orders from above. This attack promises little success at first glance because the audience seems condemned to play a subservient role. But a second look casts the scene in a different light, because the audience itself experiences a surprising emancipation – one which Hobbes enables and opposes at the same time.

The author–actor–audience triad outlined here has been explored by Victoria Kahn using the concepts of author, actor, and subject. In her outstanding essay "Hamlet or Hecuba" she writes:

> The political subject is someone who has consented to the divorce between the author and the agent, between himself and his representative. [. . .] In theatrical terms, the subject has consented to be a member of the audience and to watch – as if on a stage – the sovereign play or counterfeit his actions. [. . .] The noncorrespondence of agent and author is the source of the sovereign's power to decide.[74]

In Hobbes's model, the individual abdicates his authorship, transfers power to the state that represents him, and turns himself into a spectator or listener. One reader of Hobbes was deeply disturbed by the distinction between the representative state and the subservient spectator: Carl Schmitt. His discomfort stems from the fact that the spectator in a theater is placed at a distance from the action, which leaves him with a certain degree of autonomy. For this reason, Schmitt wants to contain and reframe the Hobbesian parallel between politics and theater. He argues that Hobbes favors the wrong kind of theater, one in which affiliation and allegiance are lost. To counter this, he evokes the old idea that the world itself is a stage, because this makes it possible to place everyone on the "platform" as fellow players: "The play was still part of life."[75] We might well ask whether Schmitt places far too much faith in the metaphor of the world as a stage. In any case, he contrasts this closed world with a situation in which the stage has assumed an independent existence as an aesthetic world in itself. Only then do the spectators "separate the reality of [their] present existence from the theatre play." Indirectness creeps into their reaction to what is happening on stage. They have "no cause and no task" now and so merely "gratify [their] aesthetic interest in the play." Perhaps they are moved, but the emotions and events they observe from a distance are actually "of no concern to them at all."[76]

If this aesthetic distance disturbs Schmitt, he clearly must take issue with Hobbes, who allows for such distance in the relationship between actor and author, state and subject. I will return later to Schmitt's attempt to overcome this distance in a total state. But what interests me right now is the question of how he exploits his reservations toward Hobbes's theatrical model of politics.

Schmitt thinks he has a strong ally in his dissociation from Hobbes: namely, Hamlet. Victoria Kahn bluntly says that, for Schmitt, Hamlet is "the anti-Hobbes."[77] But she shows that Schmitt is wrong to appropriate Hamlet, and that the attitude Shakespeare ascribes to his protagonist actually contributes to the *emancipation of the spectator* and can therefore be used against Hobbes (not to mention Schmitt). In this emancipation – as in the emancipation of the author – we once again find the outlines of an eccentric troublemaker.

Hamlet's long soliloquy at the end of Act 2 prompts Schmitt to brand him an opponent of theatrical frivolity. In this soliloquy, Hamlet is indignant that an actor could "force his soul" to strong sensations through mere "fiction" and "conceit." His eyes fill with tears, his voice breaks – "and all for nothing!"[78] According to Schmitt, Hamlet resists this inclination and "makes use of this discovery to hurl violent reproaches at himself, to reflect upon his own condition and to urge himself to action."[79]

But Schmitt's interpretation is "undermined" by Hamlet himself.[80] Shakespeare's protagonist does not move in the closed dramatic world of "historical presence and actuality" (not representation!) or in the "serious reality of the active human" to which Schmitt assigns him.[81] Hamlet is not at all averse to "the very cunning of the scene."[82] In fact, as an active agent, he decides to stage a dramatization himself – a play – as a way of accusing Claudius of his crime. Quoting Kahn once again: "It is theatrical or aesthetic form which allows for action that is not merely a repetition of the historically given."[83]

It is beyond the scope of Kahn's essay to ask how these aesthetic opportunities for action play out in the political relationship between actor and audience. But the answer is obvious: Hobbes *de facto* creates a gap between the actor and audience, a space of free play that the spectator can use – ultimately against Hobbes himself. We are familiar with this space from the theater. Spectators can be glued to what is happening on stage, they can whisper comments to their seatmates, they can be bored, they can fall asleep. They can also make sense of what they are seeing *in their own way*. And this is how the *spectator is emancipated*.[84]

Moving from theater to politics, the spectator becomes an entity with more in his repertoire than blind obedience. It is precisely because the subject becomes a *spectator* that his room to maneuver grows. Hobbes creates the conditions for this dynamic, but he tries to neutralize it at the same time by noting that the spectator or listener remains passive and is capable of doing nothing more than receiving instructions from above. But theatrical politics does offer spectators opportunities for action. They can, in their own *presence*, choose to follow the *representation* that is presented or merely proposed to them – or not. Recipients are not limited to merely absorbing and reproducing. Inside the spectator–subject there is a kind of *sleeper*, a hidden dissenter – the same eccentric troublemaker hiding in the emancipated author.

The Leviathan of the state maintains tense relations with the troublemaker – but not only because it has to fend him off at its margins, which are populated by unreasonable malcontents and madmen. Alongside the egocentric troublemaker identified by Hobbes, there is an eccentric troublemaker growing up in the belly of the Leviathan, one whom Hobbes naturally wants nothing to do with. Hobbes's great achievement lies in having made him *conceivable* nonetheless. Later on – particularly when we turn to Diderot and Tocqueville – we will find out whether and how this troublemaker has mastered the art of living.

5. The *puer robustus* of Horace – a model for Hobbes?

The contemporaries of Hobbes's *puer robustus*, that "strong and sturdy boy," include all of the other characters who, like the masterless men, roam the edges of English society. Among them are the "sturdie vacabundes" who, following a decree of 1547, were branded with the letter "V."[85] Around 1600, Sir John Popham complained about the rise of the "sturdy rogue and beggar."[86] From the same period, we have an anecdote about a "sturdy boy" who defends himself against a beating by a schoolmaster.[87] A "sturdy rebel" also searches for his place in Shakespeare's *King Henry VI* – not at the margins, however, but on the throne itself. And in *Troilus and Cressida*, a "rude son" wants to kill his father and make the world his "universal prey."[88] Many other examples could be listed here.[89]

Although he is a child of the modern age, the *puer robustus* has older ancestors. Every history has a pre-history, and every word has a history. But the pivotal word here is not the English version of the "strong and sturdy boy" but rather the Latin original: *puer robustus*.

The term *puer robustus* is not so odd and idiosyncratic that one could clearly trace its history back to a single source before Hobbes, before its grand entrance onto the stage of political philosophy. But it is also not so unremarkable and ordinary that its tracks are completely lost in the wealth of language. The *puer robustus* had a life before Hobbes.

Horace was Hobbes's favorite poet; Quentin Skinner said this, and he should know.[90] He identifies the many traces of Horace's poems and epistles in Hobbes's writing, but neither he nor other learned commentators[91] note that the *puer robustus* makes an appearance in Horace's work as well – in a context that is certainly not irrelevant to Hobbes's concerns. Admittedly, "*puer robustus*" is not identified as a quotation in Hobbes's work. We will never know whether he came up with the term on his own or was motivated by some external impetus – that is, whether Horace's *puer robustus* was listed in Hobbes's mental vocabulary book. In any case, we find a fellow in Horace's writing who is *called* the same thing but *is* actually different from his much younger namesake. His difference shines a distant light onto the stage that will be erected for the *puer robustus* in the modern age.

One of Horace's most famous odes starts as follows:

Angustam amice pauperiem pati
robustus acri militia puer
condiscat.

I want to quote two different translations before looking more closely at this verse that introduces the *puer robustus*: "Let youth, toughened by a soldier's training / Learn to bear hardship gladly." – "The boy must be toughened by hard campaigning and learn / happily to endure the restrictions of poverty."[92] It is not this verse (the start of Ode III.2) but rather the thirteenth stanza of the ode that has become famous – perhaps "all too famous."[93] The stanza relates back to the start of the ode in a way that will have to be decoded:

dulce et decorum est pro patria mori.

Dying for one's fatherland is lauded as a sweet and honorable act. The question of who looks this death in the eye and how he has been prepared to do so takes us back to the start of the poem, where we find the toughened "youth" or "boy." This is not a boy who is strong by nature, as is the case with Hobbes; his robustness is the result of military drill and training. Nonetheless, this *puer robustus* moves closer to his Hobbesian

41

namesake in his devotion to dangerous adventure and desire to lead a life under the open sky ("vitam[...] sub divo et trepidis agat / in rebus").[94] Just like Hobbes, Horace finds the combination of strength and foolishness to be worrying: "Force without wisdom falls by its own weight."[95]

The more or less well-trained youth who puts his life on the line has two potential ends in store for him: the winner's podium to which he can ascend after his glorious deeds, or the gravestone that will pay tribute to his heroic death. But Horace himself strikes a note that does not fit with the hymn to a hero's death. Correspondingly, there is more to the relationship between Horace and Hobbes than the contrast between Horace wanting to toughen the boy for war and Hobbes wanting to domesticate the toughened boy.

Horace has something in mind other than the sweet, heroic death of the strong boy. This becomes clear later on in Ode III.2, when the celebration of the youthful hero is retrospectively put in its place. A different life ideal is held up in contrast: *virtus*, a "manliness" characterized by responsibility and prudence. This mature adult is a counterimage to the *puer robustus*. Mediating between these two characters is the *puer senex*, a figure who represented the ideal combination of youthfulness and maturity in the ancient world.[96] (An Italian cultural critic inverted this figure when he described Silvio Berlusconi as a childish old man, an "eroticized *puer senex*"; one could also call him an egocentric *puer robustus*.[97])

In Ode III.2, the *puer robustus* quarrels with the virtuous citizen and, ultimately, leaves the field in defeat. In the preceding Ode III.1, we meet a third character whose life plan deviates from that of both the *puer robustus* and the virtuous citizen. Horace co-opts this character by referring to him as "I." Instead of seeking glory or accolades, instead of hoarding economic or symbolic capital, this "I" follows the "country people" who deal serenely with their external circumstances and the vicissitudes of nature. Ode III.1 ends with two questions:

> Why should I raise a lofty entrance hall
> in a new style with doorposts for all to envy?
> Why should I give up my Sabine valley
> for riches which bring more labour?[98]

Horace strikes a tone here that is clearly at odds with the heroism of the young man. In the spirit of Epicurus, he prefers a life whose joys are largely independent of external goods. (In his reinterpretation of the *puer robustus*, Rousseau describes a very similar ideal.) Horace views external goods not as a relief but as a burden. Possessing "riches" means having to defend them against external attack, an effort that causes "fear" – in the form of "Black Care" – to worm its way into this life. Glory, possessions, and fear – these key concepts in Hobbes's anthropology are preemptively held at a distance by Horace.

The *puer robustus* is therefore sandwiched between the mature "man" who follows hard on his heels (or stands on his toes) in the ode, and by the "I" of the preceding ode who only "wants enough and no more" ("desideran[s] quod satis est"). The celebration for the *puer robustus* who dies a hero's death is not called off, but it is framed by an alternative program. The way in which Horace weights and evaluates the different voices that ring out in his odes is a matter of fierce debate among his interpreters.[99] I do not want to decide this interpretational dispute, but either way it should be noted that Horace does not extol the youth's heroic death quite as martially as the young Bertolt Brecht bemoaned – or as the Nazi interpreters of Horace applauded.[100]

As mentioned, Horace's *puer robustus* is presented not as the dangerous counterfigure to the obedient subject, but as an apprentice who practices obedience and yet remains slightly cocky. If the *puer robustus* of Horace seems more assimilated than that of Hobbes, the exact opposite must be said of Horace's "I." He does not present himself as a fully integrated citizen but instead – as we have seen – nurtures his virtue on the edge of the political order. By casting doubt on dependency and obedience, the "I" himself becomes the predecessor to the *puer robustus* as a modern troublemaker.

Is it sweet to die for one's country? Other things may be sweet as well:

Dulce est desipere in loco.
A little foolishness is sometimes sweet.[101]

Horace incites his readers to vacillate between the sweetness of dying for their fatherland and the sweetness of folly. This *desipere* is a positive version of the *insipiens* who appears in Hobbes's work as a "Fool." Overall, we can embrace Horace as a great experimenter with forms of life, since foolishness (*desipere*) is at odds with the desire for insight and knowledge (*sapere*) to which Horace also gives pride of place in a human's life. *Sapere aude* – "Dare to be wise!" This motto famously also comes from Horace, and it found its way into the history of philosophy through Kant's treatise on enlightenment: "Have courage to make use of your *own* understanding!"[102] Horace clearly has a quite a lot up his poetic sleeve. He speaks of the sweet death for one's fatherland while revealing just how bitter this death actually is. He delights in levity but also values profundity and calls upon readers to make use of their own reason.

In 1780, the heyday of the German Enlightenment, Christoph Martin Wieland took two lines from Horace and threw them into a melting pot. Combining "Dulce et decorum est pro patria mori" and "Dulce est desipere in loco," Wieland created a third, exceedingly provocative sentence: "Dulce est pro patria – *desipere*." What does this mean? It is sweet to produce nonsense for one's fatherland![103] The fatherland itself is suddenly revealed to be a place not for heroic death but for nonsense. It is hard to imagine anything more insolent. I admit that Horace is far removed from the political discussion of the *puer robustus*, and none of the authors in the following sections make reference to him. But with Wieland's help, he becomes a guarantor for the modern troublemaker. Horace not only positions the death-defying youth alongside Hobbes's self-interested rebel, he relaxes institutional structures, plays with different life plans, and thus encourages those who want to explore the many lives of the *puer robustus*.

── II. ──

THE *PUER ROBUSTUS* AS A
GOOD MAN

Jean-Jacques Rousseau

1. The power and morality of the savage

Rousseau reads Hobbes and gets upset. He believes the history of human socialization as recounted by Hobbes both starts and ends in the wrong way. Rousseau thinks the state of nature beyond which, according to Hobbes, people are supposed to progress is a distorted image that essentially drags the man of nature through the mud, and that Hobbes's state is based on a contract that annuls the very liberty that makes someone a person in the first place. Since Rousseau has a different view of the tension between nature and society than Hobbes, he also takes exception to Hobbes's *puer robustus*. This fellow is a remnant of a natural state which, in Rousseau's opinion, is not at all what Hobbes imagines it to be. As an undisciplined outsider, a counterpart to a disciplinary power, the *puer robustus* seems just as dubious to Rousseau as this power itself. Rousseau tries to topple Hobbes's "horrible system" (CWR 11, 62; OC 3, 610), but he almost seems a bit dotty about the *puer robustus* himself, because Rousseau quickly pulls him from the house destined for demolition. Rousseau saves him by reinterpreting him. His reception of Hobbes is the first of many pieces of evidence pointing to the fact that the protagonist of this book is irrepressible and has more life in him than is dreamt of in our philosophy. Rousseau rehabilitates the *puer robustus* as a good savage, as I want to show in this section (section 1). He then answers the question of how this character is transformed into a good citizen (section 2). In the end, we will have to see whether this transformation is successful and how Rousseau's political order comes to terms with the troublemaker (section 3).

The *puer robustus* is mentioned by Rousseau in two places. He makes an appearance in the *Second Discourse* of 1755, which deals with the "Origin and Foundations of Inequality Among Men," as well as in *Emile*

45

from 1762. Rousseau works hard to create a new image for the *puer robustus*, and he is guided in this by the questions of power, morality, and history.

"The first crisis of modernity occurred in the thought of Jean-Jacques Rousseau."[1] Rousseau's trailblazing *Second Discourse* proves that even this nascent modernity exhibits a special virtue: the audacious ability to criticize itself. Rousseau picks a quarrel with his own era. As a thinker, he is a spoilsport, a troublemaker or "trouble-fête"[2] of a special kind; as a man, he falls out with his best friends. But this chapter is not about Rousseau himself, it is about the troublemaker he introduces in his philosophy.

Like Hobbes, Rousseau contrasts civil society with a "state of nature" which – again like Hobbes – he views more as a fictional or counterfactual countermodel than a reality tied to a specific historical epoch. Both thinkers want to review the track record of the state order by comparing it with the state of nature. The formal structure of both social theories is, therefore, identical, but there are glaring differences when it comes to the evaluation of these different states.

It would be wrong to say that Rousseau simply reverses the signs in this equation, turning the state of nature from a negative into a positive. The famous cliché of the "retour à la nature" is misleading. Voltaire's[3] taunt that Rousseau would have people walking on all fours again does not so much hit the mark as reveal Voltaire himself to be a stuffy know-it-all. The side door leading to the center of Rousseau's political philosophy can be found under the sign labeled *puer robustus*.

In the *Second Discourse*, Rousseau writes: "A wicked man is, he [Hobbes] says, a sturdy Child." Instead of directly taking exception to this theory, Rousseau curtly adds: "It remains to be seen whether Savage Man is a sturdy Child" (DI 151; OC 3, 153). With his savage man, he latches on to the sturdy child, as it were – and then grapples with the question of whether this savage man, this *puer robustus*, is wicked.

Before explaining Rousseau's answer to this question (it's *no*, by the way), I must look at the new scene he sets for the *puer robustus*. By differentiating between a natural and a civil state, Rousseau, like Hobbes, moves to the *threshold* of the political order. Hobbes needs this margin in order to precipitate a decision-making situation which legitimizes the state order from below. One could say that, for Hobbes, individuals are the *latchkey children of the state*. They are left to their own devices on the threshold, they have *no one* on whom they can rely or with whom they belong, but they carry a key that opens the door to their home: the interior of the Leviathan. By endowing individuals with self-interest and believing them to be threatened by a lack of reason, Hobbes allows for the possibility that they will throw away their key and become troublemakers. But under these conditions, they can only be evil, egocentric troublemakers.

Rousseau's seemingly harmless parenthesis – "It remains to be seen whether Savage Man is a sturdy Child" – is nothing less than an attempt to undermine Hobbes's contrast between the evil *puer robustus* and the good subject. In response to his question, he provides an intricate answer based on fundamental considerations about the man of nature and the nature of man. Rousseau moves to the threshold of society in order to gain methodological elbow room and a critical distance to the state order. He pauses there and remains *cautious* inasmuch as he examines what he sees before him. This enables him to show that people in a state of nature are not nearly as simple as Hobbes would like to believe.

I said earlier that Rousseau, like Hobbes, uses the state of nature as a methodological fiction, meaning that he does not claim people lived in this state at a particular point in time before taking the step forward into society. In this respect, the historical process through which society is formed remains in a state of suspension. It must be said, however, that this interpretation is only half right, because Rousseau plays both cards in the *Second Discourse*. On the one hand, he says a state of nature "perhaps never did exist" and he leaves aside "the uncertain testimonies of History," but, on the other hand, he talks constantly about what came first and what came later, etc., and he even manages to identify an "epoch" in history that "must have been the happiest" (DI 125, 142, 167; OC 3, 123, 144, 171).

I do not blame Rousseau for swaying back and forth between methodological fiction and historical genesis. We can take both together and say that his method consists of *methodologically perpetuating this genesis* and turning the question of whether or how one joins a political order into the Achilles heel of political theory. The state of nature cannot be dated, it is not a thing of the past and not even really a *state*; instead, it represents the flexibility that people display as they grow into society – a trait that *also*, but certainly not *exclusively*, relates to adolescence. There is a puzzling sentence in *Emile*: "Prevent the adolescent's becoming a man until the moment when nothing remains for him to do to become one" (E 232; OC 4, 518f.). What this means is that we should postpone the moment in which one's "spirits" are fixed in the process of "becoming a man."

Because Rousseau's argument is also (at least partially) based on contract theory, he, like Hobbes, must try to bring about the establishment of a political order through a clear cut, a resolution, or a feat of strength. But this does not prevent him from paying heed to the historical genesis that is part of the state-building process. In the *Social Contract* he writes: "For Nations as for men there is a time of maturity for which one has to wait before subjecting them to laws" (SC 73; OC 3, 386). In a handwritten addendum, he clarifies that by "maturity" he does not actually mean adulthood, but rather "youth" as opposed to "childhood" (SC 300; OC 3, 1466). According to Rousseau, this state of youth is characterized by the fact that one is still mentally flexible and not trapped in "prejudices" (SC 72; OC 3, 385). To be mature means to keep moving. There is a certain appreciation apparent here for the *puer robustus* and the threshold creature.

Rousseau's answer to the question of "whether Savage Man is a sturdy Child" is designed as an alternative to Hobbes. He takes Hobbes's conclusion that the strong child is evil, redirects it to the savage man, and then comes to the savage's defense. In doing so, he also pushes back against Hobbes's explanation for this wickedness, according to which a lack of reason alone is enough to lead people morally astray and induce them to cause political mischief. Rousseau offers three theses in response to the question of whether the savage man is evil, but unfortunately they do *not* fit together. In his first thesis he denies the moral capacity of the savage, and in the following two he defends it – though in very different ways.

The first thesis. According to Rousseau, savages "can do each other much violence when there is some advantage in it for them, without ever offending one another." A savage views "his kind" as merely "Animals of another species," which is why "acts of pillage" are considered "natural occurrences" (DI 218; OC 3, 219). Rousseau says that "Savages are not wicked precisely because they do not know what it is to be good; for it is neither the growth of enlightenment nor the curb of the Law" – this brings to mind Hobbes's duo of "reason" and "education" – "that keep them from evil-doing" (DI 151f.; OC 3, 154; cf. C[l] 81; C[e] 34).

Rousseau awkwardly acts as though he were opposing Hobbes by placing savages in a world on this side of good and evil. "Above all, let us not conclude with Hobbes that because he has no idea of goodness man is naturally wicked, that he is vicious because he does not know virtue" (DI 151; OC 3, 153). Rousseau is wrong. Hobbes, too, believes that those who do not even *know* virtue are in a state on this side of good and evil. He simply disputes that the man of nature can blithely appeal to his ignorance of virtue. In any case, Rousseau's first thesis is: *The savage man is neither good nor evil.*

It is fairly obvious that Rousseau does not want to leave it at that, however. More precisely, he says: "It would at first seem that men in that state [. . .] could be neither good nor wicked" (DI 150; OC 3, 152). Indifference to morality is therefore not the last that Rousseau has to say about savages. It is their very "indifferen[ce] to good and evil" – as he writes in his "Letter to Beaumont" of 1763 – that Rousseau views as evidence that "man is a naturally good being."[4] But Rousseau is *exaggerating*

48

here. It makes no sense to collapse the difference between the "amoral" person and the "good" one.[5] It is not enough to position the savage on this side of good and evil in order to claim that he is good. Moral indifference is not a virtue. For this reason, Rousseau proposes two more theses to go along with – and against – his first one, which actively push the savage in the direction of good. They require more detailed explanation – not least because, as I hinted earlier, they are incompatible.

The second thesis. In addition to the blindness to reason and morality that is shared by the savage and the child, Rousseau identifies another characteristic of the savage that Hobbes makes no mention of at all. I just quoted part of a passage from the *Second Discourse* in which Rousseau states that "enlightenment" and "the curb of the Law" have not yet taken effect on the savage. It is now time to complete this passage, as Rousseau goes on to say that the savage man is prevented from doing evil by "the calm of the passions" (DI 152; OC 3, 154). This piece of information offers an entirely new argument in defense of the savage.

Rousseau accuses Hobbes of having "improperly included in Savage man's care for his preservation the need to satisfy a multitude of passions" (DI 151; OC 3, 153f.). He rejects Hobbes's argument that the savage is overwhelmed by passions, claiming that this is unhistorical. It is only the civilized man who experiences an expansion of his economy of desire, in which expectations and disappointments escalate. If we accept Rousseau's definition that misery is a result of experiencing "privation," then the civilized man must suffer more "misery" than the savage (DI 150; OC 3, 152). The latter, according to Rousseau, does not experience the expansion of needs and emancipation of desires that run the risk of frustration in the first place. "His Desires do not exceed his Physical needs," which he can satisfy – after a fashion (DI 142; OC 3, 143). The savage has absolutely no sense of the escalation of desires that leads to disappointment, competition, and conflicts between people.[6] As a consequence of his limited horizon, he has very few opportunities to even come into contact with other people and interact with them. Rousseau's image of natural life is based not on some sort of primordial community, like a primal horde, but rather on a person who maintains no "relations" (*correspondance*) with others, is largely left to his own devices, and remains "alone" (DI 145, 139; OC 3, 146, 140). The *second thesis* in defense of the savage is, therefore: *The savage is good because he harms no one.* While the first thesis placed the savage somewhere on this side of good and evil, his position has now been shifted firmly to the side of good.

I want to explain Rousseau's second thesis in more detail by connecting his portrait of the savage to the *puer robustus*. His question of "whether Savage Man is a sturdy Child" first leads him into a discussion of the savage, while the "sturdy Child" retreats into the background. But

Rousseau does not skirt around the *puer robustus*; he brings him into his discussion at a key point. In order to do this logically, however, Rousseau must first clarify what he means by "sturdy" or "strong" and then address the issue of the "boy" or "child."

I will initially stick with the question of what "sturdy" actually means by quoting a longer passage from *Emile*:

> When it is said that man is weak, what is meant? This word *weak* indicates a relation, a relation obtaining within the being to which one applies it. He whose strength surpasses his needs, be he an insect or a worm, is a strong being. He whose needs surpass his strength, be he an elephant or a lion, be he a conqueror or a hero, be he a god, is a weak being. [...] Man is very strong when he is contented with being what he is; he is very weak when he wants to raise himself above humanity. Therefore, do not fancy that in extending your faculties you extend your strength. On the contrary, you diminish your strength if your pride is extended farther than it. (E 81; OC 4, 305)

The concept of *robustus* presented here is a balance between "desires" and "faculties," between "power and will" (E 80; OC 4, 303f.).[7] It is not about increasing one's faculties but about maintaining the proper relationship between one's own talents and the situation in which one finds oneself. It is important to remember this definition of strength or power, which I think is extraordinarily clever. It is, in fact, absurd to refer to someone as strong or powerful solely because they possess great physical strength. If they set goals that surpass their strength, they will prove to be weak. Without taking these goals into account, any talk of individual power remains abstract: "Never will your real authority go farther than your real faculties. [...] [I]t follows that the first of all goods is not authority but freedom. The truly free man wants only what he can do and does what he pleases. That is my fundamental maxim" (E 84; OC 4, 309).

Rousseau's definition of the "strong" man is much more complex than that found in Hobbes's characterization of the *puer robustus*. Hobbes defines strength as the ability to satisfy the passions that trouble man. According to Hobbes, these passions are infinite: "Man is famished even by future hunger."[8] Rousseau is not interested in a power that can increase indefinitely but ultimately prove to be a weakness; he is interested in a *proportionate* power that the savage possesses because his desires and his reality do not diverge. This is by no means merely an arrangement on a low level, where – as Schiller says – "desire [is] simple, its satisfaction easy" (CWS 8, 423). Balance is conceivable on a higher level as well:

> In what, then, consists human wisdom or the road of true happiness? It is not precisely in diminishing our desires, for if they were beneath

our power, a part of our faculties would remain idle, and we would not enjoy our whole being. (E 80; OC 4, 304)[9]

Regardless of the level on which it might materialize, the balance sought by Rousseau has a moral quality – and this links his definition of individual power to his theory of the good savage. The savage is good because he lives – because he *can* live – self-sufficiently. Of course, this is where his definition of good runs into a problem: namely, the question of how it can hold true when people no longer live their lives with "no relations" with anyone else, but instead come together in a political order. This question brings us to the limits of Rousseau's second thesis, but I want to briefly remain within the boundaries that delineate it.

Because Rousseau occupies a space on the threshold of order, he hews not to the political power of the sovereign but to the power of the individual, who is suspected – even by those who came before Hobbes – of being immoral. But Rousseau *forbids* himself to take such a derogatory stance and instead insists on a positive concept of power in the sense of authority over one's own life, an authority upon which he places moral value. This is not merely an individual morality that allows people to live their lives as they please; it is a much more demanding social morality that prevents people from *harming* anyone else as they live their lives.

If we approach the *puer robustus* with Rousseau's definition of individual power in mind, there is only one thing we can do: *welcome him*. It is precisely because this child has grown strong that he is in a position to achieve the balance described above. Conversely, in contrast to the strong child, the weak child must be vulnerable. He will only become good if he is able to match his desires to his reality. This actually goes against Rousseau's first thesis, according to which the child is still on this side of good and evil. In *Emile*, Rousseau makes explicit reference to Hobbes's *puer robustus*: "But when Hobbes called the wicked man a robust child, he said something absolutely contradictory. All wickedness comes from weakness. The child is wicked only because he is weak. Make him strong; he will be good" (E 67; OC 4 288). Those who view Rousseau as a precursor to the Romantic valorization of childhood must acknowledge that his portrait of the child is anything but rosy. Until the child has grown strong, he has much more of a tendency toward evil. It is only "in growing, one gains strength, becomes less restless, less fidgety [. . .]. Soul and body find, so to speak, an equilibrium" (E 68; OC 4, 289).

The child already has needs and articulates desires, but he does not yet have the means to fulfill them. It may seem like a favor to provide him ample opportunity to satisfy his desires, but it is actually a disservice. It places him in an artificially enhanced reality, in which the "enormous machines for happiness or pleasure"[10] run at full speed. It almost seems as though Rousseau were familiar with today's children of affluence, those modern machines of desire, when he talks about a child who behaves like a "despot" and walks all over his parents. In this context, he even manages to find words of praise for Hobbes:

> Do you know the surest means of making your child miserable? It is to accustom him to getting everything [. . .]. It is a disposition natural to man to regard everything in his power as his. In this sense Hobbes's principle is true up to a certain point. Multiply not only our desires but the means of satisfying them, and each will make himself the master of everything. Hence, the child who has only to want in order to get believes himself to be the owner of the universe; [. . .] without ever being grateful for helpfulness, he is indignant at every opposition. How could I conceive that a child thus dominated by anger and devoured by the most irascible passions might ever be happy? Happy, he! He is a despot. (E 87; OC 4, 314f., with a – not exact – quote from C[l] 95; C[e] 47f.)

Though Rousseau aligns himself with Hobbes here, it is clear why he, in a very different way to his predecessor, appreciates the *puer robustus*. The *puer robustus* represents the end point of education; he is "good" and leads a "good" life because he is able to strike a balance between desire and reality on his own.[11] He is an adult of the finest sort. In his Corsica text, Rousseau praises "the Swiss" for the fact that "their isolated and simple life made them independent as well as robust" (CWR 11, 135; OC 3, 916). The Swiss are celebrated as a kind of *enfants robustes*.

Whoever has strength of will as described above "would live happily. Consequently he would live as a good man, for what advantage would there be for him in being wicked?" (E 82; OC 4, 306). Incidentally, the connection between goodness and happiness would be picked up again two hundred years later – without direct reference to Rousseau – by Max Horkheimer: "The happy man does not have to turn malicious" – "Joy [. . .] simply makes people better. People who are happy themselves [. . .] are not so evil" (*Critique of Instrumental Reason* 33; HGS 8, 142, 149).[12]

For all of this celebration of inner strength, it must be said that there are limits to the goodness of the autarkic savage in Rousseau's second thesis. In brief, this goodness does not strengthen one's willingness to do good for others, it merely weakens one's willingness to do evil to others. Moreover, this renunciation of ill will only really functions when individuals are on their own and no one crosses them. It would certainly be wrong to claim that such an attitude fulfills all the requirements of moral goodness. The second thesis tells us only that the savage is good *within limits*. But Rousseau has yet another argument up his sleeve in favor of the goodness of the savage.

The third thesis. In his *Second Discourse*, Rousseau writes:

> There is, besides, another Principle which Hobbes did not notice and which [. . .] tempers his ardor for well-being with an innate repugnance to see his kind suffer. I do not believe I need fear any contradiction in granting to man the only Natural virtue which the most extreme Detractor of human virtues was forced to acknowledge. I speak of pity [. . .]. (DI 152; OC 3, 154)[13]

Rousseau's recourse to pity as "natural goodness" (DI 154; OC 3, 156) is also a radical rejection of Hobbes, but in a different way to his description of individual power. In Hobbes's works, good and evil – as one could say (not only) in Rousseau's terms – always come too late. Having argued that men of nature are only interested in what is good or bad *for themselves*, Hobbes makes a last-minute booking, so to speak, whereby the state provides a definition of good that settles the dispute between these self-interests and allows them to be realized within an orderly framework. Hobbes holds fast to this self-interest and derives it from a wide range of motives, intentions, and valuations. The advantage of his theory is that it does not rely on strong assumptions that attribute man's socialization to moral faculties. Rousseau pits himself against Hobbes and makes just such a strong assumption: he turns to pity. More recent critics of Hobbes's isolated view of self-interest can therefore turn to Rousseau – and they do. They draw on a wealth of empirical findings to dismantle the paradigm of *homo oeconomicus*.[14] Conversely, the supporters of this paradigm and defenders of rational choice are forced to criticize Rousseau's recourse to humanity as vague speculation.[15] As I see it, they hold the worse hand.

The savage man thus *brings something with him* when he joins society: pity. Since this sentiment has not yet been affected by competitive relationships, it appears in a purer form in the savage than in civilized man. Rousseau's third thesis is: *The savage man is good because he helps others.* He builds a bridge between solitary life in the forests and a type of socialization in which "mutual needs" are met and "social ties" are formed (DI 100; OC 3, 151). An arc can be drawn here – with certain restrictions[16] – from Rousseau to the more recent theory of recognition. Starting from the margins, from a state of nature, Rousseau wants to pave the way to social and political order and justify his claim "that *justice* and *goodness* are not merely abstract words – pure moral beings formed by the understanding – but are true affections of the soul enlightened by reason, are hence only an ordered development of our primitive affections" (E 235; OC 4, 522f.).

Taking Rousseau's second and third theses together, we can say that two "tendencies" of the savage man strengthen his morality: power and pity. *But they do not fit together.* Goodness thus becomes an ambiguous image. In both theses, Rousseau comes to the conclusion that the savage man is good, but the paths that lead him to this conclusion cannot be walked in parallel. The second thesis operates in the negative: the savage man preserves his goodness and does no harm to others only by remaining in his closed world and *not* establishing relations with anyone else. The third thesis operates in the positive: the savage man demonstrates his goodness by relating to others with a sense of pity. It does not help that Rousseau plays down the conflict between his two theses by restricting pity to the act of ensuring one's own welfare "*with the least possible harm to others*" (DI 154; OC 3, 156). Pity is thus once again reduced to the avoidance of misdeeds, a "repugnance to evil-doing" (ibid.), though there must be more to it than that.

At best, we could try to reconcile the two theses by claiming that they complement one another. In this case, the quiescent power of the savage would cause him to do no evil to others, while pity would lead him to do good for others. This complementary reading sounds appealing, but it remains contradictory. This is because the first (non-evil) attitude is based on a premise from which the second (good) attitude must *depart* if it is to stand a chance. The balance between desire and reality depends entirely on being a loner. But if you never have anything to do with other people, you cannot commiserate with them. Rousseau admits that the development of pity is "all the more energetic" (*plus énergique*) when one "identifies more intimately" (*plus intimement*) with another (DI 153; OC 3, 155). But this is certainly not the case in a state of nature.

Rousseau himself wastes no words on the dilemma into which he stumbles as he attempts to define natural goodness in the *Second Discourse*. But he seems to be bothered by it somehow, because he tries to rectify the situation in other works. To this end, he develops a strategy for a positive definition of pity that can no longer be ascribed to the savage. The concepts that play a prominent role in this endeavor are *reflection* and *relation*. The two concepts are connected.

In the *Second Discourse*, Rousseau declares apodictically that "the state of reflection is a state against Nature" (DI 138; OC 3, 138). At the same time, he says of pity that it "precedes the exercise of all reflection" (DI 152; OC 3, 155). He must assert this in order to maintain the intact, self-contained world of the savage. But Rousseau does not cling to the assumption that pity is *nothing more* than an instinctive reaction without reflection. He probably backs down here because he realizes there is no reasonable way to describe pity without any form of reflexivity.[17] The homologous reaction of compassionate individuals stems from the fact that they *understand* the behavior of others. This is the only way they can empathize or place themselves in someone else's position. And for this to be possible – as Rousseau admits in his *Essay on the Origin of Languages*

– they require the power of imagination, which is, in turn, a genuine component of human reflexivity. As if thumbing his nose at everyone who considers him the spiritual father of the Counter-Enlightenment,[18] Rousseau goes so far as to declare pity to be the offshoot of "lumiéres" (sic!) – i.e., enlightenment:

> Social affections develop in us only with our enlightenment [*lumiéres*]. Pity, although natural to the heart of man, would remain eternally inactive without the imagination that puts it into play. [. . .] He who has never reflected [*réfléchi*] cannot be clement, or just, or pitying – no more than he can be wicked and vindictive. He who imagines nothing [*n'imagine rien*] feels only himself; he is alone in the midst of mankind. (CWR 7, 306; OC 5, 395f.)

Rousseau thus insists that pity can be found even in the lone man of nature, conceding only that it remains "inactive" within him. But instead of reading pity into the isolated life of the savage, we should follow through to the conclusion that Rousseau actually reaches: that reflexivity, as the intellectual ability to discern relationships between objects, is systematically connected to the ability to form relationships between people – and both abilities come together in pity:

> Reflection [*réflexion*] is born of compared ideas, and it is the multiplicity of ideas that leads to their comparison. [. . .] Apply these ideas to the first men, and you will see the reason for their barbarousness. Never having seen anything but what was around them, they did not know even that; they did not know themselves. (CWR 7, 306; OC 5, 396.)[19]

When it comes to relation, too, the older Rousseau goes beyond the position he adopted in his earlier works. In the *Second Discourse*, he had still insisted that the solitary savage was unfamiliar not only with reflection, but also with social relations. Savages were said to live in a "state of things that allowed for almost no relations of any sort between them" (DI 158; OC 3, 161). It thus follows that people can only develop a sense of pity when they move beyond savagery. A few allusions to this can already be found in the *Second Discourse* (DI 167; OC 3, 171), but this conclusion is not drawn explicitly until *Emile*: "Thus, no one becomes sensitive until his imagination is animated and begins to transport him out of himself [*transporter hors de lui*]" (E 223; OC 4, 505f.).

With this late reinterpretation, Rousseau solves the problem he stumbled into with his third thesis. His new definition of pity, which is based on the entanglement of reflection and relation, is convincing, but in terms of his ultimate objective – to ensure goodness – it is also dangerous. By solving one problem – how can a savage be compassionate? – Rousseau lands himself in the middle of two new ones.

Because Rousseau places people in a realm of social relations that makes pity possible in the first place, *first* he must take into account that all kinds of interaction will come into play here that could result in the hindrance or "stifling" of the development of pity (DI 171; OC 3, 176). *Second*, he loses the autarky of the savage that was a bulwark against evil. Meanwhile, it remains unclear how this autarky, to which he continues to cling in *Emile*, can be maintained under social conditions. As we have just heard, the individual is "transported" into the social relations the savage had avoided, so he must "study himself in his relations" (E 214; OC 4, 493). When Rousseau finally crosses the threshold to society, he picks up a hot potato, namely, the question of how communal social life and the political order can be organized so that power and morality are reconciled.

How does the *puer robustus* fare when the problem shifts in this way? Hobbes and the other theorists who refer to the *puer robustus* may debate whether he is good or evil, but they all agree that he is a troublemaker. Rousseau is the *exception* here. In his work, we find a *puer robustus* who *is at peace with himself, harms no one and only does good for others*. He is the figure to turn to when it comes to the question of "how to go about preventing [men] from becoming [evil]."[20] Rousseau uniquely transforms the stage whose movements I am tracing in this book. He presents the *puer robustus* as someone who, in full consciousness of this goodness, actually wants to *stop* being a troublemaker. Regardless of what was done in Rousseau's name during the French Revolution, we must consider the great guarantor of revolution to actually be an opponent of it.[21] The situation that is "the best for man," Rousseau writes in his *Second Discourse*, is the one "least subject to revolutions" (DI 167; OC 3, 171). Like Hobbes, Rousseau is a lover of peace, but unlike Hobbes, he views the *puer robustus* as the messenger of peace and not its adversary. His peace is both an inner peace that prevents him from even dreaming of harming others, and an external peace that is the source of his commiseration with others.

But when the *puer robustus* joins society, he finds he cannot simply give free rein to his peacefulness. Instead, this step leads to a slap in the face. As Rousseau sees it, society is in a desolate state, and it reveals itself to be the true arena for the war of all against all, which Hobbes attributes to the state of nature: "Hobbes's error is therefore not to have established the state of war among men who are independent and have become sociable but to have assumed this state to be natural to the species [. . .]."[22] This society is dominated by "the most frightful disorder," the "most horrible state of war," in which "the usurpations of the rich, the Banditry of the Poor, the unbridled passions of all" run rampant (DI 171f.; OC 3, 176). Rousseau describes this condition most dramatically in an obscure, rarely cited passage in one of his fragments about war:

I see unfortunate peoples groaning under an iron yoke, the human race crushed by a handful of oppressors, a starving crowd [. . .] whose blood and tears the rich drink in peace [. . .]. I hear a frightful noise; what tumult! what cries! [. . .] I see a theater of murders. (CWR 11, 61; OC 3, 609)

In this society, oppressors who pervert the law for their own purposes "can punish as a rebel anyone who dares to defend it" while "all the enterprises" of the oppressors "become easy."[23] It is precisely because he is a messenger of peace that the *puer robustus* is forced to fight. He thus becomes a troublemaker after all – against his will! – and must tangle with this so-called order. However, he is very different to the egocentric troublemaker with whom Hobbes grappled. Rousseau frees the *puer robustus* from Hobbes's clutches, gives him a new twist and, in doing so, nudges the revolving stage on which he appears. His *puer robustus* is not a blinkered egoist but rather a herald, an advocate for a different kind of order – in other words, a *nomocentric troublemaker*. He is a threshold creature who uses the leeway available to him not for individual obstructionism but for political upheaval. He dares to anticipate a different order, one which he tries to understand and for which he fights – an order beyond oppression and obstructionism.

Rousseau certainly does not claim that one could be rid of the egocentric troublemaker once and for all. "Indeed each individual may, as a man, have a particular will contrary to or different from the general will he has as a Citizen" (SC 52; OC 3, 363). But this should not be the only model of life open to individuals. According to Rousseau, they can savor a wide moral repertoire that extends beyond their self-interest. The repertoire he proposes ranges from pity to justice and from natural self-sufficiency through self-love to self-legislation. What must be described now is the path to this new order, along which natural man is transformed into a citizen. It remains to be seen whether or how his great achievements – autarky and pity – will be preserved or advanced.

2. The transformation of the *puer robustus* into a citizen

The faculties that the natural man brings with him are the pity that allows him to transcend himself and the strength or power that keeps him grounded within himself. In Rousseau's works, these faculties are an exciting, suspenseful double act, and they cross one another when they are each put to the test. This makes Rousseau's effort to get from the good (pitying and autarkic) *puer robustus* to a good political order particularly difficult – especially since he does not admit to this internal tension. I now want to find out how pity fares when a political order is established, and then see what happens to the autarkic power of the individual in the social contract.

Rousseau declares that "man is by his nature sociable, or at least made to become so" (E 290; OC 4, 600). The "man of nature" joins society instead of remaining a "savage" in "the depths of the woods" (E 255; OC 4, 551). His embrace of others is driven by pity, which is a sentiment that he already brings with him, not one that develops through social life. But the natural man is endowed with more than just pity. The "sentiments" that are "suitable to our nature" according to Rousseau – such as pity – include "the love of self, the fear of pain, the horror of death, the desire of well-being" (E 290; OC 4, 600). With these natural sentiments, people relate to others but also to themselves. Rousseau expresses this doubling as a distinction between "relative" and "absolute" sentiments (E 215, 222; OC 4, 494, 505). Considering what was said in the preceding section, it is only logical for pity to fall on the side of relative sentiment. Pity with no relation to anything else would be inherently contradictory.

Pity is "the first relative sentiment [*sentiment relatif*] which touches the human heart according to the order of nature" (E 222; OC 4, 505f.). It develops in relationships based on *homology*. Those who pity others do not become entirely identical to the sufferers; as Rousseau knows, they are all too familiar with "the pleasure of not suffering" like others (E 221; OC 4, 504). But when people commiserate – or empathize in general – they place themselves in another person's situation and, in a certain respect, become the *same* as her or him: "It is not in ourselves, it is in him that we suffer" (E 223; OC 4, 505f.). Pity does not just presuppose an experience of "equality that is real and indestructible" (E 236; OC 4, 524), it makes this experience accessible in the first place. The savage believes himself to be alone in the world, and it is only when he feels pity that he even *notices* there are others to whom he is related and allows his actions to be guided by this "identification" (DI 153; OC 3, 155): "Not only do we want to be happy; we also wish for the happiness of others" (E 288; OC 4, 597).

The most prominent counterpart to pity, a natural relative sentiment, is "self-love" (*amour de soi*), a natural absolute sentiment (E 215; OC 4, 494). Self-love causes individuals to be entirely consumed with themselves, so this sentiment is associated with autarky as a type of inner harmony. But pity is also associated with another form of love. This is not "absolute love" or "self-love" but rather a "relative" or "comparative love."[24] Rousseau calls this "*amour-propre*" (DI 218; OC 3, 219). Pity thus finds itself in difficult company. It is jammed between self-love, which is an absolute sentiment but which, like pity, is natural, and *amour-propre*, which, like pity, is relational, but which is also "factitious, and born in society" (ibid.).

Unlike self-love, *amour-propre* enables people to see themselves in relation to others: "Self-love, which regards only ourselves, is contented when our true needs are satisfied. But *amour-propre*, which makes comparisons, is never content" and instead results in "emulation, jealousy, envy" (E 92, 213; OC 4, 493f.). One then adopts the "habit of measuring oneself against others and moving outside oneself."[25] When the "desire to be in the first position" becomes apparent in someone, it means this person's "love of self" has turned into "*amour-propre*" (E 235; OC 4, 523). Rousseau suggests that love of self and *amour-propre* are passions in opposition to one another, as one is "natural and good" and the other "artificial and bad."[26] But he admits that *amour-propre*, which is subject to social dynamics, can yield not only negative but also positive results in the course of the "perfectibility" (*perfectibilité*) of the individual. He therefore vacillates between the verdict that *amour-propre* is bad and the verdict that it is flexible or ambivalent.[27] Ultimately, he pulls both verdicts together by saying that it is ambivalent, but it leans toward evil:

> It is [...] this frenzy to achieve distinction [*fureur de se distinguer*] which almost always keeps us outside ourselves, that we owe what is best and what is worst among men, our virtues and our vices, our Sciences and our errors, our Conquerors and our Philosophers, that is to say a multitude of bad things for a small number of good things. (DI 184; OC 3, 189)

What happens now with the socialization instigated by the individual? It is determined by a *battle*. Pity or "benevolence" (*bienveillance*) runs up against "amour-propre," which leads to an "aversion for [...] everything that by being something prevents us from being everything."[28] The equality of pity clashes with the frenzy for distinction, the *fureur de se distinguer*.[29]

Pity enjoys a starting advantage in that it has a solid, natural basis. In its race to catch up, *amour-propre* benefits from the fact that, in the course of growing social differentiation, people find it increasingly difficult to access the pure experience of compassionate homology. Those who are occupied with self-preservation in their natural lives are the same as everyone else. This equality is Rousseau's ideal, and it is the notion behind his famous dictum that Emile will "be neither magistrate nor soldier nor priest" but "will, in the first place, be a man" (E 41f.; OC 4, 252): "Man is the same in all stations" (E 225; OC 4, 509). Once people enter society, however, they are distracted from this equality, according to Rousseau. Then they are tempted to view the poor not as fellow human beings but merely as paupers with whom they have almost nothing in common. "Why are the rich so hard toward the poor? It is because they have no fear of becoming poor" (E 224; OC 4, 507). Their motto is: "Perish if you wish, I am safe" (DI 153; OC 3, 156).

This *reality* of the differences between stations and classes goes hand in hand with the *desire* to differentiate oneself. Hobbes believes he has identified a trait bemoaned by Rousseau: that "all the pleasure, and jollity of the mind, consists in this; even to get some, with whom comparing, it may find somewhat wherein to Tryumph, and Vaunt it self" (C[l] 94; C[e] 46). Someone adopting this attitude will not just be indifferent to the miserable lot of others but will actually welcome it, because it means he will have fewer competitors. As a "relative *I*" (E 243; OC 4, 534), this individual is in a race driven by the fear of being overtaken or the pressure to catch up with his fellow competitors and pass them by. In civil society, people keep their distance from one another and focus on outdoing each other: "They all hardly know each other. How could they love each other? Each thinks only of himself" (E 46; OC 4, 258). Friedrich Schiller follows in Rousseau's wake when he writes:

> Egotism has founded its system in the very bosom of a refined society [...]. The man of the world has his heart contracted by a proud self-complacency, while that of the man of nature often beats in sympathy; and every man seeks for nothing more than to save his wretched property from the general destruction, as it were from some great conflagration. (CWS 8, 44)

This phenomenon has been examined by many different theorists, most of whom make no reference to Rousseau. We need think only of Gabriel de Tarde's analysis of "imitativeness," which is organized "according to the competition or co-operation of [...] desires and wants," or of the "emulative" or "invidious comparison" of Thorstein Veblen, or of the "mimetic desire" of René Girard.[30]

Because pity is a relative sentiment, acting upon it makes it impossible for me simply to steer clear of social entanglements. Not only am I *unable* to return to a time before "the feeling of happiness became relative" (CWR 4, 18; OC 3, 477), I do not *want* to return to it, because social relations are in my nature qua pity, and they contribute to the development of my life. This is also why I do not want to take the bait Rousseau holds out in *The reveries of the solitary walker* – namely, a love of self in which I turn my back on the world: "Everything external is henceforth foreign to me. [...] I am on earth as though on a foreign planet."[31]

What happens if, instead of turning myself into an alien, I remain in this world? My goal must be to overcome the state of disruption and disorder in which the world clearly finds itself. I am someone with a "love of order,"[32] and pity is the only means I have at hand to fight for it. Pity bears the heavy burden of having to enforce equality – the precious gift it carries with it – in a world where the *fureur de se distinguer* has run rampant.[33]

But is pity the right weapon in this fight? Rousseau has the nagging feeling that the *puer robustus*, who takes on the whole world and wants to bring order to disorder, is poorly equipped here. He therefore goes one step further than pity.

If I am driven by pity, then that is what I am: *driven*. I allow myself to be guided by a feeling. Those who feel do not *act* but are instead drawn toward things and people.[34] When Rousseau says "to live is not to breathe; it is to act" (E 42; OC 4, 253), we might add: to live is not just to feel. As someone who feels pity, I stand in the middle of a civil world in which people are in dispute with one another. As someone who feels pity, I cannot grab this world by the horns, I can only prepare myself for a situation in which I am gripped by the suffering of others. I am overwhelmed by the "multitude of objects striking [me]." And the brusque judgment that Rousseau passes on the savage in the woods – that he is too "stupid" to get by in society (E 255; OC 4, 551) – then applies to me, too. "He who in the civil order wants to preserve the primacy of the sentiments of nature does not know what he wants" (E 40; OC 4, 249). This is not to say that I have to relinquish my naturalness – but it is not enough merely to "preserve" it. As Rousseau says in his discourse on economy, "interest and commiseration must in some way be constricted and compressed in order to be activated [*activité*]" (SC 15; OC 3, 254).

When I am subjected to manifold situations in which suffering ambushes me, then "the gentle voice of nature is no longer an infallible guide."[35] I do not want to be bogged down by my commiseration nor paralyzed with emotion for the fate of a single individual. I also want to be immune to "pity for the wicked," as this would be "a very great cruelty to men" (E 253; OC 4, 548). Furthermore, I want not only to shed tears for the suffering of others but actually take action to help them. All of this leads from feelings to decisions and deeds. Reflection and reason should come to the rescue of pity. Their primary achievement, according to Rousseau, is to enforce equality. Equality should not be restricted to the homology between those who suffer and those who feel pity. It must go beyond this individual relationship and extend to others who would not even cross my mind in this blinkered sentiment: "To prevent pity from degenerating into weakness, it must, therefore, be generalized and extended to the whole of mankind. Then one yields to it only insofar as it accords with justice, because of all the virtues justice is the one that contributes most to the common good of men" (E 253; OC 4, 548).

In this quote, Rousseau speaks the word that outdoes pity: "justice." Justice explicitly crystalizes the formal principle of equality that is buried

61

within pity. There is no way for me to understand this generalized equality as long as I indulge in "unjust bias" (E 252; OC 4, 548) in my compassion for others. The more this feeling is generalized, "the more it becomes equitable, and the love of mankind is nothing other than the love of justice" (E 252; OC 4, 547). I am not just part "of another individual" but "part of [my] species" (E 253; OC 4, 548).

The agenda of the pitying man of nature must change if he wants to assert himself in society. I must be able to act – and I must gear my actions toward justice. The extent of the change required here is interpreted differently in *Emile* and the *Social Contract*. As *Emile* deals with the process of becoming a *man*, Rousseau insists here that justice develops from the natural sentiment of pity. People must "feel" this sense of equality or they "will never know it" (E 245; OC 4, 537). But what Rousseau says in *Emile* is not in accord with what he proposes at the same time in the *Social Contract*. Here he deals with *citizens* – fully developed people, in a sense – who experience equality not in their compassion but in their mutual action. Justice is cut off from the sentiment to which it is bound in *Emile*.

In the original draft of the *Social Contract*, Rousseau writes that it is "in the silence of the passions" that a person comes to an understanding "about what man may demand of his fellow man, and about what his fellow man may rightfully demand of him."[36] But if the passions are silent, pity must be silent as well. In accordance with this, the final version of the *Social Contract* speaks of "a most remarkable change in man by substituting justice for instinct in his conduct [. . .] when the voice of duty succeeds physical impulsion and right succeeds appetite" (SC 53; OC 3, 364). People are thus distanced from their nature. Rousseau clings to the equality that he now refers to as "justice," but the experience of pity, which first grants individuals a sense of equality, is cut off from this:

> But where is the man who can thus separate himself from himself and, if care for one's self-preservation is the first precept of nature, can he be forced thus to consider the species in general in order to impose on himself duties whose connection with his own constitution he completely fails to see? [. . .] Moreover; since the art of thus generalizing one's ideas is one of the most difficult and belated exercises of the human understanding, will most men ever be in a position to derive the rules of their conduct from this way of reasoning [. . .]?[37]

The goodness of the citizen is not guided by pity from the outset. Instead, this goodness manifests itself when the citizen becomes a member of an order in which the decision regarding what is just – that is, what is good – is made by equals. The "connectedness" between individuals, upon which the "public good or evil" depends,[38] does not arise naturally but rather through an active alliance. Starting with the *sympathy* of the man of nature, Rousseau ends up not with an arrangement of interests but a *synergy* of concerted actions.[39] (I will come back to this synergy with reference to Schiller, Marx, Freud, Kelsen, and Horkheimer.) Ultimately, the new order should emerge victorious over *amour-propre*, an artificial feeling fixated not on similarity but on difference.

Once this victory has been achieved, then the job of the *puer robustus* is also done. In the *Social Contract* there is no longer any threshold creature who – guided by his internal, natural compass – would take on the status quo. Instead, the *puer robustus* becomes a victim of his own success. With pity, he has paved the way for the equality that now extends beyond him and forces him to become someone else: a citizen. He can only *live* with this transformation if he is able to grow into this new role, as it were, and perfect himself within it. Rousseau naturally wants to make sure that this happens. The pivotal achievement of pity – namely, equality – should expand beyond the narrow borders staked out for it and unfold in a new political order. I join together with others and allow myself to be guided by standards that are set and shared communally.

One could say this step is essential to the political implementation of this sought-after equality. But what happens exactly when someone "separates" himself from pity, as Rousseau says, and "silences" his passions (see above)? This separation is not simply a case of the man of action rising above his feelings. It also results in the creation of an equality among active subjects that excludes all those who are not credited with the same active drive. Rousseau is not talking about random losers here; he has his sights set on a specific group. His approach to the *puer robustus*, like that of Hobbes, must be viewed through the lens of gender theory.

When Rousseau praises the drive of the citizens who come together as equals in the *Social Contract*, he is celebrating nothing other than the shunting aside of a sentiment (pity) that was coded as female in the eighteenth century. Pateman summarizes Rousseau's position thusly: "Women [. . .] cannot develop the morality required in civil society. [. . .] Women lack the capacity to sublimate their passion and are a perpetual source of disorder."[40] Rousseau himself says that, as women do not have their passions under control, they tend to "capriciousness," "infatuation" and "excess," and must therefore "never cease to be subjected either to a man or to the judgments of men" (E 370; OC 4, 710).

Rousseau's shift from pity to justice thus entails a *rejection of passion* which involves the *marginalization of women*. With their pity and the "capriciousness" ascribed to them, women – in Rousseau's critical view – bear a remarkable resemblance to the *puer robustus*. It is already clear from this that the transition from *puer robustus* to citizen is not lossless.

If masculine drive and judgment are toughened and femininity opposed, it essentially means that the promised equality generates inequality. The promised perfection of the *puer robustus*, which turns him into a citizen, is also a mutilation.

I said earlier that when the social contract is introduced, the *puer robustus* is transformed into a different character. Thus far, however, I have described Rousseau's path from nature to political order only in terms of one of the two main characteristics of the natural man: his ability to feel pity. What about the second characteristic: autarky, his authority or power over himself? Here, too, the question arises as to whether or how someone who is a member of a political community can maintain the precious autarky of the *puer robustus*.

Rousseau himself seems skeptical about this. In *Emile* he describes social attachment as "a sign of insufficiency. If each of us had no need of others, he would hardly think of uniting himself with them. Thus from our very infirmity is born our frail happiness [*frêle bonheur*]" (E 221; OC 4, 503). If this interpretation of the birth of community from the spirit of weakness were accurate, there would be no chance for the *puer robustus* to continue living in the state as the compassionate and autarkic creature he was to begin with. Instead of transformation, he would face a loss of power and of himself. But as fascinating as the notion of "fragile happiness"[41] is, it is not Rousseau's last word on the matter.

It is obvious which problem must be solved if the *puer robustus* is to complete his transformation into a citizen. As autarky is nothing other than the *sentiment absolu* of "self-love," the citizen must continue to enjoy the benefit of this self-love or he will not be a legitimate successor to the natural man. Having traced the transformation of pity into justice, I now have to see whether the natural man can assert his second main characteristic – autarky – within the social contract.

If we follow the arguments in the *Second Discourse*, the chances of this are not particularly good. In this essay, Rousseau identifies pity as the sole driver of socialization; autarky is nothing more than the inner peace or "self-love" of the isolated man (DI 154; OC 3, 156). In his later work *Rousseau, Judge of Jean-Jacques*, however, he breaks with this earlier assumption. Here, self-love is credited with being a social skill, and it is considered "very natural that a person who loves himself should seek to extend his being and his enjoyments and to appropriate for himself through attachment what he feels should be a good thing for him."[42] In *Emile*, too, self-love and sociality are said to go hand in hand:

Justice is inseparable from goodness. Now, goodness is the necessary effect of a power without limit and of the self-love essential to every being aware of itself. The existence of Him who is omnipotent is, so to speak, coextensive with the existence of the beings. [*Celui qui peut tout étend pour ainsi dire son existence avec celle des êtres.*] (E 282; OC 4, 588.)

This love of self should not be "moderat[ed]" (DI 154; OC 3, 156), as Rousseau says in the *Second Discourse*; on the contrary, it should be expanded and strengthened. It thus becomes a kind of love of all. If I want to put this love of all into practice, however, it does not mean that I should engage in some kind of universalized charity and devote myself even to those most far-removed and foreign to me. Instead, I must cleave to myself and, as a subject, love only myself as an object. Only this will ensure the closure that is crucial to autarky in the sense of total authority over oneself.

This is asking quite a lot, but Rousseau is utterly committed to this requirement, as can be seen in his somewhat enigmatic comment that one's existence "is, so to speak, coextensive with the existence of the beings." Through this total identification that turns me into an all-being, I should be able to pull off the feat of engaging in social intercourse without losing myself. Technically, this means that the *sentiment relatif* must turn into a *sentiment absolu*. If I am to cleave to myself in a collective, my self must grow larger, in a sense, and the *moi relatif* must, through a process of "alienation," become an absolute self or, as Rousseau says, a "*moi commun*" – that is, a shared or "common *self*" (SC 50; OC 3, 361). In other words, Rousseau asks me to accept the idea that *I* am *everyone*. Unlike Hobbes, he does not believe it is the state that represents the "Multitude so united in one Person"; instead, this multitude becomes a unity of its own accord.

How should I conceive of this identity that unites individuals? In a body politic, governance is organized and power is wielded. The identity in question must therefore enable people to appropriate this power while distancing and alienating themselves from their private self. To this end, Rousseau must reject the conventional description of power and subjugation, in which individuals are wedged against one another. The solution cannot be to maintain one's own power by oppressing others – because then both the ruler and the ruled would be trapped in their *moi relatif*. Rulers in particular, according to Rousseau, must continually adapt their "way of acting" to the activities of their subjects, meaning that they are dependent on them (E 83; OC 4, 308): "Whoever is master cannot be free, and to rule is to obey."[43] (This anticipates Diderot's smug criticism of the king, who is forced to heed his entourage.)

To counter the relative heteronomy that plagues both sides of the relationship between lord and vassal, Rousseau must devise a model of absolute autonomy. Only if he succeeds can he uphold his thesis of the identification of the individual with the body politic and the formation of the *moi commun*. And only then can he prevent people from being caught up in relationships marked by conflict: "All institutions which put man in contradiction with himself are worthless" (SC 147; OC 3, 464). Rousseau's solution to this contradiction is as famous as it is simple: relational dependency disappears if I am both sovereign and subject at the same time. "By contracting, so to speak, with himself," each individual becomes part of the group of "Citizens" who are "participants in the sovereign authority" as well as "Subjects" who are "subjected to the laws of the State" (SC 51; OC 3, 362):

> The words subject and sovereign are identical correlatives [*correlations identiques*] whose idea is combined in the single word Citizen. (SC 111; OC 3, 427)

> An act of sovereignty [. . .] is not a convention of the superior with the inferior, but a convention of the body with each one of its members; So long as subjects are subjected only to conventions such as these, they obey no one, but only their own will. (SC 63; OC 3, 374f.)

It is instructive to compare this reading of socialization with the author–actor–audience theory I attributed to Hobbes. Hobbes wanted to establish independence for the actor (i.e., state power as the representative of the people) and decouple him as much as possible from the authorization granted by the author (the people), thus making him the one who commands the audience (also the people). Rousseau wants to establish connections, and even identities, whereas Hobbes insists on differences. Consequently, the people *are* the sovereign for Rousseau: "Sovereignty cannot be represented [. . .]; the will does not admit of being represented [*ne se réprésente point*]" (SC 114; OC 3, 429).[44] Just as the people, in their role as author, also want to become the actor, or their own representative, they oppose the passivity of the audience. When the people submit to the sovereign – to themselves, that is – they are indeed "passive" (SC 51; OC 3, 362), but they are never merely spectators; they have the right to change from spectators into actors. In his *Letter to d'Alembert on the Theater* from 1758, Rousseau writes that people should leave the theater and assemble in a square to put on their own performance: "Let the spectators become an entertainment to themselves; make them actors themselves; do it so that each sees and loves himself in the others so that all will be better united."[45]

Rousseau's countermodel to Hobbes is dichotomous. By conflating author, actor, and audience, he prevents the state power from gaining autonomy. Because Hobbes preserves the difference between author, actor, and audience, he – unlike Rousseau – at least allows for the possibility of disturbance, i.e., that the author and audience could rise up in revolt from their marginalized position. Jean Starobinski accurately characterized Rousseau's image of unity:

> In an imaginative flight he transposes the ideal of the self-sufficient ego into a myth of the self-sufficient community. [. . .] He invents a society yet preserves the essential privileges of solitude, namely, freedom and a sense of independence. [. . .] Conceived as a single organism, all of whose parts complement one another, the community, viewed as a collective ego, works in a self-contained fashion: it never has to turn to the outside world.[46]

Rousseau, the opponent of revolution, must stage a revolution to establish order and unity. Revolution is the means of choice for overcoming the discrepancy that exists between the status quo and the desired end state. Strictly speaking, Rousseau talks about two revolutions. In the political process, "revolutions" precede the establishment of sovereign self-determination (SC 72f.; OC 3, 385), but Rousseau says that a "revolution" also takes place within the "solitary walker" that gives him a "fondness for solitude." According to this, the collective and the individual, the political and the autobiographical, are two sides of the same coin. The *moi commun* and the *promeneur solitaire* are end points of the same process, which leads from relation through association to unification. The political subject comes into the inheritance of the natural man, because the *moi absolu* of self-love lives on in the *moi commun* of the citizen who loves himself and all others. Within this collective, the autarkic power enjoyed by people in a state of nature is preserved. The *solitaire* comes into the inheritance of the natural man, of whom Rousseau says he is "entirely for himself. He is numerical unity, the absolute whole [*l'entier absolu*] which is relative only to itself or its kind" (E 39; OC 4, 249).[47]

Just as the pity of the man of nature is expected to turn into justice without being destroyed in the process, the autarkic power of the man of nature is supposed to be translated into the power of the sovereign without being relinquished. When it comes to power, too, we can say that the *puer robustus* is a victim of his own success; he gives himself up in order to find himself again as a member of the body politic. A transformation occurs in which "humankind [. . .] change[s] its way of being" (SC 49; OC 3, 360):

> Each individual who by himself is a perfect and solitary whole [must be transformed] into part of a larger whole from which that individual would as it were receive his life and his being; [. . .] weakening man's constitution in order to strengthen it. (SC 69; OC 3, 381)

This unity can now lead to a concern for the fate of others that is independent of pity. If someone in my collective is injured, I immediately perceive this to be an injury to myself, or damage to one and the same body (SC 17; OC 3, 256). Thus, the social identity of pity is supplemented and surpassed by the collective identity of the sovereign. The message of justice refined by pity is that everyone else is a person just like me. And the message of the autarkic identity that is transferred to the autonomous collective is that not only are the others *like* me,[48] I *am* actually the others in the *moi commun* and the others are *me*. I am you. You and I are we. We are a single *I*. One could say that Rousseau goes so far as to propose a collective narcissism here.[49] Just as Rousseau's equality has a dark side – the exclusion of "sentiment" and "woman" – so too does the unity of the *moi commun*. The dream of everyone identifying with this great *I* to the extent that they form a single body is actually a nightmare. The little *I*, the individual existence, is steamrolled.

What should we make of this great transformation or conversion, in which pity turns into justice and individual power turns into the power of the state? The *puer robustus* is a troublemaker interfering in a broken world; he is the herald of a new order, and once this has been established, he becomes a citizen, retires, and enjoys the peace with others of his kind. The equality that generates inequality and the unity that buries the *I* do not exactly offer the best prospects. And yet, this order does promise one thing: democracy, in which power and morality are reconciled. It is difficult to know how far to go along with Rousseau. It is handy, therefore, that he himself pauses and barbs the equality and unity he has invoked. In the end, fortunately, he does not leave the troublemaker in the lurch.

3. What does Rousseau's *puer robustus* do after his victory? Democracy and disturbance of the peace

Rousseau's attempt to make the *puer robustus* disappear after his victory is an ambitious venture, because he needs to pull off a double feat. On the one hand, he wants to get from pity to justice, and thus to an equality that holds up in the balance between one and the other. On the other hand, the power of the individual is supposed to be replaced by the sovereignty of the people, and thus by an equality that is conceived of as the unity or identity of one with the other. I encounter others whose rights I take into account in my actions, but I also have others at my side who wield legislative power together with me. As objects they are affected by my actions, and as subjects they are involved in my actions. Sometimes the focus is on the scope of rights, other times on the definition of rights. These two aspects of equality are the secret to Rousseau's democracy –

and to democracy in general. Two circles are drawn: the circle of those who are granted rights and *to whom* such rights apply, and the circle of those who *grant* the rights. For the sake of equality, democracy must try to bring these two circles into alignment. This is – to put it bluntly – *impossible*. Even after a democratic order has been established, it will never be free of trouble.

The first circle will expand and ultimately encompass everyone, because those who claim and exercise rights do so in their capacity as human beings and by virtue of their liberty. Civil rights are thus designed to expand into human rights.[50]

The second circle remains small, because legislation is tied to a collective process that demands actual participation and active cooperation. It is not possible to expand the process of political will-formation to all people.

Of course, one could try to outrun the problem and demand that human rights be guaranteed by a world state; this would have to be a political authority in which everyone was somehow involved. But this would entail just that: running, evading the issue of a discrepancy between limitless human rights and the limitation of legislation. This discrepancy is the paradox of democracy. And this paradox is not specific to Rousseau; it poses a problem for all lovers of democracy.

We know how Rousseau tries to get around the paradox of democracy. He wants to ensure the closure of the legal subject, so he views the expansion of the legal community as a false political move.[51] He thinks cosmopolitanism is *no way to create a state*, so in his treatise on economy and his considerations on Poland, he banks not on the love of one's fellow human beings, but on the love of one's country (SC 15; CWR 11, 174; OC 3, 254f., 966). Rousseau does not consistently maintain this limitation, however. After all, in the original version of the *Social Contract* he writes of a "fundamental and universal law" with which "the particular self" is "spread over the whole" (SC 161; OC 3, 329f.), and he says "there is no one who does not appropriate the word each to himself" (SC 61; OC 3, 373).[52] That little word "each" resists being limited to a selection of people, and it is the favorite pronoun of universalism.

In his moral reflections – in *Emile*, that is – Rousseau does build a bridge from the citizen to the person (meaning that a bridge can also be built from Rousseau to Kant). But in his political philosophy, Rousseau banks on a "whole" that is not actually whole at all but is, in fact, narrowly defined. Rousseau moderates universalism so that he can bring it into being on his own terms. The body politic consists solely of those who actively practice the formation of political will, and the rights they grant themselves apply only to themselves. Rousseau instructs his Corsican friends that "a purely democratic government suits a small town rather than a nation" because then civic participation is possible (CWR 11, 128; OC 3, 907). All the same, he sees democratic potential not only in the city of Geneva, but also in Switzerland, Corsica, and Poland.

In a political order where justice encompasses everyone involved and power is wielded by everyone involved, the troublemaking *puer robustus* should be able to make himself superfluous. As an egocentric troublemaker he is already played out for Rousseau in any case, but as a nomocentric troublemaker, too, he has served his purpose. A high price is paid for this peace. As a theorist of closure, Rousseau is simultaneously a theorist of exclusion; he fortifies the borders that surround his commonwealth and that – as he believes – make it possible to exist in the first place. But the presence of borders always raises the question of whether they will become thresholds that can be crossed. And disturbance inevitably follows.

Although Rousseau's stated goal is to bring about peace, he does not leave the troublemaker entirely in the lurch. Many modern theorists who oppose the tranquilization of politics believe they must therefore also oppose Rousseau. But Rousseau is *irresolute* when it comes to the self-abolition and self-transformation of the troublemaker. This comes as no surprise, since Rousseau himself was and is the uncrowned king of the troublemakers of the eighteenth century. In keeping with this, he also puts forward arguments *against the resignation of the troublemaker.* Even in a democracy, which is the goal of political upheaval, there will still be unrest. We can explore this by looking at the two strands of the political process I have just described: the granting of rights, and participation in legislation.

Harassing fire will come from those who take exception to the fact that they have been denied rights which the members of a body politic have granted to themselves *and* reserve for themselves. From the perspective of the excluded, such rights become false prerogatives; there appears to be an internal contradiction between the establishment of rights based on a person's liberty and the validity of rights that are restricted to the citizens of an exclusive, narrowly defined political pseudo-whole. This argument, which pervades the modern debate about refugees and migrants,[53] is fairly defenseless in the face of the model of democracy to which Rousseau remains loyal.

Although this disturbance harbors massive political challenges, in certain respects it remains restrained or even modest. The issue here, as I said, is about *also* claiming rights that have already been asserted; it is not about co-determining the substance of these rights through individual participation, i.e., having a voice in the formation of political will. This disturbance is not about interfering, as if one wanted to change the recipes being cooked in the kitchen, it is solely about wanting to sit at the same table. So the objection holds that there is a flaw in this kind of external reference to rights. Instead of taking on the role of active subject or participant in legislation, people content themselves with being the object or person affected.

This is not just about the granting of rights, therefore, but also about having a say in formulating those rights. Membership in the common-wealth is flawed not only when someone fails to benefit from a right, but also when they are not involved in the formation of political will. At the heart of a commonwealth we find people who also want to have a *say* or a *voice*. No philosopher is more closely associated with this argument than Jacques Rancière: "Politics exists because those who have no right to be counted as speaking beings make themselves of some account." When those who "have no part" – slaves, proletarians, women, etc. – speak up, they disturb the peace of the body politic, a community of like-minded individuals that enjoys basking in the autarky of the *moi commun*. Rancière thus accuses Rousseau of "the eradication of the part of those who have no part."[54]

Rousseau's desire to ensure the closure of the political order is indirectly apparent in his introduction of a controversial authority who is expected to come to the aid of the people: the "Lawgiver" (*législateur*; SC 68–72; OC 3, 381–4). The lawgiver is a kind of ghostwriter for the people. He is supposed to articulate their intentions and enable them to truly speak with one voice. The patronizing and paternalistic presumption inherent in this figure has been criticized many times. It seems more and more as though Rousseau wants above all to ensure the closure of the body politic, and that he accepts that excluded individuals will wander around on the edges of this intact, immune, homogeneous order. It is on account of this that he was accused of illiberalism early on, and some even claim that he paved the way for the totalitarianism of the twentieth century.[55] He has been both praised (by Carl Schmitt, for example) and criticized (by Roberto Esposito, for example) for the homogeneity of his concept of the people.[56]

But is Rousseau really *only* a theorist of homogeneity? I don't think so. For instance, one could interpret the figure of the "lawgiver" as a symptom of Rousseau's desperation to create closure due to his aware-ness of the fragility of the political order. At the risk of unduly emphasiz-ing this aspect, I want to highlight Rousseau's openness to the crises of democracy – which are always simultaneously opportunities. The closure that he favors is not as homogeneous as one might think. He does love order, but he does not delude himself that it is immune to unrest: "If we want to form a lasting establishment, let us therefore not dream of making it eternal. [...] The body politic, just like the body of a man, begins to die as soon as it is born and carries within itself the causes of its destruction" (SC 109; OC 3, 424).

71

Such destruction ruins the sense of identity that is supposed to exist between the individual and the body politic. It sounds as though Rousseau would regret this, but we can also think of him as a theorist of creative destruction. This becomes clear when we bring the dimension of *history* into play, which joins the tandem of power and morality.

The acid test for Rousseau's democracy is whether people obey the laws only out of "duty" or "interest," or whether they actually feel bound to them through the "internal assent [*assentiment interne*] of their will" (CWR 11, 175; OC 3, 961). But this assent cannot simply be given once and for all, as Hobbes imagined would be the case with submission to the Leviathan. Instead, the citizens – of Poland, in this case – should have a "continuous presence" as their sovereign (CWR 11, 186; OC 3, 975). Their initiative must be continually renewed, because nothing is as old as yesterday's presence. In the original draft of the *Social Contract*, Rousseau says:

> Today's law should not be an act of yesterday's general will, but of today's, and we have engaged ourselves to do not what everyone has willed, but what everyone now wills [. . .]. It follows from this that when the Law speaks in the name of the People, it is in the name of the People at present and not that of former times. Even existing laws only have lasting authority insofar as the People, being free to revoke them, nonetheless does not do so, which proves current consent. (CWR 4, 103; OC 3, 316)[57]

In the final version of the *Social Contract*, too, Rousseau stresses that "it is absurd for the will to shackle itself for the future" (SC 57; cf. CWR 11, 204; OC 3, 368f., cf. 424). Hannah Arendt picked up on this and accused Rousseau of "anticipating the fateful instability and faithlessness of revolutionary governments as well as justifying the old fateful conviction of the nation-state that treaties are binding only so long as they serve the so-called national interest."[58] This is an unusually unfriendly, unfair interpretation, because Rousseau – like Thomas Paine, Thomas Jefferson, and many others after him[59] – is expressing a simple, indisputable point here. The self-commitment of the political subject is tied to the historical process in which the composition of this subject changes and – as Rousseau says in his considerations on Poland – a nation works to "rejuvenate" its constitution (CWR 11, 236; OC 3, 1037). A comment from his fragments on war is relevant here: "The essence of society consists in the activity of its members and [. . .] a State without motion would be only a dead body" (CWR 11, 67f.; OC 3, 605).

A term from the recent discourse in cultural studies fits with what Rousseau has in mind here: *performance*. If the state is to avoid being "dead," it must not be a static institution; it owes much to the acts of self-legislation that have to be continually carried out anew. It *stands* on a foundation that *moves*. One could say that Rousseau "allowed for the incorporation of the Revolution, as it were, into the configuration of the state" – and it was with this theory that Ferdinand Tönnies caused a stir in the twentieth century.[60] One could also say that an "identity in progress" is bestowed upon the political order, a theory that has proven very popular in the discussion of democracy in the early twenty-first century. Rousseau himself brings movement and unrest into the order he wants to establish. The order that Rousseau has in mind is one that disturbs itself. Rousseau not only accepts disturbance, he *wants* disturbance. Democracy is nothing other than a disturbed order, an orderly disturbance. But this means that when Rousseau's *puer robustus* becomes a citizen, he does not give up the traits of the troublemaker. In anticipation of the order of tomorrow, he remains a disturber of the order of today.

Additionally, to ensure the sovereign's performance, it is not enough for citizens to vote every few years and otherwise let others make the decisions for them: "The English people thinks it is free; it is greatly mistaken, it is free only during the election of Members of Parliament; as soon as they are elected, it is enslaved, it is nothing" (SC 114; OC 3, 430). Disturbance through political performance relates not only to the redefinition of the rules of communal life, but also to the identity, composition, and reach of the sovereign, all of which continually change. The issue of who does or does not belong, who will join tomorrow and who will leave, remains open. This applies to more than just a future generation of the citizens' children. In pretentious terms, we could say that the diachronic dynamic of generations is entangled with a diatopic dynamic. New generations from nearby are joined by newcomers from afar, and the only decisive factor is whether they will *participate* as active members of the body politic.

If citizens remain troublemakers, the trouble they cause is of limited intent and effect. Political upheaval becomes suburbanized, as it were. When crisis becomes the characteristic or even hallmark of democracy itself, it shifts to the level of a change in legislation. Because change is tied to juridification, the disturbance is kept within limits. The initiative of individuals is subject to the condition that they always think of the whole right from the outset. Rousseau says that nothing speaks against laws being "revoke[d]," but this must be done with the same formality or "solemnity" (*solemnité*) with which they were established (CWR 11, 204; OC 3, 996). In other words, if citizens want to change something, they must come to a collective agreement. Until such an agreement has been reached, these citizens – their individual will notwithstanding – must adhere to the laws currently in force. They should be willing to do so because they fundamentally endorse the procedure that produced these laws – as the form in which their liberty is realized: "The Citizen consents to all laws, even those passed in spite of him." Those who refuse to formally consent to the legislative process make themselves "foreigners among the Citizens." Their best option then is to leave the "territory" in which this civic participation takes place; otherwise, their continued "residence" will be taken as a profession of their belonging or "consent" (SC 123f.; OC 3, 440).

Rousseau is ambivalent toward the abolition of the troublemaker and his complete transformation into a citizen. The troublemaker is given a considerable amount of elbow room – and yet his potential to cause trouble is conditional and limited. It is tied to the collective performance through which a political order continually reinvents itself. Rousseau has even greater reservations when it comes to disturbance by individuals who reject all ties, take matters into their own hands or laugh up their sleeves. They will always be suspected of pursuing only their own interests. Rousseau sounds almost disappointed in his fragment on war when he acknowledges the inevitable: "It is impossible to make it so that each of them does not have an individual and separate existence" (CWR 11, 68; OC 3, 606).

What Rousseau would most like to do is change horses outright and jump from criticism of the egocentric troublemaker to celebration of the nomocentric one, the founder of a new order. But between the two yawns a gap in which – following the typology of the troublemaker I outlined earlier – the eccentric troublemaker romps around. He does not enjoy the security vaunted in different ways by the egocentric and the nomocentric. Does Rousseau have any time for the eccentric? Not really. He tries to ignore him or sideline him, but now and then he foils his own plan – and this is a good thing. Hints of this can be found not in the *Social Contract*, but in other works from all phases of Rousseau's creative life.

In his *Discourse on the Virtue Most Necessary for a Hero* from 1751, the young Rousseau cannot avoid acknowledging that the "hero" *stands out*. Instead of exhibiting consideration, caution, and circumspection as a member of the body politic, Rousseau says this hero is all too often not "just, prudent, moderate" but instead tends toward "excesses." Rousseau uses the same vocabulary here that he employs in his description of the *puer robustus*. "Prudence" is depicted as the "mortal enemy of [...] all genuinely heroic acts" because it leads to temperance. Rousseau counterposes this with the hero who possesses "energy and vigor" (*de l'énergie et de la vigueur*), "bodily strength" and, above all, "strength of soul."[61] His image of the hero resembles the one Diderot will sketch in his *Encyclopédie* entry on "Genius." When the "hero" opposes the status quo, however, he does not yet link his marginal position to the self-assured anticipation of a new order. He vacillates between excellence and excess and is therefore, according to Rousseau's early testimony, a relative of the eccentric troublemaker.

Another marginal individual who can be neither dismissed nor directly integrated is ushered onto the stage in Rousseau's *Considerations on the Government of Poland* from 1772. Rousseau struggles with a detail of the Polish constitution that was a thorn in the side of many of his contemporaries: the *liberum veto*. This was the guaranteed right of every Polish delegate to veto legislation. The constitutional rule stated that this single veto could quash a bill without further ado, regardless of the size of the majority that supported it. Excessive use of this rule largely paralyzed the Polish parliament in the eighteenth century. Whenever someone felt his privileges were in danger or was willing to act as the henchman of a foreign power, he would use his veto.[62] Rousseau is surrounded by commentators calling for the abolition of the *liberum veto* (cf. the descriptions in OC 3, 1775f.). One might think he would join this choir in order to rob the individual's self-will of its power. But Rousseau does not come to this conclusion; instead, he actually suggests retaining the *liberum veto*. He couches this argument in a strange construct, however. The *liberum veto*, he says, should be restricted to cases relating to "genuinely fundamental laws" (CWR 11, 204, cf. 203; OC 3, 997, cf. 995), and it should be tied to a strict procedure. Anyone using his veto would subsequently have to explain himself to a commission and accept the commission's decision. If the commission decided that the veto was merely the expression of individual caprice and lacked any higher justification, the delegate in question would face nothing less than the death penalty (CWR 11, 204f.; OC 3, 997). Rousseau therefore expects all those who go against the majority to act in full awareness of their responsibility to the commonwealth. If they do so, they will "never need to be feared" by the state, and, indeed, they might actually save it (CWR 11, 205; OC 3, 998).

In view of the mortal risk associated with the individual veto, it would be logical to argue that Rousseau technically allows the *liberum veto* to stand but practically abolishes it through the strict conditions he places upon it.[63] The case he makes would therefore be a classic example of a paradoxical intervention. The real goal of allowing the *liberum veto* would be to ensure that decision-makers *consciously* did *not* make use of it; rather than just gritting their teeth and accepting the possibility of an undesirable decision, they would deliberately avoid bringing down a decision in the first place. This would encourage the unanimity of the citizens, upon which Rousseau places great value. According to this interpretation, the willingness to grant special power to the individual is just a cloak for the pressure to conform.

I find it hard to refute this reading, and yet it does not exhaust the potential of the *liberum veto*. After all, the "individual force" (*force individuelle*) (CWR 11, 204; OC 3, 997) of the citizen is revaluated in a daring way here. The individual can still derail the plans of a wide majority. Dissent is thus accorded an importance within the political order that Rousseau the consensus theorist would prefer to minimize. (There might be an autobiographical explanation for the special status granted to the individual, as Rousseau himself was a lone wolf who had to rely on his own power of judgment when he swam against the tide. Which he almost always did.)

Follow the paradoxical intervention argument, the *liberum veto* exists in order *not* to be used; it is an exercise in which the troublemaker hypothetically contemplates his self-destruction in order to complete his transformation into a citizen. Bearing in mind that he still has scope for dissent – however limited it may be – then the troublemaker is granted another life after the end of his first one. If he perceives his expected transformation into a citizen to be a loss of self, he can revoke it. His form of revocation is not the same as that of the nomocentric troublemaker; he does not anticipate a universal order. His response to the establishment of law is the "suspension" or "relief" of law.[64] The troublemaker operates in refusal mode and torpedoes consensus without having a fully formed alternative concept in his pocket. In doing so, he paves the way for the civil disobedience that would become a component of the radical democracy of Henry David Thoreau[65] and others in the nineteenth century. Hardly any democratic order can get by without it these days.[66]

I readily admit that, in his text on Poland, Rousseau takes only fleeting notice of the marginal, contrary individual. Even so, marginality as a personal experience is present in his mind (as someone who was himself chased, displaced, and persecuted), and he works systematically to rehabilitate those who resist integration. A glimpse at *Rousseau, Judge of Jean-Jacques* from 1777 makes this clear. In this dialog, a "Frenchman" declares that "a man who is isolated and without support [...] cannot fail to be a poisoner" (CWR 1, 205; OC 1, 924). But Rousseau uses this allegation only as a reference point for immediately taking the opposite position. The poison is, in fact, sprayed by the political order, which expects individuals to accept their abandonment. According to Rousseau, "the hatred of which J.J. is the object is not hatred of vice and wickedness, but hatred of the individual himself" (CWR 1, 175; OC 1, 885).

In *The Parasite*, Michel Serres suggested that the late work *Rousseau, Judge of Jean-Jacques* should be read not only as an autobiographical game of deception but as a "second treatise on political law"[67] – and as an objection to the idea that there could be a lossless association of individuals in a *moi commun*. Serres writes:

When he was writing of the social pact, no contradiction bothered him; everything seemed crystal clear to him. It seemed transparent to go back to a first convention; it seemed evident to him that an act of association would produce a group ego or a public persona.

But according to Serres, there is something sinister about this conclusiveness:

> The truth is that his theory was not as clear as he thought; the truth is that no one ever knew and no one knows how a unanimous agreement is formed among separate individuals. [...] Not only does he see the formation of a social pact from the outside, not only does he attest to the formation of a general will, but he also observes, through thick shadows, that it is formed only through animosity [...]. Union is produced through expulsion. And he is the one who is expelled. Is he crazy? [...] The mentally ill are not all in asylums, as people seem to think. They abound in kings' palaces, in high government positions.[68]

I said earlier that Rousseau is a theorist of closure and exclusion at the same time. And he does, in fact, draw boundaries and make exclusions for the sake of the integrity of the body politic. This is apparent in his critique of cosmopolitanism and unintegrated citizens, as well as his marginalization of women. But Rousseau only virtually moves within the boundaries he sets; in reality, he remains devoted to the troublemaker.

Hannah Arendt says that Hobbes "is the only great philosopher to whom the bourgeoisie can rightly and exclusively lay claim," as "there is hardly a single bourgeois moral standard" that he did not anticipate.[69] She describes this monopoly position with polemical intent: as a decline from the ancient ideal of republican life. She wants to restore this ideal in modern society and harks back to the Founding Fathers of America in order to do so. Rousseau, from whom Arendt keeps her distance, can certainly stand alongside them. This brings us to the widespread view that modern political philosophy is defined by two poles: liberalism and republicanism. They represent the primacy of individual interests on the one side and participation in a common cause on the other.

As fierce as the conflict between these two schools of thought may be, anyone who wades into it winds up with a rotten compromise. Rousseau's *puer robustus* can help break with this established antithesis. One of its underlying assumptions is baseless: in both cases, the starting point is something already in existence – either the individual who articulates his interests, or the institution to which the citizens belong. The argument against liberalism is that individuals only begin to take shape – meaning that they have already come out of their shell – when they develop seemingly individual needs, interests, and intentions. But it is precisely this entanglement of individual becoming and social conditions that speaks against the idea that one could, for the purposes of republicanism, specify a common ground upon which the members of a political order will engage.

The pivotal element of political philosophy is neither the individual nor the institution, but the human being as a threshold creature. This person resides in the place where affiliations and deviations are negotiated, where conflicts are fought between those who are included and those who are excluded. These conflicts do not necessarily have to end in disaster; they can also be productive. The key competency for this political dispute is found in the latchkey child of society, the *puer robustus*. Rousseau opposes the lone wolf and protects the group member; he wrangles with the egocentric troublemaker and celebrates the nomocentric one. Particularly in his later years, however, he demonstrates to his readers – and perhaps also to himself? – that the role of the eccentric troublemaker suits him best. But the theory to accompany this character is supplied not by him, but by Denis Diderot.

— III. —

RAMEAU'S NEPHEW AS A *PUER ROBUSTUS*

Denis Diderot

1. Hobbes's sublime definition

The *puer robustus* is mentioned in three places in Denis Diderot's works – and he appears under a pseudonym in a fourth. As this last appearance is especially tasty, I will leave it as a treat until the end. The year 1765 – a good hundred years after Hobbes's *Leviathan*, ten years after Rousseau's *Second Discourse* – saw the publication of the eighth volume of the *Encyclopédie*, in which Diderot summarizes the intellectual disputes of his age and pursues the cause of the Enlightenment, with which his name is associated like no other. This volume includes his lengthy article on "Hobbisme,"[1] which gives the *puer robustus* his first entrance. Much of this article consists of a translated, edited version of the chapter on Hobbes from Jakob Brucker's *Historia Critica Philosophiae*; one could even call it plagiarism, as Brucker is never mentioned as a source.[2] All the same, at the end of his article, Diderot adds his own finely balanced comparison of Hobbes and Rousseau:

> The philosophy of Monsieur Rousseau of Geneva is almost the inverse of that of Hobbes. The one thinks man naturally good, and the other thinks him wicked. For the philosopher of Geneva the state of nature is a state of peace; for the philosopher of Malmesbury it is a state of war. If you follow Hobbes, you are convinced that laws and the formation of society have made men better, while if you follow Monsieur Rousseau, you believe instead that they have depraved him. [. . .] Different times, different circumstances, different philosophies. Monsieur Rousseau writes with eloquence and emotion; Hobbes is dry, austere and force-ful. The latter saw [. . .] his fellow-citizens armed one against the other, and his country soaked with blood [. . .]. The former saw men who were versed in every sphere of knowledge tear each other apart, loathe one another, give themselves up to their passions [. . .], and conduct

themselves in a manner scarcely commensurate with the learning they had mastered.[3]

Diderot is not content to simply string Hobbes and Rousseau alongside each other like pearls on the thread of history. Which side does he come down on? His answer is that "both men were extreme," but "between their two systems there is another which may convey the truth." An *Encyclopédie* article is not the place for an author to proclaim his own truths, so Diderot only cautiously hints at the true system he seeks. Such a system, he says, must take account of the fact that in the course of the "perpetual strife" that afflicts "the human condition," the measure "of goodness and wickedness remain[s] constant." Diderot is skeptical about the advancement of "goodness" and "happiness": "All the benefits of human industry are balanced by evils, all natural evils by good works."[4]

Diderot allows Hobbes and Rousseau to compete against and immobilize one another. The reservations of the one are pitted against those of the other – and vice versa. He uses Hobbes to describe the merits of an "artificial," contractual order, only to counter this with Rousseau's objections. He depicts Rousseau's commitment to the natural life, only to immediately bring Hobbes into play against him. Objections are pelted from all sides. Diderot takes a similar tack in other works. On the one hand, he thinks civilized people living in a society are capable of all manner of "villainies" (PhS 2, 18; DOC 2, 287), but on the other hand, he views "luxury" as the "cause" not only of people's "vices" but also their "virtues" (PhS 1, 353; DOC 16, 5). This contradictory image is not actually in keeping with the progressive thinking of the Enlightenment, which the young Turgot described in such an exemplary way in 1750: "In the midst of their ravages manners are softened, the human mind becomes more enlightened [. . .]. The whole human race [. . .] goes on advancing, although at a slow pace, toward greater perfection."[5] Diderot does not anticipate steady progress, and he certainly does not expect goodness to walk off with the victory. He sees a power play and interplay between good and evil, the waves of which ripple through history.

And yet, Diderot – in his *Encyclopédie* article on "Hobbisme," in any case – does not steer a precise middle course between Hobbes and Rousseau, but instead takes an unexplained turn toward partisanship in the end. Disregarding the dark side he sees in cultivated (or "artificial") life, he believes the gradual advance of reason could shift the balance in favor of good. Following a debatable classification, it is Hobbes, not Rousseau, whom Diderot considers to be the guarantor for such a politics of small steps. His middle course thus veers to Hobbes's side.

The fact that Diderot tends toward Hobbes in this text has to do with the appeal of a character he finds in Hobbes's writing – and this brings me to the first reference to the *puer robustus* in Diderot's works. "His definition of the nature of evil strikes me as sublime," Diderot writes: "The evil man, according to Hobbes, is a vigorous child; *malus est puer robustus*. In fact, evil is the more powerful when reason is feeble and the passions are strong."[6] Here is the second reference straight away: Hobbes's definition is also mentioned in the *Encyclopédie* article on the word "robuste," in which it is once again praised as being "short, laconic, and sublime."[7] According to Diderot, we are presented with a choice. We can either believe Hobbes's "definition" to be "false," or we can follow the motto that "man becomes good to the extent that he educates himself" (DOC 15, 123).[8] Diderot chooses the second option, the package deal of reason and goodness that he finds in Hobbes's work.

Diderot's partisanship for Hobbes does not fit with his aim of creating a "true system" that should actually be equally distant from Hobbes and Rousseau. I would therefore advise against overstating this partisanship. It is simply a marker at the side of what appears to be a winding road. The twists in this road are, to a certain extent, a product of the rift between Diderot and Rousseau that occurred in 1757. Nonetheless, it is possible to conclusively reconstruct Diderot's position between and beyond Hobbes and Rousseau. This is a particularly easy undertaking if we expand our play (which would seem to make it more complex) and bring in another author.

Claude Adrien Helvétius also talks about the *puer robustus*. In his debate with Helvétius, Diderot takes the opportunity to mention the *puer robustus* a third time and provides key insights for understanding this character (section 2). But his own positive contribution to the theory of the troublemaker is found above all in *Rameau's Nephew*, where he invents a wondrous, wonderful eccentric. As mentioned at the start, the *puer robustus* will appear under a pseudonym in this dialog novel (section 3). The eponymous protagonist of the book has earned every ounce of the attention granted to him by many great thinkers; two of them – Hegel and Foucault – will have their say at the end of this chapter (section 4).

2. The *puer robustus* as a social problem or ambivalent character: Diderot beyond Helvétius, Hobbes, and Rousseau

In 1773, shortly after Helvétius's death, *A Treatise on Man, His Intellectual Faculties and His Education* was published from Helvétius's manuscripts. In the chapter entitled "Of Sociability" there is a long footnote, which reads:

81

Because man is sociable, people have concluded that he is good. But they have deceived themselves. Wolves form societies, but they are not good. [. . .] Hobbes has been reproached with this maxim: *The strong child is a bad child*, he has however only repeated in other terms, this admired verse of Corneille, Qui peut tout ce qui'il veut, veut plus ce qu'il doit. He that can do whatever he will, wills more than he ought. And this other verse of La Fontaine, La raison du plus fort est toujours la meilleure. The strongest always reason best. They who write the romance of men, condemn this maxim of Hobbes; they that write his history, admire it; and the necessity of laws proves it to be true.[9]

It is clear who is being pilloried here: Rousseau. Helvétius not only accuses him of a misguided critique of Hobbes, he actually banishes Rousseau's entire theory of the creation of human society to the shadow realm of fiction, the "romance." In his *Treatise on Man*, Helvétius is practically obsessive in his persecution of Rousseau. The hands of the man of nature, he writes, are "always imbrued in blood." "He that maintains the original goodness of men, designs to deceive them."[10] Helvétius's interpretation of the *puer robustus* follows in Hobbes's wake and is indebted to the thesis that evil arises when individuals strive against reason.

Helvétius does not merely repeat Hobbes's description of the state of nature as a "state of war,"[11] however; he modifies it slightly and thus also shifts the frame of reference for his reader, Diderot. This shift is clearly apparent in the contrast with both Hobbes and Rousseau. For all of their differences, what Hobbes and Rousseau had in common was that they each, in their own way, took individual actions as their starting point. One could say they peered over the shoulders of people who settled and meddled in the world, contemplated their moves in the game of life and then reached opposite conclusions. Hobbes thought the individual faced a choice of either attending to his needs within a legally regulated framework or relying entirely on his own strength as an evil *puer robustus*. Rousseau saw an individual who wanted to live in harmony with himself and others and who, by acting as a *puer robustus*, made sure that evil stood no chance.

Helvétius, by contrast, starts not with individual actions but with social circumstances. He approaches the *puer robustus* from above and considers him to be neither an actor nor an activist but a social problem. With this switch from activity to passivity, he categorizes the *puer robustus* as one of the pathologies to be dealt with using the social technology of the state. For Helvétius, the institutional order is not authorized by individuals – as it was for Hobbes and Rousseau – but instead remains strangely external and terribly alien to them. Helvétius claims to know what is good for them.

Helvétius's neutralization of the individual as an actor arises from his version of materialism. He presents people as creatures defined not by their actions but by their physical reactions: "Corporeal sensibility is [...] the sole mover [*moteur*] of man." – "All the sensations of man are material."[12] When Helvétius links "all our desires, and all our passions" to a natural "self-love,"[13] it reveals that he does not believe man is capable of developing on his own – because he is the plaything of endless "wants."[14] All he can do is be a good "pupil" of "every object," "all the positions" and "every incident"[15] that shapes him. To this end, he must be an apprentice not only to nature, but above all to the state, which, according to Helvétius, attends to the optimal governance of desires, tendencies, and instincts. These can be "variously modified according to the education we receive, the government under which we live, and the different situations in which we are placed."[16] (Robespierre clearly went to school with Helvétius, not Rousseau, when he says: "It would be society's masterpiece to create in man a rapid instinct for moral values which would induce him, without the delaying assistance of deliberation, to do good and avoid evil."[17])

This has consequences for the *puer robustus*, though Helvétius does not disclose them. Hobbes, Rousseau, and even Diderot are all convinced that evil is not a product of nature, it emerges only in the moment when an individual takes responsibility for his actions and chooses between good and evil. Without his own capacity to act, the individual – as Helvétius depicts him – never actually reaches this point, but instead remains a child. Helvétius's theory of society has a paternalistic slant, one that reappears in the works of the utilitarian Jeremy Bentham, who harks back to him.[18] Unlike Hobbes, Helvétius does not insist that the light of reason will eventually dawn on the rebel; he wants to turn the man of nature into a smoothly operating engine of desire.

The position argued by Helvétius is not a curiosity of the eighteenth century. Marx and Engels also hark back to Helvétius's thesis that man's "wickedness" only erupts when an incapable or malicious "legislator" falsely controls the "interests" to which he is "subordinate" (MECW 4, 132).[19] Though they want to bolster the active subject, which is not the aim of Helvétius, they nonetheless adopt his perspective on the "totality of the individual's conditions of life" and the "transformation of consciousness": "If man is shaped by environment, his environment must be made human" (MECW 4, 133, 131). Among those concerned with the "anomie"[20] of modern society, some have always sought a way out of this malaise through the social regulation of individual behavior and have thus dismantled the individual's personal responsibility. They can be found among socialists and conservatives alike.[21]

The fact that people are exposed to *situations* does not mean that they only *react* and are denied all capacity for action from the outset. Claiming that every action is a reaction leads to the elimination of the moral aspect from social life. Helvétius's thesis of man's fundamental lack of responsibility shifts the source of good and evil. People behave in a good way – *so to speak*, it should be added – when they are directed to do so by external influences. Activity, and thus moral goodness, lies with those who exert such influences:

> O! you, to whom heaven has entrusted the legislative power, let your administration be gentle, your laws sagacious, and you will have subjects humane, valiant, and virtuous! But if you alter either those laws, or that wise administration, those virtuous citizens will expire without posterity, and you will be surrounded by wicked men only; for the laws will make them such.[22]

This type of "administration" is not compatible with either Hobbes's bottom-up model or Rousseau's self-legislation. Helvétius's justification for it is that it owes its existence to a decision on the part of "heaven." But the question of how administration and education – or administration as education! – can be put into practice by people who are themselves merely creatures of sensation remains wide open in Helvétius's writing. This embarrassing gap has a good side, however: it prompts Diderot to refine his interpretation of the *puer robustus* and differentiate it from that of Hobbes and Rousseau.

Analogous to Rousseau's reading of Hobbes, we can say that Diderot reads Helvétius and gets upset. Immediately after the publication of Helvétius's *Treatise on Man*, Diderot set about writing a "refutation" of the book. The form he chose for this is strange. His text is less a systematic refutation than a running commentary in which Diderot's critical spirit is inflamed by certain passages. I can say in advance that he raises one major objection to Helvétius and picks up one small suggestion from him.

Diderot takes exception to the point I focused on in my critique of Helvétius: the shift from action to reaction. Diderot quotes Helvétius as saying "to sense is to judge" (PhS 2, 31; DOC 2, 300), a reference to the following passage from the *Treatise on Man*: "A man surrounded by an infinity of objects, must necessarily be affected by an infinity of sensations, and consequently form an infinity of judgments; but he forms them unknown to himself. Why? Because these judgments are of the same nature with the sensations."[23] Diderot then rejects Helvétius's assertion that there is a causality between sensation and judgment:

> This is a very labored conclusion, and it generally applies more to animals than to man. To move suddenly from physical sensation [. . .] to

the desire for happiness, from the desire for happiness to interest, from interest to attention, from attention to the comparison of ideas – no, I cannot agree with such generalizations. I am a man and I demand the causes that are specific to a man. [. . .] Is it really true that physical pain and physical pleasure [. . .] are the sole principles for man's actions? (PhS 2, 32f.; DOC 2, 300, 302)

The talk of "causes that are specific to a man" is particularly choice, as it indicates that Diderot believes Helvétius's fantasy of state control to be inhumane. He breaks with the notion that laws and education could "make anything" out of a man who is, by nature, "nothing" (PhS 2, 141; DOC 2, 406f.). How does Diderot's critique of this manipulation affect his interpretation of the *puer robustus*? His statement, which is the third time he references this character in his work, seems unremarkable, but it is not:

Helvétius and others translate the word of Hobbes – *Malus est robustus puer* – as "the strong child is an evil child." This is not always true; but what is always true is that the evil child is a strong child, and this is also how I would translate this word. (PhS 2, 41; DOC 2, 309)

We might initially be somewhat at a loss as to what this reversal means. But the answer soon becomes clear. Diderot does not want to linger over natural characteristics such as "strength" in order to extrapolate an individual's wickedness from them. Otherwise he would fall into Helvétius's trap of reducing man to physical characteristics. According to Diderot, there is absolutely no consequence to the fact that a child is "strong." Conversely, however, someone who is "evil" must also be "strong" in order to be effective. Diderot emphasizes the moral decisions and responsibility of man. Someone who is capable of good or evil must, first and foremost, be in a position to decide on their own actions. Otherwise, you can *forget* about judging the morality of their behavior:

If people are not free in what they do that is good or evil, then good is no longer good and evil is no longer evil [. . .], so our will is no more responsible for our volition than the mainspring of a machine is responsible for the movement it is forced to make [. . .]; each does only what he must do, as he acts in accordance with necessity. (PhS 1, 326; DOC 15, 501)

Children are the only people whom Diderot – like Hobbes and Rousseau before him – places on this side of liberty, this side of the ability to decide and differentiate. He therefore refers to them as "automata" or "little machines" (PhS 1, 334; DOC 15, 71). He accuses Helvétius of keeping people in this state by ascribing their judgment to sensations.

Laws and rules that are valid in society do not arise from a theoretical insight into the functioning of the human machine, according to Diderot, but come about in the course of practical legislation and adoption. He defends nothing less than the liberty of man: "If *liberty* is taken away, then all of human nature is turned on its head" (PhS 1, 326; DOC 15, 501).

By celebrating liberty in this way, Diderot follows more in Rousseau's wake than in Hobbes's. In fact, Diderot clearly keeps his distance from Hobbes even though he praises Hobbes's definition of the *puer robustus* in his *Encyclopédie* article. In maintaining his distance, he takes a suggestion from Helvétius (despite his criticism of him) and lops off the only serviceable point of Hobbes's argument.

Though Diderot criticizes Helvétius's *reduction* of the individual to physical sensibility, he – like every other French materialist from La Mettrie through Helvétius to de Sade and Fourier – clings to the goal that this sensibility will blossom in all of its inner diversity. He lands a punch against Hobbes here, who believed it was possible to give priority to the need for self-preservation in the realm of the senses. This was intended to set a clear target for rational deliberation, and anyone who missed this target was considered by Hobbes to be more or less a fool. For Diderot, a blinkered interest in preserving one's existence is only a small part of the "sensibility of our organs," which can be "stimulated in a hundred agreeable ways." He thinks little of those "atrabilious" people who curse all pleasures and refer to "exquisite fruits" and "delicious wines" as "bad and harmful." His terse judgment is that such people should be "confined to asylums"[24] – but not those who give free rein to their desires. The fact that an individual's diverse needs can collide with self-preservation was summed up by Roland Barthes in a stark punch line: "Sade does not like bread."[25] To soften this blow, one could say that Diderot does not *only* like bread.

Diderot's differentiated depiction of sensibility upsets the logic to which Hobbes clings. If people want and are allowed to savor a broad spectrum of sensations, it blurs the strict demand for self-preservation that Hobbes defines as a functional requirement of reason. This results in an expansion of the goals of action and a proliferation of laws and rules according to which these goals are organized and achieved. Diderot is not interested only in maximizing desires, however; unlike Helvétius, he asks how sensations bubble up on the horizon of action and liberty. And this is what makes him receptive to Rousseau's suggestions.

Diderot's relationship with Rousseau is famously – and much more extremely than his relationship with Hobbes – one of attraction and repulsion at the same time. He certainly misses no opportunity to mock Rousseau's supposed aim of sending people back into the "primeval forest" (PhS 2, 166, 323; DOC 2, 431; DOC 3, 96). But this does not stop him from following Rousseau and identifying tendencies in the life of the savage (or the child) that have moral potential in social life. Diderot says the savage has not only "been prescribed ethical teachings suitable for wolves" (DA 2, 107; DOC 11, 124), he also already has an awareness of justice and injustice "prior to any social agreement." He follows a "primitive law," which simply finds its "interpretation, expression and sanctioning" in the "written law" (PhS 2, 120; DOC 2, 387f.). (Incidentally, these comments perfectly describe one of Victor Hugo's protagonists, the Hunchback of Notre Dame.)

If the savage has moral potential, this dramatically changes the starting point for seeking access to the social and political order. Civilization does not operate on the basis of a contrast between artificial contractual order and wild nature; instead, it seeks to connect with the social competencies of the savage. In this context, it should be noted that Diderot not only cites Hobbes's evil *puer robustus*; in his "Satire against Luxury" he also rhapsodizes about the *robustes enfants* who are fulfilled by their simple actions (DOC 11, 90).

His greatest affinity with Rousseau is expressed in an early note from 1754 in an annotated copy of his *Second Discourse*. In this note, Diderot echoes Rousseau's plea for pity and warns that people could become "monsters" if this "natural virtue" were disregarded as the precursor to "social virtues." If "reason" adheres solely to self-interest or "self-love," it damages the cooperative faculties that exist in a state of nature, according to Diderot, and causes people to "withdraw into themselves" (DOC 4, 101–3). In other works, too, he criticizes the "Hobbist" who only ever thinks of himself and pits himself against others.[26] While reason is otherwise praised for staving off evil and making natural passions socially tolerable, Diderot warns that reason encourages evil and eliminates natural virtue from the individual's focus of action.

As stated earlier, Diderot tries to steer a middle course between Hobbes and Rousseau – and he repeatedly strays from it. Sometimes he follows Hobbes's definition of the *puer robustus*, other times he moves closer to Rousseau's characterization of the natural man. In one passage of his late critique of Helvétius, Diderot returns to his plan from the "Hobbisme" article to turn this middle course into the path to a "true system." He takes exception to Helvétius's notion of the perfect society and declares:

> I believe there is a goal for civilization that generally conforms far better to the happiness of man and is not nearly as far from the savage condition as one would imagine. But how can one get back to this goal when one has overshot it, and how can one come to a stop when one has reached it? I do not know. Unfortunately! (PhS 2, 166f.; DOC 2, 431)

Luckily, with Diderot's help we can say a bit more than he apparently trusts himself to say. Unlike Hobbes and Rousseau, Diderot does not set himself up as a judge who convicts or acquits the *puer robustus*. He acts more like a director who contemplates how to create and develop this role. The verdict as to whether the *puer robustus* is good or evil is *suspended* by him. This comes down to the fact that he believes evil springs from various sources. These sources are found wherever a lack of reason prevails (as Hobbes would say), but also wherever reason prevails and the natural virtue and sociability of man withers (as Rousseau would say). A "mixture of good and evil" is found on all sides (PhS 2, 126; DOC 2, 393).

This ambivalence is not an expression of confusion; it is systematically productive. It leads, namely, to a rejection of the attempt to resolve the tension between order and disturbance in a one-sided way and to seek salvation only on one side or the other. We cannot be certain that the political order will prove its goodness in its battle against the *puer robustus* (Hobbes), any more than we can trust the *puer robustus* to transform the world in a single bold move (Rousseau). In Diderot's world, there must be both an evil and a good *puer robustus* – as well as good and evil orders to which he reacts and in which he intervenes. It is not possible to judge only one of these two sides *per se*. Instead, the decisive litmus test takes place – once again – on a *threshold*. The moment of truth comes for the political order when its approach to disturbance is up for negotiation. And the moment of truth comes for the disturber not when he basks in his extravagance but when he rubs up against the political order – thereby putting this order to the test and subjecting himself to its response.

This threshold is illuminated in a work by Diderot that had a spectacular impact. According to Karl Marx, whose own interpretation of the *puer robustus* will be the subject of later discussion, the text in question is an "unsurpassed masterpiece" (MECW 43, 263).

3. Life on the threshold: *Rameau's Nephew*

Diderot was a philosopher, but he was also a novelist. Baudelaire[27] said he was the "most daring and adventurous" of all, a kind of *puer robustus* himself. His dialog novel *Rameau's Nephew* was written in the 1770s (CR 1126f.) and was first published in 1805 in a German translation by Goethe. The original French version was not published until 1891. Buried within this book is a striking reference to the *puer robustus*. At the start of this chapter, I said that he would appear once under a pseudonym, and that this appearance was something of a treat. The time has come to savor it.

In his "Hobbisme" article in the *Encyclopédie*, Diderot provides a dramatic illustration of the activities of the *puer robustus*. He takes Hobbes's claim that savage children can go so far as to "strike their Parents" and pushes it to the extreme:

> Imagine a six-week old child with the imbecility of mind appropriate to its age and the strength and passions of a man of forty. He will manifestly strike down his father, ravish his mother and strangle his nurse.[28]

Diderot uses this passage, almost unaltered, in *Rameau's Nephew*. In the verbal exchange between "Him" (the titular character) and "Me," Diderot writes:

> HIM – Everything alive, without exception, seeks to ensure its own well-being at the expense of whatever it is dependent on; and I'm sure that if I let the little savage grow up without me telling him anything, he'd want to be richly dressed, lavishly fed, prized by men, loved by women, and to want to surround himself with all the pleasures of life.
>
> ME – If the little savage were left to himself, remaining in a state of imbecility, and combining the feeble reasoning abilities of a small infant with the violent passions of a grown man, he'd wring his father's neck and sleep with his mother. (RN 78; CR 651)

In quoting himself, Diderot opens a secret door leading to an expansive new room. This room will later be occupied by Sigmund Freud, who cites this exact passage many times in his works. Moreover, the "little savage" of whom Diderot speaks here will return in the works of Hugo, Baudelaire, and Horkheimer. To be precise, the "little savage" about whom the "Him" and "Me" argue is the son of Rameau's nephew. The argument is ostensibly about education. But throughout the novel, Rameau's nephew himself plays the role of the troublemaker *par excellence*. One could therefore say that he is himself an alter ego of the *puer robustus*.

Because a "Him" and a "Me" appear in the novel, Diderot would seem to be maintaining his early resistance to the evil *puer robustus* and – in the role of the "Me" – passing judgment on a depraved descendant of Hobbes's troublemaker. It fits with this interpretation that the "Me" is considered "virtuous," someone who fulfills his "duties," while the nephew is described as "a layabout, a greedy pig, [...] a real old scumbag" (RN 40, 38, 87; CR 614, 612, 659). But the assumption that the author comes down on the side of the "Me" overlooks the subtlety with which Diderot composed his work. Thankfully, his interpreters have accepted the challenge of this subtlety and debated whether and how Diderot takes sides and who has the better hand in this game: "Him" or "Me." I will come back to this debate in a moment and try to decide it once and for all by proposing something different. But first I want to see how far we can get by simply applying Hobbes's description of the *puer robustus* to Rameau's nephew.

There is no shortage of Hobbesian ingredients to be found in Diderot's novel. The nephew is said to be "possessed of a strong constitution, a singularly heated imagination, and an exceptionally vigorous set of lungs" (RN 8; CR 586). He uses his strength to pursue his self-interest as defined by Hobbes. The nephew in Diderot's novel says:

> In nature, all species prey on each other; in society, people of all stations prey on each other too. We're forever passing sentence on each other without the law being involved. (RN 34; CR 610)

> We appear cheerful; but deep down, we are resentful and voracious. Wolves are not as hungry, nor tigers as cruel. We are as ravenous as wolves after the long winter snows; we rip to pieces anyone or anything that is at all successful. [...] You've never seen so many miserable, embittered, spiteful and ferocious beasts all in one place. (RN 49; CR 623f.)

The nephew resides not in Hobbes's state of nature but in a society that resembles this state. Not much of the strict law of the Leviathan is to be found here. Everyone goes about their own business and follows the rules for tactical reasons at best. Everyone is guided by a "wretched feeling" or has – as the original puts even more dramatically – a *diable de sentiment*, an "emotional devil" inside of them. The nephew says: "When we're in a bad mood, you should see how we treat the valets, how the chambermaids get slapped about [...]. It's what the whole of society says and feels" (RN 47f.; CR 622). The nephew is fairly untroubled by the accusation that he is "disturbing the peace" (RN 56; CR 630). To the frustration of the "Me," he basks in his indifference and is not interested in establishing a legal order. In his refusalism, the "Him" meets with all of the "layabouts" who hold their ground in a space that is not lawless, though it is lacking in order. It is not out of the question that he might do something good, but it would probably only happen by chance. When asked "What have you been up to?", the "Him" responds:

> What you, me, and everyone else have been doing: some good things, some bad things, and a great deal of nothing. And sometimes I've been hungry and I've had something to eat when I could; and having eaten, I got thirsty and sometimes I got a drink. Meanwhile, my beard kept growing, and when it did, I had it shaved off. (RN 10; CR 588)

With his indifference to rules, the nephew opens himself up to the accusation of wickedness that Hobbes levels against the *puer robustus*. This accusation is part of a package deal for Hobbes, so to speak. He says wickedness is tied to a want of reason, or a lack of understanding that it makes sense to follow the rules. Does this package deal apply to the nephew as well? The situation becomes a bit murky here. I will first look at the "Me" and then at the nephew.

The "Me" initially takes the exact same line as Hobbes when he says society must consist solely of "terrible wasters" and "terrible fools" (RN 48; CR 622). The "Me" insists on branding those who are abusive to others not only as evil, but also as stupid or unreasonable. But because we now know that Diderot believes rational people are more than willing to behave maliciously, rationality is no guarantee of a victory over evil. The "Me" also has a creeping suspicion that the bond between rationality and morality has been cut. His equally dogged and futile efforts to convince the nephew of the advantages of virtue are therefore not an attempt to admonish him to employ reason. Instead, the "Me" holds out to the nephew the promise of more happiness. The great creed of the "Me" is:

> I don't look down on sensory pleasures. I too have a palate, and it is tempted by a delicate morsel or a delicious wine. I too have a heart and eyes, and I love to see a pretty woman, I love to feel the firm round flesh of her bosom in my hands, to press my lips on hers, to feel aroused when I look deep into her eyes, and to expire with pleasure in her arms. Every so often, I am not averse to an evening of debauchery amongst friends, even quite a riotous one. But I will not conceal from you that I find it infinitely more delightful to come to the aid of someone in need, to bring a fraught situation to an end, to give a salutary piece of advice, to read something pleasant, go for a walk with a man or woman dear to my heart, spend a couple of instructive hours with my children, write a good page, fulfil the duties of my position, say some tender loving words to the one I love and receive her embrace in return. There are some things I would give anything to have done. (RN 37f.; CR 613)

The nephew is unmoved: "Well that's a sort of felicity I'm unlikely ever to be familiar with [. . .]" (RN 38; CR 614). He holds the "general principles belonging to some morality or other" to be not only "useless" and "dangerous" (RN 32, 29; CR 608, 605), but also "miserable as hell": "Come on, long live philosophy, long live the wisdom of Solomon: let's drink good wine, gorge ourselves silly on delicate morsels, roll around with pretty women, and go to sleep in lovely soft beds. What else is there? The rest is vanity" (RN 35; CR 611).

Because the "Me" cannot simply appeal to his interlocutor's sense of reason (using Hobbes), he contemplates tackling the nephew's immorality in a different way (using Rousseau). Diderot includes an extremely condensed reference to his great predecessor in his novel. The "Me" says:

91

"I do believe, in spite of the wretched, abject, vile, abominable role you play, that, deep down, you possess a delicate soul" (RN 48; CR 623). The "Me" thus offers a variation on Hobbes's verdict that the *puer robustus* finds himself in a "miserable and hateful state."[29] At the same time, however, the "Me" tries to drive a wedge between the nephew and Hobbes's man of nature. While Hobbes applies these negative traits to individuals who *remain* in a state of nature, Diderot attributes the traits to a "role" that is played – i.e., first *adopted* – in society. Evil appears to be something that is only acquired. The "Me" thus creates a space for himself in which – in keeping with Rousseau! – he can surmise that there is a "delicate soul" behind the role or façade of the nephew.

Thus, even in *Rameau's Nephew*, progression toward a deeper insight wrestles with regression to natural goodness. When the "Me" calls the nephew to order, he wavers between his goal of drumming reason into the nephew and his attempt to appeal to his social inclinations. This can be traced back to Diderot's own ambivalence regarding this question, and also to the fact that the "Me" is somewhat at a loss regarding how to handle the nephew and who he is actually dealing with here. He remarks on the nephew's "belly hanging out like Silenus's," not only hinting at the nephew's voraciousness but also comparing him with the part-man, part-animal creature from Greek mythology (RN 11; CR 588). He sees in him "a mixture of the lofty and the sordid, of good sense and unreason" (RN 7; CR 585f.).

In the field of tension between the rational and natural creature, the nephew is rather difficult to pin down. He refers to himself as an "ignoramus" and a "fool" (RN 18; CR 596), but he engages in such an elaborate war of words with the "Me" that the latter is forced to admit: "There's some sense, more or less, in everything you've just said" (RN 68; CR 641). He flaunts his animalistic existence so skillfully that one can credit him with considerable intellectual abilities: "The important thing is to go easily, freely, pleasurably, copiously and daily each evening on the chamber pot. O stercus pretiosum![30] That's the grand outcome of life whatever the rank" (RN 23; CR 601). The nephew delivers a performance of such virtuosity and wit that the "Me" grows dizzy. He has mastered the game of reflection that Hobbes's original version of the *puer robustus* – with his straightforward program of action and his lumpish brutality – would be utterly incapable of playing.

How exactly does the nephew put his obviously ample intellectual power to use? Following the Hobbesian model, we would expect a two-step process whereby he would first set a goal and then determine how to reach it. To begin with, the nephew does follow Hobbes's model: "His ruling concern is with self-preservation."[31] But when it comes to achieving this goal, he forges his own path. The "reason" credited to him does not induce him to follow the rules; instead, he is compelled by the circumstances to expertly switch roles and thus impress his benefactors. This connection between self-preservation and role play is not new. Even the "masterless man," a relative of the *puer robustus*, was closely allied with the actor[32] – and this alliance will return in Nietzsche's theory from *The Gay Science* that the "inner craving for a role and mask" is "developed most easily in [...] the lower classes," who "turn their coat with *every* wind and thus virtually [...] *become* a coat" (GS 316). In accordance with this, Rameau's nephew displays an astonishing mutability: "Nothing is more unlike the man than he himself" the "Me" notes with suspicion, withdrawing into his own ideal of life: the constancy of the becalmed spirit (RN 8; CR 585f.).

This genealogical explanation, which sees role play as a product of the need for self-preservation, is only half the story, however, because when the nephew puts on his act, something special happens to him: *he loses sight of this need – and he loses himself in the play*. He is certainly not content with merely telling others what they want to hear. The nephew lets his internal actor off the leash, so to speak, setting him – or indeed himself – free. With this move, he distances himself from natural premises and social assimilation. He employs a unique ability to reflect, one which flickers between reason and madness. This allows him to experiment with diverse forms of life, to immerse himself in their rules of play and savor their different contexts.[33] He is a master of diversion and difference.

Rameau's nephew is thus a troublemaker who not only rises above Hobbes's blinkered, bad *puer robustus*, but also develops into an attractive rival to Hobbes's reasonable subject. With his non-identity, the nephew is the secret role model for many heroes who are at the mercy of or devoted to change: "The poetical Character [...] is not itself – it has no self – it is every thing and nothing";[34] "Nothing could be more different from me than myself."[35] In light of his mutability, it is almost impossible to determine whether the nephew is evil or good – unless one considers this mutability itself to be evil. But couldn't one argue that it is a virtue of an emancipated, experimental form of life?

Because the borders between the "Me" and the "Him" get mixed up and cannot be untangled using Hobbes's tools, it becomes more important to question how Diderot himself draws these borders – and it is to this question that I will now turn. Naïvely identifying the "Me" with the author Diderot will certainly not get us very far. Anyone familiar with narrative theory will know that you are not necessarily talking about yourself when you write "I." We can assume that Diderot constructed his novel in a more sophisticated way and used it as a stage on which to argue an unexpected position, or even multiple positions.

Daniel Mornet provided a directive for interpreting the novel back in 1927, which is still valid today: "'He' and 'I,' the two characters in the novel, are, in reality, I and I; we are faced with a Diderot engaged in a fierce battle against another Diderot."[36] Ever since then, interpreters have debated how Diderot deals with this inner strife and whether one side is victorious in the end.[37] This debate has not yet been decided, but more recent scholarship has been dominated by the argument that Diderot's intention is not to clearly take the side of the "Me" or the "Him," nor to mediate between the two, but instead to map out a radical aporia that can never be overcome or overridden.[38] I am taking this position as a starting point from which to oppose it and develop my own interpretation.

This aporia is demonstrated in the antagonism between the "Me" as a "moralist true to his principles" and the "Him" as a "modern Proteus";[39] it appears as a "grand duality" between "conceptual unity" and "aesthetic irregularity,"[40] as a "dichotomy," "tragedy,"[41] or "incommensurability."[42] The adversaries meet on an equal footing; the nephew is not only the defendant in proceedings instituted by the "Me," he himself also puts the "Me" in the dock. Diderot's novel thus follows a famous model: the early dialogs of Plato, which are also designed to be aporetic.[43]

My objection to this interpretation was inspired by a comment from Mikhail Bakhtin. According to Bakhtin, the model for Diderot's novel is not the Platonic dialog but rather a different literary form: Menippean satire.[44] Putting aside the notion that this form is too esoteric or "not customary,"[45] we find that it can help us critique the aporia thesis and develop a better interpretation of *Rameau's Nephew*. According to Bakhtin, Menippean satire deals with *"extraordinary situations"*:

> Under menippean conditions the very nature and process of posing philosophical problems, as compared with the Socratic dialogue, had to change abruptly [. . .]. In the menippea there appears for the first time what might be called moral-psychological experimentation: a representation of the unusual, abnormal moral and psychic states of man – insanity of all sorts (the theme of the maniac), split personality, unrestrained daydreaming, unusual dreams, passions bordering on madness, suicides, and so forth.[46]

Bakhtin himself confirms that this characterization fits Diderot's dialog perfectly:

> Rameau's nephew in Diderot embodies and distills himself, in a wonderfully complete and profound way, all the specific attributes of an ass, a rogue, a tramp, a servant, an adventurer, a parvenu, an actor [. . .]. This is the philosophy of a person who [. . .] does not participate in [life], who has no place in it – and therefore sees it in sharp focus, as a whole,

in all its nakedness, playing out all its roles but not fusing his identity with any one of them.[47]

Bakhtin shows how Diderot's novel differs from Plato's early dialogs and why the aporia model is not applicable to it. In order for "Me" and "Him" to come into irreconcilable conflict, it would have to be possible to ascribe clearly definable positions to each of them. But this endeavor fails when it comes to both the "Me" and the "Him." The notoriously inconstant nephew is not the only one who changes position more often than some people change their shirt; the "Me" does so as well. Both characters are designed to be a "hybrid,"[48] and they act in an exploratory and experimental way.[49]

Instead of solidifying opposing bastions, we should accept that the variety on both sides is intentional on Diderot's part. He shows us a panorama of different forms of life, and he does so not with the impassive gaze of the outsider but rather as someone who surrenders to these roles himself. The novel is, to put it briefly, much too *disorderly* to be a suitable setting for aporia. While Socrates goes about diligently trying to heighten a contradiction, *Rameau's Nephew* is a celebration of effusive attacks and evasive maneuvers. The verbal slugfest is repeatedly undermined – not least in that the nephew interrupts it with various pantomimes and musical interludes. The form and content of the text complement each other in a wonderful way.

In a Socratic dialog, a topic is negotiated by people who disagree with one another, but who nonetheless share one fundamental characteristic: they are conversational partners who are united by their ability to converse. This stipulation, this closure of the realm of *logos*, speech, or reason, is neutralized by Diderot. *Rameau's Nephew* is not always about a meeting of equals, but about whether and how one enters into a debate. Diderot depicts a counterplay between sense and insanity which functions very differently than an argument between theoretical positions. It is driven by the fundamental question of whether or how one can argue at all or *come to one's senses*. This question is raised by both the "Me" and the "Him" – not only for pedagogical purposes but also, conversely, for the sake of celebrating senselessness. The "Me" thus praises the "genius" for being "usually unusual," both a role model for society and a foreign body within it at the same time (RN 10–13; CR 589–91).[50] And the nephew declares that he is both "indispensable [*un homme essentiel*]" and his "own personal little Bedlam" (RN 54f.; CR 629).

Rameau's Nephew not only depicts the counterplay between sense and insanity, it poses the question of how to transition between these two states. To pick up on this particular aspect of Diderot's novel, it is advisable to read the work not along the lines of aporia but of *liminality*.[51]

This relates to the thresholds and borders that run between (and through) the characters and that are repeatedly crossed by them. The actual point of the text is not to intensify opposing positions but to explore transitions. Lines are crossed on both sides: that of the "Me" who flirts with the irresponsibility of the genius, and that of the nephew who tips from ecstasy into razor-sharp argumentation.

On the one hand, Diderot introduces differences that are much more pronounced than those in Plato's aporetic dialogs, since *Rameau's Nephew* deals not with an argument about issues themselves but with the question of whether one is permitted to argue in the first place. On the other hand, these differences are not utterly irreconcilable objective contradictions; instead, the characters in the novel repeatedly "experiment" with permission, access, the traversing of boundaries – to cite Bakhtin's characterization of satire once again (see above). The nephew is raving one minute, reasonable the next. He is both raving *and* reasonable. As a fool, a disturbed individual, he makes himself understood and thus disturbs the convictions that the "Me" brings to the conversation.

I want to demonstrate the power of the liminality thesis by applying it to the contradiction that is the domain of the aporia thesis: the contradiction between morality and aesthetics. The fact that Diderot strives to undermine this contradiction – as well as an aporetic confrontation between "Me" and "Him" – is especially apparent in *The Salon of 1767* and his *Discourse on Dramatic Poetry* from 1758. In these texts, Diderot prepares the ground for an encounter between "Me" and "Him" and drops a valuable hint for interpreting the *puer robustus*. Instead of settling for a confrontation between the moralist and the aesthete, these texts explore their commonality.

In his *Discourse on Dramatic Poetry*, Diderot explores this commonality not on the basis of the relationship between the actor and the honest man, but between the poet and the thinker. A special skill is ascribed to both of them, and to humanity in general: "Imagination, this is the quality without which one is neither a poet nor a philosopher, nor an ingenious mind, nor a reasonable being, nor a man." A man without this trait would be "a fool [...] whose entire intellectual function would be reduced to producing the sounds he learned to combine in his youth and applying them automatically [*machinalement*] to the circumstances of his life." Diderot complains that even some philosophers become such automata: "O, how much the man who thinks the most is still an automaton!" (DOC 7, 333).[52] He calls upon the reader to cut through this fixation of terms and meanings and "pass from abstract and general sounds to less abstract and general sounds [...] until he at last arrives at a sensible representation, which is the final goal and repose of reason." What kind person dares to do this? A "painter or poet" – or a "philosopher" who is not content for his speech to be "reduced to the mechanical habit of applying combined sounds" (DOC 7, 333f.). Whoever uses his imagination to bring concepts closer to experience is acting as a threshold creature.

The interplay between the artist and the philosopher continues in Diderot's text on the Paris Salon of 1767. Once again Diderot chooses the form of a dialog here, this time between an "I" and an "Abbé." He first establishes a contrast between the imagination of the poet and the judgment of the philosopher. In a way that recalls Rousseau's *First Discourse*, Diderot ties the rise of philosophy to the demise of poetry. This is linked not only to imagination but to the "verve" of life:

> There's greater verve among barbarous peoples than among civilized peoples [. . .]. One sees the decadence of verve and poetry everywhere one looks; to the extent that the philosophical spirit has prevailed [. . .]. Reason introduces an exactitude, a precision, a method, forgive my use of this word, a pedantry that kills everything. (DA 2, 113; DOC 11, 131)

This comparison is not Diderot's last word on the subject, however, as he does identify "one happy moment, that in which there's enough verve and liberty to be ardent, enough judgment and taste to be wise" (DA 2, 114; DOC 11, 132). His embrace of this "moment" is nothing less than his final rejection of an aporia between morality and aesthetics. The "moment" is possible because the general concepts availed of by philosophy, morality, and politics are not contrary to "verve" or sensual vivification. These concepts – and ultimately language itself – carry within them a memory, as it were, of the shaky foundations on which they stand. Diderot says that this memory reaches back into childhood:

> Once, unfortunately some time ago now [. . .] we were infants. During our childhood words were enunciated to us; these words became fixed in our memories, as did their meanings in our understanding [*entendement*] [. . .]. [. . .] but in the long run we begin to use words like coins: we cease looking at their image, inscription, and border treatments to determine their value; in giving and receiving them we pay attention only to their shape and weight: and I'd say to you that it's the same with words; [. . .] without this abbreviation we'd be unable to converse, we'd need an entire day to utter and appreciate one phrase of any length. (DA 2, 115; DOC 11, 133f.)

The answer to the question of how "verve" can be recovered is thus obvious: people must mistrust the clarity based on the thoughtlessness of a life lived automatically. This liberation from implicitness, which even philosophers can and must engage in, is nothing other than a return to childhood: "And the philosopher who weighs, considers, analyzes, and breaks down, what is he doing? On the basis of suspicions and doubts, he returns to the state of infancy" (DA 2, 115; DOC 11, 134). This means there is not, in fact, a nasty rift between the "verve" of life and the "pedantry" of the intellect; instead, it is within language itself that one reaches the point at which automatic understanding and abstract generality are surmounted, and also at which the social and political order based upon this loses its power. (This motif will return in Nietzsche's comments on generality as "baseness.") Understanding is overwhelmed by the semantic richness of each word, and it reaches its own limit, the threshold between non-understanding and understanding, where meanings become fluid. This mobilizes an experience that every child has had countless times. And the person who mobilizes the child within himself in this way can be considered a *puer robustus*.

More than a few writers have followed the same line as Diderot.[53] Novalis writes that "the most educated, worldly person is so akin to the child."[54] Ralph Waldo Emerson suggests that "we do not grow old, but grow young."[55] And Baudelaire draws a connection between genius and childhood that fits wonderfully with Diderot:

> The child sees everything in a state of *newness*; he is always *drunk*. Nothing more resembles what we call inspiration than the delight with which a child absorbs form and colour. [...] The man of genius has sound nerves, while those of the child are weak. With the one, Reason has taken up a considerable position; with the other, Sensibility is almost the whole being. But genius is nothing more nor less than *childhood recovered* at will – a childhood now equipped for self-expression with manhood's capacities and a power of analysis which enables it to order the mass of raw material which it has involuntarily accumulated.[56]

Elsewhere Diderot refers to children as "automata" because they follow their natural drives and are not yet free. Here, however, he discovers a different childhood, one which he recommends to people who do not want to be automata. It is far removed from the natural compulsion for the primal scene to which those who want to break open the implicitness of their vocabulary must return. The act of becoming a child again should be understood as the perception of the moment in which an individual stands at the edge of the world. Disturbances and agreements continually emerge from this moment. And in this process, Rameau's nephew – Diderot's *puer robustus* – moves like a fish in water.

It is impossible to overstate the importance of Diderot's remarks on definition and abstraction on the one hand and movement and "verve" on the other. He anticipates what Wilhelm von Humboldt and Ludwig Wittgenstein will say later on.

According to Humboldt, the interplay of torpor and movement elicits the "partly *fixed* and partly *fluid* content of language." He describes the emergence of language as a process of "crystallization," at the end of which "the language is in effect a finished product." But this endpoint remains notional or is never reached because "regarded in its real nature," language "is an enduring thing, and at every moment a *transitory* one": "For nowhere [...] does it have a permanent abode."[57] It almost sounds as though Humboldt were quoting a remark by Diderot from *D'Alembert's Dream*[58] when he says:

> Nobody means by a word precisely and exactly what his neighbour does, and the difference, be it ever so small, vibrates, like a ripple in water, throughout the entire language. Thus all understanding is always at the same time a not-understanding, all concurrence in thought and feeling at the same time a divergence.[59]

Wittgenstein's description of the language game is essentially a continuation of Humboldt's theory of language development and change. A passage from Wittgenstein's late work *On Certainty* should suffice as evidence of this:

> It might be imagined that some propositions, of the form of empirical propositions, were hardened and functioned as channels for such empirical propositions as were not hardened but fluid; and that this relation altered with time, in that fluid propositions hardened and hard ones became fluid. The mythology may change back into a state of flux, the river-bed of thoughts may shift.[60]

If we take the insights from *On Dramatic Poetry* and *The Salon of 1767* and return to *Rameau's Nephew*, we find that morality and aesthetics – the opposition of which dominates the dialog according to the aporetic interpretation – can be traced back to a common source. The "Me" and the "Him" are poles in a process of language and living that alternates between hardening and liquefaction. Morality and aesthetics – and politics! – are part of this process. Morality involves not only the definition and establishment of norms, but also controversies in which the semantic content of concepts is mobilized and changed. And aesthetics involves not only the transgression of rules, but also tolerance of the tension between form and formlessness, work and process. And politics involves institutions and rebellions.

It is both superficially seductive and actually necessary to apply Diderot's thoughts on childhood to the *puer robustus* hidden within the character of the nephew. Through this connection, Diderot's version of the *puer robustus* takes on his final form. It becomes apparent in *Rameau's Nephew* that Diderot associates the philosopher, the artist – the

99

individual! – with the child as a threshold creature. The "Me" bemoans the fickleness of the nephew, but he himself bridles at identification with socially prescribed roles and thus returns to childhood in precisely the way described in *The Salon of 1767*. This childishness manifests itself in the nephew, too, when he willingly assimilates one moment and sabotages generally accepted classifications and arrangements the next.

Diderot's further development of the *puer robustus* can be summarized as a three-step process. In the *first* step, Diderot starts with Hobbes's definition of the *puer robustus* as the epitome of evil, but he uses Rousseau to take a fresh look at the sources of this evil, which are found not only in unreason but also in reason itself. In the *second* step, Diderot applies his characterization of the *puer robustus* from the *Encyclopédie* to Rameau's nephew, depicting him as a character who wants to ensure self-preservation through role play. But he then suspends his judgment of good and evil. The agenda of the narrow-minded, inconsiderate individual à la Hobbes is demolished by the radical self-transformation and self-alienation of the nephew, which culminates in aesthetic ecstasy. In the *third* step, Diderot does not merely ascribe to the nephew an indifference to good and evil, he actually turns the threshold creature into a positive, pivotal figure of transgression who breaks through the automatism of behaviors and rules and denounces the false peace of the status quo. In his precarious marginal position, the nephew is damageable, damaged, and damaging.

To prevent any misunderstanding: Diderot's troublemaker is not identical to the creative individual who is so eagerly celebrated by those who scorn the masses. The faulty reasoning behind this eulogy to the individual has been noted by a number of thinkers ranging from Hegel, Tocqueville, and Marx to Foucault and Rancière. Hegel views the "particular" that becomes self-sufficient in an individual as merely the counterpart to a state that operates as an abstract "universal"; Tocqueville points to the internal connection between individualism and despotism; Marx sees the isolated individual as the symptom of a ruling order that destroys social cohesion; Foucault thinks that "opposing" the individual to the state is absurd because the state itself is "individualizing," meaning that it brings forth characters who vaunt their independence; Rancière considers the breakdown of society into a "gathering of individuals" and the power of the state that elevates itself above them to be two sides of the same coin.[61]

Diderot is not among those who ensconce themselves in this opposition between state and individual. His ingenious individual remains closely tied to the existing order in two different ways. *First*, his great gift is not creativity but rather receptivity, or an openness to the world. This individual is someone whose "soul is most expansive, struck by sensations from all things, taking an interest in all that exists in nature" (PhS 1, 235; DOC 15, 35). By having his genius react sympathetically to his surroundings, Diderot gives him a feminine quality, according to the gender clichés common at the time (but unlike Rousseau, he does not believe this quality must be suppressed). *Second*, sympathy and attention enable the genius to shake up situations by "ceaselessly adding to or subtracting from the reality of things" (PhS 1, 240; DOC 15, 40).[62] As a threshold creature, the genius has a tense relationship with society, but he is also dependent on it. He can only be strong if he is not already *pleased* with himself as he is, if he does not believe he can draw on unlimited resources from within himself. This troublemaker is "in love with [. . .] becoming" (KSA 10, 593).

Diderot focuses his attention on liminality, the threshold where a social order acquires its personnel, as it were, where people engage or step away, help make the rules of the game or break them. The strategies of exclusion and inclusion, refusal and participation, are not stuck in legalistic or power-political confrontations (as is the case for Carl Schmitt, Giorgio Agamben, and many others), but instead mark historical transitions. With its liminal structure, the dialog novel *Rameau's Nephew* represents not the tightening of boundaries but their permeability, i.e., the configuration of thresholds. It thus hits on the fundamental situation of the *puer robustus*.

While Hobbes's troublemaker pits himself entirely against the world (as if one actually could!) and Rousseau's troublemaker wants to become one with it (as if that were possible!), Diderot's troublemaker sets the world in motion. Hobbes wants to take the threshold where the individual appears and the order asserts itself and turn it into a border that ensures a rigid division of labor between private interests and state power. Rousseau wants to smooth over the threshold in the *moi commun*, the grand ideal of togetherness. But neither of them ultimately do justice to this threshold, *which cannot simply be imagined out of existence.* Diderot's *puer robustus* thumbs his nose at the egocentric demands of self-interest because he stands outside of himself, but he also eschews the nomocentric anticipation of a different political order. He is neither an egocentric nor a nomocentric troublemaker, he is an *eccentric troublemaker*.[63] Diderot thus goes beyond Hobbes and Rousseau and has the *advantage* over them.

Rameau's nephew is a radical lone outsider, but he provides the template for political acts that can be described and welcomed as collective improvisation.[64] As a result, the political versions of the troublemaker who are yet to appear in this book will have to be measured against Diderot's *puer robustus*. In the loveliest passage from *Rameau's Nephew*, Diderot says of the nephew and others of his kind that

101

their character is so unlike other people's: they disrupt that annoying uniformity which our education, our social conventions, and codes of conduct have inculcated in us. If such a man is present in a group, he acts like a pinch of yeast, fermenting and giving a portion of each person's natural individuality back to them. (RN 8; CR 586f.)

4. Hegel's and Foucault's nephew

Diderot's German translator, Johann Wolfgang von Goethe, succumbed to the temptation (which has been resisted by more recent scholars) to identify the author of *Rameau's Nephew* with the "Me." In his "Remarks" on the novel, Goethe declares that Diderot "deploys all his intellectual powers to portray flatterers and spongers in the full extent of their vileness, and in the process he does not let their patrons off lightly either." "A rascal," Goethe says, is confronted in the novel with "an honest man."[65] I know of no other example in history in which the interpretations of great minds collided as rapidly and abruptly as in the case of *Rameau's Nephew*. Two years after Goethe's translation, a book was published which gave pride of place not to the "Me" but rather to the "Him," the supposed "rascal": the *Phenomenology of Spirit*. The character of the *puer robustus* thus found his way into yet another major text in the history of philosophy. Diderot's adaptation of the character was followed by that of Hegel.

It is worth mentioning another adaptation here. The nephew is given a grand entrance not only in Hegel's *Phenomenology of Spirit* but also in Foucault's *History of Madness* – and Foucault also comes down on the side of the nephew, whom he credits with an insight into the "necessary instability" of reason.[66] I want to stay with Hegel for the time being, however, before addressing Foucault.

Hegel's tribute to Diderot is clandestine; he quotes longer passages from *Rameau's Nephew* without ever mentioning the author or the work by name.[67] Hegel's judgment is crystal clear: the nephew is held up as a testament to the evolution of the spirit into a "higher consciousness," while the "Me" is declared to represent "folly" (PS 319, 318). The "Me" accuses the nephew of stupidity, but this accusation is then turned against himself. Lionel Trilling writes:

> There is no trait whatever in the character of the Nephew which he permits to be blamed or deplored. What any reader naturally understands as a deficiency in Rameau, to be forgiven or "accepted", Hegel takes to be a positive attribute and of the highest significance, nothing less than a necessary condition of the development of Spirit, of *Geist*.[68]

102

Three passages from Diderot's text are quoted or paraphrased in *Phenomenology of Spirit*. The first two relate to the nephew, specifically to his striking ability to play different roles. Hegel speaks of the "madness" of the musician, which is apparent in the fact (and thus begins the first Diderot quote) that he

> mixed together thirty arias, Italian, French, tragic, comic, of every sort; now with a deep bass he descended into hell, then, contracting his throat, he rent the vaults of heaven with a falsetto tone, frantic and soothed, imperious and mocking, by turns. (PS 317f.; RN 68f.; CR 642)

Hegel appends this quote with a paraphrase of a second passage from Diderot in which the nephew is described by his adversary, the "Me." This "Me," to whom Hegel refers as a "tranquil consciousness," observes in the nephew

> a rigmarole of wisdom and folly, [...] a medley of as much skill as baseness, of as many correct as false ideas, a mixture compounded of a complete perversion of sentiment, of absolute shamefulness, and of perfect frankness and truth. It will be unable to refrain from entering into all these tones and running up and down the entire scale of feelings from the profoundest contempt and dejection to the highest pitch of admiration and emotion; but blended with the latter will be a tinge of ridicule which spoils them. (PS 318)[69]

What Hegel has to say in his *Aesthetics* about the romantic individual can also be applied to the nephew: he is characterized by "undisclosedness," "absence of outward shape," and "lack of expression and development." "Such a heart is like a costly precious stone which catches the light only on single facets and they then shine like a flash of lightning" (HA 580).

The third passage from Diderot, which is explicitly identified as a quote in *Phenomenology of Spirit*, is found in a context in which Hegel criticizes the attempt by the "natural self" to make the "particularity" of its "nature" into the "purpose and content" of its "culture." The most that can come from this, according to Hegel, is the hardening of a certain "*kind*" of being (PS 298). It is Diderot's discussion of *espèce* that prompts Hegel to gripe about this "*kind*" of being. *Espèce* is – as Hegel quotes Diderot once again – "the most horrid of all nicknames; for it denotes mediocrity and expresses the highest degree of contempt" (PS 298; cf. RN 73; CR 647). This quote is taken from a tirade by the nephew against the suggestion made by the "Me" that he should raise his son to be a "good" or "honourable man" (RN 73; CR 647). The "Me" is presented as the advocate of a morality that is nothing more than the narrow-minded assertion of a saturated kind of being, a "tranquil consciousness" (PS 328).[70]

Hegel returns to the *espèce* in two other places in his *Phenomenology* – which brings me to the passages in which he references Diderot without the need for quotation marks. He notes that the *espèce* expresses pure "one-sidedness and peculiarity." The "existence of the good and noble" thus remains "an isolated anecdote" – and this "is the most disparaging thing that can be said about it" (PS 327, 319). The most prominent quote from *Rameau's Nephew* (which is not identified as such) can be found in the title of the chapter from which the passages cited here have been taken: "The world of self-alienated Spirit" (PS 296). This title picks up on a comment by the "Me" regarding the nephew's madcap game:

> He was completely oblivious; he carried on, in the grip of a fit of mental alienation [*aliénation de l'esprit*], of enthusiasm so close to madness as to make it uncertain whether he'd ever emerge from it, or whether we oughtn't throw him in a cab and have him taken straight to Bedlam [. . .]. He had completely lost his head. (RN 69f.; CR 642f.)

Via a detour through Rameau's nephew, the *puer robustus* therefore becomes the godfather of the theory of alienation, the impact of which ripples from Hegel through Marx to the present day.[71] Alienation is particularly associated with the troublemaker because it is not solely an affliction for this character, it is an achievement. Diderot joins the nephew's faction when – in an important, obscure passage – he says of himself: "I also know how to alienate myself from myself, a talent without which one achieves nothing worthwhile" (DOC 7, 404).[72] The nephew is not only subjected to situations in which he loses either himself or that which is particular to him (in which he is alienated, in this sense), he also actively disengages from the habits of a given way of being or *espèce*.

Following in Diderot's footsteps, Hegel refers to this process as "alienation" in the positive sense of leaping out of an established identity. The "absolute and universal inversion and alienation" achieved by the nephew is necessary for the education [*Bildung*] of the spirit (PS 316), according to Hegel – and this "*education*, in its absolute determination, is therefore *liberation*" (PR 225).[73] The "birth of liberation from the spirit of alienation"[74] takes place for the nephew – unlike for Arnold Gehlen, who coined the phrase – in an undirected, wild, excessive, and eccentric way. As a champion of transgression, he disturbs the "annoying uniformity" of life and simultaneously runs the risk of madness, which will be a topic of discussion for Foucault. (From afar, Hegel's interpretation of the antagonism between the "Me" and the "Him" recalls the contrast between the "étui-man" and the "destructive character" of Walter Benjamin.)[75]

The nephew lives out his alienation to the full by surrendering to role play. "Now he's a young girl [. . .]; now he's a priest, he's a king, he's a tyrant" (RN 69; CR 642). He acts "the admiring man, the imploring man, the obliging man" and "spends his life in positions that he has had to take up and maintain. [. . .] I look around, and I take up my positions, or I laugh at the positions I see other people taking up. I am an excellent mime artist [. . .]" (RN 84, CR 657). The "Me" actually encourages the nephew to radicalize his view. When the nephew says: "There's only one man in the whole of any kingdom who walks upright, and that's the sovereign. Everyone else just takes up positions," the "Me" responds: "The sovereign? [. . .] Anyone who needs someone is indigent and takes up a position. The King takes up a position before his mistress and before God; he dances his steps in the mime" (RN 85; CR 658). (This monarch can be seen as both a caricature of the Hobbesian sovereign, who is expected to represent the people as an actor, and a variant of the ruler who remains caught up in dependencies according to Rousseau.)

The "Me" and the nephew are not in agreement in their assessment of this role play, however – and this is important when we come to consider Hegel. While the nephew enjoys his role play, the "Me" intends it as a criticism when he claims that all the world is a stage. To counter this illusory world, the "Me" mentions a character who is supposed to be left out of such role play: "But nonetheless there is one person who is exempt from dancing the mime. And that's the philosopher who has nothing and asks for nothing" (RN 85; CR 658). Hegel takes exception to this praise for the philosopher, who is exemplified by the figure of Diogenes. This kind of withdrawal from the world, according to Hegel, leads to an individual who has relinquished his willingness to mediate and solely pursues an agenda of caring "for *himself qua* individual" (PS 319).[76] This "simple consciousness of the true and the good," in its "dull, uninspired *thought*" (PS 318f.), is poisonous to the universality with which the philosopher must engage. Such universality is exemplified by the nephew, who playfully puts himself in the position of others and represents "the self-disruptive nature of all relationships and the conscious disruption of them" (PS 321).

Hegel can only halfheartedly enjoy this playacting, however, because he believes there is a danger that the player will escape into an illusory world or take "*flight* from the real world" (PS 297). But this does not affect his assessment of the nephew, because not only is the nephew *playing*, he makes it clear in every single moment that he is *only* playing, and he thus avoids this flight from the world. By disclosing the fact of his play, he paves the way for overcoming alienation, an act that is necessary for freeing the consciousness from the clutches of reality. Though the nephew engages in the "universal deception of [himself] and others," he possesses "the shamelessness which gives utterance to this deception" and thus proclaims "the greatest truth" (PS 317). Therefore, when he surrenders to the "disunited" content and the "riches" of the characters he plays, the nephew does not make himself guilty of the "hypocrisy" that Hegel holds against actors elsewhere in the *Phenomenology of Spirit* (PS 444, 450).[77]

To counter the *espèce*, or the simply defined morality that degenerates into habit or second nature, Hegel holds up "education" – as explained earlier – by means of which the self moves beyond itself. The nephew's flexibility is, therefore, a counterpart to a "self-propelling process of formation,"[78] to the battle of the "newly emergent life" against the "shameless power" of the status quo (PW 176f.), which Hegel wants to unleash in intellectual, social, and political life.

Hegel makes an important contribution to the interpretation of the troublemaker by fitting the moral assessment of this character into the dynamics of the philosophy of history. In his first two grand entrances, the *puer robustus* was either evil (Hobbes) or good (Rousseau). But Hegel picks up on the ambivalence between good and evil that he finds in Diderot and translates it into a historical development through which the evil troublemaker is transformed into the good one. According to Hegel, the supposedly "noble consciousness" of the "Me" is nothing more than "ignoble and repudiated," which makes the "repudiated consciousness" of the nephew appear to be "the nobility which characterizes the most highly developed freedom of self-consciousness" (PS 317). This paves the way for the historical-philosophical justification of the revolutionary disturbance that Marx and Engels expect from the *puer robustus*.[79]

If Hegel could choose between the "Me" and the "Him," between *espèce* and troublemaker, he would come down on the side of the nephew. This is not to say that he would make himself comfortable by the nephew's side, however. The "nobility" or virtuousness of the nephew is only a temporary distinction. Hegel defends him with the aim of pointing out that the reckless questioning of rules is a transitional stage on the path to a higher consciousness. His acclaim for the nephew is coupled with disparagement or, to put it more positively, with an attempt to surmount or repeal his mentality.[80] As Hegel sees it, the nephew stands for "the consciousness that is aware of its disruption and openly declares it." But this consciousness not only "derides existence and the universal confusion, and derides its own self as well; it is at the same time the fading, but still audible, sound of all this confusion" (PS 319).[81] With this "fading sound," Hegel anticipates the defeat of aporetic oppositions, i.e., a dialectical development of the spirit. This development moves past both the narrow-minded torpidity of an existing order and the wild disturbance that disrupts it.

We can draw an arc here to other works by Hegel. In his *Aesthetics*, he writes: "For man is this: not only the bearer of the contradiction of his multiple nature but the sustainer of it, remaining therein equal and true to himself" (HA 240). And in *Elements of the Philosophy of Right*, he says: "The principle of modern states has enormous strength and depth because it allows the principle of subjectivity to attain fulfillment in the *self-sufficient extreme* of personal particularity, while at the same time *bringing it back to substantial unity* and so preserving this unity in the principle of subjectivity itself" (PR 282 [§260], cf. 223 [§185 Addition]).

In the end, Hegel wants to sound the death knell for both Rameau's nephew and the troublemaker. And this is the point at which I – like many others[82] – cease to follow him. Hegel desires an order that – unlike the abstract or "dead" law (PW 177) or the tranquilized *espèce* – is alive and has been fully incorporated into the lives of the individuals that belong to it. He knows that "the whole does not keep pace with the growth of the individual," meaning that "the living unity which binds the members together" will always grow "weak" (PW 176). But he believes this contradiction and division can be overcome losslessly through the synthesis of the living spirit, the spiritual life. This is the false promise behind his dialectic. It is impossible to achieve unity between universal institutions and individual ways of life – and this is precisely why the troublemaker remains alive. Everything about Hegel's eulogy to him in the *Phenomenology of Spirit* is correct – with the exception that Hegel wants it to be only temporary. Diderot has "the last word,"[83] and it is he who is proven right instead of Hegel. The "pinch of yeast" that lifts the whole continues to take effect.

Rameau's nephew fascinated Hegel, and he also fascinated Michel Foucault. Foucault says Diderot "may have been the most attentive philosopher of the eighteenth century,"[84] and, like Hegel, he gives pride of place to Diderot's skewed hero. Rameau's nephew is also the figurehead in the third section of Foucault's early work *History of Madness*. "The history that we shall write in this last part takes place inside the space opened by the words of the Nephew"[85] – it is the history of madness in the late eighteenth and early nineteenth century, in which "the relationship between reason and unreason takes on a radical new face."

Oddly, Foucault does not say a single word in his book about the appearance of the nephew in the *Phenomenology of Spirit*, even though as an apostate follower of Hyppolite, he knew Hegel's work well and mentioned him often.[86] In a radio lecture given shortly after his book was published, Foucault quoted one of the passages from *Rameau's Nephew* that was cited by Hegel.[87] It seems as though Foucault has to evade Hegel's interpretation of Diderot in order to live out his own fascination to the full. A small philological detail also speaks in favor of this evasive strategy: Foucault deliberately conceals the fact that Hegel, in his discussion of "insanity," quotes the psychiatrist Philippe Pinel, who plays an important role in Foucault's own work.[88]

Foucault wants to rescue the nephew from Hegel's dialectic and use him against it. His troublemaker does not only temporarily advance the dialectic of the spirit, he sets himself up permanently at the edge of modernity. With relish, Foucault cites Diderot's praise for the "pinch of yeast" that stirs society as well as his passages describing the nephew's crazed role play. It suits Foucault well that, in French, the terms *aliénation* and *aliénés* – estrangement notwithstanding – stand first and foremost for being exterior to oneself in the form of madness.[89] To understand exactly what Foucault expects from Diderot's mad hero, we have to trace how Foucault includes him in his history of madness and then integrate this history into the theory of the troublemaker that is developed in this book.

In three fairly clear steps, Foucault moves from Descartes through Hobbes to Diderot. According to Foucault, Descartes wants to banish "the perils of madness" through the "exercise of Reason" and drive it "underground."[90] The "unreason" of the madman is viewed by Descartes as a flaw or defect. There is something reassuring about this, because it means the madman does not possess a secret strength (such as extra-sensory impulses) but instead suffers from a weakness. He lingers in the "lurking presence of the beast" and is confined to "silence," remaining incapable of speech.[91]

Hobbes's description of the mentally ill also defuses madness in this way, but for Hobbes, the pathological madman is joined by another with a much more active presence than the one mentioned by Descartes. This madman, fool, or *homo insipiens* is dumb but not mute; he delivers wild speeches and blows the "trumpet of sedition." Foucault does not mention Hobbes's thoughts on this, but they fit perfectly with the transition he describes, through which madness "found its voice once more":[92] "But we know that this fortress of absolute tranquility, which would forever reduce madness to silence, does not exist."[93] Just as Hobbes becomes entangled in defensive combat against the foolish troublemaker, the obstructionist that follows him makes a complete return from his exile in insanity and even comes to be viewed as a champion of liberty.

Foucault is not interested in rehabilitating troublemakers as reasonable or benevolent individuals, however, but rather in casting a new light on characters who – like Diderot's hero – show signs of madness. The mental flexibility of the nephew is evidence for Foucault's thesis that madness cannot be banished to the realm of the animalistic. In opposition to Descartes, who proclaimed the "lyricism of unreason" to be "impossible," *Rameau's Nephew* marks the beginning of the "non-Cartesian nature of modern thought" and the "reappearance of madness in the domain of language."[94] Madness is no longer attributed to a deficiency;

instead, it is said to spring from reason itself. It appears as the "hidden face" of "freedom," of "history," of "becoming in man."[95]

Where once there was a great dichotomy between reason and bestiality, a space now opens up in which borders are drawn, moved, fortified, or transformed into thresholds that can be passed. Foucault is and always will be a theorist of the threshold creature or of liminality.[96] He depicts those who suffer and break under societal conditions, who behave conspicuously and are treated disparagingly. But he also describes people who not *only* retreat madly into a hermetic world but who *also* direct their barbs against the status quo: Hölderlin, E. T. A. Hoffmann, Gérard de Nerval and others.[97] Foucault could have mentioned Rilke as well: "The time of that other interpretation will come, and not one word will be left upon another, and all the meanings will dissolve like clouds and fall like rain."[98] It is not that all of these authors are simply lacking reason, like the madmen described by Descartes and Hobbes; instead, they have the aesthetic gift of being able to shift meanings and stir up the *espèce* or "milieu."[99] In doing so, they prevent "reason" from growing "bored with itself."[100] In a radio lecture from 1963 that was first published in 2013, Foucault says:

> I have the impression, if I can put it this way, that, very fundamentally, within us, the possibility of speaking, the possibility of being mad, are contemporaneous, and like twins they reveal, beneath our steps, the most perilous but also, possibly, the most marvelous or the most insistent of our freedoms.

At bottom, even if everyone in the world were rational, there would always remain the possibility of traversing the world of our signs, the world of our words, our language, of confusing their most familiar meanings, through the sole and miraculous eruption of a handful of colliding words, of turning the world upside down.[101]

Foucault is thus following the tracks of Hegel, who celebrated the "madness of the musician" (PS 317) as an ability to shift and reverse everyday habits. He even praises Hegel for rescuing "madness" in the *Phenomenology of Spirit* at least "in part" from the "zone of exclusion" to which it had long been banished.[102] But because this liberation only takes place "in part," Foucault must part ways with Hegel. Unlike Hegel, he is not content to leave madness as a strictly delineated transitional stage in the development of consciousness. He repudiates the "*homo dialecticus*," whose great achievement is said to be that he "loses [his] truth and finds it again illuminated,"[103] and he takes up residence in the confusing terrain that is "feared like a cry" and "awaited like a song," where "being achieves its limit and where the limit defines being."[104] Foucault would later refer to this as "a movement by which one extricates oneself from something, without saying anything about what one is moving towards."[105] With his interpretation of *Rameau's Nephew*, Foucault remains closer to Diderot than Hegel – and as I myself am a proponent of Diderot's eccentric troublemaker, I am also happy to follow Foucault.

Even with Diderot, the question arose as to whether a political message could be elicited from the nephew. I have tried to answer this question by taking a detour through his concept of genius, where I stumbled upon the semantic mobilization of self-interpretations and the collective improvisation of forms of life. It is self-evident to Foucault that madness has a place not only in medical discourse but in political discourse, not just because Foucault is a critic of discipline and normalization, but because he wants to turn the marginal figure into an actor.

If the madman is not ground down by obsessive thoughts or fears of persecution, he can advance to become a troublemaker. Then he will, in a sense, enjoy the crisis triggered by disruption and disarrangement. His enjoyment of this crisis depends on the accompanying critique that madness does not content itself with the "scarcely audible words of [. . .] unreason" but actually gives them "expression." In this way, Foucault says, he claims a "right of abode" and a "grasp on Western culture" that can take the form of "contestation" and lead to the "contestation of all things" in the political order.[106]

Foucault does not need to force this politicization of madness into the period around 1800. It was already a *fait accompli* for Diderot's successors. Both left- and right-leaning commentators on the French Revolution claimed that social conditions had been shaken up with an overconfidence bordering on madness.

The left-leaning faction was represented by Jules Michelet, who saw in this "beautiful folly" the strength to effect "all the progress of the world," and who, in 1847, welcomed the French Revolution as the sweet fruit of this folly:

> Who would undertake the task of following, from unknown depths to the surface, the progress of a thought? Who can tell the confused forms, the modifications, the fatal delays it has to undergo for ages? With what slow steps does it emerge from instinct to musing, to reverie, and thence to the poetical chiaroscuro! How long is its progress confined to children and fools, to poets and madmen? And yet one day that madness proves to be the common sense of all![107]

Thomas Carlyle, the right-leaning opponent of Michelet in the debate about the interpretation of the French Revolution, generously claimed in 1836 what Foucault subsequently tried painstakingly to prove: that in "every the wisest Soul lies a whole world of internal Madness," from which a "world of Wisdom" could spring.[108] But no sooner was this said than he grew discomfited by this acknowledgement of the constructive forces of madness. In his work *The French Revolution*, Carlyle quoted his earlier statement and distanced himself from it:

Rash enthusiast of Change, beware! Hast thou well considered [...] [that] our whole being is an infinite abyss, *overarched* by Habit, as by a thin Earth-rind, laboriously built together? But if "every man," as it has been written, "holds confined within him a mad-man," what must every society do; [...] "Without such Earth-rind of Habit," continues our author, "[...] in a word, *fixed ways* of acting and of believing, – Society would not exist at all. [...]." Let but, by ill chance, in such ever-enduring struggle, – your "thin Earth-rind" be once *broken!* The fountains of the great deep boil forth [...]. Your "Earth-rind" is shattered, swallowed up; instead of a green flowery world, there is a waste wild-weltering chaos; – which has again, with tumult and struggle, to *make* itself into a world.[109]

When it comes to the contrast between habit and weltering chaos, the troublemaker is in his element. Friedrich Schiller will usher him onto the stage.

— IV. —

UNLOVING CHILD, WICKED SON, STRONG SAVIOR

Friedrich Schiller

1. The *puer robustus* as a "freedman of creation"

I originally intended only to discuss the writers who specifically mention the *puer robustus*; Diderot is certainly not the last of this lot. But the temptation is too great to widen the circle and invite others into these ranks. Agitators and obstructionists, outlaws and misfits of all sorts thrust themselves into the picture, and I cannot simply ignore them. I will break ranks twice: once when I talk about Friedrich Schiller in this chapter, and later when I talk about Richard Wagner.

I can justify this breaking of ranks by saying that the rules in a book about breaking rules should not be taken all too seriously. This is not just a contrived excuse, however. I want to address Schiller – and Wagner later on – because he makes an important contribution to the conflict sparked by the character of the *puer robustus*. Schiller does not break the thread running through my narrative, he makes it vibrate like a plucked string. I am sticking with the question of power and morality, and with the troublemaker as a threshold creature who sabotages the political order or instigates historical change.

The *puer robustus* appears in the works of Hobbes, Rousseau, and Diderot – and even in those of Horace – in the context of a debate about the political and social order. The man-child is most interesting in his role as a human among other humans, not as a child of his parents. This kind of independence or liberation can only come about when the child is allowed to go his own way, or the wrong way, and when the man is recognized as a "freedman of creation."[1]

As a consequence, the career of the *puer robustus* in the seventeenth and eighteenth centuries was accompanied by a growing critique of the patriarchy – a critique that could base itself on John Locke and Immanuel Kant, among others.[2] In a patriarchy, a *special* political order is interlocked with a *special* familial order. It comprises the sovereign and subjects of a land, and it is defined by tutelage and nonage, domination and subordination. Instead of doing what his forebears tell him to do, instead of contenting himself with his status as a subject, the *puer robustus* leads a life on the threshold and questions the act of subjugation. He removes himself from the patriarchy.

Although Hobbes bemoans the existence of the *puer robustus*, he accepts the crisis of patriarchy that is the prerequisite for his appearance. Hobbes's anti-patriarchal tendencies can be seen in his critique of paternal privileges (L[e] 138–41), and in the fact that his sovereign does not function as an overpowering father figure but instead (supposedly) acts on behalf of the people. Rousseau saws away at the perch of the patriarch even more fiercely than Hobbes; his republican alliance is based on the family paradigm of brotherhood, but certainly not fatherhood.

As a student of the institute that would become known as the Hohe Karlsschule military academy, Schiller's experience of the patriarchy was bitter. On the one hand, he was exposed early on to the Enlightenment theories of his time there, but on the other hand, Duke Karl Eugen – whom the pupils were forced to address as "Father" (cf. SW 5, 239) – enforced a regimen of strict punishment and scrupulous control.[3] In *Don Carlos*, Schiller settles a score with a feudal father figure, in whom we can recognize his former school rector and territorial ruler. In the "Thalia" fragment of this play, Schiller writes: "The fear / [...] – a shuddering dread, – / Comes o'er me ever at that terrible name" (CWS 4, 127) – namely, the word "father."

To explore how Schiller entangles the crisis of patriarchy with the rise of the troublemaker, I will first look at *The Robbers*, a work of brilliance and violence by the 20-year-old writer. In no other play by Schiller does the tension between order and disturbance escalate to such an extreme (section 2). After a side glance at the short story "The Criminal of Lost Honor," I will draw an arc from Schiller's first play to his last, *Wilhelm Tell* (section 3). As we will see, elements of Franz and Karl Moor come together in the titular protagonist of this work, but the dynamics shift entirely to the political sphere. Schiller depicts Wilhelm Tell as a troublemaker who carries the key to a new political order in his pocket. It remains to be seen how people will find their way in this order, or whether the troublemaker must leave the stage once all men have become "brothers."

2. Franz and Karl Moor:
All power for me – or a different power for all?

The family story that Schiller tells in *The Robbers* is also a political story. Two sons, who have grown up to become hostile brothers, slave away for their patriarch while simultaneously grappling with a political order that has stamped out their roles for them. Franz and Karl Moor have limited ability to cope with this dual private and political challenge. They seem to stray through life. Even if Schiller was not familiar with the *puer robustus*, he uses phrases that could be applied to him: the elder Moor refers to Karl, his older son, as an "unloving child" (*Robbers* 31), and Franz, the younger, as a "wicked son" (*Robbers* 152).

The source of conflict is the home itself – not parental, in this case, but strictly paternal. Unlike other father–child dramas and stories from the time, in which the father plays both a fundamental and ambivalent role (Lessing's *Miss Sara Sampson* and *Emilia Galotti*, Diderot's *The Father of the Family*, Marmontel's *The School of Fathers* and *Error of a Good Father*), the dynamics of Schiller's plot have been transferred largely to the sons. The father is weak, but the sons remain fixated on him as if he were strong.

Franz Moor is a twice-over loser in the lottery of life. He is the second-born son, and with his "Laplander's nose," his "blackamoor's lips" and his "Hottentot's eyes," he is ugly as well: "I truly think [nature] made a heap of the most hideous parts of every human kind as the ingredients for me" (*Robbers* 33). Like the ugly Hunchback of Notre Dame, who will have his turn as the *puer robustus* later on, Franz Moor is ridiculed and despised. But unlike the Hunchback, Franz seems obsessed with the idea of his own disadvantage, which means he garners little sympathy.

Franz no longer tries to compete (positively) for the love of his father; he only wants to ensure (negatively) that his father's love for his first-born son is destroyed, to "prise a son from his father's heart" (*Robbers* 32). The second-born acts as though his father's affection meant nothing to him, as if he no longer had a father, as if he were left entirely to his own devices. In an act of desperation, he tries to neutralize the ruling patriarchal order. Franz does not position himself within the family; he is concerned only with his status as an individual in the world. In this endeavor, he essentially follows Hobbes's description of the state of nature:[4] "Each man has the same right to the greatest and the least; claim destroys claim, impulse destroys impulse, force destroys force. Might is right, and the limits of our strength our only law" (*Robbers* 33).

What Franz is describing here is nothing less than the war of all against all. According to Hobbes, this war can only end when individuals submit to a higher power; he who refuses to accept the necessity of such a power is evil – he is the *puer robustus*. Franz Moor is also evil because he rejects this insight and imagines that he has the upper hand. As a "lord" he already rules over "peasants" (*Robbers* 33), but he wants to go even further, to take his father's place and supplant his older brother. The power he seeks – unlike that of the patriarch, who bears the burden of caring for his children – is clearly a form of pure despotic rule. While Hobbes presses power-hungry individuals to enter the social contract by reminding them of their vulnerability and need for protection (L[e] 87), Franz escalates his power play. He scorns the "conventions men have made, to rule the pulses that turn the world" (*Robbers* 33). And while Rousseau mobilizes a sense of political community spirit and the social resource of pity, Franz derides the "ridiculous argument from the proximity of bodies to the harmony of minds" (*Robbers* 34).

The Robbers is a lesson in the limits of an individualistic fantasy of power. The hubris of the "monster" Franz (CWS 3, 134) becomes his downfall. Too late, he realizes that he cannot pull all the strings. When Franz tries to have Karl eliminated, his servants turn against him; the so-called *Trauerspiel* (tragedy) version of the play includes a dialog between Franz and his servant Herrmann, in which the lord vainly demands obedience. "Tremble, slave!" Franz says, more malicious than mighty. Herrmann, in turn, threatens to "invite the peoples of the earth to the table" and expose Franz as a criminal. The servant appears here as a precursor to Hegel's bondsman and a herald of the proletariat, just as Franz's egoistic power fantasy serves as a protocapitalist scenario. But this scenario leads him to a dead end: "Woe! Woe! even my creatures betray me. – The pillars of my happiness begin to crumble, and the enemy descends upon me in fury" (SW 1, 924f.).

Franz is an (almost) perfect negative example à la Hobbes, i.e., an egocentric who banks on his own strength and lingers stubbornly, contrary to all reason, in a state of nature on this side of the social contract: "Very well, then! courage, and to work! I will crush everything that stands in the way of my becoming master." (I cannot help but compare this with a few sentences posted online by Eric Harris, one of the young shooters at Columbine High School in Colorado in 1999: "I am the law. If you don't like it, you die. [. . .]. Dead people can't do many things, like argue."[5]) There is a passing indication that Schiller deviates from Hobbes, however. Franz's need for power and willingness to use violence are not simply a given, they are traced back to *suffering*. Franz has the creeping suspicion that he could have turned the corner to cooperation and joined the social order were he not internally stunted and brutalized. "And master I must be," Franz says, "to force my way to goals that I shall never gain through kindness" (*Robbers* 35). Resorting to violence and striving for power seem to be his second-best strategy, one employed for lack of a viable alternative.

The best solution would not be to come to one's senses (like Hobbes's good man) and follow the laws that would enable him to pursue his own interests within certain limits. Instead, for Schiller's good man – and even for Franz Moor, with his notion of "kindness" – faculties come into play which morally outbid the rational calculation of adherence to the law. This shows that even though Schiller places Franz Moor in Hobbes's slipstream, he himself tends to follow Rousseau.[6]

Franz Moor exhibits mere traces of the human faculties that lead to goodness. These faculties for good are more prominent in his brother, and Franz himself affirms this in a strange way. No sooner has the play begun than Franz tries to convince his father in a long speech that Karl's good disposition has changed to evil. (He does so by reading a report from an "informant in Leipzig" that he himself has forged.) However, Franz cannot avoid first describing and confirming his brother's good characteristics before chipping away at them.

He plucks at least four elements from the repertoire of the good man (cf. *Robbers* 27f.). He first mentions the "frankness that mirrors the soul in his eyes"; Franz says this sincerity has warped into "insolence" in Karl. Second, he mentions Karl's "tender feeling that melts him to tears of sympathy at any sight of suffering"; this "tenderness," according to Franz, has turned into advances of an erotic nature, an indication of a "depraved" life. Third, there is Karl's "manly courage"; this has seduced a "bold imagination" – as his brother bewails – to take criminals as role models. Fourth, Franz speaks of the "shining virtues" that befit "a model citizen"; but Franz hypocritically accuses Karl of using these virtues to lead not the citizenry, but a band of thieves.

Before talking about the young nobleman's moral decline, we must note that Karl's faculties for good fit devastatingly well with Rousseau. Schiller mentions both the "frankness" that is cultivated in Rousseau's *Confessions* and the "sympathy" that plays a key role in his *Second Discourse* and various other works. "Courage" is one of the first goals of education in *Emile*, and civic "virtues" are the basis of the *Social Contract*. The 20-year-old Schiller did not have all of these connections in mind, but the astonishing correlations here encourage me to include *The Robbers* in this book.

Franz Moor represents the evil *puer robustus* as depicted by Hobbes – with a slight variation in that he employs violence because his kindness is too weak. By contrast, Karl Moor – based on the portrait painted of him by his brother – has the faculties to be the good *puer robustus* that we know from Rousseau. We must therefore ask a different question of Karl than of Franz. The question is not why or how someone on the threshold

116

of society refuses to *become* good (which, in a Hobbesian context, means obedient), but rather why or how he *loses* his goodness. What tips the scales here is not the weakness of reason, but hurt feelings.

At the beginning of the play, Karl finds himself in a situation that is still compatible with Rousseau. His associates are not entirely savory characters, but he consorts with them primarily because he holds "healthy nature" against "ridiculous conventions" (*Robbers* 36). For Schiller, "nature" is not just the guarantee of Karl's goodness, it is his battle cry against the "law." While Franz bristles at the "conventions" (see above) that curtail his individual power, Karl grapples with the agreements and rules of a despotic order. In a draft of an ultimately discarded scene that would have appeared at the start of the play, Karl imagines himself to be a "great man" who takes up the struggle against this order:

> Why are there despots? Why should thousands upon thousands writhe beneath the whims of *one* belly and hang on its every flatulence? – The law makes it so. – Curse the law that slows to a snail's pace what could have been an eagle's flight! The law has never made a great man, but freedom leaps the palisades of convention and breeds colossi and extremities. (SW 1, 918)

Karl suspects that his dream of freedom could breed "colossi and extremities." But why does he assume the law is entirely hostile to him? His assumption is based not only on the alienation of the man of nature from the political order, but on personal disappointment. This is where Rousseau and Schiller part ways. The latter has Karl despairing of the law of the *world* because he despairs of his *father*. When his brother Franz deceives him into believing that his father has disowned him (*Robbers* 42), Karl takes this (with negligent credulity) to be the truth, and he loses his faith in the world: "All so happy, all kin through the spirit of peace! the whole world one family, a father there above – a father, but not mine – I alone cast out, I alone set apart from the ranks of the blessed [. . .]" (*Robbers* 99). Disappointment can make Karl evil only because, for him, the good in the world is inextricably bound to the goodness of his father. Political law is conflated with the law of his father. Because Karl believes he has been deceived by his father, he takes revenge not on his father but on the world:

> Oh, then catch fire, manly resignation, be as a ravening tiger, gentle lamb, and let every fibre stiffen to hatred and destruction! [. . .] So let me forget sympathy and human feeling! I have no father now, I have no love now, and blood and death shall teach me to forget that I ever held anything dear! Oh, my amusement shall be the terror of the earth [. . .]. (*Robbers* 48f.)

As the head of his band of robbers, Karl plays the role of "a monster on this glorious earth" (*Robbers* 99) and compares himself with Milton's Satan (CWS 3, 249). When he ultimately realizes that he has been driven into battle through the intrigues of his brother, he briefly indulges in the ecstatic fantasy that he could once again be "pure as the heavenly aether" and have "peace" return to his soul (*Robbers* 156). But he has already committed countless crimes, and Karl allows the violence to escalate to dispel any doubt that he is beyond salvation and deserves the maximum punishment. Looking back, he laments that he "called it revenge and right" to "make the world a fairer place through terror, and uphold the cause of justice through lawlessness"; "Oh, childish vanity – here I stand at the limit of a life of horror" (*Robbers* 159).

It is notable that he refers to his crimes as "childish," as they truly are the acts of a child or boy who has grown wicked but, by gaining an understanding of his wickedness, comes to appreciate goodness in the end. This can be seen in his willingness to submit to the law. The maximum penalty he chooses is not to seek death by his own hand but to hand himself over to the "law" for punishment:

> But still something remains that can reconcile me to the laws against which I have offended, and restore the order which I have violated. They must have a sacrifice – a sacrifice that will make manifest their invulnerable majesty to all mankind – and I myself shall be the victim. For them I must surely die. [...] I shall go and give myself up into the hands of the law. (*Robbers* 159f.)

Karl, the "unloving child" – unlike Franz, the "wicked son" – takes the audience on an emotional roller coaster ride. An irascible but, one suspects, good-hearted youth rails against his conventional peers, and ultimately against everyone and anyone – or, as Hegel says with a shake of his head, against the "general state of the world" (HA 179). Karl then rashly and overzealously blunders into a major disappointment that drives him to savor his wickedness to the full. In the end, he wants to offer up a sacrifice that will serve "all mankind," an act that brings to mind the ultimate sacrifice that Jesus made as the scapegoat[7] for "all mankind." The birth of universalism from monotheism is re-enacted here. What started in the family becomes a matter for all mankind. In his judgment of himself, Karl internalizes the law and, in doing so, levels criticism against an instrumental interpretation of the law, according to which the "evil man" will only accept laws for the sake of personal advantage – an interpretation that encourages today's rational choice theorists to hark back to Hobbes.[8]

Because Karl Moor lives out his desperation with no regard for the consequences or the people concerned, he effectively becomes a universal villain. The judgment passed on him therefore goes beyond merely

118

settling a family feud or punishing an ordinary criminal; it represents the punishment of a crime against humanity, a universal atonement. Good and evil themselves are at stake here. The themes of power and morality that are woven into the character of the *puer robustus* once again come together here. The escalation of power and violence also increases the possibility of a transformation into the greatest good: "Perhaps the greatest villain is not farther removed from the most upright man than the petty offender; for the moral forces keep even pace with the powers of the mind [. . .]" (CWS 3, 135).

The "law" to which Karl delivers himself up is still the law of the status quo, i.e., that of the society he rejected as being despotic. But it receives Karl's stamp of approval nonetheless because it makes the right decision, at least this one time, in its judgment against him. Punishment is meted out to the person who knows he has led an improper life. In accepting this law, Karl opposes his brother, who has set his sights on becoming the "master" and seeks to battle everyone on his own. With his reference to "all mankind," Karl is anticipating – however vaguely – a legal order that speaks on behalf of this mankind and that remedies the defect of merely consolidating the "palisades of convention" (see above).

It is worth including Schiller in the history and theory of the *puer robustus* because, in *The Robbers*, he brings together the same two troublemakers I found in Hobbes and Rousseau: Franz, the egocentric troublemaker, is contrasted with Karl, the nomocentric troublemaker. The one who wants all power for himself wrestles with the one who wants another power for all. (The eccentric troublemaker is nowhere to be found in *The Robbers*.) But it is also worth including Schiller because his description of the genesis of good and evil, which culminates in the two main characters, is different than that of Hobbes and Rousseau.

The wickedness that surfaces in Franz and at least partially in Karl Moor is not the expression of a lack of reason for Schiller, as it is for Hobbes, but it is also not the result of incorrect socialization, as it is for Rousseau. Instead of the Hobbesian birth of wickedness from the demon of foolishness, or Rousseau's story of wickedness as the fruit of self-love, *The Robbers* depicts the birth of wickedness from disappointment. Evil is given a back story: it springs from the vicissitudes of life. These include discrimination and rejection, which can rouse pity but can also trigger self-satisfaction, self-righteousness, and self-administered justice. This is particularly clear in Schiller's story "The Criminal of Lost Honor," which was published five years after *The Robbers* in 1786 and is, in many respects, a counterpart to his first play:

> The friend of truth [. . .] can no longer be surprised to see the poisonous hemlock thriving in the same flower bed where otherwise only healing

herbs blossom, to find wisdom and foolhardiness, vice and virtue, together in one cradle. ("Criminal of Lost Honor" 40)

It is almost as if Schiller were anticipating Mao Zedong's comment that China's soil would produce both fragrant flowers and poisonous weeds. If good and evil are not tied to fixed traits in an individual, then no one can ever tell someone else outright that they are good or evil. The edifying contrast between the "unloving child" and the "wicked son" begins to wobble. One also cannot insist that people start out evil and become good (Hobbes) or start out good and become evil (Rousseau). The moral status of the troublemaker is once again up for debate.

Christian Wolf, the titular protagonist of "The Criminal of Lost Honor," believes himself, like Franz Moor, to be at a disadvantage in the lottery of life (of beauty, of wealth, etc.). Also like Franz Moor, he tries to achieve success as a thief. He futilely seeks "fraternal unity" ("Criminal of Lost Honor" 51) among criminals, but in the end the power of the law turns against him.

Schiller's short story is an important companion to *The Robbers* because it explores the reasons for the emergence of the troublemaker in more detail. It is not, as in the case of the brothers Moor, just about personal disappointment and political disenfranchisement, both of which have their origins in patriarchy. Here, economic deprivation also plays a role. When the "criminal" Christian Wolf is released from prison, he is "turned away" by everyone and cannot even find work as a day laborer or swineherd. It is not "vanity" or "recklessness" that drives him to poaching again; it is "dire poverty."[9] Beneath the evil *puer robustus*, who breaks the rules in pursuit of an individual advantage, and beneath the good *puer robustus*, who breaks the rules in anticipation of a different, universal order, we find a type who might be considered their poor relation. The "loss" that such individuals suffer leads them to "become aliens in [their] own homeland – and often in [their] own homes."[10] Schiller grants them the emergency right to break the rules. This right takes effect when the universal order fails to guarantee that an individual can provide for himself.

Schiller is expanding on an idea from Hobbes here, who also permits the rules to be broken for the sake of self-preservation. When someone "as if in a great famine [takes] the food by force, or stealth, which he cannot obtaine for mony nor charity [...] he is totally Excused" (L[e] 208). This situation, which is considered an exception by Hobbes, is given more attention by Schiller, and it eventually moves right to the center of Victor Hugo's and Marx's depictions of the impoverished masses. The perpetrator profile in "The Criminal of Lost Honor" therefore combines economic deprivation with the social experience of missing out and

120

the desire to show everyone. Economic, political, and private motives become muddled and intensify the conflict.

Thus far there has been much talk of conflict and crisis in the political order, but not much about finding a way out of this crisis. Schiller does not stop at the breaking of rules, however; he takes the next step, which leads from transgression, sedition, and resistance to a new order. In *The Robbers*, this next step is only counterfactually indicated in Karl's invocation of the "law." The criminal of lost honor does not even reach this point and can only hope in vain for the "mercy" of the prince.[11] The step is not taken in earnest until Schiller's last drama.

3. Wilhelm Tell's journey from loner to league founder

In the play *Wilhelm Tell* from 1804, Schiller makes a triple jump from the old order, via the transgression of rules, to the establishment of a new order. The old order unmistakably follows a Hobbesian schema: there is a king who is feared by all but who also "protects" his subjects, and when young Walter asks why the people do not have "the courage to protect themselves," his father Wilhelm Tell responds: "The neighbor there dare not his neighbor trust" (CWS 4, 66). In this old world, it is the sovereign who prevents the war of all against all. A new order is to be established not for the benefit of "all mankind," as Karl Moor imagined it, but for the benefit of Switzerland. What Tocqueville had to say about Switzerland also applies to *Wilhelm Tell*: "The stage may be small but there is greatness in the play."[12]

"Who shall deliver you?" the Baron of Attinghausen asks anxiously on his deathbed – and the subjects who no longer want to be treated as children respond: "Ourselves" (CWS 4, 86). This self-deliverance is to be achieved through the creation of an order based on a union or contract, in which the people "[rule] themselves in peace" (CWS 4, 48). But these happy days are not yet here, and the revolution proves to be risky. The transition from one order to another inevitably results in a crisis and a lawless, unlegislated state. The *we* who is supposed to rule does not even exist yet; the political subject is still in the process of being formed. The Swiss who swear an oath to the confederation can swear to it only as a static ideal. They lack the necessary destructive, creative energy. "Oh, when will come deliverance to this devoted land?" (CWS 4, 14). There is no answer to this question for the time being, so a counter-question is asked instead: "Without him [a savior], what have you power to do?" (CWS 4, 85). This question is posed by Hedwig, Wilhelm Tell's wife.

Because the confederates-to-be are not capable of using force themselves, they need someone to do it for them. They find their savior in

Wilhelm Tell – who, in the first part of the play, however, clearly belongs neither to the old existing order nor to the new imagined one. He is not concerned with the rules and regulations of the emperor, but he also does not want to get involved with the union of confederates. That Tell has what it takes to be a savior is initially far more unlikely than the usual glorification of him would suggest. To begin with, he is depicted as someone who, astonishingly, bears more resemblance to Franz Moor than to Karl.[13] Tell is an individualist, something that becomes abundantly clear in his dispute with Stauffacher:

> *Stauffacher.* Much might be done – did we stand fast together.
> *Tell.* When the ship founders, he will best escape who seeks no other's safety but his own.
> *Stauffacher.* And you desert the common cause so coldly?
> *Tell.* A man can safely count but on himself.
> *Stauffacher.* Nay, even the weak grow strong by union.
> *Tell.* But the strong man is the strongest when alone. (CWS 4, 22)

Tell is reluctant to belong to anything; he is a loner who believes he can afford to be alone because he is strong. Like the evil *puer robustus*, he relies only on himself. And yet he is far from wicked; wickedness in the *Tell* play, unlike in *The Robbers*, is embodied by a single character: the imperial governor Gessler. Tell acts on his own account, but he lays claim to goodness. He proves this not through obedient compliance or confederate solidary, but through the fact that he is attached to others in pre-political sympathy. "Tell rescues the lost sheep from yawning gulfs," he says, and then asks rhetorically: "Is he a man, then, to desert his friends?" (CWS 4, 22).[14] He thus moves further from Hobbes's *puer robustus* and Franz Moor and closer to Rousseau – though only the Rousseau who harks back to pity, not the Rousseau who anticipates the social contract. This feeling is more resilient in Tell than in Karl Moor, whose "tenderness" quickly wears out. Tell feels connected to others from the outset, without finding it necessary to join together with them through a particular attitude, action, or effort. He can therefore remain alone without closing himself off from the world. He resembles Rousseau's savage who insists on autarky but devotes himself to others when the occasion arises.

If we were to stick solely with sympathy and charity, we would be assigning virtues to Tell that were coded as feminine at the time. Rousseau clearly emphasizes this female side in the compassionate *puer robustus* – and the step he takes from pity to justice can be attributed to his misogyny and opposition to anything he considers feminine. Adam Smith blatantly expresses the link between sympathy and femininity: "Humanity is the virtue of a woman."[15] Tell is not Schiller's only protagonist to appropriate this female-coded feeling – Don Carlo is another prime example: "A tear is man's unerring, lasting attribute," he declares, and the king "whose eye is dry was ne'er of woman born!" (CWS 4, 157).

This is not far removed from the sentimental man's thirst for action, however. Tell has a thirst for action in abundance, and this gives rise to the psychological puzzle of how the sympathetic or feminine(?) side of this troublemaker can be reconciled with the fact that he is a loner and ruffian who declares "murder" to be his "business" and turns "the milk" – mother's milk? – "of human kindness" into "rankling poison" (CWS 4, 93, 91f.). Tell almost seems to have a split personality. But there is a simple solution to this psychological puzzle. Tell is sympathetically good by nature, not by his *own doing*, which is why he can blithely and brazenly *do* whatever he likes. He kicks over the traces but never loses his internal compass. Because Tell, on this side of his recklessness, is possessed of a morality rooted in a natural characteristic, he has mastered the art of navigating the discrepancy between the old and new order with instinctive certainty. He is in no danger of going or being led astray. This is the key to the humanity or super-humanity of this hero.

One could also say this is the trick Schiller uses to solve a systematic problem arising in the transition from the old order to the new. Those who make this transition oppose the existing law in anticipation of a future law, the legitimacy of which they can only allege and ultimately certify by staking their life on it. This is the tremendous challenge facing a nomocentric troublemaker. "He enters" – as the young Hegel says in *The Spirit of Christianity and Its Fate* – "on the battlefield of might against might and ventures to oppose his adversary." In this "struggle for right there is a contradiction," because the insurgent opposes the existing right, which is "a universal," with the new right, which is "also a thought, though a different one": "life is in conflict with life" here.[16] At the moment of upheaval, everything hangs in the balance. The old order is no longer self-evident, but the new order is still striving for legitimacy because, for the time being, it is suspected of being the fantasy of an outsider.

The friends of revolution among Schiller's contemporaries tried to justify the uprising in anticipation of its legitimate goals. According to Johann Benjamin Erhard, the "rightfulness" of a revolution cannot be based directly on a "right," it can only declare some future right as its goal and measure itself against the goodness of this future right. Therefore, "an insurrection that arises for the purpose of asserting human rights [. . .] is sacred and a triumph of humanity."[17] Tell takes a different route. He absolves himself of the need to anticipate an unreliable future and allows himself to be guided by something already in existence, something he should be able to count on: natural goodness.

Even Rousseau doubted that this goodness was as rock-solid as Schiller would lead us to believe in his portrait of an infallible hero. But it is the goodness of the individual hero that Schiller thinks will spill over to all of society, so he follows Rousseau in depicting a transition from sympathy to synergy. In the end, Tell founds the political union and is transformed from an outsider into a brother. The arc from Schiller's first drama to his last can therefore be interpreted as a shift from a real pair of brothers to an ideal brotherhood.

How does Tell manage this feat? Since he is initially independent of both the emperor and his fellow countrymen, he has the scope to act for the benefit of his inept friends: "But when your course of action is resolved / Then call on Tell; you shall not find him fail" (CWS 4, 22). Word of his special status has even reached his adversary and eventual victim, Gessler, who says as much when they meet shortly before the apple is shot: "I had been told thou wert a visionary, – / A wanderer from the paths of common men. / Thou lovest the marvellous" (CWS 4, 69). In his encounter with Gessler, Tell behaves like a pigheaded man who does not see the big picture at all and is even willing to risk endangering his own son: "Think you, had I a mind to use my strength, / These pikes of theirs should daunt me?" Tell asks, refusing to doff his cap to Gessler. Those loyal to the emperor shout "Rebellion! Mutiny!" As the conflict with Gessler escalates, Tell – as he himself says – gets worked up "from inadvertance" (CWS 4, 67f.). And yet it is precisely this escalation on which the Swiss are depending.

Tell starts off as an odd loner, then challenges the old powers and uses force to prove himself a strong savior and creator of the "league" (CWS 4, 46). "Tell is the fulfiller and secret head of the league, not although but because he is not a member of it."[18] Switzerland's national hero reveals himself to be a threshold creature. Tell stays within striking distance, has no time for deliberation, seeks conflict, and makes things happen. As a master of the exceptional state, he is a precursor to the cowboy or lone ranger whose "destiny is to defend society without ever really joining it."[19] Tell is also a predecessor to Richard Wagner's heroes, who do not really belong and who intervene in the action from the outside. While cowboys and Wagner's heroes keep their distance to the very end, however, Tell is transformed from the "founder" (CWS 4, 109) into a member of the league. When this league becomes a reality, the Swiss can say "We are free men" (CWS 4, 100) – and they view this liberty not as arbitrary freedom but as self-legislation:

The old is crumbling down – the times are changing –
And from the ruins blooms a fairer life. [...]
And freedom waves her conquering banner high!
Hold fast together, then – forever fast! [...]
That league may answer league, when comes the hour to strike.
Be one – be one – be one – (CWS 4, 87f.)

124

This league is brimming with the spirit of Rousseau, which leads Schiller into the same situation that confronted Rousseau in the *Social Contract*. If Tell goes from being the founder to a member of the league, it means that he has done his job and left his old identity behind him – just as Rousseau's *puer robustus* ultimately becomes a victim of his own success. Once the conversion to the new order is complete, everyone belongs together and no one drops out. Having brought the *puer robustus* to menacing life in *The Robbers*, Schiller now banks everything on moving history forward to the point where the *puer robustus* can be taken out of service. Love changed to hate, and now evil turns to good. The "just man" was "devour[ed]" by the "wicked" (*Robbers* 84), and now the situation is reversed. We can precisely describe the requirements necessary for this.

One necessary condition for someone like the *puer robustus* to enter the scene is the existence of something like historical development. Even Hobbes allows for this (however grudgingly), because it would otherwise be impossible for him to talk about the disparity between the intellectual and physical development of the *puer robustus*. Rousseau expands on and revaluates this idea of evolution toward perfectibility. For all that Hobbes and Rousseau act very differently, the new order they preach is based in one way or another on the (self-)elimination of the *puer robustus*. Disturbance, transgression, and the fight against the existing order are initiated by a threshold creature whose days are numbered. This is especially true of Schiller's "league," which has to rid itself of history for all to "be one – be one – be one –."

History is most apparent in the passing of generations. This is where difference is generated – and difference is a thorn in the side of unity. The becalming of historical dynamics at the end of *Wilhelm Tell* must therefore also be the end of the generation game. Schiller describes this as the transformation of men into "brothers." The self-salvation that is enacted in *Wilhelm Tell* culminates in the equalization of those who join together in the league. That which can only be said counterfactually in *The Robbers* – "how good and how pleasant for brethren to dwell together in unity" (*Robbers* 153) – is suddenly within reach. And that which is imagined in Schiller's "Ode to Joy" and was set to music by Beethoven in the final movement of his Ninth Symphony – "Every man becomes a brother"[20] – is brought to the stage as a political order in *Wilhelm Tell*.

There is no place in this brotherly alliance for the troublemaking *puer robustus*. We come to a deuce and a draw in which no one can be the *Other*. There are no foreign bodies in this body politic. The league will succeed provided that everyone who participates in it belongs to a single generation. Their coevality is sealed in that the brothers trace back their self-definition to a *single* moment shared by everyone: the moment in which they joined together. They become brothers by virtue of the oath they swear or the contract they conclude; they are not just brothers, but twins or multiples who see the light of day all at once, in a kind of precipitate delivery. Because they owe their self-definition to the memory of this union, they remain ageless in a sense.

But there are still two sources of irritation here. First, it is embarrassing that all the talk is of "brothers" and men, as if women were no part of this union. This is absurd not least because the women in *Wilhelm Tell* make an important contribution to the victory of the Swiss. But unlike Goethe in *Iphigenia*, for example, Schiller keeps them confined to the back room of history. Second, it is puzzling how one could speak of brothers but never mention their father. As a rule, a father is just as indispensable as a mother if there are to be brothers (or sisters) in the first place. But a father has no place in a league that casts itself as a single generation.

As a student at the Karlsschule, shortly before he completed *The Robbers*, Schiller gave a speech on "Virtue Considered in its Consequences," in which he rhapsodized about the harmony of a social order that "turns the infinite spirit world into a single family and so many myriads of spirits into so many sons of *one* all-loving father" (SW 5, 283). It is just a small step from this "single family" to the vision of brotherhood in the "Ode to Joy." In the ode, men are brothers because they are God's creatures: "Brothers – o'er the stars unfurled / Must reside a loving father."[21] But this harmonistic view of the earth as a unity populated by a large group of brothers or children ultimately leads nowhere, because the fatherhood that looms like a shadow over this brotherhood cannot simply be wished out of the world. If the brothers, in their role as sons, continue to deal with their fathers, then they will continue to have what it takes to be the *puer robustus*, whether he goes astray (as Hobbes sees it) or he rattles the prevailing order (as Rousseau sees it).

A strictly conceived league of brothers cannot allow itself to simply *forget* the fathers. The brothers must be able to include them somehow – but in a way that eliminates their generational difference at the same time. There is a solution, as elegant as it is odd, that enables the brothers to guarantee the congeniality, coevality, and contemporaneity upon which their union depends: they must become their own fathers, they must *identify* themselves with them. Jean-Paul Sartre gets to the heart of this eccentric idea: "We are brothers in so far as, following the creative act of the pledge, we *are our own sons*, our common creation."[22] The brothers attempt to reach this state not by following a (traditionally paternal) model as *offspring*, but by anticipating this model, by begetting the law and thus delivering themselves into the world.

Behind Schiller's fraternal league we find Rousseau's social contract, in which the citizen is sovereign and subject at the same time. For a male citizen, the difference between the father (which this citizen is) and the son (which he also is) shrivels away. Schiller expresses this circular relationship precisely: "And this alone shall be the freeman's duty / To guard the empire that keeps guard for him" (CWS 4, 48). The brothers will always be united if they no longer fight for their father's affections but are themselves the father instead. This dual role should prevent historical, generational dynamics from gaining momentum and giving the *puer robustus* a foot in the door again.

Looking at Rousseau, I tried to show how the troublemaker thwarts this kind of union and fusion. Sometimes Rousseau himself brought the troublemaker into play, but sometimes the troublemaker reappeared against Rousseau's explicit wishes. Schiller, too, sends mixed signals that herald the defense of the league while also professing its fragility. His plays "deal repeatedly with conspiracies, rebellions, uprisings, factions or whatever terms are used for this."[23] One could argue that the uprising in the *Tell* play is a way of escaping this political unrest once and for all. But the appeal of this league of brothers has something hypocritical about it. A source of irritation creeps into the celebration of brotherhood: namely, the generational relationship that keeps the political challenge of historical dynamics in play.

This insecurity manifests itself not as a rebellion that continues to brew, but as an inconclusiveness regarding the replacement of the old world. One symptom of this is that *Wilhelm Tell* is positively teeming with father figures who should really no longer exist. We can draw one final arc here from *The Robbers* to *Wilhelm Tell*. Even in Schiller's first play, the father leads a nearly spectral existence; he contributes to the escalation of events more through indecisiveness than mercilessness and becomes a plaything for projections. One could subtitle this play "The Tragedy of the Lost Father"[24] and not – as Schiller considered doing – "The Lost Son" (SW 1, 913).

If *The Robbers* can be read as a play about the deflation of fathers, *Wilhelm Tell* deals with their inflation. This stands in strange contrast to the celebration of brotherliness. As if pushed through a revolving door, one father after another – or men who would like to assume the role of father – is ejected onto the stage: Baron Attinghausen, the "common parent" (CWS 4, 88); Rudenz, who wants to "inherit" what is his (CWS 4, 88); the emperor and his representative, Gessler (CWS 4, 96); John of Swabia, who commits "parricide" on the emperor (CWS 4, 105); Walter Furst, who refers to his son-in-law Wilhelm and his grandson Walter Tell as his "children" (CWS 4, 74); and, finally, Wilhelm Tell himself, who is greeted by his wife with these words at the end of the play:

127

Boys, dearest boys! your father comes to-day.
He lives, is free, and we and all are free!
The country owes its liberty to him! (CWS 4, 109)

It is precisely because Schiller wants to distill the purest form of this fraternal league that he cannot prevent a small, distressing (though not dirty) secret[25] from creeping into the drama: namely, that this league – as a new, intact political order – reaches its limits when it comes up against the relationship between generations, or the process of historical change. This is illustrated by the historical event that Schiller was commenting on in dramatic form with his *Wilhelm Tell* play: the French Revolution.

When Jean-Sylvain Bailly, president of the National Assembly, declared on June 20, 1789, in the context of the Tennis Court Oath, that "la famille" was now "complète,"[26] he specifically meant a family consisting only of brothers, a people of equals who belonged together. But the course of the French Revolution casts doubt on whether such a fusion of the political community under the banner of brotherhood can actually succeed. Psychoanalytically informed historians[27] of the French Revolution have clearly revealed the centrifugal forces and destructive energies at work in the politics of the league of brothers. I will return to the Oedipal abyss that opens up when a father figure is internalized when I talk about Freud later on. There is something rotten about the artificial construct in which the brotherhood encloses itself and becomes entirely self-absorbed. The difficulties that confronted Rousseau's *Social Contract* return with a vengeance in both the French Revolution and in Schiller's work. The forces of destruction come from the outside and work away on the inside.

The challenge that comes from the outside is easy to explain. The same objection that was raised against a social order based on contract theory can be raised against the fraternal league. In short, not everyone who belongs to this order will always be present, and even if it were possible to drum up every current member, new members would join all the time.[28] The league of brothers claims an ever-constant, evergreen status for itself. Whatever tricks contract theorists devise to incorporate newcomers on a precautionary (virtual, optional, preemptive, or whatever you want to call it) basis, they still dream of the zero hour that David Hume[29] revealed to be an illusion back in the mid-eighteenth century. Hume said it was certainly possible to imagine an order following the model of the social contract, in which everything was newly defined, without consideration for "ancestors" and their "laws." But this would only work if "one generation of men [did] go off the stage at once, and another succeed" – again, all at once. This mechanism might regulate the passing of generations among butterflies, Hume said, but not among people, whose "society is in perpetual flux." People are not butterflies. Hume's "flux" is of interest here not as a natural phenomenon but as a process of transmission between old and new, or old and young. As long as this process continues – and there is no way to stop it – the construct of the brotherhood remains ideological. This means the character of the *puer robustus* will continue to wander through history.

Attacks from the outside are not the only establishment woes facing the band of brothers. The league also disintegrates from the inside. Destructive forces are unleashed when the brothers perform the audacious trick required of them for the sake of their success – the trick of identifying themselves with their father, or becoming their own father. By declaring themselves the sovereign, they subjugate themselves and demand their own obedience. To ensure closure – as Schiller writes in the fourth of his *Letters on the Aesthetical Education of Man* from 1795 – "the individual *becomes* the state" (CWS 8, 40). Even if the league of brothers is not at risk of external attack, this form of identification is fragile and – just like Hegel's synthesis of the individual and the universal – it is disrupted by internal division.

We can see this if we turn Schiller against himself and recall the systematic discontinuity in his *Letters on the Aesthetical Education of Man*. While Schiller initially wants to accomplish the transition to a rational and legal order by means of aesthetic experience, in the end he distances himself from the state order. The riposte to his maxim from the fourth letter, that the "individual *becomes* the state," can be found in his twenty-seventh and final letter, in which he declares that "it is impossible for the general to issue from the individual" (CWS 8, 89). With these words, Schiller lodges a protest against Rousseau's *moi commun*.[30] The individual, who cannot make himself universal, places limits on the league of brothers. The individual's identification with the state would have to be lossless for each person to be so melded with their identity as their own sovereign that they would gladly accept their own commands as their innermost desires. But internal dissent remains between the individual as sovereign and as subject.[31] Subjugation inevitably goes hand in hand with a feeling of subjection and surrender; it is accompanied by a lack of understanding. And the creature who was supposed to have been excluded from this order crawls out once again: the *puer robustus*. He continues to play a key role in the play for power.

— V. —

THE *PUER ROBUSTUS* AS
VICTIM AND HERO

Victor Hugo

1. Quasimodo as a monkey gone wrong

Near the west portal of the Cathedral of Notre-Dame de Paris, there once stood – according to an account by Jacques Du Breul from the year 1612 – a wooden platform upon which people could place foundlings. The devout were supposed to leave alms there for the poor infants, and "good people" were encouraged to take the poor children and raise them "as their own."[1]

The events said to have transpired there after the Sunday service on April 5, 1467, are recounted not in that old report, however, but in the novel *Notre-Dame de Paris, 1482* by Victor Hugo. It was on this day that a "very restless small mass" was found on the wooden platform near the cathedral, which roused the "intense curiosity" of many churchgoers. They puzzled over what "sort of living creature" it might be. "That's not a child," one said – and the others chimed in:

> It's a monkey gone wrong.
> It's a real monster of abomination, this so-called foundling.
> I imagine [. . .] that it's a beast, an animal, the offspring of a Jew and a
>   sow. (ND[e] 153ff.; ND[f] 235–7)

The "creature," which was "at least four years old," screeched like a banshee and had red hair and only one eye, the other having been covered by a large wart. No sooner had the churchgoers suggested burning it as if it were the spawn of the devil than a young priest picked it up, said "I adopt this child" and disappeared. A lay sister in a gray frock whispered that the priest was perhaps a sorcerer, but the priest was already gone and did not hear the slander (ND[e] 154ff.; ND[f] 237–9).

Because this April Sunday, the first Sunday after Easter, is known as "Quasimodo Sunday" in the church calendar, the priest christens his new

130

pupil Quasimodo. In doing so, as Hugo writes, he perhaps also wants to imply that this being was only roughly or approximately ("à peu près" or "quasimodo") human, that the "poor little creature" was "unfinished and incomplete" (ND[e] 162; ND[f] 245).

"Now, in 1482, Quasimodo had grown up" and "was about twenty years old" – and it is in this year that Victor Hugo sets the events of his *Notre-Dame* novel, which he published in 1831 when he himself was barely 30. After rising rapidly in the hierarchy of the church, the priest Claude Frollo has secured the position of bell-ringer at Notre Dame for his adoptive child, and the cathedral becomes "his nest, his home, his country, his universe." But Quasimodo is still ugly, and to top it all off, he has gone deaf. His relationship with the world is like one big misunderstanding, so he withdraws to his bells and prefers to haunt the furthest and highest corners of the church (ND[e] 163, 173; ND[f] 245f., 257). (Ugliness is a trait Quasimodo shares with Schiller's Franz Moor and the "Criminal of Lost Honor"; it is the external grounds for exclusion and denigration.)

When Quasimodo does dare to venture outside, there is only one role available to him: that of the monster, the ogre. Without having to make any effort or disguise himself, he wins a competition for the ugliest grimace during a folk festival, and the description of him provided on this occasion is truly frightening. The wart over the eye, the "horseshoe mouth," the "irregular teeth, with gaps here and there like the battlements of a fortress," the "calloused lip, over which one of those teeth protruded like an elephant's tusk" –

> The grimace was his ordinary face. Or rather his whole person was a grimace. A large head bristling with red hair; between his shoulders an enormous hump [...]; big feet, monstrous hands; and with all that deformity a certain air of fearsome energy, agility, and courage [...]. He looked like a giant, broken into pieces and then badly mended.

"Oh! the ugly monkey," one of the spectators says. "As wicked as he's ugly," adds another, while a third remarks, "He is the devil" (ND[e] 58f.; ND[f] 120ff.). Victor Hugo's characterization of Quasimodo culminates in the sentence: "*Malus puer robustus*, says Hobbes" (ND[e] 166; ND[f] 249). This explains what prompted me to include one of the strangest, saddest heroes in world literature in the ranks of this book. Quasimodo is also a *puer robustus* – and what a *puer robustus*!

Indeed, what kind of *puer robustus* is this Quasimodo? As Hugo writes, he leads an "unsociable" life (ND[d] 164; ND[f] 248). The tremendous physical strength that this character wields without rational control makes him a danger to others. Hugo thus adheres to the image of the evil man provided by Hobbes, and he adopts other elements of

Hobbes's theory as well. In what is known as the *Reliquat*, Hugo's posthumously published notes on the novel, directly after the entry "*Malus
puer robustus* (Hobbes)" we find the phrase "Homo homini monstrum,"[2]
which is also used in the novel (ND[e] 286; ND[f] 393). In the drafts of
his *Cromwell* play, which were written almost contemporaneously with
the novel, Hugo notes: "*Homo homini lupus*, said Hobbes."[3] Although
the *Notre-Dame* story is set in the fifteenth century, Hugo's research on
the seventeenth century, on Cromwell and Hobbes, flowed into his work
on the novel. The Hobbes quote in *Notre-Dame* is not a one-off.

At best – or at worst – there is only one argument to be made against
the thesis that Quasimodo is a *puer robustus*. One could absolve him
of evil on account of his intellectual backwardness, just as Hobbes and
many of his successors granted a place on this side of good and evil to
the child who follows his passions. Even Hugo says of Quasimodo: "His
face showed no sign of shame or blushes. He was too far from the social
state and too near the state of nature to know what shame was" (ND[e]
250; ND[f] 348). If it were not possible for Quasimodo to understand or
"know" morality, then the charge of evil would go up in smoke because
he would be an innocent, inculpable man.

This would be an acquittal based on a lack of accountability – but
Hugo does not ultimately reach this verdict, nor would Hobbes evaluate
Quasimodo's case in this way. In fact, several things speak against branding the bell-ringer as a child or cretin. First, unlike a weak child, this mus-
cleman is actually capable of committing crimes, a fact that is morally
relevant from the consequentialist perspective that Hobbes brings to bear.
When passions run wild in an adult, the adult – unlike a small child –
becomes a danger to others. Second, we can assume that an adult, even
one like Quasimodo, could prove himself in society – by allowing himself
to be tamed, if nothing else. Anyone who refuses, anyone who reveals
himself to be an obstructionist, winds up in the drawer that Hobbes has
set aside for strong – and wicked! – boys.

Hugo appears to have modeled Quasimodo precisely on the type of
character referred to by Hobbes as a *puer robustus*. But appearances
are deceiving. In the course of the novel, the judgment that was initially
passed on the Hunchback – that his lack of reason leads to a lack of
morality – is repudiated. Quasimodo is actually a *puer robustus* who
deviates from Hobbes's template in an explosive way. Two points are
worth noting here. First, Hugo offers a new reading of the genesis of
wickedness (section 2). And second, he goes beyond individualistic
interests in the Hobbesian sense and describes a social dynamic between
Quasimodo and the other main characters in the novel (his adoptive
father Claude Frollo and the Gypsy woman Esmeralda) which, in the
end, turn the Hunchback into a good hero (section 3). Quasimodo the

medieval monster thus becomes the forebear of the moral and political troublemakers of the nineteenth century. We encounter them in Hugo's own novel *Les Misérables* (section 4) as well as in the works of Honoré de Balzac and Charles Baudelaire (section 5).

2. The birth of wickedness from humiliation

The Hobbes quote in *Notre-Dame* particularly stands out, but we should not conclude from this that Hugo remains fixed on Hobbes's interpretation of the *puer robustus*. In the end, he allows Quasimodo to grow out of his violent wickedness without relying on the use of reason as a control mechanism, as Hobbes did; I will talk about this moral emancipation in the next section. Hugo also deviates from Hobbes when he describes the genesis of Quasimodo's wickedness by clarifying why the behavior of his *puer robustus* is initially *malus*. He offers two explanations for this.

First, Hugo ponders the connection between ugliness, foolishness, and wickedness. He says Quasimodo's psyche is trapped in a "defective body" that distorts and confuses his access to reality, so his thoughts can never be anything other than "wild" or simply "idiotic" (ND[e] 165f.; ND[f] 248f.; cf. ND[e] 78f.; ND[f] 145). Quasimodo's physical condition – his combination of deformity and monstrous strength – impacts not only his intelligence but also his morality. "He was in fact vicious because he avoided people; he avoided people because he was ugly. [...] His strength, so extraordinarily developed, was a further cause of viciousness" (ND[e] 166; ND[f] 249).

In these lines, we can hear an echo of Hobbes's theory of the connection between insufficient intelligence and wickedness. But a new aspect also comes into play here. Hugo speculates that Quasimodo's body – the damaged, mutilated vessel for his soul – has destroyed his intellectual, emotional, and moral faculties. The idea that both idiocy and wickedness can be traced back to such outward physical factors is not found in the same form in Hobbes, but it does appear in the French Materialism of the eighteenth century, in the works of Helvétius, for example. According to this thinking, the *puer robustus* is a problem inherent in the material itself, as it were, so manipulating the material – through the optimized regulation of physical and mental processes, or through behaviorist training – can eliminate the problem. It is not the Hobbesian anti-nature (namely, the superior, disciplinary state power) that is deployed against the monster; it is nature itself, which can be readjusted. Whether Hugo stays true to this interpretation remains to be seen.

Second, Hugo provides an explanation for Quasimodo's wickedness that starts at a very different point and moves further from Hobbes than

133

the first one. Directly after the passage I have just looked at and the *puer robustus* quote, Hugo writes:

> Besides, to be fair to him, his viciousness was perhaps not innate. From his earliest steps among men he had felt, then seen himself the object of jeers, condemnation, rejection. Human speech for him always meant mockery or curses. As he grew older he had found nothing but hatred around him. He had caught it. He had acquired the general viciousness [*méchanceté générale*]. He had picked up the weapon with which he had been wounded. (ND[e] 166; ND[f] 250)

When Quasimodo learns the language of "mockery" and "curses" from his fellow human beings, he seems to be a descendant of Shakespeare's Caliban: "You taught me language, and my profit on't / Is I know how to curse." Hugo describes Quasimodo's wickedness as an adaptation. It reflects the "general viciousness" of the society that punishes him with contempt. This thesis is a counter-program to both Hobbes and the French Materialists. In accordance with this, it is not when existing passions break free without the necessary control and discipline that evil arises. The focus is not on qualities *derived from nature*, but – as we saw earlier with Schiller – on the *social genesis* of aggression. Hate springs from disappointment, violence from sadness. Quasimodo may be "vicious," but only because he is a child of his time, the unloved member of a society who has been painfully pinned down in the role of the pariah, the outcast. The *puer robustus* thus becomes a *victim*.

Hugo never tires of telling us that Quasimodo – at least initially – is "vicious." But he encourages the reader to feel for him, to regret the "humiliation," the "contempt," the "disgust" he faces, and to appreciate his hapless attempts to connect with others (ND[e] 78; ND[f] 145). Various interpretations of Quasimodo's wickedness therefore stand side by side in the novel. The *first interpretation* is based on materialistic or naturalistic premises and focuses on the effects that Quasimodo's stunted locomotor system and sensory apparatus have on his intellectual capabilities and moral attitudes. The *second interpretation* is based on social-philosophical or social-psychological premises and focuses on the effects that social ostracism and exclusion have on an individual's inner life. One could say that the underdog turns into the bad boy. Following this second interpretation, Quasimodo does not move through society as a savage or an untoward, unadapted foreign body; instead, he holds up a mirror that would allow this society to see and be shocked by its own behavior if it wanted to. Like Rameau's nephew, Quasimodo reflects "what the whole of society says and feels."

Looking at the novel as a whole, there is no doubt that Hugo leans more toward this second interpretation than the first. It would also be scarcely credible for Hugo the Romantic to conduct an experiment in his *Notre-Dame* novel that revolved around the quasi-technical modification of nature. In general, Hugo follows more in Rousseau's wake than in Hobbes's, since even the former attributed wickedness not to natural passions that would culminate in violence if left uncorrected or uncontrolled, but instead to social conditions.

Hugo does not stick to Rousseau's narrow definition, however, whereby evil is specialized, as it were, in the offensive, aggressive pursuit of one's self-interest. Instead, in Hugo's work – and that of others – another social space opens up (one which Hugo himself does not illuminate), in which so-called evil is a response to injuries and humiliations of all sorts. Evil hovers over the political order like a shadow that cannot be shaken off. Sometimes good and evil mix together, "beauty and the beast," *la belle et la bête*. Hugo discovers just such a mixture in Hobbes's contemporary Cromwell: "It was a complex, heterogeneous, multiple being, made up of all sorts of contraries – a mixture of much that was evil and much that was good."[4] Hugo breaks fresh ground with an insight that I am adopting for myself. He positions evil within a mental and social dynamic that takes us far beyond Hobbes and Rousseau, whose approaches are negatively and positively fixated on the nature of man.

Leaving aside the fact that Diderot applies his description of the *puer robustus* word for word to Rameau's nephew, Quasimodo is probably the first literary figure whose creator explicitly links him to Hobbes's *puer robustus*. The innovative, idiosyncratic wickedness of Quasimodo, which is not encompassed by Hobbes's and Rousseau's descriptions, can be more precisely defined by looking to two other literary figures, however. One comes from Hugo's first novel, the other from Mary Shelley.

The eponymous protagonist of *Hans of Iceland* is not referred to as a *puer robustus* by Hugo, but he is another successor to Hobbes's character nonetheless. After committing a terrible crime, Hans is brought before a court, where he introduces himself as follows: "I am Hans of Iceland [. . .]. I have committed more murders and lighted more fires than all of you ever pronounced of unjust judgments in your whole lives. [. . .] I would drink all the blood which flows in all your veins with the keenest pleasure. It is my nature to hate men, and my mission to destroy them." When Hans is asked "for what object" he committed "so many crimes," he bursts out laughing and says: "There was something in me which impelled me to do it."[5] Though Hans fits outwardly with Hobbes's description of the strong boy, he demolishes the schema of passions that Hobbes envisages for the evil man. Hans is driven not by economic self-preservation or social self-assertion but by his passion to "drink all the blood." His wickedness springs from a deep hatred for the world, but one which remains strangely baseless. It is not until he creates the character of Quasimodo that Hugo links this hatred to injuries suffered previously.

The next relative of Quasimodo is a creature conceived by an engineer of dubious talents: the artificial monster from Mary Shelley's *Frankenstein*, the first version of which was published in 1818, a good ten years before Hugo's *Notre-Dame* novel. Shelley has the monster speak a line in a moment of rare insight that Hugo could have given to Quasimodo: "Misery made me a fiend."[6] Franco Moretti correctly identified this miserable being as the embodiment of the working class, and he interpreted society's fear of him as the fear of the bourgeoisie.[7] It is not until Frankenstein rejects his own creation and casts him out that the creation hits back. For Shelley, as for Hugo, wickedness springs from injury. It is borne not by the egoist stubbornly asserting his own demands, but by the individual who has been denied an ego or identity and who strikes back with the courage of desperation. The monster's wickedness is its revenge for acknowledgment denied. The problem with this revenge, however, is that it remains blindly tied to whatever it is directed against. Such a vengeance would never be embraced by a troublemaker who uses the threshold as a springboard for a new movement, only by someone who is trapped in the status quo. Does Quasimodo also remain stuck in his hatred for the whole world?

3. Moral emancipation

Up to this point, we have pondered how Quasimodo's wickedness might have come about and looked at Hugo's different answers to this question, which go beyond the boundaries marked out by Hobbes, Rousseau, and the French Materialists. For the time being, I have accepted the premise that Quasimodo is, in fact, evil. Hugo, however, does everything he can to unsettle this apodictic judgment. He ties the question of evil to an analysis of the network of relationships to which Quasimodo belongs and in which he is feared, or perhaps also valued.

Hugo's scenario therefore fits with the approach I have taken in this book, because I am not interested in the isolated observation of an individual who may be mature or immature, capable of morality or amoral, good or evil (or somewhere on this side of good and evil). What I am interested in are the transitional arrangements or entry requirements that apply when one grows into or joins a society. The question of morality is thus tied to the question of power and history, making it rather pointless to speculate solely about Quasimodo's mental state.

Hugo was not a political philosopher, he was a novelist. His book depicts a late-medieval world, a wild jumble of arbitrary acts and claims to power. It would be excessive to foist a theory of political order on the *Notre-Dame* novel. And yet, from the social relations described by Hugo we can derive premises to be applied to the political sphere. The ultimate question here is whether or how marginalized and disenfranchised individuals can overcome the wickedness that is attributed to or acted out by them. The answer to this question can be found by looking at the development of the two relationships that dominate Quasimodo's life. Enter Claude Frollo, his adoptive father, and Esmeralda, the Gypsy girl.

"There was, however," Hugo writes, "one human being whom Quasimodo excepted from his malice and his hatred for the rest, and whom he loved as much as his cathedral, and perhaps even more. That was Claude Frollo" (ND[e] 171; ND[f] 255). Just as Quasimodo's wickedness seems diabolical or bestial, the love with which it is contrasted appears not to be a human virtue:

> Finally, and above all, it was gratitude. Gratitude taken to such extreme limits that there is nothing with which we can compare it. It is not a virtue of which the finest examples are to be found among men. We shall say, then, that Quasimodo loved the archdeacon [Claude Frollo] as no dog, no horse, no elephant ever loved its master. (ND[e] 172; ND[f] 256)

Who is this man to whom Quasimodo devotes himself? The relationship between the two starts, as we know, with a good deed: Frollo takes pity on the foundling. Frollo is introduced as a man of science who also has merits as an educator. One year before adopting Quasimodo, Claude Frollo's parents were claimed by the plague, leaving his little brother "abandoned in his cradle." Claude Frollo, who had just turned 19, took in his brother and became, as Hugo writes, "a new man": "He realized that there were other things in the world besides the speculations of the Sorbonne and Homer's poetry, that man has a need for affection, that life without tenderness and love is just a dry, creaking, destructive piece of machinery" (ND[e] 159f.; ND[f] 242). A secondary theme in the novel is, therefore, the relationship between two very different boys: Claude's brother Jehan and his foster son Quasimodo. Jehan perfectly embodies the image of the "spoiled" child that Rousseau described in *Emile* (ND[e] 294; ND[f] 400), making him the civilized, decadent counterpart to the supposedly evil savage. (At the end of the novel there is a fratricide when, in his attempt to protect Esmeralda from a mob of attackers, Quasimodo also kills Jehan.)

Claude Frollo takes on the task of instilling a sense of discipline and order in Quasimodo. Unlike Hobbes's state, which assumes this task as an institution, Frollo turns it into a personal mission. But as he raises Quasimodo over the years, he undergoes dramatic personality changes that undermine his legitimacy as a disciplinarian. These changes are rooted in the characterization of the 19-year-old Frollo mentioned earlier. He begins to doubt science – and he longs for love. These urges develop in a devastating way. Doubt leads Frollo into the depths of the occult science of alchemy, and his desire for love is not satisfied by his pity for Quasimodo, it turns into blind lust and an entirely unrequited passion for Esmeralda. She completes the triangle of relationships that dominates Hugo's novel.

Esmeralda's fate is tied early on to that of Quasimodo, though neither of them know it. As a little girl she is stolen from her mother by two "gypsy women" from "Lower Egypt" (this is how they are referred to in the novel); in place of her daughter, the frantic mother finds "a kind of little monster" in the nursery – the same "monster" that will be left outside the Cathedral of Notre Dame (N[e] 233, 231; N[f] 329). One of the "gypsy women" has rejected Quasimodo and stolen Esmeralda to become her foster mother instead. Like Quasimodo, the young girl is depicted as someone far removed from so-called civilization, though in her case this results in goodness from the outset. She is compared to a "delightful animal, gentle, intelligent, witty" (ND[e] 277; ND[f] 382).

The relationship between Esmeralda and Quasimodo begins with a welter of emotions. On account of an "indecent assault against the person of a loose woman" – namely, Esmeralda – Quasimodo is brought before the court and sentenced (N[e] 214; N[f] 307). The sentence is carried out immediately: he is flogged and publicly pilloried. Esmeralda mingles among the rabble subjecting Quasimodo to its abuse, and when she approaches him, he expects her to "add her blow like everyone else" (N[e] 252; ND[f] 350):

> Without a word she approached the victim [...], and taking a gourd from off her belt, she gently brought it to the poor wretch's parched lips. Then from that eye, which up to then had been so dry and burnt up, a big tear could be seen slowly rolling down that misshapen face, so long distorted by despair. (ND[e] 252; ND[f] 350f.)

In this moment, thanks to this humane, compassionate gesture, Quasimodo develops a third stance, a third sentiment to accompany his seemingly diabolical or bestial hatred for humanity and his seemingly super- or sub-human virtue of loyalty to Claude Frollo: affection for Esmeralda. Having previously enjoyed Claude Frollo's pity as a foundling, he now receives Esmeralda's pity as well – a pity we are familiar with from Rousseau's man of nature. Quasimodo will later say, "A drop of water and a little pity, that's more than I could repay with my life" (ND[e] 397; ND[f] 527).

In the course of the novel, Quasimodo winds up in an extremely difficult moral conflict. Frollo, whose wish is Quasimodo's command, becomes the enemy of Esmeralda, whom he timidly loves. When Esmeralda decisively rejects Frollo like a *puella robusta*, Frollo's campaign of seduction turns into one of destruction. Quasimodo's educator becomes a criminal. The man who once took a *puer robustus* and introduced him to the world is revealed to be *malus* himself.

How should Quasimodo react to this? The predicament places the Hunchback in a situation which – if he were a *puer robustus* in the original Hobbesian sense – he should not actually be at all *equipped* to deal with, seeing as he must lack moral maturity and reason. At most, he could continue on as before and remain loyal to Frollo to the bitter end, or he could helplessly and senselessly sway back and forth between his passions. Hugo describes this in a touching and vivid way: "For the rest, the poor bellringer did not know what he, Quasimodo, would do, what he would say, what he wanted. He was filled with fury, and filled with fear. The archdeacon and the gypsy clashed in his heart" (ND[e] 531; ND[f] 687).

The conflict that has become an affair of the heart for Quasimodo does not percolate through him like a desolate torpor; he is not merely a moral failure who is at its mercy. Instead, Victor Hugo equips his hero with an ability that belies the very definition assigned to him: the Hobbesian definition of the *puer robustus*. Quasimodo neither adheres blindly to his loyalty, nor does he switch sides and shift his dull allegiance from Frollo to Esmeralda, becoming her tool or fighting machine. He instead experiences a process of education or moral emancipation. In the course of this, the contrast between the rational Frollo and the irrational Quasimodo, with which the novel opens, is straight-out reversed. Of Frollo, Hugo now says "his reason" was "almost wholly destroyed" (ND[e] 382; ND[f] 511). The sleep of reason produces monsters. And Quasimodo is said to be able to take "counsel within himself, with a better and speedier line of reasoning [*avec un raisonnement meilleur et plus prompt*] than might have been expected of so ill-organized a brain." He manages to piece together his view of things from "countless details" and decide the moral conflict for himself (ND[e] 442, 530; ND[f] 579, 686).

The rest of the story is quickly told. Frollo carries his destructive actions too far and accuses Esmeralda of an attempted murder that he himself tried to commit, which results in her being taken to the gallows. Quasimodo rescues her from the hangman's clutches and takes her to the sanctuary of the church, but he can only give her a short reprieve. In the cathedral, Esmeralda is assaulted by Frollo, her worst enemy. Quasimodo manages to push him from the tower of the cathedral, but he can neither save the girl nor prevent her death. In the final chapter of the novel, the title of which is "Quasimodo's Marriage," Hugo recounts the posthumous union of the two. He writes that years later, in the cellar where the bodies of the executed had been deposited, their skeletons were found in a close embrace (ND[e] 539; ND[f] 700).

With Frollo's moral downfall and Quasimodo's moral emancipation, the (Romantic) reversal of fronts is complete. Hugo depicts this in the way Rousseau taught him to. The man of science is no guarantee of progress; he barricades himself against goodness, loses himself in lust, and forfeits all sense of reason in the end. The church, supposedly the bastion of morality and order, sows the seeds of evil. It is the uncivilized man who goes against this, proving and asserting himself as a moral being – the same man who feels compelled to say of himself that he is "something dreadful, neither man nor beast" (ND[e] 396; ND[f] 527). Quasimodo, the supposedly evil *puer robustus*, is the only one to stand by the innocent Esmeralda.

The "beast" becomes a good man – and a predecessor to the good revolutionary. Shortly after completing his *Notre-Dame* novel, Hugo wrote a profile of the Comte de Mirabeau, in which this hero of the French Revolution is described using the same vocabulary that was applied to Quasimodo – namely, that he is a "miscarriage," a "monstrous man" who becomes the orator of the people on the basis of these very traits.[8] Hugo thus leads the troublemaker from the fifteenth into the eighteenth century. But Hugo also identifies troublemakers among his direct contemporaries, and in doing so – as we are about to see – he forges a link between the moral fable of Quasimodo and the political battles of the nineteenth century.

4. The street urchin as a *puer robustus*

As a beast who becomes a man, a brutal, one-eyed ogre who is purified through charity, the Hunchback of Notre Dame is a creature of the Middle Ages, not the modern era. He lives in a world of passions, of love and hate, not a world of interests.[9] And yet, Quasimodo fits with the liberated individuals of the nineteenth century – thanks to a little trick on the part of Victor Hugo. Since he is introduced as a foundling, this hero is disembedded right from the start. No sooner has he entered the world than he is already alienated from it. He starts life on the very threshold occupied by Hobbes's individual, who must choose between good and evil, assimilation and scandal. By construing Quasimodo as a threshold creature, the *Notre-Dame* novel takes on a modern slant and offers an opportunity to bridge the divide between the heroic monster of the novel and Hugo's present day.

Among Hugo's contemporaries, it was almost considered good form to make reference to the *puer robustus*. Alexis de Tocqueville, who (like Hugo) was a member of the National Assembly in 1848 and (like Hugo) was sidelined after the coup by Napoleon III, discovers the *puer robustus* among the uncouth masses in Europe and the impetuous pioneers in America. Marx and Engels, whose critique of the French emperor surpasses that of Hugo in his polemical pamphlet *Napoléon le Petit*, find and celebrate the *puer robustus* among the proletariat. And in his *Notre-Dame* novel – which is positively brimming with contemporary references[10] – Hugo himself provides a hidden clue to the continued existence of the *puer robustus* in the present day. On the face of it, this clue does not even relate to Quasimodo himself, but as we are about to see, it keeps him in the game:

> A group of children, those little barefoot savages who have always run around the Paris streets under the eternal name of urchins, *gamins*, and who, when we were children too, threw stones at all of us when we came out of school in the afternoon, because our trousers were not ragged, a swarm of these young rascals ran to the crossroads [...]. (ND[e] 87; ND[f] 156)

This *gamin* has what it takes to be a contemporary, since Hugo says he has "always" existed, in the fifteenth and certainly in the nineteenth century. (I would add that these "little [...] savages" can also be found in the eighteenth century in Diderot and in the twentieth century in Freud and Horkheimer.) Hugo gives these street urchins their first appearance in *Notre-Dame*, and they enjoy a prominent return in his great novel *Les Misérables* from 1862. Looking back, Hugo ensures that the modern traces found in his medieval hero Quasimodo – the *puer robustus*! – remain clear to all. In *Les Misérables*, Hugo summarily declares the Hunchback of Notre-Dame himself to be an "urchin" (M[e] 486; M[f] I, 743), thus certifying the equivalence between the *puer robustus* and the gamin. Both are threshold creatures who keep their distance from the political order, rove around, come together and drift apart again, break existing rules or make new ones for themselves. How does Hugo describe the life of the gamin?

> This specimen heckles, jeers, sneers, likes a good brawl [...], fishes in the sewer, hunts in the cesspool, digs gaiety out of muck, lashes the highways and byways with his verve, [...] wallows in dung and comes out of it covered in stars. [...] Anarchy begins and ends in the gamin. This wan child of the working-class faubourgs of Paris lives and grows, ties himself in knots and "pulls through" in suffering, a thoughtful witness to social realities and human affairs, and he doesn't miss a trick. [...] Whoever you are, you who go by the name of Prejudice, Abuse, Ignominy, Oppression, Iniquity, Despotism, Injustice, Fanaticism, Tyranny, watch out for the wide-eyed gamin. This little kid will grow up. (M[e] 479f.; M[f] I, 736f.)

When he speaks of gamins, Hugo is not just talking about children who roam the streets before their lives begin in earnest. The existence of the gamin is not an episode; the "little kid will grow up," but throughout his life he will carry around the question of where he belongs and what he can hold on to. This child is not a brief preliminary stage preceding the citizen or subject, he is the true representative of a people suffering under "despotism" and "injustice." "Man's debasement through the proletariat, woman's demoralization through hunger, the wasting of the child through darkness" – the interrelated "problems of the century" are, according to Hugo, symptoms of a world in which "social damnation exists, through laws and customs, artificially creating hell at the heart of civilization" (M[e] xxxvii; M[f] I, 31). It is not just the gamin who is a threshold creature but the entire people. It is pushed to the margins by those in power, even though it represents the very heart of society. The prominent role of the gamin incorporates the idea of the "people as a child" (*le peuple enfant*; M[e] 486; M[f] I, 748; cf. ND[e] 248; ND[f] 346).

With this idea, Hugo is pulling on the same rope as the historian Jules Michelet, who believes there are two characteristics of the child to be found in the people: the feeling of playing a game whose rules or "formulas" it did not make, but also the strength or "happy energy" it puts into "seek[ing]" its language and finding it.[11] This description is exquisite, as it fits seamlessly with Diderot's celebration of "verve" and his suggestion that the philosopher "returns to the state of infancy." Hugo accentuates the unspoilt nature of the people as a child in accordance with Michelet's thinking, just as he previously praised the natural goodness of Quasimodo in accordance with Rousseau's thinking. The "*gamin de Paris*," Hugo notes, "is more or less intact on the inside":

> He has horrible teeth because he is malnourished and his stomach suffers, but he has beautiful eyes because he has wit. [. . .] He is strong on French boxing. There is nothing he could not grow into. He plays in the gutter and rises up out of it in revolt; his effrontery persists in the face of grapeshot; he was once a little guttersnipe, he is now a hero; [. . .] This child of the quagmire is also a child of the ideal. (M[e] 482, 486; M[f] I, 741, 747)[12]

Quasimodo is robust, and so is the gamin: "The fist is not a bad way to achieve respect, either. One thing the gamin most likes saying is: 'I'm strong as all get-out, I am!'" His strength is one thing he has in common with Hobbes's *puer robustus*, but what about his goals? "He is like Tantalus when it comes to two overriding ambitions that constantly elude him: to overthrow the government and to patch up his pants" (M[e] 484f.; M[f] I, 745f.). This clever piece of political and economic information takes Hugo's gamin beyond the original Hobbesian *puer robustus*. Hobbes believes there is but a single motif to be found in the rebel: the personal advantage he expects to gain by seizing power for himself. But the gamin has more than just an economic agenda that compels him to maximize the benefit for himself and violate the rules of the state. He also has a political agenda that is nourished by his "freethinking anarchy" (M[e] 484; M[f] I, 744) and is indifferent to any private advantage:

> To attempt, to brave, to persist, to persevere, to be true to oneself, to tackle destiny in hand-to-hand combat, to flummox catastrophe by fearlessness before it, to now confront unjust power, now deride intoxicated victory, to hold steady, to stand firm – that is the example the people need, and the light that galvanizes them. (M[e] 490; M[f] I, 753)

Hugo's novelistic intervention has theoretical weight. He essentially develops a counter-model to Hobbes's construct of communal life based on contract theory. As we know, there were two steps to Hobbes's strategy. Man was supposed to view himself as an individual who pursued his own private interests, and he was supposed to realize that he would benefit from the neutral power of a state to ensure justice and peace. Hugo believes both steps go in the wrong direction. Man is maimed when he is reduced to an individualistic concept of himself, and the state becomes a danger when it is elevated to untouchable heights. According to Hugo, the state order should be open to appropriation and change from below. Hugo's opposition to Hobbes becomes blatantly obvious when, in *Les Misérables*, he provides a description of the social contract that is not based on Hobbes but could instead qualify as a textbook version of Rousseau's model:

> From the political standpoint, there is only one principle: the sovereignty of man over himself. This sovereignty I have over myself is known as Liberty. Wherever two or more such sovereignties gather together, the State begins. But in this gathering together, there is no abdication. Each sovereignty concedes a certain portion of itself to form the common right. [. . .] The point of intersection of all these aggregate sovereignties is known as Society. [. . .] Hence what is known as the social bond. Some say social contract [. . .]. (M[e] 977f.; M[f] II, 566)

"The twentieth century," Hugo boldly predicts, "will be happy"; it will be the century in which this state of political liberty will be achieved, a state representing nothing less than the end of history: "You could almost say: There will be no more events" (M[e] 978; M[f] II, 567). The idea behind the *puer robustus* emerges like a distant dream, the idea that the historical dynamics that bring him forth will settle down at some point.

143

Hobbes's image of total state stability could be viewed as preparation for this, as could (in a different way) Rousseau's and Schiller's permanent union. Many authors will pick up on this idea before it eventually becomes something like the official theory of post-history in the twentieth century.[13] This diagnosis of the end of history then takes on a melancholy note, however, meaning that the troublemaker who resists this end will become attractive once more.

Leaving behind Hugo the visionary and returning to Hugo the contemporary, we still feel the appeal that the troublemaker holds for him. At least, Hugo does not want to relegate him to the corner of evil any more than Rousseau or Diderot before him. His gamin is an ambivalent figure, both a champion of freedom and villain. "They were savages, yes; but savages of civilization. [...] They looked like barbarians yet they were saviors. They reclaimed the light wearing the mask of night" (M[e] 700f.; M[f] II, 161f.).[14] The gamin is credited with the ability to oppose his oppressors, but he is also in danger of going astray: "The gamin is a national treasure [*grâce*] and, at the same time, a disease," Hugo says (M[e] 486; M[f] I, 748). Ultimately, however, this ambivalence lists to the side of good. I first want to show the conditions under which the "disease" of the gamin breaks out before we meet the good gamin.

The dual agenda of the gamin, as quoted earlier, is to "overthrow the government and to patch up his pants." In political terms, he does not represent rebellion for the sake of personal advantage, he represents – to put it melodramatically – the fight for a better world. He becomes diseased when he loses this political perspective and begins to pursue his economic interests alone. Then the gamin falls back into Hobbes's original definition of the *puer robustus*, to a certain extent: "When a man has hit rock bottom [...] then all horrors may break loose. Despair is penned in by the flimsiest walls, all of them opening onto vice or crime."– "Sometimes the stomach paralyzes the heart" (M[e] 611f., 1017; M[f] II, 27, 625).

Hugo sees this reduction to economics in the wickedness of the pauper, whom we encountered in the form of Hobbes's starving man and Schiller's "Criminal of Lost Honor." But the ego trip is also an option for those who occupy the upper echelons of society, or those who want to reach them. Hugo depicts this pattern of behavior in a character named Montparnasse:

A lugubrious creature, that was Montparnasse. Montparnasse was a mere boy, less than twenty years old, with a pretty face, lips like cherries, lustrous black hair, the brightness of spring in his eyes; he had all the vices and aspired to all the crimes. Digesting what was bad gave him a craving for what was worse. [...] The cause of all this adolescent's assaults was the desire to look slick and expensive. (M[e] 596; M[f] I, 909)

144

Individuals may be forced to turn to evil from a fear of hunger on the one hand, or from a desire for "elegance" on the other; the latter turns Montparnasse into a "killer" (ibid.). When aspects such as fashion and luxury are included in the characterization of this egocentric *puer robustus*, his gender classification changes as well. Just as Montparnasse displays markedly feminine traits in the description quoted above, many writers blamed the breakdown of society on extravagant women who indulged in luxuries; Balzac and Zola are prime examples of this.

Hugo is heavily engaged in the battle against the wickedness of luxury. He has his main character in *Les Misérables*, Jean Valjean, meet Montparnasse and harangue him. Valjean's strategy is instructive in terms of the theory of the *puer robustus*, as he not only waylays Montparnasse with moral admonishments, he also tries to appeal to Montparnasse's economic and individualistic logic – following the rational choice argument used by Hobbes: "Woe to the man who wants to be a parasite! [...] To become a villain is not easy. It's easier to become an honest man" (M[e] 757f.; M[f] II, 244). The fact that this argument has no effect on Montparnasse is significant, both in Hugo's novel and far beyond it. It shows once again that there is no dominant economic strategy when it comes to weighing the advantages of breaking the rules or following them. In terms of self-interest, it is not always counterproductive to break the rules, since opportunities often arise to cheat others and get away with it. Hobbes's strategy for pacifying the troublemaker is demolished in the world of Hugo's novel – and in the world of the nineteenth, twentieth, and twenty-first centuries.

When Hugo links wickedness to both impoverishment and enrichment and finds "rabble" – as he writes in 1841 – on "all levels of society,"[15] he is taking precisely the same line as Hegel, Marx, and Engels, who also distinguish between two types of "rabble" or "lumpenproletariat." They all denounce the narrow-minded egoism of the poorest as well as the self-serving mentality of the rich. This maps out a solution that can keep the troublemaker from evil: he must be protected from the two economic diseases of hardship and greed. For Hugo, the only route to good politics and the synthesis of power and morality is through the resolution of the social issue.

How can the historical shift that leads to this synthesis be arranged? Hugo needs a subject of history who represents the emancipation of the people, a leading figure who has what it takes to be a good troublemaker and is not trapped by the economic agenda of struggling for existence or for a place in the sun. In his quest for such a leading figure, Hugo comes across the counter-figure to Montparnasse and his gang: the good gamin. He gives this character a grand entrance in *Les Misérables*. His childish young hero is named Gavroche. Gavroche is "only a step away"[16] from

145

Quasimodo, the Hunchback of Notre Dame: "This boy never felt as good as when he was on the streets. [. . .] His parents had thrust him at life with a good swift kick in the pants. He had quite simply taken wing. [. . .] He had no roof over his head, no bread, no fire, no love, but he was jubilant because he was free" (M[e] 491; M[f] I, 755f.).

Gavroche is based on the most famous gamin in cultural history, the boy whom Eugène Delacroix immortalized in his painting *Liberty Leading the People* when he placed him next to Marianne, the freewheeling heroine of freedom.[17] The painting depicts a scene from the July Revolution of 1830 in Paris. The gamin stands on the barricade boldly brandishing his pistols, and he is perhaps slightly shocked by his own courage. At his feet lie the bodies of his comrades-in-arms. This is the gamin whom Hugo introduces in *Les Misérables*, and to make sure that readers notice the connection to Delacroix's painting, he explicitly says that Gavroche, his good gamin, stood on the barricades with a "musket" during the 1830 revolution (M[e] 906; M[f] II, 462).

One highlight of the novel is Gavroche's final appearance during the failed June Rebellion in Paris in 1832. Gavroche enters the unprotected area in front of the barricade on the rue de la Chanvrerie to empty the cartridge pouches of the dead and supply the rebels with fresh ammunition. The gunsmoke lying "as thick as fog" in the street obscures the view of the enemy soldiers: "They went on firing at him and they went on missing him." Gavroche evades countless shots like a dancer defying gravity. It seems as if nothing can touch him, as if he were undead or undying, an angelic messenger of salvation: "The insurgents, breathless with anxiety, followed him with their eyes. The barricade trembled; he sang. This was not a child, it was not a man; it was a strange fairy larrikin [*gamin fée*]. You would have said the invulnerable dwarf of the mêlée." Hugo expresses Gavroche's extraordinary appearance by describing him as a gender-hybrid being. This "fairy," this small, superhuman hero, is *puer robustus* and *puella robusta* alike.

But the sad truth is that even Gavroche is not invulnerable. In the end, a bullet brings him down: "They saw Gavroche totter, then he crumpled. The whole barricade let out a cry; but there was something of Antaeus in this pygmy. For a gamin to hit the pavement is like a giant hitting the ground; Gavroche had only fallen the better to rise again; he stayed sitting there on his haunches" – and then "a second bullet from the same sniper cut him off": "That great little soul had taken wing" (M[e] 997ff.; M[f] II, 596–9).

Without wanting to talk down this magnificent scene, I would savor the emotion here with caution. The "great little" troublemaker is described as an oddly otherworldly, saintly figure, a good spirit.[18] Goodness is celebrated, but it vanishes in a dream. In this Romantic dream of a new beginning, the gamin appears not as a boy at the mercy of the world but as an enraptured savior. (In Wagner's Siegfried, who could be described as an unsettled, unsettling relative of the gamin, this tendency will be intensified.) Hugo does not believe, however, that the strength of this child, who rises from the "quagmire" to become an "ideal," is enough for salvation – any more than the childlike people for whom he is a symbol can rely on its own strength. The compliments Hugo pays to the gamin therefore have a flip side. If the people is a child, we can assume that it is naïve and clueless. It requires pedagogical support.[19]

"To attempt, to brave, [. . .] to stand firm" – as we have heard, this is supposed to be the stance of the troublemaker who has his eye not only on personal advantage but on noble political goals. And yet, Hugo refrains from setting him up as a capable political actor, a subject of history. Instead, he counts on public instruction for moral reformation. The prime example of this in *Les Misérables* is Gavroche's older brother in spirit, Jean Valjean, who, after many missteps and aberrations, eventually focuses on doing good. Lurking behind this esteem for the child and the idea of educating the people, we find the condescension of the guardian, however. Those who consider themselves educators – as Hugo does – are also entitled to declare the people to be immature if necessary. Hugo plays this card in June 1848 when he, like Tocqueville, distances himself from the rebels, whose "heroism," as he sees it, springs from "depravity."[20]

5. The relatives of the street urchin: Balzac's real man and Baudelaire's little savage

Trying to keep up with the *puer robustus* and all of his transformations and relations is exhausting. I do not want to let up, however, so having traced an arc from the bell-ringer to the street urchin, I now want to visit two other relatives whose competition keeps things lively: the *gaillard*, Honoré de Balzac's real man, and the little savage of Charles Baudelaire. As his older and younger colleagues, Balzac and Baudelaire heckle Hugo from right and left. The royalist Balzac wants to take the troublemaker to task, while the revolutionary Baudelaire is a troublemaker himself. We can count on both of them to extinguish the Romantic light that Hugo casts over the scene.

The counterpart to Hugo's gamin in Balzac's fictional world is the *gaillard*. He appears in several novels in the *Comédie humaine* under the name of Jacques Collin or his alias, Vautrin. Balzac does not grant him the moral bandwidth of Hugo's gamin, which makes the gamin seem willing to do evil but inclined to do good. A good troublemaker is an oxymoron for Balzac. Jacques Collin a.k.a. Vautrin is a "bit of a lad [*fameux gaillard*]"; he has "broad shoulders, a powerful chest, bulging muscles," is "cold-blooded" and bound to wind up in "hell" in the "dark little corner where naughty children [*les enfants méchants*] are sent." He has a skull "with bronze ramparts against which the will of others is flattened out," he is one of the "fellows who put themselves above everyone else, even above the law," he wants to become "like a cannon-ball," and he is a "dangerous" man who is "permanently at war with society."[21] Balzac says this fellow has "nerves" with the "metallic hardness of a savage's" and "all the capacities that a savage needs."[22] It sounds as though Balzac were talking about the *puer robustus* when he counts Vautrin among the "heroes of evil-doing," those "giants of skill and cunning" who are, at the same time, like "children" and "wild animals."[23] The *gaillard* says:

> Here is my past life in three words. Who am I? Vautrin. What do I do? What I like. Let's leave it at that. [. . .] I am good to those who are good to me [. . .]. But, by jingo, I can be devilish nasty to those that annoy me or whose faces don't fit.[24]

Hobbes's war of all against all enters the picture when this *gaillard* says that the people who "struggle" to "succeed at any price" will "devour each other like crabs in a pot."[25] Balzac's conservative social criticism is directed against both the disorder of economic competition and disorder in the form of political unrest. He wants to eliminate disturbances and smooth over differences. In one lovely passage from *A Harlot High and Low*, Balzac compares society to the "water of the river" which is troubled by the "mutinous [*mutiné*]" or "rebellious [*rebelle*]" wave, by the "vortex [*tourbillon*]" of the "diabolical man." In the end, the "action of social forces" in the "general mass" is expected to swallow up this turbulence as if it had never existed in the first place.[26] In Balzac's wildest dreams, there is no swell to disturb the smooth, flat surface of society, upon which the satisfied gaze of God rests and is reflected. (Balzac would not have been pleased to hear John Stuart Mill compare society to Niagara Falls.)

Balzac's novels, however, testify to concerns that this pacified world might lose the people that could sustain it. Balzac fuels the terrifying suspicion that the world consists solely of criminals. He stumbles across a series of depraved subjects who integrate themselves in a *juste milieu* that has nothing *juste* about it anymore. Collin a.k.a. Vautrin pursues a seemingly respectable career – if rising from the role of informant to head of the Parisian secret police can be considered such. But unlike Hugo's protagonists, Collin's path in life does not represent personal, political, and moral development, but rather a virtuoso swapping of roles between the "general to the convicts"[27] and those who move sinuously in the waters of a decadent society.

When Balzac introduces Collin/Vautrin, his choice of words is strikingly similar to Hobbes's description of the *puer robustus*. And yet, Balzac's troublemaker, like that of Hugo, steps out of the Hobbesian framework, which is why it is productive to compare Balzac, Hugo, and Hobbes. Balzac encounters a rule violation without calculation, a feat of strength driven by an indignation both fundamental and unfounded. The *gaillard* is therefore more like Hans of Iceland than Montparnasse, who is interested only in his personal advantage. The portrait of this *gaillard* from Ernst Robert Curtius's *Balzac* book of 1923 is still fitting:

> Vautrin [...] is a criminal on a grand scale who walks his dangerous path in full awareness. He takes pleasure in playing his game against everyone else. He is sustained by the feeling of superiority of the man "who has examined the things of this world and realized that there are only two options open: dumb obedience or revolt." [...] Vautrin does balk at eliminating the lives of those who obstruct his plans. But he is never driven to commit his crimes by lowly motives of acquisitiveness. [...] The guiding principle behind his career as a rebel is something more profound: not a craving for gold, not a desire for evil, but the satisfaction of the thirst for power: "j'aime le pouvoir pour le pouvoir, moi!"[28]

Like Hobbes, Balzac grapples with the "protest" of the "*state of nature* against society." And again like Hobbes, Balzac encounters "malefactors" who are "so denuded of reason [...] that they become utterly childish."[29] But when the *gaillard* flouts the law, he does so not like Hobbes's individual or like Franz Moor, for the sake of a petty quest for personal advantage, however misguided. He therefore also deflects Hobbes's strategy for pacifying him. He is indifferent to the promise that his economic interests will be met if he swaps his stubbornness for subservience. Hobbes's state power can do nothing to counter Vautrin's grasping for "power" as an end in itself. Balzac thus provides distorted evidence for the thesis that has emerged from the history of the troublemaker. This troublemaker cannot be reduced to an egocentric type; he questions power and wages war against an order that he views as an affront to liberty. Although Balzac cannot endorse this rebel, the troublemaker's fight against the *juste milieu* exerts a strong, sinister power of attraction over the author.[30]

Like Hugo, Balzac goes further than Hobbes in that his troublemaker challenges the entire existing order. But the moral growth and purification of the troublemaker, as illustrated by Hugo in the characters of Quasimodo and Jean Valjean in *Les Misérables*, is alien to Balzac. He takes no stock in ascribing noble motives to the troublemaker who grasps for power. He renounces miracle cures by luminaries and entrenches himself against the troublemaker by viewing him solely as a criminal.

Balzac radically escalates the alternative between "obedience" and "revolt" (see above), and he argues for obedience. He sees salvation only in the past, in the return to an old order in which power was centralized, monarchist, and glorified by Christian morals.

It is not Balzac's conservatism that I want to wield against Hugo, but rather his escalation and intensification of political conflict. Hugo's image of society seems oddly fuzzy and mawkish compared to Balzac's, which turns out to be more sober and uncompromising. The conservative Balzac shares this chilly view with another writer: Charles Baudelaire. I want to look at Baudelaire because he illuminates even more clearly the weaknesses in Hugo's treatment of the troublemaker, and he opens the door to the continued existence of the *puer robustus*.

How does Baudelaire join the *puer robustus* game? Think back to one of the epithets Hugo uses to characterize the gamin: the "little savage." This lightly thrown word weighs heavily because, as mentioned, it harks back to the "little savage" that was Diderot's sobriquet for the *puer robustus*, and it looks ahead to the "little savage" who will appear in the work of Sigmund Freud as Oedipus and in that of Max Horkheimer as a fascist. But right now I am interested not in the long career that the *puer robustus* pursued under this alias, but in the appearance of the "little savage" in Baudelaire.

Baudelaire is one of the many writers who do not mention the *puer robustus* by name but who could actually be a *puer robustus*. He was a rebel on the barricades in February and June 1848 and was therefore involved in the second uprising that Hugo described as one of the "popular coups d'etat" that "must be put down" (M[e] 962; M[f] II, 542). It is reported that in June 1848, Baudelaire held "wild speeches, arrogant and bombastic, he swaggered and blustered," and his hands smelled of gunpowder.[31] Much like the title and composition of his collection of poems *The Flowers of Evil*, he vacillated between good and evil, the divine and the satanic. (Carl Schmitt would take careful note of Baudelaire's frenzied activity in his fight against evil.)

One of Baudelaire's most abysmal texts – which, incidentally, was published in 1862, just like *Les Misérables* – bears the harmless title of "Cake." Here the author slips into the role of a wanderer who is enjoying nature and feels "at perfect peace with [himself] and with the universe." He appears to follow Rousseau in his belief in the good man of nature, the good *puer robustus*. "Those newspapers that claim man is born good" suddenly seem "not so ridiculous" to him. All of this is, as one might suspect, sheer irony, but it gives Baudelaire the opportunity to abandon his belief in goodness in a spectacular fashion.

When the wanderer stops for a break on his country walk, a "little creature" crosses his path, "ragged and disheveled, whose hollow eyes,

150

savage and as if imploring, were fixed on the piece of bread" the wanderer is about to eat. It is not hard to view this "creature" as a gamin who has wound up in the countryside. No sooner has the boy accepted a handout than he is "bowled over by another little savage" – here comes the *petit sauvage*! – "who seemed to come out of nowhere, and so perfectly similar to the first that he could have been his twin brother." But the similarity between the two poor boys leads not to fraternal unity but to fratricidal strife. (It is not Marx but Freud who sends his regards here.) "Together they rolled about in the dirt, fighting over the precious prey, neither one apparently willing to give up half to his brother." This is a fight over property that breaks out in a natural idyll, a fight between the seemingly "legitimate possessor of the cake" and the "usurper." The battle between the two boys drags on "far longer than their childlike stature would seem to have predicted"; it is fueled by the implacability of unreason or desperation, which also prevents the *puer robustus* from becoming a respectable member of society. In the end, this battle is literally fruitless, since "when finally, worn out, gasping for breath, bloodied, they stopped [. . .] there was in fact nothing left to fight over; the piece of bread had disappeared, dispersed into crumbs [. . .]." Baudelaire remarks: "So there is, then, a superb country where bread is called *cake*, a delicacy so rare that it is enough to engender a literally fratricidal war!"[32]

This scene is a gem. It depicts a fight over goods in which good is unthinkable. Baudelaire rejects the ironically invoked belief that "man is born good" as if it were a poisoned chalice. In the space of just a few lines, he switches from the Rousseauian scenario of natural peace to the Hobbesian scenario of the war of all against all – though any resolution through the artificial peace of the Leviathan is denied.

Using Baudelaire's story as a contrast medium, Hugo's handling of the gamin emerges with crystal clarity. For Hugo the Romantic, the gamin is not trapped in an obdurate struggle; he has a future, one which Baudelaire's "little savage" gambles away. If any liberation is to be possible for the latter, it can only be achieved under difficult conditions, without the support of Hugo's luminaries. "Baudelaire [. . .] speaks to the terrible sadness of the age."[33]

The idea of a liberation in which this sadness is both expressed and overcome is the subject of Baudelaire's famous text "Assommons les pauvres!" – "Let's Beat Up the Poor!" The handout bestowed upon the "little savage" by the wanderer in "Cake" is withheld here by a man who encounters a beggar outside a tavern. He is goaded by a "Demon of combat" who whispers to him: "the only man who is worthy of liberty is the man who knows how to take it" – whereupon he starts brutally beating the beggar. The feint of the flaneur is an incitement to resistance:

Suddenly [. . .] I saw this antique carcass turn itself around, and attack me with an energy that I would never have suspected in such a broken-down machine; and, with a look of hatred that seemed to me to *augur well* [*bon augure*], the decrepit old rogue threw himself on me, blackened both my eyes, knocked out four of my teeth, and [. . .] beat me flatter than plaster. With my strong medicine [*énergique médication*], I had thus given him back both his pride and his life.[34]

Timothy Clark says "Let's Beat Up the Poor" is a "commitment, self-destructive and despairing, to a revolution of and by the people."[35] According to Baudelaire, liberation cannot be limited to the alleviation of material need and to "egoistic happiness" – in the sense of economic progress in which people are "americanized by [. . .] zoocratic and industrial thinkers."[36] *(He thus positions himself against Hobbes.)* It does not serve the cause of political liberation to compassionately succor the poor, nor can such liberation extend solely to dedication to "public happiness," which Baudelaire maligns in "Let's Beat Up the Poor!"[37] A different order cannot be decreed nomocentrically; instead, according to Baudelaire, the resistance of the beggar merely "augur[s] well." *(He thus positions himself against Rousseau.)* The troublemaker is left with the role of the eccentric who suffers from his acute marginal position, because this non-place gives him no clear view of what is to come. He moves, as Baudelaire writes in *The Flowers of Evil*, like a bat that has lost its sense of orientation: "When earth is changed to a dank prison cell / Where, like a frantic bat inside its cave, / Hope scrapes its fragile wings upon the wall / And knocks its head against the rotting roof,"[38] then the individual who is entangled in and who tangles with the world is incapable of specifying good objectives or the party of good. *(He thus follows Diderot.)* Instead of stylizing the troublemaker as a do-gooder, Baudelaire relentlessly turns evil into good – and vice versa. He sees "Christ" on the side of the rebels on the "barricades" but at the same time feels a satanic "love of crime."[39] Political conflict escalates sharply in his work – and is also characterized by deep uncertainty. Baudelaire has no time for whitewashing emancipation and coupling self-liberation to an educational program. He does not trust the lofty pedagogue who could define the educational objectives. *(He thus positions himself against Hugo.)* For all of this hostile opposition and comparison, my sympathies are with Baudelaire.

Baudelaire reviewed *Les Misérables* right after it was published, and just a short time before he had devoted a chapter of his "Reflections on Some of My Contemporaries" to Hugo. At first glance, Baudelaire seems to be full of praise. He writes of the "notes of love" Hugo expresses "for the poor who are crushed in the cogwheels of society": "*Les Misérables* is then a book of charity, an astounding call to order of a society too enamored of itself and too little concerned with the immortal law of brotherhood."[40] Baudelaire raises no objections to this brotherhood in his journalistic commentary from the revolutionary year 1848.[41] But he is bothered by the fact that Hugo, the evangelist for "fraternal affection," takes on the role of "father" and "protector"[42] whether he is writing about Quasimodo or the gamin. This dual brother/father role serves no one well, Hugo no more than Schiller, because then – as implied – engagement is mixed with condescension.

Baudelaire sees an internal connection between "hyperbolic charity" and disdain.[43] Hugo wants to help the miserable and is prepared to patronize them in order to do so. He adopts the superior position of the father in politics, just as he claims the superior position of the author in literature. Because his brotherhood is crossed with paternalism, he persists in viewing troublemakers from the outside. Hugo sees them, according to Baudelaire, as "children in [. . .] need of protection or consolation," which can only be granted to them by someone "strong."[44] These children are presented as weak figures, not as active threshold creatures. Mind you, Baudelaire is bothered not by Hugo's focus on that which is childlike (Baudelaire does this himself), but by the fact that Hugo's categorization is ultimately disparaging.

I am not yet ready to ask whether or how the energy of the miserable could be unleashed. This will be a topic for Marx and Engels. In the next chapter I will look at a troublemaker who fits with Hugo in a different way. Just as a childlike beginner is embraced as a troublemaker in *Les Misérables*, this chapter features a child who boasts of setting the world on fire. His name is Siegfried.

SIEGFRIED, FOOLISH BOY

Richard Wagner

1. The contract as a crime against nature

When it came to Schiller, I allowed myself an exception to the rule of dedicating entire chapters only to authors who have some connection to Hobbes's *puer robustus*. What follows – as previously announced – is a second exception: Richard Wagner. Though he does occasionally mention the "state of nature," this does not make him an expert in political philosophy. He is unlikely to have read Hobbes. One could say he had better things to do – such as composing the Ring Cycle. But his writings on politics and aesthetics leave no doubt that he had considerable theoretical ambition and skill.

I do not feel too guilty about including him out of turn here because Wagner took the issue at stake in the debate about the *puer robustus* and, with overwhelming precision, he made it his own. In the Ring Cycle, he attacks the idea that power can be regulated and distributed by means of contracts (section 1). To counter this world trapped in contracts, Wagner offers up a hero who is expected to kick-start the dynamics of history and ensure the goodness of power (section 2). As we will see, Siegfried plays the role of a *puer robustus* or, to use Wagner's own words, a "brave boy." Stupidly, his recipe for success is stupidity (section 3).

The great theme of order and disruption is channeled and sorted in the Ring by a single simple contradiction: the one between nature and contract, *physis* and *nomos*. Wagner sounds the attack on the artificial order, and the subsequent disturbance occurs under the banner of nature. Wagner wants to bring an end to "treacherous treaties / shameful agreements" (*Ring* 108). He bemoans the "confusion" that distances man from "nature" and drives him to "self-laceration" (WPW 2, 169): "When the learned physician is at the end of his resources, in despair we turn at last to – *Nature*" (WPW 1, 55).

In essence, Wagner's critique of the world of "treaties," which plays a key role in the Ring, can be read as a reply to the contract theories developed by the political philosophers of the seventeenth and eighteenth centuries. Because these theories declare the formation of the contract to be the key scene, they perforce focus on the threshold where individuals decide whether to cooperate. At the same time, they try to eliminate the complexity of this situation. They therefore provide seemingly irresistible incentives for entering into the social contract, either by depicting the state prior to this contract as a horror (Hobbes) or by basing the formation of the contract on a natural tendency toward cooperation (Rousseau).

Wagner is interested not in the transition that takes place at this threshold but in the contradiction that comes to a head here. He places nature and contract in opposition to one another.[1] The contract concluded by Hobbes's interest-driven individuals becomes the hostile representation of an artificial order for Wagner. To counter this, Wagner holds up a primordial life that is supposed to differ agreeably from the Hobbesian state of nature and that is to be preserved or restored. Wagner thus moves closer to Rousseau's concept of the state of nature, though without following Rousseau down the path leading to the social contract.

To ensure continuity with the discussion thus far, I will focus on the opposition between contract and nature that Wagner takes from political theory and wields against it. I am leaving aside the fact that, in his battle against the contractual world, he looks not only to the worldly aspect of nature but also to an otherworldly, (quasi-)religious salvation.[2] Wagner virtually revels in the contrast between contract and nature in all four parts of the Ring Cycle. To knock out just a few pieces of evidence for this:

- The naturally innocent Rhine maidens guard a treasure without having the faintest clue that it attracts the desires of all those who want to use it in contractual transactions; for them, the gold is a bauble.
- Wotan's wife Fricka is the representative of artificial convention; she rails against the "lustful" (*Ring* 99) breaking of contractual bonds.
- Siegmund's and Sieglinde's incestuous love is based on a natural attachment that is a *skandalon* in a world of contractual relationships.
- Brünnhilde intercedes on behalf of the lovers and asks her father, Wotan, for his understanding.
- Alberich and Mime use contracts to cheat others.
- Hagen refuses to partake in the oath of brotherhood between Siegfried and Gunther because this binding obligation would curtail his individual freedom of action and freedom of contract.

The list of examples could go on and on.

155

How does Wotan, who should actually be lord of these proceedings, fit into all of this? In the Ring he is presented as a gloomy god. He plays a decisive role in the Rhine gold being snatched from the depths of the water and unleashing its baleful power in the world of men. Alberich, who makes no secret of his greed, sees in Wotan a kindred spirit and notes that Wotan is committing an offense against the creation entrusted to him, "against all that was, / is, and shall be" (*Ring* 57). Wotan throws himself into the search for personal advantage, driven by the idea of the "bargain" (*Ring* 19) that has become dissociated from involuntary "nature" and is based on settling, convention, or "caprice" [*Willkür*] (WPW 1, 25f., 69–72). "What you are / you became by your bargains," Fasolt says, eager to learn (*Ring* 24).

In *Richard Wagner in Bayreuth*, Nietzsche writes that Wotan is a god who "binds himself through contracts, loses his freedom, and becomes entangled in the curse that is inseparable from power" (NCW 2, 329). In *The Valkyrie*, Wotan becomes ever more ensnared in this world; he is swayed by his wife, Fricka, who doggedly insists on adherence to contracts – "To her I had to surrender!" (*Ring* 110) – and yet, in the end, he is happy that Brünnhilde speaks out against the artificial order and champions nature, thus saving Sieglinde and the child she is carrying. This child, who will be named Siegfried, grows up to become Wotan's finest adversary. Or perhaps, in the figure of Siegfried, Wotan finally finds someone who can, in his stead, complete the task that is actually incumbent upon him, which he has failed to do: to destroy the world of contracts. At the end of *Twilight of the Gods*, Brünnhilde calls after Wotan:

> Not goods, not gold,
> nor godly splendor; [. . .]
> not treacherous treaties,
> shameful agreements,
> not the dissembling convention
> of hard law:
> blessings in desire and suffering
> come – from love alone. (WPW 6, 363)

Meanwhile, Brünnhilde has devoted herself as a lover to Siegfried, to whom the old world of contracts is alien, and who proves his affinity with nature by understanding the language of the birds – a tongue bound by no terms (*Ring* 207, 217–19).

The world of contracts against which Wagner declares war in the Ring Cycle is a world in which he conflates politics and economics. In doing so, he glosses over the difference between political socialization and material interests that is so precious to Rousseau, and he anticipates Carl Schmitt's critique of liberalism. According to Wagner, the "*Quiet* and *Order*"

156

ensured by the state come "at the cost of the most despicable outrage on human nature" (WPW 2, 187). The state is said to tear people from their natural bond with one another and offer itself up as a stage for "forceful or intriguing individuals." These individuals are guided only by "egoism" and try to increase their "booty" through contractual agreements (WPW 2, 192; WPW 1, 167). (Marx takes the same line at almost the same time.)

As economic individuals, people judge their interaction with others based on what they themselves get out of it in the end. In Wagner's early essay "How Do Republican Efforts Stand in Relation to the Monarchy?" from 1848, he writes: "It is a matter of debate [...] whether money should be granted the power to twist the beautiful free will of man into the most repugnant passion, into penuriousness, usury and criminal cravings. This will be the great struggle of liberation for a deeply debased and suffering humanity."[3] "Shattered segregation" (WPW 1, 90) characterizes the life of every protagonist in the Ring who succumbs to the allure of the gold – and nearly all of them do. The proceedings on the stage are thus "stalled" at the same "crossroads" that Wagner believes dominates all of "modern society," namely, "wholesale Speculation" (WPW 1, 42): "The Nibelung's fateful ring become (sic) a pocket-book, might well complete the eerie picture of the spectral world-controller" – by which he means money, the "demon strangling manhood's innocence" (WPW 6, 268).

If Wagner were to assign a home to this monetary "demon" in the real world, he would probably choose England. After visiting London in 1877, he said: "This is Alberich's dream come true."[4] His tirades are directed against "English banker[s]" (WPW 1, 42), but also against Jews.[5] Richard's grandson Wieland Wagner appropriately updated this idea and asserted that the demon of money had moved from England to the USA: "Valhalla is Wall Street."[6] In 1942, Joseph Alois Schumpeter wrote: "The stock exchange is a poor substitute for the Holy Grail."[7] Later on we will return to the financial crisis of 2008, which Wagner's remarks seem to have anticipated.

2. External salvation

How can the world escape the egocentric crisis in which it finds itself? The Ring Cycle is not a submissive exercise in waiting for salvation; it is an experiment that sounds out the options available to individuals who no longer trust in divine guidance.[8] They are expected to free themselves from the clutches of business arrangements and social commitments. Wotan longs for this different kind of life, but it is completely beyond his reach. The god has been disavowed, and he hands the reins to another: "Only a free Will, independent of the Gods themselves, [...] can loose the spell; and in Man the Gods perceive the faculty of such free-will," Wagner writes in an early version of the "Nibelungen-Myth" from 1848 (WPW 7, 302). What is needed is someone who will free himself from the old world. But his freedom must not be the kind that is exercised in this world – namely, the freedom of choice and freedom of contract that Wagner denounces as a sham.

In his letter to Karl August Röckel from January 25/26, 1854, Wagner develops a concept of freedom that is not based on a contrast with nature (like the Kantian one) but is instead derived directly from it: "One thing counts above all else: freedom! But what is 'freedom'? is it – as our politicians believe – 'licence'? – of course not! Freedom is: *integrity*. He who is true to himself, i.e. who acts in accord with his own being, and in perfect harmony with his own nature, is *free*."[9] Freedom should therefore not manifest itself in situations where a decision is to be made; it should be interpreted as the liberation of forces of will, the goodness of which has apparently already been established. To evade his imagined relativistic bogeyman, Wagner creates a counter-figure in the form of a hero who is said to possess the highest degree of inner certainty in all that he does. Siegfried is granted the power to turn the political and economic world upside down.

Wagner poses the question of power in a radical way. He is not interested in the distribution of power within a world that follows certain rules, but in the power to bring this world to an end and put another in its place. Disruption expands to become the salvation and redemption of a world in which people have entered into artificial arrangements and are trapped in self-willed, self-obsessed plans. The early Nietzsche was quite taken with the idea of Siegfried as the "marvelously rigorous archetype of youth," the "free, fearless human being" who stands "in opposition to all tradition" and brings about a "change in direction and goals" (NCW 2, 264, 329; KSA 8, 267). Wagner is looking for an Archimedean point, a place outside of this world from which the outsider can move the levers and go on the offensive. He believes he has found this place in nature, and he wants to draw upon this as he intervenes in history.

But what is meant by "nature" in this case? The appeal to *nature* is notoriously vague, since the (*one* true) natural life cannot be pinned down. As we saw with Hobbes and Rousseau, many different forms of life can be considered natural. This blurs their opposition to artificial or social life. It is especially helpful to look back to Rousseau in order to find out where Wagner puts his own new twist on the concept.

In his *first step*, Wagner goes along with Rousseau. Just as Rousseau – unlike Hobbes – attributes the natural gift of pity to humanity, Brünnhilde is seized by pity for Siegmund and Sieglinde in the key scene of *The Valkyrie*, and she allows herself to be guided by it from that point on in her battle against the artificial world of contracts.[10] And just as Rousseau surpasses pity with justice and charity, Wagner makes charity, in the form of all-around devotion, into a component of a political vision. (Thomas Mann will follow Wagner's thinking here.) Wagner contrasts the "stiff political union of our time, upheld alone by outward force," the "statutory 'norm of standing,'" with the "*free* communions of the Future," the "vital relations" between people (WPW 1, 203; WPW 2, 163). The principle of equality that Rousseau attached to pity is also picked up by Wagner in his essay from 1849 entitled "The Revolution": "Annulled be the fancy that gives One power over millions, makes millions subject to the will of one, the doctrine that One has power to bless all others. Like may not rule over like."[11]

In his *second step*, however, Wagner goes in a different direction. Instead of developing "relations" and "communions" along the lines of political equality – like Rousseau – he tries to trace these back to a common, natural foundation. In brief, Wagner follows the cliché of the "return to nature," but he does not follow its originator, namely, Rousseau himself. His approach to the modern world operates on the basis of a simple opposition between artificial decline and natural achievement. In *The Art-Work of the Future* from 1850, Wagner writes: "The real Man will therefore never be forthcoming, until the true Human Nature, and not the arbitrary statutes of the State, shall model and ordain his life" (WPW 1, 71). Wagner speaks of an "evolutionary process of Nature *in Man himself*" (WPW 1, 79) and dismisses the "erroneous supposition that men must needs be what our wilful notions, abstracted from the Past, dictate that they *should* be." In return, he invokes the "certain knowledge, that they require alone to be what by their very nature they *can* be, and *therefore shall and will be*" (WPW 1, 265).

But this "can" and "shall" is not for everyone, according to Wagner. Only Siegfried is capable of performing this feat of strength in the name of nature. Released from the "rule of the gods," guided by the "instinct [*Unwillkür*] of the individual," Siegfried can perform the deed "the gods are forbidden to do" (WPW 2, 183; *Ring* 101). Even while Sieglinde is still carrying him in her womb, Siegfried is viewed by Brünnhilde as "the noblest hero of all." He is the "laughing hero," the "boldest of men," the "bravest of men in the world," the "mightiest of men," an "overjoyful man" (*Ring* 137, 240, 259f., 287, 315). Wotan says:

Since I love him,
I must refuse to help him;
he stands or he falls
unhelped by me:
gods rely only on heroes. (*Ring* 195)

In the context of this book, it must be mentioned that Wagner developed his Siegfried character based on the Oedipus myth; Oedipus himself will make an appearance as the alter ego of the *puer robustus* in the chapter on Freud. Wagner sees pure men of nature in both Siegfried and Oedipus, and this leads him to a surprising acquittal of the "great-hearted Oedipus." The moral reproach and (self-)blame that make the Oedipus story a tragedy in the first place are repudiated by Wagner, who assigns them to the artificial world of contracts. The fact that Oedipus unwittingly falls in love with his mother is described by Wagner as an innocent attachment or "natural instinct [*Unwillkür*]" (WPW 2, 186, 182). As evidence of the naturalness of this love, Wagner mentions its fruitfulness – e.g., that healthy children are born of it. He steers clear of all moral conflict by claiming that Oedipus – like Siegfried – is simply following the call of nature. This twist becomes ideological at the moment in which Wagner absolves the call of nature from all critical consideration and places a moral seal of approval upon it. If we read Wagner together with Freud, we find that he provides an example of the "lie of the heroic myth" (SE 18, 137).[12]

Siegfried must deny his social origins in order to block all relationships that could lead to psychoanalytic or socio-theoretical analyses. Like Oedipus and the Hunchback of Notre Dame, Siegfried is a foundling – and he *must* be in order to be the hero who comes out of nowhere. His supposed lack of a past and lack of relationships is a precondition for Siegfried's great feat. He has no baggage and is, as Bernard Williams aptly puts it, a "vacuum."[13] Siegfried is "in perfect harmony with his own nature" (see above), but despite his ability to understand the language of the birds, this harmony is not primarily a mimetic performance of adaptation and integration; instead, it is a harmony with himself, an empty form of self-assertion against the world he opposes. Siegfried is a troublemaker who sets historical dynamics in motion by playing the role of a pseudo-stranger. He must appear just as suddenly as the sprouting of the human "mushrooms" that Hobbes proposes as a methodological fiction, or the emergence of the human "butterflies" that Hume criticizes. To bring about a new beginning, Siegfried must be removed from history and society.

This fantasy of exterritoriality is something Siegfried has in common with other Wagner characters. Lohengrin, for example, can only fulfill the role of savior because he comes from the outside and does not belong to the commonwealth in crisis: "A wonder! A wonder! A miracle has happened, / an overwhelming, strange, unheard-of wonder! / We greet you, hero sent by god!" (*Lohengrin* 56f.). Parsifal also owes his redemptive power to the fact that he has no background. Gurnemanz asks, "Where are you from?" and Parsifal responds, "I don't know." – "Who is your father?" – "I don't know." – "Who sent you this way?" – "I don't know." – "Who gave you the bow?" – "I made it myself." Gurnemanz calls Parsifal a "dullard," but this ignorance is his greatest asset because it means he can stand before the world as an "innocent fool" (*Parsifal* 133, 135, 155). He is immune to all entanglements and all erotic temptations. He does not want to "unite" with Kundry, he does not want his "soul's salvation" to be wangled or "kissed away" by her (*Parsifal* 197). As Hanns Eisler aptly noted, he offers "salvation from outside, from 'above.'"[14] This idea of a new beginning, which could also be described as a revolution from outside or from above, thus joins the political theories of revolution that descend into the lowlands of history – as Marx and Engels try to do – in order to track down the political troublemaker.

3. The hero as child and dullard: Siegfried's recipe for success

In the Ring, Siegfried takes on the role of the revolutionary – a role played by Wagner himself during his time as the court Kapellmeister in Dresden, and one that he also admired in others. What Wagner wrote about Mikhail Bakunin, his companion in his Dresden days, also applies to Siegfried: "Everything about him was on a colossal scale, and he had a strength suggestive of primitive exuberance."[15] Siegfried also fits into the typology of the revolutionary that Mona Ozouf developed based on the French Revolution. Ozouf distinguishes between a "spontaneous" ("energetic") and a "directed" strategy of rebirth or regeneration for humanity, and she links these variations to different models of revolution based either on a "wondrous" event or on "painstaking" effort.[16] Siegfried obviously has to be placed on the side of spontaneity.

Siegfried's talent as a revolutionary was emphasized not only by Wagner but also, before him, by an author who will have much to say later on in this book: Friedrich Engels. This coincidence is too wonderful to ignore. In 1840, at the age of 20, Engels published a newspaper article entitled "Siegfried's Native Town," which functions as a prelude to Wagner but also, and above all, to the appearance of the proletarian as the *puer robustus* in the later works of Marx and Engels. In this early work, Engels is naturally referring to the original version of the Siegfried character from the *Nibelungenlied* when he writes:[17]

What is it about the legend of Siegfried that affects us so powerfully? [...] Siegfried is the representative of German youth. All of us, who still carry in our breast a heart unfettered by the restraints of life, know what that means. We all feel in ourselves the same zest for action, the same defiance of convention [...]; we loathe with all our soul continual reflection and the philistine fear of vigorous action; we want to get out into the free world; we want to overrun the barriers of prudence and fight for the crown of life, action.

Though Siegfried's opponent was a "dragon," the young Engels – very much like Wagner later on – feels called upon to engage in a revolutionary battle against a new monster, the "state" that "suppresse[s] every free movement":

> Police for thinking, police for speaking, police for walking, riding and driving, passports, residence permits, and customs documents – the devil strike these giants and dragons dead! [...] Perhaps a friendly Morgan le Fay will make Siegfried's castle rise again for me or show my mind's eye what heroic deeds are reserved for his sons of the nineteenth century. (MECW 2, 135f.)

For Siegfried's total new beginning – or, as one could disparagingly say, for his beginnerdom – certain conditions must be met. He will only have what it takes to be a hero if he is a *child* and a *dullard*. In these two roles, Siegfried fits perfectly with the model of the *puer robustus* defined by childishness and unreason – but for Wagner (unlike Hobbes), this characterization marks him out as a savior. Siegfried is referred to as a "brave but foolish boy," an "insolent boy," "bold, youthful, and fearless, unknown to [himself]," an "obstinate boy" (*Ring* 175, 205, 206, 212). Wotan sees in him a "youth of dauntless daring" who is "unhelped by Wotan" (*Ring* 224). Brünnhilde revels in "extreme joy":

> O radiant youth!
> O glorious hero!
> My proudly fearless,
> brave, noble boy! (*Ring* 243)

Siegfried, as Susan Sontag remarked, is "a high-spirited, childlike brute under the protection of the gods."[18] He is capable of the "deed that will free our world" (*Ring* 225) only as long as he is and remains a child. This child stands not for attachment or dependence here, but rather for a person who has no past and therefore claims a special position at the start of everything. Presuppositionlessness, which is actually just "forgetfulness" (NCW 2, 313, 318), is praised as a revolutionary virtue.

"Children! create something *new*! something *new*! and again something *new*!" Wagner wrote to Franz Liszt on September 8, 1852.[19] The confrontation between the old and new world coincides in the Ring with the confrontation between Wotan and Siegfried. It is formulated most briefly in the previously mentioned letter that Wagner wrote to Röckel on January 25/26, 1854: "Wodan" – as he is called in the letter

– "resembles *us* to a tee; he is the sum total of present-day intelligence, whereas Siegfried is the man of the future whom we desire and long for but who cannot be made by us, since he must create himself on the basis of our own annihilation."[20] Siegfried is conceived as a counter-figure to the man of the present, who is personified not only by Wotan but also by Wagner himself. An American Wagner scholar[21] noted in the late nineteenth century that Wotan is a "degenerative millionaire," which brings to mind Theodor Fontane's harsh judgment of the composer himself: "He is entirely Wotan, who wants money and power [. . .] and constantly cheats to this end."[22]

In order for Siegfried to remain a child, he must use autosuggestion to cast himself as a rank beginner or cast off the historicity that is inscribed in the *puer robustus*. He must somehow avoid the realization that he does not, in fact, come out of nowhere, that he does have a (pre-)history. The fact that he is considered an "orphan" (*Ring* 166), as Mime says, comes as a welcome relief to him because it means he does not have to deal with the past. As Mime's foster child, however, Siegfried is not immune to longing for his true parents and driving himself into the ground in his search for them. This question troubles him, as becomes clear in his long quarrel with Mime (*Ring* 162–8). But the lessons Siegfried takes from this quarrel – namely, how he manages to assert his beginnerdom against the passing of generations and history – are telling.

Siegfried initially has an easy job of it with Mime, his substitute father. He simply refuses to take Mime seriously and does not allow Mime to curb his fantasies of new beginnings and power. By rejecting Mime, he begins – as Adorno's polemic rightly has it – to "[falsify] the condition of the disinherited [man] [. . .] as the unmutilated one."[23] Siegfried turns himself into a man of nature by artificially excluding himself from society. The natural state upon which he prides himself is, therefore, not something given but something created, an artificial product. Siegfried employs two strategies to secure his own personal zero hour: a negative strategy for warding off the past and a positive strategy for seizing power in the present and future.

First, Siegfried suppresses his curiosity about his true father. He manages to do this by drawing a rather simple conclusion: "My father, how did he look?" Siegfried asks, only to answer immediately: "Why, of course, like his son!" (*Ring* 202). Take note of how the genealogy is turned around here: it is the father who looks like the son, not the son who looks like the father. Siegfried thinks he knows himself and can therefore co-opt his father as well. By basing his conclusions solely on himself, he lays claim to a complete new beginning for himself. The disrespect he has rehearsed in his interactions with Mime serves him well in his first encounter with Wotan – in a scene in which he rebels against the old god as if he were a caricatural cross between Prometheus and Oedipus (*Ring* 228, 230):

> When all my life
> there stood in my path
> an aged fellow;
> now I have swept him away. [. . .]
> Ho! Ho! So you'd stop me!
> Who are you then
> to say I can't go on?

Second, the fatherless Siegfried believes he can define his new home, his own world, entirely through his own efforts. As befits the veiled indifference with which Siegfried shapes his father in his own image, this home is entirely freed from the pull of the past: "In the world I'll find my home," Siegfried says, meaning that he can be at home anywhere (*Ring* 167). This power to position himself wherever he wants is impaired only by his grief for his mother: "Ah, how this son / longs to see his mother!" (*Ring* 202). After Brünnhilde – whom Siegfried initially almost takes to be his mother – has been found, however, this grief recedes into the background. He creates a second home with his mother-wife. Just as Parsifal crafts his own bow, Siegfried is confident that he himself can do whatever needs to be done. "Meat I roast for myself" (*Ring* 159) he says proudly. In this, he seems to be a relative of the self-made man. But what sets Siegfried apart from the self-made man is his stupidity.

Siegfried is not just a boy but a "foolish boy" at that. The Rhine maidens speak of him disparagingly: "He thinks he is wise, / he thinks he is strong, / but he's stupid and blind as a child!" (*Ring* 312). One of Siegfried's defining traits is his "shallow simplicity";[24] he is a "dupe" with a "ready-made heroic pose."[25] This hero does not have the faintest idea why he does anything, but this instinctively makes him the executor of fate. Stupidity does not lead Siegfried astray, it allows him to fulfill his task.

Once Siegfried gains access to the Nibelungen treasure, he haphazardly grabs not only the ring but also the Tarnhelm, a magic cap that becomes essential to the rest of the story. After regarding his loot "meditatively" (really!?), he says: "I know not their use" (*Ring* 211). "No teacher here could be found" – this is his justification for not yet having learned to fear (*Ring* 212). It is only this unlearnedness that enables him to conquer the giant Fafner: "Only his folly / can serve in his need!" (*Ring* 183). In the meantime, Siegfried becomes an easily manipulated marionette in Hagen's hands,[26] but this is the very reason the coveted ring can be secured and finally taken out of circulation in the end. It is not actually through his own deeds or misdeeds that Siegfried terrorizes his

164

environment. He moves and functions like a sleepwalker. His lack of a clue is his recipe for success, and the further he pushes it, the more his childishness becomes puerile, his cheekiness brazen.

Wagner wants the contradiction between nature and contract to represent a fight between good and evil. But there is a peculiar and indeed harrowing upshot to this confrontation. In the case of Siegfried, the force of good is found in a protagonist who actually stands on this side of good and evil, where there is no real negotiation, where nature rules and foolishness prevails. As nature's mouthpiece or henchman, he is not *beyond* all doubt, but any doubt is beyond him.

How does Wagner fit with the theory and typology of the troublemaker I have developed in this book? What role does he play in the context of political philosophy? Stupidity is a trait that his hero – as mentioned – shares with Hobbes's original version of the *puer robustus*, who has only a "childish disposition." But Siegfried's lack of insight does not cause him to be stuck – like the *puer robustus* – in an egoism that Hobbes considers unreasonable and self-destructive. According to Wagner, stupidity is an attribute that equips his hero with a natural imperative and redemptive power. He rejects the Hobbesian alternative that says an individual must be either an evil dissenter or a good contractual partner. By reaching out to the whole, Wagner's troublemaker rises above all the egocentric troublemakers who operate as freeloaders, scroungers, and so on.

This inevitably brings him closer to the *puer robustus* of Rousseau who operates nomocentrically, a troublemaker who anticipates and identifies with a different political order. Wagner seems to be familiar with this idea when he says that only "in the completest absorption into the commonality of those who differ from him can [man] ever be completely *what* he is" (WPW 1, 99). But we should be cautious with this classification. The nomocentric troublemaker cannot and does not want to be anything other than a *creature of the future*. From his vantage point on the edge of the status quo, he anticipates a vision that guides him and mobilizes him to action. Such an audacious plan is alien to Wagner's hero, who obstinately remains in repose in his own presence. I should add that this is precisely why a chasm also opens up between Siegfried and Diderot's eccentric troublemaker, who dances on the edge of the political order and remains suspended there.

Wagner's relationship with the other troublemakers in this book can also be illustrated in terms of the different interpretations of childhood with which they are associated. Wagner's celebration of his childish hero stands in sharp contrast to the critique of childhood as a state of immaturity that is a key element of Hobbes's campaign against the *puer robustus* (and to which we will return in the works of Alexis de Tocqueville and Benedetto Croce). Childhood is celebrated not only by Wagner, however,

165

but by many of the other authors who appear in this book, including Rousseau, Diderot, Emerson, Baudelaire, Hugo, and Michelet, i.e., advocates of the nomocentric and eccentric troublemaker alike. They turn the crudity of the child into a *capability* or skill. Strictly speaking, for Rousseau it is "youth" and not "childhood" that harbors the critical potential for a natural life and that is held up against the individual's entanglement in society. Diderot, Emerson, and Baudelaire interpret the contrast between childhood and adulthood as a contrast between liquefaction and hardening – and they make a case for the former. Michelet describes the productive conflict of the child who is at the mercy of existing rules and who simultaneously mobilizes his "energy" against them. And Hugo sees in this conflict both an opportunity for change and a danger of simplemindedness.

Celebrating childhood is not dubious in itself; what matters more is *how* it is celebrated. All of the authors mentioned believe there is a moment of crisis in childhood that should be interpreted positively, in the etymological sense of *krisis* and *krinein*, as an opportunity for differentiation and decision. In this moment, people do not belong to the status quo wholesale, but they remain connected and exposed to it. It is this fragile, precarious status of the threshold creature that is abrogated in Wagner's celebration of childhood. He transforms the threshold into an apparently stable place, into its own world. In his disconnection from the world, Siegfried most resembles the gamin who appears as a boyish "fairy" in Hugo's work. But unlike Hugo's childish hero – who lights the way to a different, better life, but only as an ignis fatuus – Siegfried embarks on a historic mission. He presumes to have the absolute power to create a natural order out of nothing. The phrase "nomos of the earth" suits Wagner at least as well as it suits Carl Schmitt. Like the other troublemakers, Siegfried chafes at an existing order that appears to him as a world of contracts. But he draws his energy not from this friction, but from a source that seems to bubble away reliably within him: nature.

Siegfried does not cross the finish line as a beaming victor in the Ring Cycle. The world is saved from the capital subverting it and the ring is taken out of circulation, but both Siegfried and Brünnhilde must lose their lives for this to happen. In the opera, Siegfried merely prepares the ground for a new order; it is left up to the public to actually restore society. The public is responsible for completing the work of redemption in a way that remains true to the narrow-minded specifications of its hero.

Wagner might talk about "union," "Communism," "the common-being of *Mankind*," and "*free* communions," but what he really means is society's return to a state of nature (WPW 1, 166, 99, 261, 203). It should be sufficient for individuals to achieve awareness of nature for themselves, just as Siegfried does. Siegfried's posthumous victory is realized when people follow him in binding themselves to the "Earth-Nature" that is the "prime condition of their existence, their life and handiwork" (WPW 1, 261). They do not reach an agreement amongst themselves but are instead united or unified by delivering society up to nature. It might be more fitting to speak of pseudo-nature here, because its power can be a front for almost anything as long as it fulfills this single criterion: it must be appreciated *hors discussion*, beyond any doubt, in a virtually predetermined and harmonious way. This means the "union" of individuals must be nothing less than a total fusion. The only people then left in existence are those who are "what by their very nature they *can* be, and *therefore shall and will be*" (WPW 1, 265).

To qualify this, it should be said that Wagner himself hints that this total fusion is not necessarily the end of history. His hints relate primarily to the character of Brünnhilde.[27] She actually has what it takes to be a *puella robusta* who confronts Siegfried, because her own battle against Wotan's world of contracts manages to do without the short circuit between stupidity and nature. But Wagner never gives her the chance to fight this battle; instead, he delivers her up to Siegfried. (It is strange that many of the authors examined here actually create strong female characters, but they begrudge these characters their strength. In the case of Wagner, this applies to Brünnhilde in the Ring and to Elsa in *Lohengrin*, but it is also true of several of the female characters or disguised female heroes in the works of Schiller and others.)

As a troublemaker who is expected to bring about the total fusion of humanity, Siegfried is a precursor to the fascist troublemakers who are indiscriminately lumped together in the *Volksgemeinschaft* or "people's community." To modify a phrase from Wagner – "The error of the philosopher became the madness of the masses" (WPW 1, 260) – we could say that the error of the composer will become the madness of the masses. Error and madness feed on their access to a source of power outside of society itself. This strategy relies on a disturbance that disturbs and destroys the social interplay of order and disturbance *as such*. Those who act as the henchmen or executors of such a power speak with *one* voice and act in the interest of *one* goal. They appear as a bloc, a mass, and can therefore be called *massive* troublemakers. They bring us to the nadir of the history and theory of the troublemaker. I will come to them when I talk about Schmitt, Strauss, Schelsky, and Horkheimer, as well as the fundamentalists of the present day. But the next troublemaker to take the stage is not the one who gives himself up to the masses, it is the egocentric troublemaker who gains the upper hand in the course of the expansion of democracy and capitalism. This *puer robustus* owes his appearance to Alexis de Tocqueville.

— VII. —

THE *PUER ROBUSTUS* BETWEEN EUROPE AND AMERICA

Alexis de Tocqueville

1. The birth of the *puer robustus* under the yoke of despotism: Tocqueville's first insight

"It cannot be doubted," Alexis de Tocqueville writes in the second volume of *Democracy in America*, "that the moment when political rights are granted to a people who have, until then, been deprived of them is a moment of crisis, a crisis often necessary, but always dangerous." He continues:

> The child inflicts death when he is unaware of the value of life; he takes property from others before knowing that someone can rob him of his. The common man, at the moment when he is granted political rights, finds himself, in relation to his rights, in the same position as the child vis-à-vis all of nature. In this case the celebrated phrase applies to him: *Homo puer robustus.* (DIA 2, 392; O 2, 274)

These lines were published in 1835, four years after the *puer robustus* appeared in Victor Hugo's *Notre-Dame*. This is not the only time Tocqueville grants this character (still "celebrated" at the time!) an appearance. He next mentions the *puer robustus* around 20 years later, which brings him – historically speaking – into line with Wagner and with Marx, who will be the focus of the next chapter.

I want to hold off on his later references to the *puer robustus*, however, and initially look only at this single passage in which he mentions Hobbes. It comes from a book in which Tocqueville, just 30 years old at the time, holds up American democracy as a model for his fellow countrymen and all Europeans.[1] In this book, he investigates the circumstances that help or hinder the emergence of democracy. One of his concerns is the "common man" who struggles to exercise his "political rights" in his role as a *puer robustus*.

168

Although Tocqueville expresses these concerns in a book about America, they relate first and foremost to the situation in Europe. The question of why the *puer robustus* proliferated in the Old World leads to Tocqueville's first great insight (section 1). His praise for the New World does not prevent him from criticizing it as well, however (section 2) – and this criticism grows sharper in later years, when he formulates a second insight into the theory of the troublemaker, one intended specifically for the USA (section 3). In the end we shall see whether Tocqueville's critique of the *puer robustus*, the man-child, fits together with his fascination with the thrill of the new (section 4). Is he sympathetic to the good troublemaker? To answer this question, I will confront Tocqueville with the theories of John Stuart Mill and Friedrich Nietzsche.

Tocqueville makes life easy for his readers. Unlike his predecessors, each of whom put their own twist on the *puer robustus* and gave him a new identity, Tocqueville depicts the *puer robustus* exactly as Hobbes intended. Both Tocqueville and Hobbes describe a fellow who is unable or unwilling to set and follow rules. He has no time for the political order and gives free rein to his "blind, greedy, vulgar passions" (*Recollections* 103/O 3, 850; cf. DIA 2, 392; O 2, 274). Incidentally, Tocqueville is not alone in this description. A few years earlier, in 1831, the royalist Narcisse-Achille de Salvandy had attributed a destructive "energy" to the "lower classes" and characterized the people as "multitudinous fantastical tyrants" to whom "Hobbes's definition" of the "strong child" (*enfant robuste*) could be applied.[2] And after 1840, the phrase *puer robustus* would be used to describe the people or the workers by a variety of other authors – Marx being just one of them.[3]

Unlike Rousseau, Tocqueville does not celebrate the inner calm of the good *puer robustus*. Unlike Diderot, he does not flirt with a *puer robustus* who sets the world in motion like a pinch of yeast. Unlike Schiller, he feels no sympathy for the troublemaker who breaks the law. Unlike Hugo, he finds no moral compass within the *puer robustus*. Unlike Wagner, he does not seek to turn the brave boy into a savior who will upend the old world. Tocqueville describes the *form of life* of the *puer robustus* exactly as Hobbes does. But he does not leave it at that. In addition to *describing* the strong boy trapped by his "passions," he *explains* the boy's *life circumstances* and thus answers the question of how he came to be what he is.

Tocqueville does not divide history into a state of nature and a state of society, as Hobbes does. He is more interested in the transitions between social orders, to which people have always been exposed, and in the "necessary, but always dangerous" crises (see above) that emerge in the course of this. Like Sigmund Freud after him, he draws a parallel between social development and a person's individual becoming:

A man is newly born; his first years pass obscurely amid the pleasures or occupations of childhood. He grows up; manhood begins; finally the doors of the world open to receive him; he enters into contact with his fellow men. Then, for the first time, you study him and think that the seeds of the vices and virtues of his mature years can be seen developing in him. If I am not mistaken, that is a great error. Go back to the beginning; examine the child even in the arms of his mother. (DIA 1, 45f.; O 2, 29)

We saw this blunt contrast between childhood and maturity in Hobbes's work as well. But Tocqueville's discreet appeal to "examine the child even in the arms of his mother" is actually highly charged. Applied to the development of society, it means that we should also pay attention to the "arms" that encircle the people, or the conditions that surround them. This enables Tocqueville to provide a new explanation for the fact (which he does not dispute) that the *puer robustus* is incapable of political self-organization.

Tocqueville argues that immaturity, ineptness, and unwillingness *in politicis* are attitudes or bad habits acquired by people when they are not free. This brings Tocqueville to his *insight regarding the birth of the* puer robustus *under the yoke of despotism.* "In despotic States, men do not know how to act, because they are told nothing," he says (DIA 4, 1083; O 2, 738). They have scope to act only in their "private life" and thus never learn how to "use that freedom" (DIA 2, 421, 328; O 2, 353, 214). "A nation that asks of its government only the maintenance of order is already a slave at the bottom of its heart. The nation is a slave of its well-being, and the man who is to put it in chains can appear" (DIA 3, 952; O 2, 654).

For Tocqueville, therefore, Hobbes's all-powerful sovereign who maintains order and subjugates people is no longer part of the solution; he is part of the problem. The problem, in this case, is that heteronomy stunts people's capacity for self-determination. Tocqueville says that when he sees a "people" on the edge of anarchy, he is "tempted to believe that for them despotism would be a benefit. But these two words will never be found united in my thought" (DIA 2, 366; O 2, 257f.).

In Tocqueville's Europe – the setting for despotism – the powerful and powerless are entrenched against one another. As result, the subjects or citizens-to-be are blocked from positive identification with their political institutions. The only power they know is a state power that rules over them from above. According to Tocqueville, this applies even to as innocuous an area as administration. Because this administration is patronizing, because people are "accustomed to finding an official constantly at hand" who sets the rules, it is difficult for the people to strive

170

assiduously for self-administration (DIA 1, 155; O 2, 102). Europe is therefore also a breeding ground for the *puer robustus*. Wherever despotism alienates people from politics and restricts them to the satisfaction of private needs, dissatisfaction takes the form not of political engagement but of "pointless damage" (DIA 2, 391; O 2, 273).

Tocqueville argues in a Hobbesian way by depicting the *puer robustus* as a narrow-minded, antisocial type. But without openly stating it – or perhaps even noticing it – he lays a Rousseauian argument on top of this, one that fits with the observations of Schiller and Hugo. According to this argument, the *puer robustus* trapped in his passions is a child of his time, a symptom of a societal state. Contrary to Hobbes, Tocqueville claims that despotism is what makes it impossible for people to be anything other than slaves or raging troublemakers. But unlike Rousseau, Tocqueville does not try to put a positive spin on the *puer robustus* and recruit him for the cause of liberty. The fellow is still his bogeyman.

The behavioral patterns of despotism are tenacious in Europe; they can only be "destroyed slowly," as Tocqueville puts it so beautifully, "deep within souls" (DIA 4, 1022; O 2, 701). All the same, it is necessary to break through them and thus vanquish the *puer robustus*:

> So when you say to me that laws are weak, and the governed, turbulent; that passions are intense, and virtue, powerless; and that in this situation you must not think about increasing the rights of democracy, I answer that, because of these very things, I believe you must think about it; [. . .] Incontestably the people often direct public affairs very badly; but the people cannot get involved in public affairs without having the circle of their ideas expand, and without seeing their minds emerge from their ordinary routine. (DIA 2, 392, 398; O 2, 274, 279f.)

Tocqueville seeks to explain the origin of political immaturity, and he is naturally also interested in the outcome of this immaturity. But "there is nothing harder than apprenticeship in liberty" (DIA 2, 393; O 2, 275). The people face a problem previously identified by Machiavelli: "[For] that people is nothing other than a brute animal that, although of a ferocious and feral nature, has always been nourished in prison and in servitude. Then, if it is left free in a field to its fate, it becomes the prey of the first one who seeks to rechain it."[4] As long as the people remain trapped in political immaturity, they can only become a *puer robustus*, who finds no favor in Tocqueville's eyes. Liberation is arduous, and the political subject who can make the transition from despotism to democracy will not fall from the sky. Where on earth will we find him, where will he prevail?

2. Praise for America and a warning against the Wild West

"How is it," Tocqueville asks, "that in the United States, where the inhabitants arrived yesterday on the soil that they occupy, [. . .] that each person is involved in the affairs of his town, of his district, and of the entire State as his very own?" (DIA 2, 387; O 2, 271). The reason for this, he believes, is that the battle lines have not yet been drawn between the subject and the state. The conditions under which citizens could exercise and enjoy their political rights had been met to a far greater extent in the USA than in Europe.

When Tocqueville speaks of the free "inhabitants" of America who "arrived just yesterday on the soil" of their country, however, he displays a startling ignorance or arrogance. He acts as though these "inhabitants" were the only people there – as if there were no American Indians and also no slaves. The political participation he celebrates is not really open to *everyone*, only to those who have been granted civil rights. What Tocqueville has to say about the people excluded from society is a mixed bag to say the least. Regarding Native Americans he resorts to whitewashing, claiming that the European immigrants had dealt with them "calmly, legally, philanthropically, without shedding blood" and had left them to their wild freedom (DIA 2, 547; O 2, 393). When it comes to relations with the "Black race," though, Tocqueville reaches a different conclusion. According to his classification, slaves – unlike the Indians – are part of America's (unjust) legal order, so he cannot simply treat their oppression as an external affair. Tocqueville laments that "Blacks" are kept in a state of political immaturity, much like the *puer robustus*, and he speaks out against slavery. But he is concerned that these emancipated people might not be able to handle their liberty (DIA 2, 552–5; O 2, 419–21). In this respect, his assessment of "Blacks" resembles his assessment of Algerians, whom he says are still in a state of "infancy."[5] He voices the same reservations against of all these people that he expresses against the inept, unruly lower classes in Europe.

In the closed world of the white immigrants, on the other hand, everything is rosy: "America is the only country where we have been able to witness the natural and tranquil development of a society" (DIA 1, 47; O 2, 30). Tocqueville says that the people in America practice liberty both vigorously and prudently. They organize their self-governance without needing the Leviathan. Tocqueville admires Americans for *living* their political maturity to the full. Like Max Weber[6] will do later, he emphasizes their passionate engagement in countless "associations," in which they share and pursue political, social, religious, and cultural goals (DIA 3, 896; O 2, 620f.).

172

With his talk of "tranquil development," Tocqueville indicates that he interprets the development of the USA as an anti-revolutionary project in which people grow in line with their requirements, or simply grow up. There is no need to fear that they will act rashly – something that cannot be said of the European masses. In Tocqueville's view, it is a stroke of historical luck that the despotism that drives someone to become a *puer robustus* has never existed in America. While Europe is buffeted by storms and rocked by wars, on the other side of the Atlantic he feels only the gentle tailwind of history, which fosters the reconciliation of power and morality within a democratic order.[7] Like Victor Hugo, Tocqueville wants the people to go through a process of education or maturation; and like Hugo, he is occupied by the question of how it is possible for historical change to be free of trouble – and free troublemakers.

Even before Tocqueville, there had been controversies in America itself regarding the extent to which the people could be trusted with their own emancipation and ability to self-organize. Looking at this debate between the Founding Fathers can help us trace the inner-American disturbances that were not hidden from Tocqueville. The dispute involved Alexander Hamilton and James Madison on one side, and Thomas Jefferson – "the most powerful apostle democracy has ever had," according to Tocqueville (DIA 2, 426, cf. 323; O 2, 300, cf. 229) – on the other. Tocqueville's rejection of the idea that people should be protected from themselves through a kind of well-meaning despotism identifies him as an acolyte of Jefferson.

Madison and Hamilton wanted to take precautions against the people's immaturity, which they saw as a threat to the political order. They (essentially) recommended preventive measures against the *puer robustus* who lay dormant within each citizen, and they hoped to carefully nudge political decision-making away from the will of the people.[8] Jefferson considered this an attempt to make political immaturity into a permanent state, and he opposed the notion of countering the danger of anarchy, the "bellum omnium in omnia," by concentrating power – i.e., "despotism." (This criticism is remarkably relevant in the context of current surveillance debates.) To Jefferson, the "thought alone" that the stability of the "government" should be based on the citizens' "fear" of its power was "treason against the people." His critique was directed at Hobbes, though he is not mentioned by name.[9] Jefferson connected the democratic project to historical processes of education, re-education, and further education. For him, history was tied up with the question of power and morality – just like the *puer robustus*. In his *Notes on the State of Virginia*, Jefferson countered the proponents of stability by invoking Condorcet's (and Rousseau's) concept of *perfectibilité*: "Every government degenerates when trusted to the rulers of the people alone. The people themselves therefore are its only safe depositories. And to render even them safe their minds must be improved to a certain degree."[10]

Tocqueville declares "perfectibility" to be a matter that concerns all of humanity,[11] but since development had halted elsewhere, the model he holds up here is America, where "all have an intense faith in human perfectibility" (DIA 2, 600; O 2, 435). Like Hobbes, Tocqueville – who coined the term "individualism" – grants people a sense of "particular" or "individual interest" (DIA 3, 881, 919–23; O 2, 612, 636–8). But unlike Hobbes, he believes this interest unfolds in the enjoyment of both private and political liberty. His model of perfectibility has two prongs consisting of self-directed economic activity and political self-determination. It is worth mentioning these two prongs because, as we are about to see, there is a tension between them that impedes the "tranquil development" of democracy in America.

At first glance, Tocqueville seems to simply repeat the classic liberal dogma of a synergy between politics and economics, between political and private happiness. And he does, in fact, talk of a "close bond and a necessary connection between [. . .] liberty and industry" (DIA 3, 950; O 2, 652). In keeping with this, he (like John Stuart Mill[12]) flirts with the notion that there is not only a socialist but also a liberal vision of a classless society which enables the economic and political development of all people (cf. DIA 2, 394, O 2, 276).

But Tocqueville is not naïve enough to be written off as a dutiful disciple of classical liberalism. His sensitivity to conflict weakens slightly when he comments on the situation of American Indians and African Americans, but it does not abandon him altogether when it comes to the tensions erupting within the nascent democracy of the USA. He sees such tensions in the agonal relationship between politics and economics. With respect to inhumane working conditions in factories, Tocqueville warns that economic inequality undermines democratic cooperation between equals.[13] At the same time, he worries that economic ambitions could derail the enthusiasm for "political liberty" (DIA 3, 893f., cf. 950; O 2, 620, cf. 652). According to his diagnosis, the pursuit of private interest and "love of well-being" have become "the national and dominant taste" of the Americans (DIA 3, 934; O 2, 643). Tocqueville is not alone in thinking this. As early as 1787, the judge and politician Edmund Pendleton had warned his compatriots against the "fatal passion for sudden riches" that could "extinguish every sentiment of political and moral duty."[14]

Tocqueville's praise for the "tranquil development" of American democracy suggests that the *puer robustus* who was making mischief in Europe could not gain a foothold in America. And yet there were disturbances nonetheless – caused by people who scorned cooperation and participation. Therefore, when searching for the American version of the *puer robustus*, we must start not with despotism, which *excludes* people from political activity, but with the people who deliberately *renounce* political activity in a democracy. They presumably have better things to do – such as ruthlessly pursuing their own enrichment. These saboteurs of the political sphere are born not of need but of greed, not of discontent but of cockiness. A lack of opportunity for political development is not the only factor in this attitude; such an attitude can escalate even in a country that offers such opportunities in abundance.

So the *puer robustus* who was initially found primarily in Europe makes his way to the USA after all. Tocqueville tries to reassure himself by claiming that the fellow is not ubiquitous. He distinguishes between good and bad Americans, between democratic citizens and the *puer robustus* – and between east and west:

> Why, in the East of the Union, does republican government appear strong and well-ordered, why does it proceed with maturity and deliberation? [. . .] Why, in contrast, do the powers of society in the West seem to move haphazardly? Why, in the movement of affairs, does something disorderly, passionate, you could almost say feverish, reign that does not herald a long future? (DIA 2, 497f.; O 2, 356f.)

His answer:

> It is in the East that the Anglo-Americans have contracted the longest use of the government of democracy, and that they have formed habits and conceived ideas most favorable to maintaining it. Democracy there has little by little penetrated customs, opinions, forms; you find it in all the details of social life as in the laws. [. . .] In the West, in contrast, a part of these same advantages is still lacking. Many Americans of the states of the West are born in the woods [. . .]. Among them, passions are more violent [. . .]. (DIA 2, 498; O 2, 357)

According to Tocqueville's interpretation, even in America (though only in the Wild West) there are characters who are simply narrow-minded and uncivilized. He is clearly disconcerted by the advancement of these primitive fellows:

> The Americans who withdraw from the shores of the Atlantic Ocean in order to plunge into the West are adventurers impatient with any kind of yoke, greedy for wealth, often cast out by the states where they were born. They arrive in the middle of the wilderness without knowing each other. There they find to control them neither traditions nor family support, nor examples. Among them the rule of laws is weak, and that of mores is weaker still. So the men [. . .] are inferior in all ways to the Americans who inhabit the old limits of the Union. (DIA 2, 603; O 2, 438)

175

This image of the Wild West was not borne of prejudice; it reflected reality. The murder rate was "fifty to several hundred times higher" in the west than in the rest of the USA, and "the causes were right out of Hobbes," meaning that the legal order was not sufficiently enforced.[15] The pioneers, to quote a song by Adam Ant, were the "Kings of the Wild Frontier." They created their own empire. These "young wild" men[16] were obstinately self-interested because they had not yet come to the realization that they shared a destiny – a realization that nurtures the spirit of political liberty and counteracts the temptation to devote oneself to personal enrichment. The pioneers were said to "expect nothing so to speak from anyone; they are always accustomed to consider themselves in isolation, and they readily imagine that their entire destiny is in their hands" (DIA 3, 884; O 2, 614). (Leo Strauss and Helmut Schelsky would return to this rugged individualism later on – both of them, astonishingly, putting a positive spin on it.)

Tocqueville's aversion to the pioneers is so extreme that he bluntly advises against the westward expansion of the USA. He says such an expansion would endanger the elaborate and precious interplay between individualism and communal relationships upon which the USA was founded. "The Americans rejoice when contemplating this extraordinary movement" toward the west, but Tocqueville believes they should instead "consider it with regret and fear" (DIA 2, 611; O 2, 445). When these lines were published – they can be found in the first volume of *Democracy in America* from 1835 – the development that Tocqueville feared was just starting. This makes the depth of his concern all the more remarkable.

In the first section of this chapter, I pointed out that there are two elements to Tocqueville's interpretation of the *puer robustus*. He adopts Hobbes's *description* of the *puer robustus*, which emphasizes his blind, passionate nature, and he supplements this with a new *explanation* that identifies this behavior as a consequence of despotism. But when Tocqueville finds the *puer robustus* in America, his explanation falls apart. It no longer fits, because despotism held no sway in America.

At this point, there are only two lines of argumentation open to Tocqueville. He could content himself with Hobbes's description, according to which some people are simply foolish and savage by nature, or he could stick to his innovative ambition to provide social reasons for the rise of antisocial behavior. To do this, he would have to readjust his analysis and investigate the special circumstances that promoted the emergence of the *puer robustus* in the USA.

Tocqueville opts for the path of least resistance. He depicts the pioneers as narrow-minded philistines who are simply not mature enough for the political achievements of the USA. This attitude is evident when he speaks of the "violent passions" of those who are "born in the woods" (see above). Tocqueville seems to find confirmation of his disparaging judgment when he looks beyond the western USA and turns his attention to South America. There, he believes, men of nature who are incapable of cooperation are on the verge of seizing power. He is backed up in this by Hobbes's warning against the war of all against all:

> We are astonished to see the new nations of South America stir, for a quarter century, amid constantly recurring revolutions; and each day we expect to see them recover what is called their *natural state*. [. . .] The people who inhabit this beautiful half of a hemisphere seem obstinately bound to eviscerate themselves. (DIA 2, 366; O 2, 258)

Carl Schmitt will eventually trump Tocqueville's Hobbesian description of the Wild West and South America by declaring in 1950 that Hobbes's state of nature had taken root all over the "New World."[17] Tocqueville's loyalty to Hobbes in his assessment of the American west – which he claims is inhabited solely by mischief-making men of nature – is a serious weak point in his argumentation. Westward expansion was driven not just by a few backwoodsmen; the pioneers were supported by the same people on the east coast of America whom Tocqueville credits with having clean hands. Henry David Thoreau was right when he said that "California [. . .] is the child of New England."[18]

What would happen if, in his analysis of America, Tocqueville tried to maintain his high standard of argumentation and find concrete social reasons for the political sabotage of the pioneers? Then he would not have to tell the story of the birth of the *puer robustus* under the yoke of despotism, but rather the story of his birth from the spirit of capitalism. He shies away from this in *Democracy in America* – but he does not leave it at that. It is often said that, after his brilliant early work, Tocqueville turned his back on the subject that had occupied him in his youth.[19] But in essays and letters from the period around 1850, he gives the *puer robustus* another grand entrance and develops a second great insight into the theory of the troublemaker.

3. The birth of the *puer robustus* from the spirit of capitalism: Tocqueville's second insight

On September 12, 1848, Tocqueville gave a speech before the Constituent Assembly in the Palais Bourbon, which he intended to be a grand plea for individual liberty. In this speech, he holds up the USA as a bright counter-image to his compatriots:

> There you will find a people among whom conditions are more equal than they are among us; where everything emanates from and returns

to the people, and where nevertheless each individual enjoys a more complete independence and greater liberty than in any other time or any other country on earth, an essentially democratic country, I repeat, the only democracy that exists in the world today, the only truly democratic republics that history has ever known.[20]

Here Tocqueville invokes the ideal for which he believes the New World – or at least the founding states on the east coast – stands: the ideal of political and private liberty. "No other country in the world," he enthuses in a speech given in Cherbourg in March of the same year, "can provide us with such useful examples or inspire such legitimate hopes. In America, the republic is not a dictatorship exercised in the name of liberty; it is liberty itself, the authentic, true liberty of all citizens."[21] In his search for a society that is not simply a marketplace or experience machine but a political project, Tocqueville once again finds what he is looking for in the USA. By contrast, he complains about the "great [. . .] offense" of the ministers in France who "wish only to play on the chord of private self-interest in men."[22] *Enrichissez-vous* was the slogan making the rounds in France.

Tocqueville's new views are easily reconciled with his early book on America. Depoliticization and the pure pursuit of private interests were still considered the domain of Europe. Tocqueville commends the USA – at least when he wants to set his fellow countrymen right – as a country working to counter this development. But letters addressed to his American friends after 1850 reveal his growing doubts about his initial assessment of the nation.

On December 4, 1852, Tocqueville declared the annexation of new territories in the west to be a symptom of a "spirit of [. . .] plunder";[23] on December 11 of the same year he warned that American democracy had to combat the "spirit of adventure and conquest," the "excessive pride in its strength, and the passions of youth" that it had brought forth itself; on September 19, 1855, he bewailed the "violent, intolerant, and lawless spirit" spreading across the USA;[24] and on October 14, 1856, he wrote:

> But what scares me is [. . .] this race of desperate gamblers that your prosperity, in a land that is still half-empty, has brought forth, a race that combines the passions and instincts of the savage with the tastes, needs, vigor, and vices of civilized men. The world, I think, has never seen anything like it before. Who can say where this might lead you if they ever gained the upper hand in your affairs?[25]

It is worth pausing over this last letter to Theodore Sedgwick, as Tocqueville moves beyond his earlier, rather weak position here. The developments he eyed suspiciously in the USA are no longer blamed only on factors rooted in the natural, savage constitution of man, but also on factors that first come into play when man becomes civilized. While he spoke disparagingly of the "passions" of coarse adventurers in his work on America from 1835 to 1840, he now views the pioneers as hybrid characters in which nature and civilization mix together.

This systematic progress brings us to the second great insight that Tocqueville contributes to the theory of the troublemaker. Having identified the *puer robustus* as a child of despotism in his first insight, he now takes a fresh look at the situation in America. He describes the *puer robustus* not just as a narrow-minded man of nature who lacks what it takes to become a responsible citizen, but also as the champion of a new "civilized" type of person who maximizes his private gain and believes himself so clever that he can keep his distance from the state order. This character has laid claim to the future, and he is the premature child of a breed of people who think little of political cooperation and all the more of economic ruthlessness. Tocqueville thus arrives at his *insight into the birth of the* puer robustus *from the spirit of capitalism.*[26]

His argument is more sophisticated than that of Hannah Arendt, incidentally, who blames the demise of political liberty solely on the impoverished Europeans who had come to the USA in the nineteenth century with their animalistic desires and childish disposition in search of the "promised land."[27] Following Tocqueville's schema, we could say that Arendt turns the old European *puer robustus* into the culprit who, after emigrating to the New World, found he had nothing better to do than undermine the political ideals of the USA. This reeks of arrogance toward both the poor and the social issue. Tocqueville himself is not entirely free of such arrogance; in his dispute with Pierre-Joseph Proudhon, for example, he complains about the "consumption" and "material passions" of the poor.[28] But while Arendt absurdly suggests that the pursuit of profit is alien to the middle classes, Tocqueville attacks the "civilized man" without regard for his class.

If I continue to make reference to the *puer robustus* when talking about Tocqueville's later works, at least I cannot be accused of foisting this character upon him against his will. Tocqueville himself mentions him in three letters he addressed to American and English friends on August 29, September 1, and September 4, 1856, three years before his death. In these letters, Tocqueville not only speaks of undesirable developments in the far western USA, he also claims such developments have spilled over to the entire country. "Viewed from this side of the ocean, you have become the *puer robustus* of Hobbes," he says apodictically in the first letter: "Being so, you upset all of the friends of democratic liberty and delight all of its opponents."[29] In the second letter he writes:

179

I have passionately wished to see a free Europe and I realize that the cause of liberty is more compromised now than it was at the moment of my birth. I see around me nations whose souls seem to weaken as their prosperity and physical force grow, nations that remain, to borrow Hobbes's phrase, robust children who deserve only to be treated by means of the stick and the carrot. Your America itself, to which once turned the dreams of all those who lacked the reality of liberty, has, in my view, given little satisfaction to the friends of liberty for some time.[30]

And finally: "I must say that America is a *puer robustus*."[31] Theodore Sedgwick, one of Tocqueville's recipients, sent an interesting reply which was not published until 2009. Sedgwick writes:

Your observations on the subject of our affairs do not surprise me, since there is enough room for even more severe reproach. [. . .] For almost three generations [. . .] we have only had the most complete and striking prosperity. We have lost our simplicity and modesty, not to mention our virtue. I believe that we shall be punished by this great hand that holds the reigns (sic) of the universe.[32]

What kind of punishment could the Americans face for the misdeed of which they stand accused? The demise of their democracy and the loss of their political liberty – the only "true" liberty, according to Tocqueville (see above). And what would take their place? Tocqueville imagines two possible scenarios.

If the development of private liberty is unchecked and everyone relies solely on their own "force," believing that they hold their "entire destiny" in their own hands – to use Tocqueville's words – then everyday life becomes an anarchic competitive struggle, the war of all against all as conjured up by Hobbes. America seems to have avoided the punishment of anarchy, but thinkers have been warning against it nonetheless ever since Tocqueville's time. An arc can be drawn here from the theory of social "anomie"[33] through the tragedy of the commons[34] to current analyses of unfettered capitalism.

Besides anarchy, there is another conceivable scenario, and if the former is exemplified by Hobbes's war of all against all, the latter fits with Hobbes's rule by the Leviathan, in which political liberty is surrendered but state power prevents any ruinous conflicts in the realm of private liberty. Tocqueville had previously painted this scenario in lurid colors – and this brings us back to his book *Democracy in America*. Tocqueville seems to have had the Leviathan in mind when he warned against the rise of a new despotism. This despotism dominates a world in which people

180

spin around restlessly, in order to gain small and vulgar pleasures with which they fill their souls. Each one of them, withdrawn apart, is like a stranger to the destiny of all the others [. . .]; as for the remainder of his fellow citizens, he is next to them, but he does not see them; he touches them without feeling them; he exists only in himself and for himself alone.

Because these people have lost all interest in political liberty, they are not concerned if an "immense and tutelary power" rises over them. This power is "absolute, detailed, regular, far-sighted and mild. [. . .] It likes the citizens to enjoy themselves, provided that they think only about enjoying themselves" (DIA 4, 1249f.; O 2, 836f.). Hobbes's subject is just another man-child, like the *puer robustus*. Under this new despotism, people do not reach the "manhood" of a self-determined life; they remain fixed "irrevocably in childhood" (DIA 4, 1250; O 2, 837). As Shakespeare aptly puts it, they are in love with their "own obsequious bondage."[35]

This scenario, too, could be said to have retained its sense of threat since Tocqueville's time. The arc here stretches from the legend of the Grand Inquisitor recounted by Dostoyevsky in *The Brothers Karamazov*, through the "last men" who, according to Nietzsche's vicious characterization of them in *Thus Spoke Zarathustra*, enjoy their "little pleasure for the day" and their "little pleasure for the night" and therefore want "the same" (PN 130), to Francis Fukuyama's *The End of History and the Last Man*, which vacillates between optimism and disillusionment.[36] The *puer robustus* is tamed in the comfort zone of the affluent society and enters a kind of sleep mode. But it takes just the touch of a button – the opportunity for some quick and dirty business, say – to rouse him again. Marx, Freud, Carl Schmitt, and others will sing a wretched song of this – and during the financial crisis of 2008, the song will become a scream.

We could say that Tocqueville's America saw the start of an open race between political and private liberty. This race has continued to the present day, and the starting whistle has since been heard elsewhere as well – maybe all over the world. Many examples bear witness to this, but I will limit myself to just a few from the American context:[37] Josiah Royce wrote a critical history of the California pioneer days and called for "loyalty"; Woodrow Wilson attacked the power of trusts in his book *The New Freedom*; John Dewey set social liberalism against *laissez-faire* liberalism; Hannah Arendt claimed that the political liberty of the Founding Fathers had been replaced by the "futile antics of a society intent upon affluence and consumption"; Lyndon B. Johnson conjured up the vision of a great society and Ronald Reagan delivered the economically liberal counterprogram; Michael Walzer described the fragile coexistence of the economic and political "sphere"; and Albert

181

Hirschman analyzed how citizens oscillated between public and private interest. The list could go on.

Taking stock of the current situation, it seems impossible to call an end to this race between private and political liberty and declare a winner. The balance of power is constantly shifting. It should come as no surprise, then, that both Tocqueville's portrait of the American *puer robustus* and his description of the new despotism are hot topics even now. A feeling of invincibility, social disconnection, ruthless enrichment, a thirst for adventure and playfulness are standard issue in the sociotope of Wall Street today. The debate about political disenchantment and the question of whether we now live in a postdemocratic or populist age instead of a democratic one follow in the footsteps of the new despotism scenario. In this respect, we can say that Tocqueville does not have the final word on the birth of the *puer robustus* from the spirit of capitalism, but he provides a key that still works perfectly when we seek to understand and evaluate the crises of capitalism and democracy.

Following Tocqueville's thinking, the *puer robustus* merely plays the role of the bad boy or egocentric troublemaker in all of these scenarios. He is partly to blame for American democracy going to the dogs, as it were, in the nineteenth century – or, to use Hegel's words, going to the "private citizen" who pursues "particular interests" and "look[s] to the universal only in order to obtain private satisfaction."[38] In brief, what this American is accused of – by Hegel and Tocqueville alike – is having forgotten the state. He fulfills all the criteria that Hegel attributes to the "rabble" who have lost sight of the bigger picture and think only of themselves. Neither Hegel nor Tocqueville equates Americans with rabble, but we do find such a comparison in the works of Heinrich Heine, who refers to America as an "enormous freedom prison [. . .] where the most repugnant of all tyrants, the mob, exercises its crude sovereignty!": "Oh Freedom! you are a bad dream!"[39] In the wake of Hegel and Heine, Karl Marx will also unleash his fury on the mob. He will not refer to this mob as a *puer robustus* – like Tocqueville – but will instead reserve this title as an honorific for the historical figure who fights the mob: namely, the proletarian. I mention all of this to draw attention to the fact that the script for the *puer robustus* does not end with the arrival of the politically disenchanted, egocentric troublemaker. He still has a grand future ahead of him. In closing, I want to see whether Tocqueville – despite having only negative things to say about *puer robustus* so far – ultimately gives the troublemaker a chance.

4. Life as a revolution and experiment: Tocqueville, Mill, Nietzsche

Tocqueville knows of only one *puer robustus*: the evil one. This means that, unlike Rousseau, Diderot, Hugo, and others, he cannot directly reference this character to explore the potential of the good troublemaker. And yet he does recognize such potential, and he harbors sympathies for nonconformists and eccentrics. To finish this chapter, I want to look more closely at these sympathies and return to the question from the end of the chapter on Rousseau: namely, what role the troublemaker might play in a democracy.

Our search for the good troublemaker is relegated to the threshold where the interplay between adaptation and deviation takes place. As this threshold also represents the border between childhood and adulthood, it invites the deliberate perpetuation of childhood – in the spirit of Diderot and Baudelaire, or in the spirit of Nietzsche: "Once you were young – now be so fittingly!" (NCW 8, 200; cf. *Human* 81). Tocqueville balks at this. He bemoans the "excessive pride in [. . .] the passions of youth" in America and pits (good) adults against (bad) children. In his opinion, the "people as a child" of whom Victor Hugo spoke would do well to grow up fast. The ambition to achieve political liberty is associated with maturity, while the *puer robustus* acting on his own authority and the children lulled by the state are associated with immaturity. Consequently, the only decisive aspect of childhood and youth is that they eventually pass. (Tocqueville is sending his regards to Horace from afar, who contrasted manly virtue with the *puer robustus*. Around a hundred years after Tocqueville, Benedetto Croce would adopt this position as well.)

Tocqueville's cautionary attitude toward the troublemaker is in keeping with his reservations about historical upheaval. He hits a low point in his policy of stability when he declares the preservation of power to be an end in itself in the fight against historical unrest. He reaches this conclusion after the revolution of June 1848, the bloody suppression of which he vehemently defends: "This society, [. . .] in which everything is wavering and weak, needs not so much a well-organized and wise power as any power at all: without it, it is liable to dissolve."[40]

For all that Tocqueville loves order (just like Rousseau), he is repeatedly unfaithful to it (also like Rousseau). On these occasions, he climbs out of the "conservative"[41] drawer in which he has made himself at home. Ultimately, his relationship to historical change is divided, and thus so is his approach to those who usher in such change: troublemakers. As a counterfigure to the bad *puer robustus*, Tocqueville holds up not only the mature adult, but also another character, whose youthfulness is scandalizing:

> So, in the United States, do not look for uniformity and permanence of views [. . .]. What is found there is the image of strength, a little wild, it is true, but full of power; of life, accompanied by accidents, but also by activities and efforts. (DIA 1, 155f.; O 2, 102f.)

This person that Tocqueville admires – "wild" and "full of power" as he is – recalls the *puer robustus* but also rises above him in a positive way. The effusive, ebullient individual is set against the swaggering, short-sighted one. Tocqueville not only assigns Hobbes's evil *puer robustus* to a new position, he gives him competition – or *gives him grief* – with a different kind of youthful individual. Tocqueville does not provide us with a complete model of the good troublemaker, but he acknowledges and needs both types: an egocentric troublemaker whom he criticizes, and an eccentric troublemaker with whom he sympathizes. In the second volume of *Democracy in America* from 1840, we find an impassioned argument for "innovation" as a form of "trouble":

> Will I dare to say it amid the ruins that surround me? What I dread most for the generations to come is not revolutions. [. . .] When I see [. . .] the love of property [become] so anxious and so ardent, I cannot prevent myself from fearing that men will reach the point of regarding every new theory as a danger, every innovation as an unfortunate trouble, [. . .] and that they will refuse entirely to move for fear that they would be carried away. [. . .] You believe that the new societies are going to change face every day, and as for me, I fear that they will end by being too invariably fixed in the same institutions, the same prejudices, the same mores; so that humanity comes to a stop and becomes limited; that the mind eternally turns back on itself without producing new ideas; that man becomes exhausted in small solitary and sterile movements, and that, even while constantly moving, humanity no longer advances. (DIA 4, 1150f.; O 2, 781f.)

In this remarkable passage, Tocqueville describes the dark sides of saturation, which to him appear even more threatening than the revolution he so distrusts. He distances himself from a self-contained world that would be dominated by the *espèce* that is the scourge of Diderot and Hegel, and he opposes the hatred of innovation that Hans Kelsen will later brand as "misoneism." Leaving the safe confines of theory, we discover the innovation-happy American so prized by Tocqueville in a TV spot that is far more than just an advertisement – namely, in Apple's *Think Different* campaign of 1997:

184

Here's to the crazy ones. The misfits. The rebels. The troublemakers. The round pegs in the square holes. The ones who see things differently. They're not fond of rules. And they have no respect for the status quo. You can quote them, disagree with them, glorify or vilify them. About the only thing you can't do is ignore them. Because they change things. They push the human race forward. While some may see them as the crazy ones, we see genius. Because the people who are crazy enough to think they can change the world, are the ones who do.

Should we really go so far as to embrace every demented, disrespectful rule-breaker? Or can we clearly separate the good disrupters from the bad? Tocqueville's answer to these questions remains guarded. He calls the American troublemaker "enterprising, adventurous, above all an innovator [*novateur*]" whose entire life "happens like a game of chance, a time of revolution" (DIA 2, 643f.; O 2, 471). Tocqueville talks about revolution, but he robs it of its horrors by relating and restricting it to the life of an individual. This mitigates the disturbance, which affects not a collective but only a single person.

This individual disturbs himself. He is *at odds* with himself, annoyed with himself and is even prepared to secretly *hate* himself.[42] He becomes an alien in his society, either because he is alienated from himself as a member of this society or, as Diderot and Hegel would say, he dares to engage in "mental alienation." Anyone at a remove from himself winds up in an internal outland of his own making, so to speak. This also means that his *elsewhere* arises from an act of repulsion and departure that is always a continuation. His innovation does not come out of nowhere. Tocqueville's self-revolutionary is not a cocky beginner, a savior from a strange land like Wagner's heroes, but he is also not a pure, angelic child like Gavroche, whom Victor Hugo elevates above the entangled, desperate, dirty people. Personal revolution is not an absolute beginning or triumphant zero hour for Tocqueville, it is a threshold situation. The self-revolutionary moves on the edges of a society that Tocqueville calls "stationary" (*stationnaire*) (DIA 4, 1142; O 2, 775).

Tocqueville rejects the notion that there could be a society in which rules and forms of life were completely congruous. But by individualizing revolution, he sets a limit on the potential disturbance it could cause. He would be content with a more colorful and lively society, and he dodges the question of whether or how the eccentric troublemaker could take political action. There is a serious weakness in his theory here.[43] Tocqueville celebrates individual flexibility, but his political ideal is an order in which true adults cooperate reliably, a "republic without struggle, [. . .] a sort of *consensus universalis*" (DIA 2, 634; O 2, 463). (In this respect, Jürgen Habermas is his disciple.)

185

On the political level, Tocqueville is rather more suspicious of disturbance – to the extent that, for the sake of protecting this consensus, he is vexed by the "continual changeability of legislation" that exists in a "republic." According to him, this "instability" makes the republic "an inconvenient way to live in society" (ibid.). Although Tocqueville is an admirer of Jefferson, he falls short of Jefferson's model of a democracy characterized by internal strife. Jefferson is a friend of "rebellion"; he considers "constitutions and ordinances" that are unalterable to be undemocratic and says: "The Creator has made the earth for the living, not the dead."[44] Tocqueville's tranquilized republic also differs dramatically from the model of democracy proposed by his famous American contemporaries, the triumvirate of Henry David Thoreau, Ralph Waldo Emerson and Walt Whitman. To illustrate this, allow me to quote just a few lines from Whitman's *Leaves of Grass*:

> What do you think endures?
> Do you think a great city endures?
> Or a teeming manufacturing state? or a prepared constitution? [. . .]
> Away! these are not to be cherish'd for themselves,
> They fill their hour, the dancers dance, the musicians play for them,
>   [. . .]
> All does very well till one flash of defiance.
> A great city is that [. . .]
> Where the men and women think lightly of the laws,
> Where the slave ceases, and the master of slaves ceases,
> Where the populace rise at once against the never-ending audacity of
>   elected persons,
> Where fierce men and women pour forth as the sea to the whistle of
>   death pours its sweeping and unript waves, [. . .]
> Where children are taught to be laws to themselves [. . .][45]

Make what you will of Whitman's ebullient democracy (I will return to it later with the help of Thomas Mann). Whitman himself somewhat put the brakes on his ebullience in his work *Democratic Vistas*. But this comparison with Whitman clearly reveals the weakness of Tocqueville's political theory. His "republic without struggle" seems oddly static, and it comes uncomfortably close to the conformist society in which the tamed *puer robustus* has made himself at home. Tocqueville's description of the troublemaker is *productive* in that it is geared not toward heroic intervention against the status quo, but toward the act of working on oneself, toward self-disruption and self-transformation. But it is also *problematic* because it grinds down the troublemaker's sharp political edges.

I now want to go beyond Tocqueville's description of the eccentric troublemaker in order to thoroughly explore this troublemaker's political potential. To this end, I will bring in two other thinkers who are also shaken by the frightening vision of conformity, but who grant the troublemaker a more proactive role: John Stuart Mill and Friedrich Nietzsche. To be precise, they are spooked by the warning against *Chinese conditions* – a warning that comes from Tocqueville himself. China appeared to Tocqueville to be a static countermodel to the dynamic West – a comparison that is odd today, but one that seemed obvious at the time. Tocqueville said that China was dominated by "a singular type of immobility" (DIA 3, 786; O 2, 558) that could be traced back to the waning of its historical, generational change, its loss of critical potential and a blind adherence to the established order:

> The Chinese, while following the path of their fathers, had forgotten the reasons that had guided the latter. They still used the formula without looking for the meaning; they kept the instrument and no longer possessed the art of modifying and of reproducing it. So the Chinese could not change anything. They had to give up improvement. They were forced to imitate their fathers always and in all things [. . .] (DIA 3, 786; O 2, 558)

According to Tocqueville, even "the men of democracies" were becoming "Chinese": "Their youth is lost and their imagination grows dim [. . .]; and when they are finally able to do extraordinary things, they have lost the taste for them" (DIA 4, 1122f.; O 2, 762). This leads him to make a comparison between "faint-hearted and soft citizens" on one side and "an energetic people" (*peuple énergique*) on the other (DIA 4, 1276; O 2, 848). Tocqueville was probably not thinking of Plato when he made this comparison, but it could almost be a quote from *Phaedrus* (239c), in which the delicate, mild boy (*malthakos*) is compared to the tough, strong one (*stereos*).[46] (Even in Plato we find a forerunner to the *puer robustus*!)

Mill and Nietzsche appropriated this warning against Chinese conditions. While Mill openly admits to taking this argument from Tocqueville, Nietzsche keeps quiet about it. (In his posthumously published writings, there is only a brief comment in which he counts Tocqueville among the "finest minds"; KSA 11, 442.) In this sorely neglected triple constellation of thinkers, I am interested in the types of eccentric troublemakers that Mill and Nietzsche employ to combat torpor.

Mill discusses Tocqueville's *Democracy in America* in a long, two-part review, the second part of which was published in 1840. Nietzsche read this second part in the German edition of Mill's *Collected Works*, and he heavily annotated his own copy of it. Nietzsche also read Mill's *Civilisation* essay from 1836 and *On Liberty* from 1859 in just as much depth.[47] To remain true to my three-point constellation, in the following

I will refer exclusively to quotes from Mill that were highlighted by Nietzsche.

In his review of Tocqueville's work, Mill insists that "servility" and "Chinese stationariness" were rampant in Western societies, too.[48] In his essay *On Liberty*, he bemoans the disappearance of those "men of strong bodies or minds" who could barely be kept under control in "some early states of society," and whose "rebellion" had to be vanquished in a "hard struggle" through the "power" of the "social principle" by means of "law and discipline."[49] Mill endows these "men" not just with "strong bodies" but also – unlike Hobbes's *puer robustus* – with "strong minds." (Incidentally, Mill mentions the *puer robustus* – though only in passing – in the French summary of a lecture he attended at the age of 14 in Montpellier.[50])

That old-time rebellion was, according to Mill, brought to a halt by the "relaxation of individual energy: or rather, the concentration of it within the narrow sphere of the individual's money-getting pursuits."[51] It is capitalist society, therefore, that has tamed and civilized the troublemaker – and Mill protests against this. The people have grown inert, he says, and they do all that they do "because it is the custom," meaning that they are not truly acting but merely functioning as "automatons in human form." They cultivate "conformity," as Mill sees it, and shun "eccentricity" as much as they shun "crimes":[52] "That so few now dare to be eccentric, marks the chief danger of the time." – "But these few are the salt of the earth; without them, human life would become a stagnant pool. [...] If they are of a strong character, and break their fetters," society might warn against them because they are "'wild,' 'erratic,' and the like," but it would do so "much as if one should complain of the Niagara river for not flowing smoothly between its banks like a Dutch canal." Mill has no time for "social reformers" who view eccentrics only as a "rebellious obstruction."[53]

Following his Tocqueville-inspired criticism of conformity, Mill turns his attention to the phenomenon dodged by his French predecessor: namely, disturbance as a political act. He allows the eccentric troublemaker to leave the individualistic playing field to which he was relegated by Tocqueville. Mill's deliberations are impressive, but they also reach a limit that Nietzsche moves beyond.

The political troublemaker pits himself against the state. As an eccentric, he grapples not only with himself or his contemporaries, but with the *center* of the political order. (To clarify Mill's position here, I will draw on his *Utilitarianism* essay from 1861 and make an exception by using quotes not highlighted by Nietzsche.) Mill notes that "the law [...] may be a bad law" – and not only does he justify opposition to such laws, he actively opposed them himself. Together with his friend and future wife, Harriet Taylor, he fought against women's discrimination, and he also took a stand against capitalist property rights, which he said led to "social inequalities" and were actually an "injustice" that he branded "tyrannical." The "history of social improvement" is characterized by "transitions" which, according to Mill, include the "breach of law." Although he was anything but a revolutionary, he believed that breaches of law are often the "only weapons" that have "any chance of succeeding" against "pernicious institutions"; even the "most illustrious benefactors of mankind" had employed such weapons.[54] Disturbances such as this can take place even in a political order that calls itself democratic, according to Mill, because they are directed against despotism in all of its forms, including the "despotism of custom," the "tyranny of the majority," and the "*régime* of public opinion."[55] (These last quotes and all following ones are from passages highlighted by Nietzsche.)

Unlike Tocqueville, Mill does not want to tranquilize the political sphere and turn it into a "republic without struggle"; instead, he returns to the threshold where rules are called into question. This threshold is not only the entry point to an ordered society, it is the site of a recurrent loop of critique and confrontation. If "nothing was ever yet done which some one was not the first to do,"[56] then every breach of rule or law is a step taken without the security of a rope team. It is in the nature of the eccentric troublemaker to break out and not immediately build up. This makes him fallible and vulnerable, but it also protects him from presuming himself to be a ventriloquist for a better world that does not yet exist and of which he has no concrete image.

While Tocqueville keeps the political troublemaker at arm's length, Mill approaches him with a combination of open arms and minor reservations. First, he wants to give the troublemaker the benefit of the doubt, without any schoolmasterly judgment: "In this age, the mere example of nonconformity, the mere refusal to bend the knee to custom, is itself a service."[57] Instead of appointing conformist "automatons" who have abdicated their moral responsibility to serve as judges over the troublemaker, Mill generously wants to stamp the troublemaker with a seal of approval. Conformists are expected not just to put up with the troublemaker, but to welcome him as an eccentric.

This sweeping escape clause actually makes Mill somewhat uncomfortable, because it cancels out the distinction between destructive and constructive "refusal." Furthermore, Mill believes "there are but few persons [. . .] whose experiments, if adopted by others, would be likely to be any improvement on established practice."[58] He therefore rushes to add a caveat to his welcoming embrace. The criterion for a good troublemaker is that he must ultimately be acknowledged by others – however hesitantly or belatedly.[59] This means the nonconformist must somehow prove to be of use to society. Mill is concerned with rehabilitating him while simultaneously relaxing his relationship with the social order.

This is where we encounter a degree of inconclusiveness in Mill's thinking. The simple question is: who is taking advantage of whom? If the conformist is incited to change by "assuming" or adopting eccentric impulses, does he thus prove his willingness to disturb himself? Or are eccentrics subject to a schoolmasterly review, in which some of their experiments will be praised or tolerated while others are hushed up or prohibited? Mill leaves these alternatives hanging.

There is one model of the eccentric troublemaker that moves past Mill's vacillation between inclusion and exclusion and breaks with the moral consensus that Mill wants to continually reestablish. This radical model is advocated by Friedrich Nietzsche. He has actually already been in play here since, as explained earlier, almost all of the above-mentioned quotes from Mill were highlighted by Nietzsche in his copy of Mill's works. But the time has now come to let Nietzsche speak in his own words.

The differences between the two philosophers are vast;[60] Nietzsche famously referred to Mill as a "*typical blockhead*" (KSA 12, 362). But Nietzsche does not keep Mill at arm's length. In fact, counterparts to many of the Mill quotes mentioned above can be found in Nietzsche's works. Tocqueville's grand alternative between Chinese conditions and energetic life was passed on from Mill to Nietzsche.

Among the Chinese, Nietzsche remarks in *The Gay Science*, the "capacity for *change*" had "become extinct centuries ago" (GS 99). But now this "Chineseness" could be found worldwide: "A small, weak, dawning sense of well-being" that "spreads over everyone equally" might be "the last image that humanity has to offer" (KSA 9, 73; cf. KSA 9, 452f., 458, 547, 626; NCW 8, 128f., 303). To counter the "weak characters without power over themselves," Nietzsche presents the "full human beings overloaded with power and consequently active of necessity," those "magically incomprehensible and unthinkable" individuals (GS 233f.; NCW 8, 230, 94): "Man is still changing – he is in progress" (KSA 9, 458). This life in progress is laid out and lived out by Nietzsche – as it is by Mill and certainly by Ralph Waldo Emerson – as an "experiment" (NCW 5, 249; cf. KSA 13, 492). This life experiment takes a jab at the status quo. "The dangerous and uncanny moment" – but also the most enticing moment, for Nietzsche – "has been reached when the greater, more diverse, more comprehensive life *lives over and beyond* the old morality" (NCW 8, 176). The troublemaker proceeds to scatter the herd of last men.

It is clear how this troublemaker should be morally assessed from the viewpoint of the status quo. Anyone who dares "chart a new course" must reckon with "the severest disapproval from all representatives of the morality of mores," who will consider him "evil" (NCW 5, 12; cf.

NCW 8, 232). The following two sentences from Mill and Nietzsche are almost identical:

> If [. . .] life is reduced *nearly* to one uniform type, all deviations from that type will come to be considered impious, immoral, even monstrous and contrary to nature.[61]
> The more a feeling of unity with one's fellow humans gains the upper hand, the more people will become uniform, and the more strictly they will consider any difference to be immoral (KSA 9, 73).

Anyone who takes the troublemaker's side is tempted to simply turn the spear of judgment around and – together with Mill – welcome him as a benefactor. The following passage from Nietzsche's work *Dawn* appears (only!) at first glance to be another variation on Mill:

> One has to retract a great deal of the abuse that people are wont to heap upon all those figures who broke the spell of a custom with a *deed* – in general, they are branded criminals. Anyone who has ever overturned an existing moral law has always, heretofore, passed initially for a *bad person*: but afterward when, as it happened, the law could no longer be propped up and people acquiesced to the fact, the evaluation began a gradual transformation – history concerns itself almost exclusively with these *bad people* who have later been *pronounced good*! (NCW 5, 20; cf. *Human* 232; GS 234f.; NCW 8, 231f.)

But this passage actually reveals the decisive difference between the two authors. Nietzsche is not happy about this retrospective endorsement; instead, he wants to provoke an overall mistrust in these fluctuating judgments. Neither the established order nor the outsider gets the moral seal of approval from him. He is interested not in reinterpreting evil as good, but rather in fundamentally questioning all moral labels. In *The Genealogy of Morals* he writes: "We need a *critique* of moral values, *the value of these values must itself first be questioned*" (NCW 8, 212).

This "critique" revolves around the relationship between morality and power. Nietzsche believes that morality, as the totality of commandants and laws, is not a stronghold of good that stands alongside the apparatus of power; it actually shares in this power. There is power in the universality of laws and of "concepts" themselves that result in a leveling out or "baseness" (NCW 8, 181). A "machinery" of "generalization" kicks in, producing "a great and thorough corruption, falsification, reduction to superficialities" (NCW 8, 274; GS 300).

This moral power has a paradoxical effect. If it turns individuals into people who simply take orders, then they become passive entities or victims. This ultimately means they can no longer be considered moral actors. Therefore, regardless of the substance of any given law, the form of the law itself harbors a moral problem: a "hatred of the human," a "counterwill against life" (NCW 8, 349). "The lack of personality always takes its revenge: A weakened, thin, extinguished personality that denies itself is no longer fit for anything good" (GS 283). In the end, this lack of personality causes morality to be "eliminated [. . .] as well" (NCW 8, 96). Society then becomes a "state" that is "the coldest of all cold monsters," "where the slow suicide of all is called 'life'" (PN 160, 162). Helvétius, whom Nietzsche accuses of taming the "dangerous man" (i.e., the *puer robustus*; NCW 8, 131), tried to make society into just such a smoothly functioning apparatus, and the later Schelsky will develop a very similar program.

According to Nietzsche's argument, there is no weight to the accusation that the outsider is immoral. Those who follow the rules are not moral in and of themselves; they simply drift through life as well-functioning automata. But this is certainly no reason to cackle gleefully at the dismantling of morality. For all of his martial posturing, Nietzsche assures us in *Ecce homo* that he is "no moral monster" (*Ecce Homo* 3). Nietzsche's critique of morality is important to the theory of the troublemaker not because it *does away with* morality but because it *puts pressure on it*. I interpret – and defend – his position as immanent critique, a demand for a different kind of morality. For instance, he refers to "*herd-animal morality*" as "only one kind of human morality, beside which, before which, after which many other, above all *higher* moralities are possible or should be" (NCW 8, 97). "Morality acts to prevent the rise of new and better mores: it stupefies" (NCW 5, 20).

These other mores, the "virtue that is moraline-free" (PN 570) for which the troublemaker stands, are an alternative to the "morality of unselfing oneself" which clings to "the law and the general delight in lawfulness and obedience" (*Ecce Homo* 63; GS 234). But what is Nietzsche's countermodel to the unselfing of oneself? It seems logical simply to counter it with "self-glorification." Unfortunately, this is precisely the conclusion drawn by Nietzsche: "The noble kind of human being feels *itself* to be value-determining, does not need approval [. . .]: such a morality is self-glorification" (NCW 8, 171). But such glory does not get us very far. Just as individuals must not "become hung up on a person" or "a fatherland," according to Nietzsche's prudent council in *Beyond Good and Evil*, they must not become "hung up on [their] own detachment" (NCW 8, 42f.). In other words, embracing the cult of your own exceptional position ultimately makes you dependent on everyone you consider to be beneath you and to whom you harbor an aversion in your "ressentiment" (NCW 8, 262). Nietzsche's "Übermensch" does not believe it is his job to celebrate small victories and get the better of others. Incidentally, this is why Georges Sorel's idea[62] that Nietzsche's "*master*" can be found in America's self-made man – i.e., the American *puer robustus* à la Tocqueville – is misleading.

This ambiguous "self-glorification" should really be replaced by the "self-overcoming" that Nietzsche insists is his "strongest characteristic" (KSA 10, 112). Only then is it possible to take up a plausible counter-position to the morality of the law. Nietzsche's eccentric troublemaker refrains from acting as the legislator of himself; he stands alongside the "Columbus Novus" of Nietzsche's poem of the same name, the "homeless" representative of a "spiritual nomadism" (KSA 10, 34; GS 338; *Human* 263). His life is one of external insecurity and internal uncertainty. He thus occupies a space delineated by Diderot's *Rameau's Nephew* and Foucault's *History of Madness*:

> Every individual action, every individual way of thinking provokes horror; it is quite impossible to fathom all the many things that, through the whole course of history, precisely those more unusual, select, and original intellects have had to suffer because they were always perceived as evil and dangerous, because, in fact, *they perceived themselves as such*. (NCW 5, 12)

> *Provided they weren't actually mad*, all those superior people who were irresistibly compelled to cast off the yoke of any sort of morality and to devise new laws had no choice other than to drive themselves, or to pretend, to madness – and indeed this applies to innovators in all spheres and not merely those of priestly and political caste [. . .]. (NCW 5, 15)

If we take the outsider's uncertainty seriously, then this state of being "beyond-the-law" is not just a "prerogative of the most powerful" (NCW 8, 261), as Nietzsche suggests; instead, it describes the position of the person on the margins who risks self-abandonment on account of his marginality. He can *crack up*. As long as he does not destroy himself in the process, Nietzsche's outsider will turn his spear on the status quo – and this spear is sharper than either Tocqueville or Mill expected. It is not limited to private life (as it is for Tocqueville), nor is it a positive factor in humanity's advancement (as it is for Mill). According to this interpretation, the outsider is morally and politically valuable not because he provides materially valuable impetus, but because he fulfills a critical function.[63] His message to the political order is this: You have only earned the right to be considered moral *if you have subjected yourself to me*. Otherwise you are nothing more than a well-oiled machine.

The political order is thus called upon to question itself and set itself in motion. To put it another way, power is only moral when it becomes historical. This is the conclusion reached by Nietzsche's most important twentieth-century disciple, Michel Foucault. Foucault uses the term "normalizing society" to describe the conformism opposed by Nietzsche; to counter it, he suggests the innocuous but productive concept of "political historicism." This concept takes a swipe at Hobbes's, Hegel's, and Marx's strategy of tranquilizing or ending history, and it refers to a dynamic constellation of "power relations" or "infinitely dense and multiple [...] political struggles" that continue in an open-ended way.[64]

Nietzsche's (and Foucault's) contribution to the theory of the troublemaker is productive but also disappointing. Nietzsche does not resign himself to the inconclusiveness that brings Mill to a halt: namely, whether an established political order should pass judgment on welcome innovations and harmful invectives, or whether it should generously put up with disturbances. Only the latter approach comes into consideration for Nietzsche. But he lets down everyone tormented by the burning question of how, specifically, disputes are to be decided in this interplay between order and disturbance. This question relates to both the type of disturbance (to what extent can the law be broken?) and the outcome of the conflict (where does this self-overcoming lead?).

According to Nietzsche, the crucial factor in each case is that there should be an "enhancement of the feeling of power" and "yes-saying [...] to life" (*Will to Power* 290; *Ecce Homo* 46). Foucault supplements this with the vague, pluralistic comment that the "multiplicity of force relations" should not only be analyzed but also strengthened.[65] If we do not want to leave it at that, the only thing to do – and at least it's doing something! – is take a pragmatic view of political change and look to the negotiation processes that take place in such conflicts. They are not a necessary evil but rather the shining hour of politics.

In connection with this, we should recall Diderot's contribution to the theory of order and disturbance, according to which the dispute does not take place discursively or dialectically within the tidy confines of conversation, but instead spills over its borders or thresholds. People are involved in this dispute with their minds and their bodies, as speaking, acting, feeling, suffering human beings. Nietzsche invites people to engage in this dispute, but he does not really participate in it himself. This may have something to do with his outsize reservations toward potential opponents, but also toward potential allies. As he sees it, the representatives of the order with whom he would have to duel are incapable of giving satisfaction, and it is pointless for a free spirit to seek allies because "community of any kind somehow, somewhere, some way makes us – 'base'" (NCW 8, 190). However radical Nietzsche's troublemaker is, he can be dealt with calmly by the defenders of the established order. They will hardly ever be bothered by him. His "sublime malice" (NCW 8, 284) remains oddly abstract.

Many of Nietzsche's countless early readers threw themselves into the struggles of the age all the same, taking up a variety of different positions when they did so. Even the great socialist Jean Jaurès could not reconcile himself to Nietzsche's reticence. In a lecture in 1902, he told his dumbfounded audience that Nietzsche's hero, the "Übermensch," was none other than the "proletariat."[66] For all that this leap in logic is wrong, it is true that a different troublemaker has stormed onto the stage – not an obstructionist, not a great loner, but a collective. It is time to introduce the *puer robustus* of Marx and Engels.

— VIII. —

THE *PUER ROBUSTUS* AS A REVOLUTIONARY

Karl Marx and Friedrich Engels

1. The people is by far the most dangerous

The *puer robustus* makes three appearances in the works of Karl Marx and Friedrich Engels.

First: On September 12, 1847, the *Deutsche-Brüsseler-Zeitung* published an article entitled "The Communism of the *Rheinischer Beobachter*." In this essay, Marx polemicizes against the curious suggestion of the *Rheinischer Beobachter* newspaper that a grand reconciliation between the people and the king could soothe the rampant unrest of the time:

> We merely wish to make some well-intentioned comments to those gen-
> tlemen who would like to rescue the apprehensive Prussian monarchy
> by means of a somersault into the people. Of all political elements the
> people is by far the most dangerous for a king. [. . .] The real people, the
> proletarians, the small peasants and the plebs – this is, as Hobbes says,
> *puer robustus, sed malitiosus*, a robust, but ill-natured youth, which
> permits no kings, be they lean or fat, to get the better of him. (MECW
> 6, 233)

Second: In a series of articles on "The Bourgeoisie and the Counter-Revolution" that appeared in the *Neue Rheinische Zeitung* in December 1848, Marx addresses the arrangements made between the bourgeoisie and the monarchy, and he knows who can thwart them:

> The Crown is ready to sacrifice the aristocracy to the bourgeoisie, the
> bourgeoisie is ready to sacrifice the people to the Crown. Under these
> circumstances the monarchy becomes bourgeois and the bourgeoisie
> monarchical. [. . .] The *bourgeoisie was convinced* that evidently only
> one obstacle stood in the way of its *agreement* with the Crown, [. . .]
> and that obstacle was the people – *puer robustus sed malitiosus*, as
> Hobbes says. The *people* and the *revolution*! (MECW 8, 163, 165)

196

Third: In 1892, many years after Marx's death, Engels wrote a long preface to the English edition of his book *Socialism: Utopian and Scientific*. In this preface, he discusses the power struggles between the aristocracy and bourgeoisie in seventeenth-century England and describes the strategies used by the different parties to "[keep] down the 'lower orders', the great producing mass of the nation." He says the aristocracy relied on blatant power interests and adopted a "new [irreligious] doctrine": "With Hobbes it stepped on the stage as a defender of royal prerogative and omnipotence; it called upon absolute monarchy to keep down that *puer robustus sed malitiosus*, to wit, the people" (MECW 27, 293).

Franz Mehring seconded Marx and Engels, his role models, and lauded the "people" as the "*puer robustus sed malitiosus*, the robust and malicious boy who, on March 18, 1848, kneaded the 'original dough' of the legitimate monarchy with rough fists and broke the sword of the prince of Prussia."[1] The cat is out of the bag: the *puer robustus* is the revolutionary subject. The worker was commonly referred to as an "enfant robuste" at the time, and Marx and Engels turned this into a positive attribute.

Marx and Engels do not mention the *puer robustus* in their main works, but they use him as a byname for their main protagonist: the people or the proletariat. The *puer robustus* can therefore help us get to the heart of their theory – and to discover the heart defect to be found there. Two decisive and seemingly unrelated innovations bring Marx and Engels into the history and theory of the troublemaker: they transform the *puer robustus* into a collective, and they make him the protagonist of a philosophy of history in which evil changes to good.

Their *first* innovation is that the *puer robustus* appears in their works not as an individual rogue, reject, or rebel, but rather as a class of people that wants to topple the political order. We have not encountered this before in the meandering history of this character. Granted, even the predecessors of Marx and Engels found troublemakers in the coarse masses; the "masterless men" of Hobbes's age were followed by the "valiant beggars," "strong beggars," "sturdy beggars," "strong and mighty vagabonds," "rufflers," and "chamberdekens" of eighteenth- and nineteenth-century England. They were joined by lawless drifters in France ("dealers and *chambrelans*") and by the revenants of the *puer robustus* in the USA who were castigated by Tocqueville.[2] But a mass phenomenon is not the same as a collective subject. From Hobbes to Tocqueville, the mass appears not as a unified entity capable of joint action, but as an incohesive "heap" in which everyone seeks their own fortune. Egocentric troublemakers break the rules, but they do so for themselves alone. Even those who break away from Hobbes to explore the eccentric or nomocentric potential of the *puer robustus* continue to focus on the individual.

This applies to Rousseau, whose (good!) *puer robustus* starts out alone and abdicates just as the transformation into a *moi commun* is about to take place. The same applies to Diderot, who elevates the outsider to an artist. And the situation is no different with Schiller, Hugo, and Wagner, who present the outsider as a broken hero (Karl Moor, Quasimodo) or a fantastic luminous being (Tell, Gavroche, Siegfried).

Marx and Engels set themselves against this powerful backstory by bringing the *puer robustus* onto the stage of world history as a revolutionary collective subject. They present neither a strong nor slight individual, but rather an entire class. Their casting of the *puer robustus* sends a new signal – but there was, of course, a prelude to this signal. For example, if they had wanted to, Marx and Engels could have invoked the Abbé Raynal as their predecessor. A close companion of Diderot, Raynal said as early as 1770 that it was only a matter of time before the "mine" that had been placed "under the foundations of our tottering realms" was detonated. The fuse would be lit by the "hatred between the craven men who possess all riches and the strong, even virtuous men [*hommes robustes, vertueux même*] who have nothing to lose but their life."[3] The collective *puer robustus* of Marx and Engels therefore stands on the shoulders of the collective *hommes robustes* of Raynal – and his *hommes vertueux* are, in turn, the children of Rousseau's good *puer robustus*. Raynal goes so far as to describe the music of the struggle of the "rebels" for liberty as the "sound of breaking chains," thus anticipating the "chains" that Marx and Engels expect the proletariat to lose (MECW 6, 519).[4] Marx and Engels want to advance this struggle for liberty – in which the people will "slaughter its tyrants" and "change the form of government to which it was victim for centuries"[5] – by serving as the directors of the proletarian collective subject that is about to take the stage.

By referring to the *hommes robustes* as also being *vertueux*, Raynal paves the way for the moral revaluation of the revolutionary collective subject. This brings me to the *second* innovation that Marx and Engels contribute to the theory of the *puer robustus*. Until now, this theory has been dominated by the antithesis between evil (Hobbes) and good (Rousseau), or by an ambivalence between the two (Diderot). In Hegel's interpretation of *Rameau's Nephew*, this ambivalence was at least perceived as a development in which evil changes into good and the violation of the political order becomes a venture to establish a different order. The *puer robustus* himself has thus far been denied success, however, even when he manages to make the switch from evil to good (as he does in Hugo's work, for example). But Marx and Engels adopt Hegel's dialectic and bank on the victory of their *puer robustus*: the people. They pit the supposedly evil but ultimately good people against a state order which – unlike the one envisioned by Hobbes – can lay no claim to being good itself. The breach of order must be more than an act of individual caprice so it can be freed from the stigma of evil. It is the product of historical struggle for Marx and Engels, who do not hold with the "salvation from outside" with which Wagner hopes to delight an ailing humanity.

Honesty demands that we acknowledge the negativity – that is, the wickedness – of the violence that accompanies revolutionary struggle. Revolution cannot be legitimized at the *drop of a hat*. The irony with which Marx and Engels speak of the *puer malitiosus* should not blind us to the fact that they are dancing over a chasm of justifications. You can't make an omelet without breaking eggs, and you can't rise up against an unjust regime and fight for a better world without spilling blood. Such an uprising has to be legitimized and – it is important to add – it can be legitimized, but the bar for legitimation is set high. And legitimacy certainly cannot be achieved by following Leo Trotsky and chalking up the "horrors" of revolution as "incidental expenses of [...] historical development" – as necessary transaction fees, in other (economic) words.[6]

Marx and Engels face two challenges. They have to find a collective that makes for a suitable subject of history and force for revolution, and they have to justify the historical-philosophical revaluation of this subject, meaning that they must also legitimize the upheaval caused by this new *puer robustus*. The two problems merge into one for Marx and Engels, so their proposed solution is already mapped out: they establish a collective subject that acts not only for itself but in the name of all humanity, and in doing so, they legitimize this subject at the same time. As they move toward their goal, Marx and Engels break with the individualistic self-image that has come to dominate bourgeois society (section 2). They must grapple with the lumpenproletariat that gets in their way as they attempt to mobilize their collective subject (section 3). But this does not stop them from trying to hoist the proletariat into the saddle as a legitimate force for revolutionary change, the vanguard of a better world (section 4).

2. The fight against dependence and separation

Marx's collective subject kicks against the individualism that has come to dominate bourgeois society. But before this individualism is *dismissed*, it is *welcomed*. Before we can sound the attack, we must listen to Marx's eulogy for the bourgeoisie. Marx lauds the bourgeoisie for dissolving "all fixed, fast-frozen relations" and causing "all that is solid" to "[melt] into air" (MECW 6, 487). It has succeeded in abolishing the "*previous ties*" to all that was "spontaneous" (MECW 35, 489; cf. MECW 5, 73; MECW

28, 206, 415, 530). In the *Grundrisse* (*Outlines*), Marx unmistakably depicts this "process of dissolution" as a liberation (MECW 28, 426). His talk of "free workers" obscures and ridicules their actual lack of freedom, but it encapsulates their disengagement from "all *conditions restricting production*" and thus anticipates the "total, universal development of the productive powers" that Marx desires (MECW 28, 427, 439; cf. MECW 35, 489f., 504f.). "Production on the basis of exchange value [. . .] along with the universality of the estrangement of individuals from themselves and from others," Marx says, "now also produces the universality and generality of all their relations and abilities" (MECW 28, 99). This also creates an opportunity to develop a free relationship with nature, according to Marx.[7] He thinks as little as Hobbes does of the kind of liberty that is far-removed from society, in which individuals fight for self-preservation and are at the mercy of natural compulsions.

This is the source of Marx's primary objection to Max Stirner, who depicts the individual as a lone warrior taking on society. As an advocate of "egoism," Stirner by definition falls back on Hobbes's state of nature: "Take hold, and take what you require! With this the war of all against all is declared. I alone decide what I will have."[8] Marx opposes this egocentric troublemaker, but it must be noted that his critique of individualism does not lead him to dismiss the individual as such. He does not want to *replace* the individual with the collective subject, he wants to lead the individual to the collective subject. The "kingdom of freedom" that represents the convergence of Marx's thought offers the individual an opportunity for self-realization in a community (MECW 24, 324; MECW 37, 807).

The bourgeois individual is the solution to one problem – liberation from natural compulsion – but he immediately becomes part of a new problem. Specifically, he remains stuck "at a definite historical stage of development" which "cripples" freedom and makes the communal enjoyment of life inaccessible (MECW 5, 439, 437; cf. MECW 5, 432f., MECW 35, 365). The most impressive critique of this bourgeois individual can be found in Marx's essay "On the Jewish Question" from 1843. In this work, Marx depicts a society that revolves around the "*egoistic, independent* individual" à la Hobbes, who is passed off as a "real" man "*in the proper sense*" (MECW 3, 167f.; cf. 162). These individuals are bound by certain rules. They must act as if they initially existed "independent" of society, only "entering" it in order to enjoy the "security" of the contractual framework that dominates it.[9]

Like many other critics of contract theory, Marx – and I am in agreement with him here – attacks the influential notion that people can get along losslessly with one another as individualistic parties to the social contract. We hear this kind of critique not only from Marx but from the conservative camp as well. For example, Thomas Carlyle complained in 1843 that each person was "girt in with a cold universal Laissez-faire: [...] imprisoned in a deaf, dead, Infinite Injustice": "We call it a Society; and go about professing openly the totalest separation, isolation. Our life is not a mutual helpfulness; but rather, cloaked under due laws-of-war, named 'fair competition' and so forth, it is a mutual hostility."[10]

In his critique of a world in which everyone flounders "in the icy water of egotistical calculation" (MECW 6, 487), Marx brings two key words into play: "separation" and "dependence" (MECW 3, 162, 104). They form a diabolic pair. Individuals are led to believe that, thanks to "separation," they could independently choose the kind of contractually regulated "dependence" to which they will submit. But they are actually weak, lost characters who abandon themselves to the world of contracts and competition and wind up in a state of "*all-round* dependence" (MECW 5, 51, 46; cf. MECW 28, 94).[11] The catchword that Marx summons up to counter both dependence and separation is "association" (MECW 3, 162). Association is expected to draw people out of their isolation and entanglement in contractual obligations and give them access to a society in which they can indulge freely in relations with others while fully coming into their own.

Just as the bourgeois individual marks a "definite historical stage of development" (see above), Marx says the rights granted to this individual are special as well. They serve solely to protect the individual from assault by others. The "liberty of man as an isolated monad, withdrawn into himself" entails a "right of man to liberty" that is understood to be only "the *right* of this separation, the right of the *restricted* individual" (MECW 3, 162f.). In his essay "On the Jewish Question," Marx thus launches a fundamental critique of human rights:

> None of the so-called rights of man [...] go beyond egoistic man, beyond man as a member of civil society, that is, an individual [...] separated from the community. In the rights of man, he is far from being conceived as a species-being; on the contrary, species-life itself, society, appears as a framework external to the individuals, as a restriction of their original independence. (MECW 3, 164)

These human rights, according to Marx, are tailored to an individual's economic activity in a capitalist system (cf. MECW 35, 186). They explicitly do *not* liberate people but instead keep them trapped in an attitude that leads them to believe they can only develop in opposition to others, not along with them.

Because the state believes it has a responsibility to guarantee human rights[12] that serve the purposes of contractual freedom in the classical liberal sense, it becomes an abettor of capitalism. The law underlying the contractual regulation of working conditions, for example, offers ample opportunity to deprive workers of their rights. It is as one-sided and unfair as a law that "forbids both rich and poor to sleep under bridges and to steal bread," as Anatole France noted with irony.[13] Marx – in contrast to the social democratic leader Ferdinand Lassalle – insists that workers should expect nothing from the state legal order.[14] This is because the state deals with workers not as humans, only as individuals. It protects human rights only insofar as they are contractual rights (MECW 24, 91–9).[15] As a countermove, Marx suggests that people should seek self-realization in a collective, and he flirts with the notion that the state could die out.

On a critical note, it should be said that Marx underestimates the contribution that civil society makes to positive socialization or "association." This is evident in Marx's sweeping claim that human rights cement the reduction of human beings to individuals. Much (or indeed all) of the evidence suggests that Marx is painting a distorted picture of the substance of these human rights. The most astute critique comes from Claude Lefort, who demonstrates that the right to freedom of opinion, for example, does not protect opinion solely as a form of property or as *my opining*. Instead, it encompasses and insists upon a public sphere in which people have "a right to public speech and thought" and are able "to step out of [themselves] and to make contact with others, through speech, writing and thought."[16] According to Lefort, this right is not characterized by "separation" but instead carries within it a positive definition of collective institutions. In keeping with this, even bourgeois society enables individual socialization and participation. At the same, the collective that Marx holds up in opposition to individualism must not be entirely at odds with the status quo. Marx's contrast between the bourgeois world and the "kingdom of freedom" is too simple. In the end, Marx has to be more bourgeois than he would like.

I have described how Marx *accepts* the individualization enforced by civil society as a starting point, then *criticizes* the diminished form of social life to which this individualization is tied. But how do people reach the point of saying enough is enough? When we look for the troublemaker who stirs up the status quo, we find the workers whose special role I have deliberately avoided discussing until now.

If truly everyone is entangled in the "bellum omnium contra omnes" described by Hobbes and cited by Marx (MECW 41, 381; MECW 28, 93; cf. MECW 4, 375), then this "war of all against all" must conceal a very different kind of warfare: "class warfare."[17] As is so often the case, Marx follows Hegel's thinking here. In the introduction to Hegel's essay on the German constitution (1800–2), Hegel describes a society divided between those who revel in their "bad conscience" and make "property

[. . .] into an absolute" and those who are left only with "suffering." In *Elements of the Philosophy of Right* from 1821, Hegel writes:

> On the one hand, as the association [*Zusammenhang*] of human beings through their needs is *universalized* [. . .] the *accumulation of wealth* increases [. . .]. But on the other hand, the *specialization* [*Vereinzelung*] and *limitation* of particular work also increase, as do likewise the *dependence* and *want* of the class which is tied to such work. (PR 266 [§243])

> In these opposites and their complexity, civil society affords a spectacle of extravagance and misery as well as of the physical and ethical corruption common to both. (PR 222 [§185])

Marx sharpens this theory of social "polarization,"[18] which reveals that Hobbes's talk of the "multitude" or amorphous mass of individuals is an ideology: "Society as a whole is more and more splitting up into two great hostile camps, into two great classes directly facing each other: Bourgeoisie and Proletariat" (MECW 6, 485). In this polarized society, those who savor their liberty when entering into the social contract come up against those to whom the conditions of the contract are dictated. Bourgeois "individuals who developed under the conditions of the ruling class" think they are free to decide on the dependencies they will accept as contractual partners; they believe separation creates a safe space in which they can insist upon their liberty (MECW 5, 78). The workers, on the other hand, are forced to participate in the world of contracts without the ability to make productive use of the interplay between alternately retreating from and participating in this world. Their attack on the capitalist order can therefore be interpreted as a dual struggle against both dependence *and* separation. Unfortunately, Marx does not clearly point out this dual agenda.

Against dependence. According to the bourgeois socialization model, dependence on natural compulsion is supposed to be replaced by people's dependence on one another. The latter is said to have the advantage of being negotiable; people should enter into dependencies, but they should also be able to free themselves from them. Among the workers, however, this transformation of dependency does not function. The workers wind up in new dependencies while remaining trapped in the old ones, and they have to grapple with natural compulsions at the same time. This naturally suits the bourgeoisie just fine. Workers who are denied liberation from natural life are a prime example of what Foucault refers to as "biopolitics."[19] They are "children of the earth [ripped] away from the breast on which they were raised," but they continue to fight for sheer survival. Because they have no access to nature as an "immediate source of subsistence" (MECW 28, 206), they must rely on socialization – in the form of selling their labor power – to satisfy their natural needs (MECW 35, 187).

The proletariat appears to be a hybrid, "at once purely social, purely historical" and yet somehow "outside society and history."[20] It is tossed back into the "*want*" that characterizes its "local being" – back into "all the old filthy business," as Marx dramatically puts it (MECW 5, 49). Strictly speaking, this "filthy business" is not old at all; it is new, because while the individual man of nature is expected to be capable of self-preservation – at least according to Rousseau – "the proletarian is helpless; left to himself, he cannot live a single day" (MECW 4, 376). In capitalist production, Marx says "labour is used to make a worker out of the human being still in the making, the completely immature human being, the *child*" – the outcome being that the worker is "a neglected child" (MECW 3, 308). Before standing on the stage of history as a valiant *puer robustus*, he must work up the courage to fight.

The worker's helplessness, according to Marx and Engels (and others as well[21]), harbors the impetus for revolutionary mobilization. The liberty that is codified in contract theory and – following Marx's narrow-minded interpretation – in the rights of man does not even touch the workers. They are denied the possibility – or spared the folly! – of gearing their lives toward bourgeois liberty, which seems to be nothing more than a taunting fiction. Social dependency thus loses the lure of free negotiability. Since the bourgeois-capitalist order does not keep its promise of liberty, its business model is untenable. The pressure to lead a contract-bound life is unbearable for the workers. This sets the stage for the troublemaker, who breaks with this life.

The fact that workers were reduced to a state of nature can explain why they were viewed in the nineteenth century as a source of threat emerging not from society at all but from nature itself. The workers appear on the threshold of society as enemies, as Others, not like human beings at all but like a "great animal."[22] Hegel is not alone in referring to the poor as a "raw mass," a "crude, blind animal."[23] Honoré de Balzac's warning against "wild animals" and Victor Hugo's encounter with the "savages of civilization" were mentioned earlier. And Thomas Carlyle came across "frightful men, or rather frightful wild animals [. . .]. Hunger they have for all sweet things; and the law of Hunger: but what other law? Within them, or over them, properly none!"[24] (This topos has recently appeared again: after the unrest in inner-city London in the summer of 2011, the *Daily Mail* referred to the rioters as "wild beasts."[25])

These apparently inhuman, pre-human poor are despised, feared or pitied depending on the writer's inclinations. But the marginal position occupied by these wild, brutal people can be interpreted positively as well. This reinterpretation starts by acknowledging their unbridled strength – a strength we have seen before in the *puer robustus*. In 1843, the early socialist Edgar Bauer wrote:

> The naked savages are among us [. . .]. Within the states, an abyss that has hitherto spewed disdained flames will open up, and with a shock that will cause our aristocratic edifices to tremble and collapse in on themselves, it will send forth the multitudes of oppressed against an egoism protected by rights and laws.[26]

Engels, too, stresses that the vitality of "barbarians" is needed to "rejuvenat[e] a world labouring in the throes of a dying civilisation" (MECW 26, 255f.). Once they have been spewed out by society, the workers are estranged from it, which is why they can turn around and confront it. I will critically analyze this confrontation in the last section of this chapter when I look at Marx's concept of the "species-being" (*Gattungswesen*).

Against separation. So far, I have traced how the idea of an individualistic self-image is spoiled for the workers because the dependency in which they have become entangled takes on intolerable dimensions. However, there is a flaw in the collective that they form. This collective is not defined in positive terms; instead, it is a natural, perhaps even lumpen mass driven by utter privation. For a revolutionary collective subject to get off the ground, the workers must not only overcome their dependence, they must be capable of joining together and rejecting their separation. This separation goes hand in hand with the promise that individuals will not be entirely at the mercy of political and economic liabilities, but can instead react to dependencies and enter into them as necessary from a position of their own. As long as people believe this promise, they will remain deaf to the call to join a collective – because "each," as Marx says in allusion to Bentham, "looks only to himself" (MECW 35, 186).

When workers sell their "own labour capacity," they are technically operating as separate individuals. But the liberty granted to them here is illusory. The worker is pulled into a process in which "he no longer belongs to himself but to capital" (MECW 30, 261). Because the workers must expend their "*life power as much as possible without interruption*" for capitalists, they essentially forfeit all of their individual autonomy. Any downtimes that might interrupt their work serve a single, predetermined purpose: the reproduction of their life or labor power (MECW 28, 220). The back room and elbow room created by separation, which is complementary to dependence, thus shrivels away to nothing.

One example of this is the disintegration of the private household. The "compulsory work for the capitalists" that "every member of the workman's family, without distinction of age or sex" must perform has caused the "home" to become an empty space (MECW 35, 398): "The husband works the whole day through, perhaps the wife also and the elder children, all in different places; they meet night and morning only, all under perpetual temptation to drink; what family life is possible under such conditions?" (MECW 4, 424). Among the workers, bourgeois separation deteriorates into desolate loneliness.

This does not rule out the possibility that workers will stubbornly insist on this separation in the belief that it gives them a purely individual space in which to improve their situation. Then they will cling to the autonomy they are actually forced to relinquish and try to gain some kind of advantage for themselves from their weakened position. This weakness leads them to take on weak opponents – not the capitalists, in other words, but the others who are just like them. Just such an about-turn can, in fact, be seen among the workers: "Each is in the way of the other, and each seeks to crowd out all who are in his way, and to put himself in their place. The workers are in constant competition among themselves" – and Engels believes "this competition [...] among themselves is the worst side of the present state of things (MECW 4, 375f.). Under such conditions, it is out of the question that the "mass" of workers would "unite" (MECW 6, 492).

On this side of the contract theory quarrels that arise in competitive situations, we can say that workers are pulled into the production process neck and crop. But their total absorption – like the radical experience of dependence – can actually generate the impetus for revolutionary mobilization. This starts when the workers realize they are living their lives in a state of "cooperation" or "*interconnection*" under the spell of "a power alien to them": "Once they enter into the labour process, they are already incorporated into capital, and their own cooperation is therefore not a relation into which they put themselves; it is the capitalist who puts them into it. Nor is it a relation which belongs to them; instead, they now belong to it" (MECW 30, 261). Because the workers are closed off from the experience of autonomy and separation, they can only view themselves as members of this cooperative. They *are* nothing else. It would seem as though they have become "one level mass of broken wretches past salvation" (MECW 20, 148). But even if Richard Wagner's "salvation from outside" fails to materialize, they are not pinned down in desperation.

What exactly does this "cooperation" represent? It follows the rules set by the despotic capitalist, which is why the workers view it "not as their deed"; it appears to be a "solidarity of defeat," not a "solidarity of action" (MECW 30, 312; MECW 30, 10). And yet, this is precisely what it is: solidarity. *Because the workers are barred from retreating into a state of separation*, because they are utterly at the mercy of the labor process, they identify with the only thing left to them: their cooperation. "When the labourer co-operates systematically with others, he strips off the fetters of his individuality, and develops the capabilities of his species" (MECW 35, 334). Marx takes account of this experience by speaking of the "twofold nature of the process of production." As he explains, this is "a social process" on the one hand and "a process for creating surplus value" on the other (MECW 35, 337). The "labour process" can therefore develop a dynamic that is uncoupled from exploitative capital, resulting in the "metamorphosis" of the workers (MECW 30, 261). In their *Manifesto of the Communist Party*, Marx and Engels take this argument across the finish line:

> But with the development of industry the proletariat not only increases in number; it becomes concentrated in greater masses, its strength grows, and it feels that strength more. (MECW 6, 492)

> The advance of industry, whose involuntary promoter is the bourgeoisie, replaces the isolation of the labourers, due to competition, by their revolutionary combination, due to association. The development of Modern Industry, therefore, cuts from under its feet the very foundation on which the bourgeoisie produces and appropriates products. What the bourgeoisie, therefore, produces, above all, is its own grave-diggers. (MECW 6, 496)

The revolutionary collective aims to improve upon a so-called liberty in which everyone is pitted against everyone else by offering true liberty under the banner of cooperation. In the final section of this chapter, I will return to Marx's theory of the self-organizing collective under the heading of the *Gemeinwesen* (community).

Marx's critique of dependence and separation allows him to pave the way for the appearance of the revolutionary collective. This critique sends mixed signals, however. In the struggle against *dependence*, the revolutionary collective goes on the offensive because it has – to put it bluntly – been ejected from society and degraded to the point that it is merely a creature of nature; it is an alien force that sets in motion the gears that should liberate the workers from their privation. The struggle against *separation*, on the other hand, aims to replace bourgeois socialization with a better kind under the banner of "association." The proletariat wrestles with its material living conditions – and with the social conditions to which it is subjected. As we will see at the end of this chapter, this dual agenda is the actual source of the difficulties Marx encounters in defining the revolutionary collective subject.

The question is not just whether Marx's concept is systematically convincing, however, but also whether it is historically effective. There is one obvious potential barricade to the revolutionary mobilization of the workers: if they succumb to the temptations of an individualistic model of life, they will think they have better things to do than revolt, and then they will fail to heighten their class consciousness and join together in a collective.

3. The lumpenproletariat as the spoilsport of the revolution

When it comes to the development of class consciousness among the proletariat – and among the bourgeoisie! – individualism remains a burden. Marx uses a special epithet to describe the workers who succumb to the temptation of individualism: they become members of the "lumpenproletariat." These people are not fit to create a state, and certainly not fit to start a revolution.

Interestingly, Marx applies this word not only to the lower but also to the upper classes. He takes this concept of the dual lumpenproletariat from Hegel, though he could have referred back to any number of other writers, including Victor Hugo.[27] Following Hegel's model, a "rabble" forms at both ends of the social spectrum, among rich and poor alike. The impoverished rabble is said to react to its "feeling of rightlessness" by making "itself rightless" and considering itself "exempt from the obligations" imposed upon it by the state. The lack of rights from which it suffers turns into a freedom from rights that it exercises ruthlessly.[28] Hegel's favorite example of this – one which was mentioned by Kant and Goethe before him and Marx after – are the "*lazzaroni* of Naples" (PR 266).[29] But this is not the full, terrifying picture, because Hegel laconically adds: "There is also a rich rabble."[30] Like its poor cousin, this rabble is an "aggregate of private persons"[31] who are indifferent to the political order: "Wealth is a power, and this power of wealth can easily become a power over the law. [...] One can say it is depraved that the rich man considers everything to be permissible."[32] The rich and poor rabble alike revel in rejecting the "public order" and "laws of the state" and allowing themselves to be guided solely by their "*subjective ends and opinions*" (PR 18). If everyone has the option of doing this, it means everyone is "*latently rabble*."[33]

As with Hegel's rabble, we find Marx's "lumpenproletariat" in both the upper and lower strata of society. As I intend to spend more time looking at the poor lumpenproletariat, which is the real spoilsport of the revolution, I – unlike Hegel – will start by looking at its rich counterpart.

Marx first notes that capitalists avail themselves of the political order by enforcing measures and rules that benefit themselves. This includes the destruction of corporative institutions and the previously mentioned enforcement of contractual freedom. "The executive of the modern State is but a committee for managing the common affairs of the whole bourgeoisie" (MECW 6, 486). But it is not just that the "political power" of the state is used by one class for "oppressing" another (MECW 6, 505). Because capitalists abide by the law solely for tactical reasons, they are themselves tempted to undermine the political order they dominate if it would be to their advantage. Marx observes the *"disintegration"* of "a [...] bourgeoisie held together by great common interests" (MECW 11, 112) and finds wonderfully dramatic words[34] to describe this tendency:

> Clashing every moment with the bourgeois laws themselves, an unbridled assertion of unhealthy and dissolute appetites manifested itself, particularly at the top of bourgeois society [...]. The finance aristocracy, in its mode of acquisition as well as in its pleasures, is nothing but the *rebirth of the lumpenproletariat on the heights of bourgeois society.* (MECW 10, 51)

> The whole turpitude of the capitalist regime [...] broke loose unfettered. At the same time an orgy of luxurious debauch, meretricious splendour, a pandemonium of all the low passions of the higher classes. This ultimate form of the governmental power was at the same time its most prostitute, shameless plunder of the state resources by a band of adventurers, hotbed of huge state debts, the glory of prostitution, a factitious life of false pretences. The governmental power with all its tinsel covering from top to bottom immerged in mud. [...] This was the state power [...] in its supreme and basest reality, which the Paris working class had to overcome, and of which this class alone could rid society. (MECW 22, 536)

Marx is repulsed by this "gang of shady characters," the "rapacious" rich rabble that pushes itself all the way "to the head of the administration" (MECW 11, 196). But his disgust is mixed with joy at the idea that capitalists themselves are eroding the system from which they profit. In doing so, they make it easier for the working class to bring the system down. As we have just heard, Marx sounds confident about the success of this undertaking. But the working class that he wants to mobilize against the "finance aristocracy" and prostituted "state power" continually disappoints him. This is apparent in the historical events that Marx wrestles with: the failure of the June Days uprising in Paris in 1848, Louis-Napoléon's coup of 1851, and the suppression of the Paris Commune of 1871. The search for the revolutionary subject, the collective *puer robustus*, is arduous not only because of the supremacy of capital but because the proletariat does not act the way Marx imagines it will.

This brings us to the counterpart to the "finance aristocracy": the poor version of the lumpenproletariat. It takes the blame for weakening the workers' movement, and it serves as a versatile whipping boy for Marx.[35] He offers two interpretations of the lumpenproletariat which are, unfortunately, contradictory. One comforts him, and the other keeps him awake at night. The lumpenproletariat is alternately presented as a relict of the past and an opponent of the present.

In the *Manifesto of the Communist Party*, Marx and Engels character-ize the "lumpen proletariat" contemptuously, but rather casually, as an example of the "passively rotting mass thrown off by the lowest layers of old society" (MECW 6, 494). It gets by under its own steam, but this steam inevitably generates very little power. Marx consoles himself with the thought that this lumpenproletariat is just a remainder of a long-gone epoch in which "the propertyless man" was only "a vagabond, a robber and a beggar" (MECW 29, 121f.; cf. MECW 35, 723). What Marx is referring to here – though he does not explicitly name them – are the mas-terless men of early-modern England. While the proletariat is integrated in the production process and can be organized, the lumpenproletariat wanders around on the margins of society. (Antonio Gramsci notes this point in 1934 in his analysis of "subaltern social groups."[36]) Marx thinks little of this disorderly marginal group and instead banks on society being polarized between the bourgeoisie and the proletariat.[37]

This is why Marx must also take on Mikhail Bakunin,[38] who declares this marginal position to be a virtue and thus places his revolution-ary hopes in this very same "lumpenproletariat," in the "millions of uncivilized, disinherited, wretched, and illiterate." Like his companion in Dresden, Richard Wagner, who keeps Siegfried free of the taint of history, Bakunin celebrates the "virginity" (*vierge*) of the lumpenproletariat, which has no truck with "the whole bourgeois culture." It is said to be "powerful enough on its own" to turn the entire world upside down.[39] This assumption is nothing but "schoolboyish rot" according to Marx. He accuses Bakunin of wanting to place the "social revolution" in the hands of backward groups – ultimately perhaps even "Slav agricultural and pastoral peoples" – and instead recommends starting from the "definite historical conditions of economic development" (MECW 24, 518). The maladjusted obstinacy of the lumpenproletariat treasured by the anarchist Bakunin is, in Marx's view, a product of the fact that it exists far from the central battleground of industrial production. The lumpenproletariat is not of this world and therefore cannot affect it. In this respect, the lumpenproletariat belongs to the past.

But is this really true? What about the contemporary proletariat? Marx feels increasingly let down by the proletariat; he struggles with disap-pointment and bemoans its lack of fighting power. What this means is that he finds the character traits of the lumpenproletariat – which he actually believes to be an anachronistic marginal phenomenon – reflected in the most recent version of the proletariat itself. In *The Eighteenth Brumaire of Louis Bonaparte* from 1852, he wrestles with the sad question of why the "Paris proletariat" was largely "unresisting" when it surrendered to the despot (MECW 11, 146, 108). What his answer boils down to is that it had adopted the individualistic attitude of the lumpenproletariat. Just like the other usual suspects – the "vagabonds, [...] rogues, moun-tebanks, *lazzaroni*" and the "small-holding peasants" who cling to their private property – the workers appear to be an "indefinite, disintegrated mass, thrown hither and thither" in which each person acts in "isolation" instead of engaging in "mutual intercourse" (MECW 11, 149, 187).

Its privatization strategy is what aligns the lumpenproletariat with the social developments of the day, as just such an individualistic battle was raging at the time. According to Marx, the French workers failed to act as a revolutionary subject, a collective *puer robustus*, because they took on this petty battle as their own cause. By "forgetting the revolutionary interests of their class for momentary ease and comfort, they renounced the honour of being a conquering power" and "surrendered to their fate" (MECW 11, 146). They became a "mass" formed solely "by simple addition of homologous magnitudes, much as potatoes in a sack form a sack of potatoes" (MECW 11, 187). "The 'lumpenization' of a class is its return to the strict conservation of itself and, at the same time, its decom-position into a mere aggregation of individuals."[40] Depoliticization was additionally encouraged by the "industrial and commercial prosperity" enjoyed by the workers at the time of the coup of Napoleon III, which led them to either keep quiet or play along (MECW 11, 146). "*Trade was excellent,*" Engels noted sourly in February 1852 (MECW 11, 214).

Marx and Engels vacillate between wanting to relegate the lumpenpro-letariat to the past and viewing it as an all-too-contemporary phenom-enon. The former approach keeps the lumpenproletariat on the margins, while the latter sees it spreading through the ruling system. But what they describe as a creeping decline of the working classes into the lumpenpro-letariat could be interpreted another way, namely, as "the passage of the revolutionary into the bourgeoisie": "Many revolutionaries have been seen to abandon their old intransigence when they found themselves on the road to fortune."[41]

This bourgeoisification theory turned the workers' inhibition toward revolution into a burning issue for Marx, because it meant that the class war might fall through altogether. This would be the case if there were only a single class left: the bourgeoisie. Even before Marx, Tocqueville thought he had discovered just such a classless society in the USA. Western industrial societies since Marx and Tocqueville could be described as having developed in this direction. Workers flout the notion of class consciousness, know no comrades or kindred spirits, adopt an individualistic model of behavior, and swim (rather poorly) with the tide of bourgeois society. They live in conditions that are perhaps just as precarious as those of the "rag-pickers, knife grinders, tinkers" (MECW 11, 149; cf. 35, 637f.) – or perhaps not.[42]

When workers enter into this wager, they are following a strategy recommended by Max Stirner: "Only from egoism can the rabble get help."[43] In place of the revolutionary subject celebrated as a *puer robustus* by Marx and Engels, we get the indestructible egocentric troublemaker, the *puer robustus* of Hobbes. The omnipotence and "fever-phantasies" of Stirner's "young man" are transformed into the power fantasies (however illusory they may be) of the man who wants to command "things and thoughts according to his heart's pleasure."[44] This "man," as Marx notes, believes he now "has the whole world in his pocket and has nothing more to trouble him" (MECW 5, 127). The rebel settles down.

If the behavioral model of the lumpenproletariat becomes a bourgeois mass phenomenon, the margins of society where the egocentric trouble-makers roam must *swell*. We can visualize this as the margins bloating until the middle of society is completely absorbed and obliterated by them. The rich and poor lumpenproletariat bump up against each other here, and everyone muddles along somehow. Once this state has been reached, the diagnoses of Machiavelli ("the world is all crowd") and Nietzsche ("everything has become mob")[45] are proven true. This, then, results in a state referred to by Gustave Flaubert as a "voyoucratie" and by Thomas Carlyle as an "aristocracy of rogues."[46] In France, power was seized by someone Marx aptly calls the "*chief of the lumpenproletariat*": Napoleon III (MECW 11, 149; cf. 195f.). Silvio Berlusconi, Donald Trump and many others will follow in the footsteps of this "chief."

The image painted by Marx in his 1852 essay on the *Eighteenth Brumaire* almost perfectly matches that of the "new despotism" conjured up by Tocqueville in 1840. This despotism is like a lid on the pot of an economically flourishing society, in which individuals indulge in a sense of private well-being, come to terms with their disenfranchisement and erode the political sphere. They accept their "political nullity," as Hegel would say (PW 151). Tocqueville's and Marx's critique of this depoliticization fits into a simple schema:

- Both oppose the egocentric troublemaker who appears as an evil *puer robustus* in Tocqueville but as a lumpenproletarian in Marx.
- Tocqueville contrasts this character with citizens who live in a "republic without struggle," thus trying – in vain, as we have seen – to neutralize the troublemaker.
- Marx contrasts the lumpenproletarian with the proletarian, whom he embraces as a good *puer robustus*. In anticipation of a different social

212

order, Marx positions the proletarian as a nomocentric troublemaker, as we are about to see.

The politicization and depoliticization debate that raged in the nineteenth century (and continues today!) can therefore be reconstructed as a dispute concerning the role of the *puer robustus*, who appears alternately as an enemy and an exemplar. Marx now has a duty to deliver: he has to explain what kind of non-lumpenized, non-mobified self-awareness the proletariat is expected to develop. He has to show how the model of the revolutionary collective subject is actually *livable*.

4. The revolutionary subject as a species-being or community-being

How does the proletariat go on the offensive? When does it get its turn to play the troublemaker? In his essay "On the Jewish Question," Marx notes:

> Only when the real, individual man re-absorbs in himself the abstract citizen, and as an individual human being has become a *species-being* in his everyday life, in his particular work, and in his particular situation, [. . .] and consequently no longer separates social power from himself in the shape of *political* power, only then will human emancipation have been accomplished. (MECW 3, 168; cf. MECW 3, 184f.)

Marx is downright pushy in his insistence on the "individual" and his "particular" situation here. This brings me back to the point I discussed at the start of the second section of this chapter, namely, that the revolutionary subject is a scion of bourgeois society, and this society revolves around the individual. According to Marx, the "emancipation" of this subject is supposed to be achieved by means of a shift from "abstract citizen" to "species-being." This puzzling keyword stands for the collective he is seeking.

But what exactly is a "species-being"? To answer this question, we have to look at this phrase favored by Marx (MECW 3, 159, 164; MECW 28, 420) in the company of another word he also likes to use: "community" (MECW 3, 155, 164, 204, 296, 298). Marx does not mean a community in the usual sense of a collective or congregation; he is instead referring to the fact that each person is a community-being, i.e., a creature who can or does live communally. The "species-being" (*Gattungswesen*) and "community-being" (*Gemeinwesen*) bring me back to the thread running through the depiction of the workers' struggle against "dependence" and "separation."

213

In his sorely neglected study *From Mandeville to Marx: The Genesis and Triumph of Economic Ideology*, Louis Dumont sees this conceptual pairing – which Marx throws together rather carelessly – for what it actually is: a problem. Dumont says that these two words stand for "two views of man" that can be "contrasted."[47]

"Generic or universal essence" (i.e., "species-being"), according to Dumont, refers to people who, from the outset, are admitted to a social order and who emerge from it; as evidence of this, he holds up Marx's sixth thesis on Feuerbach, which states that man is "the ensemble of the social relations" (MECW 5, 4). Every single person is therefore not, first and foremost, an individual but rather an example of a species. Dumont believes that the "social or common being," by contrast, represents a person who connects with others as an individual, meaning that communality is not a given but must first be created; his proof of this is Marx's comment that "the *other* person as a person has become [. . .] a need" for the individual, so in this respect "he in his individual existence is at the same time a social being" (MECW 3, 296).

Dumont passes unequivocal judgment on this comparison. He praises the interpretation of man as a "species-being," referring to it as a valuable insight; this insight makes Marx a point of reference for the "holism" Dumont himself advocates. Within the idea of the "community-being," on the other hand, there lurks an "individualistic view of man," according to Dumont, which results in social "relations" being derived from the individual's needs, interests, and whims. In this respect, Marx remains attached to the doctrine of liberal economists and bourgeois revolutionaries who reduce "society [. . .] to a means for individual ends."[48]

Dumont's reference to the "contradiction"[49] inherent in the dual "species-being"/"community-being" is valuable, but I believe his judgment is misguided. Man is a species-being *in any case*, without any effort on his part and perhaps even without his knowledge. It is a static trait. The dynamic development of relationships, by contrast, comes into play with the community-being. This process is certainly not tied to individualistic premises for Marx, as Dumont believes. According to Marx – and in contrast to Hobbes and the ranks of economists into which Dumont wants to force him – individuals do not start out with interests that they then bring to others. Instead, they only really find themselves when they open themselves up to others while simultaneously leaving behind their inner individualist. The fact that such a process is taken into account in the community-being seems to give it an advantage over the species-being, particularly in contrast to Dumont's thesis. Armed with this insight, I now want to critically analyze how Marx's worker appears to be a species-beings on the one hand and a community-being on the other.

This will result in two very different proposals for imagining the revolutionary collective subject.

The species-being. If a worker is "the ensemble of [his] social relations," what exactly do these relations do to him? Under the conditions of capitalism, as we have seen, he is relegated to a state of natural "want", i.e., to the existence of a creature of nature. There is no longer *this* worker or *that* one; instead, all workers are species-beings in the sense that they are people driven to the brink of an animalistic life. The description of the proletariat as a species-being is thus closely tied to the notorious immiseration thesis that Marx initially supports but then rejects. (It should be said straightaway that there are good reasons for his late departure from this theory, regardless of whether you want to use Marx against himself or reject him altogether.)

In the *Economic and Philosophical Manuscripts*, Marx says: "The human being had to be reduced to this absolute poverty in order that he might yield his inner wealth to the outer world" (MECW 3, 300). This state of deepest alienation is supposed to veer into a state of highest development. The "crisis" – of this Marx and Engels are "certain" – is always followed by the "revolution" (MECW 10, 510). Marx explains the immiseration thesis in his drafts of the *Critique of Hegel's Philosophy of Law* from 1843 and *The Holy Family* from 1845:

> Where, then, is the *positive* possibility of a German emancipation? *Answer*: In the formation of a class with *radical chains*, [...] a sphere which has a universal character by its universal suffering and claims no *particular right* because no *particular wrong* but *wrong generally* is perpetrated against it; which can no longer invoke a *historical* but only a *human* title; [...] a sphere, finally, [...] which, in a word, is the *complete loss* of man and hence can win itself only through the *complete rewinning of man*. This dissolution of society as a particular estate is the *proletariat*. (MECW 3, 186)

> Since in the fully-formed proletariat the abstraction of all humanity, even of the *semblance* of humanity, is practically complete; since the conditions of life of the proletariat sum up all the conditions of life of society today in their most inhuman form; since man has lost himself in the proletariat, yet at the same time [...] through urgent, no longer removable, no longer disguisable, absolutely imperative *need* [...] is driven directly to revolt against this inhumanity, it follows that the proletariat can and must emancipate itself. But it cannot emancipate itself without abolishing the conditions of its own life. It cannot abolish the conditions of its own life without abolishing *all* the inhuman conditions of life of society today which are summed up in its own situation. (MECW 4, 36f.)

215

Michael Hardt and Antonio Negri pull off the same sleight of hand as the early Marx when they write in their all-too-influential book *Empire*: "There is World Poverty, but there is above all World Possibility, and only the poor is capable of this."[50] The seductive power of the immiseration thesis lies in its ability to breezily answer the question of how revolution can come about and be justified. It ties together the two great innovations that Marx brings to the theory of the troublemaker in a peculiar way. First, immiseration is expected to mobilize the masses, who have nothing to lose. They will then form a powerful collective subject. Second, the revolutionary action of this subject will be legitimate, because the subject will be fighting a battle against inhumanity itself. I want to track this dual strategy and show where it runs aground.

Workers in a capitalist society are driven to the margins; they belong to this society in the manner of people who do not belong. If they want to escape their "absolutely imperative *need*" and their "estrangement [...] from themselves" (MECW 4, 37; MECW 28, 99), they cannot simply ensure their self-preservation on their own; instead they must grapple with the roots of their need, which are embedded in the level of "universality," in the organization of the conditions of production. Therefore, the war they wage can only be a supra-individual or "justifiable war" (MECW 22, 351).

According to Marx, the unique characteristic of this class is that it is "not a class" anymore (MECW 3, 186; cf. MECW 6, 212). It does not lobby on its own behalf – employing what Hegel calls the "violence of the specific against the specific"[51] – but instead advocates a new version of the aspiration formulated by Hegel in his *Elements of the Philosophy of Right*: to "lead a universal life" (PR 276 [§258], cf. 237 [§205]). Engels says "the historical mission of the modern proletariat" is an "act of universal emancipation" that extends beyond its own destiny (MECW 24, 325). The existential struggle of the proletariat coincides with the preservation of the species-being. This is what changes evil into good. As a *puer robustus*, the proletariat is in no way *malitiosus*.

Étienne Balibar stresses that "resistance and rebellion [...] have nothing to do with corporatist protest, with the defense of a particular interest (such as wage interest versus profit interest); on the contrary, they should *defend* the *universal* against its own limitation and negation."[52] Balibar rightly points out that the claim to universality takes on a new form with the proletariat. It is not about abstract rights, as it is with the bourgeoisie – rights which apply to everyone as a "phrase" but certainly do not benefit everyone in the same way (cf. MECW 5, 439, 46f., cf. 87f.). Instead, it is about a kind of lived universality that is realized on the level of the "existing 'production of life'" (MECW 5, 54).

To use my categorization, Marx's proletariat belongs to the group of nomocentric troublemakers who herald a new order. They do not think only of themselves in an egocentric way, nor do they think beyond themselves in an eccentric way. Marx's *nomos*, the new law, is not supposed to be something that is set, however, but something that is given. As a species-being, the proletariat does not merely think in universal terms, it actually *is* "the universal in action."[53] Like Rousseau before him and Badiou after him, Marx does not believe the people are dependent on representatives (cf. MECW 3, 184); instead, in their pure presence, they are entirely fulfilled by themselves and their agenda.[54] In order for the workers to play their part as a species-being, their universal agenda must be transformed into flesh and blood, so to speak.

In *The Holy Family*, we find a "famous"[55] but questionable line about the proletariat as a collective subject, one which I would like to look at in more detail. "It is not a question of what this or that proletarian, or even the whole proletariat, at the moment *regards* as its aim. It is a question of *what the proletariat is*, and what, in accordance with this *being*, it will historically be compelled to do" (MECW 4, 37). In this sentence, we find the sore that poisons the theory of the collective subject as a species-being. This sore is found in the relationship between being, regarding, and doing.

What Marx and Engels are describing here is a direct transition from what the proletariat *is* to what it *does*. The intermediate step of *ideas* or intentions – upon which every single theory of action depends in order to distinguish *action* from *behavior* – is edited out here. Marx and Engels prefer to leave the potentially misguided intentions of the poor to one side. While Georg Lukács eagerly seized upon the sentence just quoted,[56] Jacques Rancière critically skewered it: "The proletarian is someone *who has only one thing to do* – to make the revolution – and who *cannot not do that* because of what he is." Rancière's double negative – the "prolétaire [. . .] qui *ne peut pas ne pas la faire*"[57] – harbors a critical point that I want to hone even further.

Imagine a person who asserts that "it is simply not possible for me not to do this." One could certainly respect this person and credit them with acting on the basis of firm convictions (*ideas* even!). It would be different if someone said "I cannot not breathe because I am what I am." Of course, Marx, Engels, and their defenders avouch that what they call *being* does not represent one's natural existence alone. It instead encompasses the worker's entire "actual life-process," his "conscious being" (MECW 5, 36). But everything comes down to precisely what it means to say – as in the above-mentioned sentence from *The Holy Family* – that the proletariat "*is*, and [. . .] in accordance with this *being*" is "compelled" to act.

The sentence immediately following this reads: "Its aim and historical action is visibly and irrevocably foreshadowed in its own life situation as

217

well as in the whole organisation of bourgeois society today" (MECW 4, 37). Marx and Engels therefore insist that the "being" or the "real premises" (MECW 5, 31) of the workers *dictate* what they do. They are kept on a short leash, and they only do the right thing because they have no other choice. Their consciousness exclusively serves the purpose of registering a command. The collective subject is expected to accomplish its "tremendous insurrection," the "most colossal event," without being thwarted by the desires and ideas of the workers (MECW 10, 67; MECW 11, 110).

In order to clearly establish the revolutionary agenda and sidestep the workers' fickleness and their lumpenproletariat tendencies, Marx and Engels derive the need for the act directly from necessity. The goals, means, and methods of revolutionary action are set not *by* the workers but *for* them. This results in a paradox. The collective subject – which is understood to be a species-being – is expected to get by without having its own ideas or desires. Since this contradicts the very concept of an active subject, the proletariat secretly becomes a *collective object*.

As long as Marx and Engels cling to the logic of the species-being, they remain trapped in a fairly dismal choice between real subjects who are led astray by their idiosyncratic ideas and an ideal subject who gets by without such ideas but is only expected to function automatically instead of taking action.

On the one hand, Marx and Engels hardly miss an opportunity to complain about the fact that the actually existing proletariat does not meet their expectations. "What is the rabble worth if it has forgotten how to fight?" (MECW 38, 513) Engels asks in exasperation. On the other hand, the ideal proletariat evaporates into an imaginary entity, the very "spectre of Communism" that is mentioned purely ironically at the start of the *Manifesto of the Communist Party* (MECW 6, 481). Marx and Engels want their communists to be alive and kicking. But sadly, the simulacra of bourgeois ideology that they criticize are spectral, and the ideal proletariat they hold up in contrast to the "paralyse[d]" people (MECW 11, 125) is also an unembodied specter. As a collective object[58] it simply cannot exist – and it therefore joins the "inverted Schlemihls" of whom Marx speaks, the "shadows that have lost their bodies" (MECW 11, 125). The actually existing people does indeed fight battles as a *puer robustus*, but it does so with a self-image that has nothing to do with the definition of the revolutionary species-being.

As stated earlier, the theory of the species-being forms an ill-fated alliance with the immiseration thesis. Only the latter – as mentioned – is rejected by Marx himself, and not least by many Marxists. In light of this, it is necessary to set out on new paths in search of the revolutionary col-lective subject. These new paths are also required because the historical development of the second half of the nineteenth century did not actually lead to the escalating destitution anticipated by Marx. Capitalism did not do Marx the favor of intensifying social contradictions to the extent that workers were driven into a fight against dehumanization. Marx therefore has to distance himself from his immiseration thesis in order to keep the class war on track.[59]

This distance is called for on both historical and systematic grounds, because the immiseration and species-being arguments do not lead to the establishment and legitimization of a revolutionary collective subject. But we have not yet said all there is to say about Marx's troublemaker. The proponent of revolution still has another arrow in his quiver. After all, Marx talks not only about the "species-being" who is supposed to pay for the switch from "absolute poverty" to "inner wealth," he also talks about "community" or the community-being. Perhaps this will take us down a path that does not lead to a dead end.

The community-being. In 1864, the revolutionary poet Georg Herwegh composed his *Bundeslied*, an anthem celebrating the founding of the General German Workers Association:

Man of labor, awake!
And recognize your power!
All gears will stand still
If your strong arm wishes it. [. . .]
Break the double yoke atwain!
Break the hardship of slavery!
Break the slavery of hardship!
Bread is freedom, freedom bread![60]

The phrase "double yoke" is both poignant and productive. Herwegh is juxtaposing a natural misery (the "slavery of hardship") and a social misery (the "hardship of slavery"). We would do well to differentiate the two parts of this "double yoke." Marx's argument that the proletariat is a "species-being" can be categorized under "slavery of hardship," because it is tied to the idea that people's immiseration reduces them to creatures of nature. The "hardship of slavery," by contrast, is open to an interpretation centering on the "power" of the actor. (For Herwegh, however, this is – yet again – the power only of the "man.") The focus here is not just on material hardship but on the deprivation experienced by people who are hindered in the development of their actions. If we turn toward them, we cannot possibly keep their ideas – in the sense of the "species-being" of Marx and Engels – at arm's length. This brings me to the notion of the "community" or community-being. It is flagged up most clearly in Marx's commentary on James Mill from the year 1844:

Since *human* nature is the *true community* of men, by manifesting their *nature* men *create*, produce, the *human community*, the social entity, which is no abstract universal power opposed to the single individual, but is the essential nature of each individual, his own activity, his own life, his own spirit, his own wealth. (MECW 3, 217)

It is worth comparing this with a passage from the first draft of Rousseau's *Social Contract*. Rousseau writes: "Certain it is that the word *mankind* [*genre humain*] offers the mind only a purely collective idea which does not assume any real unity among the individuals who constitute it." This comment can be directed toward Marx's species-being – and it is directed against an abstract collective. In contrast, Rousseau adds that each person has a "sentiment of common existence [*existence commune*]" which gives him or her a "universal motivation" to "act for the sake of an end related to the whole."[61] Following the distinction I make, the species-being takes a turn here to become a community-being. Only when the workers organize themselves will they sense the "power of the united individuals" (MECW 5, 81). Marx, like Rousseau, presents himself as a theorist of *synergy* here. What he points to – as explained in the second section of this chapter – is the pivot from "separation" to "association": "In the real community the individuals obtain their freedom in and through their association" (MECW 5, 78).[62]

Unlike the brash sleight of hand that turns the worker into a species-being, this path is actually traversable. If Marx takes this path, however, he must pay a price for it. To be precise, he has to accept and trust in the workers' self-organization. Although he struggles with it, he does start to move in this direction. In *The Civil War in France* from 1871, for example, he defends the "Communal Constitution" (the local self-determination of the communes) against suspicions that it is part of a sectarian struggle against "over-centralization." In a very Rousseauian and not particularly internationalist way, he trusts this institution to "[restore] to the social body all the forces hitherto absorbed by the State parasite feeding upon [...] society" (MECW 22, 333).[63] Marx is absolutely prepared to give the actually existing workers the benefit of the doubt. In August 1844 he wrote to Ludwig Feuerbach: "You would have to attend one of the meetings of the French workers [*ouvriers*] to appreciate the pure freshness, the nobility which burst forth from these toil-worn men" (MECW 3, 355). These "*ouvriers*" cannot be female, but they can be "pure"! And the "nobility" he sees in them can be read as an echo of the "nobility" that Hegel found in the "repudiated consciousness" of the *puer robustus*. In Marx's *Economic and Political Manuscripts*, we find a similar, though less rapturous, vote of confidence:[64]

220

When communist *artisans* associate with one another, theory, propaganda, etc., is their first end. But at the same time, as a result of this association, they acquire a new need – the need for society – and what appears as a means becomes an end. In this practical process the most splendid results are to be observed whenever French socialist workers are seen together. Such things as smoking, drinking, eating, etc., are no longer means of contact or means that bring them together. Association, society and conversation, which again has association as its end, are enough for them; the brotherhood of man is no mere phrase with them, but a fact of life, and the nobility of man shines upon us from their work-hardened bodies. (MECW 3, 313)

This is Marx strolling across the frozen lake that separates him from the mundane ideas of the workers. But the ice is thin, and Marx himself has brought the thaw. There is a danger that it will shatter and break his connection to the workers. At least three cracks are apparent in the passage just quoted. *First*, we can assume that Marx's comment about drinking, smoking and talking being "enough" for the members of the workers' association is not meant as a compliment. *Second*, we should also be wary of his goodwill toward "communist artisans," as in another passage he viciously mocks the radical artisans known as "Straubingers": "The fellows are horribly ignorant and, their condition in life being what it is, completely unprepared. [. . .] [W]ages remain constantly at the same wretched level" (MECW 38, 87; cf. 579). *Finally*, even his praise of "brotherhood" is tempered,[65] because elsewhere Marx complains that it promotes "pleasant" and "sentimental" tendencies (MECW 10, 57f.), and Engels says it reeks of Wilhelm Weitling's brotherly affection, which leads to "sentimental starry-eyed love" (MECW 26, 320).

Just as Marx and Engels are half attracted to and half repelled by this "brotherhood," they generally struggle with all questions pertaining to the self-understanding and self-organization of the workers. This also applies to the question that comes free, so to speak, with the issue of "brotherhood" – namely, the question of women. A quote by Marx from a letter of 1868 is enlightening here: "Everyone who knows anything of history also knows that great social revolutions are impossible without the feminine ferment. Social progress may be measured precisely by the social position of the fair sex (plain ones included)" (MECW 43, 185). I am interested not in the politically incorrect conclusion to this quote, but rather in the contradiction inherent in it. In the first sentence Marx refers to women as a source of "ferment," much like Diderot calls Rameau's nephew a "pinch of yeast." But this is immediately followed by a denial that women play an active role, as the next sentence describes them not as ferment but as an indicator – like litmus paper, one might say. They are not subjects who bring about progress; they serve only as objects against which this progress can be "measured." Here and elsewhere, Marx's views on the role of women remain inconclusive.

Marx clears a path for women's emancipation, which – like the liberation of the individual – starts with capitalism: "Modern industry, by assigning as it does an important part in the process of production, outside the domestic sphere, to women [...], creates a new economic foundation for a higher form of the family and of the relations between the sexes." Marx thinks communism will tap this "source of humane development" (MECW 35, 492f., cf. 405). In keeping with this, one might expect women to be involved in enhancing the profile of the revolutionary subject. But Marx does not foresee the existence of a *puella robusta*. His revolution is and remains a "shock of [male] body against body" (MECW 6, 212). Only in the new world that has been brought forth by manly revolutionaries will both "true manliness" and "true womanliness" – whatever that might mean – be able to unfold (MECW 4, 439).

The composition and inner constitution of the collective that Marx and Engels embrace as a "community" gives them cause for concern – because they must come to terms with the historical contingencies of the revolutionary subject. This relates to a wide range of gender roles, mentalities, and cultural identities. The older Engels seems prepared to acknowledge such contingencies. In August 1889, after he has begun to lose hope, he witnesses a dockworkers' strike in London and writes enthusiastically to Eduard Bernstein:

> Hitherto the East End had been in a state of poverty-stricken stagnation, its hallmark being the apathy of men whose spirit had been broken by hunger, and who had abandoned all hope. Anyone who found himself there was lost, physically and morally. And now, this gigantic strike of the most demoralised elements of the lot, the dock labourers, not the regular, strong, experienced, relatively well-paid men in steady employment, but those who have happened to land up in dockland, the Jonahs who have suffered shipwreck in all other spheres, starvelings by trade, a welter of broken lives heading straight for utter ruin and for whom Dante's words, '*lasciate ogni speranza, voi che'entrate*' might be written up on the dock gates! And this dully despairing mass of humanity who, every morning when the dock gates are opened, literally fight pitched battles to be first to reach the chap who signs them on – literal battles in the competitive struggle of the redundant workers amongst themselves – that mass, haphazardly thrown together and changing every day, has successfully combined to form a band 40,000 strong, maintain discipline and inspire fear in the powerful dock companies. It is something I am glad that I have lived to see. For *this* stratum to be capable of organisation is a fact of great significance. (MECW 48, 364f.)[66]

Engels does something incredible here: he resorts to viewing the lumpenproletariat – which he has disdained his whole life – as revolutionary material. He wants to grant it a sense of "organization"; he is counting on this mass. In 1895 he writes: "Where it is a question of a complete transformation of the social organisation, the masses themselves must also be in on it, must themselves already have grasped what is at stake" (MECW 27, 520). It almost looks as though he were allowing the revolutionary subject to actually be a *subject*. But Engels remains a spoilsport, because he continues to interpret any comprehension or understanding on the part of the masses as merely the acknowledgment of a task that has already been defined. In this respect, he is no less paternalistic than Hugo.[67] The revolutionary subject may no longer appear to be the object of an "imperative" historical necessity that dictates what must be done, but it still suffers from a learning disability and requires education and instruction – following the strict specifications of the Party. The community disintegrates into a mass that simply takes orders – but it does not *have* to be this way.

In summary, we can say that when Marx and Engels search for a subject that acts as a species-being, they come up empty-handed because this subject *cannot exist*. Their ideas about it are neither attainable nor viable. But when they search for a collective subject that acts as a community formed through "association," they strike gold. In this case, it comes down to what the proletariat imagines for itself, not just what it "is." Its process of self-understanding is more unordered and unpredictable than Marx and Engels would like. All the same, the community has the merit of being politically constituted of its own accord. This can be seen in the small and large struggles in which people thrash things out, agree on goals, form a political will, and take action. In doing so, they develop the ability to self-organize and create relationships or "associations," regardless of how narrow their field of vision may be.

The two models of the revolutionary subject that get caught in Marx's and Engels' net can also be compared in terms of the relationship between politics and economics. The interpretation of this relationship is a matter of fierce debate among scholars. *Some* complain that Marx *shifts* the battlefield from politics to economics. *Others* claim that Marx maintains a connection between politics and economics and is thus capable of thinking about the political in a new way. This interpretive dispute can be described and decided by looking at the difference between the species-being and the community.

Evidence for the *first interpretation* includes Marx's opinion that the proletariat should appropriate the relations of production and instrumentalize the state as an "organ" (MECW 6, 504; MECW 24, 94), as well as Engels' prediction that the proletariat would "*[seize] political power*," abolish "the State as State," and finally replace "the government of persons" with "the administration of things" (MECW 24, 320f.). Engels correspondingly moves "the whole machinery of state [. . .] into the museum of antiquities" (MECW 26, 272).[68] According to Jacques Rancière, this leads to a devaluation of politics, to a "metapolitics" that denounces all "politics" as a "lie" and contrasts it with "a reality that is called society" or "a *beyond* of politics": "From the metapolitical point of view, it designates the performer of the real movement of society who denounces the democratic appearances of politics and is supposed to cause them to be blown to smithereens."[69] Rancière is following Claude Lefort's critique of the "lacune du politique," and thus Marx's "refusal to think in political terms."[70] As I see it, this refusal is rooted in Marx's fixation on the *species-being* who is expected to succeed in enforcing its agenda without any process of self-understanding. It is supposed to have a political effect, but it can itself only be unpolitical in the strictest sense. The *community* must be defended against this tendency that dominates Marx's works, and this is precisely what Rancière does with his definition of the political dispute that revolves around participation and exclusion, around the "part of those who have no part."[71]

The second interpretation invokes Marx's early position that the "political state" is "annihilated" in a liberated society (MECW 3, 30). This annihilation is not supposed to bring an end to politics, however; it is supposed to free politics from the clutches of the state. Étienne Balibar, for example, believes that Marx is absolutely not advocating an economistic metapolitics but instead wants to transform the concept of the political itself. In accordance with this, action on the economic level becomes an indispensible element of political action.[72] The transformed meaning of the political is expressed when Marx says that "every class struggle is a political struggle" and every "social movement" is always a "political movement" (MECW 6, 493, 212). Following Balibar, Miguel Abensour claims that "the State is not the last word of the political," and he criticizes "the division of political existence and social exist-ence." Referring to Lefort's "savage democracy," he makes an appeal for an "insurgent democracy."[73] However, this generous interpretation of Marx's pivot toward economics does not explain the practical organi-zation of the collective, which is expected to regulate its political and economic affairs in a single blow.

There is only one decisive point here: with these two interpretations, Marx's critics and defenders wind up agreeing, one way or another, that they do not conceive of the collective subject as a species-being; they all come down on the side of the community instead. Proponents of the first interpretation believe there is an urgent need to strengthen this community in a way that goes beyond Marx's delicate suggestions, and that goes against his pivot from politics to economics. It seems to me that they find strong evidence for their critical interpretation in Marx's texts. Proponents of the second interpretation, on the other hand, try to rescue Marx as a theorist of community and put him to use in a new defense of the "political." There are only (or at least) a few passages in his works upon which they can base their arguments. I am satisfied with the finding that all of these interpreters – arguing for or against Marx – seek a point of access to the collective subject that is geared not toward the species-being but toward the community.

This finding has a consequence that is unpleasant for Marx but beneficial to the theory of the troublemaker. It puts pressure on the revolutionary collective subject right at the point where its claim to universality is at stake. It cannot and does not want to boast that it speaks with the pure voice of humanity in its role as a species-being. Instead, the collective subject – as a community – sticks to its self-will and its particular agenda. It responds to the prevailing law – the injustice from above – with a revolutionary breach of law. It anticipates a different law and strives to change the political order, but its efforts are based on a forward-looking aspiration, not on a dictum set in stone, e.g., the assertion that, in any case, the proletariat can only achieve good things in the name of humanity.[74] As a community-being, the collective subject presents itself as a revolutionary, but a skeptical, cautious one. Alexander Herzen found wonderful words to describe this in 1850:

> Social thought now at work is such that every step towards its realization constitutes an egress! And that is the difficulty! Where to? What lies beyond those walls? Fearful void, space, freedom ... How to go on without knowing where? How to lose without the hope of gain? If Columbus had reasoned this way he would never have set sail. [...] Of course it would have been easier if people could have merely moved from one *hôtel garni* to another still more comfortable, but unfortunately there is no one to prepare the new apartments. The future is even more uncertain than the sea: there is nothing in sight and it will turn out to be such as people and circumstances will make it.[75]

Herzen – alongside Marx, Bakunin, and others – is one of the main characters in the great trilogy *The Coast of Utopia* by the English playwright Tom Stoppard. What Herzen says at the end of this trilogy is too lovely to go unmentioned here: "History knocks at a thousand gates at every moment, and the gatekeeper is Chance." The motto is simply "to go on, and to know there is no landfall on the paradisal shore, and still to go on."[76] Like the *puer robustus*, Herzen is a revolutionary troublemaker standing on a threshold: the temporal threshold between present and future.

Marx is aware of this threshold, but he approaches it with ambivalence. On one hand, he moves the troublemaker to a future in which he is expected to have escaped the entanglement that clouds his view and causes him to stumble around in the dark. Marx audaciously declares that the working class is "really rid of all the old world" (MECW 5, 73). On the other hand, Marx believes this class inevitably remains trapped in the old world that it must overcome: "The present generation [. . .] has not only a new world to conquer, it must go under in order to make room for the men who are able to cope with a new world" (MECW 10, 117; cf. MECW 22, 335f.). This means the "present generation" has, at most, only a faint idea of the goodness of the future that has been heralded. And this is not enough to be certain of one's own goodness. (This problem will return in Togliatti's discussion of the "unhappy consciousness".)

I said earlier that the species-being is conceived as a nomocentric troublemaker whose law is dispensed as a given. This was the source of its legitimacy – which crumbled to pieces, however. The community-being also presents itself as a nomocentric troublemaker, but it fares better. In contrast to the eccentric troublemaker, it insists on going all out and confronting the status quo with a new order. It therefore faces similar challenges to the people described by Rousseau and the league described by Schiller. This revolutionary is not good by virtue of some inner quality, nor can it justify its goodness in anticipation of a distant, strange world. Instead, it has the duty to exemplify – within the limits of what is feasible – the *other* that can become good. The ability to justify the revolution as a "*real* movement" (MECW 5, 49) hinges on whether it has the strength to integrate, expand, and universalize this movement – i.e., on whether the collective can expand beyond a small circle of first movers. With this stipulation in mind, cynics of violence don't stand a chance. But it would be impudent to want to develop hard criteria for judging historical struggles. This is not possible on the drawing board of theory.

If we want to make the revolutionary nomocentric troublemaker as strong as possible, we must *weaken* him and acknowledge that he is entangled in the present. We also have to push him closer to the eccentric troublemaker – closer than Marx and Engels would like. Political protest is dependent on popularity, and this applies not only to Mill's troublemaker but also, in a different way, to Marx's revolutionary. This point will once again become a flashpoint in the Marxist interpretations of the revolutionary and the *puer robustus* of the twentieth century, in the works of Togliatti and Mao. But first I want to turn to a theorist who banks not on the economy but on the economy of desire and who introduces the *puer robustus* not as a revolutionary collective but as part of a family constellation. As we will see, Sigmund Freud's contribution to the theory of the troublemaker is at least as political – and at least as productive for political philosophy – as that of Marx and Engels.

THE *PUER ROBUSTUS* AS OEDIPUS

Sigmund Freud

1. The little savage

If someone had asked Sigmund Freud whether he was familiar with Hobbes's *puer robustus*, he probably would have shaken his head. And yet, Freud is one of the authors who has earned a place in this book. The bridge between the *puer robustus* and Freud is slender, but it is also strong. It does not lead directly from Hobbes to Freud but instead swings past Diderot. Freud refers to the *puer robustus* without realizing it, and he does so at a key point in his theory.

As a refresher: Diderot presented the *puer robustus* in his *Encyclopédie* article on "Hobbisme" and described him even more dramatically than Hobbes himself. He then repeated this description almost word for word in *Rameau's Nephew*. Here is the decisive passage again: "If the little savage were left to himself, remaining in a state of imbecility, and combining the feeble reasoning abilities of a small infant with the violent passions of a grown man, he'd wring his father's neck and sleep with his mother."

Freud came across this passage in 1912 while reading Otto Rank's book *The Incest Theme in Literature and Legend*.[1] He repeatedly returned to it over the course of many years: in his *Introductory Lectures on Pyscho-Analysis* (SE 15, 208), in his comments on the trial of the alleged patricide Philippe Halsmann (SE 21, 251) and in his posthumously published "Outline of Psycho-Analysis" (SE 23, 192).[2] Thus the *puer robustus* who was transformed into a "little savage" by Diderot takes the stage once again in Freud's work and undergoes yet another transformation – to become Oedipus. Freud uses this very passage from Diderot to characterize Oedipus, and this is precisely why he is fascinated by it.

The invention or discovery of the Oedipus complex can be dated fairly exactly. It is attested in Freud's famous letter to Wilhelm Fliess from October 15, 1897:

> A single idea of general value dawned on me. I have found, in my own case too, [the phenomenon of] being in love with my mother and jealous of my father, and I now consider it a universal event in early childhood [. . .]. If this is so, we can understand the gripping power of *King Oedipus*, in spite of all the objections that reason raises against the presupposition of fate [. . .]. The Greek legend seizes upon a compulsion which everyone recognizes because he senses its existence within himself. Everyone [. . .] was once a budding Oedipus in fantasy.[3]

Three words in this quote demand special attention: "I," "everyone," and "Oedipus." Jealousy toward one's father and infatuation with one's mother are Freud's own experiences as revealed through self-analysis. Freud universalizes them as an "event in early childhood" that affects everyone. As historical evidence for this universality, Freud mentions how posterity has been captivated by the Oedipus drama (cf. SE 4, 262).

Freud has his work cut out for him with Sophocles' original Oedipus, however, because there is actually nothing to indicate that this Oedipus has a more or less conscious desire to kill his father and sleep with his mother. The Greek template also draws no connection between the two actions which might imply that father and son were in competition for the woman.[4] These differences between the Sophoclean and Freudian Oedipus are what make the Diderot quote so dramatically important. In the span between Ancient Greece and Viennese Modernism, it is a unique statement[5] that anticipates Freud's escalation of the Oedipus myth in an exemplary way. In this quote, we find both the assumption of an instinctive intent – the so-called "own Oedipus wish" (SE 23, 192) – and the package deal of patricide and intercourse with one's mother.

Freud believes Diderot's portrait of the "little savage" must be interpreted in light of the "difference between the primitive and civilized worlds" (SE 23, 192). But this contrast between nature and civilization is much less applicable to Diderot's hero, with his considerable cultural competencies, than to his predecessor, the Hobbesian original: the *puer robustus* who obstinately insists on his natural freedom.[6]

In fact, the arguments of Hobbes and Freud largely run parallel to one another. Like Hobbes, Freud believes that the "liberty of the individual" (Hobbes would say "natural liberty") was "greatest before there was any civilization," though this is not a liberty that one should "defend" or savor (SE 21, 95). Like Hobbes, Freud uses the model of the "social contract" (SE 23, 82) to describe how individuals join a civil or cultural order.[7] "Violence" is "overcome" through "the transference of power to a larger unity" (SE 22, 205), i.e., to the state, which holds the monopoly on

229

violence (SE 21, 112f.). Hobbes and Freud both declare that civilization places restrictions on individuals while simultaneously opening up new opportunities for development. As a counterimage to this state, we find in the works of both Hobbes and Freud individuals who act aggressively in the interest of self-preservation. According to Freud, aggression drives people to "exploit" another's "capacity for work without compensation, to use him sexually without his consent, to seize his possessions, to humiliate him, to cause him pain, to torture and to kill him. *Homo homini lupus*. Who, in the face of all his experience of life and of history, will have the courage to dispute this assertion?" (SE 21, 111). Freud also speaks of the "struggle of all against all" (SE 13, 144), but he takes the liberty of never even mentioning Hobbes, and he also deviates from him in a significant way.

The aggressive self-preservation that dominates Hobbes's model of the state of nature loses its prominent position in Freud's analysis of the "complicated structure of our mental apparatus" (SE 21, 78). Freud identifies instincts having to do with the "preservation, assertion and magnification of the individual" (SE 22, 96; cf. SE 18, 50f.), but also those that push aside the "interest [. . .] of self-preservation" (SE 18, 77). In human beings, these instincts – which originally served to ensure the survival of the species – are said to develop into the wide range of sexual desires, "emotional ties" (SE 18, 91), and the "community of feeling" that play a key role in the "structure of human society" (SE 22, 212). These dispositions, which I will discuss later in the context of Freud's concept of democracy, are designed not to establish boundaries between the "I" and others but to eliminate such boundaries altogether.

This leads to a simple argument that cements the superiority of Freud's description of the transition from nature to civilization over that of Hobbes. In brief, this argument says that self-preservation starts *too early* with Hobbes. Hobbes skips the question of how a *self* or an *I* that identifies and pursues its own interests is formed in the first place: "The adult's ego-feeling cannot have been the same from the beginning," Freud writes, turning his attention to the task of defining the conditions for ego "development" (SE 21, 66).[8] With this genealogical view, Freud not only goes against Hobbes, he goes against everyone who believes human society is composed of complete, fully developed individuals (for a critique of this, see p. 260). A key element of the Hobbesian definition of the *puer robustus* – which Hobbes only reluctantly permitted – thus emerges in full force here: *history*.

Whether or how Oedipus, the "little savage" or the *puer robustus* can find a place in society is determined not by an isolated decision or contract, but rather by a complicated socialization process whose highways and byways, detours and dead ends need to be explored. This socialization process relates to how people grow up – and how they grow into a political order. By establishing a connection between the generation game and political change, Freud addresses the very problem expressed by the *puer robustus*. The phenomena of adaptation and resistance, and of inclusion and exclusion, crop up again in the figure of Oedipus or the "little savage." For this reason, disciples of Freud, such as Siegfried Bernfeld and August Aichhorn, examined all kinds of troublemakers.[9] In a short but important essay entitled "Family Romances," Freud writes: "Indeed, the whole progress of society rests upon the opposition between successive generations" (SE 9, 237). He wonders how his reinterpreted generation game can lead to a positive outcome – this being the disappearance of Oedipus the "little savage." In fact, Freud does say that "forgetting" (SE 4, 262) the Oedipus complex is a possibility, as is its "destruction and [. . .] abolition" (SE 19, 177).

I am interested in how Freud's social psychology can benefit political philosophy, and specifically in the question of which model (or models) of a political order are tied to his conception of the generation game. In answering this question, I will encounter the alternative between democracy and dictatorship, which Freud interprets in a rather unorthodox way (section 2). I will then compare the character of Oedipus, who is at the heart of this interpretation, with the previously discussed versions of the *puer robustus*. Finally, I will throw myself into the dispute regarding political order and disturbance that flared up among Freud's immediate successors: Walter Lippmann, Paul Federn, Hans Blüher, Thomas Mann, and Hans Kelsen (section 3).

2. Democracy and dictatorship

"But surely infantilism is destined to be surmounted. Men cannot remain children forever," Freud says. However, "the path from the infant [. . .] to the civilized man is a long one," he warns, and "many human young" can "go astray" (SE 21, 49, 52). It initially seems far-fetched to claim that the phases of the Oedipus complex experienced by a child could have any relevance to political philosophy. But Freud disagrees. By equating "children" – the "primitives of the present day" – with "savages" (SE 18, 117; SE 23, 82), he draws a parallel between individual and social development. In *Totem and Taboo*, Freud writes:

At the conclusion, then, of this exceedingly condensed inquiry, I should like to insist that its outcome shows that the beginnings of religion, morals, society and art converge in the Oedipus complex. This is in complete agreement with the psychoanalytic finding that the same complex constitutes the nucleus of all neuroses, so far as our present knowledge goes. It seems to me a most surprising discovery that the problems of social psychology, too, should prove soluble on the basis of one single concrete point – man's relation to his father. (SE 13, 156f.)

A lengthy debate has raged over the question of whether the development of the individual, which, according to Freud, takes place in an Oedipal constellation, can be used as a template for the "cultural development" of humanity as a whole. The anthropologist Bronislaw Malinowski provided the decisive commentary on this back in 1924, in an essay first published in Freud's own journal, *Imago*. His critique of Freud culminates in the sentence: "It appears necessary [. . .] not to assume the universal existence of the Oedipus complex, but in studying every type of civilization, to establish the special complex which pertains to it."[10] In accordance with this, the Oedipal constellation is not the key to the entire history of humanity, but it may be the key to a specific historical epoch. When Freud deigns to speculate about society's emergence along the lines of the Oedipus complex (SE 21, 144; SE 23, 83f.), his deliberations are not very productive from a scholarly point of view. And yet it is worth engaging with his fundamental thoughts, because while they do not help us understand the prehistory of humanity, they do provide a better understanding of the contemporary society to which Freud belonged. His Oedipal constellation fits perfectly with this society, which was characterized by political and private patriarchy – and its crisis.[11] Freud's analysis contributes to our understanding of the relationship between order and disturbance by foregrounding the themes of power, morality, and history in a new way.

Freud believes he is saying something about the prehistory of society, but instead of demanding an empirical basis for this statement, we can interpret it as a psychological-political thought experiment. The experiment starts with Freud imagining a situation in which the "pressure that civilization exercises" has not even begun to take effect yet. He essentially returns to Hobbes's natural world, in which anyone "may without hesitation kill [. . .] anyone else who stands in one's way," or "carry off" someone else's "woman" or "belongings" (SE 21, 15). But Freud foresees a different end to this power struggle than Hobbes. According to Freud, it is possible for one person to seize "all the means to power" and establish himself as a "violent primal father" (SE 21, 15; SE 13, 142, cf. 148). It is worth noting that Freud uses a thoroughly male schema here; his prehistory reflects his real status quo, which is male-dominated.

The "primal father" does not herald the birth of a true political order, however, but only a preliminary stage: "In this primitive family one essential feature of civilization is still lacking. The arbitrary will of its head, the father, was unrestricted" (SE 21, 99f.). Where arbitrariness reigns, all rules and regulations are just game pieces that the ruler can move around at will. The tension between order and disturbance is not yet in sight. It gradually comes into view when we realize that there is an expiration date on the regime of the "primal father." His power, to put it briefly, is undermined by history. He has to contend with (real or symbolic) sons who are themselves predispositioned to become fathers. This dynamic is much more obtrusive than the dynamic between a lord and his vassal or slave. In the generation game, one person is what the other person will become. The relationship between father and son is dominated by opposition and equality at the same time. The son is under his father's command – and is on his way to becoming just like his father.

Looking now to the son – Oedipus, that is – we can see that his identity is actually split: he is puny and great at the same time. *On the one hand*, he identifies with his role as an underling and awaits both the deeds performed by his father and the orders issued by him. Even though Freud's starting point is a "violent primal father" (see above), this father's deeds can also serve the purposes of "protection, care and indulgence" (SE 13, 144). So the son can, to a certain extent, come to terms with his puniness or impotence. *On the other hand*, he can also have designs on his father's greatness and identify with him as a superior or potentate. This split identity gives rise to the son's "ambivalent emotional attitude" toward his father, the "ambivalence" of the "father-complex" that Freud frequently mentions in *Totem and Taboo* (SE 13, 129, 141, 143, 145, 151). This attitude vacillates between a "readiness to submit to" his father and a "bitterness against [his] father," between "admiration" and "hatred" (SE 13, 148, 129). And slowly but surely, Oedipus the troublemaker who challenges his father's dominance comes into play.

The relationship between father and son remains undisturbed as long as power changes hands smoothly at the right moment. This is highly unlikely, however. There is always a threat of massive carnage: other father-rulers might develop greater appetites when one of their colleagues resigns, several sons might fight for power, and the relationships between fathers and sons and their respective mothers, daughters, and wives are always potentially explosive. But for an Oedipal disturbance, the most decisive situation is when father and son clash with one another. From the perspective of social theory, things get interesting when multiple sons rise up in revolt against their father. They might do so when they can no longer withstand their ambivalence toward their father and their hatred prevails over their love. This then leads to the father's downfall or death: "United, they [have] the courage to do and [succeed] in doing what would have been impossible for them individually" (SE 13, 141).

How should we assess this uprising in light of the theory of order and disturbance? On the one hand, we can say the sons want to empower themselves and place themselves in their father's position. On the other hand, we can interpret their behavior as a revolt, in that they are rebelling against oppression. Max Horkheimer makes the splendid point that it is not clear whether the sons "pursue power as one pursues loot or criminals."[12] And there is, in fact, a huge difference between someone grabbing power as if it were "loot" and someone attempting to neutralize it as if it were a criminal entity. As we will see, Freud thinks that both interpretations – the appropriation of power as well as its abolition – are conceivable, but he favors the first one. Based on these premises, he derives his approach to the theory of dictatorship and democracy.

As mentioned, Freud sticks with the first interpretation, according to which the disturbance caused by the sons is merely a preamble to the accession of a new ruler. He struggles to view the sons' resistance as an act of emancipation. In his Dostoevsky essay, he writes: "You wanted to kill your father in order to be your father yourself" (SE 21, 185). And in *Totem and Taboo*, the sons' hatred for their father is attributed to the fact that he is an "obstacle to their craving for power" (SE 13, 143), a craving that drives each one of them. Freud points out that a difficult problem arises when power is transferred to the next generation. The sons will initially stick together in pursuit of their common interest, which keeps them united in a cooperative game; but once they succeed – and kill their father – this same interest will "divide" them again (SE 13, 144). This is because each son will be seized by the desire to take power himself. The result is an inheritance dispute, a fight over the line of succession, which ends when a new father figure asserts himself and everyone else must submit to him again. In accordance with this, the sons' commonality in their struggle against their father is also their doom.

In terms of the theory of the troublemaker, it is naturally of critical importance whether, in resisting their father, the sons remain stuck in (egocentric) power interests, or whether they take the second option mentioned above and withdraw from the whole power play. There is an indication in Freud's work that such withdrawal is possible: namely, in the sons' feeling that they are working together to achieve something. This social experience breaks with the dominant strategy of power and impotence described above, which is geared entirely toward the father–son relationship. Such an experience is tied to the moment of the struggle against power – and to the fact that it is declared to be absolute and detached from its pre- and post-history. Then it is not a case of *one* father being eliminated in this moment and replaced by *another*; instead, the father that is eliminated is the *only* father that is even conceivable in this moment.

234

To put it another way, the ambivalent identification in which the sons are trapped – identification following the schema of inferiority and superiority – takes a timeout. The sons lose their ambivalence and no longer view themselves primarily as sons or would-be fathers but rather – as Freud himself says – as individuals borne by "social fraternal feelings" (SE 13, 146). In this interim period they form a "fatherless society" (SE 13, 149), a term coined by Freud that will have far-reaching effects.[13] (We have already encountered fatherlessness and brotherhood – and the associated devaluation of women – in Schiller's *Tell* play, for example.) But Freud does not count on the long-term stability of the "fatherless society"; he views it as an example of a "leaderless" and thus "fleeting" group (SE 18, 93; cf. 83, 85) which will seek a new ruler or someone of "overmastering strength" (SE 13, 144).

Taking these two scenarios together, we can see that Freud clings to the power play between father and son on the one hand, while foreseeing the creation of a "fatherless" world and "fraternal feelings" on the other. It is important to note that he makes liberal use of the vocabulary of political theory to characterize these scenarios. Specifically, he employs two key words: dictatorship and democracy. The "primal father" – and, one might add, the son who replaces him and has "seized all the means to power" – plays the role of the "dictator" (SE 21, 15) for Freud. The sons who abandon the play for power and powerlessness during this timeout wind up forming a "fraternal clan" that practices what Freud refers to as "democratic equality" (SE 13, 148). These words suddenly reveal the political ambition behind Freud's interpretation of the generation game. They become even more weighty when we consider that democracy and dictatorship are referred to rarely and usually only fleetingly in Freud's works. (He mentions the "democratic mode of thinking of Jews" [SE 8, 112], concedes that the Christian church has a "democratic strain" [SE 18, 94], and considers "conservative democracies" to be important opponents of fascism [SE 23, 55]; I will come back to his two important comments on "dictatorship".)

The prospects are not yet all that great for deriving insights into the state of modern society from Freud's thought experiment. His models of dictatorship and democracy seem fairly simple and remain closely tied to familial constellations. But there is more to it than that. Freud uses the dynamics inherent in the Oedipus complex to further refine these political models. He focuses mainly on the dynamic in which the father's domination is contested, broken, and renewed. Freud's important finding here is that even if the son succeeds in murdering his father and taking his place, he will not delight in his victory. Instead, he will find himself in an Oedipal conflict which Freud characterizes using the terms "triumph and mourning" (SE 21, 186). Oedipus must mourn his victory because

235

patricide is an offense not only against his father but also, as Freud sees it, against the part of his ambivalent identity that comprises a subservient admiration for authority or a "longing for the father" (SE 13, 148). He thus injures himself – or a part of himself – by his own hand; to a certain extent, he himself suffers the death he brings about. Therefore, after his crime, he is overcome with "remorse" and "a sense of guilt" (SE 13, 143). These feelings might even precede the crime and prevent him from carrying it out.

The appeal of the notion of setting oneself up as a triumphant ruler thus begins to fade, because the son not only has to bring down his old father and prevail over his brothers; he has to kill his own old ego, which is imbued with a willingness to obey. How can he pull off the feat of toppling the father-tyrant without suffering these disastrous consequences? He can do so by breaking the cycle of this power struggle, by refraining from striking out as Oedipus (a.k.a. "the little savage," a.k.a. the *puer robustus*) and instead installing a "*substitute* for his father" or a "father-surrogate," toward whom he continues to cultivate a submissive attitude (SE 13, 129, 150; cf. SE 18, 137).

The symbol of this new authority, according to Freud, is the "totem" that is reinforced with "taboos." This, as he bluntly declares, is where "human morality has its beginning" (SE 13, 144, cf. 159): "The taboo-observances were the first 'right' or 'law'" (SE 21, 101). The *history* that Freud depicts as a struggle for *power* culminates in the *morality* attributed to the new authority recognized by the collective of sons. This brings an end to the arbitrary rule in which, according to Freud – and Hobbes before him – there are "no judgements of value: no good and evil, no morality" (SE 22, 74).

The development that leads from totem and taboo to morality, right, and law is summed up by Freud in a brief sentence: "The super-ego is the heir of the Oedipus complex and represents the ethical standards of mankind" (SE 20, 59). The super-ego is also referred to as the "depersonalized" father (SE 20, 128). The power to which the individual must submit has not been abolished; it has been neutralized and juridified. With this, the transition from the generation game to the political order is complete.

The violent ruler to whom everyone originally submitted is referred to by Freud – as we have just heard – as a "dictator." If power is preserved in a sublimated form, however, then the political order that arises from the Oedipus complex must still have the characteristics of a dictatorship. The father is dead, but he has also triumphed. Freud does, in fact, return to the concept of "dictatorship" in connection with higher cultural development. He does so at a politically charged point in time. In 1933, Freud wrote to Albert Einstein: "The ideal condition of things would of course

236

be a community of men who had subordinated their instinctual life to the dictatorship of reason" (SE 22, 213). In his *New Introductory Lectures on Psycho-Analysis* from the same year, he wrote:

> On the other hand intellect – or let us call it by the name that is familiar to us, reason – is among the powers which we may most expect to exercise a unifying influence on men – on men who are held together with such difficulty and whom it is therefore scarcely possible to rule. It may be imagined how impossible human society would be, merely if everyone had his own multiplication table and his own private units of length and weight. Our best hope for the future is that intellect – the scientific spirit, reason – may in process of time establish a dictatorship in the mental life of man. [. . .] The common compulsion exercised by such a dominance of reason will prove to be the strongest uniting bond among men [. . .]. (SE 22, 171)

Incidentally, the phrase "dictatorship of reason" was used by various authors even before Freud, including Carl Schmitt, Heinrich Mann, Joseph Roth, and Hans Kelsen.[14] In Freud's work, it refers to the idea that the "strongest bond" (see above) that connects people is diverted, as it were, through a role installed above them as a higher authority. It represents a compulsion that has become "rational," one which does not confront people externally but is instead internalized or assimilated by them. What this means is that the dictatorship is actually exercised by the people themselves.

This idea fits perfectly with political philosophy before 1800.[15] Freud brings us back to Rousseau's thesis that the individual is both his own "sovereign" (Freud would say "dictator") and his own "subject." "If we must be ruled, then we only want to be ruled by ourselves," writes Freud's conversational partner, Hans Kelsen, describing Rousseau's position in a nutshell.[16] Immanuel Kant directly anticipates Freud's idea when he bases sovereignty not on the will, as Rousseau does, but on reason, which is supposed to rule over nature – even one's own: "If he lives among others of his own species, man is *an animal who needs a master.*"[17] According to Kant's famous dictum, even "a nation of devils (so long as they possess understanding)" is capable of "setting up a state."[18] The dictatorship of reason is directed both inwards and outwards. It represents both the self-mastery of each individual and the mastery of everyone who steps out of line. In both cases, it is the "little savage" who must be subdued.

There is a small caveat here, however, because Freud advises a certain degree of restraint in the dictatorship he proposes. "Reason" must also be capable of "giv[ing] man's emotional impulses [. . .] the position they deserve" (SE 22, 171). If it fails in this, then it will wind up exercising a form of self- and external control that gives the super-ego "sadistic" traits (SE 21, 136, cf. 185). If we attempt to strengthen our understanding of and respect for emotions, we are led – once again, in the context of eighteenth-century political philosophy – to the objections that Friedrich Schiller raised against Kant. What Freud calls a "dictatorship of reason," Schiller calls a "monarchy of reason."[19] If this monarchy lacks the necessary restraint, Schiller says it will "[hold] in hand all free movement," exercise "violence against our drives," "destroy" our "feelings", and solidify itself in a "state" that wants to "crush under foot such a hostile individuality."[20]

At this point, it becomes clear why a schism developed in the reception of Freud, dividing his interpreters into a right-leaning and left-leaning faction. The right-leaning faction focuses – roughly speaking – on the development of the super-ego, which represents social rules, and that of the ego, which consciously adopts these rules as its own. The left-leaning faction emphasizes – roughly speaking – the repressive traits of the "dictatorship of reason" and wants to bring imagination to power.

I do not want to align myself with either of these interpretations, as they are both founded on a blinkered assumption. Both factions base their arguments on a contrast between control mechanisms on one side and instinctive life on the other. Following this template, the only social relationships that receive attention are those that are organized *vertically*. The focus narrows to the individual who either complies with the social rules *or* breaks with them. There is no doubt that Freud himself suggests such a narrowing of focus; his work is pervaded by comments that support this vertical or hierarchical interpretation. "Everything [is] the father–son relationship" – this sentence is spoken by a fictional interlocutor, whom Freud does not contradict (SE 21, 22). And yet, he strikes different tones as well. It is time to give them a hearing, and when we do, the (tyrannical or rational) dictatorship will be joined again by democracy, which thus far has flickered to life only in a brief moment of "fraternal feelings."

In his letter to Einstein entitled "Why War?", Freud uses the vertical schema of the "dictatorship of reason," which he says could "unite" people "even if there were no emotional ties between them" (SE 22, 213). Following this argument, horizontal relationships are dispensable. But there is an important addendum to this thesis:

> The community must be maintained permanently, must be organized, must draw up regulations to anticipate the risk of rebellion and must institute authorities to see that those regulations – the laws – are respected and to superintend the execution of legal acts of violence. The recognition of a community of interests such as these leads to the growth of emotional ties between the members of the united group of

people – communal feelings which are the true source of its strength. (SE 22, 205)

With this statement, Freud intellectually teeters on the brink. While he says that political unity derives from individual interests in the legal order, he also believes the "true strength" of this collective lies in the "emotional ties" that come to life within it. If we lean toward the second part of this argument, we move away from the vertical interpretation of social relationships to which Freud's model – as depicted thus far – is indebted.

Freud himself acknowledges that there is an entire spectrum of "emotional ties" that "operate against" aggression and ultimately even war. First, he mentions "relations [...] towards a loved object," which can exist without a "sexual aim" and thus without the associated claims to ownership and competition. And second, he mentions the "emotional tie" as a "means of identification." This is followed by a decisive sentence: "Whatever leads men to share important interests produces this community of feeling, these identifications. And the structure of human society is to a large extent based on them" (SE 22, 212). He is no longer talking about ties that gear individuals toward a higher authority, but about forms of communal relationships that are structured horizontally.

In psychoanalysis, "identification" is clearly defined as the "earliest expression of an emotional tie with another person," one which "plays a part in the early history of the Oedipus complex" (SE 18, 105), meaning that it does not emerge from this complex but precedes it. When Freud emphasizes that such "identifications" or a "community of feeling" are important to the "structure of human society," he holds out the encouraging prospect that social relations and the political order based on them are not necessarily bound to the logic of domination and rebellion that characterizes the Oedipal conflict. Instead, these relations are distinguished by a quality that Freud refers to with the momentous phrase "democratic equality." Independent of Freud, Albert Ogien and Sandra Laugier say: "The spirit of true democracy [...] is that of horizontality."[21]

The fact that identification is categorized as a pre-Oedipal phenomenon arouses the suspicion that we are dealing with undifferentiated early-childhood impulses that have little bearing on political questions. We might think of vague feelings of community as subsequent forms of pre-Oedipal identification and thus defer to Freud's recommendation that they be overcome by means of Oedipal logic. But this would be too easy.[22] When a sense of identification develops in social life, it not *only* leads to sinister phenomena, it also evolves into a wide range of vital relations. At this point we have to turn Freud against himself, since he remarks once in passing: "In the individual's mental life someone else is

239

invariably involved, as a model, as an object, as a helper, as an opponent" (SE 18, 69). In light of this range of vertical as well as horizontal relations, we have to ask: should all of these roles that the Other can play be shoved into the Oedipal drawer? The answer is no.

It is necessary to leave Freud for a moment and survey the repertoire of social relations in which people relate to one another in an identifying way – that is, in which the Oedipal hierarchy does not come into play. The defining feature of these relations must be that they are immune to turning into competitive relationships in which there are, in the end, only winners and losers, rulers and the ruled.

We can distinguish between two types of identification that meet this requirement. The first represents a relationship between people in which there is no object of desire (a commodity, a third person, etc.) that could become a reason for dispute. This identification contents and fulfills itself with the shared experience of commonality. The second type of identification focuses on relationships in which different people do relate to a single object, but they are free of exclusive claims to ownership. I refer to these two types – as mentioned earlier in the chapter on Rousseau – as *sympathetic* and *synergetic* forms of identification.[23] In the former case, the focus is on a shared feeling or a shared landscape (*pathè*), while identification in the latter case refers to a shared task or shared work (*ergon*). I want to explain these two types in more detail and show that Freud is prepared to accept the existence of these phenomena, although he does not give them the attention they deserve.

The classic definition of *sympathetic* identification was formulated in the Scottish moral philosophy of the eighteenth century. Adam Smith interprets "sympathy" – which goes beyond "pity" – to be every form of emotional accord. This "fellow-feeling" involves responding to the experience of others and sharing their joy or pain.[24] Although Freud does not address this philosophical interpretation of sympathy, it is an important template for his theory of identification. Gabriel Tarde pushes sympathy closer to Freud when, in *The Laws of Imitation*, he invokes Smith and attributes imitation to sympathy, which he calls the "primary source of sociability."[25] Freud then invokes Tarde, but he unfortunately ignores Tarde's reference to sympathy and instead subordinates imitation to the Oedipal dynamic (SE 18, 88). Freud views sympathy only as a mechanical reaction that steers behavior in a collective and is defined – as he says, quoting McDougall – by the "principle of direct induction of emotion by way of the primitive sympathetic response" (SE 18, 84).

Freud certainly has opportunities to expand his narrow view of sympathy, but he lets them pass him by. For example, in a letter to Freud from November 9, 1912, Lou Andreas-Salomé talks of a "demand for sympathy" on the part of the individual, the frustration of which is a cause of neurotic behavior. Andreas-Salomé systematically outlined her thoughts on the "expression of sympathy" and the "demand for devotion" in an important *Imago* essay from 1914, but Freud never responded to it.[26]

Incidentally – or perhaps not so incidentally at all! – it must be said that the entire discourse on sympathy ranging from Adam Smith through Georg Simmel to Lou Andreas-Salomé is tied up with the gender-based theory that women are sympathetic beings. When it comes to sympathy as identification, the situation that fits best in Freud's repertoire is one that Smith mentions as a paradigmatic case of sympathy, namely, the relationship between mother and child.[27] In Freud's work this appears only as the relationship between "mother and son," in which an "unchangeable affection, unimpaired by any egoistic considerations" is acted out (SE 15, 206; cf. SE 21, 113).

Mothers in particular and women in general are depicted by Freud only as objects of desire, not as subjects in relationships. Freud holds fast to this discrimination, even when he admits that a woman's "passive" behavior is probably due to the "influence of social customs" (SE 22, 116). Freud's apostate disciple Otto Rank noted critically that a "state system administered by men" is aimed at "the ever wider exclusion of woman."[28] Since Freud cements this exclusion in his Oedipal model of society, he is not interested in exploring the continued male *and* female existence of these early "identifications" and unegotistical relations in social and political life as a whole. All the same, Freud's invocation (as impassioned as it is vague) of an "eternal Eros" that could satisfy humanity's "communal life" should be interpreted as a kind of want ad aimed at sympathetic identification (SE 21, 145).

Synergetic identification, unlike sympathy, has received scant philosophical attention, but it has been addressed recently – without being mentioned by name – in debates about collective intentionality. Synergy is established when people join forces in relation to a common cause. They pull together (in the same direction!) and pursue a shared goal. They are all *at work* together. (Marx's theory of "community" is based on this very synergy.) While sympathy is intransitive, synergy is transitive. Unlike sympathy, synergy can only be comprehended by talking about the goals and aims that people set in their actions. Smith's fine talk of "fellow-feeling" can easily be reinterpreted to fit with synergy. Disastrous competition is avoided here as long as these goals *can* only be pursued communally or people only *want* to enjoy them communally. Certain games can only be played together, and some experiences have to be shared with others. "'I' that is 'We' and 'We' that is 'I'" – this expression from Hegel is the motto of synergy (PS 110).[29] Synergetic relations are also underestimated by Freud – but they are not ignored. Synergy as a form of identification corresponds with the "community of feeling"

241

(SE 18, 91) and "democratic equality" (SE 13, 148) in Freud's repertoire, which distinguish the band of brothers in the moment this band ceases to (once again) be torn apart by internal conflicts.

The similarities and differences between sympathetic and synergetic relationships must be explored in more detail, though it is beyond my scope to do so here. Such an exploration would revolve around the relationship between the theory of sympathy, which was developed primarily by Scottish moral philosophers, and the concepts of brotherhood and solidarity that evolved in the late eighteenth and the nineteenth century.[30]

One might argue that the potential of non-Oedipal identifications and communal relationships should not be overestimated. Experiences of sympathy or synergy can be undermined by competition and power plays. I certainly do not want to deny this – on the contrary, I want to emphasize it. But this does not invalidate the forms of identification described above, it simply reveals that they are part of a person's inherently contradictory social repertoire, which is put to use in the charged relationship between order and disturbance.

One thing is absolutely clear: Freud's Oedipus complex does *not* encompass the entire spectrum of social dynamics, in which history, power, and morality – or, in Freud's particular case, the progression of generations and the political order – relate to one another.[31] Freud offers only an incomplete description of this dynamic, which I am tracing in this book by following the thread of the *puer robustus*. Not only is his model the product of an age in which the dominance of private and political patriarchy was reaching its limit, it is also fixated on the logic of domination and subjection and on the man as the ruling power.

Freud's social psychology leads to a main peak and a secondary peak, as it were. The main peak is the idea of the "dictatorship of reason," in which people themselves authorize the entity to whom they submit. After Oedipus initially appears as the troublemaker who wants to topple the ruler and take his place, despotic rule is transformed into the rule of law, a state in which the nomocentric troublemaker both proves and abolishes himself. This model is limited by its fixation on hierarchical, vertical relations in which the "ego" has more to do with the "super-ego" than with another "ego."

But this main peak hides a secondary peak, which Freud refers to only briefly, and even snidely. The "democratic equality" that has already been mentioned multiple times hints at an alternative to the "dictatorship of reason." It brings into play a horizontal interaction in which the ego relates to others on an equal level.[32] This does not yet represent an independent model of political order, but it does prevent the "dictatorship of reason" from solidifying into a closed world. To put it another way, this is what makes the "dictatorship of reason" into – a democracy.

The political order is drawn into a process in which power positions are reshuffled and the hierarchies themselves are undermined, creating room for a wide scope of action. This brings the troublemaker back onto the scene.

The thesis I want to pin down here is that the task of political theory is not to *choose* between vertical hierarchy and horizontal equality but to make this highly charged relationship *productive*. Freud refrains from doing this. Starting from his systematic premise that the Oedipus complex monopolizes social relations, he outlines a hierarchical political order that, with a stroke of luck, will be a dictatorship of reason. The greatness and the limitation of his work is that he held on to this systematic premise with all of his might. Freud's Oedipus interpretation bears a close factual connection to other versions of the *puer robustus*; I want to reveal this connection by briefly looking back at these other versions.

Hobbes/Freud. The "super-ego" that demands compliance and must take non-compliance into account fits with Hobbes's finding that the disciplinary power of the state will face individuals who are contemplating ruthlessness. Freud writes:

> There are countless civilized people who would shrink from murder or incest but who do not deny themselves the satisfaction of their avarice, their aggressive urges or their sexual lusts, and who do not hesitate to injure other people by lies, fraud and calumny, so long as they can remain unpunished for it. (SE 21, 12)

Freud's social psychology not only serves as a travel guide through the "dark continent" (SE 20, 212) of the subconscious; it is also a road map through the centers of power of bourgeois society, which are teeming with the revenants of the *puer robustus* whom Hobbes wanted to bring under control.

Rousseau/Freud. I have already pointed out that the structure of Rousseau's social contract, in which the citizen is both sovereign and subject at the same time, anticipates Freud's theory of domination as self-mastery. But Rousseau not only banks on vertical self-rule for his theory of communal life, he also mobilizes the sympathetic and synergetic potential that Freud acknowledges only in passing. The ability of the *puer robustus* to harmonize desire and reality, which Rousseau praises, anticipates the balance between the pleasure principle and the reality principle as outlined by Freud.

Diderot/Freud. Since Diderot's *puer robustus* – i.e., Rameau's nephew – serves as a model for Freud's Oedipus, their relationship is naturally particularly close. From Freud's perspective, the nephew expertly navigates the border between neurotic and aesthetic fantasy. Conversely, when Diderot (like Hegel) targets the normality of the *espèce*, he is taking aim at figures who reappear in Freud's work in the form of compulsive characters, and who do not just follow rules but submit to them in a "masochistic" way (SE 21, 136). To use a peculiar phrase from Freud, they are guided not by morality but by an *Übermoral* or "excessive morality" (SE 13, 160).

Hugo/Freud. Hugo's novel *Notre-Dame de Paris* is a rich source of material for psychoanalytic theory. The struggle between the bestial yet deeply humane Quasimodo, the intellectual and sadistic Frollo, and Esmeralda, the beautiful wild girl and compassionate mother-woman, plays out in Freud's Oedipal triangle. But it ultimately moves beyond this Oepidal constellation, because the deaf Quasimodo pricks up his ears (so to speak) just when Freud's attention lapses: namely, when sympathy enters the picture. Instead of being merely an object of psychoanalytic study, Hugo's hero becomes a good student of Rousseau.

Tocqueville/Freud. Since Tocqueville's *puer robustus* takes the form of an American pioneer, among other things, it makes sense to mention Freud's dismissive judgment of America,[33] where he thought the super-ego was being dismantled, resulting in "damage to civilization" (SE 21, 116). According to Freud's interpretation, which was picked up by other authors,[34] defiance of authority in the USA (not just among the pioneers) was developing into a mass phenomenon. Freud's biting commentary certainly does not do justice to the emancipatory desire for liberty in the USA, but it does accurately describe the narcissistic smugness found there, which brings the Oedipal game to an end.[35] Instead of rubbing up against others and rising to challenges, people suffice themselves, do whatever they want, and think they're great. (One politician who has perfected this narcissistic model of behavior is Donald Trump.)

Marx/Freud. Freud (unlike his disciple Paul Federn, whom I will discuss in a moment) does not concern himself with the question of whether the proletarian revolution can be interpreted as an Oedipal bid for liberation. But he does stress that those who are disenfranchised cannot be expected to comply with the law. He therefore opposes not the "great animal" of the proletariat – as one might expect in light of his conservative concept of civilization – but the ruling class of exploiters:

> If, however, a culture has not got beyond a point at which the satisfaction of one portion of its participants depends upon the suppression of another, and perhaps larger, portion [...] it is understandable that the suppressed people should develop an intense hostility towards a culture whose existence they make possible by their work [...]. It goes without saying that a civilization which leaves so large a number of its participants unsatisfied and drives them into revolt neither has nor deserves the prospect of a lasting existence. (SE 21, 12)

Freud is not far removed from the proletarian *puer robustus* of Marx and Engels when he expresses an understanding for why "suppressed people" would revolt against this so-called "civilization."

Having compared Freud with the other authors examined in this book, one could also ask whether Freud is perhaps not just the father-figure of psychoanalysis but also a *puer robustus* himself.[36] But I now want to look beyond Freud as a person and turn to the early reception of his works, when other writers tried to put more of a political spin on this thinking.

3. Politics after Freud: A debate between Walter Lippmann, Paul Federn, Hans Blüher, Thomas Mann, and Hans Kelsen

Freud's followers and contemporaries pulled his theory into the political struggles of their time and argued about the lessons that could be taken from them for dealing with order and disturbance. The field of tension between dictatorship and democracy that Freud opened up in his own unique way became perilously relevant in the first decades of the twentieth century. The debate about Freud, which expanded into a political debate, revolves around questions that can be easily classified – because Freud leaves nothing to be desired when it comes to the clarity of his premises.

To put it briefly, Freud uses one exclamation mark and one question mark. He places a large exclamation mark over the political hierarchy that grows out of the Oedipus complex. He calls upon readers to tolerate the ambivalence of this hierarchy, i.e., to think of the urge to rule and to submit as two sides of same coin and, ideally, to reconcile them through self-mastery. But he adds a small question mark as well: Is there a form of social life and politics that cuts across this hierarchy? Along with the vertical father–son axis, is there a horizontal axis of "fraternal feelings" or "love"?

Freud's two premises delineate the field in which his followers and contemporaries move. If they stick with the Oedipal model, they have to grapple with the question of how to approach the hierarchy built into it. Do they tolerate its ambivalence, or do they escalate its inherent conflict and turn it into a fight for or against authority? If, however, they stick with the question mark that Freud himself places after his model, they will want to assert claims to equality and communality in political life. Each route gives rise to different approaches to understanding disturbances. In accordance with Oedipal logic, disturbances are bound tightly to the struggle for power. But following the thread of "fraternal feelings," they promise an escape from Oedipal logic. I want to show how thinkers responded to Freud's two premises in this debate by looking at Walter Lippmann, Paul Federn, Hans Blüher, Thomas Mann, and Hans Kelsen.

Walter Lippmann. In the course of his long life, which lasted from 1889 to 1974, Lippmann played a wide variety of roles. He started out as an enthusiastic reader of Henri Bergson and Sigmund Freud, worked for US president Woodrow Wilson as a young man, and later invented the concept of "public opinion" and helped usher into the world the school of "neoliberalism" at a famous colloquium in Paris in 1938.[37] But in Richard Sennett's book *The Corrosion of Character*, he was posthumously crowned an opponent of the neoliberal destruction of the community.[38] He is considered one of the most influential American commentators of the twentieth century.

The young Lippmann, who is the sole focus of our discussion here, was captivated by the philosophy of life and psychoanalysis. Thanks to his German background, he had no difficulty immediately reading Freud's latest publications in the original language, and he did not hesitate to apply Freud's theses to the current situation in the USA. His debut book, *A Preface to Politics* from 1913, received a positive review in *Imago*, in the same issue that featured the final section of Freud's work *Totem and Taboo*. "The book," wrote Ernest Jones, who would later be Freud's biographer, "can be recommended wholeheartedly as an impressive attempt to apply modern psychological insight and intuition to the problems of sociology and statecraft."[39]

In this book, Lippmann picks up on Freud's theory of taboo and complains that American society is dominated by "routineers" who cling "in a panic" to "taboo" as a "merely negative law."[40] But this law does not fit with a democratic society, "for the more self-governing a people becomes, the less possible it is to prescribe external restrictions." Lippmann notes with satisfaction that "the sterile tyranny of the taboo" had already contracted its "final illness."[41] This opens up the prospect of a radical questioning of hierarchies. "The American dream," Lippmann wrote in 1914, "may be summed up, I think, in the statement that the undisciplined man is the salt of the earth."[42] (This is a thinly veiled quote from Mill, and it inevitably brings to mind Diderot's remark that Rameau's nephew was like a "pinch of yeast" that set society in motion.)

The question of how Lippmann deals with Freud's premises is easy to answer. He sticks to the Oedipal opposition introduced by Freud, but he resolves the ambivalence envisaged within it. He comes down on the side of the younger generation and celebrates the "effervescence" of the young men who launch an attack on the moribund political order.[43] In essence, Lippmann provides nothing short of a characterization of the *puer robustus*. "The institutions of the past" against which such men fight, according to Lippmann, "are like the fresh eggs of the past – good while they are fresh."[44]

The fight against taboo institutions is, as Lippmann says with reference to William James, the "moral equivalent of war." What he means is that martial desires are redirected toward a valuable new task: storming the bastions of tradition. "Hardihood" is required here, and any trace of "feminism" is disruptive.[45] The Oedipal attitude of Lippmann's young men is apparent only in their fight against paternal authorities, not – as is the case with Freud – in their competition for women as sexual objects. In his later books, incidentally, Lippmann would mitigate this male narrow-mindedness and declare the emancipation of women to be a critical component of his political program.[46]

Is there a political order that would appeal to this martial youth? Lippmann does not bank on the Kantian, Freudian model of a dictator-ship of reason – and he takes exception to American democracy, which he believes had been so closely tied to institutions by the Founding Fathers that it was deaf to the young people's call for change: "Had they written the Constitution in the fire of their youth, they might have made it more democratic." Lippmann wants to make politics "alert to a process of continual creation, an unceasing invention of forms to meet constantly changing needs."[47]

He hints at a shift here from the vertical to the horizontal, which would transform the Oedipal fight against taboo into a communal project dedi-cated to the permanent restructuring of the democratic order. But unfor-tunately, Lippmann never really moves beyond the battle between the young savages and the status quo. He is content merely to release natural "impulses, cravings and wants" to stimulate politics. "Like dynamite," however, these "energies of the soul" are "capable of all sorts of uses."[48]

Lippmann foresees the emergence of various dissenters and disrup-tors, not all of whom he wants to endorse. Along with heroic democrats there are, as he complains, radical workers who commit "terrorism," "insurrectionists," "marauding bands," etc. All the same, Lippmann praises Karl Marx for having imposed a strict organizational structure on actionism.[49] In any case, Lippmann remains fixated on the lower half of the Oedipal constellation, where he finds the taboo-breaker (or good *puer robustus*) on one side and the terrorist (or evil *puer robustus*) on the other. How a state can be made from this is beyond him.

Lippmann's Oedipal revolt was short-lived. In his very next book, *Drift and Mastery* from 1914, he distanced himself from "chronic rebellion,"[50] and in *A Preface to Morals* from 1929 he countered the creative man of nature, the hero of his earlier model, with the ideal of "maturity."[51] (In a way, he was converted by Tocqueville.) Although the political references to Bergson's "creative evolution" and Freud's Oedipus appear clumsy and generalized in Lippmann's first book, they deserve attention. His concept of the Oedipal struggle for liberation is not only a precise, one-sided reac-tion to Freud's interpretation of politics as a generation game, it is also a way of approaching the point at which influential theories of politics in the twentieth century part ways. On the one hand, Lippmann's critique of the government machine has been picked up by all those who want to liberate individuals through maximum deregulation and the dismantling of institutions. It is fitting, in this regard, that in 1938 Lippmann presented himself as an advocate of economic liberalism. On the other hand, the motifs introduced by the young Lippmann reappear in the works of political theorists who couple a critique of institutions to the participation of individuals in a "strong democracy."[52]

Paul Federn. Of all the early, politically engaged followers of Freud, Paul Federn (1871–1950) particularly stands out. In his paper *On the Psychology of Revolution: The Fatherless Society* from 1919, he throws the caution of his teacher – the "greatest psychologist"[53] – overboard and interprets the revolutionary activities after the end of World War I as a promising step toward a "fatherless society." Federn takes his key phrase from Freud's *Totem and Taboo*, though without explicitly mentioning this.

Federn starts with Freud's *first premise*, according to which the father–son relationship and the institutions derived from it establish a hierarchy that brings with it an irresolvable, inevitable ambivalence between power and submission. Like Lippmann (to whom he does not refer, however), Federn cannot tolerate this ambivalence in the Oedipal constellation. Instead, he welcomes the downfall of the father, the "sudden collapse of all state authorities" after the end of the world war.[54] Like Lippmann, Federn restricts himself in his analysis of the Oedipal constellation to the relationship with the paternal authority; the role of the mother, or the relationship between men and women in general, remains unexplored. He sticks closer to Freud than Lippmann does, however, and finds traces of the ambivalence highlighted by his teacher even among revolutionaries. After successfully toppling their father, they seem disoriented and overcome by "inner confusion." Their old "feelings of reverence for the state order" are initially replaced solely by a new "wrong way" of living.[55]

In Federn's work, the different versions of the *puer robustus* appear in the guise of good and bad revolutionaries. The "*destructive* tendencies of revolution" are apparent above all in the "gigantic strikes" which, according to Federn, are nothing more than an expression of a rejectionist attitude. For Federn, these strikes – along with the "terror" he considers to be a "sign of weakness" – reflect a negative fixation on paternal authority.[56] It is notable that Freud also emphasizes the destructive tendencies of revolution in his sole reference to Federn's *The Fatherless Society* (SE 18, 98).

But Federn does not want to accept the continued existence of "parricidal" obsessions.[57] To counter them, he calls for good revolutionaries to escape the disastrous tension between authority and anti-authoritarian rebellion. This is when he turns to Freud's *second premise*. His critique of a political hierarchy shaped by the Oedipus complex is linked to the search for a power that can "work against the effect of the father–son configuration." Federn throws to the wind his teacher's warning against the unreliability of the "fraternal community" and claims that it is "progression to move from the fatherlessness of society to the principle of brotherhood."[58] According to Federn, the socialist "councils organization" breaks with the logic of the "patriarchal order" and leaves behind both revolutionary patricide and the accompanying desire for a father. Federn welcomes "fatherless fellows" as representatives of a new political order[59] in which – as he dramatically puts it – "the soul of humanity [. . .] might become a more beautiful one." This "new state" is supported by the "strength of the need for union among peers who are of like disposition or like mind" and by a "mutual, continual consensus."[60] The foundation of this "restless, 'fatherless society'"[61] is a distant but extremely worthwhile goal from Federn's point of view.

As I see it, Federn's deviation from Freud is systematically productive in that he reevaluates the forms of communal relationship that Freud himself treated rather shabbily: the "group spirit" or "democratic equality" of brothers. While the Oedipal hierarchy is unilaterally dominant in Freud's work, Federn makes the opposite mistake of turning the horizontal order of the "fatherless society" into an absolute. He does not want to mobilize and dynamize the generation game – as does Lippmann; he wants to neutralize it. The sons are reinterpreted as brothers who are actually no longer allowed to have a father. (Schiller's problem returns here.)

Hans Blüher. If Walter Lippmann and Paul Federn can be considered unofficial members of the youth movement, Hans Blüher (1888–1955) is one of its spokespeople. To call him a colorful figure would be an extreme understatement.[62] Like Lippmann's *A Preface to Politics* and Federn's *Psychology of Revolution*, Blüher's *The Role of Eroticism in Masculine Society* received a positive review in Freud's journal *Imago*.[63] Like Lippmann and Federn, Blüher rejects Freud's *first premise* – the inescapable ambivalence of the Oedipal constellation – and comes down unilaterally on the side of the younger generation. "The youth have lost faith in the generation of their fathers and teachers," Blüher noted, and he joined the front line in "the struggle of youth against age."[64]

Blüher had the opportunity to look critically at the "*Oedipus situation*" in the journal *Imago*, and unlike Lippmann and Federn, he stood by Freud's full description of the triangular relationship between father, mother, and child. The (implicitly male!) "youth" not only confront their father, they also become acquainted with the "*feeling of matrimony*" in "their own nursery."[65] As long as youngsters are trapped in the fight

249

against their fathers, they inevitably remain fixated on the woman and mother who belongs to this father. As a result, the youngsters focus their attention on the opposite sex and become susceptible to the seductions of women. According to Blüher's peculiarly militaristic scenario, society faces the threat of an "invasion of women," "*invasion of girls*," or "occupation by girls."[66]

Blüher does not just want to tip the balance in the Oedipal constellation in favor of the younger generation, he ultimately wants to do away with the whole model. This means that the struggle against the father must culminate in "indifference"[67] toward him – and that, through radical "anti-feminism,"[68] man must also rid himself of the woman upon whom he remains sexually dependent in the Oedipus complex. "Woe betide the man who succumbed to a woman!" Blüher wails. His verdict: "Woman did not invent the state," she aspires "only to family."[69]

It is inevitable, therefore, that Blüher would embrace Freud's *second premise*: the community of brothers. While Freud foresees a quick end to this community, Blüher must stabilize it to prevent the brothers from remaining trapped in their desire for a father and divided by their competition for women. The brothers can only escape both the father *and* the woman, according to Blüher, by taking their cue from a reference made by Freud himself in *Totem and Taboo*: the reference to the "homosexual feelings and acts" that occur in "bands of males" (SE 13, 144, 141). This point is also mentioned in correspondence exchanged between Freud and Blüher.[70] Blüher's position is already so extreme that it is impossible to escalate it any further. According to him, the only future for politics is with homosexuals, as only with homosexuals can politics succeed as an "*attempt to break through the system of age groups*," i.e., the generation game.[71] In place of the *puer robustus*, we find a homoerotic youth.

While the father figure becomes superfluous for Federn because the brothers join together in political solidarity, this figure is forgotten altogether for Blüher because a *Männerbund* (male association) forms instead. Blüher considers this special form of "man-manly" eroticism to be the condition for the possibility of politics as a "principle of association" that "*goes beyond the family.*"[72] One of Blüher's most influential sentences is: "There is *one* great Eros that rushes deep beneath the human state."[73] Thomas Mann will pick up this idea – as we will soon see.

In connection with this, Blüher harks back to Heinrich Schurtz's ethnological study on *Age Groups and Male Associations*, which received a good deal of attention in its time. He rhapsodizes about the "house of men" in which "the political intellectuality of the male sex" would come to light through public deliberation.[74] It almost sounds as though Blüher were thinking of a republican assembly here. But he firmly rejects the idea that the male association is "democratic" and aims instead at a very

different concept of politics. The state that accompanies the male association must be a place of total fusion, of an "ecstatic or solemn event." This
is the only way it can assert itself against the "bourgeois character" of
the individual and the family man.[75] Instead of ambivalence, instead of a
back and forth between power and impotence, rule and riot, assimilation
and aberrance, Blüher envisages a community in which closure becomes
an exhilarating feeling.

When this fusion is total, then everyone speaks with one voice, but
there is one who speaks the loudest, as it were. This person absolutely
must not be a father, not even a "better kind of father,"[76] but instead
someone who presents himself as a "male hero" and "leader." The connection with this leader should be free of the ambivalence inherent in
the relationship with a father. "To be a people means: to follow," Blüher
says – but the leader is one of us.[77] What we are faced with here is a form
of association that could be described as a bad version of "pre-Oedipal"
identification – and Adorno described it in just this way: as "malicious"
or "repressive egalitarianism."[78] For Blüher, collective identity emerges
not in a positive way through the exploration of commonalities, but in
a negative way through the exclusion of those who are considered alien.
This is apparent everywhere we look: in his antisemitic diatribes,[79] his
discrimination against the relationship between man and woman, etc.
The identification underlying the fusion of the male association has
violent tendencies.

All the same, it is not enough merely to shake our heads at Blüher.
He is a product of the collapse of the generation game in Germany
around 1900, and motifs from his work crop up wherever this game
grinds to a halt. The lasting impact of Blüher's ideas can be seen not
only in the variety of male associations in Weimar and Nazi Germany,
but also in some peer groups from more recent times who seek salvation
in self-imposed isolation.[80] Above all, Blüher's peculiar position serves
as a distorting mirror that reveals the systematic problems with Freud.
Because Freud neglects "social fraternal feelings" due to his fixation on
the Oedipal constellation, and because he does not explain "democratic
equality" in any detail, Blüher has an easy job of reinterpreting these
"fraternal feelings" in his own way and, ultimately, straying down a path
toward "man-manly" synchronization. A father is no longer conceivable
here, but neither is a fight about rules or regulations, nor a debate about a
common cause. The path leading from Blüher to fascism is short – all too
short.[81] But this is not the only direction in which his ideas lead.

Thomas Mann. As stated earlier, there is much to be said for shoving
Blüher into a historical cabinet of curiosities. But we should resist
this temptation, not least because Blüher inspired Thomas Mann to
write a key line in his speech "On the German Republic" from 1922,

in which the 47-year-old Mann initiated his late political turn toward democracy. This sentence reads: "Eros as statesman, even as a creator of states, is an old, trusted idea, which in our times has recently been skillfully advocated anew."[82] If Mann had inserted a footnote here, it would have referred to the line from Blüher that was mentioned earlier: "There is one great Eros that rushes deep beneath the human state." This also brings us back around to Freud, who invokes "Eros, which holds together everything in the world," without any sexual limitation, as a force for understanding and peace between people (SE 18, 92; cf. SE 21, 145; SE 22, 212). In Thomas Mann's essay for Freud's 70th birthday in 1929, this "Eros" plays a key role – a fact that Freud registers with some discomfort.[83]

This is an indication of how Thomas Mann relates to Freud. He leaves aside the inner ambivalence of the Oedipal generation game, or so it seems, and tries to make the political order (democracy, in this case!) independent of it. Mann does not abide by Freud's *first premise* of rational self-mastery, but rather by his *second premise*, and he tries to make "Eros" socially acceptable, as it were. While in 1923 Heinrich Mann was defending the "dictatorship of reason," analogous to Freud's hierarchical model, his brother was advocating the opposite model at almost exactly the same time.

It is a bit perilous for Thomas Mann to refer not directly to Freud but rather to Blüher's "great Eros," because in doing so he lands himself with the model of a male association that wants to be everything imaginable – just not "democratic." What Mann means in 1922 when he talks about a democratic Eros – essentially contradicting Blüher – can only be understood in contrast to the earlier position he took in his *Reflections of a Nonpolitical Man* from 1918.

In this earlier book, Thomas Mann stays in Bühler's neighborhood, at least in terms of his critique of democracy. Although he ascribes erotic associations to democracy, he says democracy is – to put it briefly – dominated by a false Eros, namely, that of woman: "What would a humanity be that had lost its *masculine* component?" Mann asks rhetorically. And: "One hardly understands democracy if one does not understand its feminine touch."[84] This is obviously not meant as a compliment; it is meant as a reproach – as an objection to any effeminacy and to the loss of a willingness to defend and sacrifice oneself. For the Thomas Mann of 1918, this feminine democracy has "something un-German, anti-German" about it: "Away, then, with the alien and repulsive slogan, 'democratic!' [. . .] Germany as a *republic*, as a virtue-state with a social contract [. . .] – this would be a fright!"[85] Turning away from women, from feminized men and from "merchants and literati" entails turning toward the world of the "warrior."[86]

When Thomas Mann read the recently published second volume of Blüher's *The Role of Eroticism in Male Society* in 1919, he noted: "As for myself there is no doubt in my mind that 'even' the *Betrachtungen* [*Reflections*] are an expression of my sexual inversion."[87] (In Blüher's work, "inversion" stands for homosexuality.) The politics that Mann maps out in his *Reflections* is thus erotically charged – not feminine, like democracy, but (to use Blüher's term), man-manly.

In 1922, Mann revised his judgment of democracy and also changed its gender-based, erotic coding. It is not that he suddenly approved of the democracy he had previously considered a feminized, unheroic political order. Instead, his advocacy relates more to a democracy that is connected with masculine eros. It is only because Mann can cling to this eros and apply it to democracy[88] that he makes such a decisive case for the republic. He rejects as "nonsense" the notion that "Eros as statesman" can only be effective in a system under a single leader, as Blüher claims.[89] According to Mann's new interpretation of it, eros can also – and especially – live in a democracy in which liberty stands not only for hierarchical self-mastery but for free discourse among equals, for the pleasure taken in others, and for mutual exchange.

This changes what Thomas Mann could offer the *puer robustus* – if he made reference to him. The role of the fiend or obstructionist who refuses to submit is no longer the only role open to him. The *puer robustus* can now give his propensity for violence the noble sheen of the warrior. Moreover, he is a strong candidate for the role of a political hero who unites two ideals of democracy: association among equals, and the ability to change or transform – or, generally speaking: equality and liberty. Both ideals pay homage to eros, according to Thomas Mann.

For his erotic democracy project, Thomas Mann calls upon two sources whom he himself characterizes as a "wonderful pair"[90]: Novalis and Walt Whitman. Both interpret eros as "sympathy."[91] They see in eros a proto-democratic pleasure that allows one to open oneself up to others in equality and unison. Unlike Sigmund Freud and Heinrich Schurtz,[92] who link sympathy to the strong cohesion of homogeneous groups, Thomas Mann creates a kind of escape clause for romantic sympathy, because the relationships borne by it are not limited from the outset.

This form of association thus strikes a blow against ossified institutions or – as Novalis says – against "mechanical administration."[93] Novalis relates eros or sympathy to "the rapturous feeling of freedom, the unlimited expectations of a more potent sphere of action, the pleasure in what is new and young, the informal contact with all fellow citizens, the pride in human universality, the joy in personal rights and in the property of the whole community, and the strong civic sense."[94] Thomas Mann sees in Novalis "an almost American freshness," which he believes is brought fully to light in Walt Whitman's "erotic and all-embracing notion of democracy" and his "social eroticism."[95] Mann presents himself here not as a republican of reason but as a republican of emotion.

If Thomas Mann democratizes Blüher's political eros, he still follows the homosexual interpretation of community that Blüher introduces in his variation on Freud's thinking. Among the most daring passages in the speech "On the German Republic" are those in which Mann claims there is an inner connection between democracy and homosexuality. He credits the latter with having the advantage that "sexual polarity proves inoperative," enabling "like with like" to become joined in "passionate communion."[96] Novalis is less of a model for him here than Whitman, who mentions "staying close to men and women" but prefers to talk about "manly attachment" and the "manly love of comrades."[97] (It is curious that Mann's positive references to Whitman's homoerotic democracy were swept under the table as being objectionable in the first American translation of "On the German Republic."[98])

We could attribute Mann's male fixation to an autobiographical agenda, take umbrage at the fact that there is no place for women in his democracy, and leave it at that. But on this side of such limitations and objections, I am interested in what prompts Mann to declare liberty and equality to be a male privilege. His reasoning emerges systematically from a premise that Mann takes from Freud.

In Freud's model, as mentioned, there are only two possible positions for a woman. On the one hand, she is presented as the object of male desire and the cause of rivalry between men. On the other hand, she is presented as a creature of nature whose responsibility is limited to procreation. Reduced to the status of an object, woman is denied entry into the space of equals which opens up in a republic; and as a creature of nature, she is denied the capacity for politics. Freud says: "Women represent the interests of the family and of sexual life. The work of civilization has become increasingly the business of men" (SE 21, 103). Thomas Mann's republic has homoerotic characteristics because he accepts Freud's premise that there is an Oedipal asymmetry between the sexes which reflects the ideological distribution of power in society. His model of democracy, therefore, is indeed based on communal feelings, but it cements the inequality that exists in this community of a halved humanity.

Before I turn my attention to Hans Kelsen, I want to cast a sideways glance at one reader of Thomas Mann who demonstrates how the relationship between order and disturbance was given a National Socialist twist. Alfred Baeumler, who would later become the leading Nazi philosopher, alongside and ahead of Ernst Krieck, responded with enthusiasm in 1920 to Mann's *Reflections of a Nonpolitical Man* and was motivated by this book to develop a new "historic-heroic world view."[99]

In a speech on "The Academic House of Men" from 1930, Baeumler reckons with Mann's democratic turn – in an oddly horrifying way. His first step is to starkly contradict Mann's text and act as though Mann's "erotically" charged "democracy" were still directed at the "relationship with woman," as it was in the *Reflections*.[100] Then, in his second step, he can protect the "relationship between man and man"[101] (which he praises as the basis of National Socialist politics) from any homoerotic charge – despite the latent or blatant homosexuality of the Nazis. His third step is to construe the "development of humanity" as the development of men[102] and couple the "male association" to the "martial nature" of the "German."[103] And for his fourth step, he reinterprets the troublemaker: the rebellious youth movement is transformed into a Nazi strike team that has set off not "for itself" but "for Germany."[104] In this devotion to total unity, we encounter a character I refer to – as explained in the introduction and the chapter on Wagner – as a *massive troublemaker*. This fighter who merges and synchronizes with the mass will make another appearance in Horkheimer's critical analysis, and he will return again in the form of a fundamentalist in the twenty-first century.

Hans Kelsen. To conclude this chapter, I want to turn to the legal scholar and philosopher Hans Kelsen (1881–1973), which brings me back into Freud's immediate orbit. The close personal exchange between the two began in 1911 and reached its peak in lengthy discussions held during a summer vacation in 1921; in 1927, both of them signed an election announcement for the Social Democrats.[105] By introducing Kelsen, I am also contrasting Baeumler the Nazi philosopher with a defender of democracy who was driven into exile by the Nazis. I hope Kelsen can provide a conclusive answer to the systematic question that has given me nothing but a bloody nose – if I may say so – with the authors I have looked at thus far: How is it possible to withstand the tension between the vertical dimension of politics (the establishment of institutions) and its horizontal dimension (the mobilization of communities) and turn it into something productive? How is it possible to avoid getting stuck in swaggering protest (Lippmann), fleeing from history into a "fatherless society" (Federn), letting the community degenerate into a total fusion (Blüher) or turning it into an erotic playground where equality remains a male privilege (Thomas Mann)?

Kelsen's intensive involvement with Freud is a little-noticed aspect of his work.[106] Not only is it documented in several essays that Kelsen wrote for *Imago*, it also permeates his programmatic texts on democracy, most of which were published in the 1920s. Unlike the authors examined thus far, Kelsen tries to reconcile Freud's *first premise* – which couples the political order to the verticality of the Oedipus complex – with his *second premise* – the value of horizontal communal feelings in politics.

Freud himself makes only a rudimentary attempt to address this doubling by distinguishing between two types of "groups" or masses: a hierarchically organized mass that he believes is "capable of subsisting" (SE 18, 121), and an egalitarian, anarchic mass that is doomed to collapse. In Kelsen's lecture on "The Conception of the State and Social Psychology" from 1922, he objects to Freud's reduction of the question of political order to this kind of group psychology perspective.[107] Freud, who was in the audience at this lecture, responded – as we know from the minutes of the discussion – with the defensive argument that he had "not dealt with" the "problem of the state" on account of its "complexity," and with the offensive argument that the theory of the "mass" was thoroughly suited to the analysis of "associations" of all kinds, particularly as their political variants in the form of the "state" still seemed rather "archaic."[108]

As Kelsen sees it, Freud presents him with an alternative between a vertical and a horizontal concept of the collective. He speaks – with a clarity not found in Freud's work – of the "dual [...] bond of the members with one another and with the leader."[109] (It is important to remember that while Kelsen uses the word *Führer* [leader] in this text, the term had not yet been tainted by totalitarianism in 1922.) If we want to use Kelsen to determine the requirements for the *democratic* organization of this collective, there is something we clearly must take exception to here: the fixation on leadership, which Freud derives from his Oedipal interpretation of the generation game and uses to counter the instability of the order of brothers.

In his treatise on "God and the State" from 1923, Kelsen once again gets to the heart of this alternative. On the one side, the individual knows himself to be part of "a whole [...] which is therefore felt to stand over oneself, the mere part, as something higher, [...] and towards which a feeling of dependence must therefore ensue." On the other side, the "*social* experience" relates to the "individual consciousness [...], bound up with other beings, who [...] are felt by him to be similar in kind, to be comrades."[110] With tremendous precision, Kelsen tests the repertoire that is available for these two interpretations of the collective and the political order.

Regarding the hierarchical organization of social life, Kelsen sticks to Freud's homology between the familial father-authority and the "founding father" or "Divine Father."[111] This substitute father also appears in a depersonalized form as a "totem," a "guiding idea" or an "ideology."[112] But how does democracy relate to this concept of political order, which has been derived from paternal authority? Freud suggests that we should view the idea of "popular sovereignty" as the internalization of authority, through which the people imagines itself to be the ruler. And Kelsen also says that, in a democracy, the people don a "totemic mask" and appropriate the power of the totem for themselves. But Kelsen believes this image is misleading, and for good reason – because the people and the sovereign absolutely do not merge in a democracy.[113]

Kelsen opposes the complete identification of the individual with the state, in which the individual gains freedom only as part of a "collective," or in which it is actually only "the personified state that is free."[114] This critique of the idea that the state should be imputed with a "life," in the sense of a "macroanthropos," is what distinguishes Kelsen from Rudolf Smend's state integration, from an autocratic or totalitarian "state-self" and even from Rousseau's *moi commun*.[115] Only in light of his criticism of the merging of individuals into a single "self" does it become clear that one word in particular deserves attention in the following dictum from Kelsen – namely, the word "we" in the plural: "*l'état, c'est nous*."[116]

Appropriating or internalizing paternal authority is not at all conducive to democracy as Kelsen conceives of it. He has to break with the logic behind Rousseau's popular sovereignty and Freud's "dictatorship of reason." This puts Kelsen in a difficult position, however. If he cannot accept the internalization of the father- or leader-figure and its transformation into democratic self-leadership or self-mastery, then the only option available to him – or so it seems! – is to conceive of democracy as a "fatherless society." Then, at best, he has a choice between viewing it as a leaderless clan of brothers, as Freud does, or upgrading it to a council democracy, as Paul Federn does. Without mentioning either teacher or student, Kelsen refers to the very controversy fought out between the two when he writes in 1933:

> Democracy, on the whole, is a soil unfavourable to the ideal of a leader, because it does not favour the principle of authority as such. And so far as the archetype of all authority is the father, since that is the original experience of authority, democracy – in Idea, that is – is a fatherless society. It seeks, so far as possible, to be a leaderless association of equals.[117]

This sounds as though Kelsen were coming down on the side of Federn. But it is important to note his interjection here: he says that democracy is a fatherless society "in Idea." And *only* in idea, one might add. Kelsen operates with a contrast between the idea or ideology of democracy on the one hand and its reality on the other. He is interested in the latter, and Federn's suggestion is not suited to it, according to Kelsen. Kelsen does not want to base democracy on institutions that function as a paternal authority, but he also does not view it as a "leaderless association." How does he forge his own path here? To counter Federn's zero hour of self-foundation, he looks to a historical process of integration, subordination, and reorganization. His defense of real as opposed to ideational democracy therefore incorporates a theory of institutions that are open to change. This democracy represents not an absence of leaders but a multiplicity of them:

> Democracy is marked out by the fact of a more or less rapid turnover in the leadership. In this decisive respect it is thoroughly dynamic in character. A steady upstreaming occurs from the community of the led into the position of leadership.[118]
>
> This means that the creation of many leaders becomes the central problem for real democracy, which – in contrast to its ideology – is not a leaderless society.[119]

In brief, Kelsen fights a battle against the primacy of the vertical.[120] He relativizes the vertical relationship between the leader and those who are led in that the leaders multiply and relate to each other horizontally. Additionally, the installation of democratic leaders is traced back to horizontal processes of opinion- and decision-making among the citizenry. All of these processes are inconceivable without an experience of equality that runs counter to the conditions of super- and subordination. For this horizontal pivot, Kelsen can follow up on what Freud calls the "community of feeling." He even avails himself of "Eros, who holds everything together in the world" – in "the widest sense of the word, not merely [. . .] including sexual love" – to explain the relations and ties between people.[121] But unlike Freud, Kelsen does not stop at a sweeping appeal to "Eros," which quickly finds itself disadvantaged in the face of Oedipal logic. Instead, he wants to concretize the experience of communality and put it to political use for the benefit of democracy. This is apparent in his essay on "State-form and World-outlook," which was published in Germany in 1933, the very year in which democracy was being done away with there. The following quote is spectacular in this regard:

> If we ask what type of character it is which corresponds to such a political attitude, in which the longing for freedom is modified by the sense of equality, it is obviously that person in whom the experience of his own self is not so elemental, not so utterly different from all other experiences, the experiencing of all others, the experiencing of the not-self, that this self would be incapable of honouring in fellow-feeling the claim of the thou to be also a self, to be also acknowledged as such. It is the type of personality whose basic experience is the *Tat twam asi*, the man who, when he looks across at another, hears a voice within him saying: That is you. This kind of personality recognises himself again in the other, experiences the other a priori, not as something essentially alien, not as an enemy, but as an equal and therefore a friend [. . .]. It is the type whose ego-feeling is relatively subdued, the type of the sympathising, peace-loving, non-aggressive man [. . .].[122]

258

It is necessary to provide a short explanation here. The phrase *Tat tvam asi* comes from Hinduism and – as Kelsen weaves into this quote – it means "that is you." This expression encapsulates the message in this passage. In what was to be his last battle for democracy on German soil for some time, Kelsen links the theory of political and legal institutions to the image of the democratic "type," the democratic individual. The political experience he ascribes to this type is based on nothing other than sympathy, or the "intrinsic equality"[123] in the relationship between I and you. A theory of socialization or communal relationships is embedded in this, one which breaks free of the Oedipal logic that allows people only to submit to the law or elevate themselves to the position of lawmaker. State institutions derive their authority from their ability to respond to that original "intrinsic equality" through the creation of legal equality. Equality precedes the law, not the other way around. Active – or, to use my terminology, synergetic – participation in legislative processes is founded on sympathy.

Kelsen does not hesitate (or should we say shy away?) when it comes to exploring and defending experiences of equality even in what is actually considered to be Freud's domain: the realm of sexuality. He grapples not only with Federn's "fatherless society," as we have seen, but also with the equality or similarity of kind that is said to distinguish a homoerotic community, according to Blüher and Mann. In a long essay on "Platonic Love" from 1933, Kelsen expresses doubts about this and points out that Platonic eros is no guarantee of equality, but instead is tied up with the "will to power over men."[124] Kelsen looks beyond Plato to deliberate on the present day. It almost sounds as though we were reading Hans Blüher when Kelsen describes an "eternal youth" who demonstrates a "strikingly conservative, even reactionary tendency" and a hatred of "democracy."[125] Kelsen's accusation is directed against all notions of political community characterized by homology and homogeneity. He says that such communities – including the homoerotic male association – employ a "social scheme" of "inequality." This is based on "hostility" toward others or the excluded – be they women, so-called gentrified men or other groups.[126]

Kelsen argues for the abolition of limits on the experiences of equality between people. He is concerned not only with taking both sexes into account but also, more radically, with loosening sexual classifications and acknowledging the "bisexual disposition" of human beings (cf. Freud SE 19, 31ff.; SE 21, 105). This disposition does not represent "an inversion but a redoubling, a broader development of the sexual impulse." Kelsen writes laconically: "That the masculine and feminine principle can appear in different proportions in concrete individuals, [. . .] is a fact [. . .] already known to Parmenides."[127]

259

In the context of law and politics, Kelsen is wrestling with hierarchy – even on the psychological level, with the Oedipal axis between father and son representing the masculine model of domination. Kelsen spent many years seeking an exchange with Freud, the underlying reason for which is closely tied to the *puer robustus*: Kelsen's dynamic image of democracy ultimately represents an eminently historical concept of the political order and the vicissitudes of human life as a whole. In Kelsen's work, we encounter neither those oddly familyless, faceless members of the fatherless society, nor those individuals who, in accordance with the fictitious primal scene of contract theory, come to the negotiating table as fully-formed beings. From Kelsen's perspective, this idea of an "original creation of the social order" is not compatible with the "social experience" of human beings, who are always "born into" their life circumstances and then proceed to work on the "development" and "alteration" of them.[128]

Kelsen's consideration of history involves acknowledging the fact that institutions exist – and realizing that they are not untouchable: "The unity or the whole of the state is not a dormant condition but a continually renewed process, not a static but a dynamic unity [...]. The legal order [...] is an 'eternal process in which the state continually creates itself anew.'"[129] The legal scholar Hermann Heller follows the same line: "Every human organization continues to exist by continually coming into existence."[130] With this view, Kelsen and Heller become antagonists of Carl Schmitt in the Weimar Republic and pioneers of the theory of democratic "iteration."

In his theory of the state, Kelsen repeatedly asserts the existence of what can be described as a generation game, an interplay between order and disturbance. He thus takes exception to Rudolf Smend's attempt, in his concept of the integrative state, to simply subsume "children" and treat them "*as if*" they had always had a "part" in the existing order. Kelsen rejects the idea of presenting the state order as something "done and dusted" – as he says – and sealing it off from impulses emanating from elements that are not entirely integrated.[131] This acknowledgement of threshold creatures extends not only to internal outsiders (i.e., children) but also to strangers, to others. This is connected with Kelsen's surprising praise for the "Soviet constitution" from 1920, which, as he says, does not treat "those foreign to the state" as "downright outlaws" but instead grants them civil rights.[132] (The fact that the prospects were not great for actually exercising these civil rights in the Soviet Union does not impact the value of Kelsen's call for inclusion.)

If we were to search for a word that encapsulates what Kelsen opposed with all of his might, we would find it in his book *Society and Nature* from 1943. The (unfortunately somewhat unwieldy) word is "misoneism." This word, which Kelsen borrows from Lucien Levy-Bruhl, can be defined as a hatred of the new, a "conservatism" in which "the dead rule over the living."[133] Kelsen was not familiar with the *puer robustus* – or, like all readers of Freud, he knew him only in the guise of Oedipus. But anyone who has devoted himself to the fight against "misoneism" can be considered a *puer robustus* who has freed himself from Freud's Oedipal circle.

In summary, we can say that Kelsen does an exemplary job of picking up on the central points raised by Freud and discussed by the long list of other authors analyzed here. In Kelsen's work, Freud's highway and his byway – the "dictatorship of reason" on one side and the "social feeling of community" on the other – converge. We could also say that Kelsen manages to reconcile Freud with Freud himself. In doing so, he does not settle for making a case for youth (as Lippmann does) or arguing for an exit from the generation game in favor of the brotherhood (as Federn does). Kelsen refuses to restrict the experience of equality to a male community, a restriction that Blüher and Mann pursued in very different ways. Unlike Blüher and in a different way to Thomas Mann, he casts the light of freedom and democracy over the political order. His theory of democracy, as Oliver Lepsius says, is "exemplary even today."[134]

In the Weimar Republic, Kelsen found himself fighting a losing battle. If we follow him into exile in America, we run into a kindred spirit, John Dewey:

> The relation of individual freedom to organization is seen to be an experimental affair. [...] Organization tends [...] to become rigid and to limit freedom. In addition to security and energy in action, novelty, risk, change are ingredients of the freedom which men desire.[135]

In the "creative democracy" proposed by Dewey, the conflict between "authority and freedom," "stability and change" appears to be transformed into a harmonious pendular movement.[136] In the earlier chapters on Rousseau and Schiller, I showed that the *puer robustus* faces the prospect of a victory that could make him a victim of his own success – namely, he could pave the way for a political order in which disturbance is well-liked. The prediction that the *puer robustus* would disappear turned out to be premature earlier. But could there be, in the democracy of today or tomorrow, something like a disturbed order or an orderly disturbance? Then the exception represented by the *puer robustus* would no longer cease to exist; then it would be possible, as Bonnie Honig puts it, "to de-exceptionalize the exception."[137]

This idea is ahead of its time. *Historically* we can say that this special type of democracy did not even get its foot in the door in the early twentieth century. Tensions did not ease in politics; they ratcheted up.

Systematically this means that we still have to contend with Hobbes. The individual who wants to win and is in danger of losing, who steps out of line and is pushed out of line, is still in the game. The state continues to exist – as does its discontents.

— X. —

ANARCHISTS, ADVENTURERS, YOUNG ROWDIES, AND LITTLE SAVAGES

Carl Schmitt, Leo Strauss, Helmut Schelsky, and Max Horkheimer

1. Blossoming in dark times: Hobbes *da capo*

Following the *puer robustus* through the centuries feels somewhat like a godparent looking on with concern as their charge is drawn ever deeper into the turmoil of history. While he started as an outsider caught between good and evil, madness and foolishness, violence and genius, other leading roles were offered to him later on. He has appeared as an American and a proletarian, he has been called Siegfried and Oedipus. The *puer robustus* is deployed in a game whose rules are continuously changing. In this and the following chapter, the *puer robustus* will face his last two tough rounds. They take us into the force fields of National Socialism and Communism.

Looking first to National Socialism, our gaze immediately falls on something repellent: the gangs of thugs which – as befits Hobbes's definition of the *puer robustus* – represent a combination of brute strength and clouded reason. As troublemakers with totalitarian backing, they are, admittedly, only distant cousins to the outsiders and threshold creatures I have primarily dealt with so far. But with the help of Max Horkheimer, I want to go deeper into the critical analysis of (proto-)totalitarian associations that started with my examination of Hans Blüher and Alfred Baeumler. This chapter is not intended as a contribution to the mass sociology of fascism, but is instead dedicated to questions such as how the *puer robustus* fares in the debates about political philosophy in the 1930s and 1940s and how these debates were influenced by the father of this character: Thomas Hobbes.

The political philosophy of those dark years was characterized by a tremendous fascination and love–hate relationship with Hobbes. He owes his presence to the ambivalence he was thought to embody. He represents radical individualism – and the unease this engenders. His legacy is the absolutized power of the state – and the unease this engenders. Hobbes, naturally, wants nothing to do with this ambivalence; he wants to bring both sides together in a solid unit and identify a disposition in the individual that leads to the affirmation of the power of the state. His bridge between the individual and the state was expected to withstand the heavy weather of history. But the philosophical surveyors who inspected this bridge in the twentieth century found extensive damage, and they set out to repair it. In doing so, they opened up an extremely dangerous construction site, because if the foundation stones of this bridge – the state and the individual – are engineered in just a slightly different way, then the ground on which they are supposed to be laid shifts, causing the entire structure to totter.

Many theorists were repelled by Hobbes's individualism while simultaneously being attracted to his absolutization of the state – a state they no longer wanted to justify by falling back on individualistic motives, however. In this way, Hobbes, when perceived selectively, became the warrantor of totalitarianism. But he was also invoked as an opponent of totalitarianism, because both his individualism and his peace-loving state function as a bulwark against collective warmongering. This results in alternating polarizations.

The 1930s and 1940s saw Hobbes scholarship flourish in dark times. Important contributions to the philosophical discussion included Max Horkheimer's *Origins of Bourgeois Historical Philosophy* (1930), Leo Strauss's *The Political Philosophy of Hobbes* (1936), Carl Schmitt's *The Leviathan in the State Theory of Thomas Hobbes* (1938) and Helmut Schelsky's doctoral thesis on *Thomas Hobbes* (1939). In France and England, the relationship between Hobbes and totalitarianism was fiercely debated by Vialatoux (1935), Capitant (1936), Taylor (1938), and Collingwood (1942), among others.[1]

Hobbes was not only the subject of philosophical deliberation, however; he was also an important point of reference in standard works as varied as Franz Borkenau's *The Transition from the Feudal to the Bourgeois Worldview* (1934),[2] Talcott Parsons' *The Structure of Social Action* (1937)[3] and Franz Neumann's analysis of fascism, *Behemoth* (1942), in which Hobbes's peace-keeping state is held up against the "non-state" and the "lawlessness" of the Nazis.[4]

In the same period we find Hannah Arendt's essay on Hobbes, "Expansion and the Philosophy of Power" (1946), which was incorporated almost unchanged into her book *The Origins of Totalitarianism* (1951).[5] Though he is never mentioned, Hobbes also had an indirect effect on Sigmund Freud's *Civilization and Its Discontents* (1930) as well as Norbert Elias's *The Civilizing Process* (1939), in which the "threat which one person represents for another" is contrasted with the state's "stable monopoly of force."[6] This tremendously diverse discussion is framed on one side by Ferdinand Tönnies's book on Hobbes, expanded editions of which were continually published until 1925, and on the other side by Michael Oakeshott's influential introduction to *Leviathan* (1946), which was, to a certain extent, the start of the postwar period for Hobbes.[7]

The fascinating history of this Hobbes boom, which has yet to be written,[8] is of interest here only insofar as it impacts the character of the *puer robustus*. It stands to reason that this history would be enlightening in this respect, because the generation problem was escalating at the same time. This was a moment in which the political order was set in motion and came under fire, and the dynamics of history – in the form of the "problem of generations"[9] – made their massive effects felt for better and for worse.

In the following I will focus on the philosophical contributions of Schmitt (section 2), Strauss (section 3), Schelsky (section 4), and Horkheimer (section 5) that are particularly relevant to the question of the *puer robustus*. I will pay special attention to their works from the Nazi period, though it is also worth looking at their development after 1945. As authorities on the Hobbesian oeuvre, all four authors were naturally familiar with his work *De cive*, in which the *puer robustus* first appears. However, the *puer robustus* is only mentioned by name and discussed by Leo Strauss (SGS 3, 259). Max Horkheimer, however, does speak of "little savages" (AFT 373), using the nickname invented by Diderot for the *puer robustus* and adopted by Sigmund Freud. (It should be noted that Étienne Balibar mentions the "famous metaphor" of the *puer robustus* in his interpretation of Carl Schmitt, but he does not go into any further detail.[10])

Schmitt, Strauss, Schelsky, and Horkheimer grapple in different ways and for different reasons with the concept of individualism that was passed down from Hobbes. Ferdinand Tönnies, the nestor of more recent Hobbes scholarship, pressed this subject upon them. He viewed individualism not as a characteristic of man in a state of nature but as a peculiarity of bourgeois society. Referring to the preface to *De cive* in which Hobbes introduces the *puer robustus*, Tönnies writes:

> The idea that the war of all against all does not reflect chiefly, much less exclusively, the position prior to the civil state, but also or even essentially the position within the civil, orderly, peaceful state is being sounded as early as *De Cive*. Not, however, in the text of that work but in the preface to the reader, which Hobbes wrote later.[11]

The critical analysis of individualism spearheaded by Tönnies would continue under the headings of "egoism" and "atomism" (Horkheimer), and "relativism" and "liberalism" (Strauss, Schmitt, Schelsky). Even if one could make the *puer robustus* – that "madman" and "rebel" (Hobbes) – see reason in his own well-understood self-interest, there would still be no way, so the thinking goes, to establish a state with him. This thinking is shared for different reasons by all four of the authors mentioned.

2. Carl Schmitt on the total state and its enemies

As the motto for his work *The Value of the State and the Significance of the Individual* from 1914, Carl Schmitt chose a line from Theodor Däubler: "First comes the command, the people come later." And a note in his *Glossarium* from 1951 reads: "With each newborn child, a new world is born. For God's sake, then each newborn child is an aggressor!"[12] Schmitt stands on the threshold of a political order where people are either docile or refractory, and where the *puer robustus* roams around. There are two questions to clarify here: How does Schmitt conceive of the political order that takes shape in the form of the state? And what is to be done about the troublemaker who threatens it?

Schmitt believes the state is in trouble – and he wants to save it. Two factors are responsible for this "crisis,"[13] according to Schmitt. One damages politics from the inside and is called liberalism, and the other damages politics from the outside and is called economics. They are intimately intertwined because they share the same root: individualism.

As Schmitt sees it, liberalism is devoted to "individual freedom," which is interpreted as a negative freedom, i.e., as freedom from the state or a freedom "unconnected with the State."[14] The "political practice" of liberalism is said to lead not to its own "positive theory of state, government, and politics"; instead "there exists [...] only a liberal critique of politics" which makes the modern state look better the weaker it is. The "anti-statal kernel" of liberalism, according to Schmitt, hollows out the power that the state needs to wield against external and internal enemies.[15] In a parliamentary democracy, liberal anti-politics has the effect of reducing the formation of political will to the trade between lobbies, "party coalitions," and "big capitalist interest groups," to the "'daily compromise' of heterogeneous powers and alliances."[16] Finally, democracy shaped by liberalism presents a caricature of the people as the sovereign who, "through total privatization," has gone to the dogs – or to the individual, to be more precise. In 1929, Schmitt complained that "the sovereign disappears [...] in the voting booth," where the people live out their "uncontrollable mass desires and ressentiments," and in 1933 he wrote triumphantly: "The *election* from below [...] comes to an end."[17]

266

In Schmitt's view, politics as a "clash of opinion" is simply an out-growth of the economics of "competition"[18] which revolves around naked self-interest. Following this thinking, liberalism tries to "subju-gate" the political sphere "to economics," which ultimately leads to a "world without politics":[19]

> Today nothing is more modern than the onslaught against the politi-cal. American financiers, industrial technicians, Marxist socialists, and anarchic-syndicalist revolutionaries unite in demanding that the biased rule of politics over unbiased economic management be done away with.[20]

The demise of politics in the clutches of economics can be felt not only on the side of the state, but also on the side of individuals. They develop a "state of mind which finds the core categories of human existence in production and consumption."[21] With this polemic, Schmitt is not only calling for the power of the state to be strengthened, he also wants to show that the liberal promotion of the individual does a disservice to humanity. Someone who – as Schmitt says, quoting Däubler – is fixated on his "individual happiness" will be shut off from the "great and won-drous moments" in life, which he would experience in "devotion to the cause" and "losing himself in the task."[22] Schmitt suggests that people should bid farewell to liberal individualism and distance themselves from the "duality" of the "contrast between the *State* and the free *individual person*, between statal *power* and individual *freedom*, between *State* and State-free *society*, between *politics* and the apolitical *private*, therefore irresponsible and uncontrolled." The path to "surmount[ing] the liberal-democratic system"[23] leads, in the end, to the identification of the person (or the German) with the "total state" or the "total leader-state," and to a concept of democracy in which the individual is conquered and the homogeneity of the people, the *demos*, is assured.[24]

In his diagnosis of the crisis, Schmitt not only mentions the erosion of state power, he also notes that human experience is shrinking to a "material reality."[25] This second point is often overlooked by scholars, but it is of particular interest to the emergence of the troublemaker. In Schmitt's early works in particular, the fixation on "material reality" is often described by means of a theological category, namely, the triumph of the "worldliness of immediate natural life and unproblematic con-creteness."[26] If we describe this worldliness as presence, we can see how it leads to the erosion of the state. This presence, namely, barricades itself against representation – and this word is Schmitt's placeholder for the state order and for the order of the world as a whole. Its most reliable bastion is the Catholic Church, the steward of the next world in this world. Its "superiority over the matter of human life," Schmitt wrote in 1923, cements its "superiority over an age of economic think-ing." A world without representation, according to Schmitt, is an image of ultimate abandonment, and one of its manifestations is a "world without politics" (see above). What is generally referred to as politics – in parliamentarianism, for example – appears to Schmitt to be an absurd degenerate form of representation; and he views the council democracy as the nadir of anti-representational modernity.[27]

At this point, I must address a controversial passage from one of Schmitt's most extreme National Socialist works. In *State, Movement, People*, he defines "leadership" as "a concept of the immediately present and of a real *presence*."[28] It would seem as though Schmitt were betray-ing everything he previously said in favor of representation. Hitler, in the role of leader, is pulled into the realm of worldliness (or so it appears) in which people are trapped and occupied with their needs. Is this meant to be a criticism? Or is Schmitt throwing his state-theoretical defense of representation overboard for the sake of supporting National Socialism?

Both suppositions are wrong. Hitler's "presence" is construed by Schmitt not as a case of lingering in "material reality" (see above) but as the arrival of a higher power in the world. While the Catholic Church reveres Jesus Christ as someone who entered the world in order to represent God's power, Schmitt interprets Hitler's arrival as the moment in which this power is not merely surmised but actually represented in *presence*. Basically, Hitler is another Jesus Christ. His seizure of power is an Advent. Schmitt can rely on Hitler himself to support this interpreta-tion. In 1926, Hitler said that Jesus was the "greatest champion in the fight against the Jewish world enemy" and "the greatest warrior who ever lived on the Earth." "The teachings of Christ," he proclaimed, had been "fundamental to the struggle against the Jews, the enemy of mankind, for millennia," and it was now time for his works to be "completed."[29] At the infamous conference organized by Schmitt in 1936 on "Judaism in Legal Studies," Schmitt quoted directly from *Mein Kampf*: "Hence today I believe that I am acting in accordance with the will of the Almighty Creator: *by defending myself against the Jew, I am fighting for the work of the Lord*." For Schmitt, Hitler is Christ arisen to continue the "struggle against Jewry."[30]

It is tempting to turn away from this in horror, but I must mention it because it casts a light (or rather, a shadow) on Schmitt's interpretation of Hobbes – and unless I am mistaken, scholars have overlooked this point until now. When Schmitt defines the Jesus–Hitler alliance as an instance of a power representing something higher availing itself of presence, he makes Hobbes the third party in this union by praising Hobbes's willing-ness to base state representation on theological foundations. He points to Hobbes's sentence "Jesus is the Christ" as "the axis of the conceptual system of thought of his political theology."[31]After 1945, however, Schmitt restricts himself to the connection between Jesus and Hobbes and sweeps Hitler under the table.

But Schmitt is unable to entirely co-opt Hobbes for his position – and this is especially clear when it comes to the issue of "representation," which, as I demonstrated in the chapter on Hobbes, is critically important to the definition of the troublemaker. In Hobbes's work, representation concerns the tangled relationship between the people as author and the sovereign as actor, i.e., as the representative or agent of the people. Hobbes initially deploys the people as author, but he disempowers them in order to establish the sovereign as the representative or actor whom the people merely watch. I described this model as the author–actor–audience theory and saw in it the potential to take a critical turn, to dynamize the political. The representation game can lead to emancipation or disturbance on the side of the people if they reclaim their original position as author or interpret their role as spectator in an active way.

This finding can now be used against Schmitt. His thoughts on representation and presence are so wrong and ill-fated because, from the outset, they deny the internal game that Hobbes had taken into account. For Hobbes, representation stands for something higher, and power is supposed to break through into presence from above, based on something that is not of this world: "Power is not something evil, it is something entirely alien."[32]

One point highlights the difference between Hobbes and Schmitt particularly clearly. It emerges from the famous sobriquet that Hobbes gives to the Leviathan: it is a *"Mortall God"* (L[e] 120). This turn of phrase sounds as though it would fit with Schmitt's theological overloading of state representation, but it actually reveals the chasm between Schmitt's theological representation and Hobbes's political one.

For Hobbes, this mortal god is situated "under" the true god and is connected to him in some way. But it is not this supreme lord to whom people owe their "peace and defence," but rather their man-made *"Mortall God"* (ibid.). Schmitt notes: "That the state is characterized as 'god' has no particular meaning in Hobbes' construction of the state."[33] Much to his displeasure, Hobbes's *"Mortall God"* remains a pseudogod, an authority constructed by people. Since the state is the work of man, as Hobbes sees it, Schmitt says it can be nothing more than a "gigantic mechanism in the service of ensuring the physical protection of those governed."[34] This critique of the state as a "mechanism" can be found not only in Schmitt's work, incidentally, but also in *Mein Kampf*.[35]

Schmitt accuses the *"Mortall God"* of a weakness that I would actually consider a strength: namely, that Hobbes's political order does not demand total subordination. In Schmitt's view, this makes it not more human, but more vulnerable. It runs the risk of being brought down by troublemakers.

One minute Schmitt credits Hobbes with a potential that is directed against the secularization of state power, and the next he complains that Hobbes remains stuck in worldliness. There has been much debate about whether or how Schmitt's attitude toward Hobbes, whom he calls a "brother,"[36] changed from the early 1920s until his last essay on Hobbes in 1965.[37] In the late 1930s, Schmitt attributed the different tendencies in his interpretation of Hobbes to an ambivalence in Hobbes himself – to his "indecisiveness." Schmitt says that, on the one hand, Hobbes traces the state back to the interests of individuals and abandons it to ruin, but on the other hand he valorizes the sovereignty of the state and sees in it "much more than the sum total of all the participating particular wills." Following Schmitt's reading, Hobbes wants to surmount the individual-istic preconditions of his contract theory and achieve a "totality of the state," but he does not succeed.[38] Schmitt might say of him that he was someone who started off wrong but wanted to end up right.

In this book, I am trying to interpret the relationship between order and disturbance by looking at the triad of power, morality, and history. Schmitt fits into this schema in that he couples the power of the state to the preservation of morality,[39] namely, to the fight against the evil in man. The fact that he makes a mockery of this fight with his personal dedication to National Socialism is of more than passing importance here. Be that as it may, Schmitt says that at the "core of the political idea" there should be an "exacting moral decision": "Every political idea in one way or another takes a position on the 'nature' of man and presupposes that he is either 'by nature good' or 'by nature evil.'"[40]

Over the course of many years, Schmitt was repeatedly drawn back to this alternative, or to the question debated between Hobbes and Rousseau in their judgment of the *puer robustus*. Schmitt has to reject the Enlightenment slogan that "man was by nature ignorant and rough, but educable,"[41] because if this education were to succeed, people might become so "good" that they would no longer need any state.

From Schmitt's point of view, the balance between power and morality cannot be achieved through a historical process or through progress. This is why Schmitt also struggles with Hegel's dynamization of the question of good and evil, which Hegel famously also links to Rameau's nephew and thus to the *puer robustus*. According to Schmitt's critique of Hegel, "world history" does not make a suitable "world court" but instead leads to a "process without a last instance."[42] He insists that people cannot overcome evil of their own accord. The "tremendous feat" of taming "a sea of unbridled and blinkered egoism and the basest instincts" can, Schmitt believes, only be achieved by the state, the "highest moral

270

authority" which stands above "all subjectivity." It keeps control of "a chaos that is irrepressible at its core, namely, within individuals."[43] The "total state" (see above) is able to fight this battle most resolutely, according to Schmitt, and can therefore claim to represent the greatest good.

Because Schmitt weds power to morality in the state, he cannot help but view troublemakers as enemies who are considered evil – no matter how good they themselves may want to be. Schmitt takes on four types of troublemaker. The most radical type opposes the state in principle, regardless of the form it might take. Two other types appear on the margins of states that display the modern weaknesses bemoaned by Schmitt. And a fourth type enters the scene after the state has already been shaken to its very foundations. It is time to discuss Schmitt's battle against *anarchists*, *egoists*, *Jews*, and *partisans*.

Anarchists. Someone who believes in "the goodness of man's nature" might not hurt a fly. But this person is a threat to the state nonetheless, because they flatly deny the state's justification for existence and claim that people can manage their coexistence without its help. The anarchist's "radical denial of state" arises from his "belief in the natural goodness of man."[44] It is based on the seamless expansion of the idea that what is good *for me* is good *for you* and also good *for us* and *for humanity*. Schmitt has great respect for this troublemaker, the *anarchist*, because he views him as an enemy on an equal footing, someone who denies power as totally as Schmitt affirms it.[45] Of Mikhail Bakunin, he writes:

> Bakunin's intellectual significance rests, nevertheless, on his conception of life, which on the basis of its natural rightness produces the correct forms by itself from itself. For him, therefore, there was nothing negative and evil except the theological doctrine of God and sin, which stamps man as a villain in order to provide a pretext for domination and the hunger for power.[46]

Schmitt praises Bakunin for not shifting from the political to the economic, as he complains that Marx did when he "followed his opponent, the bourgeois, into economic territory."[47] Marx's successors went even further in gearing socialism toward the satisfaction of the workers' needs and ultimately subordinating politics to economics. The same tendency is apparent on the opposing side, among capitalists, about whom the younger Schmitt had very few nice things to say.[48] But the anarchist vision of domination-free socialization entails more than just an accumulation of individual beneficial effects. For this reason, the anarchist is Schmitt's fiercest opponent – and yet the two are in agreement when it comes to the critique of economic individualism, whether this is found among workers or capitalists. (It is important to add that this agreement

271

also has a repugnant side, as both Schmitt and Bakunin pepper their critique of individualism with antisemitic tirades.[49])

Schmitt's examination of the anarchist – and the other three troublemakers – is of interest here not as an issue specific to *him*, but only insofar as the theory of the troublemaker can draw its own conclusions from it. I believe we can distinguish between two different interpretations of the anarchist here. This first is justifiably rejected by Schmitt, but the second withstands his attack.

According to the first interpretation, the anarchist trusts himself to be able to develop the "correct forms" (see above) of political life on his own, i.e., to pull a new world out of his hat. But he plays down the fact that he is capable only of a negative, polemical achievement. Although anarchy only makes sense as a rejection of domination, Bakunin and his fellow anarchists presume to have the competence to bring about a positive positing, a total new beginning. This is also the source of the similarity between Bakunin and Wagner's Siegfried. Following this interpretation, the anarchist does not operate as a threshold creature who challenges a political order; he exaggerates his role and acts as though he could create a new world.

Contrary to Schmitt, however, the second interpretation of the anarchist remains intact. According to this interpretation, the anarchist opposes domination in the negative, critical sense just mentioned but – since *archè* means both rule and origin, after all – he also opposes any claim to bring about a total new beginning. This anarchist survives anarchism as a historical phenomenon, and he survives Carl Schmitt's critique of him. He is a troublemaker who shows up in politics whenever hierarchies need to be opposed. This fits with Emmanuel Lévinas's attempt to distinguish anarchy from "anarchism" and construe anarchy as a protest against the "principle" of the *archè*: the anarchist "can only disturb the State [. . .]. The State then cannot set itself up as a Whole."[50]

Egoists. Even if the state manages to vanquish the anarchist troublemaker, it is not entirely in the clear. Schmitt warns that the state will nourish troublemakers like a viper in its bosom if it is incorrectly positioned – which, in his view, means too weak. These particular troublemakers do not strive for the anarchic liberation of society as a whole, however; they cannot and do not want to consider themselves morally good, because they are concerned only with themselves. They are egoists.

How should the state defend itself against them? Here, Schmitt refers to Hobbes again and complains that he is too accommodating to the egoist. As Schmitt would have it, Hobbes's proposed solution to the "difficult problem of fitting the rebellious and self-seeking man into a social commonwealth" is "that the rebellious fierceness and obstinacy of individuals must be overcome with the help of reason or intelligence."[51]

The most important evidence for this thesis is Hobbes's discussion of the unreasonable *puer robustus*, to whom Schmitt does not directly refer, however. He attributes Hobbes's interpretation of evil to Enlightenment "rationalism,"[52] which does not exonerate individuals from evil, but which claims that evil can be overcome. The state that adopts this view delivers itself up to individuals who, for the sake of their own interests, are prepared to affirm the political order and are therefore – at least superficially – good. But the accelerant is still within the reach of parasites and freeloaders. Relying on the unreliable goodwill of egoists abases and weakens the state, as Schmitt sees it. A passage from *The Value of the State and the Significance of the Individual* from 1914 illustrates this:

> The great, transpersonal organization is not the work of individuals; it does not fit into the array of means and ends of however many people; it is inconceivable that man's egoism, surpassing itself of its own accord, could have erected a superhuman structure as a means of achieving its purposes, only to be immediately hurled back from its grandeur into nothingness. Purpose is no more the creator of law or the state than the sun can be defined as a fire lit by freezing savages to warm their limbs.[53]

For both Hobbes and the adherents of modern liberalism, the state does not represent anything higher; it is instead the tool of someone lower, namely, the "freezing savages" or men of nature who jostle against one another under its protective roof. But Schmitt believes the state is supposed to come "from above."[54] This is why he does not want to count on the egoist; he wants to fight him. From Schmitt's perspective, Hobbes's attempt to tranquilize the egoist is like playing with fire: "The dawn of the day when the great leviathan can be slaughtered" and "break down because of rebellion and civil war" is "already visible" to Schmitt.[55]

Schmitt's depiction of the egoist is plausible. His objections to the theory that a stable order can be derived from the self-interest of individuals alone fit well with the critique of the rational choice model that I developed earlier. All the same, we should be wary of Schmitt's warning against the egoist. Schmitt actually *welcomes* this egocentric troublemaker in the most heinous way because it allows him to cobble together an argument for the total state that he wants to deploy against the egoist. The total state *needs* an egoistic enemy so that it can depict the liberal state as a weakling. The egoist is thus a secret agent for totalitarianism.

It would interfere with Schmitt's argument, however, if it emerged that the self-image of the individual were actually split, meaning that the individual was not *just* an egoist. This kind of split or mixture of moral motives can be found in many other relevant characters, including Tocqueville's American and the poor European who vacillates between the proletariat and the lumpenproletariat. The egoist whom Schmitt describes as both the child *and* the gravedigger of the liberal state has lost any sense of division. He is, as Schmitt says (quoting Baudelaire), nothing but *satanic*.[56] If evil comes from below, then good cannot also come from below; it can only come from above. It is from this argument that Schmitt derives the authority of the state. The state responds to the compulsive behavior of the egoist by using compulsion to "refound" and "reform" him.[57]

Jews. The "chaos that is irrepressible at its core, namely, within individuals," which Schmitt wants to oppose using the state order, appears not only in egoists pursuing their own self-interest. Schmitt follows Hobbes in arguing that this chaos also entails a confusion of languages, society's semantic disorder. Hobbes eliminates this disorder by entrusting the state with the task of going over the heads of individuals to define what is good. The state not only has political authority, it also has semantic authority. I have looked critically at the plausibility of this feat of language philosophy elsewhere. But Schmitt dreams of this feat as well, and he adopts Hobbes's thesis that the war of all against all can also erupt as a war of words. In *State, Movement, People* from 1933, he interprets the fact that "every word and every concept soon become contentious, uncertain, vague and unsteady" as a sign of liberal confusion:

> We demand [...] commitment without which all the guarantees and freedoms, all the independence of the judges, and above all, that "creativity" would be but anarchy and an especially noxious source of political dangers. We seek a commitment which is deeper, more reliable and more imbued with life than the deceptive attachment to the distorted letter of thousands of paragraphs of the law.[58]

The state becomes weak, according to Schmitt, not only when it is reduced to individual interests, but also when it refrains from controlling a person's vocabulary down to "the tiniest fibre of his brain,"[59] i.e., from unifying or synchronizing everyone's world view. However, Schmitt seems to harbor some doubt about whether the chaos of the "distorted letter" (see above) can be successfully combatted through acts of state alone. He therefore tries – at least in his strict National Socialist phase – to tap other sources of ensuring unity.

To this end, he invokes the "ethnic identity [*Artgleichheit*] between leader and following," i.e., the "ethnic identity" of a "people." Without this, Schmitt warns, "a total leader-State could not stand its ground a single day."[60] On this basis, "rules and norms" are transformed into "essential elements of a [...] community and its concrete order and formation of life."[61] This leads Schmitt to think about "the idea of race," which "at the Congress of the National-Socialist German Jurists at Leipzig in 1933 [...] was time and again highlighted in the Leader's forceful closing speech, in the riveting addresses of the Leader of the German Legal Front, Dr. Hans Frank, and in the distinguished specialized reports, as for instance, that of H. Nicolai."[62] With this, Schmitt's third troublemaker is pulled onto the battlefield. Anyone who disrupts the people's race-based "ethnic identity" is an "internal enemy" in the form of an "alien"[63] – a Jew.

In his Hobbes book of 1938, Schmitt talks about the supposed subversive effect of Jews. He notes and complains that the Hobbesian sovereign is reluctant to employ his semantic power of definition. This sovereign insists on uniformity only when he believes his own preconditions, his peacekeeping power as such, is under threat. The rest is, in short, *irrelevant* to this state. Only the "actions" of an individual are "totally subject to the law of the land," wrote Reinhart Koselleck, characterizing the Hobbesian position (entirely in the spirit of Schmitt, unfortunately); but "his mind remains free, 'in secret free'. From here on the individual is free to migrate into his state of mind." Koselleck views this "exoneration" of the individual as a "burden" for the state.[64] Schmitt himself identifies a "rupture" here. With its "differentiation between inner faith and outer confession," the "political system of the *Leviathan*" creates a breeding ground for a "seed of death" resulting in a "sickness unto death."[65]

According to Schmitt, Hobbes's "Jewish" interpreters are responsible for promoting the spread of this sickness. By placing freedom of thought and belief beyond state control more rigorously than Hobbes, Spinoza is said to cement a "revolutionary state-destroying distinction between religion and politics," sentiments and behavior, "inner and outer."[66] Schmitt's portrayal of Jews thus goes beyond the antisemitic cliché that stigmatizes them as stubborn egoists. He claims they have also infiltrated the state legal system and weakened it so that they can survive within it as "a different kind."

Unlike his opposition to the anarchist and egoist, there is not much we can learn from Schmitt's fight against this third troublemaker – other, perhaps, than that this fight is essentially directed against the eccentric and therefore unintentionally attests to his continued survival and strength. A fragment from Nietzsche fits well here:

> Those who *blaspheme God, the immoralists*, the nomads of every type, the artists, Jews, musicians – at bottom, all disreputable classes of men –
> We have raised ourselves to the level of *honorable* thoughts; even more, we *determine* honor on earth, "nobility" –
> All of us are today *advocates of life. (The Will to Power*, p. 71)

Partisans. After the defeat of National Socialism, Schmitt believed the state was headed straight for ruin. "The epoch of statehood is now coming to an end. There is nothing more to be said about it," he wrote in the foreword to the 1963 edition of *The Concept of the Political*.[67] This "end of statehood" is the focal point of his later works on international law, in which he regularly criticizes any interference in the sovereign rights of individual states – ranging from the intervention of other states in the American Civil War to the role of the League of Nations.[68] Schmitt saw this as evidence of another stage in the triumphal march of economics, as he believed that international intervention in the internal affairs of other states was increasingly based on free-floating non-state or pre-state interests.

In essence, he occasionally assumes positions that could be directly adopted by more recent critics of globalization. He thought it was no longer true that the economy was subordinate to the circumstances of the state, in the sense of *cujus regio, ejus economia*, but that the "world interventionism" of the USA instead represented the "highly modern reversal, *cujus economia, ejus regio*."[69] In Schmitt's view, internally the state had become a quasi-economical source of protection that pacified its citizens, while externally the borders of the state were perforated by economic entanglements.

The demise of the state should technically result in the demise of the troublemaker who works away at it. But in searching for remainders of the political, Schmitt comes across a character who does not fit into this image of global pacification: the partisan, about whom he wrote a book in 1963. Schmitt's fourth kind of troublemaker now enters the scene. One could say that Schmitt must criticize the partisan because the partisan attacks the state. But one could also say he must praise the partisan because the partisan attacks the state. This is no more of a paradox than Schmitt's respect for the anarchist. As long as the partisan attacks a state, there must still be a state to be attacked – much to Schmitt's relief. A genuinely political agenda is what unites the partisan and the anarchist and what distinguishes them both from the egoistic troublemaker, who only pursues private interests.

Though Schmitt thinks otherwise,[70] Schiller's bandit chief Karl Moor could potentially be considered a partisan. Schmitt himself chooses Mao Zedong as one of his examples, whose own approach to the *puer robustus* will be discussed later on. One of Schmitt's interlocutors, the Maoist Joachim Schickel, suggested the following interpretation: "During the Cultural Revolution in China, the Party – in practice, the establishment of the Party, namely, the institutionalized, regularized, de-totalized Party – was destroyed and completely reformed. I would say that this was the act of Mao Tse-tung as a partisan; a properly partisan act." Carl Schmitt responded: "Very well, there is no other way to interpret it."[71] Interestingly, Schmitt's model of politics is dominated by the same extremes that apply to Mao. He vacillates between the unconditional claim of the partisan, who focuses not on himself at all but rather on a larger good cause, and the unconditional, absolute authority or "character of wholeness" that the "total state" – and, in Mao's case, the "*Party*" – claims for itself. Schmitt thus also praises Mao's sense of "real enmity," which he links to Hobbes's interpretation of war.[72]

Is this partisan an example of man's "evil nature" which the state – if it existed – would have to combat?[73] Schmitt's thesis of the "end of statehood" means that partisans cannot be judged to be evil in advance. After all, the state power, which claims to be the guardian of morality, is moot. Unlike robbers or "pirates," partisans continue to operate as if they were involved in a truly moral confrontation. They stake a claim to "legitimacy" and place themselves under a "moral compulsion":

> [Partisans] feel compelled morally to destroy these other men, i.e., as offerings and objects. They must declare their opponents to be totally criminal and inhuman, to be a total non-value. Otherwise, they are nothing more than criminals and brutes. The logic of value and non-value reaches its full destructive consequence.[74]

The most important word in this quote is "value" because, by using it, Schmitt emphasizes how fragile the conditions are under which the partisan can claim legitimacy. This talk of "values," according to Schmitt's later work *The Tyranny of Values*, is the symptom of a world in which the morality (and thus legitimacy) of actions stems solely from what people posit as being moral. He attributes values to a non-binding "subjectivism."[75] The partisans' deficit of justification merely reflects the deficit of the institutions they oppose, because they, too, are engaged in an "eternal war of words," compared to which Hobbes's "war of all with all" looks "truly idyllic." The Earth that has been transformed into this "paradise of values" appears to Schmitt to be "a hell."[76] He himself withdraws from this world, which is no longer dominated by the battle between good and evil, but only by the arbitrariness of posited values.

In the case of this last troublemaker, the partisan, it is worth using Schmitt to argue against Schmitt. In support of Schmitt, we could say that the partisan is, in fact, compelled to pass moral judgment on his opponent in order to justify his actions. In opposition to Schmitt, we could say that this moral stance does not invalidate itself if there is a subjective element to it. It absolutely cannot do without such an element. Subjective does not mean arbitrary or random; what we are talking about here are claims to validity made by subjects who look beyond their own particularity and their own welfare. Schmitt accuses Hegel of turning world history into a "process without a last instance," but we can hold on to this phrase and turn it into a positive. Perhaps there is no last instance or final authority, but there is a process in which people seek what is right, and in which laws are made and broken. And in spite of Schmitt's apocalyptic scenario, this process has continued to the present day.

3. Leo Strauss on the closed society and adventurers

Who was Thomas Hobbes? According to Leo Strauss, he was "that imprudent, impish, and iconoclastic extremist, that first plebeian philosopher, who is so enjoyable a writer because of his almost boyish straightforwardness, his never failing humanity, and his marvelous clarity and force."[77]

Who was Leo Strauss? He was – as he put it in a thinly veiled autobiographical lecture in 1941 in New York – a "nihilist" as a young man. In the 1920s, this "young nihilist" was filled with "a desire for the destruction [. . .] of *modern* civilization" and attracted to "the chaos, the jungle, the Wild West, the Hobbesian state of nature."[78] This sounds suspiciously like the *puer robustus*, particularly as Tocqueville used precisely this name to refer to the pioneers in the American west.

There is no getting around the thought that something is not quite right here. Hobbes and Strauss were not disturbers of the peace, they were guardians of order. If Hobbes is an extremist and Strauss a nihilist, they cannot be in the service of evil; their work of destruction must serve a higher purpose. In fact, Strauss eventually abandons nihilism and takes pains to say: "The question concerning the right order of living together [. . .] urges itself, in view of the reigning anarchy, on every impartial person" (HCR 137). Strauss's brotherhood with Hobbes ultimately stands under the banner of order after all. What we must find out is how Strauss gets from nihilism to the "question concerning the right order" and how his answer to this question affects the titular protagonist of this book, the notorious obstructionist. As we will see, Strauss passes even harsher judgment on the *puer robustus* than Hobbes does himself. And there are illuminating weaknesses in his judgment.

When Strauss held his autobiographical lecture in New York, he was an exile who had been driven out of Germany by Hitler. But the young Strauss in the Weimar Republic had different concerns. He found himself confronted with a world in which the liberal individual had triumphed. What the nihilistic "young Germans [. . .] hated" – as he said in retrospect – was the "prospect of a world in which everyone would be happy and satisfied," a world that appeared to them to be "the greatest debasement of humanity."[79] The hero of this world, the individual, counted on his ability to use the political order without disturbance – even from himself – as a framework for his own economic activity.

Tocqueville and Nietzsche had earlier described such a depoliticized, amoral world in their dark visions of a "new despotism" and the "last men." Strauss makes reference to both of these thinkers[80] and confesses that "Nietzsche so dominated and bewitched me between my 22nd and 30th years" – between 1921 and 1929, that is – "that I literally believed everything that I understood of him."[81] In Nietzsche's posthumously published essay entitled "The Greek State" from 1872 (which the young Strauss could not have known but certainly would have appreciated), the 28-year-old Nietzsche railed against

> those truly international, homeless, financial recluses [...], who, with their natural lack of state instinct, have learnt to misuse politics as an instrument of the stock exchange, and state and society as an apparatus for their own enrichment. The only countermeasure to the threatened deflection of the state purpose towards money matters from this quarter is war and war again: in the excitement of which at least so much becomes clear, that the state is not founded on fear of the war-demon, as a protective measure for egoistic individuals, but instead produces from within itself an ethical momentum in the love for fatherland and prince, indicating a much loftier designation. ("The Greek State," p. 171)

In "German Nihilism," Strauss operates on the basis of an opposition between "open" and "closed society."[82] This refers to a distinction made by Henri Bergson, which was later picked up by Karl Popper in *The Open Society and Its Enemies*, as well as by Victor Turner in the form of a contrast between "communitas" and "structure."[83] Unlike Bergson, Strauss believes the "open society" of liberalism is "morally inferior," a "meeting ground of seekers of pleasure, of gain, of irresponsible power, indeed of any kind of irresponsibility and lack of seriousness."[84] He comes down on the side of the "closed society" and, in doing so, implicitly takes a stand against theorists of democracy such as Hans Kelsen, Hermann Heller, and John Dewey.

Where does the *puer robustus* fit into this scenario? Nietzsche's "financial recluse" is not a bad epithet for Hobbes's and Tocqueville's versions of this character, but the wickedness they denounce seems to have gone missing from those who want to maximize their pleasure and profit. Such troublemakers have sown their wild oats and finally realized they can best pursue their self-interest by following the rules of the contract theory game.

But the *puer robustus* is not entirely toothless. According to Strauss, the "open society" has a parasitical relationship with the "closed society"; it lacks any strength of its own to ensure cohesion, and it therefore secretly feeds on the remainders of the old morality. Its victory is based on "hypocrisy."[85] As a consequence, the law-abiding behavior of its individuals is unreliable. The *puer robustus* – as described by Hobbes and many others – maintains a permanent place in the back of each person's mind. The existing order is nothing but poorly disguised disorder, what Thomas Carlyle refers to as "anarchy, *plus* a street-constable."[86] Strauss writes:

> Our situation is characterized by a fundamentally limitless anarchy, there is absolutely no generally binding norm anymore [. . .]. And the *question* is: can this anarchy be overcome, and how can it be overcome? (SGS 3, 630)

> This whole modern world is coming apart at all the seams. (SGS 3, 433)

> Modern man is [. . .] fit to be buried.[87]

With this last sentence, Strauss presents himself not only as the gravedigger of modernity but as the midwife of the non-modern man. "Only in view of *unrest* [*Unruhe*], only *in* unrest, if not indeed in revolts [*Unruhen*] can that understanding of man be gained from which the right created for the satisfaction of man can be understood" (HCR 141). It would be wrong to throw this "unrest" into the same pot as American "restlessness" (DIA 3, 944; O 2, 648) or other innovation-happy attitudes. Strauss may toy with the thought of following the "century of the child" with an "age of the adolescent," one who "doubt[s] seriously [. . .] the *principles* of modern civilization" and is no longer impressed by "the great authorities of that civilization."[88] But he does not consider coming down on the side of the new against the old and welcoming the *puer robustus* as a good rebel – just as he makes no attempt to restore a tradition grown fragile. (His critique of Edmund Burke's conservatism makes this clear.[89]) Strauss is not protesting in order to take sides in a historical dispute between old and new; his is a protest against surrendering to this historical process, a protest against "historicism."[90] In accordance with the triad of morality, power, and history, this means Strauss does not want to surrender to the vagaries of historical development; he wants to oppose them by holding up an order in which power sets moral standards.

Strauss's justification for nihilism and the way in which he finally moves beyond the stance of the "young nihilists" is starting to emerge. This nihilism is not "absolute," it is directed in a "specific" way against a civilization that has succumbed to history,[91] and it is supposed to pave the way for a "movement from the supremacy of history towards the supremacy of nature."[92] This recourse to the nature of man is the "most important and least developed of Strauss's themes,"[93] and I will take a critical look at it in a moment, since this nature is what Strauss believes makes the "closed society" of the political order accessible. "Self-sacrifice," "courage," and "seriousness" are the attitudes appropriate to

it.[94] Strauss eerily juggles with contemporary role models for this attitude. In his New York lecture of 1941, he mentions Ernst Jünger's eulogy
for the "warrior" and Carl Schmitt's theory of the "*Ernstfall*" ("serious
moment") on the one hand, and then Winston Churchill's "blood, sweat,
and tears" speech on the other.[95]

Strauss wants to fight the battle against liberalism on the highest level,
and this leads him to Hobbes. In a review published in French in 1933, he
wrote: "Hobbes is the founder of liberalism; and hence whoever wishes
to engage in either a radical justification or a radical critique of liberalism
must return to Hobbes" (HCR 122). He is less restrained in his review of
Carl Schmitt's *The Concept of the Political*, which had been published a
year earlier in German: "A radical critique of liberalism is thus possible
only on the basis of an adequate understanding of Hobbes."[96] In a letter
to Gerhard Krüger, Strauss says with a shake of his head: "How can a
sensible person, a *philosopher*(!), be liberal or justify liberalism? [. . .] The
upshot is a complete lack of orientation in the 'trends in current thought,'
in which 'everything' is philosophically possible" (SGS 3, 404).

Strauss grapples with Hobbes at the end of his book *Spinoza's Critique
of Religion*, in *The Political Philosophy of Hobbes* (which first appeared
in English in 1936), in various essays and reviews, and in his long chapter
on Hobbes in *Natural Right and History* from 1953. He looks back to
the start of liberalism while looking forward to its end, which Strauss
happily anticipates in 1933: "As world history will soon have brought
liberalism to an end everywhere, the great and true problems can finally
be understood again" (SGS 3, 428).

The ambivalence that is the secret to Hobbes's great influence in the
1930s is viewed by Strauss much as it was viewed by Carl Schmitt.
Strauss depicts Hobbes as the person who clears the way for liberalism –
and makes life difficult for it at the same time. This duality corresponds
to the "indecisiveness" highlighted by Schmitt. But unlike Schmitt,
Strauss starts his analysis not with the theory of state power, but with
morality. Hobbes's ambivalence can be summed up as follows according
to Strauss's diagnosis: *On the one hand*, Hobbes ascribes to individuals a
wild mixture of drives that are morally relevant. To prevent these drives
from leading to chaos, the state order must take action – meaning that
this order functions primarily as a bulwark against evil and cannot be
interpreted as an extension of individual interests. *On the other hand*, as
Strauss interprets it, Hobbes swings around to focus on these individual
interests and tries to derive the state order from them. The first strategy is
anti-liberal, the second is liberal.

In his Hobbes book, Strauss develops convincing arguments against
a more recent influential trend in scholarship, whereby the justification
of state sovereignty based on contract theory is attributed *exclusively* to

281

morality-free self-interest. Hobbes's concept, according to Strauss, does not begin and end with the rational choice strategy that one employs to maximize one's own "utility" under the umbrella of the state.[97] Instead, self-interest is only one element of a person's comprehensive, morally relevant repertoire for Hobbes. In his early book *The Political Philosophy of Hobbes*, Strauss shows how Hobbes initially takes account of the honor and courage of "aristocratic virtue" but, over the course of time, increasingly pushes this to the background (PPH 50, 114f., 126). In view of this competition, the interest in self-preservation loses its monopoly position as a "fundamental fact"[98] and cannot be considered "the norm of universal ethics" (HCR 128f.). In his later essay "On the Basis of Hobbes's Political Philosophy," Strauss invokes other moral motives, such as "kindness" and "charity," which can, under certain circumstances, come into "conflict" with the "demand of civil obedience."[99]

The evolution from self-interest to the state is further hampered, as Strauss sees it, by the fact that people are compelled by drives stemming not from the realm of good but from the realm of evil. In particular, this includes "vanity": "If man by nature finds his pleasure in triumphing over all others, then man is by nature evil" (PPH 13). Vanity seduces people into overestimating their strength and resisting subjection; it accompanies obedience like a dark shadow. Hobbes's approach to vanity resembles his approach to the noble virtues, according to Strauss: He "puts vanity more and more into the background" (PPH 14) and, in the end, wants to incite people to move from self-interest to obedience. As Strauss summarizes it: "By trying to give reasons for unqualified submission to authority, Hobbes makes impossible unqualified submission to authority."[100] In other words, if submission must be unqualified, it is actually a waste of time to summon up reasons for it. But this is precisely what Hobbes believes is necessary – and thus he concedes that submission is not a sure bet. The state cannot rely on individuals; it must assert itself in its struggle against them.

Hobbes is strongly inclined to avoid this battle, according to Strauss, and to cling to the seemingly elegant solution that individuals are devoted to the state of their own accord.[101] This brings us to the liberal Hobbes. "His final word" is that if the subjects "rightly understood [their] own desire for private gain," they would "unconditionally obey the secular power" (PPH 118). "Competition," "striving after power," and "animal appetite" would then proceed along the tranquilized pathways of the political-economic contract society (PPH 14).[102] The recalcitrant would be tamed. Wickedness is not fundamental; it is only a misunderstanding. Strauss believes a political order that comes about in this way is morally deficient and – as Carl Schmitt and others would agree – politically unstable. "Calculation and self-interest are not strong enough as social bonds."[103] I am on board with Strauss's diagnosis – but not with the treatment he suggests.

Morality, according to Strauss, can only be assured if, instead of looking to the support of individuals, the state becomes the absolute power that counters all evil "rebellious" tendencies.[104] The state should not only manage individual interests, it should itself be "good" in the highest moral sense. "Affluence does not cure the deepest evils," Strauss says[105] – and he thus argues more fiercely than any other interpreter of the *puer robustus* that the state must assert itself against a person who is "by nature evil." Strauss claims that the liberal Hobbes shies away from the very "assumption of his theory" that would justify the power of the state (PPH 13). He writes: "Oppression is coeval with society, [...] because men are bad. [...] One would have to say that man is by nature bad if, to quote Hobbes, this could be said without impiety [*sine impietate*]" (cf. C[l] 80; C[e] 33).[106] Here Strauss is alluding to the very passage in which Hobbes talks about the *puer robustus*. In Strauss's review of Hobbes from 1933, he explicitly mentions the *puer robustus* and incorporates him into the argument just outlined:

> Vanity and fear characterize the two opposite ways of human life. To vanity – the outlook of the physically grown-up man who is still only a puer robustus [strong boy] – there corresponds the natural ideal of the happiness of man: the dream of triumph, of conquest, of mastery over all men and thereby over all things. Fear – the concern of homo adultus [adult man] – is in accord with the outlook of defense, of a modest life, of working in the rank and file. It is to the opposition so understood, which is never again developed as purely, as deeply, and as frankly as it is by Hobbes, that one must go back if one wishes to understand the ideal of liberalism, as well as socialism, in its foundations. For each battle against the political in the name of the economic presupposes a preceding depreciation of the political. (HCR 135)

The *puer robustus* is presented as someone who lets politics go to the dogs and, as Hobbes says, "surpasseth in rapacity and cruelty the wolves, bears, and snakes."[107] Strauss's defense of the state boils down to the argument that the state must gear itself toward good *and* that only the state is capable of enforcing this good. In accordance with the moral grounding of politics that Strauss takes from Hobbes and intensifies, the state is virtually obliged to have an abundance of power if it is to remain victorious in the struggle against the *puer robustus*.

Strauss goes very far – too far – in his attempt to defend this abundance of power. This is particularly clear in an infamous letter he wrote to Karl Löwith on May 19, 1933, while in exile in Paris. To rescue the state from liberal decline, he says, it is necessary to look to "fascist, authoritarian, *imperial* principles" (SGS 3, 625).[108] Here we have a victim of the Nazi regime casting out the devil by Beelzebub. In the battle against rebellious obstinacy and individualistic self-interest, he seeks the backing of a fascistically consolidated state power. This is a consequence of the fact that Strauss's interpretation of the *puer robustus* remains entirely fixated on the character's wickedness, and it carelessly pushes aside all of the efforts made by Rousseau, Diderot, Hugo, and others to rehabilitate him.

We can be bewildered by Strauss's decision, in 1933, to choose "fascist principles," of all things, to employ in the fight against evil. But it would be too lazy to simply reject him on account of his description of the situation in 1933, just as it would be too lazy for us to console ourselves with the knowledge that he would later count himself among the "friends and allies of democracy."[109] We can learn an important lesson from Strauss here. It relates to his understanding of the state and the rebel, and thus to his special approach to the question of order and disturbance in political philosophy that guides the thinking in this book.

Like clutching at the straw that I hope will save me from dismissing Strauss, I cling to the valuable distinction he makes in his critique of Schmitt: the distinction between "dangerous" and "evil." Strauss notes that when Schmitt speaks of "evil," he actually just means "dangerous" – or, more precisely, dangerous to the state.[110] By shifting from "evil" to "dangerous," Schmitt's state loses the moral claim that is supposed to be tied to power, as Strauss bemoans. This is the source of his complaint that such a state remains a mere positing and is therefore just as arbitrary as the liberalism that Schmitt – like Strauss, in his time – opposes.[111] Arbitrariness on a large scale stands in opposition to arbitrariness on a small scale. Meanwhile, no one knows who is right, because it is purely a matter of decision. The state's demonstration of power is only justified, according to Strauss, when the state is truly good and the individual against whom it is directed is truly evil. "Politics is the pursuit of certain ends; decent politics is the decent pursuit of decent ends."[112]

Strauss suspects that everything is not *automatically* above board when a republic is defined by changing majorities and opinions. No one would blame him for his doubts. He is loyal to the state only to the extent that the state's intended "good" corresponds to "the truth about man and society."[113] "Just government is government which rules in the interest of the whole society, and not merely of a part."[114] Justice and goodness prove themselves, according to Strauss, in the transcendence of individual narrow-mindedness. Consequently, it is not "self-realization" but only "self-denial" that can promote a "non-mercenary morality" in politics.[115] This attitude leads people to pursue a goal that is larger than themselves. It opens them up to the experience of "the sublime."[116]

284

By basing the goodness of the state on truth, Strauss makes politics dependent on philosophy. The latter can be counted on to have an understanding of the iron laws of "human nature" in all of its "unchangeability."[117] How such insights into human nature can be gained remains unelucidated, but the praise for democracy that Strauss finally brings himself to express is ultimately based on the fact that its guarantee of liberty benefits those philosophers who strive for truth and thus stand for "human excellence."[118] That this liberty also happens to be granted even to those who remain stuck in mediocrity is something he tacitly accepts.

Strauss explicitly stresses, however, that the state is not *always* good. This implies that he must be aware of circumstances in which a radical critique of the state would be permitted or even required. But far be it from Strauss to endorse such a critique. He does say: "There will always be men [...] who will revolt against a state which is destructive of humanity or in which there is no longer a possibility of noble action and of great deeds." But he thinks little of "revolutionary or subversive activity"[119] and believes that those who have had the benefit of a philosophical education could not be anything other than "politically moderate": "They are not subversives, [...] they are not irresponsible adventurers but good citizens."[120] What makes Strauss the enemy of the rebel and thus the enemy of the good version of the *puer robustus*? He mentions two reasons for the caution he advises; the first sounds defensive, the other offensive. Strangely, as we are about to see, these two reasons do not fit together – they actually contradict each other.

For something like rebellion to be permissible at all, according to Strauss, it must be morally superior to the state against which it is directed. And it must justify this superiority through philosophical insight. This brings Strauss to the *defensive* finding that such an insight is *inaccessible*. The insurgent who believes himself to be in the right can only be a "boaster" or a "sectarian."[121] By warning against the rebel's tendency to overestimate himself, however, Strauss is shooting himself in the foot. This is because access to the truth is denied not only to the troublemaker, but to *everyone*. Strauss says that there is a supremacy of "problems" over "solutions": "But wisdom is inaccessible to man. [...] [W]e are not competent to be judges."[122] Anyone surprised by Strauss's desire to base politics on an understanding of the "nature" of man now finds Strauss falling back on the Socratic motto of knowing that we know nothing.

With his defensive call for tentativeness, Strauss almost sounds spiritually akin to Isaiah Berlin. Strauss would clearly not stand for such a comparison, as he accuses Berlin of being a relativistic liberal.[123] He therefore cites a different argument against rebellion, one which puts him on the *offensive*. This argument does not content itself with the inadequacies

285

of human knowledge to quell the exuberance of rebellion, but instead invokes a certainty that should be reason enough for the state to crack down on rebellion with an iron fist.

According to Strauss, because the actions of the state are focused solely on the "form of laws," these actions aim at generalization and thus already fulfill a necessary condition of morality.[124] Like Kant, Strauss considers the regular nature of the state to be a proto-moral quality. Strauss refuses to believe that an individual venture could claim a validity beyond private opining. All he sees in rebels is treachery and a self-satisfied delight in destruction. In other words, he acknowledges only Franz Moor, not Karl Moor. Strauss's verdict that protest is inevitably "evil" must be held up against John Dewey's thesis that it should be considered a "competing good."[125]

There is a strange passage in the essay "What Is Political Philosophy?" which does not really seem to fit with Strauss's aversion to the rebel that I have just criticized:

> There exists a very dangerous tendency to identify the good man with the good sport, the cooperative fellow, the "regular guy" [. . .]: by educating people to cooperate with each other in a friendly spirit, one does not yet educate non-conformists, people who are prepared to stand alone, to fight alone, "rugged individualists."[126]

This text from 1954–5 strikes a very American tone. Strauss's plea for the nonconformist recalls Tocqueville, Mill, and Ralph Waldo Emerson ("Whoso would be a man, must be a nonconformist").[127] And considering his early criticism of individualism, Strauss's praise for the "rugged individualist" is also surprising; this praise is shared, incidentally, by Helmut Schelsky, who, in 1946 – perhaps as a courtesy to the American occupying forces – expressed admiration for the "pioneers of the frontier" with their "weatherproof individualism."[128]

Strauss is not otherwise as benevolent toward dissenters as in the passage just cited. The precondition for his eulogy is a limitation: namely, that disturbance should not take place in the political sphere but should instead be restricted to the "private"[129] attitude of the individual. Strauss thus takes the sting out of this disturbance – much like Tocqueville does with the self-revolutionary. The nonconformist is presented as the alter ego of the philosopher who stands at the edge or above the community and enjoys an unobstructed view of truths that remain hidden to the people entangled in their own interests. Strauss is the sole author analyzed in this book who allows the outsider to exist only as a privileged figure: a philosophizing "gentleman."[130]

4. Helmut Schelsky on power and young rowdies

The career of the scholar who is the focus of this section could be described as a resocialization measure that turned a savage into a supporter of the state. Helmut Schelsky's earliest relevant text here is the Nazi polemic *Sozialistische Lebenshaltung* ("Socialist Ways of Life") from 1934, in which the 21-year-old brownshirt railed against "individualism" and celebrated the formation of a "*Volksgemeinschaft*" ("community of the people").[131] Schelsky studied under Arnold Gehlen and Hans Freyer, who also became Nazis. In 1939 he qualified as a university lecturer with a dissertation on Thomas Hobbes, a paper that was almost unsurpassed at the time in its academic sterility and ideological neutrality. It was not published until decades later. After 1945, Schelsky focused on empirical social research and became one of the most influential German sociologists of his generation based on one topic in particular: youth. Having experimented with rebellion as a young student, he turned his attention to the *Halbstarken*, or young rowdies. In the end, he came to view the youth not as a disruptive element or source of unrest, but as a generation in early retirement which had submitted to democracy. Schelsky's path leads from a "revolution from the right" to praise for "restoration."[132]

Schelsky's connection to the other authors covered in this chapter is palpably clear. He shares his enthusiasm for National Socialism with Schmitt; he grapples with Schmitt and Strauss in his interpretation of Hobbes; and after the war he maintained a tense but productive rivalry with the Institute for Social Research led by Horkheimer, one highlight of which – as we will see at the end of this section – was a surprising reference to Adorno.

While scholars have already analyzed the relationships between Hobbes, Schmitt, and Strauss, this triangle of authors has not yet been expanded into a quadrangle by including Schelsky – or indeed a pentagon by including Horkheimer.[133] Schelsky's path from joining the National Socialists, through his interpretation of Hobbes, to his later studies of the sociology of youth, offers an opportunity to bridge the gap between Hobbes and the political theory of the late twentieth century. Implicitly, as we will see, the *puer robustus* is everywhere.

Hobbes is not mentioned in the young Schelsky's text on *Socialist Ways of Life*, but this work can easily be read as an attack on the Hobbesian doubling of individualism and state power. "Individuals," Schelsky says, are preceded by the "community of the people" that is the "precondition" for "all of their actions," and their "will" develops through their "continual deferral of selfish goals and drives."[134] Schelsky cites Hitler's comparison between "material egoism" and "a spirit of sacrifice."[135]

287

He not only goes after individualism, however; he also goes after the state. Schelsky consorts with the faction within Nazi ideology which – unlike Carl Schmitt, for example – subordinates the state to the people. And he once again invokes Hitler to do so: "The state is a means to an end." Schelsky rejects as "reactionary" those "currents" which – invoking Hegel – view the state as "God present in this world," and he counters them with a focus on the "life of the people" as a truly "revolutionary [...] attitude."[136]

Both individualism and the institution of the state are contrasted with a community which – like Blüher's and Baeumler's male association – represents a *total fusion*.[137] Schelsky's National Socialism stands not so much for totalitarian institutions as for the excitation of the masses, the lock-step performance of the people. The energies inherent in revolution, rebellion, Oedipal protest, etc., are not civically domesticated, they are channeled by the movement. Anyone who does not participate must reckon with punishment. The harshest quote from Schelsky's early text is: "It is true socialism for the people who do not fulfill their obligation to the *Volk* or who actually harm it to be neutralized or even destroyed."[138] The *puer robustus* here is forced into the role of *Volksschädling* ("pest harmful to the people").

Schelsky retrospectively describes his own development almost as if he had spent his time sobering up in a drunk tank. He says Hans Freyer urged him to pursue strict philosophical work and suggested the topic of "the relationship between power and right" in Hobbes.[139] Looking back, in the late preface to his Hobbes text, he remarks that, at the time, he had "naturally [...] not been an opponent of National Socialism, but rather an adherent with a very subjective interpretation of its substance" (TH 8).

What Schelsky retains from his National Socialist beginnings, but also from his study of German idealism under Gehlen[140] and Freyer, is "an activist conception of humanity." He "seats the nature of man [...] in becoming," in "the deed." Schelsky interprets "power" as "the power to do" and declares that the significance of the "will to power" has "always been misunderstood" in the interpretation of Hobbes's theory of the state (TH 30f., 84, 114). According to Schelsky, Hobbes should be viewed as "an 'activist' thinker" (TH 14), and Schelsky wants to follow Hobbes's lead in this. Schelsky invokes two philosophers as warrantors for his interpretation. The first – unsurprisingly – is Nietzsche, whose "will to power" is pushed in the direction of Hobbes. The second – very surprisingly – is John Dewey, whose pragmatism is said to be "largely in accordance" with Hobbes.[141]

Activism wields polemical power against all theories that justify the state order by making recourse not to activity but to an "original being"

288

(TH 113), a particular nature of man, whether this nature is construed as weak and needy, "dangerous" (Carl Schmitt), "evil" (Leo Strauss), or communal (Aristotle).[142] It is clear from this that Schelsky bows out of the fundamental discussion of whether man is "evil" or "good." Such a discussion undermines the possibility of "transformation" and self-formation that is open to individuals and enables good and evil to be reinterpreted (TH 283, cf. 195f.). "Man is by nature neither good nor evil, but powerful."[143] In terms of the triad of power, morality, and history, we can say that Schelsky relegates morality to the back row (TH 196), while he interprets power in an activist way, conceives of it as a historical process and approves of it. In connection with this, Schelsky refers multiple times to the preface of *De cive* in which the *puer robustus* first appears, without ever mentioning or acknowledging the fellow himself, however (TH 331, 420, 427f.).

Schelsky's marginalization of morality pits him against Strauss, while his dynamization of power pits him against Schmitt. If individuals are not considered an ongoing danger or source of evil, this topples the argument for a strong state that Carl Schmitt employs on the basis of political theology and that Leo Strauss employs on the basis of moral philosophy.[144] But Schelsky continues to be occupied by the question of "*Who brings about the order?*" (TH 401). If man is what he does and what he makes of himself, the state order must prove to be the work of man. (Schmitt argues the opposite: "The state is thus not a construct that people have made for themselves; on the contrary, it makes a construct of every person."[145]) The "ingenuity" of Hobbes, according to Schelsky, was to derive the creation of the state from human actions and thus "establish a *concept of the political* without explaining it on the basis of the state" (TH 108, cf. 79). Access to the state comes from the bottom up, according to Schelsky's activist interpretation of Hobbes, so Schelsky must return to the threshold where the wheat is separated from the chaff, the *puer robustus* from the law-abiding citizen. On the one side are those who are "*dangerous to the state*" and "antagonistic to the state," those who – on account of their "excessive self-esteem" as Schelsky says, using a nice quote from Hobbes[146] – want to get by on their own (TH 429, 432, 190). And on the other side are those who work in a way that supports or shapes the state.

By choosing the bottom-up approach, Schelsky moves closer to the much-discussed position that rule abidance is a product of the benefit calculation of individuals who are, as Rudolf Smend says, characterized by their "deepest inner non-participation in the state."[147] But Schelsky drives a wedge – in a different way to Leo Strauss – between Hobbes and the rational-choice interpretation of rule abidance. Schelsky believes the utilitarian interpretation overlooks the "achievement of the Hobbesian concept of power," which does not gear human action toward some external benefit or commodity but instead tries to "increase" it as a form of "consummation" or "passionate activity," as Schelsky writes, quoting Dewey[148] (TH 123, 163).

I share Schelsky's critique of utilitarianism, but I am somewhat nervous about it. There is nothing about the critique itself that could lead to totalitarianism, but Schelsky is on the starting blocks and getting set to draw his own political conclusions from this critique – making it dangerous to move ahead with his argument.

Schelsky does not want to relegate the enemy of the state to the corner of evil, as Leo Strauss does. Instead, he believes he can convict him of a "false self-view" or a false life. The troublemaker "contradicts himself" in that the way he acts is damaging to this action itself, or to his "power to do" (TH 341f.). People damage and limit their display of power when they pit themselves against others and *wrestle* with them (cf. TH 156f.). To maintain full consciousness of their own power, they must *eliminate* discrepancies and disagreements. They can achieve this by identifying with the state in "total devotion" (TH 418). "The discovery of this character of power to establish conviction, discipline and order is one of the deepest insights of the Hobbesian philosophy of power" (TH 387).

To counter the inclination to become a *puer robustus*, Schelsky holds out the promise that, through identification with the state, a person will gain access to a "communal action" which "sets him on the path to his perfection" (TH 195, cf. 130, 330). With this phrase, which sounds more like Rousseau than Hobbes, Schelsky turns against one of the best-guarded convictions of Hobbes scholars: that, in Hobbes's contract theory, submission to the sovereign is compensated with the acquisition of individual rights. But according to Schelsky, such rights would once again sow seeds of discord in the fusion of individuals with the state: "The fight is not about rights at all, but about the survival of the state; [Hobbes] wants to convey this realization [. . .] to everyone involved" (TH 427).

The exegetic debate about whether Schelsky's reading of Hobbes is accurate does not interest me here. I will say, however, that I believe it is incorrect, as Hobbes does promote individualistic advancement under the umbrella of the Leviathan, and he defines the liberty of the individual – contrary to Schelsky's assumption – largely as a negative liberty, i.e., as "an *absence of the lets, and hinderances of motion*" (C[l] 167; C[e] 125; cf. L[e] 91).[149] But how shall we evaluate Schelsky's proposal independent of Hobbes?

It is easy to see where Schelsky stumbles as he moves from individual action to the total state. There is an increase in power, but it can no longer be attributed to people personally; instead – as Schelsky traitorously admits – there is a "transferral of power" (TH 417) to the state leadership. The achieved unity is based on an "identity fiction," making it merely a "fictitious unity" (TH 395, 367).[150] The price of activism is that the individual person is no longer allowed to be an actor. He is relegated to "fealty" (TH 330). Schelsky's solution destroys itself on the path from the power of the individual to the power of the state.

This brings the *puer robustus* out of his defensive position. As an individualist, he is shunted to the margins by Schelsky. But because he does not surrender to the state, he is actually the only person left to be an activist. As a result, anyone who insists upon their own activity or power must take on the character traits of the *puer robustus* and become a source of unrest. There is indeed a form of political order that welcomes such unrest, but it is not Schelsky's *Volksstaat* ("people's state") – it is democracy alone. The troublemaker who hinders the autonomization and unification of state power is, consequently, a special friend of the state: namely, a friend of democracy.

As I said, Schelsky developed his interpretation of Hobbes in a kind of drunk tank. He was foaming at the mouth in 1934, but then he cleaned himself up. He provides a dry justification for a state based on leadership and fealty – nothing more, but also nothing less. After 1945, he faced time in another drunk tank. He wanted to take his leave of National Socialism and befriend the democracy of the postwar period. The first sign of his success appeared in 1946 in the form of his text on "The Peoples' Desire for Liberty and the Idea of the Planned State" – a very interesting conglomerate of old and new, narrow-mindedness and openness, which I can unfortunately only address very briefly here.

Just as the earlier Schelsky had celebrated "communal action," the later Schelsky continued to oppose the liberal Hobbes: "There exists neither 'the' state nor 'the' individual, there is only a social whole."[151] But he moves this "whole" away from National Socialism and spins it off in various new directions. Instead of setting up a contradictory package of "will" and "fealty" that is supposed to keep the troublemaker down, as he did in his Hobbes text, Schelsky now tries to reconcile the idea of the state with that of liberty. He is thus faced with the important new task of defining this liberty in such a way that the troublemaker cannot use it against the state.

On the one hand, Schelsky again refers to John Dewey and says that the world is "an incomplete, nascent world with an uncertain future, but it is geared towards people taking action and pitching in," i.e., toward "liberty." In connection with this, he can even imagine a "rebirth of liberalism," which he previously harshly criticized. Like Dewey – and unlike Leo Strauss – Schelsky sticks to the position that good and evil are "a matter of experiment" and can only be determined through a process; he talks of the "moral justification of the *experiment*."[152]

291

On the other hand, this open evolution and experimentation in political life runs the risk of dissolving or destroying the institution of the state, which is why Schelsky wants to put the brakes on the activist. He alludes multiple times to Carl Schmitt, such as when he warns against "satanic insurgency."[153] People are expected to act as "teammates" within a fixed framework, and not, like the *puer robustus*, as spoilsports.[154]

Schelsky's solution – if we can call it that – is to weaken and restrict liberty. We find evidence of this in his thesis that "liberty" consists of "the creation of certain living conditions." This shifts the perspective from the actor to the state, which establishes an orderly framework for a safe life. Liberty thus deteriorates – as Schelsky is astonishingly willing to admit – into lack of concern: "Ultimately, it does not come down to the citizen's liberty vis-à-vis the state, but to the welfare and happiness of the people."[155]

This is traitorous in terms of political ideas because Schelsky is affiliating himself with Ernst Forsthoff and Rudolf Smend who, in the Weimar period, were at the farthest right edge of the political spectrum, and who subsequently exerted a strong influence on the self-conception of the young Federal Republic of Germany. As a result, a geographical and intellectual distance opens up between Schelsky and both Dewey, with his "creative democracy," and Kelsen, with his concept of dynamic democracy, which had been conceived as an alternative to Smend's celebration of political integration even before 1933.[156]

One decisive consequence of Schelsky's pivot from liberty to welfare was that he turned away from activism and ended up with a paternalistic version of the very utilitarianism he had previously bitterly opposed. He now welcomed the economization of politics.[157] This pivot was sealed in his later works, particularly *The Skeptical Generation* from 1957. In this book, he bids farewell to the revolutionary fantasies of the youth movement[158] and, implicitly, from his own activities around 1933. He refers critically to Karl Mannheim, who characterized the youth as the "pioneers in building up a new world" and the key to a "dynamic society" and "militant democracy." Mannheim portrayed the new generation as an innate outsider, like the *puer robustus*; he said it came "from without," like other groups who "live on the fringe of society," such as the "oppressed classes" and the "unattached intellectuals, the poet, the artist."[159] Schelsky firmly rejects this idea. A life on the threshold seems horrific to him. As Schelsky sees it, the basic requirement of youth is to overcome "behavioral uncertainty" and to retreat to a "home."[160] According to Schelsky, young people just want to belong. What his teacher Hans Freyer meant as a bitter reproach in 1931 now fit perfectly with Schelsky's concept: "We just want things to get better for us. To get our due. We just want in. We just want – to get older."[161]

Schelsky sees in "the youth of today" a "political and organizational passivity." But he believes this is a *good* thing. In place of "collectivist active transformation" there is "adaptation," a "*privatist*" orientation and the "need for authority." What the youth "generally demands of the state is that it should establish and maintain peace and order."[162] Schelsky supports the grossly overblown but personally seductive theory that the youth, and the entire population, has been depoliticized. He claims they have a "permanent consumer passivity towards politics."[163] With his reference to a "person's fundamental desire for order, peace, permanence and continuity,"[164] we find that Hobbes's hour has come once again. The reduction to the private sphere, which is where the Leviathan ultimately leads, and the depoliticization that Tocqueville depicts in his nightmare image of the "new despotism", are presented as an ideal in Schelsky's later work. In place of the political dynamic between the "generational fronts,"[165] we find a society of people who are apparently all the same age or ageless, all of whom fall into line. Like David Riesman, upon whom Schelsky bases his argument here, Schelsky emphasizes the ambivalence of political abstinence, but this is still more preferable to him than "political adventure."[166]

Schelsky's diagnosis can be plotted along two axes, the construction of which I have repeatedly addressed in this book. The first relates to the *generation question*. Plotted along this axis we find Hobbes, Tocqueville, and Freud appealing to people to grow up in the right way, as well as Rousseau, Diderot, and Hugo defending the threshold situation of the child. With his fight against the troublemaker, the later Schelsky reveals himself to be a narrow-minded advocate of adulthood. He even goes so far as to reframe young people – with their desire for peace and quiet – as quasi-adults.

The second axis along which Schelsky's diagnosis can be plotted is the *gender question*. In 1934, the young Schelsky depicted an activist who was swamped with masculinity (taken to mean combat readiness); in the postwar period, however, he described how this character was tranquilized through the "public services" offered by the welfare state. In other words, the savage man is subdued by a woman who appears in the form of a caring mother. Schelsky *likes* this, though his teacher Arnold Gehlen remarked with bitter irony (and, thankfully, with a reference to Hobbes): "The Leviathan thus increasingly takes on the traits of a dairy cow." Gehlen foresaw the downfall of the state in this development: "When a state collapses, men lose their value – and this condition could also be referred to as liberty."[167]

The idea that democratic freedom goes hand in hand with the defeat of man is a cliché from which we should quickly distance ourselves. All the same, it is worth looking at Schelsky's position in the context of earlier stages of gender theory. It is important to remember that even Hobbes's original Leviathan was interpreted as an authority that appeared male–female, paternal–maternal, punitive–caring. Gehlen's "dairy cow" was therefore already on the scene in Hobbes's work. Anyone who submitted for the sake of preserving their life was said to act in a quasi-feminine way, while those who threw security to the wind were said to act in a quasi-masculine way.

When the *puer robustus* assumed the form of the nomocentric troublemaker in the period after Hobbes, this masculine stance was entirely associated with the role of the hero. It was presented as a virtue of political self-determination, while both the obedient subjects and, increasingly, the egocentric troublemakers were pushed into the female corner. There was a precious secret hidden in this scenario, however: the fact that this heroic troublemaker was female-coded in a decisive way. He wanted to meet with approval, and – in the works of Rousseau, Schiller, and even Freud – he therefore exhibited a quasi-feminine, socially acceptable sympathy. This femininity came into play in a different way in the playful, eccentric troublemaker who, according to Diderot, distinguished himself by sympathetically placing himself in the position of others and using his sentiments to "commiserate" with everyone.

Schelsky is neither willing nor able to juggle all of these clichés, much less to break through them. He clings to simple templates to ensure a sense of order in his thinking – and in the world after World War II. This order emerges in his about-face from activism to the satisfaction of needs. The turnaround took place in Germany, the nation of the economic miracle, as well as other Western countries that were on their way to joining the affluent consumer society.

In the 1950s, events took place that did not really seem to fit with Schelsky's thesis of youth in early retirement. He had to grapple with them in *The Skeptical Generation* – if only to defuse the explosive material within them. It was a time of wild unrest – in cinema, in music, on the streets. It is beyond the scope of this book to provide a history of everyday life and youth culture after 1945, so I want to mention just three outstanding examples of new kinds of disturbance in the political order: the movies *The Wild One* (1953) with Marlon Brando and *Rebel Without a Cause* (1953) with James Dean,[168] and *Absolute Beginners*, a novel about life in London by Colin MacInnes (1959),[169] which was later filmed with David Bowie.

In Germany, the break with satisfaction took the form of what were known as the *Halbstarken* riots. Between 1955 and 1958, there were around 100 "large-scale riots" in Germany in which 50 to 1,500 young people wreaked violent destruction.[170] The year 1956 saw the release of a corresponding film, *Die Halbstarken* (translated into English as *Teenage Wolfpack*), with Horst Buchholz. The teenage rowdies' favorite pastimes – smashing cinema seats, breaking off car mirrors, and beating up passers-by – do not make for the most glorious chapter in the history of the troublemaker. The rowdies let loose until they had vented their spleen. Their mischief often only lasted for a night, and after 1958 the hubbub died down fairly quickly. This does not mean, however, that youth protest came to an end – on the contrary.

In order to categorize Schelsky's approach to this youth protest as a continuation of his involvement with National Socialism and his inter-pretation of Hobbes, it is necessary to say a few words about the teenage rowdies in Germany and slot them into the history of the troublemaker. Contemporary accounts depicted these rowdies as close relatives of earlier versions of the *puer robustus*: the masterless men of Hobbes's age, the *gaillards* and gamins of Balzac and Hugo, the politically inca-pable European lower classes of Tocqueville, Hegel's rabble and Marx's lumpenproletariat, etc. Even in their name, the *Halbstarken* (literally, the "half-strong") exhibited the robustness of the *puer robustus*, the "strong and sturdy boy." It is worth quoting from early characterizations of the *Halbstarken* because they illustrate the kinship between these teenage rowdies and the *puer robustus* in a striking way:

> The "*Halbstarke*" is the young person "gone astray." "Gone astray" is a nicely illustrative phrase. To go astray means to go wrong; the one who has gone astray has entered life in the wrong way.[171]

> [He is] a strong-boned animal with a mighty power of resistance, thick and close-knit brows over deep-set eyes, with a boxer's nose and big white teeth [. . .], a young barbarian, a barbarian of the present day [. . .], a child, but dangerous.[172]

There is a dual perspective in these characterizations which runs through the entire history of the *puer robustus* right from the start. The focus is sometimes on troublemakers who are shifted to a realm beyond society and declared to be creatures of nature, and sometimes on how the social order deals with deviations. While Hobbes and, to a certain extent, Tocqueville describe the *puer robustus* as an irrational creature of nature who is alienated from society, Schiller and Hugo are interested in the social origins of the troublemaker. This duality also appears in reference to the working and dangerous classes of the nineteenth century: some-times they are presented as wild animals by nature, sometimes it is said that barbarous conditions are what turn them into barbarians (regarding Tocqueville and Hugo, see above, pp. 168, 130).

This controversy was reignited by the *Halbstarken*. On the one hand, the teenage rowdies were seen as an example of a "reversion to a wild type," one which tears through the thin "blanket of civilization" and says:

"We are, it seems, only civilized people on notice."[173] On the other hand, there were doubts about whether the violence arose from the failure of civilization, as if from a power failure. This led some scholars to wonder if the violence was actually the result of civilization itself: "The youth stands abandoned and unfulfilled in the jungle of modern life."[174] Helmut Schelsky took this tack. He observed "a breakout reaction among the youth, which is unplanned but rooted in vital needs and directed against the manipulated satisfaction of modern life and against the unassailable pressure of conformity in modern society," against "the cotton wool of manipulated humanity."[175]

Schelsky was less disturbed by the teenage rowdies than some of his agitated contemporaries, however – and this relates to the fact that he integrated them into his image of society, in which the thirst for exploits had dried up. He did not think the teenage rowdies were even capable of true exploits; all he saw in them was an "emotionally driven eruption."[176] This is easier for the state to pacify than deliberate protest or targeted action. If the teenage rowdy is merely driven, then he is not an actor, and he makes for a rather sad troublemaker. But even one of Schelsky's close colleagues, who spoke of "eruptive action," doubted that Schelsky was right with his tranquilization strategy.[177] This doubt fed into a strange poem, one still worth reading today, which appeared on September 2, 1956, in the German tabloid *Bild am Sonntag*:

> You made us half-strong because you are weak! [. . .]
> Are we not distorted reflections of your phony existence?
> We make public noise and run riot,
> but you struggle mercilessly in hiding,
> one against the other. [. . .]
> For each one of us who makes noise,
> show us one of you who is good in silence [. . .].
> The strong go into the jungle and cure Negroes
> because they despise you, as we do.
> Because you are weak, and we are half-strong![178]

If Schelsky read these lines, they must have triggered mixed feelings in him. This is because the "strong" in question here resemble the activists from his Hobbes text, while the "weak" are like the needy, tranquilized citizens who expect the state to manage their "public welfare." I have to use Schelsky against Schelsky here, because I find myself in the embarrassing position of fishing activism out of the compromising context of his Hobbes text of 1939 and defending it in order to hold it against the later Schelsky.

Schelsky thinks himself safe because the activism of the *Halbstarken* is not an *objection*, in the strictest sense, but is instead *wordless*.

Incidentally, these "speechless rebels"[179] had many successors. Their significance – contrary to Schelsky's thinking – lies in the fact that they thwart the minimization of action that Schelsky thinks he sees *and* that he wants to encourage.[180] Action cannot be eliminated from the world. It would be a mistake to vindicate only those troublemakers who step forward with a complete program, a fixed concept, a long to-do list. As a threshold creature, the troublemaker cannot be chastised for not being fully formed and not knowing what to do.

In accordance with this, the *Halbstarken* – again contrary to Schelsky – take on political significance.[181] It is true that, at first glance, they appear apolitical and thus do not even attract attention in a society plagued by "permanent consumer passivity."[182] And yet, the *Halbstarken* deviate from this consensus in an odd way. The disturbance they cause is not based on the calculation of benefit otherwise prevalent in society. The rioters frankly indulge in their "uselessness"; they are active but "unproductive."[183] They deviate from a politics that has dissolved into economics.

The rapid demise of the *Halbstarken* protests would seem to confirm Schelsky's thesis that society can be permanently tranquilized and depoliticized. But in light of the ongoing youth protests in Germany and throughout the Western world, we have to laugh and shake our heads at Schelsky's prediction in his book *The Skeptical Generation* from 1957:

> Come what may, this generation will never be revolutionary, will never react to things in a blaze of collective passion [. . .]. In all that is so popularly referred to as world-historical events, this youth will be *a quiet generation* [. . .]. A generation that has set its sights on survival. [. . .] Nothing could be more wrong than to interpret these protests against social adaptation as the precursor to a radical political or social youth "movement."[184]

Schelsky's prognosis was completely wrong. His empirical research into this "quiet generation" was based on people born between 1930 and 1940. They included many leading figures in the student movement that would start just a few years later.[185] This generation made the transition "from 'half-strong' to strong protest,"[186] and Hannah Arendt welcomed the resurgence of action by calling out to the student movement that "acting is fun!"[187] In opposition to Schelsky, we can therefore say that the "awareness of a fully-formed world being at one with itself"[188] crumbles as soon as Schelsky has declared it to be a *fait accompli*. Society's internal outsider does not retire after all; the *puer robustus* remains ready to make another appearance.

I now want to jump on the springboard that will take me to the section dedicated to Max Horkheimer. This springboard comprises an unusually lengthy, nearly page-long quote in *The Skeptical Generation* taken from

Horkheimer's companion, Theodor W. Adorno. This reference is unusual because while there was certainly interaction between Schelsky and the Frankfurt School, there was also a high degree of mutual animosity.[189] The quote is from a "memorandum" by Adorno in which he talks about people afflicted by what he calls "concretism." I will cite just a few lines from Adorno's text:[190]

> It is as if these people had appropriated the paternal "It's none of your business, you silly boy," the "Leave the thinking to those who have learned how to do it," so thoroughly that they forbid themselves any impulse not geared towards the tangible and concrete. [...] A shrinkage of the power of imagination and memory, of foresight and of hindsight, is found without exception among such people. What is respectively their "own" [...] precedes any interest in the "alien" in the broadest sense. [...] Instead of a persevering *I* that is identical to itself, there is adaptation to the situation.

Schelsky is interested in Adorno's "very apt [...] term 'concretism'" and remarks:

> One can see in it a crass egoism and vulgar materialism that makes it impossible to think beyond the current situation, to look at the whole picture or to experience intellectual obligations – that, in fact, leads to pure profiteering and hedonism as life goals, if not straight to criminality. We then have before us "those bruisers of the so-called practical life" (Seidelmann) that are quite typical of this generation and are not especially gratifying.

Mind you, one "can" view all of it in this way, Schelsky says. "One must," however, "see" it differently, as he goes on to say: "A negative assessment of this mental attitude among the youth [...] is out of the question."[191] He adopts Adorno's description but upends the assessment of it. Just as he himself withdrew to a drunk tank after 1945, so to speak, he praises the postwar youth for their withdrawal from the "world of illusions, of ideologies" and the triumph of "the positivism of life security," of sobriety and objectivity.[192] His partisanship for "reality" is ideological, however. Behind Schelsky's praise for "concretism," there is an objectivity connected to a compulsion, to total discrimination against the immaterial, supposedly unreal sides of life. These include not only dreams and fantasies but also non-economic values and ideals. Schelsky's peaceful citizens fundamentally lack the ability to advocate for any particular values. In one of his few public statements about Schelsky, Horkheimer wrote in 1961: "A skeptical generation is no more immune to participation in misdeeds than is one of believers."[193] Even in apathy, the deed as misdeed lies dormant.

5. Max Horkheimer on the authoritarian state and little savages

Max Horkheimer, too, pulls Hobbes into the political and philosophical abyss of the twentieth century. But he does so as the member of a different political camp – not as a Nazi collaborator like Schmitt and Schelsky, nor as a conservative exile like Strauss. His involvement with Hobbes starts with the book *Beginnings of the Bourgeois Philosophy of History* from 1930, and Hobbes also haunts various essays from Horkheimer's time in exile, including "Egoism and the Freedom Movement" from 1936 and "The Authoritarian State" from 1940. As with Schelsky's works, Hobbes plays hardly any role in Horkheimer's sociological and socio-philosophical studies after 1945; but we will see that, beneath the surface, these studies – much like Schelsky's works – still relate to the *puer robustus*. Horkheimer was naturally familiar with Hobbes's *De cive*, and he was also familiar with Diderot's encyclopedia article on "Hobbisme" (HGS 9, 129f.), in which the *puer robustus* makes an appearance. Horkheimer does not mention the *puer robustus*, but he does talk about "little savages" (AFT 373) – without, however, naming Diderot as the source of the phrase.

The fact that Horkheimer's theoretical assumptions and goals have little overlap with the other authors in this chapter does not preclude him from reaching similar conclusions. In his works – as in the works of Carl Schmitt – Hobbes's state is presented as a mechanism or a machine (BPS 337–43; HGS 9, 107). Somewhat clumsily, Horkheimer simply lumps Hobbes in with the early materialists (BPS 343; HGS 9, 121). From a social technology perspective, the "rebel" (BPS 345; cf. HGS 9, 126) is merely a bad scientist on his own behalf. *The person who disturbs is disturbed* – according to Hobbes he suffers from a deficit of reason, and according to Helvétius he is not a receptive "pupil" of his own circumstances.[194] But according to Horkheimer, the "revolution" or "rebellion" that Hobbes views as "the absolute and most terrible crime, the crime *par excellence*, as it were" cannot be considered an expression of simple unreason (BPS 349, 345; HGS 9, 127). In light of the social inequalities that Hobbes downplays in his "myth of the contract" (BPS 349), the "rational justification for obedience" comes to nothing – so it is perhaps high time for some disruption (cf. HGS 5, 330f.). Contrary to Hobbes, Horkheimer believes the number of rebels surpasses that of idiots, as they have multiplied since Hobbes's time.

I have pointed out several times – including at the start of this chapter – that the modern theory of the state and the theory of the individual have the same origins. *A state seldom comes alone.* The entire complex is up for debate here: the Hobbesian duo (odd couple? power couple?)

of state and individual. In the works of Hobbes, the state forces the dissolution of ranks and the disembedding of individuals in order to ascribe rights and duties to them under the umbrella of a new unity. Schmitt, Strauss, and Schelsky believe that Hobbes's formation leaves a flank unprotected. By playing on the threshold, Hobbes lands himself with a sense of estrangement between the individual and the state, which can degenerate into obstructionism.

To close this gap, other thinkers have imagined a total state (Schmitt), defended a closed society (Strauss) or banked on welfare services from the state (Schelsky). While they all cling to order and want to save the state from the individual, Horkheimer looks to disruption. He, too, labors away at the Hobbesian duo of state-and-individual – but mostly at the individual. While the other three authors blame this individual for weakening the political *order*, Horkheimer believes the individual weakens the *disturbance*. He seeks an entity that combats the "authoritarian state" in its various guises as "integral statism" and "state capitalism."[195] But he encounters people who are individualistically deformed. The unruliness of the hangers-on, Mafiosi and similar fellows remains blinkered, and the political potential of the troublemaker is weakened. Horkheimer's search for this potential proves difficult for two other reasons as well. The first has to do with Marx, the second with Hitler and Stalin.

Marx was on the hunt for a revolutionary collective subject, and he thought he had found it in the *puer robustus* of the proletariat. At the same time, he noted with disappointment that this proletariat was increasingly becoming a "lumpenproletariat," meaning that the workers were falling back on the economic self-interest they were actually supposed to have transcended. Horkheimer finds it difficult to connect with Marx here because he views Marx not only as a critic of depoliticization, but also as a precursor to socialistic economization, according to which "future forms of society" are judged "solely according to their economy."[196]

Historical events further complicate Horkheimer's search for the political troublemaker. He is reluctant to speak of revolution because he sees that the Russian revolution led to Stalinism, and that National Socialism presented itself at least in part as a revolutionary movement. (Alfred Baeumler, for example, praises the "masculine-active, deliberately acting, *revolutionary*" view of history.[197]) Stalinism and National Socialism have coiled themselves around the vocabulary of revolution as the epitome of political disruption.

Horkheimer responds to the compromised revolutionary with a critical review of the various concepts circulating around him. He describes a revolutionary who is a placeholder for "nature" or "youth" representing the good core of humanity (BPS 55, 87; HGS 5 341), who appears as the "creator of [his] own destiny" and of a new world (BPS 98), or as the protagonist of the philosophy of history who completes his task just in time.[198] If we stick with the troublemakers who have appeared in this book, then the first kind fits with Rousseau, the second with Richard Wagner's Siegfried, and the third with Marx and Engels. Horkheimer does not expect terribly much from any of these concepts of the revolutionary, and his depressing summary of the situation is further intensified because he believes these conventional revolutionaries have been joined by yet another, one who gives him the chills. Horkheimer's description of this new type of revolutionary is his most valuable, critical contribution to the theory of the troublemaker.

As mentioned earlier, Horkheimer is familiar with the well-established thesis of Marx and others that people who are pinned down in their role as individuals can no longer summon the strength for political disturbance. *But he realizes that this thesis is not true.* Admittedly, these people cannot bring about the emancipation through political disruption that Marx would like to see. But another kind of disruption runs rampant instead – and it is quite terrifying. To put it briefly, Horkheimer describes this as a disturbed disturbance, i.e., a disturbance that allies itself with the political order.

In his essay "Egoism and Freedom Movements" from 1936, Horkheimer starts with a finding that seems to have been taken directly from Marx's essay "On the Jewish Question": "The nature of the isolated individual is itself a dubious topic for anthropology. This isolated individual is not the same as human beings in general, which is supposed to be anthropology's frame of reference" (BPS 50f.). It is precisely this individual, as Horkheimer shows, who finds himself in a relationship with others and with himself that is the source of the terrible disturbance just mentioned.

A deep sense of strangeness creeps into the *relationship between* this individual *and others*, according to Horkheimer. Regardless of whom the individual encounters, the other person remains alien (cf. BPS 95f.). "All who are drawn into this world develop the egoistic, exclusionary, hostile sides of their being" (BPS 52). In a posthumously published note from 1939/40, Horkheimer describes this in dramatic terms:

> The bourgeois individual can only be understood in light of his dogged resolve to embrace this egoism. His entire education boils down to him learning to despise himself if he acts differently. Then he is weak, pathetic, crazy. [...] At the end of the world, he reveals himself to be what he has ultimately become: blind to everything beyond his own narrowest objectives – the enemy. (HGS 12, 278f.)

While Carl Schmitt positions the state against the "internal enemy," Horkheimer describes a society consisting solely of enemies: "In reality the

301

enemy is everywhere and nowhere."[199] Hobbes is praised in the *Dialectic of Enlightenment* for having "denounced harmony,"[200] and Horkheimer does exactly the same. He sees a society made up purely of troublemakers. Their closest relatives are "criminals": "The radical isolation and the radical reduction to an unchanging, hopeless nothingness are identical. The human being in jail is the virtual image of the bourgeois type."[201]

Is it even possible to withstand the feeling of being alienated from and hostile toward everyone else? In his *relationship with himself*, the individual finds this unbearable. The message associated with this – that he should be able to muddle through on his own – sounds like a hollow, scornful demand. The more commonplace the experience of actual powerlessness, the "more pitiful the individuals of the masses [...] appear to themselves" (BPS 98). They become enemies of themselves. They hate themselves for amounting to nothing and achieving nothing. This drives them to struggle with their self-image, and it mobilizes the very development that leads to havoc – or, more precisely, to "Heil Hitler."

The troublemaker that Horkheimer has in mind is something new. He is different from the proletarians who discuss their goals and attempt to implement them as a "community," and he is also different from the American pioneers and the "lumpenproletariat,"[202] who are concerned only with scrounging up something for themselves. In any case, he has nothing to do with the friends of deviation (Diderot), adventure (Nietzsche), or "social eroticism" (Thomas Mann). This new troublemaker has no intention of raising his head, because he is sick of himself. He is driven not by "self-determination" but by "self-abasement" and "self-contempt" (BPS 98). He is far removed from humanity's "self-realization" (Marx); instead, this "individual of the masses" (see above) overcomes himself through self-abandonment or, as Horkheimer says, referring critically to a term from Joseph de Maistre, through "self-negation" (HGS 5, 324).[203] He shakes off all trace of individuality – and can then be defined only as a mass being. By wading into battle against established society, this mass being becomes a *massive troublemaker*.

This troublemaker hastily leaves his marginal or threshold situation and replaces inner and outer alienation with total assimilation. While Schelsky's activist development of political will only tips over into self-negation at the end, following Horkheimer's explanation this self-negation is an important element of the mobilization of the masses by the National Socialists. You can engage in damage and destruction, but you are not really doing it yourself, not in your own name, but rather as part of a mass with a higher calling. The Nazis said as much in one of their pamphlets: "We are and we act? No! *It – 'it' – is and acts in us*."[204]

A desire for subjugation is woven into this type of disturbance. It is, as Adorno brilliantly puts it, what drives those "rebels who, crashing their

302

fists on the table, already signaled their worship for their masters."[205] In Wilhelm Reich's book *The Mass Psychology of Fascism* from 1933, with which Horkheimer is in agreement "on many points" (BPS 399, note 144), Reich writes: "The more helpless the 'mass-individual' has become [. . .], the more pronounced is his identification with the führer (sic)." This is referred to as "national narcissism."[206] The affirmation of the totalitarian collective can only be assured when everyone is cast from the same mold and is of the same type. They are not only formally equivalent as individuals, they fuse together into a synchronized mass. This confirms, however, that they themselves are "a nullity."[207] The Nazi slogan that readily confirms this is: "You are nothing, your *Volk* is everything!"

Those who want to give the troublemaker the benefit of the doubt are put off their goodwill by the Nazi hordes. Horkheimer refuses to write off the troublemaker as such in the face of National Socialism, but he shows how and why a *disturbed* disturbance can come about. It stems not from the self-awareness of those who can withstand and perhaps even relish their threshold situation, but rather from the self-negation of those who cannot bear their alienation.

Keeping Horkheimer in mind, if we look back at Carl Schmitt, it is obvious how he exploits the alienness of individuals in order to promote their integration into the "total state." Individuals must become a "nullity" in order for Schmitt to allocate them to a new unity and hype up the shared "ethnic identity" of the leader and his followers. Unlike other contemporary interpreters of Hobbes, Horkheimer does not mobilize the state order against rebels or adventurers, he describes how this order itself becomes fascist and turns the troublemaker into its fighting machine.

Horkheimer talks not only about Nazi thugs but also, as mentioned earlier, about "little savages" (AFT 373) – and he in no way equates the two. The latter make an appearance in his essay on "Authoritarianism and the Family Today," which was published in 1947. This is both a companion piece to the American studies on the *Authoritarian Personality* by the Institute for Social Research from 1950 and a postscript to the studies on *Authority and Family* from 1936.

In this essay, Horkheimer looks at the desolate situation of the individual in capitalist society and detects within him – even, rather audaciously, in the American version of him – "opinions which might be regarded as potentially fascist" (AFT 368). To be precise, he describes a combination of two such "opinions." Following my categorization, we could say that *massive* disturbance, in which individuals relish their subjugation, is linked (also and especially in the USA) to *egocentric* disturbance, in which individuals ruthlessly do their own thing. As Horkheimer sees it, the "little savage" has not opted for just one of these two disturbances, like the Nazi thug; instead, he combines absorption in the mass with stubborn willfulness in a half-baked way. Lacking a "consistent independent ego," he takes refuge in a "gang" and "behaves as a scheming little adult" who always has to "look out for himself" (AFT 367, 373, 360). He is trapped in the "glorification of authority *per se*, without any specific idea of the end which the authority is supposed to serve," and he simultaneously revels in being "hardboiled" and having a "lust for power" (AFT 368, 367, 371). This "configuration of submissiveness and coldness" gives free rein to a "sado-masochistic character" (AFT 368f.).

In one passage, Horkheimer highlights only the second, egocentric side of the "little savages" and notes: "In a cold and inscrutable world, they suspect everybody of being their enemy and leap at his throat. They revert to the cynical principle of early bourgeois philosophy, *homo homini lupus*" (AFT 373). In the smallest of spaces, this passage brings together the *homo homini lupus* popularized by Hobbes with the "little savage" who serves as an epithet for the *puer robustus* in Diderot, who instigates the war of all against all in Baudelaire, and who is an epithet for Oedipus in Freud.

In general, Horkheimer's "little savages" can be described as *hybrid* characters. They pursue the self-interest to which they are relegated, and they are driven by their hardship or their discontent. Insofar as they feel alienated from themselves, they are driven by a longing for the mass in which they feel strong. This mixture of the egocentric and the massive troublemaker is not necessarily contradictory. The "little savages" can live out their hybrid identity by pursuing aggressive interests under the protection of a mass that often forms only on an *ad hoc* basis. They partially do their own thing and partially devote themselves to the mass, but their devotion never goes so far that – like fascists – they are prepared to surrender themselves and die for their people.

Recent history is shot through with such hybrid troublemakers, who feel great and goad each other on in groups, and who therefore display a mixture of egocentric and massive elements in various proportions. They made an appearance in the London riots of 2011[208] and in the violent and sexist clashes on New Year's Eve in Cologne in 2015.[209] But it is not only in the anonymity of the street that we find characters who could be interpreted as a combination of the egocentric and massive troublemaker – they are found on the big political stage as well. Their most prominent representative is named Donald Trump.

Horkheimer focuses on the threshold where people enter society in either the right or wrong way, and he asks which opposing forces could keep the "little savages" from carrying out their misdeeds. Specifically, he makes reference here to the synergetic and sympathetic forms of socialization that I discussed in the context of Rousseau and Freud (see pp. 63,

241). In his essay on "The Authoritarian State" from 1940, Horkheimer argues synergetically. He speaks of "free association," i.e., of a collective subject that is strictly opposed to the fascist mass, and writes: "Dread in the expectation of an authoritarian epoch does not hinder the resistance."[210] In "Authoritarianism and the Family Today" from 1947 and in his later references to Schopenhauer's "pity" and "freedom from egoism" (HGS 7, 251, 248), however, he sticks with sympathy. The refuge of sympathy is the family, to which Horkheimer – despite being aware of the pathologies – ascribes the "dream of a better condition for mankind."[211] What the little savages "suffer from is probably not too strong and sound a family but rather a lack of family" (AFT 373). Horkheimer sees in the family an "element of social cement" (AFT 361), and he thus misses the opportunity to conceive of it as an agent of historical change – that is, to discover the threshold situation within it, where people undergo a process of becoming.

In the 1950s, Horkheimer was afflicted by a despondency that induced him to reject and betray this process of becoming. This is apparent in the frontal attack on the young Jürgen Habermas that Horkheimer launched in a letter to Adorno from September 27, 1958. Horkheimer accuses Habermas of uncritical enthusiasm for "revolution" that leads to "terror" and claims that Habermas "praises dictatorship, even if unintentionally."[212] One of the lines that Horkheimer takes from Habermas's incriminated essay "On the philosophical discussion of Marx and Marxism" would have suited him well in earlier years – and it suits me well to use it to bring my Horkheimer commentary to a close: "Society is always a society that must be changed."[213]

In the debates during the Nazi era, the troublemaker barely stood a chance. The individual who had been freed to act as an egocentric or eccentric troublemaker was viewed as a corrosive element. The nomocentric troublemaker was declared to be the enemy and was, at best, considered a partisan to be combatted. The massive troublemaker appeared in their stead, either entering into a hybrid relationship with the egocentric troublemaker or wreaking his own havoc in his desire to submit. But what happens to the troublemaker in a communist setting?

— XI. —

GOOD SPIRITS AND
POISONOUS WEEDS

The puer robustus *in Italy in 1949 and
China in 1957*

1. Togliatti's New Year's message to his comrades

Fascism has been defeated. The revered party leader returns from exile in Moscow, dedicates himself to political reconstruction, is severely wounded in an assassination attempt, and sends his comrades a New Year's message which is published on January 1, 1949, in the newspaper *L'Unità*. Palmiro Togliatti speaks:

> The imperialists [...] are concerned and unsettled by one thing above all – and this is the power, the strength and combat readiness of our great party. [...] *Puer robustus et malitiosus* – our party is young, strong and not to be outwitted. You can count on that! [...] We are the party upon whom it is incumbent to stand by the people in its need, by teaching it to resist, to fight its enemies and to unite in order to defend bread, freedom and peace and to conquer the future.[1]

Some contemporary readers of this message seem to have been puzzled by the invocation of the *puer robustus*.[2] Togliatti thus found himself having to explain the Latin phrase, which he had initially simply quoted from memory – with a misspelled "malitrosus." After some research in the parliamentary library, he passed on the information that the phrase had originally come from Hobbes and could also be found in Friedrich Engels' *Socialism: Utopian and Scientific*. In that context, however, it was aimed not at the Communist Party but at the people in general. Engels was therefore behind the appearance of the *puer robustus* in Italy – and he also inspired the character's appearance in China, which I will talk about later (section 2). Following the tracks of the *puer robustus* will take me from Italy to the Far East – and then back to Europe, where I will finally take on Alain Badiou, the most influential Maoist of our day (section 3).

In his New Year's message and follow-up explanations, Togliatti emphasized the strength of youth; he toned down the adjective *malitiosus*, defining it as the gift of being able to slyly and mischievously thwart the intrigues of one's opponents. For Togliatti – as for Marx and Engels – the *puer robustus* is a good person whom others simply believe to be evil. If it were still necessary to do so, the indestructibility of this character could be demonstrated by his repeat appearances in Italian parliamentary debates and newspaper articles following the New Year's greeting of 1949. But Togliatti does more than just provide a footnote to Marx and Engels; he gives the *puer robustus* a twist which is significant in its substance, particularly in contrast to the fellow's appearance in Beijing just a few years later. This twist concerns how the troublemaker relates to organizations and institutions.

Togliatti concedes that by embracing the *puer robustus*, he is embracing not the people but the party; he is, therefore, someone who is worried about the strict organization of the revolutionary collective. At the same time, he joins in the choir of voices praising young people as the pioneers of a new world. The relationship between the party and the youth was somewhat dicey, however – especially in post-Fascist Italy, where there was not only the usual gap between party discipline and youthful exuberance, but also a deep sense of alienation between the communists and the younger generation, with whom they had practically no contact during the long years of Fascism. When Togliatti returned from exile, he found himself on a political threshold that seemed predestined for the appearance of the *puer robustus*. But the pathos of a new beginning was tinged with postwar exhaustion. Togliatti's allusion to the *puer robustus* was, therefore, an expression of political optimism under difficult circumstances. It speaks in his favor that Togliatti was acutely aware of the difficulty of this new beginning, which he analyzed in 1947 in his important text on "The Moral Crisis of Italian Youth."

In this essay, Togliatti anticipates the thesis of his New Year's greeting, which says that politics is intimately connected to the question of youth. He objects to an essay by Benedetto Croce, in which "the idealistic philosopher attends to the problem of youth, but only to deny that it exists. There is a youth, of course, but it would be absurd to believe – so says Croce – that it has a particular function or mission in the nation. The only thing the youth has to do, its only mission or function, is to grow up!"[3] Togliatti refers to this as a bad "joke," as a blindness to the fact that the "problem of youth" crops up not only in private life but also on the "collective" level, in the "political, moral and social" realm. According to Togliatti, the youth as a whole stands for the difference between the status quo and a "new world," between reality and "dream":[4]

Youth does not live on common sense alone, and I would say that humankind cannot live on it. It requires momentum, dreams, enthusiasm, and I think it also requires illusions and errors, all of the things that common sense denies and condemns. Going beyond the bounds of sober common sense has always been the task of those who want to be the ferment of innovation in the world – and this is what the youth represents.[5]

In his obituary for Togliatti in 1964, Jean-Paul Sartre wrote: "When reading Togliatti's speeches and writings, one word jumps out again and again: *new*. Everything is always *new* for him. In every situation, what happens first is something new, something unforeseen."[6] It is the tension between order and disturbance that defines politics as Togliatti sees it. He does not peddle the cliché of impetuous or innocent youth, but instead directs our attention to the dramatic threshold from which the rules of the political order can be called into question – the threshold where the *puer robustus* resides. This is the systematic significance of the package deal of youth and politics.

When Togliatti calls upon the youth to savor the enthusiasm of the new, however, he is confronted with an unpleasant predecessor, one which seems to have made similar advances to the youth – namely, Fascism. We need look no further than Joseph Goebbels' praise for "this youthfully Fascist Italy," which he said was "filled to bursting with creative power."[7] The myth of youth that Togliatti wants to revive is stained and bloody; the reality he faces is a post-Fascist youth that is sick of this myth. It is not dreams and ideals that Togliatti encounters, but disillusioned "reserve" and emotional "coldness." Disenchanted, he quotes from submissions to an essay contest that had been organized by young Italians: "We guard ourselves against enthusiasm." – "What saddens our souls most of all is the absolute impossibility of devotion to a dream."[8] Schelsky and Adorno witnessed the same disenchantment and reification among the postwar youth in Germany. Togliatti therefore struggled to revive the *puer robustus* of Marx and Engels as a revolutionary subject for political mobilization after 1945. (The relationship between the Communist Party and the youth would remain troubled in later years, as can be seen in Pier Paolo Pasolini's impressive, shockingly party-friendly poem "The PCI to the Young!" from 1968 – and the debate surrounding it.[9])

Among his contemporaries, Togliatti was known for studding his texts with allusions to the Western educational canon. In addition to mentioning the *puer robustus et malitiosus*, he alludes to Søren Kierkegaard and Heinrich Heine in his text "The Moral Crisis of Italian Youth." These references help illuminate the environment around the *puer robustus*, as both of them deal with the threshold creature as a political subject who challenges the established order and struggles with insecurity.

In view of a youth that is tangled in the past and hesitant about the future, Togliatti turns to Kierkegaard's concept of the "unhappy consciousness." The young are unhappy, Togliatti says, because their hopes are "encumbered by shackles" that keep them "chained" to the Fascist past.[10] He falls prey here, however, to an instructive misinterpretation of Kierkegaard's (and, indirectly, Hegel's) definition of the "unhappy consciousness." In the original version, unhappiness arises from a sense of non-identity that causes the mind to shift its focus to the past or future, thus "absenting" itself from itself. Kierkegaard writes: "So the unhappy one is absent. But one is absent either when living in the past or when living in the future."[11] In this respect, as Kierkegaard (but certainly not Togliatti!) sees it, even those who are hopeful are unhappy because they distance themselves from themselves and their present.

The unhappy hopefulness that Togliatti overlooks is, in fact, central to the experience of the troublemaker. As a threshold creature, he cannot help but look beyond what currently exists and suffer under the discrepancy between the status quo and another possible life. His skill is his ability to withstand the tension between entanglement in the present and the audacity of the future, to affirm his own non-identity and translate this tension into a dynamic in which he transforms himself – and perhaps also leads all of society to undergo a transformation or conversion. If the troublemaker thinks he is above Kierkegaard's "unhappiness," then he is overestimating himself. He would be living *beyond his means*, throwing himself entirely at the future and imagining that he had a handle on it. This would turn him into a guardian of revolution or one of the false utopians that Alexander Herzen so pointedly criticized. Unfortunately, it must be said that Togliatti's party was not immune to this exaggerated opinion of itself.

Togliatti's complaint about the "unhappy consciousness" shows that he, like Marx and Engels (though for different historical reasons), struggled with the revolutionary subject's lack of vigor. Also like Marx and Engels, he wanted to mobilize this subject with the help of the party, promising that the "party" would not work against "liberty" but instead bring about "liberation" from the individualistic tendencies of "capitalist society."[12] Togliatti thus compares the Communist Party with a good spirit, *una specie di genio*, alluding to the spirit that Heinrich Heine discovered walking behind him one night in Cologne around 100 years earlier. Like his allusion to Kierkegaard, Togliatti's allusion to Heine is enlightening. He makes reference to the following lines from *Germany: A Winter's Tale*:

309

I was thoughtfully strolling along the streets,
And back of me he came,
[...] I turned and said:
"Now tell me by what right
You follow my footsteps everywhere
Here in the desolate night?
We always meet when thoughts of the world
Are sprouting in my heart,
When inspiration fires my brain
And flashes of lightning dart. [...]
But he replied in a monotone [...]:
"I am no scarecrow, no ghost of the past [...].
I'm of a practical character: [...]
I find no satisfaction
Till thought becomes reality;
You think, and I take action."[13]

Togliatti exhaustively describes Heine's nighttime scene and comments on it with the words: "We, too, have this kind of spirit at our disposal. It is our organization."[14] He praises the Communist Party as a good spirit that will turn the dreams of humanity into reality. But unfortunately, Heine's irony passes him by. For Heine, it is nothing other than a ghost, a "singular guest,"[15] that is responsible for reality and vigor. The subject that is supposed to perform the liberating deed does not actually exist. Once again we encounter one of the figures that Marx referred to as "shadows" without "bodies," as "inverted Schlemihls" (MECW 11, 125), and once again we are dealing with a desperate search for a subject that might actually have the power to act. (Derrida would probably have been delighted by Heine's interplay between ghosts and go-getters if he had taken notice of it while writing his book *Specters of Marx*.)

If Heine's irony had not passed Togliatti by, he would have faced the question of whether the Communist Party, which wanted to turn dream into reality, had the characteristics of a specter. The ghastly aspects of Togliatti's party were held in check, but not those of the Communist Party of China, which came to power in 1949, the same year Togliatti wrote his New Year's message to the Italian people. Again and again, people rebelled against this power. One of them called himself a *puer robustus*. He was not a party member, he was a dissident.

2. Mao Zedong and Tan Tianrong on fragrant flowers and poisonous weeds

One of the rare ideological thaws in Maoist China took place in 1956 and 1957. Mao Zedong proclaimed the slogan "Let a hundred flowers bloom, let a hundred schools of thought contend."[16] To combat resistance from within the party,[17] he launched a campaign aimed at renewing the party and society as a whole, and he called for the open discussion of contradictions and conflicts. Bureaucracy and dogmatism were pilloried. On March 12, 1957, Mao declared:

> "To give free rein" or "to impose restrictions"? This is a question of principle. Letting a hundred flowers bloom and a hundred schools of thought contend is a fundamental as well as a long-term policy. It is not a temporary policy. [...] The opinion of the Party Center is that we can only "give free rein" and "not impose restrictions." [...] To give free rein is simply to allow everyone to express his or her opinion freely so that he or she would dare to speak up, dare to criticize and dare to contend; it means being unafraid of mistaken arguments or poisonous things. [...] So far, rather than being too free, it has not been free enough; we should not be afraid of giving free rein, nor should we be afraid of criticism or poisonous weeds.[18]

A hundred flowers and poisonous weeds – the political interplay between order and disturbance continues with new metaphors, under new conditions. Mao celebrates the "dictatorship of the proletariat" and the "people's democratic dictatorship,"[19] but he also seems not merely to tolerate outsiders and troublemakers, but actually to welcome them. His Hundred Flowers campaign resonated with intellectuals who, as young people during a different spring, had revolted against the empire in the May Fourth movement of 1919.[20] Mao himself had stood alongside them at the time, and now they once again sensed change and raised their voices.

Mao was especially popular among the students at Peking University. They founded a Hundred Flowers Society, published a newspaper called *The Democratic Baton*, created a "democratic garden" as a forum for open discussion, and erected a "democracy wall" next to the university dining hall. The many posters that were pasted there offered a "feast for the eyes," as one daily newspaper put it.[21] Another contemporary report said: "In Peking University with its glorious revolutionary tradition, more than 8,000 young people had become inflamed with enthusiasm."[22] The whole university was mobilized, the whole world was reeling. A democratic spring! One of many – a predecessor to the Prague Spring,

311

the protests on Tiananmen Square from April to June 1989, and perhaps even the Arab Spring of 2011 and future springs yet to come.

The Chinese student uprising of 1957 – and the Hundred Flowers movement in the narrowest sense – can be dated fairly precisely.[23] On May 19, protest broke out. A big-character poster announced: "The time has come / for us, the youth, / to raise our voices and sing. [. . .] / Let us expose all the feelings in our heart / to the light of the sun. / Let criticism and accusations / rain down on the heads of the people like a storm."[24] Just a few weeks later, on June 8, the spring was interrupted by an unseasonable freeze. The extent of the unrest had surprised and alarmed Mao, and the disturbance was quelled. The so-called rightists were purged, and around 400,000 people were sentenced or exiled. But this future had not yet been foreshadowed back in May.[25]

On May 20, 1957, a 22-year-old student spokesperson named Tan Tianrong[26] pasted his first poster to the wall. He took what represented the limit of liberalization for Mao and cheekily turned it into a positive: the title of his text was "Poisonous Weed." Tan's message started with a quote from Heraclitus, according to which "all old men should meet their death" and "governance of the city should be handed over to beardless young men"; the message ended – or culminated – with the signature "Puer robustus sed malitiosus." With these words, the author of this wall newspaper confirmed that the fundamental political question of modern society – the question of order and disturbance in the light of power, morality, and historical change – had moved beyond the borders of the Western world.

With his wall newspaper, Tan had unwittingly composed the perfect counterpart to Togliatti's New Year's message, which had referred to the Communist Party of Italy as a *puer robustus*. Togliatti stood in the slipstream of communism's founding fathers and grappled in a post-Fascist, newly democratic Italy with the question of how his party could get the future on its side. Eight years later, a student in Beijing came along and drove a wedge between the communist authorities and the youth. But this is about more than just a struggle between young and old; it is about the status of the troublemaker in the context of socialism, in which both the collective uprising of an oppressed class and the extravagance of the individual are supposed to be things of the past.

In China, the proletariat – the embodiment of the *puer robustus* according to Marx – was added to the list of winners in world history and found itself confronted with a *puer robustus* of a different sort, one who disputed the other's victory, or at least took the shine off it. You might be curious (at least, I hope you are!) as to why a student in Beijing chose the *puer robustus* as his role model around 300 years after Hobbes. But before I satisfy this curiosity and talk about Tan Tianrong and his texts, I have to explore the environment in which he moved and find out how Mao prepared the field in which both a hundred flowers and poisonous weeds would grow.

Mao's "hundred flowers" slogan was propelled by the fear that, barely ten years after the triumph of communism, Chinese society was facing stagnation. His campaign was directed against the bureaucrats in the party ranks, and its purpose was to involve the people – among whom so-called "democratic parties"[27] and various other special-interest groups were active – in the advancement of society. Mao wanted to mobilize energies that might otherwise have remained untapped and to encourage people flirting with non-compliance to help establish the people's republic instead. His invitation was directed primarily, though not exclusively, at artists and scientists whom he expected to make an important contribution to the country's progress.[28]

Mao claimed that this blooming and contending would not lead to "disorder,"[29] but he was not so naïve as to believe that the hundred flowers would come together of their own accord in a natural harmony or "symphony."[30] He said it was inevitable that "poisonous weeds" would sprout up alongside the "fragrant flowers"; he had borrowed this contrast, incidentally, from Qu Yuan, one of his favorite poets (4th century BCE).[31] Alternatively, Mao could have made reference to the Soviet educator Anton Makarenko, who described children as "flowers" who should develop into valuable "fruit" and not "common weeds."[32] Furthermore, Mao could have referred to Schiller's talk of "healing herbs" and "poisonous hemlock" growing in the same flower bed, or to Baudelaire, who, in arranging the order of poems in *The Flowers of Evil*, grappled with the question of whether the collection should culminate in the invocation of the devil or of God.[33]

How did Mao deal with the "poisonous weeds" that sprouted alongside the fragrant flowers in the wake of his generous invitation? Analyzing his texts from the years 1956–7, we find four different answers to this question. They are inherently contradictory and can be arranged in ascending order according to the degree of goodwill that Mao musters up for the weeds. The answers can be categorized under four headings: criminalization, regulation, conflict, and critique.

Criminalization. The first and most infamous justification for Mao's invitation to everyone to speak up "freely" (see above) is that when you "lur[e] out the snakes,"[34] when the enemies of the state make themselves known, it is easier to persecute and eliminate them. In fact, Mao did say (though not until the first counter-campaign in the summer of 1957): "Only when demons and ogres are allowed out of the cage can they be destroyed; only if the poisonous weeds are allowed to come out of the soil can they be pulled out."[35] Even during the Hundred Flowers movement,

313

many activists expressed concern that the party was encouraging open discussion only to gain access to opposition groups. Their concerns were justified.[36]

Regulation. According to the second justification for the encouragement of uncontrolled growth, Mao wanted to have a sympathetic ear for non-conformist, critical opinions so that factual grievances could be identified and redressed. This was supposed to channel and regulate the discontent of the population. Mao turned on the functionaries who feared even "small, small democracy" in factories and organizations,[37] proclaiming: "We must be closely linked to the masses. [If we are] divorced from the masses, [if we] practice bureaucratism, we will surely be given a beating."[38] Mao had learned his lesson from the debates in the Soviet Union following Stalin's death in 1953 and from the Hungarian Uprising of 1956.[39]

Conflict. The third justification for Mao allowing poisonous weeds to grow is based on an agonal conception of politics. According to Mao, conflicts would arise not only in the age of class war but also in socialist society. Patronizing criminalization and regulation were not enough to combat this, because the fight would continue. Mao said:

> Only when there is distinction and struggle can there be development.[40]

> Without opposition, there will not be struggle. Only that which emerges from struggle can withstand the test.[41]

> Truth emerges out of struggle with error. Beauty emerges out of comparison with and struggle with ugliness. Good deeds and good people emerge out of comparison with and struggle with evil deeds and evil people. Fragrant flowers emerge from the comparison with and struggle with poisonous weeds.[42]

It was actually not clear from the outset what the outcome of this struggle would be. Stinging nettles had won out over roses in the past. But Mao was confident of victory. He sought conflict primarily to strengthen the fighting power of communism:

> [To fear disorder] is to lock ourselves up in a room, close our eyes, close our ears. That would be very dangerous. [. . .] Our purpose is precisely to get people to think for themselves, to convene forums, to discuss things. Perhaps many weird arguments would come up; I think that the more weird arguments, the better. Just don't let yourselves be locked up, blockaded. Marxism was created and developed out of the struggle with forces that opposed it, and it must continue to develop even now.[43]

The purpose of the poisonous weeds was to keep the fragrant flowers in shape, as it were; they would be nourished by the opponents they vanquished. In connection with this, Mao made numerous comparisons that

314

essentially defined the poisonous weeds as a fortifier or supplement. He pointed out that farmers hoe weeds and use them as fertilizer for useful plants.[44] He also made comparisons with vaccination, whereby one draws strength from fighting against a pathogen:

> It is precisely in the midst of others' criticism and in the storm and stress of struggle that Marxists can temper and develop themselves and expand their [strategic] positions. To struggle with erroneous ideas is like getting vaccinated; under the effects of being inoculated with a vaccine, one will develop greater immunity [against disease]. Things nurtured in greenhouses cannot have strong vitality.[45]

Like the toxin in a vaccine, the weeds appear in a weakened state, which is why there is no need to worry about the outcome of the conflict. It is worth mentioning that Carl Schmitt – unsurprisingly – favors this agonal interpretation. He did not know that one of the rebels of 1957 had adopted the Hobbesian insult "*puer robustus*" as an honorific, but he commented on "poisonous weeds" as follows:

> For years, it has always left a deep impression on me when I read in Mao that one must let weeds grow when one notices that hostile groups are forming in one's own camp. One must let the weeds grow; then it is easier to distinguish them, then it is easier to rip them out, and then there is more and better fertilizer. This is interesting in terms of the concept of the political.[46]

Critique. The fourth reason for Mao to show consideration for poisonous weeds relates to critique in the highest sense – namely, *krisis* as a process of distinguishing and deciding in the counterplay of order and disturbance. This reading deserves special attention because, unlike the other three strategies, this one does not clearly attribute the fruitful and the poisonous, good and evil, to different entities. Mao conceded that there could be a debate about what should be considered good or evil: "Since there are problems, it's good to have a bit of disturbance. [...] When problems occur, both sides should be looked at."[47] – "It is difficult to distinguish fragrant flowers from poisonous weeds."[48] European Maoists such as Alain Badiou[49] like to quote Mao's praise for unrest, but the more exciting aspect is that it recalls Thomas Jefferson's dictum that he approved of "a little rebellion now and then." This also makes it conceivable for evil to turn into good, a transformation we are familiar with from the history of the *puer robustus*. In his most important text from the Hundred Flowers period – the famous speech "On Correctly Handling Contradictions Among the People" – Mao said:

> To determine whether something is right or wrong frequently takes a trial period. In history, new and correct things often could not win

recognition from the majority of people at the start, and they had to move forward by twists and turns in struggle. People tend to deny correct things, good things, as fragrant flowers at the outset; instead, they regard them as poisonous weeds. [. . .] [It] is still a common occurrence for newly emerging forces to be held back and for reasonable opinions to be suppressed. [. . .] Also, in defining what a fragrant flower is and what a poisonous weed is, the various classes, strata, and social groups are each able to have their own criteria.[50]

This quote reveals the complexity of the debate around good and evil. In the toned-down published version of this speech, Mao mentions Copernicus and Darwin as examples of "weeds" who had turned into "fragrant flowers"; in the original version, he also mentioned Jesus and Martin Luther.[51] The point of view that will ultimately prove to be good is not determined from the outset; it only emerges, according to Mao, through "free discussion."[52] When this understanding of critique is placed alongside the strategies discussed earlier – criminalization, regulation, and conflict – the latter three appear comparatively narrow-minded.

Imagine for a moment that Mao were an advocate *only* of critique. He would then seem to deviate from his own teaching. The debate about whether something is good or evil would become a key component of politics itself. The legitimacy of power would be jeopardized and called into question. The contradictions that arose in society would lead to a process with an uncertain outcome, in which no participant, no group, and no committee could claim the truth for itself. Everyone would be involved in this process; no one would stand above it. This would, in essence, invalidate the Communist Party's monopoly on truth. The political order would have to be liberal in a radical sense. And the *puer robustus* could hold out hope of being recognized as a hero.

Mao made a case for *also* engaging in critique, but he would never draw from this the conclusions just mentioned. For the sake of the other strategies that he continued to employ against the "poisonous weeds," he had to keep the back-and-forth of social contradictions in check. Mao could not permit the existence of diverse initiatives with equal rights or an open-ended answer to the question of good and evil.

To reconcile his first three strategies with his fourth one, Mao used a trick. He abruptly made a distinction between "two types of social contradictions": "those between the enemy and ourselves, and those among the people." And he emphasized: "They are two types of contradictions completely different in nature."[53] Poisonous weeds might indeed grow here and there, among the people itself and among the enemies of the people. But Mao reserved the right to deal with these contradictions in different ways. "Regarding those who are obviously counterrevolutionaries and saboteurs of the socialist cause, the matter is easy; [simply] depriving them of their freedom of speech will do." But when it came to "erroneous ideas among the people," Mao had to take a different approach and employ "the method of discussion, criticism, and reasoning."[54] He dreamed of a time when there would "no longer be any enemies" – either because they had been converted, or because they had been eliminated.[55]

There is explosive force behind the comparison of these two methods. On the one hand, "discussion, criticism, and reasoning" are considered elements of a political debate in which even fixed ideas about good and evil can be shaken. On the other hand, the scope of permitted "criticism" is restricted to contradictions within the people. Mao thus erected a dividing wall between the people and its enemies. This dividing wall is not made of paper, but it can be moved. The kicker is that Mao himself decides where it should be placed.[56]

Mao's argument therefore leads to a bad end. Members of the people will have their criticisms heard and can participate in the reinterpretation of good and evil. But this membership is decided not by the fixed law of citizenship, for example, but by the party – the very same institution against which such criticism might be directed. Take the troublemaker Tan Tianrong, for example. Was he a member of the people or an enemy of the people? There is, conveniently, a clear answer to this question. Foreign Minister Chen Yi described the relationship between the people and Tan as a "contradiction [. . .] between ourselves and the enemy."[57] An allegedly open discussion was permitted within a closed circle, the scope of which was defined by the regime as it saw fit. A comment made by Merleau-Ponty in a different context fits wonderfully here: "We thus see the birth of a very singular institution: official criticism, a caricature of permanent revolution." All that does not align with this official criticism, *"all that is other is an enemy."*[58]

There are, therefore, two opposing tendencies in Mao's model of politics. On the one hand, he calls for critique and even uproar, and he recommends a recurrent (he suggests every three years[59]) revolutionary overhaul of institutions. On the other hand, he introduces an ideological distinction between the people and the enemy, which channels this mobilization and ensures the people's synchronization. One could say that, in a contradictory way, Mao clamps together the positions of two theorists who have almost nothing in common and to whom he himself never refers: the positions of Georges Bataille and Carl Schmitt. On the one hand, Mao's concept of revolution bears characteristics of the unleashing of energies that fascinates Bataille.[60] On the other hand, his contrast between the people and the enemy of the people corresponds to Carl Schmitt's fundamental political distinction between friend and

317

enemy – in this case, the internal enemy.[61] (While Mao ignores Schmitt, the reverse is not true; see p. 276f.)

In forcing together these different theoretical motifs, however, Mao distorts them beyond recognition and winds up with something that has catastrophic consequences for political theory and practice. He encourages the synchronization of revolutionary energies (in opposition to Bataille), and he undermines the state (in opposition to Carl Schmitt) by mobilizing the masses. The Hundred Flowers movement was crushed by Mao because it resisted synchronization. Political movements were permitted, but their revolutionary energies had to be approved by the regime; then these energies could be turned against the internal enemy.

This paved the way for a historical event that combined the mobilization of the masses with the elimination of the internal enemy: the Cultural Revolution after 1966. The Cultural Revolution put Mao's extermination of poisonous weeds from 1957 back on the agenda. One literary work strikingly depicts the terrible game that was played with fragrant flowers and poisonous weeds in those years: the novel *Brothers* by Yu Hua.[62] The role of the revolutionary who generously reaches out to the people is played in this novel by Blacksmith Tong, who settles a fight between boys by proclaiming: "You are all the blossoms of our nation." But this strategy of openness is trumped by events that divide the population in two, with the "red-armbanders" on one side, the people wearing "dunce caps" and the "class enemies" on the other. The violence takes its course. "Class enemy" Song Fanping is beaten to death by "red-armbanders," or the Red Guards. As Mama Su watches them turn away from the body triumphantly, she thinks: "*They are not human!* [. . .] *How can people be this vicious?*"

Compared to the Cultural Revolution, the Hundred Flowers period of 1956–7 left a relatively light mark on history. But from the viewpoint of political philosophy, this movement is far more valuable than its infamous successor. The social change that took place in this period – unlike the years after 1966 – was not driven by synchronization and collective agitation. Instead, the followers of the Hundred Flowers movement accepted Mao's invitation to openly engage in critique, to speak out in diverse voices. For them, the question of what was a fragrant flower and what a poisonous weed was open-ended.

What exactly did the representatives of this movement say? What did Tan Tianrong, the physics student and diligent reader of philosophical texts, actually say? Here, at long last, is the text of his first wall newspaper, which he titled "Poisonous Weed" and signed *puer robustus sed malitiosus* and then pasted to the wall of Building No. 26 at Peking University on May 20, 1957.[63] As this text has previously only ever been published in Chinese, it is worth quoting in full here, in all of its complexity.

318

Poisonous Weed
"Every adult in Ephesus should die and governance of the city should
be handed over to beardless young men." Heraclitus[64]

At the moment, the contest between a hundred schools of thought and
the blooming of the hundred flowers is still miles removed from us, the
uninformed youth. There is no system of censorship in our country. But
the complete lack of knowledge about Marxism among the editors of
every newspaper – such as the *People's Daily*, the *China Youth Daily* and
the *Journal of Physics* – their inability to understand anything of dialectics, and the vast stupidity that fills their metaphysical brains create
a 10,000-mile-long Great Wall, behind which the truth is sealed off.
Here is an example: After 1895, Marxism – in accordance with an iron
necessity – turned into its opposite, an initial negation. This fittingly led
to a 62-year hegemony of two related lines of thought within the international communist movement, namely, revisionism and dogmatism.[65]
In the article "More on the Historical Experience of the Dictatorship of
the Proletariat," however, all of this is traced back only to "man's ideological condition."[66] If this is not naked idealism, what is it?

The text about "Spring" by Wei Wei[67] is not only meaningless
and contradictory, it is simply mentally muddled. It is inconclusive and
confusing, but it is treated like the last word on the Xu Jin problem.[68]

Physics, which is overflowing with superstitious quibbles and
employs untruths and far-fetched analogies to compensate for its errors
(also known as "original thought"), is already facing its downfall. Li
Zhengdao and Yang Zhenning have robbed physics of its last remaining
glory, and yet the *Journal of Physics* still talks about these metal layers
and cylinders – what a waste of time![69]

This cannot be tolerated any longer. I suggest the following:

1. We students in Peking should be allowed to produce and publish our
   own cross-disciplinary scientific journal.
2. A lecture series organized by the students will be introduced so that
   we can prove to the world we are not just a few "students with the
   three virtues"[70] (also known as "idiots," "excellent students" or
   "cogs in the machine" – all the same thing, in any case) and we are
   not censoring our thoughts. The youth of China also includes tens
   of thousands of "intelligent and good-looking young people." They
   are persistent and determined, they are bursting with talent, they
   are dazzling. At the sight of them, the international capitalists, who
   happen to be eating, drop their knives.

You stare.
You smile.
You are speechless.
You furrow your brow.

You grit your teeth.
You nod.

All of this is correct. The only thing you should absolutely avoid is becoming furious. You must avoid the state or the automatic reflex that instinctively drives you to reject ideas with which you are not familiar. Otherwise, you would fit better in Shanghai Zoo than Peking University. So, farewell!

Puer robustus sed malitiosus.

On May 20, 1957, Tan Tianrong – a "medium-sized man with glasses" and "gentle eyes" – stood next to his wall newspaper and answered questions from other students. When asked about the meaning of the Latin signature, he responded: "These are the words of the English philosopher Hobbes; you would have known that had you read Engels' book *Socialism: Utopian and Scientific*."[71]

Tan Tianrong was not alone. His fellow campaigner, Long Yinghua, argued that in addition to a five-year plan for socialist industrialization, there should be a plan for socialist democratization. The student Lin Xiling gave a speech in which she referred to a "liberal Western thinker" who had said: "I may not agree with what you say, but I will defend to the death your right to say it." There were boos and cheers from the assembled listeners. Liu Jisheng wrote: "I want to ask, ask and ask!" Rong Di, writing in another wall newspaper, characterized Tan Tianrong as Don Quixote, fighting for "justice and humanity" while being "misunderstood" by his contemporaries.[72] Many other examples could be mentioned. On June 24, 1957, after the counter-campaign had already begun, Tan wrote half-apologetically and half-recalcitrantly:

> My dear friends, allow yourselves to be embraced. Never doubt our great Chairman Mao, and always support us. Never doubt the Communist Party. [...] Never doubt Marxism. It will eradicate dogmatism in the course of its theoretical development. [...] We young students can lay the tracks ourselves. We can drive motorcycles ourselves. Can we not then also overcome the current difficulties? All is well. There is no reason to fear. [...] I will swim against the tide and never give up. [...] Whenever you encounter something new, it is not enough to sniff at it, you must think about it and get used to it. [...] Think about it, my future friends! [...] *Puer robustus sed malitiosus.*[73]

And in a letter to Shen Zeyi entitled "What are we fighting for?", he wrote:

> We are not misanthropists. [...] We have racked our brains to figure out how to find our place in life. [...] We are fighting for a humane society.

320

[. . .] How can you misunderstand the affection we feel for the party and for socialism, and the pain we feel when the party makes mistakes? Socialism is our highest ideal, and we need no hints from the outside to strengthen our belief in this ideal. But in view of the events of recent days, we must accept that we stand in contrast not to socialism but to a deformed socialism [. . .]. We oppose the Chinese version of the Beria regime, which bases its power on bloodshed, incarceration and deceit.[74]

With this last jab at deformed socialism, Tan was referring to Lavrentiy Beria, long-serving chief of Stalin's intelligence service. While Mao claimed to be opening up politics unlike Stalin, Tan provocatively argued that Maoism was beginning to move closer to Stalinism. He insisted that the renewal or reorientation of the party must take place under the banner of "democracy and freedom." The kind of renewal that would take the form of mass mobilization and blind destruction during the Cultural Revolution was not what he had in mind.[75] In his "Fragmentary Thoughts on May Fourth"[76] – i.e., on the democratic protest of 1919 – this Chinese *puer robustus* addressed the tense relationship between old and new and discussed various models of dealing with order and disruption:

Old ways die slowly, the new is born slowly, without haste, one thing comes after the other – this is evolution.
The new is already there, the old defends itself against being swept away, the new can wait no longer and destroys the old – this is revolution.
Destruction is unavoidable when development encounters an obstacle. [. . .] The new is necessary for development to be possible. This is why the youth is always revolutionary and the revolution is always the youth. [. . .]
When the revolution has achieved victory, the new becomes the old and a new type of new arises. But the old stands in its way and says: "A long journey has led me here, and I cannot accept that my sweat and my blood have been shed for nothing. I will stay and make myself comfortable." The new says: "Your comfort is my torment, you are delaying the end of my journey" – and it destroys the old. This game is played again and again. This is also why the revolution never appears to achieve victory.

With his theory that the process of renewal had no end, Tan was not acting as a wanton advocate of permanent revolution; he was describing a state of affairs that Rousseau, Jefferson, Diderot, Tocqueville, and Kelsen had pointed out in different ways before him. Remarkably, this young physics student from Beijing can hold his own with those representatives of classical political philosophy. Like them, he stresses the discrepancy between a political institution and the population for

321

which it is responsible. This discrepancy exists regardless of whether the institution elevates itself above its subjects as an alien power (Hobbes) or serves as the tool of a powerful minority or ruling class (Marx). But it fundamentally applies to the extent that an institution that represents the will of the people distinguishes itself from the presence of this people.

Later on, in his "Thoughts on May Fourth," Tan returns to the distinction between evolution and revolution and discusses the various forms in which the dynamics between old and new can play out. He also revises his earlier thesis of a youth that is necessarily revolutionary:

> When the old, which was just now still new, does not simply celebrate the past [. . .], when it quickly withdraws after it has left its trace – is that not also glorious? [. . .] The thesis that "the youth is always revolutionary" is true only assuming that "the old will never be prepared to give it space." [. . .] If the old ways die slowly, the new will also be born slowly, one thing steadily follows the other. On this day, as history takes its normal course, there will no longer be any need for the exceptional circumstance of revolution. [. . .] This brings us back to the topic of change and chaos. Change is steady development, chaos is destruction through revolution. If one wants to avoid chaotic destruction, one must seek steady change. When that which should change does not change, then change will be brought about through destruction.

Tan's sympathies clearly lay with evolution; he viewed revolution as an emergency solution that becomes unavoidable when the old clings to power. He felt emboldened by Mao to use the blossoms of the hundred flowers for criticism. But there was growing concern in the party that the reins of control were slipping from its hands. In a crisis meeting convened on June 6, 1957, there were warnings that students and other groups were joining together, causing the situation to "worsen": "For the masses are also dissatisfied with the Party today. . ." – "The problems brought to light have far exceeded the estimate."[77] On June 8, as mentioned, the party changed tack. Mao, who had completely underestimated the "vast reservoir of discontent that had been built up,"[78] felt that things were going too far and decided to deal with the poisonous weeds using only three of the four previously mentioned strategies: criminalization, regulation, and conflict. The well of criticism was capped.

Tan Tianrong – together with his comrade and lover Lin Zhao (who would be executed in 1968[79]) – was the most prominent student to be persecuted as a rightist in the campaign in the summer of 1957. He was the only one whom Mao mentioned and attacked by name in a speech from July 1957.[80] In the *China Youth Daily* he was identified as one of the main founders of "The 100 Flowers Society," who had "exploited the innocence, the impetuosity" of the youth.[81] A long list of accusations was leveled against him. It was said that he wanted to destroy socialism, was part of an international anti-communist conspiracy, engaged in extreme individualism, wanted to establish his own army, etc.[82] In July 1957, Tan wrote in a text entitled "Failure":

> I used to have a precious plant. It had a bud, but it never bloomed. Impatient, I tore it open. Then, I watched it wither day after day. [. . .] I also had a dream. I didn't like it because it was vague. I tore it to bits, carelessly. Then, awake, I kept waiting, hoping for another dream. In vain. So I lost both chances. I can't seem to have the good dream I dream about.[83]

In 1958, Tan Tianrong was sent to the Xingkaihu camp in barren northeast China, where he remained until 1968. He spent the following decade as a laborer in his hometown of Xiangxiang; in 1978 he was rehabilitated and allowed to teach physics again; and from 1986 to 1996 he was a professor at Qingdao University.[84]

I want to end this section with an epilogue that revolves around flowers as well as a father and son. The father is named Ai Qing and was one of the most important Chinese poets of the second half of the twentieth century. The son is named Ai Weiwei and is one of the most important artists of the present day.

In February 1957, the same month in which Mao gave his speech on "contradictions among the people" and proclaimed the Hundred Flowers slogan, Ai Qing wrote the text "The Gardener's Dream." It is a commentary on the flowers and the weeds that have been mentioned so frequently in this section:

> There are several hundred roses in the garden, so that the gardener can see roses all year long. His friends throughout the country know that roses are his pride, and they send him all sorts of roses whenever they can. [. . .] In full blossom, the roses, all of the same form but colored variously, give the garden a flourishing vitality. Yet it's a little monotonous. [. . .] One night he dreams: He is trimming the withered twigs from his roses when he sees many flowers entering his garden. It seems to him that every kind of flower in the world has come there. The flowers look at him sadly, with tears in their eyes.

Ai Qing gives a voice to these other flowers: the peony, the water lily, the jasmine, the orchid. They complain in different ways that they are neglected, their beauty is disregarded or their friendship scorned.

Each having expressed herself, the flowers say in unison: "To be understood is a kind of happiness." The roses speak last: "We're desolate. If we could live together with our sisters, we would be happier." Another of her sisters says: "To be someone's favorite is blissful, but we've been alone a long time. Behind the backs of the fortunate there is endless complaining."

Then all the plants disappear. Waking, the gardener is depressed. He walks to and fro in the garden, thinking: "Each plant has its own will to live. Each has a right to put forth its blossoms. My prejudice has made all flowers unhappy, and it's narrowed my vision of the world day by day. Lack of comparison is confusing my mind. [. . .] From now on, my garden will be a place for all flowers. Let me live more wisely. Let all flowers blossom according to their seasons."[85]

These lines require very little decryption. They celebrate difference, debunk the supposed diversity of the varicolored roses, criticize a closed world in which one is deaf to requests and complaints from outside, and bemoan the damaging effect of uniformity on one's own thought.

Ai Qing was Tan's comrade in suffering. He, too, participated in the Hundred Flowers movement, though not as a student but as a famous poet. In 1958 he was sent to Labor Camp 852, very close to Tan Tianrong's camp Xingkaihu. The following year he was interned in a camp in Xinjiang in China's far northwest.[86] "After 1957, I was cut off from everything. It was like living in a coffin," Ai Qing said in retrospect.[87] He was not rehabilitated until 1978 – by none other than the new strongman, Deng Xiaoping, who had himself led the anti-rightist campaign in 1957.[88] Ai Qing was allowed to publish again, and he felt optimistic: "Now people are saying, for example, that '100 flowers are blooming and 100 schools of thought contending.' That used to be a slogan, but it was never put into practice. But now people have started to make it a reality."[89]

The fact that the growth of these flowers would continue to be curtailed – despite Ai Qing's hopes – is demonstrated by the fate of his son, Ai Weiwei, who was born in Beijing in 1957, shortly before his father was banished. Ai Weiwei has not only personally experienced the limits of openness in today's China, he has also made the defeat of the Hundred Flowers movement into the subject of an artwork that was displayed in various locations in 2009–10. The most extensive and famous display was in the Tate Modern in London in 2010, when 100 million porcelain sunflower seeds were spread out in a thick layer on the floor of the museum's main hall. Every single seed had been crafted by hand, making each as unique as the different flowers in the garden his father had written about in 1957. But "like Mao's metaphorical flowers," these seeds were also destined to "never bloom."[90]

3. From China back to Europe: We can forget Alain Badiou

I hope I have dispelled any notion that the Hundred Flowers movement was a distant, isolated chapter of history. The dissent that erupted between Mao and the students expressed the full force of the tension between order and disruption; it revolved around different forms of disruption between conflict and critique, evolution and revolution, as well as around the different strategies employed by the ruling order to deal with troublemakers.

Mao was not only the Great Chairman in China, he was a leading figure for many Western European leftists. Consequently, his approach to "contradictions among the people" and to the *puer robustus sed malitiosus* was imported to the continent where this *puer robustus* originated. What is notable about the reception of Mao in Europe, however, is that the Hundred Flowers movement and Tan Tianrong's "poisonous weeds" have played no role – quite unlike the Cultural Revolution,[91] a mass movement that wreaked havoc in its fixation on a supposed enemy. The fact that the Cultural Revolution was celebrated by many activists and theorists in the 1970s as an anti-statist act of liberation[92] would have been water under the bridge were it not for Alain Badiou, who recommends it as a model for present-day protests against globalized capitalism. To end this chapter, I want to talk briefly about Badiou, one of the most influential theorists in recent radical social criticism, and explain why I have no time for him.

Badiou invokes the Cultural Revolution and treats the Hundred Flowers movement rather dismissively.[93] There are systematic reasons for this, since the protest movement of 1957 would spoil the revolutionary game he wants to play – a game that would be disrupted by the cries for democracy that were voiced in 1957. There is, however, one point of reference from 1957 that Badiou would not want to go without: Mao's speech "On Correctly Handling Contradictions Among the People," which was mentioned earlier. Badiou draws on this "altogether innovative text"[94] in order to systematically analyze revolts and revolutions as well as the "discernment of good and evil"[95] – i.e., the very same questions that concern me as they relate to the *puer robustus*, whom Badiou snubs.

In nearly all of his texts, Badiou proposes a thesis of difference, dissent, and revolt that is found in a similar form in the works of many other theorists – a thesis which, incidentally, I *agree with*. According to this thesis, politics – or, as many people prefer to say, "the political" – does not go hand in hand with the theory of the state; instead, it emerges in the conflict between the state and that which the state excludes or repudiates, that which eludes the state, that which is lacking in the state or which simply does not exist for the state.[96] Many versions of this thesis exist, and the devil is in the details.

What exactly does Badiou's version look like? We can categorize his argument using the major themes behind the theory of the troublemaker – history, power, and morality – which he combines in a curious way. He insists on *history* by placing dialectical movement on a permanent footing. In the course of historical dynamics, *power* is supposed to be transferred from the state to the masses. Their actions thus receive a *moral* seal of approval. I want to analyze this triple step more carefully.

History. The fact that Badiou insists on historical dynamics is fine by me. But in describing these dynamics, he runs into argumentative difficulties. According to Badiou, the fundamental incompleteness of history arises from the interplay of social contradictions – in other words, from his theory of dialectics. He is picking up on Mao's interpretation of Lenin here. Mao praised Lenin for having referred to "unity" as being "conditional, temporary, transient, and relative" while referring to the "development and movement" of opposites as "absolute." "All processes of the world," as Lenin himself wrote, are to be conceived of "in their 'self-movement,' in their spontaneous development, in their real life."[97] Using Mao, Badiou extends this dialectic beyond the contrasts in bourgeois society and claims that social contradictions would continue to exist even in a socialist society such as China.

But what does it actually mean to grant primacy to the "self-movement" and "spontaneous development" of "real life"? It simply means that this movement itself eludes unification. It is comprehensible only in particular moments. For this reason, it is impossible to conceive of history as anything other than a pluralistic event in which numerous "self-movements" take place, which express themselves, relate to each other, and struggle against one another. This is where Badiou's argument runs into trouble. Badiou refuses to acknowledge this plurality and brands it a bourgeois misunderstanding.[98] To put it briefly, Badiou first dynamizes history, then he channels it. He ties the political subject to a "collective destiny" in which "each person's life joins in the History of all, without any hiatus."[99] He celebrates the pure presence of a "massive popular event" which is not thwarted by self-distance or self-representation.[100] This collectivization of historical processes is then eviscerated by Badiou for his theory of power.

Power. The processuality of history is compacted in mass events, according to Badiou, but it is not channeled to the extent that the collective solidifies into a higher institutional unity. As a consequence, Badiou must always be at loggerheads with the state, regardless of its type. Even within a state that is "formally a 'proletarian' state," Badiou believes that "the class struggle continues, including forms of mass revolt."[101]

This means that "the socialist state" in China cannot be "the policed and police-like end of mass politics," but should "on the contrary [...] act as a stimulus for the unleashing of politics, under the banner of the march towards real communism."[102] The Cultural Revolution is celebrated by Badiou because it instigates the transfer of power from the state to the movement. It brings historical development closer to the moment in which – in the words of Engels, so often cited by Badiou – the state "dies out of itself" (MECW 24, 321) or, to put it more innocuously, "withers away."[103] For the state to die out, others must come to life. Badiou believes that "Mao's innovative, collectivist project" known as the Cultural Revolution resulted in

> the unprecedented mobilization of millions of workers and youths, a truly unparalleled freedom of expression and organization, gigantic demonstrations, political assemblies in all places of work or study, brutal and schematic debates, public denunciations, the recurrent and anarchic use of violence including armed violence, and so on.[104]

In his rather enthusiastic depiction[105] of the Cultural Revolution, Badiou once again refers to Mao's speech from the spring of 1957, in which Mao addressed various historical contradictions. Badiou thinks he can classify the Cultural Revolution as an expression of "contradictions *within the people*"; he explicitly distinguishes it from "the terrorist model of resolving contradictions *with the enemy*."[106] This is the nadir of his argumentation. By defining the Cultural Revolution as an expression of internal contradictions, he acts as though it had availed itself only of the methods Mao had specifically defined for dealing with such contradictions: namely, "free discussion" and "criticism." This whitewashes the brutality of the Cultural Revolution. Furthermore, Badiou does not concern himself with the infamous trick Mao used in his distinction between contradictions among the people and contradictions with the enemy. This trick – as explained earlier – involved placing a movable wall between the two types of contradictions. In the blink of an eye, a member of the people – such as Tan Tianrong – could be turned into an enemy to be persecuted mercilessly. This strategy became routine during the Cultural Revolution. Badiou simply sweeps this aside.

Moving away from the specific case of the Cultural Revolution, Badiou appears to follow a strategy that could be called the empowerment of the troublemaker. As long as the troublemaker is an outsider standing on the threshold of the political order, he is forced to justify his self-determination in relation to power. He does so by egocentrically invoking his own interests, eccentrically undermining the ruling power, or nomocentrically setting himself up as a participant in a different power. In Badiou's autonomization of "mass revolt" (see above), all of these strategies collapse together. The threshold on which the troublemaker finds himself expands to become a lawless space. Historically, we see this in the fact that the "revolutionary youth" in China was officially "guaranteed a form of impunity" during the campaign unleashed by Mao, which Badiou believes to be reasonable.[107] He dreams of an undisturbed disturbance – which is a contradiction in itself. Badiou does the troublemaker a disservice by generously allowing him to be entirely sufficient unto himself. In doing so, Badiou denies him the elixir of life that he can only find on the threshold between order and disturbance and in the productive tension with the status quo. By attributing the uprising of the entire people to the unharnessed, wild troublemaker, Badiou ultimately paves the way for his moral-philosophical legitimation.

Morality. Badiou argues that the Communist Party of China "derives its legitimacy only from as complete an exposition as possible of the way *it* is negated by the action of the masses who rebel against it."[108] Following this line of thinking, the state only indirectly has an opportunity to be good itself – namely, by doing away with itself, delegating its power and releasing its goodness elsewhere, in the self-movement of the empowered masses. With his talk of "legitimacy," Badiou makes concessions to the moral vocabulary I am using here, but in the end he seems to reject this vocabulary. Regarding the Cultural Revolution, he writes:

> The theme of total emancipation, practised in the present, in the enthusiasm of the absolute present, is always situated beyond Good and Evil. This is because [. . .] the only known Good is the one that the status quo turns into the precious name for its own subsistence.[109]

But this thesis of an extra-moral space of revolt is terribly contradictory. Badiou is essentially falling back on an argument already found in Hobbes. According to this, the distinction between good and evil is made within the "status quo," which is why the troublemaker can only be situated outside of both the established order and morality. I have already demonstrated why this argument is misguided using the example of the "Hobbesian howler." The moral claims to validity that are raised by outsiders extend beyond the outsiders themselves. Badiou does two different things here – which is why he winds up contradicting himself. On the one hand, he insists on situating turmoil in an extra-moral space; on the other hand, he describes this turmoil using an expression that is deeply impregnated with morality: "emancipation." For Badiou, turmoil should be super-good or über-good, so to speak; it is beyond comparison and justification. The revolutionary gives himself the nod and pats himself on the back. And that which is praised as "emancipation" withers into a power grab, or the "violence of the specific against the specific" (Hegel, *Werke 1*, 459).

328

How can an emancipation worthy of this name be differentiated from the corrupted "emancipation" of Badiou? The former obviously represents a process of emerging from a state of bondage or disenfranchisement. It involves someone (a group or an individual) fighting against the prevailing conditions that are causing suffering. The nub of this formal description is that, because these conditions are imposed from above, they unleash suffering that not *only* affects the "someone" who rebels against them. In striving for emancipation, this someone is acting in a space also occupied by others. The individual or group who rebels is grappling with something that does not just affect them personally. (In this respect, they differ from someone suffering from heartache, for example, who struggles to get over it and break free. We would not refer to this process as emancipation.)

When people strive for emancipation, they take action as people affected by a circumstance, but they inevitably have others in mind as well who are also experiencing the same lack of liberty. They dedicate themselves to a cause that is greater than them alone. They thus assert a claim to universality that they will defend and want to justify. Their engagement must have the potential to resonate with others, to trigger the kind of "enthusiasm" that Kant felt in connection with the French Revolution. Badiou is not interested in the response from others; he ascribes "enthusiasm" to the Cultural Revolutionaries themselves.[110] They make a show of what they do and are sufficient unto themselves.

Both Marx's "species-being" and "community-being" could claim – in different but equally plausible ways – to look beyond themselves. But in Badiou's apparently extra-moral celebration of emancipation, the revolutionary collective absolves itself of this claim. It is wrapped up entirely in itself and emerges in the course of a "creation *ex nihilo*" as if "from nothing."[111] Formally speaking, therefore, Badiou's praise for the Red Guards is identical to Richard Wagner's eulogy for Siegfried. I do not mean that as a compliment. The revolutionary guards were at least as "foolish" as Siegfried.

"Forget Badiou!" recommends Olivier Assayas, director of the brilliant film *Carlos the Jackal*.[112] I am happy to take this advice, but before doing so I want to draw two final conclusions from my critique of Badiou. One comes from looking back, the other comes from looking forward.

Looking back, this critique of Badiou reveals that our fixation on the Cultural Revolution and neglect of the Hundred Flowers movement needs to be revised. I naturally make this recommendation in the service of remembering the *puer robustus* who appeared in 1957. The choices he makes – in terms of history, power, and morality – differ in every respect from those of Badiou. This *puer robustus* interprets history solely as an open-ended process and has no use for the seizure of power by a militant group. He struggles with the question of what is right and wrong, good and evil, and he does not shirk the responsibility of having to justify the protest he stages.

Looking ahead, we can say that whoever wants to act as a troublemaker or embrace others as troublemakers must guard themselves against Badiou as if against a false friend. Badiou celebrates the unleashing of the revolutionary subject, which can only end in violent caprice or – as Slavoj Žižek says in connection with the Cultural Revolution – in "pathetic outbursts."[113] The uprisings or "massive popular events" (see above) that Badiou longs for in the struggle against capitalism will end in disaster if they follow his guidelines.

Žižek's critique of Badiou gives rise to a further point that allows us to embed the discussion of Maoism in the theoretical framework that stretches across this book as a whole. Žižek describes Mao as a "Lord of Misrule," a leader who chips away at himself.[114] What he is talking about is Mao's aim to neutralize the state and its rules through the Cultural Revolution. Mao's characterization as a "Lord of Misrule" – which, incidentally, Žižek takes from Jonathan Spence[115] – is a highly charged historical allusion. It refers, namely, to a carnival figure from the early modern period. The "Lord of Misrule" was the big shot of deregulation, a master who temporarily suspended all rules and undermined himself, and thus a counterfigure to the regulating Leviathan.[116] During the Cultural Revolution, the carnivalesque chaos turned deadly serious. The rule of the "Lord of Misrule" was extended indefinitely, as it were, and his counterpart, the state Leviathan, was dismantled.

With carte blanche to do whatever they wanted, the Red Guards – I am following Žižek again here[117] – revealed themselves to be close relatives of a seemingly distant group of individuals who also simply do whatever they want. The carnival image blurs and expands, and the state of lawlessness is suddenly defined not just by the revolutionary guards, but by different – and yet similar – characters. According to Žižek, these are the individuals who simply do their own thing under the reign of a new "Lord of Misrule" – namely, unfettered capitalism. To use my terminology, they are egocentric troublemakers who are apprentices or masters in the game of economic deregulation – just like the poor or rich lumpenproletariat described by Marx.

The *puer robustus* emigrated to China, as did the "lumpen or *liumang* proletariat." In 1988, the journalist Yi Shuihan used this phrase to refer to a new "parasitical [...] mentality" that was widespread in China, one which combined the ruthless pursuit of "personal benefit" with a disregard for "all laws and principles."[118] This fits with a polemic by the Chinese literary critic He Xin from the same year:

The religion of the Chinese today is cheating, deceit, blackmail and theft, eating, drinking, whoring, gambling and smoking. [...] We think any honest, humble gentleman a fool and regard any good person who works hard and demands little in return as an idiot. Crooks are our sages; thieves and swindlers our supermen [...]. There are no greater cynics than the Chinese people.[119]

Badiou's Red Guards, who are situated beyond good and evil, and the new supermen in China (and elsewhere) thus prove to be creatures cut from the same cloth. They are political and economic versions of a *puer robustus* who impassively lets loose and whose disruption has lost or revoked any connection to the existing order. I have absolutely no use for this undisturbed disturbance. But some general questions remain: How do the troublemakers of today make their voice heard in political practice and theory? How do they take action? I am looking for the *puer robustus* on the current playing field, battlefield, and field of tension between democracy and capitalism – and I am coming to the end.

— XII.—

THE *PUER ROBUSTUS* TODAY

1. No end to history

The *puer robustus* has not appeared under his own name in recent times. But because he has taken on so many roles and cropped up in so many different worlds over the centuries, it is easy to recognize him in many contemporary figures. As I was writing this book and telling friends and colleagues about the *puer robustus*, nearly everyone had a new example of him to share: "There's another one!" But I am not collecting figures for a contemporary gallery; I am trying to determine how to systematically take our thinking about the troublemaker a step further. With the audacity that might be permitted at the end of such a book, I will say this much: *The current situation is shaped by a battle that the* puer robustus *is fighting with himself.* The adventure story I have told in this book ends on a rather wild note. The scene is populated by a variety of troublemakers who differ radically. They come into conflict with one another while simultaneously taking on the political order in their own individual ways.

By analyzing this conflict, I am strictly remaining within the framework outlined by the history of the *puer robustus*. I am looking only at modern societies as political, legally constituted orders that are being infiltrated or challenged. This final chapter will, therefore, not deal with failed states as self-service stores for oligarchs or gateways for francs-tireurs – and also not with civil wars around the world. I must also resist the urge to trace the career of the troublemaker in spheres outside of politics and political theory, even though he plays important roles there. We can see this in theoretical discussions about (post-)avant-garde art and creativity, as well as in economic debates about disruption and innovation. (Which, incidentally, have long been connected to one another; the "creative destruction" of Schumpeter's entrepreneur can be traced back to the "self-overcoming" of the Nietzschean "artists of life," for example.[1])

332

Before turning to the current political struggle, we must recall a time in which it was popular to believe that this struggle was actually *over*. Think back to the year 1989. Demonstrators in East Germany were shouting "We are the people!" The Berlin Wall fell. The Eastern Bloc crumbled. The Cold War came to an end. It was undoubtedly the troublemaker's finest hour – and, if we are to believe some of the commentators of the time, his finest hour was also his final hour. The dream that the great struggle could be resolved for all time became a prediction in the summer of 1989, when Francis Fukuyama declared that the clash of ideologies had been decided by the victory of the West, thus bringing history to an end.

Fukuyama took the idea of the end of history from Kojève and Hegel, but he was actually just turning the early-modern tandem of economic and political liberalism into a capitalist-democratic double act: "We might summarize the content of the universal homogenous state as liberal democracy in the political sphere combined with easy access to VCRs and stereos in the economic."[2] To put it less flippantly: in this world, "freedom," "democracy," and "free enterprise" (what an odd combination!) were expected to be acknowledged as "universal values."[3]

Fukuyama has since backtracked on his prediction, but it is still worth trying on his old eyeglasses and looking at the future – i.e., our present day – from the perspective of 1989. Then we can see how things could have turned out, or perhaps how they have turned out in some cases. What we see is a world entering a "homogenous state" and pursuing the great tranquilization of the troublemaker. This tranquilization affects every different version of the troublemaker: the egocentric, nomocentric, eccentric and massive troublemaker alike. There are, therefore, four troublemakers to be *normalized*.

With the victory of capitalism, the *egocentric* troublemaker moves into the mainstream of society. The contentious figure becomes a leading figure who sheds all that is disruptive and objectionable.[4] The egocentric does not need to resort to brute force to brutally assert his interests. When everyone can own "VCRs and stereos" (today we would have to say smartphones), then there is no need for a war of all against all.

The *nomocentric* troublemaker is offered an opportunity for incorporation. In a democracy in which disruption comes factory installed, cooperation is open to him and there is no need for subversion. He seems able to moderate his audacity without negatively affecting his ambitions. He can continue to anticipate a different order, but in the context of democratic opinion- and decision-making, he must seek support for it.

The *eccentric* troublemaker is normalized by moving closer to the egocentric. Instead of spurning the "self" and self-interest – his original mission – he transforms the desire for transgression and self-alienation into the *fureur de se distinguer* (Rousseau; see p. 59). He tries to use his distinctive characteristics to score points with other market participants and boost his human capital. This troublemaker becomes a member of the creative class.[5]

The *massive* troublemaker is weaned off his martial attitude. He is kept away from the altar on which he would have sacrificed himself for a higher cause, but he is welcome to swim with the tide, join the Love Parade, and have fun. Apart from that, his individualization runs smoothly.

The effects of this fourfold normalization can be felt everywhere. But at the same time, things are coming apart at all the seams. The crystal ball in which Fukuyama foresaw an ideal world at the end of history has shattered on the stone floor of reality. And the troublemakers are crawling out of their holes and denying that they were ever pacified.

2. The egocentric troublemaker and the financial crisis

The financial crisis of 2008 proved that the egocentric troublemaker is very much alive. Instead of coming to terms with being normalized, he seized the opportunity for deregulated enrichment, triggering a crisis in which many people would be done out of their livelihoods and several nations would be brought to the brink of the abyss.

The first troublemakers that come to mind here are straightforward criminals such as Bernie Madoff, master of the Ponzi scheme (damages: 65 billion dollars), and the UBS rogue trader Kwemi Adoboli (damages: 2 billion dollars). But more interesting than the unlawful acts committed by individuals or even institutions are the speculative transactions that stayed within the legal bounds of the financial market. It was the mass occurrence of such transactions that led to the crisis, and these transactions were not hindered but rather enabled by rules that had been stretched beyond recognition. People succumbed to mass suggestion or autosuggestion and either ignored risks or tried to outsource them. One popular game was to palm off toxic securities on others, collect a commission for them and, parallel to this, rake in high profits by betting on a slump in the price of these same assets. Lloyd Blankfein, CEO of Goldman Sachs, viewed this in retrospect as normal "market-making."[6] Anyone not turning the wheel of huge returns was considered *pretty stupid*. Two UBS traders talked about criminal business practices as follows:

> *Trader A:* these are wicked dogs at the pm [precious metals] desk. Sick what they're doing, haha.

Trader B: 1.1 mio up [profit] on the day, beautiful.
Trader A: hohohoho.[7]

In the documentary *Inside Job*, Frank Partnoy, a professor of law and finance in San Diego, describes the temptation to come off the field as a winner and leave behind scorched earth – the classic scenario of the egocentric troublemaker: "You're gonna make an extra 2 million dollars a year – or 10 million dollars a year – for putting your financial institution at risk. Someone else pays the bill, you don't pay the bill. Would you make that bet? Most people who worked on Wall Street said, sure, I'd make that bet."[8] Looking back, Warren Buffett, the uncrowned king of investors, compared the goings-on before the financial crisis with a fabulous ball that comes to a bad end:

> Well, when there's a delusion, a mass delusion, you can say everybody is to blame. I mean, you can say I should have spotted it, you can say the feds should have spotted it, you can say the mortgage brokers should have, Wall Street should have spotted it and blown the whistle. I'm not sure if they had blown the whistle how much good it would have done. People were having so much fun. [. . .] There's plenty of blame to go around. [. . .] There's no villain.[9]

No one had to feel like a "villain" at this big party, like someone who was disturbing the order – and if anyone did, it was only those who ruined the atmosphere by refusing to play along. It was not until the morning after the party that the shock went through the financial system, global economy, and political institutions. In essence, what we have here is the behavioral model that Tocqueville saw among the American pioneers in the mid-nineteenth century. This kinship between the Wild West and Wall Street was confirmed by someone who was as intimately familiar with capitalism as Warren Buffett, though in a different way: Larry Hagman, who played the ruthless businessman J. R. Ewing in the legendary television series *Dallas*, said in 2011:

> The Ewing men mentally live in a lawless no-man's-land. They're businessmen but they act like cowboys fighting over land, cattle or gold. [. . .] *Dallas* showed the "asshole side" of capitalism. J.R. doesn't believe in anything but making money. It's his religion. And he was a prophet in his way. He always embraced the unscrupulousness of capitalism that we're suddenly surprised by today. What J.R. did with Ewing Oil is happening everywhere today. The banks have taken the whole world for a ride. Me included.[10]

I do not want to put a fox in charge of the henhouse by taking a lesson from those who – like foxes in a henhouse – did the damage themselves.

But it is enlightening to see how these foxes, the representatives of the financial world, engaged in rhetorical damage control as soon as they heard the farmer approaching. Alexander Dibelius, head of the German operations of Goldman Sachs at the time, was asked in 2009: "Is there criminal energy in your industry?" His response was: "No, but there are isolated cases, like Bernie Madoff, that were able to thrive in fertile soil." The only interesting aspect of this is, of course, the "fertile soil":

> Viewed in retrospect, some things in our industry look greedy, self-involved and out of touch with reality, as if the society around it were absolutely irrelevant. And I admit that, on the whole, we have not managed to deal with the expectations that this society places in us – as an individual, as an institution, as an industry.[11]

In March 2009, Wendelin Wiedeking, then CEO of Porsche (five months before he resigned), who was occupied at the time with the business of taking over Volkswagen by means of loans and highly speculative options, declared:

> We are currently experiencing a fundamental crisis of meaning that marks the end of financial capitalism. [. . .] Companies that only run after short-term financial key figures, such as shareholder value or quarterly returns, must now recognize that they have worshipped a false idol. [. . .] We have to focus on customers and their desires again. And we have to fulfil our responsibilities to our employees and to society.[12]

Both of these (hollow) statements mention the word "society," which – ever since Margaret Thatcher's proclamation of 1987 ("There is no such thing as society"[13]) – should actually be counted among the victims left in the wake of the march toward neoliberalism. There is satisfaction to be taken in the fact that something like "society" is still allowed to exist according to Dibelius and Wiedeking. But it appears to be an endangered species now; it is disturbed, threatened, has perhaps even been shaken to its very foundations. Because the financial crisis has had massive consequences beyond the economic sphere, it stands apart from the normal crises that are as common in capitalism as wildfires are in the forests of California. But what exactly is meant by "society" here? It is a makeshift placeholder for the non-economic, for everything outside of financial capitalism. This "outside" interests me only in a certain respect, one which is determined by the subject of this book. I am interested in the financial crisis as a disturbance in the political order – in this case: in democracy.

Representatives of many different camps all agree that economics and politics have drifted apart. The crisis in their relationship is attributed to the fact that the economy has long operated on a global scale, while politics remains largely national. International entanglements are limited by national sovereignty – and this sovereignty is the basis of democratic political orders. The discrepancy between economics and politics has serious repercussions for the calculated actions and profit expectations of the egocentric troublemaker.

As long as this troublemaker was forced to act within a state order, he could still – as Sigmund Freud noted – "injure other people by lies, fraud and calumny" in the "satisfaction" of his "avarice." But to "remain unpunished," he would have to corrupt the state. He could not evade the state; he could only try to bend it to his will. The example of this held up by Marx was post-1848 France, when "governmental power" lay in the hands of a "band of adventurers" who plundered the state.

Instead of carrying out the laborious work of destruction, the egocentric troublemaker of today has a much more convenient option: he can turn his back on the order intended for him and seek the "satisfaction" of his "avarice" elsewhere. This results in a dramatic shift in power. Disturbance no longer involves intervening in the political order but rather abandoning it. The political order cannot be *indifferent* to this, however, because the troublemaker does not simply disappear without further ado. When he leaves the boundaries of the political order, he takes whatever he can with him. The most harmless examples of this are legal and illegal forms of capital flight, all of which benefit from the impotence of politics.

Some of what I have just said may sound as though nationally bound democracies are the poor, noble victims of free-floating streams of capital. If this impression were allowed to stand, however, we would have a terribly distorted image of the situation. This is because the underdog is not forced to play the role of victim – he can also play the role of collaborator. In keeping with this, capitalism not only breaks or abandons the borders of a nationally constituted political order, it also seeks a connection with this order. Democracies practically throw themselves at capitalism in the hopes of ensuring or increasing the prosperity of their members by making concessions to capital. This causes the relationship between politics and economics to list to one side. The asymmetry of power is apparent in the fact that some banks are said to be "systematically important" or "too big to fail." Politics pays the penalty for its own actions – namely, for delivering itself up to egocentrics who are the engine of economic dynamics, thus weakening itself in the process.

Compared to the classic tranquilization strategies for the egocentric troublemaker that we know from Hobbes, a shift takes place here in burdens and benefits. Economic actors no longer follow the rules for the sake of their self-interest; instead, the rules are adapted to this self-interest. In terms of domestic policy, this means that deregulation is flagged as the royal road to the greatest possible prosperity for the greatest possible number of people. In terms of foreign policy, states offer themselves up as service providers for global capital flows and try to attract them or keep them in the country with tax breaks and location-specific advantages. Politics and economics thus form a hybrid, and the political order makes itself dependent on economic dynamics that harbor considerable potential for disturbance. This potential is amplified on all levels – through the financial market deregulation authorized by the state, through the proliferation of "luxury fever"[14] in the general population, etc.

In the event of a crisis, capital has the option of changing its mode of disturbance and becoming a parasite on politics instead of a saboteur. It then seeks the protection of the state, which has chained its destiny to economic spirals of accumulation and consumption and has become susceptible to blackmail in times of need. Though Lehman Brothers was not saved from bankruptcy in 2008, what the CEO of one of the world's largest hedge funds said in the 1990s still generally holds true: "If I get in big trouble, the Fed will come and save me."[15] Ultimately this gives rise to the familiar combination of the privatization of profit and socialization of loss. Criticism of this has been voiced even deep in the right-wing camp. Thatcher biographer and conservative journalist Charles Moore wrote two sensational articles in 2011 – "I'm starting to think that the Left might actually be right" and "Our leaders have lost faith in the powers of their people" – in which he said:

> The global banking system is an adventure playground for the participants, complete with spongy [...] flooring so that they bounce when they fall off. The role of the rest of us is simply to pay.[16]

> Thus "globalization", which ought to mean free trade throughout the world, turns out to mean a system in which big banks take the gains of international success and taxpayers in each nation affected bear the cost of any failure. The banks only "come home" when they have run out of our money. Then our governments give them more.[17]

The roles of political saboteur and political parasite, both of which are open to the capitalist threshold creature, can be categorized by repurposing a word that found its way into social scientific discourse in the 1990s: *glocalization*. What this means is that globalization does not lead directly to the homogenization of everyone's living conditions because there is an inbuilt countereffect. Globalization "involves the creation and the incorporation of locality."[18] This dual development takes both harmless and harrowing forms. The appreciation of local customs is harmless, but the hardening of ethnic identities leading to a clash of civilizations is harrowing.

In the above-described strategies employed by capital, we find that capital has its own version of glocalization. Capital leverages globalization by operating across borders, or by not acknowledging borders at all. But it also avails itself of localization – not only by developing special markets but (to use Charles Moore's apt phrase) by coming "home" when necessary and being cosseted by the nation state, as if by a mother. The tension between globalization and localization, which will accompany me through the rest of this chapter, offers variable options to the egocentric troublemaker. The glocal double bind poses no dilemma for him; in fact, it allows him to have his cake and eat it too. Alongside this capitalist winner, however, we find a large number of economic individuals who barely scrape by. Their diagnosis is: "I am me, you are you, and *something's wrong*."[19] If you just play along and do your job, you are more likely to be one of the losers in this glocalized world than the capitalist troublemaker, who manages to keep all of his balls in the air as he juggles the two orders.

The nomocentric and eccentric troublemakers are confronted with the glocal double bind just as the egocentric troublemaker is, though in a very different way. They experience it as a "democratic paradox."

3. The eccentric and nomocentric troublemaker – and the democratic paradox

A crisis seldom comes alone. The financial crisis is linked to a chain of other events that have rattled the world in recent years. These events are tied up with experiences of terror, but also excitement. George Magnus, the former Chief Economist of UBS who earned an impressive reputation in 2007 when he warned of the coming financial crisis, speaks in this context of a "crisis convergence."[20] Humanity has wound up on a roller coaster of history, where the highs and lows sometimes alternate so quickly that even a hardened theme park enthusiast would feel the urge to flee.

I now want to return to that vision of the end of history, of the global triumphal march of capitalism and democracy. With this economic-political double act, the West has beguiled the world, sparked hope, fomented hate, produced winners and losers. The West has not achieved victory – and it has landed itself with its own huge problems. I am quoting Francis Fukuyama again here because his slow departure from the neoconservative idea of the end of history has led to his growing awareness of the inner woes of democracy. In 2016 he said:

> The financial crisis was disastrous and was managed abysmally. It frightened people deeply, many lost their jobs, and now there is a feeling

of uncertainty and instability. We're realizing that democracy is not a sure-fire success. We have to continually renew our institutions.[21]

Fukuyama is correct in saying that the financial crisis led straight to a democratic crisis. But this crisis will not be resolved simply by improving political "institutions."[22] It is not enough to demand from democracy a decisive reaction to the financial crisis, because this word – *reaction* – erroneously implies that actually existing democracy stands counter to capitalism as an independent entity. But democracy is not an independent order; it as – as we have seen – a political-economic hybrid that has compromised itself by facilitating ruthless enrichment, exploitation, and exclusion. Regardless of whether the political order labors away at its impotence, participates in power in cooperation with the economy, or sets itself up as a friend and helper to ailing financial institutions – in any case it will find itself in the midst of a crisis of legitimacy, or even an existential crisis. Within this "crisis," however, democracies can also become "self-critical."[23] Then they must be defended against themselves, which simply means that *they must be disturbed*.

In the previous section I hinted that the current interplay between order and disturbance could be categorized as a case of "glocalization." In accordance with this, we can also make a distinction between the global, external aspect of the democratic crisis and its local, internal aspect.

The *external aspect* relates to the appeal that democracy has in those parts of the world where dictators, autocrats, theocrats, or single parties hold the power. This appeal is tarnished by debacles such as the nation-building attempts following the wars in Afghanistan and Iraq. It would be caricaturizing the problem to act as though democracy as an export commodity could be strictly isolated from the other messages that the West sends out into the world. This is already apparent on the political level, where power politics and interest-driven politics take their place alongside the democratic agenda. But in keeping with the economic-political double act of the West, these mixed signals extend far beyond the political sphere.

We can see this clearly in the Arab Spring. On the one hand, it proves that the promise of democracy has the power to mobilize people in other countries. On the other hand, the pre-history of the Arab Spring includes developments that have nothing to do with the glad tidings of democracy. For example, the Arab Spring was unleashed in part by a local food crisis – and investigating the roots of this crisis takes us far from democracy, all the way back to the expansion of the financial markets and thus to the crisis of 2008. The financial crisis affected the trade in raw materials and resulted in extremely volatile food prices. This at least partially explains the supply bottlenecks in the so-called "Third World."[24] It is perhaps no coincidence that Mohamed Bouazizi, whose self-immolation triggered the "Arabellion" at the end of 2010, was a vegetable seller.

The mixed signals mentioned earlier consist of the fact that the West plunges countries such as Tunisia or Egypt into a crisis by means of capitalism, while simultaneously priding itself on having inspired this crisis as a movement for more democracy. The brutal awakening from the democratic dream in the Arab world testifies to the perseverance of autocratic regimes, but also to the signs of wear on the vision of democracy. Now that fundamentalist movements are growing popular not only in the Middle East and Africa but even in Europe, the ball is back in the West's court.

The *internal aspect* of the democratic crisis in Western societies can – like its external aspect – be explained on the basis of the mixed signals sent by the economic-political double act. They can be set alongside each other and against each other under the headings of exclusion and inclusion.

All across the political spectrum, from left and right alike, we hear warnings against the consequences of growing economic inequality. Francis Fukuyama says it is "bad for democracy," and Thomas Piketty declares it to be "incompatible" with the "principles" of "modern democratic societies."[25] Democracy suffers from the fact that an economically privileged class dominates the political decision-making process.[26] Everyone on the lower rungs of society not only lives in precarious or oppressive economic conditions; they are forced to be mere spectators to the power play in the political sphere. Economic inequality expands into political exclusion, even though there should be no place for this in a democracy – at least not for those who enjoy the privileges of citizenship.

This political exclusion is exacerbated by another development pointed out by Wolfgang Streeck: When a state has to turn itself into a "debt state" to cover expenses driven up by the economic crisis, it makes itself dependent on the "set of interests" of private and institutional investors. The "trust of creditors" then becomes an important criterion for the success of the state. As a result, the state is no longer accountable only to its "citizens" but also to another "reference group."[27] In deferring to the demands of this group, the state will make decisions that pass by the people as a sovereign. These decisions are usually especially explosive for those on the lower rungs or outer edges of society, including many immigrants and children of immigrants.

The political inclusion that is baked into the principle of democratic participation is undermined by the economic developments mentioned above, but it also suffers from internal problems of its own making. As soon as this inclusion – i.e., the membership of all citizens in the body politic – is asserted particularly aggressively, it starts to look threadbare. France is a good example of this. In France, the prospect of democratic participation is tied to the creation of a neutralized public sphere in which each citizen is nothing more than a pure republican subject. Participation in this sphere comes at a significant cost. The people must be willing to abandon parts of their own identity for the sake of political inclusion. This is why the headscarf debate harbors much greater potential for conflict in France than elsewhere.[28]

The idea of the republican subject – which, according to Rousseau, goes hand in hand with alienation in a positive sense, with self-loss and self-gain – loses its attraction when the higher meaning of this sacrifice is lost, when the political subject no longer has any say. In the revolutionary manifesto *The Coming Insurrection*, written by an "Invisible Committee," we read that "in France, the relentless, age-old work of [. . .] the power of the state [. . .] grinds down any solidarities that escape it until nothing remains except citizenship – a pure, phantasmic sense of belonging to the Republic. The Frenchman, more than anyone else, is the embodiment of the dispossessed, the destitute."[29]

When it is no longer possible to derive a positive identity through participation in the democratic order, people are relegated to existence on the margins of society and forced to determine which resources they can use to assemble an identity. One of the solutions available to people on the edge of the political order is already obvious: they can adopt a counter-identity that enables them to mentally decouple themselves from the order that is giving them the cold shoulder. I will return to this in the next section when I talk about fundamentalist disturbance.

But first I want to look at the eccentric and nomocentric troublemakers. Unlike the massive troublemaker, they do not try to take refuge in a closed world. Furthermore, their relationship with the political order is not instrumental, as it is for the egocentric troublemaker. They do not ask how they can escape or outsmart the political order. Unlike their two hostile brothers, the eccentric and nomocentric troublemakers do not maintain a nominal distance from the political order; they critically slave away at it. They relate to the political order in a mode of transgression or transformation.

In the present day and recent past – the period to which I am limiting myself here – there has been no shortage of disturbances. I do not want to squeeze all of them into pigeonholes. I first want to mention three dramatic disturbances – not to analyze them in detail, but to use them as a foil for determining how they differ from the disturbances that are especially enlightening when it comes to dealing productively with the crisis of democracy.

- Los Angeles, April 29–May 4, 1992: Following the acquittal of four policemen who nearly beat Rodney King to death during his arrest, riots break out during which 55 people die and around 2,000 are injured.
- Paris, October 27–November 16, 2005: After two youths fleeing from the police are electrocuted by power lines, a riot erupts in the *banlieues*, during which around 9,000 cars are set alight.
- London, August 6–11, 2011: After a man named Mark Duggan is shot by the police, demonstrations and looting take place in London and many other cities, resulting in total damages of around 200 million British pounds.

This type of violence is triggered by similar events and can almost be called up at the touch of a button. Such violence is popular with the Invisible Committee mentioned earlier, whose manifesto *The Coming Insurrection* not only badmouths ATTAC[30] and countless other left-wing initiatives as if they were the class enemy, but also welcomes the "flames of November 2005" in the *banlieues* as "joyous fires" and signs of "a decade full of promise":

> This whole series of nocturnal vandalisms and anonymous attacks, this wordless destruction, has widened the breach between politics and the political. No one can honestly deny the obvious: this was an assault that made no demands, a threat without a message, and it had nothing to do with "politics." One would have to be oblivious to the autonomous youth movements of the last 30 years not to see the purely political character of this resolute negation of politics.[31]

I would prefer to live with the accusation of being "oblivious" than to affiliate myself with this eulogy. For all that these uprisings denounce the mendacity of "politics," they are a poor tool for realizing the "purely political" (regarding the theoretical background of this distinction, see p. 325f.). If the uprisings are indeed political, then they are political in an "antipolitical" way.[32] The rioters are fighting against their abandonment on the margins of society, but with their violence, they are – like the *Halbstarken* before them – announcing only *that* they exist, not *what* they stand for or even what they stand *against*. According to Žižek, "opposition to the system" in the Parisian *banlieues* was reduced to a "meaningless outburst" in which "(self-)destructive violence" was the only response to the state's demand that everyone "[play] by the rules": "The protestors' violence was almost exclusively directed against their own. The cars burned and the schools torched were not those of richer neighbourhoods; they were part of the hard-won acquisitions of the very social strata from which the protestors originated."[33]

I want to prevent *disturbance* from collapsing into *destruction*. I will therefore focus on actions that bear the hallmarks of what could be described as *excess*. This excess can manifest when disturbance itself takes a form (or is *performed* as a form of life) that veers off from the status quo instead of remaining shackled to it with destructive energy. This is the business of the eccentric troublemaker. But this excess can also be found when the goal of the disturbance is to point to something beyond what is happening in the here and now. This is the business of the nomocentric troublemaker.

There are two reasons for me to look at these two types together in this section and treat them both as political troublemakers. First, the history of the *puer robustus* has revealed that the nomocentric trouble-maker can take his systematically strongest form when he moves closer to, or even merges with, his eccentric counterpart. The fight for a better future requires a guarantee in the present; this is apparent even in Marx's theory of revolution. Second, recent protests have been lacking in grand scenarios for the future. The nomocentric troublemaker is thus keeping a very low profile. Surprisingly, this analysis is shared by the *Economist*, the journalistic vassal of capitalism; by Slavoj Žižek, one of its harshest critics; and by Giorgio Agamben, the factotum of doom. In an article entitled *Rebels Without a Cause* (in allusion to the old James Dean movie), the *Economist* writes: "There is a hole at the heart of the new protest movements." Analogous to this, Žižek sees in these movements a "pregnant vacuum," and Agamben diagnoses an "absence of determinate contents in their demands."[34]

Various explanations have been proposed for this vacuum, and I only want to mention them here without weighting them. The protests might have lost their content because, in a market society, all provocations are co-opted as attempts at distinction and utilized in a socially accept-able way. The French collective of authors known as Tiqqun caustically summed up this co-optation as follows: "A revolutionary is not a revo-lutionary, but costume jewelry."[35] Or the opponent faced by the trou-blemakers might be so overpowering that it not only dominates reality but even co-opts the imagination. Or the "vacuum" might be connected to the rebels' prudent reluctance to dictate goals rather than generating them through collective protest – however far they get with it.

I take the view that the political troublemaker of today is breaking apart into a *local* and a *global* type – and that it is extremely difficult to bring the two types back together. I want to demonstrate this using three examples. The first example represents local mobilization, the second represents an attempt to combine local and global concerns, and the third represents a purely global operation. The names associated with each of these exam-ples are Barack Obama, Occupy Wall Street, and Edward Snowden.

It may be overdoing it to mention Obama in a book about trouble-makers; after all, he is an ordinary politician who won a few elections and was, for a time, president of the most powerful country in the world. And yet his first election campaign in 2008 was anything but ordinary, and his "victory" – as even Slavoj Žižek shockingly concedes – was "not just another shift in the eternal parliamentary struggle for a majority" but rather "a sign of something more."[36] As it is part of democracy's agenda to declare the troublemaker to be an honorary member, so to speak, it is worth looking at political processes that take place in the context of the political order – an order that is partial to disturbance.

Obama's campaign was characterized by what appears in retrospect to be an almost kitschy enthusiasm, an eruption of democratic energies in the general population which can also be seen as a counterpart to the financial crisis. Following Albert Hirschman's wise observation from 1982, we can view this as one of those moments in which "exit" turns into "voice":

> Large numbers of people grow up with the feeling that the existing social and political order is not subject to change or that, in any event, they are powerless to bring such change about. The sudden realization (or illusion) that I can act to change society for the better and, moreover, that I can join other like-minded people to this end is in such conditions pleasurable, in fact intoxicating, in itself. [. . .] Secondly, there is the [. . .] pleasurable experience: not that *I* can change society, but that my work and activities in the public arena change and develop *me*, regardless of any real changes in the state of the world that I might achieve.[37]

Obama's first election campaign (independent of his presidency) has earned its place in a book about troublemakers based on a single sentence from the many speeches Obama gave on his way to the White House. This particular sentence, which he spoke on February 5, 2008, in Chicago, stands out like an unforgettable face in the crowd: "We are the ones we've been waiting for."[38] What an odd thing to say! Imagine coming across someone at a train station who has been watching the trains come and go for hours, and when you ask him what he's doing, he responds: "I'm waiting for myself." You would shake your head and walk away. So why did Obama's audience burst into cheers upon hearing this sentence? Why did they feel encouraged by him in a peculiar way?

Obama's line challenges or invites us to distinguish between an old and a new *I* or *we*. What stretches before us is a relationship between present and future, between past and present. We are waiting for something yet to come, or we have long awaited something that is just now arriving (namely, ourselves). In this respect, the sentence fits with the USA and with democracy in general, both of which are in love with becoming.[39] It looks to the future, but not in the sense of executing a predefined game plan or life plan. Instead, "waiting" demands patience and humility. Those who wait are dependent on something not entirely at their command; they must be prepared to be surprised. In this case, the surprise is that we will be different, we will become a different *we*.

This gives us a precise, formal description of the attitude I have found in the eccentric troublemaker in this book. He goes beyond himself without knowing where this will take him. We can therefore consider Henry David Thoreau to be a predecessor to Obama: "Not till we are lost [. . .], do we begin to find ourselves."[40] We do not pull ourselves out of a hat as "self-made men," we do not pat ourselves smugly on the back; we distance ourselves from our own status quo and allow ourselves to be guided by the idea of a different life that lies ahead of us.

The sentence "We are the ones we've been waiting for" is, therefore, also a fitting way of describing what has been referred to as "inner migration" in this book. It encompasses historical dynamics based on the procession of generations, and also the life change that each person undergoes both for themselves and as part of a social body in motion. A connection can also be sensed here between the inner migration of the eccentric troublemaker and the external migration confronting Western democracies. Bonnie Honig writes: "Every day [. . .] new citizens are born, others immigrate into established regimes, still others mature into adulthood. Every day, established citizens mistake, depart from, or simply differ about their visions of democracy's future and the commitments of democratic citizenship."[41] Every day, democracy encounters the troublemaker.

While Obama's line "We are the ones we've been waiting for" seems, at first glance, merely to reveal a special relationship between identity and time, there is a political point to it. It expresses reservations toward the validity and legitimacy of institutional premises and can thus be viewed as a revival of the "experimental," "creative" democracy promoted by John Dewey.

In Obama's case, however, the disturbance is kept in check. The political energies he tapped were unleashed in the carefully calculated run-up to an election, in a national or, to use my wording, local context. The formation of political will was based on a clear division of labor between the ones advocating for a person and a program and the one striving for executive power. The *we* waiting for a better *we* stands in relation to an *I* – the future president – to whom this *we* entrusts itself. Once again, we encounter the distinction between author and actor that plays a key role in representative democracy. Even though Obama banked on the *we* in his election campaign – think back to his slogan "Yes, we can" – effective power was still shifted from the people to its highest representative. At a campaign rally for Obama, for instance, talk show host Oprah Winfrey could not resist proclaiming: "He is the one!" She was alluding to a key scene in the film *The Matrix*, in which Neo rises from the dead, like Jesus, and his followers whisper reverently: "He is the one."

After Obama's campaign movement got bogged down in institutional work, disruptive potential bubbled up elsewhere. The Occupy movement, for example, represents civil disobedience, nonviolent resistance, disturbance of the public order, and perhaps even – if we are to believe its spokesperson David Graeber – the "revolutionary transformation of society."[42] One might argue that both the Obama enthusiasm and the Occupy movement quickly went up in smoke, but it would be terribly cynical to wrinkle one's nose at dashed hopes after the fact.

The protests that flared up in New York and elsewhere in 2011 operated on the basis of an opposition between Main Street and Wall Street. It was directed against the power of the economic sphere and the political institutions that were seen as its appendages. According to Graeber, the protest involved "refusing to elect leaders that could then be bribed or co-opted."[43] This co-optation is part of the hybrid structure of the political-economic order, which I addressed in the second section of this chapter. A democracy that can be pressed into this hybrid structure and damaged as a result is a democracy that, according to Graeber, must be saved from itself: "According to the official version, [. . .] 'democracy' is a system created by the founding fathers, based on checks and balances between president, Congress and judiciary." "Almost anyone else" would define democracy as "collective self-governance by popular assemblies."[44] Graeber is posing a systemic question here, one which revolves around a struggle between two concepts of democracy that are mutually exclusive. In the call for mass demonstrations in the USA on May 1, 2012, the vision of a different, true democracy was expressed:

> We dare to look forward to a world when the borders that divide us will be made meaningless, to the birth of [a] genuinely democratic culture of communities managing their own resources for the common good, and where the value and dignity of no human being on this planet is considered inferior to any other.[45]

These lines represent a new version of the phenomenon I analyzed under the heading of "glocalization." It is a double-barreled vision: "Nurses, bus drivers, and construction workers" are, according to Graeber, fighting for the establishment of "democratic self-governing communities" on the one hand and "the dissolution of national borders" on the other.[46] It is odd that Graeber does not concern himself with the problems inherent in this dual goal, or the tremendous tension between local and global issues. Local communities would be overwhelmed if they had to take on transnational responsibilities and conquer global political challenges. Two other theorists who sympathize with the Occupy movement offer a less naïve analysis than Graeber: Slavoj Žižek and Judith Butler. Both of them spoke to Occupy demonstrators in October 2011 and addressed the relationship between local resistance and global change on later occasions as well.

Žižek gave a speech in New York on October 9, 2011, which he subsequently used as the basis for two texts in which he expanded on his thoughts; I will primarily be quoting from these texts in the following.[47] Žižek is interested in defining the possibilities of political disturbance and the revolutionary upheaval of society in a positive way: "The taboo has been broken, we do not live in the best possible world; we are allowed, obliged even, to think about the alternatives." Žižek, like Graeber, imagines the political order that the troublemaker must attack to be a democracy that has gambled away its legitimacy through its "marriage" to "capitalism." His opponent, therefore – to use my terminology – is the political-economic hybrid.

In brief, Žižek rejects the possibility of a divorce between democracy and capitalism, or the idea of reclaiming the autonomy of the political sphere and giving it primacy over the economy. He does not believe it is possible, within a "democratic-liberal framework," to "democratize capitalism, to extend democratic control to the economy, through the pressure of mass media, parliamentary inquiries, stronger regulation, honest police investigations, and so on." Žižek tries to show why this cannot work by harking back to Marx. According to his argument, democracy is *not made* for controlling the economy because it has, from the outset, been complicit in a division of labor with capitalism. It grants people political rights but ensures their private rights at the same time, and by exercising these rights, people become individuals who ultimately wear themselves out in competitive relationships.[48] The triumphal march of egocentric troublemakers during the financial crisis was simply the climax of this development. Žižek writes: "Democratic mechanisms [. . .] are themselves part of the apparatus of the 'bourgeois' state that guarantees the undisturbed functioning of capitalist reproduction."

Žižek draws the same conclusion from this as Marx: "If we want genuine improvement," what we need "is not political reform, but a change in the 'apolitical' social relations of production." Žižek must therefore be especially pleased that the Occupy movement is not directed primarily against political institutions but against the economic center of power that is Wall Street. But he is caught out by the same problem I referred to in the chapter on Marx – namely, that the collective struggle for a change in relations requires some kind of internal organization, meaning that it cannot help but be considered political. Unfortunately,

Žižek tells us almost nothing about what form this politics should take – only that it is best to steer clear of democracy.

Žižek's rejection of democracy – or of the idea that it could be something different than it is today – is not only rooted in democracy's weakness with respect to capitalism. He mentions another reason as well, which gives me the opportunity to relate his position to my new interpretation of glocalization. This second reason emerges in his debate with the conservative journalist Anne Applebaum, who serves as his whipping boy (or girl), in a manner of speaking. Applebaum is an avowed proponent of a conventional representative democracy with "elections, political parties, rules, laws," etc. Much to Žižek's delight, Applebaum herself hints that a democracy that can function "only within distinct borders" is threatened by decline:

> A "global community" cannot be a national democracy. And a national democracy cannot command the allegiance of a billion-dollar global hedge fund, with its headquarters in a tax haven and its employees scattered around the world. [...] Although I still believe in globalization's economic and spiritual benefits – along with open borders, freedom of movement and free trade – globalization has clearly begun to undermine the legitimacy of Western democracies.

Žižek is justified in saying there is a "truly weird gap" in Applebaum's argument. After verbosely describing the enfeeblement of democracy, the best she can come up with is to demand that the demonstrators engage with the "process" mandated by the existing "political system." This ultimately dooms the protest to be meaningless, as Žižek sees it, because the "political system" within which this protest is supposed to be expressed is, "according to Applebaum's own account [...] precisely *not* up to the job."

The problem is that Žižek blindly follows the thesis of locally blinkered democracy and simply draws a different conclusion from it than Applebaum. He views democracy not as an arena to which the protest should kindly limit itself, but as an obstacle the protest must surmount in order to become global and face down capitalism as an opponent on equal footing: "Badiou hit the mark with his [...] claim that 'Today, the enemy is not called [...] Capital. It's called Democracy.'"[49] Really? What Žižek has to say about the organization of a global revolutionary disturbance is shockingly vague. He talks about a "communist struggle" as a "positive universal project shared by all participants," and about a reconceived "dictatorship of the proletariat."[50] Ernesto Laclau's criticism of Žižek from the year 2000 is still valid: "The difficulty with assertions like this is that they mean absolutely nothing. [...] His anti-capitalism is mere empty talk."[51]

349

Has Žižek had second thoughts recently? In texts written in the wake of the terrorist attacks in Paris in 2015, he deigns to defend the "European emancipatory legacy" and suddenly sees the good side of "fundamental human rights" and the "welfare state."[52] Perhaps he himself knows how to reconcile his praise for such democratic achievements with his democracy-bashing, but I unfortunately do not.

While Graeber's definition of political disturbance amounts to a *naïve* reproduction of democratic communities, Žižek describes political disturbance as a *cynical* dismissal of democracy. The one handles political glocalization by ignoring the tensions within it, while the other splits it in a way that pits global protest against local democracy. He thus fails to do justice to the global potential inherent in democracy itself. This becomes apparent when we put aside these naïve and cynical depictions and look at the *critical* depiction of political disturbance presented by Judith Butler. Two weeks after Žižek, on October 23, 2011, Butler spoke to the demonstrators in Zuccotti Park in New York:

> We would not be here if elected officials were representing the popular will. We stand apart from the electoral process and its complicities with exploitation. We sit and stand and move and speak, as we can, as the popular will, the one that electoral democracy has forgotten and abandoned. But we are here, and remain here, enacting the phrase, "We the people."[53]

As her emphasis on the physical presence of the demonstrators shows, Butler is less disparaging of the local aspect than Žižek. But she by no means neglects the global aspect. In her book *Notes Toward a Performative Theory of Assembly* from 2015, Butler returns to the collective experience of assembly and – like Graeber, but in a different way to Žižek – operates with a "struggle" or "battle" over different concepts of democracy. Alongside democracy as a "political form" whose institutions represent the people, she holds up a democracy based on the "principle of popular sovereignty" or the real will of the people.[54] This second type largely corresponds to what Graeber calls a "self-governing community" and the strain of democratic theory represented by Rousseau in the context of this book. Just as Rousseau believes that the popular will cannot be represented losslessly, Butler differentiates the will of the people from representative democracy:

> So, something that must fail as representation, and that we might call [...] nonrepresentative, [...] becomes the basis of democratic forms of political self-determination – popular sovereignty, distinct from state sovereignty [...]. [It] is a way of *forming* a people through acts of self-designation and self-gathering [...].[55]

The phrase "We, the people" from the Declaration of Independence was enthusiastically invoked by Butler in her speech in New York in 2011, but in her later book she subjects it to critical analysis. Butler points out an aspect that Rousseau had identified before her: namely, that those who say "We, the people" are indeed talking about the people, but they themselves *are not* the people. If they claimed to be, they would be living beyond their means. Someone is always missing from the people – and in the case of Occupy, there were quite a lot of people missing from the 99 percent on whose behalf the demonstrators wanted to speak. The people who sustain democracy cannot be assembled in their entirety in the here and now; they are, in the strictest sense, not to be found.[56] What this means is that the people exhibit the unreliable and elusive aspects of the *puer robustus*. Regarding the protests in New York, Butler says:

> Such gatherings are not the same as democracy itself. We cannot point to one provisional and transient gathering and say, "that is democracy in action," and mean that everything we expect of democracy is emblematized or enacted at such a moment.[57]

The cry of "We, the people" thus proves to be in need of elaboration. It requires a postscript – namely, that it is *not true*. The funny thing is that this postscript in no way devalues the exclamation itself. In fact, the two things belong together. People want to express their will in a democracy, and when they do so as political beings, they are not making claims that are particular to them but are instead addressing the *whole* and speaking as a *we*. This assertion goes hand in hand with the knowledge that one is looking beyond oneself and beyond the collective that is currently present. One both is – and is not – "the people." Anyone who drops the second part is arrogating to themselves a self-contained identity that does not exist. Butler therefore also rejects the idea (and, implicitly, the arguments of Badiou, and Hardt and Negri) that "democracy" is the "event of the surging multitude."[58] Furthermore, her analysis aims to make it possible to distinguish democratic protests from political assemblies in which the claim "We are the people" is merely a form of hollow self-affirmation. (After all, this slogan was used not only by the civil rights activists in Leipzig in 1989 but also, as Butler herself mentions, by the radical right-wing Pegida demonstrators in Dresden in 2015.[59])

Democracy amounts to more than just political movements, but it also cannot get by without them. It has such movements to thank for crises in which a body politic continually redefines its "identity in progress."[60] The "critical function"[61] of these crises is nothing other than the function of the troublemaker. This is where Butler departs from Graeber (whom she does not mention, however), who celebrates the self-governing community as a pure, self-sufficient alternative to representative democracy. It is also where she departs from Žižek (whom she also does not mention), who wants to replace democracy with a universal mass movement.

Butler devotes her attention to the tension inherent in democracy. In accordance with this, democracy relies on assemblies in which the people is present as a body politic, meaning that democracy is – as Butler says, "in one sense" – "emphatically local." Additionally, democracy must extend beyond this assembly and cannot confine itself to the boundaries of a closed community; its aspirations can therefore only be "global."[62]

Glocalization constitutes a double bind for capitalism, as explained in the previous section, and capitalism puts this to expert use by simultaneously scrounging for local advantages and seizing global opportunities. Democracy also has to confront glocalization; it is certainly not merely defensive or helpless in the face of the global, as Applebaum believes. One of the many theorists who have reflected upon this democratic glocalization is Hannah Arendt, who addressed it in her thesis on the tension between "popular sovereignty" and "human rights." On the one hand, democracy is localized "between people [...] acting and speaking together"; on the other hand, it installs rights that apply not just to selected citizens but to people who have been granted the "right to have rights."[63]

If we side with Butler and many others (in opposition to Graeber and Žižek) and stand by the idea of an inner tension in democracy, we must acknowledge that the double bind of glocalization does, in fact, pose a serious problem for democracy, unlike for capitalism. An impressive number of political philosophers have described this as the "democratic paradox."[64] The paradox is that democracy is based on a political subject, but at the same time it extends beyond this subject. These two sides wrestle with one another, and they cannot come into their own without some loss. This is where we see the processual, plastic, iterative character of democracy.[65]

One special form of this idea can be found in the influential suggestion of sociologist Robert Ezra Park from 1928, who proposed that "marginal man," "migrant," and "stranger" were models for the democratic, "emancipated individual" who is supposed to be able "to interrupt the routine of existing habit and break the cake of custom," i.e., to actively initiate "periods of transition and crisis."[66] Another special form of this idea is apparent in the widely discussed notion that Europe has an "eccentric identity," meaning that it is itself, but at the same time it cancels itself out through its universality.[67]

The democratic paradox initially reveals itself in conflicts on the level of institutions, but since I am interested in disturbance and not in order, I will not analyze this in any detail. Some of the aspects that could be discussed here include the preservation and demise of sovereign rights, the tension between democratic will-formation and transnational legislation, the relationship between nation states, transnational organizations and NGOs, refugee policies, etc.

But because we are dealing with a true democratic *paradox*, I believe any attempt to solve this paradox is pointless. Such attempts have been made *on the one side* by authors – on both the right[68] and the left[69] – who want to couple democracy to the nation in a consistent way. Any goals extending beyond this are viewed not as an inherent tendency of democracy but as something that harbors the danger of a reversion to chaos or to Hobbes's state of nature.[70] (Many such voices were heard in the German and European debates about the refugee issue in 2015–16.) *On the other hand*, it is also ridiculous to assume that a "transnational democracy" could be realized without loss within an orderly institutional framework.[71] Democracy is pulled back and forth between its ambition to dissolve borders and its demand for a community of participation. If disturbances occur as the democratic paradox unfolds, I believe they are not just inevitable but actually desirable.

The political order cannot escape the democratic paradox, nor can the nomocentric or eccentric troublemaker. When it comes to the question of how he should intervene or attack, the troublemaker is torn between (over-?)estimating the "incipient or 'fugitive' moments" of local actions and (over-?)extending himself in the interest of "realizing greater ideals of justice and equality."[72] Mind you, this is no cause for dejection, but it does limit his leeway and narrow the range of decisions available to him. The troublemaker does not sit at the negotiating table with everyone else; he remains outside, standing on the threshold. He is doomed to operate *either* locally *or* globally. I want to briefly outline these two separate strategies, which will bring me to Edward Snowden.

When the troublemaker acts locally, he fights to transform a political order that surrounds him every day. He wants to inflict wounds on it or leave traces that will eventually cause this order to change. He practices what James Holston, in his case study of Brazil, refers to as "insurgent citizenship." Holston meticulously describes the tension-filled processes between the "insurgence of the local" and the institutions of the state. In doing so, he warns against making a strict distinction between civil society and the state – because such protests typically reveal the permeability of the border or the accessibility of the threshold between the two spheres.[73] The troublemaker appears and disappears, resists and falls into line, but his integration does not need to be a defeat; with a stroke of luck, it can be a testament to his success. In this fluctuation between maintaining an outsider position and intervening to bring about change, eccentric and nomocentric motives merge into one. Holston describes this disturbance in a particularly lovely way:

Insurgence describes a process that is an acting counter, a counterpolitics, that destabilizes the present and renders it fragile, defamiliarizing the coherence with which it usually presents itself. Insurgence is not a top-down imposition of an already scripted future. It bubbles up from the past in places where present circumstances seem propitious for an irruption. In this view, the present is like a bog: leaky, full of holes, gaps, contradictions, and misunderstandings. These exist just beneath all the taken-for-granted assumptions that give the present its apparent consistency.[74]

Are people who put up local resistance disconnected from the big wide world around them? Do they fundamentally aim too low for nomocentric concerns? Certainly not. To answer the question of how far resistance can penetrate a network of global connections, there are two maxims to choose from. One says that a drop in the ocean changes nothing. The other says that a butterfly flapping its wings in the Amazonian jungle can unleash a tornado in Texas. As is generally the case with such phrases, they do not tell the whole truth, which lies somewhere in between. The exact location is not determined by philosophers; it can be found in socio-scientific fieldwork, and perhaps even in works of art (such as Nigel Cole's 2010 film *Made in Dagenham*, which tells the story of female Ford employees fighting for equal pay, or Matthew Warchus's film *Pride* from 2014, about the alliance between Welsh miners and gay and lesbian activists).

When the troublemaker acts globally, then he comes from the outside, to a certain extent, not from below. To cope with the task of tackling an order that is almost untouchable, he makes himself intangible. When the power of the political order extends to every nook and cranny, when this power is *everywhere*, he responds by being *nowhere*. He cannot be settled, or even locatable. Geoffroy de Lagasnerie analyzed this new form of resistance in his interesting book *The Art of Revolt*. According to Lagasnerie, the global troublemaker seeks the protection of "anonymity" and thus rejects a classic requirement of the political public sphere: that people answer for their words and deeds and show their face. This requirement tends to be met by those who practice civil disobedience and, through their struggle, confirm their membership in the state they are challenging. But in light of the superior power of the political order, the global troublemaker believes he is justified in *disappearing*. A willingness to accept "responsibility" would unreasonably endanger him. He rejects "interaction" and "reciprocity" in order to "liberate [himself] from the demand of entertaining a relationship with those with whom [he stands] in conflict."[75]

When the troublemaker evades the "order of the law" that wants to take hold of him, in a radical sense, it means that he is contesting the state's jurisdiction over him and coupling his struggle against the state to the loss of his membership in it. He takes his statelessness into account. One of the main figures in Lagasnerie's book serves as a good example of how protest can escalate in this way: Edward Snowden. Snowden is one of the global troublemakers who, according to Lagasnerie, is "mounting an attack on the heart of the juridico-political system":

> In fleeing, migrating, and explicitly refusing to stand before the justice of "their" country (is it still even their country?), they reject national or political belonging and the manner in which it has been imposed on them. [...] As such, the practice of flight calls into question what one could call the *national structures of revolt and politics*. [...] Snowden [...] is committed to a practice of desubjugation that has led him to stop belonging to his nation [...]. This was less an act of disobedience than an act of resignation.[76]

Though I can go along with Lagasnerie's description of the global troublemaker in this respect, I am bothered by the fact that he underplays the sad or painful side of this revolt and its inner shortcomings. The "joy in being nobody," as dreamed of in *The Coming Insurrection*, is really no joy at all.[77] Lagasnerie *glorifies* his hero by presuming that he can "choose [his] own community."[78] This in no way corresponds to the actual options available to Snowden in his Russian exile, for example – but it is also neither reasonable nor desirable as an ideal, counterfactual scenario.

Lagasnerie says: "Belonging to a state should be rethought – in terms of choice, not constraint."[79] Here he invokes libertarian arguments such as those of Robert Nozick, which recommend that individuals maintain a solely instrumental relationship with the state. Lagasnerie thus falls into an individualistic trap in which his global troublemaker suddenly takes on egocentric characteristics. This troublemaker wants to find a state that benefits him, so he can only judge the people he lives with in this state based on whether or not they also benefit him. (We can see this kind of instrumental relationship in Julian Assange's treatment of his colleagues, if we are to believe the reports of the people affected.[80])

The local and the global troublemaker embody the two halves that break apart – and that must break apart – in political resistance today. If democracy operates under the conditions of glocalization, then the battle against the injustices within it cannot be fought *all at once* on both the global and the local level. The shortcomings of the global troublemaker thus complement those that plague the local troublemaker. While the latter cannot escape the *partiality* that ties him to the situation around him, the former cannot escape his *impartiality*. He is doomed to placelessness, and thus to loneliness.

4. The massive troublemaker and fundamentalism

At the start of this chapter, I said that Western societies were currently characterized by a struggle between different troublemakers. Therefore, in analyzing the relationship between order and disturbance, it is inappropriate to present oneself simply as a partisan *either* of order *or* of disturbance. Instead, everything depends on the type of order and the type of disturbance.

Troublemakers are found on the threshold of the society from which they are excluded, to which they are opposed, or on which they turn their backs. In this position, they can be in a passive and/or active mode. They can suffer from exclusion, but they can also take measures to dissociate themselves. Some are denied the invitation to play along, and others spurn such an invitation. In the end, sometimes the people themselves do not know the extent to which their marginal position is imposed or desired. The troublemakers living a precarious, fragile existence on the threshold of society have an identity problem. Their identity is necessarily *relative*, meaning that they cannot define themselves without reference to what repels them – and they have to consider every possible variation along the passive–active spectrum: that they are being rejected, that they feel rejected, or that they are deliberately rejecting their environment.

The *egocentric* troublemaker solves his identity problem by acting solely on the basis of self-interest and striving to outfox the political order. The *eccentric* troublemaker transcends both the political order and himself; he flouts his identity but is just as critical of the existing order as the *nomocentric* troublemaker, who holds out the prospect of a different order and boldly identifies with it in anticipation of its existence. The *massive* troublemaker who was introduced in connection with fascism tries to solve his identity problem by *crossing out* the aspects of his identity that are relative and claiming to belong entirely to a closed collective.

We have a depressing modern example of the fascist troublemaker. The year 2011, the *annus mirabilis* for the Arab Spring and Occupy Wall Street, was also an *annus horribilis*. On July 22 of this year, the Norwegian fascist Anders Behring Breivik murdered 77 people in Oslo and on a nearby island, including many young people at a social-democratic summer camp. In a lengthy document that Breivik circulated with the title *2083 – A European Declaration of Independence*, he railed against the "mass importation of Muslims," called for the elimination of "all traces of Liberal Modernity" and rhapsodized over a "pan-Nordic union."[81]

But the massive troublemaker appears not only as a fascist, but also (generally) as a *fundamentalist* and (specifically) as an *Islamist*. These

356

types cannot be forcibly aligned, but they do exhibit formal similarities. They link their identity to a disturbed disturbance in which the connection to the status quo is broken and a new kind of closure is put in place. Two steps lead to this disturbance, which ends in destruction.

I have just made the general point that a wildly varying mixture of passivity and activity, of imposed and effected isolation, is found on the threshold. This mixture can be toxic – and the toxin's *first* step is to infect the outsider's status as a victim. The decisive factor is not just the extent to which the outsider *is* a victim, but the extent to which he *feels* like a victim and embraces this trait. Being a victim and seeing oneself as a victim are not necessarily the same thing. I can be overwhelmed by my powerlessness, but I can also exaggerate it, indulge in a sense of futility and ignore the opportunities for participation that are actually open to me. This exaggeration of the victim role is perversely *seductive*. The advantage of it is that it relieves me of the effort of taking the initiative myself. I can blame my circumstances entirely on the situation in which I find myself. A well-known psychological mechanism is at work here, one which involves the shifting and unloading of responsibility.

This first, entirely defensive step paves the way for the *second*, entirely offensive step. The ruling order confronts me and even creeps into me; it has made me what I *am*. But *I* am actually not this being at all, because I am merely a victim, so the being has apparently come into existence without my involvement or responsibility. ("*Proximally,* it is not 'I', in the sense of my own Self, that 'am', but rather the Others, whose way is that of the 'they'.[82]) Because this being is a stranger to me, I can claim a different identity for myself, one which is decoupled from the overpowering political order. Regardless of what I then *do*, at least *I* am the one doing it, while my life prior to this was merely that of a victim. But this doing is too much for me alone, so I seek the backing of a larger cause. This turns me into a warrior who is beyond reconciliation and understands nothing but victory or defeat. A great schism occurs.

These two steps are familiar to us from the movement patterns of the most active massive troublemaker at the moment: the Islamist. Of course, he can only be discussed in this book if his genesis can be traced back to the self-made problems of Western societies[83] – and these problems include the switching of roles from victim to perpetrator that I have just described. This idea was corroborated by the French rapper Jo Dalton – among many others – who was personally acquainted with some of the *Charlie Hebdo* attackers in Paris in January 2015: "If you make people victims, they will become butchers."[84] In many cases, this victim–perpetrator switch is accompanied by a double aggrandizement: you are a victim, but you additionally stylize this status.[85] You not only act, you go for the big blow. From a feeling of being utterly neglected, you make the decision to take on the whole world.

The question of why so many Islamist attackers – in London, Boston, Paris, Brussels, etc. – have come from the heart (or, more accurately, the margins) of Western societies has been intensively investigated by reporters and social scientists alike using various methods.[86] I want to look at the history of just a single Islamist troublemaker here, a case that has been nearly forgotten today, but that contains all of the ingredients that will reappear all too often later on.

Khaled Kelkal was "one of the main protagonists of the wave of Islamist terrorism that hit France in the summer of 1995."[87] After an attempted attack on the Paris–Lyon high-speed train route, investigators tracked down Kelkal, who skirmished with the police and was shot dead on September 29 of the same year. In a long interview conducted with him in 1992 by the social scientist Dietmar Loch and subsequently published in *Le Monde*, his life plays out like a drama in five acts.[88]

- *Act 1: Socialization.* Kelkal, who was taken to France from Algeria at the age of two, does well in school. The teachers show an interest in him, and the pupils are diverse: "We got along fast."
- *Act 2: Discrimination.* The boy from the *banlieue* is unable to cope with the move to high school (*lycée*). He feels there is a "giant wall" separating him from his fellow students, "the rich": "I had the skills to succeed, but I couldn't find a place for myself because I sensed that total integration was impossible. Forgetting my culture, eating pork – I couldn't do it. [. . .]. I reached a point where I thought, 'What are you doing here?' instead of saying, 'It's good this way, it's for you, it's something to work on.'"
- *Act 3: Delinquency.* Kelkal describes his exit from the system and his path to criminality as if it were a move to Hobbes's state of nature: "I could only count on myself." – "When you steal, you feel free, because you're playing a game. As long they don't catch me, I'm the winner. [. . .] You either lose or you win. But it's true: this path leads to nowhere." Kelkal is arrested and sentenced to several years in prison. But he does not remain isolated. On the streets of his neighborhood and in prison, he forms an "alliance" with others who are fed up (*"il y a un grand ras-le-bol"*) and want to annoy society (*"emmerder la société"*).
- *Act 4: Segregation.* Looking back, Kelkal views his crimes as a crude act of "vengeance" in which he reflected the very bogeyman image that society had of him: "You want violence, we'll give you violence." (He behaves like Victor Hugo's Quasimodo, who initially only reflects the "hatred" that his "environment" displays toward him.) Kelkal escapes this "vicious circle," as he says, when he discovers an order

in which everything "has its place" and has "a meaning": Islam. "I am neither Arab nor French, I am Muslim. [...] There are no races anymore, there is nothing at all, everything is extinguished, there is unity, we are united."

• *Act 5: Terror.* The final act in the genesis of this Islamist takes place just three years after the interview on which this chronology is based. Kelkal, who in 1992 was still dreaming of finding support in a total spiritual "unity" and, at the same time (glocally!), of opening a small business in Algeria, remains trapped in a fight that he views as a battle between two worlds. He becomes a terrorist.

To put it in terribly prosaic terms, there is a disastrous interplay here between push and pull factors. The push drives people to the edge – particularly those who do not know where they belong, who are disembedded just like the masterless men of Hobbes's era. The Kelkals of this world are especially easy to push away when they simultaneously feel a pull and are drawn toward a new goal. In the early phase they operate in a "reactive"[89] way, meaning that they relate to something negatively. Then they start to deny this relation. Working in a very different way to the global troublemaker who was discussed in the previous section, the outsiders who become Islamists cut their connection – however disturbed it may be – to the order in which they live. They seek to "destroy the Grayzone,"[90] the intermediary world between unbelievers and supposedly pure doctrine. They act as though they had nothing to do with the status quo, as if they were alien, external enemies.

If this new "unity" – about which Khaled Kelkal rhapsodized – is to succeed in its immunization effect, it must be *massive*: flawless, intact, all of a piece, with no openings that could allow for excursions or connections. The pull factor of this unity will only be effective if it is specially tailored to the requirements that must be fulfilled by a total counterworld. It is not a product of tradition, it does not already *exist*, it must first be *constructed*. In concrete terms, this results in Islam being twisted and deformed. It can no longer rely on specific cultural practices[91] or social life contexts, because these are not accessible to all those struggling to get along somewhere on the margins of Western society. An Islamist must never feel forsaken, he must always – ideally or virtually – have access to a "new universal community" of like-minded people: "Modern Islamic radicalism [...] is a global space."[92] This means there is also an Islamist form of glocalization. It functions in the short-circuit between small local groups and the so-called Holy War being waged worldwide.

As with fascists, we find a disturbed disturbance among Islamists. This disturbance coincides with the unconditional affirmation of an order. A reactive, relative identity is replaced by an absolute identity. The idea of "total fusion" arose in connection with fascism, and important analyses of modern fundamentalism and Islamism have moved in the same direction. Scott Atran speaks of an "identity fusion," a "wedding" of "personal" and "collective identity."[93] Michel Wieviorka says that violent perpetrators rush to identify themselves as the "hyper-subjects" of a higher authority, in whose name they act.[94] Compared to this great subject, their own puny existence seems negligible, so in the end the Islamist is not making much of a sacrifice when he becomes a suicide attacker. But the rewards of death are all the greater, as death promises definitive, irrevocable admission to a perfect order. The "neo-community" thus becomes a "necro-community," a community of death.[95] The massive troublemaker destroys others as well as himself.

5. The little savage and the populism of Donald Trump

In view of the terrorist attacks that have left their bloody mark on the early twenty-first century, there is a growing appreciation for calm and order. Up until now, the Hobbes years have outnumbered the anti-Hobbes years in this century. More often than not, rattled nerves and uncertainty have caused people to long for a state which – as Hobbes promised in *Leviathan* – can guarantee "peace and defence." The times have been rare when a rotten, false peace has been terminated, the desire for disruption has bubbled up and people have mobilized the "chaos in [themselves] to be able to give birth to a dancing star."[96]

If we compare the fundamentalist attacks of "globalized Islam" and the economic processes of the globalized economy, we encounter massive differences, but also effects of eerie similarity. Both of them, to put it simply, lead to a fear of the loss of the local. They undermine the reliability of lifeworlds and people's ability to define these themselves. "What we have come to call a globalized world harbors fundamental tensions between opening and barricading, fusion and partition, erasure and reinscription."[97] It is notable that the special political order currently dominating the Western world struggles to act as a protector of the local in the face of such attacks. Democracy wants to guarantee that people can shape and define their life circumstances on their own. It takes people's fears and concerns seriously, but it is not prepared to respond to them in a way that would cause it to surrender itself. This is what would happen if security surpassed all other goals and the "closed society" that has already been mentioned multiple times was actually established. Instead, the proponents of democracy are suspicious of Hobbes's promise of peace and order because – as we may recall from Rousseau and Tocqueville – they sense within it the danger of despotism.

Democracy is tied to processes of inner renewal, and thus to inner estrangement or strangeness. It also insists on external openness, because with an exuberance of human rights it transcends its own boundaries. Democracy does not take sides in the relationship between the global and the local; it stands in the middle. It is – in self-assured terms – designed and made for people who are not just at home but also *on the move* – toward themselves and others. Specifically, this also means that democracy finds itself forced to loosen its historically strong connection to the nation state so that it can confront the globalized economy on a halfway equal footing.

If democracy occupies an intermediary position as described above, it means that a gap must open up in the political spectrum where local fears and concerns can escalate. And if democracy then loosens its close connection to the nation, it must take into account that this nation will become what is referred to in chemistry as a free radical: it will be open to new connections. In concrete terms, the nation will thumb its nose at democracy and fall prey to nationalism and populism. Appreciation for democracy will then be replaced by the dream of the defense or restoration of an intact world. The nationalist and populist movements currently running rampant are staging a battle against various global tendencies: global terror, global streams of money and goods, migration and refugee movements, transnational political institutions, etc.

Although populism takes on the massive troublemaker in the guise of the fundamentalist terrorist, it has a frightening amount in common with him. They are hostile brothers. Both populism and fundamentalism are dominated by conceptions of themselves as intact, closed identities and ideal total orders. Even in the populist camp we find massive troublemakers wanting to undermine or eliminate democracy. Unlike Islamists, however, these populists do not occupy the margins of the society; they come right from the center of it – a center they view as a pitfall in which they might lose themselves. In order to become misfits, they must undergo a transformation which follows a specific pattern or ritual. They escape – and they engage.

On the one hand, they abandon the ruling order or they feel abandoned by it, so they signal their distance from it. (Ethnologists refer to this as removal, economists as divestment.) On the other hand, populists use this distance to gain elbow room and gather impetus for their own movement. They want to go on the offensive and use their contempt to punish, attack, and topple the political order. The history and systematics of the troublemaker provide a perfect template for this ritual, this double movement – namely, Horkheimer's "little savage." He withdraws from the political order by banking everything on his ability to get by on his own, and he intervenes by becoming part of a mass that grasps for power. The original version of this little savage is the egocentric-massive troublemaker.

Whether it is a historical coincidence or necessity – in either case, it is notable that the most prominent and successful populist politician of the present day is an almost uncanny match for Horkheimer's model of the little savage. I cannot resist the temptation to explore this match to the full, which is why this section about populism will focus on Donald Trump. I will talk about his egocentric-massive agenda in a moment, but first I want to make some general comments about his status as a troublemaker.

In accordance with the ritual just described, a populist leader must present himself as an outsider who comes from the middle. Donald Trump not only plays this role, he exaggerates it. Despite his wealth, he poses as a man of the people and takes up the struggle against the so-called "system," which is a political-economic complex. In an ad that aired on November 7, 2016, right before the US presidential election, Trump said: "A global power structure [. . .] is responsible for the economic decisions that have robbed our working class."

There are, of course, good reasons to doubt that Trump is serious about his marginal position. (For example, when Trump said "power structure" in this ad, a picture flashed up of Goldman Sachs CEO Lloyd Blankfein – but this did not stop Trump from giving influential positions to many people with Goldman Sachs connections after his election.) The decisive factor, however, is that Trump has been extremely effective in presenting himself as an outsider who comes from the middle. He is a reflection of a big disconnect between the population and its democratic institutions.

Even before Election Day 2016, a commentator asked a question that is really the key question: "Is Trump a Bumbling Incompetent or a Canny Disrupter?"[98] This points to two aspects that are actually constitutive of the outsider. To those who stand on the margins, the practices and routines of those who belong are unfamiliar and unknown. This is what makes the outsider look "incompetent." But those who stand on the margins are also in a position to break rules that have become second nature, as it were, to those who participate and play along. This is what makes the outsider a "disrupter."

It fits with this disruption that Trump himself, his staff, and even many commentators have availed themselves of the entire vocabulary of protest, uprising, revolt, and even revolution. The crassest example of this is a comment from Trump's former senior advisor, Steve Bannon: "Lenin wanted to destroy the state, and that's my goal too. I want to bring everything crashing down, and destroy all of today's establishment."[99]

The talk of disruption is somewhat confusing, however, because this concept is rooted in an economic development that Trump has vowed to fight: namely, the radically globalized new startup economy of Silicon Valley, which seeks to break open established structures. In this respect, one disruption has been pitted against another. As a troublemaker, Trump is not only taking on the established order, he is also taking on those who are proud to count amongst their ranks "the crazy ones, the misfits, the rebels, the troublemakers."

It is not exactly flattering, but it is almost inevitable that Trump, the political newcomer and self-declared outsider, would be accused of incompetence. He employs two strategies to counter this accusation. First, he argues that his lack of experience in office is an advantage because it makes him impartial. In an interview with Fox News on May 17, 2016, he commented on controversial statements made in previous TV debates, admitting: "I mean, my whole life is a debate, but I have never actually debated before." Second, he argues that it is high time for the state to be run like a business, and he claims that he can compensate for his inexperience in the work of government with his record as an entrepreneur.

But in attempting to execute his planned disruption of the system, Trump stumbles over his incompetence. Insider reports from the first rather chaotic days of his presidency claimed that Trump was acting like a "feckless" or "clueless child" in the White House.[100] Many of his appearances during the election campaign and in the first phase of his presidency fit this pattern – especially when his childish thoughtlessness was accompanied by adolescent recklessness. We need only think of Trump's comments about women, which he plays down as "locker room talk," or of the delight he takes in sweeping insults, or of the terribly childish feeling of omnipotence on display when he signs his executive orders.

One particularly enlightening episode took place early in the election campaign, when Trump referred to the moderator Megyn Kelly as a "bimbo." A commentator pointed out that while the word "bimbo" fits the cliché of the dumb blonde in English today, it can actually be traced back to the Italian word for boy (*bambino, bimbo*), and it was adopted by the English language in early twentieth century to refer to an "unintelligent or brutish male." This led to the suggestion that the word should be applied to Trump himself; in this sense, he is the bimbo.[101]

This unexpectedly brings together all of the elements that were part of Hobbes's original definition of the *puer robustus*. The *robustus* applies to the strength or power that Trump likes to demonstrate, especially in economic and sexual respects. (Incidentally, this unites him with one of his closest relatives in the political arena: Silvio Berlusconi, who has himself been referred to as a *puer senex*.) The *puer* fits with Trump as a "bimbo" who often seems rather adolescent in his position as an uncouth outsider.

Puer in the sense of a "childish mind" or Hobbes's "want of reason" fits with the accusation that Trump is "incompetent" or "clueless." When it comes to both Hobbes's *puer robustus* and Trump, however, it is a matter of debate whether one might require a strange mixture of narrow-mindedness and cleverness to break the rules. This is why Trump has been called not only "incompetent" but also "cunning."

The startlingly close correspondence between Hobbes's *puer robustus* and Donald Trump suggests that Trump is precisely the type of trouble-maker Hobbes has set his sights on: the egocentric troublemaker. This categorization does fit – but only to a certain extent. As hinted at earlier, Trump has two faces. He is an egocentric-massive troublemaker – and, as we are about to see, this is critical to his success as a populist.

His *first face*, the one that Trump mainly showed during the election campaign, is actually that of the egocentric troublemaker. As a rascal and a trickster, he throws all conventions to the wind and follows the motto of "rules are for losers."[102] It is impossible to forget Trump's response in the televised debate of September 26, 2016, in Hempstead, New York, when Hillary Clinton accused him of having paid absolutely no federal income taxes, at least during the years for which his tax returns were publicly available. His spontaneous reaction both confirmed this suspi-cion and robbed it of its edge: "That makes me smart." The exploitation of every available loophole seems to be the achievement of an individual who is interested primarily in one aspect of state regulations: how he can undermine them. Moreover, Trump violates every rule of what, according to basic moral standards, is considered good behavior; he makes deroga-tory remarks about people with disabilities, about the mothers of fallen soldiers, etc. His cult of rule-breaking extends so far that Trump will conveniently forget, misrepresent, or completely twist statements that he himself has made, without ever accounting for this behavior. He feels obligated to no one and to nothing, not even to himself. And anyone who believes reliability is a virtue is driven to despair.

Like Hobbes's *puer robustus*, Trump banks on his own strength and sets up the world as his battlefield. This attitude fits with Hobbes's description of war in a state of nature, with Tocqueville's image of the American pioneers as "adventurers" with no time for "laws" or "mores," and even with the rich rabble of Hegel and Marx. Trump made the fol-lowing comment back in 1981: "Man is the most vicious of all animals, and life is a series of battles ending in victory or defeat. You just can't let people make a sucker out of you."[103] And in an interview with Fox News on May 17, 2016, he declared: "I view myself as a person that – like everybody else – is fighting for survival." Trump is not gritting his teeth in resignation at the cut and thrust of life, however; instead, he is fueling the fire of the war of all against all in pursuit of a single goal, which he formulates in the closing words of his book *The Art of the Comeback*: "Victory, victory, victory!"[104]

The egocentric troublemaker is additionally ordained for something higher in the figure of Trump. Trump is interested not just in an economic battle with other benefit maximizers, but in a political battle against an institutional order. Unlike Hobbes's *puer robustus*, however, he wants to represent good, not evil. This is only possible, of course, if the moral relationship between rules and breaking them can be turned around. If the order is evil, if "the system is rigged," then disturbance is no longer dishonorable but honorable.

Trump credits the rule-breaker with tricking or leveraging a corrupt system, and he himself appears to be a moral hero. He thus becomes a role model for all those who feel abandoned by the state or the whole world and believe that they should be allowed to see everything through on their own. They demand carte blanche, or even a seal of approval, for everything they do. In accordance with the popular American motto that taxes are theft, this might also apply to illegal employment; and following the broad interpretation of the Second Amendment to the Constitution, it might ultimately even apply to vigilante justice.

With his *second face,* Donald Trump presents himself as more than just an egocentric troublemaker. It is easy to understand why he needs another face – especially after having taken office. After all, it would not be terribly constructive if his followers emulated him by thinking only of themselves and excelling as loners. Then the extent of their enthusiasm for Trump would be summed up by a comment from one of his supporters: "He may be an asshole, but he is *our* asshole."[105] Even the positively reinterpreted and re-evaluated egocentric troublemaker remains tied to an agenda of self-assertion that is limited to the individual. Strictly speaking, a president would be superfluous in this case. The second face that Trump shows is not simply that of a politician representing state interests; it is still that of a troublemaker, but one who is leaving behind his egocentric identity.

Trump's supporters may try to emulate him, but they also expect him to achieve something that fundamentally distinguishes him from them. Trump has to convince his supporters that he is "one of us," but he must also be able "to 'do it for us,'" i.e., to take the reins and do something for his supporters that only he can do.[106] The collection of individuals getting by more or less successfully is thus transformed into a collective, a *we* that places special expectations on Trump's *I*. This is no longer about an alliance between warring individuals and their buddy Trump; it is about a contrast between these ordinary individuals and an extraordinary leading figure.

Trump himself provides a precise description of this transformation in the relationship between him and the people, between *I* and *we*, in an important speech given on October 13, 2016, in West Palm Beach, Florida. First, he establishes a well-known opposition between movement and system: "Our movement is about replacing a failed and corrupt – now, when I say 'corrupt,' I'm talking about totally corrupt – political establishment, with a new government controlled by you, the American people. [. . .] This election will determine whether we are a free nation or whether we have only the illusion of democracy, but are in fact controlled by a small handful of global special interests rigging the system." Here Trump is apparently addressing the *we* of the people and not talking about himself. Viewed in isolation, these sentences are nothing other than a plea for the empowerment of the citizens and the restoration of a democracy that has been all but eliminated in the USA through the rule of an alliance of political elites and special interest groups. The plea is dramatized when he declares the upcoming election to be a matter of shaping the country's destiny: "This is not simply another four-year election. This is a crossroads in the history of our civilization that will determine whether or not we the people reclaim control over our government. [. . .] This is our moment of reckoning as a society and as a civilization itself. [. . .] We will end the politics of profit. We will end the rule of special interests." Trump provisionally counts himself among this *we* and declares himself to be part of the people. "I [. . .] know that it's not about me," he so humbly claims. "It's about all of you and it's about our country. [. . .] It's about all of us together as a country."

But then comes the twist that determines everything. Trump makes it clear that he does not believe the people are capable of handling this enormous task. This is why it is all up to him: "I'm the only one that can fix it." – "I will make it good. I'll bring back our jobs." Trump offers himself up as a leader who will guide the people into a bright future: "Many of my friends and many political experts warned me that this campaign would be a journey to hell [. . .]. But they're wrong. It will be a journey to heaven." On the way to this heaven, all the representatives of the corrupt system will attempt to trip him up: "They would stop at nothing to try to stop me." Trump says he is prepared to suffer through all of these attacks and to resist them: "I take all of these slings and arrows gladly for you. I take them for our movement so that we can have our country back." These words (loosely based on Shakespeare's *Hamlet*) dramatically change the relationship between the American *we* and the Trumpian *I*. Trump will not, in fact, liberate the people from the powerless state in which, according to his interpretation, they find themselves. On the contrary: they will remain in need and wait helplessly for someone to rescue them and take them along on this "journey to heaven." It was not lost on most commentators that Trump arrogantly compares himself to Jesus Christ in this speech. He will allow himself to be wounded on behalf of the people, he will endure the arrows shot at him and the stones thrown at him. (We cannot overlook the fact that Hitler also compared himself to Jesus.) A statement made at a press conference on January 11, 2017, also shows that he believes he has authority from on high: "I will be the greatest jobs producer that God ever created." In an interview with Fox News on November, 3, 2017, Trump said: "I am the only one that matters."

Trump's *I* pushes itself ahead of the American *we* and makes the *we* dependent on him. In doing so, incidentally, Trump sets up a contrast with the campaign slogans that accompanied Barack Obama's path to the presidency: "Yes we can" and "We are the ones we've been waiting for." When Trump speaks of the *we*, he eliminates the plurality that actually makes it what it is. This is the only way the *we* can be represented and embodied by a singular *I*. He creates a political fusion, a total unity, in which he speaks and acts on behalf of everyone.

Trump is therefore a prime example of a disturbed disturbance. His disturbance is short-circuited with an order that is assumed to exist and be in need of defense: the greatness of America, which must be restored. Trump is thus acting not just as an egocentric troublemaker here, but as a *massive troublemaker*. Having made it into the White House, he can go about undermining democracy from on high. His allegation that the USA has been operating under "the illusion of democracy" is reflected back at him. Under his rule, the illusion remains in place – and is even intensified. If Trump promotes any kind of democracy at all – and the word rarely passes his lips – then, at best, it resembles the distorted image that Carl Schmitt had in mind when he tied democracy to the "homogeneity" of the people.

Since the first appearance of the massive troublemaker is historically associated with the rise of fascism, the obvious question here is whether Trump should also be considered a fascist – and this question has been answered in the affirmative by commentators on the right and left alike.[107] Distortions often arise when current political developments are identified with fascism, because too little attention is paid to the historical differences. Furthermore, although the massive troublemaker was invented by fascism, he is certainly not exclusively tied to it. In my view, there are both similarities and differences between Trump and the fascist leaders of the past.

One important *similarity* is the short-circuit between the individual leader and the people, which goes hand in hand with the transition from plural to singular that was described earlier. The total closure of the mass always works on the basis of exclusion. This exclusion affects people who are not absorbed into the unity of the *I* and the *we* and who resist such closure. Trump unabashedly expressed this in his first press conference after taking office, on February 16, 2017. On the one hand, he evoked the unity of the people: "It's all about unification. We're unifying the party and hopefully we're going to be able to unify the country." On the other hand, in the very same press conference Trump brusquely disclaimed such inclusion and employed a selective concept of "the people," which is, incidentally, a "core claim" of populism.[108] In this specific case, it was representatives of the press that Trump claimed were not part of the people (on other occasions he has mentioned Muslims). On February 17, 2017, Donald Trump tweeted: "The FAKE NEWS media (failing @nytimes, @NBCNews, @ABC, @CBS, @CNN) is not my enemy, it is the enemy of the American People!" When Trump speaks of enemies of the people in this way, it structurally corresponds to a totalitarian way of thinking – one found not only in fascism, incidentally, but also in Maoism. Thus, we also have John McCain's laconic response to Trump's tweet: "That's how dictators get started."[109]

One important *difference* between fascism and the Trump regime can be illuminated on the basis of a character trait mentioned in countless psychological profiles and portraits: Trump's narcissism. He is driven by his ambition to elevate narcissistic self-affirmation to a collective experience in which the *I* merges with the greater whole. "The rise of Donald Trump [. . .] marks the fusion of populism and narcissism."[110] He loves himself, and he wants to be loved by everyone else just as much. In this respect, he would probably have a good deal of sympathy for Mae Holland, the protagonist of Dave Eggers' novel *The Circle*. When she finds out that her popularity among her co-workers lies at 97 percent, she is "devastated."[111]

The ambition to be loved by everyone initially appears to fit with the "national narcissism" that Wilhelm Reich spoke of in connection with fascism. But there is a kind of built-in brake system with Trump – because he is not just a massive troublemaker, he is also an egocentric one. It is not the collective of the American people, but rather the narcissistic subject of Trump himself around which everything revolves – and should continue to revolve. Trump has returned to the same themes over and over again for years – such as a concern with America's greatness in international showdowns – but he resists defining a fixed ideological identity for the American people. Because the collective is not organized and defined as a total collective, it will not develop into an entity that narcissistically relates to itself. Instead, the narcissism remains tied to Trump as an individual. He rarely misses an opportunity to demonstrate that his new policies bear his signature – a signature that can look different from day to day. Unlike fascist leaders, but exactly like the biggest egoist in the history of philosophy – namely, Max Stirner – Trump places "enjoyment of the world" in the service of "self-enjoyment."[112]

This individualistic or egocentric caveat is also apparent in Trump's interpretation of the relationship between leader and people. Unlike the totalitarian leaders of the twentieth century, he does not rely on rituals of physical or mental synchronization, on mass demonstrations or radio broadcasts. In brief, Trump banks not on the collective performance but on the individual show. He orchestrates this show as a series of sensations. He puts something out into the world – and the world waits with bated breath to see what he will do next, what surprise he has up his sleeve. One aesthetic element that Trump uses especially effectively is the cliffhanger, which enables him to monopolize attention for what is to come. The most significant example of this comes from the last televised debate prior to the election, on October 19, 2016, in Las Vegas. When asked whether he would accept the result of the election, he refused to answer and instead said: "I will keep you in suspense." Since taking office, this cliffhanger strategy has entered everyday politics and turned it into a sequence of erratic actions, tweets, and other coups.

Trump's populist political style can be analyzed more precisely by applying the author–actor–audience theory that was developed in connection with Hobbes's theory of representation. In accordance with this, Trump considers himself empowered by the people, as the "author," to represent them as their president-"actor." As the main actor on the political stage, he believes his responsibility is to captivate the people who are his "audience." To do this, he must satisfy their consumer needs, keep the tension high, and prevent people from changing the channel. Trump's connection to the people derives not from processes of will-formation, but from the media spell he casts to keep the people trapped in a state of pure receptivity. This results in a fusion between *I* and *we* in which – to put it painfully bluntly – there is no longer any room for one thing: democracy. Trump and many other populists act as troublemakers who weaken or destroy the political order of democracy.

We can assume that in the coming years in the USA (and elsewhere), a battle will be fought between populism and democracy. This battle represents a new chapter in the history of order and disturbance. The first hostilities have already been reported. On his path to power, Trump launched a frontal assault on the "rigged system" of the political order. But the early days of his presidency were characterized by classic conflicts that were not disturbances in the strictest sense, but rather procedures within a democratic order; executive orders were reviewed by the courts and discussed in legislative processes, etc. The disdain Trump had previously expressed for these institutions only came through in passing – such as when he referred to a judge who had ruled against his travel ban as a "so-called judge" in a tweet from February 4, 2017. We can be cautiously optimistic about this president's lack of ability to transform the system through a revolution from above. It is clear, however, that there is more to the democratic process than ensuring that institutional checks and balances – specifically between the president, Congress, and the courts in the USA – will continue to function. This process must also involve a lively back and forth, a debate between institutions and citizens.

Democracies head south when governance takes on an independent existence, when participatory processes atrophy and when people act solely as private individuals. It would perhaps be more honest to say that such political orders are no longer democracies at all, they are forms of gentle despotism like those Tocqueville believed would proliferate in a depoliticized consumer society. Maybe the only positive thing to take from Donald Trump's election is that he does not exactly fit into the pigeonhole of gentle despotism. By invoking "government by the people," part of the famous phrase from Abraham Lincoln's Gettysburg Address, he highlighted the citizens' self-determination – and then abused it. It has become apparent that the citizens are not indifferent to this self-determination, and it now remains to be seen whether they will notice Trump's abuse.

Whether a country is a democracy or a populist regime is determined by whether its citizens want to be spectators at a one-man show or want to take their authorship seriously and put it into practice. The fight against populism is a fight against the monopolization of the broadcaster and a fight for the reconquest of the political stage, from which the voices of the citizens – and, as Hans Kelsen pointed out, the voices of a variety of democratic leaders – ring out. If this stage were to become the site of debate and disturbance in the future, it would not surprise me – and it would please me.

6. On the threshold

As we reach the end of this adventure story, this theory of the troublemaker, one might hope that I could come up with an ideal: with the *right* kind of troublemaker. But there is no such hero to put on a pedestal and admire. The troublemaker is an opportunist. He is attached to the occasion, the *kairos*. All the same, we can generally tell when his deeds become misdeeds: namely, when he elevates himself above the opportunity and denies the threshold situation in which he finds himself. Then he is only doing his own *thing* or only fighting for a *cause*; then he is simply an ego or a mass.

Of the many threshold creatures who appear in this book and have influenced their respective times and places, I have become especially fond of one troublemaker in particular: Diderot's nephew, who brings movement to society like a pinch of yeast. He looks to the moment of opportunity – his own life being the greatest opportunity! – because his yeast will remain dry and dormant unless the conditions are right. I am confident that the *puer robustus* who chafed against and was strengthened by a wide variety of situations in the past will find more good opportunities to take the stage and take action in the future. The troublemaker's adventure story will continue. But my imagination alone is not capable of developing moves for the disruptions to come. A social imagination is needed for this, a political imagination that emerges on the main squares and the margins of the world.

Sometimes these places seem unremarkable. We can gripe about a storm in a teacup, but not about a storm in our living room. Just such a storm is depicted in a play that is considered "one of the great pages of bourgeois culture: on a par with Kant's words on the Enlightenment, or Mill's on liberty."[113]

A husband. A wife. An argument. What is at stake is their future – and that of society as a whole. Helmer, the husband, wants to force his wife, Nora, to be "first and foremost [. . .] a wife and a mother." Henrik Ibsen portrays the fight between the two in his drama *A Doll's House*:

> *Nora*: I believe that first and foremost I am an individual, just as much as you are – or at least I'm going to try to be. [. . .]
> *Helmer*: You are talking like a child. You understand nothing about the society you live in.
> *Nora*: No, I don't. But I shall go into that too. I must try to discover who is right, society or me.
> *Helmer*: You are ill, Nora. You are delirious. I'm half inclined to think you are out of your mind.
> *Nora*: Never have I felt so calm and collected as I do tonight.[114]

In this drama, not only are the rules within an established order negotiated, the order itself is called into question. The "reshaping of social conditions"[115] for which Ibsen said he would work is initiated here by a woman – a *puella robusta* – who is at risk of losing herself. Nora does not even know whether she is already a person or has yet to become one. She must wrest her humanity from Helmer – no, from society itself. Her struggle takes place on a literal threshold: Nora is about to leave her matrimonial home, and in the end she slams the door shut behind her.

The slamming of a door – a sound that fits well with this book. You can hear it when the door shuts, but also when it is pushed open.

NOTES

Comments on citations

For frequently cited works, I use abbreviations that are decoded in the List of Abbreviations. For quotations from works that play a key role in my argument, I cite both the original edition of the work and the translation (where available). In all other cases, I cite only one edition of the work. The English versions of foreign-language works are always cited in the body of the text where available; this is generally not the case in the notes. Emphases in quotations were always in the original.

Epigraphs

Emerson, *Essays & Lectures*, p. 1108 ("The Conduct of Life"); for an explanation, see
    p. 13.
Fleisser, *Gesammelte Werke*, Vol. 1, p. 265 ("Der starke Stamm").

Introduction

1 Bakhtin, *Problems of Dostoevsky's Poetics*, p. 173; "Forms of Time and of the Chronotope in the Novel" in *The Dialogic Imagination*, p. 115.
2 Wittgenstein, *Culture and Value*, 74e. The quote "I don't know my way about" naturally also comes from Wittgenstein, *Philosophical Investigations*, 55e.
3 Simmel, *On Individuality and Social Forms*, p. 196.
4 Bakhtin, *Problems of Dostoevsky's Poetics*, p. 73; cf. Bakhtin, "Forms of Time and of the Chronotope in the Novel," p. 248.
5 Hegel, *The Science of Logic*, p. 106.
6 Regarding "liminal entities," see Turner, *The Ritual Process: Structure and Anti-Structure*, pp. 94–130. I want to thank Anna Rosa Thomä for talking about thresholds with me.
7 As mentioned by Sextus Pompeius Festus; see Agamben, *Homo sacer*, p. 71.
8 Ibid., pp. 17, 153, 83; Agamben, *Means without End*, p. 35; cf. Thomä, "Der 'Herrenlose,'" pp. 975f.
9 Agamben, *The Coming Community*, p. 85.
10 Cf., e.g., Agamben, *Homo sacer*, p. 131.
11 Rancière also complains that Agamben "misses the logic of political subjectivation"

in that he distinguishes between the "spheres" of those who belong and those who are excluded and ignores the "interval" in which the "capacity for staging scenes of dissensus" unfolds; Rancière, "Who is the Subject of the Rights of Man?", pp. 77–8. A similar position is held by Del Lucchese, *Tumultes et indignation*, p. 76 (with reference to Machiavelli, Spinoza, and Foucault).

12 Foucault, *Ethics: Subjectivity and Truth*, p. 315 ("What is Enlightenment?"); Foucault, *History of Madness*, p. xxix (from the preface to the first edition).

13 Hall, "The Emergence of Cultural Studies and the Crisis of the Humanities," p. 23.

14 Goethe, *The Essential Goethe*, p. 581 (from *Wilhelm Meister's Apprenticeship*, 1795–6).

Chapter I. The *puer robustus* as an evil man: Thomas Hobbes

1 Strauss, *Spinoza's Critique of Religion*, p. 94.

2 The early English translation that was published in Hobbes's lifetime is used in the two major editions of his works: the old Molesworth edition, and the *Clarendon Edition of the Philosophical Works of Thomas Hobbes*, cited here as C[e]. Richard Tuck, editor of the volume *On the Citizen* in the series *Cambridge Texts in the History of Political Thought*, complains that the earlier translator "worked in an extremely slapdash manner," and Tuck therefore supplies an entirely new translation; cf. Hobbes, *On the Citizen*, p. 11: "An evil man is rather like a sturdy boy, or a man of childish mind." For a critique of the assumption that the early English translation was published with Hobbes's consent, cf. Tuck's editorial remarks, ibid., p. xxxvi; for an opposing viewpoint, cf. Warrender's argument in Hobbes, C[e] 6–8. I consulted Tuck's new version, but I have stayed with the old, popular version – not least because this was the origin of the effective history of the *puer robustus*.

3 Shakespeare, *Complete Works*, p. 1293 (III.3).

4 Calderón de la Barca, *The Great Theater of the World*, p. 54.

5 The importance of this annotation is emphasized by the founder of modern Hobbes scholarship; cf. Tönnies, "Hobbes and the Zoon Politikon," pp. 49f.

6 Regarding this passage, cf. Tönnies, *Thomas Hobbes*, p. 109; Agamben, *Homo sacer*, pp. 36, 105; Manow, *Politische Ursprungsphantasien*, p. 203.

7 Power, *Experimental Philosophy*, p. 192; cf. Shapin and Schaffer, *Leviathan and the Air-Pump*, p. 304 (though it is quoted incorrectly there).

8 See, e.g., Goldsmith, "Picturing Hobbes's Politics?", pp. 234f.; Bredekamp, "Thomas Hobbes's Visual Strategies," pp. 29–60; Skinner, *Hobbes and Republican Liberty*, p. 99; Manow, *Politische Ursprungsphantasien*, pp. 55–79. (I say male or female American Indian in the text because the sex of the figure is a matter of debate among scholars.)

9 Emerson, *Essays & Lectures*, p. 1108.

10 Sophocles, *Antigone*, p. 63, line 88.

11 Durkheim, *The Division of Labor in Society*, p. 310.

12 Schmitt, *The Leviathan*, p. 31; Schmitt, "Der Staat als Mechanismus bei Descartes und Hobbes" [1936/37], in: *Staat, Grossraum, Nomos*, pp. 139–51, here p. 140; cf. Esposito, *Communitas*, p. 23.

13 Tönnies, *Thomas Hobbes*, p. 229.

14 For a critique of Hobbes's "'instrumental' notion of reason," see Larmore, *The Autonomy of Morality*, p. 93.

15 "Truly the greatest" benefit is "that we can command and understand commands"; cf. Hobbes, *Man and Citizen*, p. 39 (*De homine*, X.3)/*Opera*, Vol. II, p. 91.

16 Gauthier, *Morals by Agreement*, p. 10: "In Hobbes we find the true ancestor of the theory of morality we shall present [. . .]. To the conceptual underpinning that may be found in Hobbes [. . .], we seek to add the rigour of rational choice"; cf. Gauthier, *The Logic of Leviathan*.

17 The intellectualist strategy pushes Hobbes in the direction of Kantian rationalism; the amoralistic – and by far most influential – strategy relies on rational choice; the strategy based on ethical goals takes various forms and is less firmly established than the other two. My characterization of the first two strategies follows that of Samantha Frost, who could also be considered a representative of the third strategy; cf. Frost, *Lessons from a Materialist Thinker*, p. 10; for a slightly divergent precursor to this schema, cf. Frost, "Faking it," p. 31.

18 Frost, *Lessons from a Materialist Thinker*, p. 109, cf. p. 10; Esposito, *Communitas*, p. 14.

19 Kant, *Lectures on Ethics*, p. 149.

20 I am following an argument made by Pettit, *Made with Words*, p. 64.

21 Hobbes, *English Works*, Vol. IV, p. 209 (*De corpore politico*, VIII.12).

22 Hobbes refers to both culpable rebels and mentally incompetent individuals as "Madmen" (cf. L[e] 208), even though he should actually make a strict distinction between the two. In the later Latin version of *Leviathan*, he solves this problem by simply leaving out the mentally ill (L[l] 469). He takes a similar approach elsewhere, where the Latin version mentions only the individual "qui mentis compos non est," or who is accountable but not of sound mind (L[l]♦249; cf. by contrast L[e] 113]). Foucault would have delighted in this reinterpretation.

23 Foucault, *Abnormal*, pp. 33f. Foucault rarely makes reference to Hobbes, unfortunately – and as far as I can determine, he does not mention Hobbes at all in his discussion of madness. Regarding the "war" that Hobbes believes is a threat "even when the State has been constituted [. . .] that wells up in the State's interstices, at its limits and on its frontiers," cf. Foucault, *Society Must Be Defended*, p. 90.

24 Springborg (in "Hobbes's Fool the *Insipiens*, and the Tyrant-King") argues convincingly that the Latin counterpart of *insipiens* lends theoretical weight to Hobbes's discussion of "the Foole."

25 A short essay about this character was recently published, however: Shell, "Stalking *Puer Robustus*: Hobbes and Rousseau on the Origin of Human Malice." The *puer robustus* is mentioned in passing in the stimulating account by Naville, *Thomas Hobbes*, pp. 211–13.

26 Hobbes's treatment of the fool has become an acid test for the controversy between the rational choice approach and its critics. For advocates of the *first* position, cf., e.g., Gauthier, "Three against Justice: The Foole, the Sensible Knave, and the Lydian Shepherd"; Gauthier, *Morals by Agreement*, pp. 165–70; Kavka, "The Rationality of Rule-Following: Hobbes's Dispute with the Foole"; Hoekstra, "Hobbes and the Foole." Advocates of the *second* position sometimes try to distance Hobbes from rational choice theory and sometimes turn against both. For the first variant, cf. Lloyd, *Morality in the Philosophy of Thomas Hobbes*, pp. 295–355 (chapter on "Fools, Hypocrites, Zealots, and Dupes: Civic Character and Social Stability"); for the second variant, cf. Larmore, *The Autonomy of Morality*, pp. 95–7. I stand closer to the second group, though I do not believe Hobbes is a rational choice theorist. I want to thank Charles Larmore for the long discussion about Hobbes's fool.

27 The rational choice theorists' strongest argument against the fool involves moving away from the individual case (as Gauthier and others suggest) and making compliance itself the dominant strategy in terms of self-interest. In keeping with this, it would be unwise to violate the meta-rule that one must follow the rules. But even faithfulness to this meta-rule is conditional. In terms of self-interest, nothing speaks against *occasionally* being unfaithful to it.

28 Cf. Zaitchik, "Hobbes's Reply to the Fool," p. 247: "The point of the Fool's objection [. . .] was not that unilateral violation of covenant is generally advantageous or rational but rather that it might sometimes be."

29 It is missing the point to believe that Hobbes is criticizing only the "Explicit Foole" (cf. Hoekstra, "Hobbes and the Foole," pp. 623–8), because he even calls the

rule-breaker who remains hidden a "Fool." There is no justification for doing so, however.

30 Elias, *The Civilizing Process*, pp. 367, 370. One can interpret Elias's work as a sequel to Hobbes's political philosophy as directed by Freud.

31 Regarding these two diseases, cf. Rancière, *The Names of History*, p. 20.

32 Cf. Macpherson, *The Political Theory of Possessive Individualism*, pp. 98f.

33 Booth, *In Darkest England and the Way Out*, pp. 11f.

34 Regarding Moses Wall's position, which can be gleaned from a letter to John Milton from May 19, 1659, see Masson, *The Life of John Milton*, Vol. 5, p. 602; cf. Hill, *Intellectual Origins of the English Revolution Revisited*, pp. 265f. – Regarding the improbability of uprisings by the poor, cf. Locke, *The Works*, Vol. 4, p. 71; cf. Macpherson, *The Political Theory of Possessive Individualism*, pp. 223f. Regarding the comparison between the poor and the rich and the danger to justice that emanates from the latter, cf. Rousseau, CWR 9, p. 301 (*Letters Written from the Mountain*)/OC 3, 890. Regarding the weakness and gullibility of the poor, see Mercier, *Tableau de Paris*, Vol. 3, p. 288 (chapter: "Émeutes"); cf. Farge, *Fragile Lives*, p. 227. Regarding the unnecessary fear of "insurrections of the proletariat" cf. Mommsen, *The History of Rome*, Vol. 3, p. 311; cf. Croce, *Historical Materialism and the Economics of Karl Marx*, pp. 112f.

35 Foucault, *Society Must Be Defended*, p. 194.

36 Hobbes, *Behemoth*, *English Works*, Vol. 6, pp. 320f. This quote plays an important role in the divergent interpretations of Hobbes by Tönnies and Strauss; cf. Tönnies, *Thomas Hobbes*, p. 268; Strauss, *The Political Philosophy of Hobbes*, pp. 117f. Tönnies sees it as a premonition of capitalist conflicts, while Strauss believes it indicates that Hobbes wants to protect the bourgeosie from unreasonably overestimating its power.

37 Sade, *Justine*, pp. 37ff. The reference to Sade as a critic of Hobbes comes from Naville, *Thomas Hobbes*, pp. 217f.

38 Foucault, *Society Must Be Defended*, pp. 108f.

39 Unfortunately, the "masterlesse" man is also overlooked by those who are avowedly attached to marginal figures. Jacques Derrida, for example, wrote an entire book about "rogues," the "nonbrothers," the "excluded or wayward, outcast or displaced, left to roam the streets," and yet he ignores the masterless and Hobbes's description of them; see Derrida, *Rogues*, p. 63. The same can be said for Susan Buck-Morss, who analyzes the threat of bourgeois society from below in *Hegel, Haiti, and Universal History* but only mentions the masterless in passing; see Buck-Morss, *Hegel, Haiti, and Universal History*, p. 104, which references Linebaugh and Rediker, *The Many-Headed Hydra*, p. 18.

40 Vives, *Concerning the Relief of the Poor*, p. 8. Regarding Vives's works in England, cf. Travill, "Juan Luis Vives: The *De Subventione Pauperum*," p. 169.

41 Mullaney, *The Place of the Stage*, pp. 21f. Cf. Agnew, *Worlds Apart*, p. 50; Beier, *Masterless Men*; Jütte, *Poverty and Deviance in Early Modern Europe*, pp. 12, 80, 165–7, 187–90; Thomä, "Der 'Herrenlose'"; regarding the spread of this character to America, cf. McClay, *The Masterless*.

42 Cf. Filmer, *Patriarcha and Other Writings*, pp. 1–4; Thomä, *Väter*, pp. 30f.

43 Hobbes, *The Elements of Law Natural and Politic*, p. 44; regarding Hobbes's "critique of romance," cf. Kahn, *Wayward Contracts*, p. 143.

44 Regarding the difference bewteen Filmer and Hobbes as well as "Hobbes' criticism of the natural basis of father-right," cf. Pateman, *The Sexual Contract*, pp. 45f.

45 Rancière, *The Names of History*, p. 19, see also ibid., p. 21.

46 Pettit, *Made With Words*, pp. 89, 107–11.

47 Regarding the "Hobbesian howler," cf. Appiah, *Experiments in Ethics*, p. 197.

48 Personal letter from Appiah, August 15, 2014.

49 Regarding Caliban as the "paradigmatic *infans* who marks the threshold of what is human," cf. Trüstedt, *Die Komödie der Tragödie*, p. 116.

50 Shakespeare, *Complete Works*, p. 1077 (I.2).
51 Rancière, *Disagreement*, pp. 77f.; Esposito, *Communitas*, p. 27.
52 Cf. Hume, "Of the Original Contract"; Hegel, *Elements of the Philosophy of Right*, §75, pp. 105–6; Mill, "On Liberty," *Collected Works*, Vol. 18, p. 276; Marx, *Grundrisse*, p. 83; Nietzsche, *Human, All Too Human I*, p. 238; Durkheim, *The Division of Labor in Society*, pp. 149ff.; Weber, *Economy and Society*, p. 729; Dewey, *The Early Works*, Vol. 1, p. 231 ("The Ethics of Democracy").
53 Schmitt, *Der Wert des Staates und die Bedeutung des Einzelnen*, p. 85. Hobbes is not mentioned in this book.
54 Schmitt, *Staat, Grossraum, Nomos*, p. 147 ("Der Staat als Mechanismus bei Descartes und Hobbes").
55 Foucault, *Society Must Be Defended*, p. 96.
56 Regarding the contract as a "latent conflict" and "only a truce, and a fairly precarious one at that," cf. Durkheim, *The Division of Labor in Society*, pp. 152, 302.
57 Ankersmit, *Aesthetic Politics*, p. 18; Bristol, *Carnival and Theater*, pp. 120f.; Pitkin, *The Concept of Representation*, pp. 23–37; Pye, "The Sovereign, the Theater, and the Kingdome of Darknesse," p. 86; Kahn, "Hamlet or Hecuba," p. 79; Skinner, "Hobbes on Representation," p. 160; Vieira, *The Elements of Representation in Hobbes*, p. 143.
58 For the founding act behind principal-agent theory, cf. Jensen and Meckling, "Theory of the Firm," pp. 308f.
59 Cf. Agnew, *Worlds Apart*, p. 102: "Hobbes's sovereign [. . .] was indeed a 'player-king.'"
60 Ankersmit, *Aesthetic Politics*, p. 271.
61 Regarding this "epoch-making answer," cf. Skinner, "Hobbes on Representation," p. 177.
62 Pye, "The Sovereign, the Theater, and the Kingdome of Darknesse," p. 91.
63 Frost, "Faking It," p. 47, with a quote from L[e] 111f.
64 Frost, "Faking It," pp. 45–7.
65 Regarding theatrical role-play as the "model" for Hobbes's political attempt to "alienate" individuals from their "private self," cf. Ezrahi, "The Theatrics and Mechanics of Action," p. 307.
66 Frost, *Lessons from a Materialist Thinker*, p. 166. By tying the actions of the state too closely to the individual's mandate, however, Frost underestimates the power shift in favor of the state that operates in Hobbes's theory of representation.
67 Pye, "The Sovereign, the Theater, and the Kingdome of Darknesse," p. 91.
68 Cf. Castoriadis, *The Imaginary Institution of Society*, pp. 102f.; Taylor, *Modern Social Imaginaries*, pp. 23–48.
69 Spinoza, *Theological-Political Treatise*, pp. 254f.; cf. Balibar, *Spinoza and Politics*, pp. 27f.; Balke, *Figuren der Souveränität*, p. 220.
70 Cf. Sreedhar, "Hobbes on Resistance."
71 Agnew, *Worlds Apart*, p. 103; Mullaney, *The Place of the Stage*, pp. 44–9.
72 Mullaney, *The Place of the Stage*, pp. 49–51.
73 Plessner, "Zur Anthropologie des Schauspielers," p. 417.
74 Kahn, "Hamlet or Hecuba: Carl Schmitt's Decision," p. 79.
75 Schmitt, *Hamlet or Hecuba*, pp. 35, 41.
76 Ibid., p. 37.
77 Kahn, "Hamlet or Hecuba," p. 84.
78 Shakespeare, *Complete Works*, p. 308 (II.2).
79 Schmitt, *Hamlet or Hecuba*, p. 37.
80 Kahn, "Hamlet or Hecuba," p. 85.
81 Schmitt, *Hamlet or Hecuba*, pp. 38, 40.
82 Shakespeare, *Complete Works*, p. 308 (II.2).
83 Kahn, "Hamlet or Hecuba," p. 86. Menke, independently of Kahn, comes to a similar conclusion in *Tragic Play*, pp. 138–43, 153 (regarding the transition from "reflective spectator" to "practical question").

376

84 I am, naturally, following Rancière here, *The Emancipated Spectator*, pp. 13–17, even though he does not deal with Hobbes in this text. Rancière also does not mention that Carl Schmitt writes about the emancipation of the actor (without endorsing it, of course); cf. Schmitt, *Hamlet or Hecuba*, p. 37.

85 In addition to "V," the letters "R" for rogue and "F" for fugitive or falsity were also common; cf. the wealth of evidence in Beier, *Masterless Men*, pp. 159f.

86 Cited in Linebaugh and Rediker, *The Many-Headed Hydra*, p. 20. This book is a treasure trove of references to the "outcasts of the nations of the earth," as the authors put it, quoting Daniel Horsmanden from the mid-eighteenth century (ibid., p. 201). Cf. also Heller-Roazen, *Enemy of All*, p. 141.

87 Barker, "Introduction," p. lxv.

88 Shakespeare, *Complete Works*, p. 533 (*King Henry VI, Part 3*, I.1), p. 1160 (*Troilus and Cressida*, I.3).

89 Cf. Hill, *Puritanism and Revolution*, pp. 221, 232f.; Pugliatti, *Beggary and Theatre in Early Modern England*, pp. 4, 7, 36–49; Fumerton, *Unsettled*, pp. 4–32, 47–59.

90 Skinner, *Visions of Politics*, Vol. 3, p. 42: "Of all the ancient poets, Horace was unquestionably Hobbes's favourite." Regarding direct quotes from Horace in Hobbes's writing, cf. ibid., p. 43, note 40.

91 In the two most recent annotated editions of *De cive* (the major edition from Clarendon Press and the corresponding volume in the series *Cambridge Texts in the History of Political Thought*), there is no mention of Horace in relation to the *puer robustus*.

92 Horace, *The Odes: New Translations by Contemporary Poets*, p. 163; Horace, *The Complete Odes and Epodes*, p. 77. The first translation is by Robert Hass, the second by David West.

93 Maleuvre, "Les Odes Romaines d'Horace, ou un chef-d'œuvre ignoré de la cacozélie (presque) invisible," p. 64. Regarding the reception of this verse, cf., e.g., Kantorowicz, "*Pro patria mori* in Medieval Political Thought."

94 Horace, *The Odes: New Translations by Contemporary Poets*, p. 162.

95 Horace, *The Complete Odes and Epodes*, p. 82 (III.4).

96 Cf. Curtius, *European Literature and the Latin Middle Ages*, pp. 98–101 ("Boy and Old Man"); Eyben, *Restless Youth in Ancient Rome*, pp. 9–11.

97 Belpoliti, *Il corpo del capo*, p. 157.

98 Horace, *The Complete Odes and Epodes*, p. 77; for the following quotes in the text, ibid. pp. 76–7.

99 A "tension" or "dichotomous stance" is expressed in the plurality of life choices according to Schenker, "Poetic Voices in Horace's Roman Odes," p. 161. By depicting the *puer robustus* as someone eager for war and willing to die, Horace is describing a "thought process" from which he distances himself according to Jameson, "*Virtus* Re-Formed: An 'Aesthetic Response' Reading of Horace, *Odes* III 2," p. 227. A similar position is taken by Lohmann, "'Dulce et decorum est pro patria mori.' Zu Horaz c. III 2," p. 354, and Koselleck, *Begriffsgeschichten*, p. 230. For a critique of the relativization of heroism, cf. Welwei and Meier, "Der Topos des ruhmvollen Todes in der zweiten Römerode des Horaz."

100 Riedel, "Zwischen Ideologie und Kunst," pp. 394–8 (regarding Brecht and Horace), 411f. (regarding Nazi interpretation of the sweet hero's death).

101 Horace, *The Odes: New Translations by Contemporary Poets*, pp. 294f. (IV.12).

102 Horace, *The Epistles of Horace*, p. 14f. (*Epistle* I.2); cf. Kant, *Practical Philosophy*, p. 17 ("An answer to the question: What is enlightenment?").

103 Wieland, "Patriotischer Beitrag zu Deutschlands höchstem Flor," p. 153. The reference to Wieland comes courtesy of Koselleck, who (incorrectly) cites the phrase *Dulce est pro patria desipere* and calls it a "transformed quote from Horace"; cf. Koselleck, *Begriffsgeschichten*, p. 226. Strangely, he overlooks the fact that Wieland is playing not only on "Dulce [. . .] est pro patria mori" but also on "Dulce est desipere in loco." He

therefore misses Wieland's point and fails to realize that Horace had already countered the heroic death of the *puer robustus* with "sweetness" of another kind.

Chapter II. The *puer robustus* as a good man: Jean-Jacques Rousseau

1 Strauss, *Natural Law and History*, p. 252. I do not follow Strauss's interpretation of the substance of this crisis, but it is beyond my scope to address the problem of "modernity" here; cf. Thomä, *Totalität und Mitleid*, pp. 47–56; Thomä, *Vom Glück in der Moderne*, pp. 220–56.

2 Guillemin, "Jean-Jacques Rousseau, trouble-fête." This phrase is picked up by Schmitt, *Theory of the Partisan*, p. 22.

3 Rousseau, *Correspondance complète*, Vol. 3, p. 157 (letter from Voltaire to Rousseau dated August 30, 1755).

4 Rousseau, CWR 9, 28 ("Letter to Beaumont")/OC 4, 935f.

5 Unfortunately, Starobinski, *Jean-Jacques Rousseau*, pp. 294f., argues for this kind of dedifferentiation. Esposito causes a different type of confusion by claiming that Rousseau's theory that the savage is not evil is the actual "*pointe*" of Rousseau's critique of Hobbes; cf. Esposito, *Communitas*, p. 45. But it is not so much a *pointe* as a weak point.

6 Cf. Rousseau, SC 153 ("On the General Society of Mankind")/OC 3, 281f.; Rousseau, CWR 4, 40 ("Political Fragments")/OC 3, 479.

7 In Heinrich Meier's German edition of the *Second Discourse*, Meier quotes a line from the Roman historian Justin to which Rousseau refers (as Grotius and Pufendorf did before him), and which he uses as the template for his theory of the balance between desire and reality: "They [the Scythians] do not covet gold and silver to the same degree as other people. They live on milk and honey. [. . .] The frugality of their lifestyle is also the source of their equity, as they do not covet the possessions of others; a craving for riches is found only where they are put to use" (*Diskurs über die Ungleichheit*, 140).

8 Hobbes, *Man and Citizen: De Homine and De Cive*, p. 40 (*De homine*, X.3)/*Opera*, Vol. II, p. 91.

9 In his late work *Rousseau, Judge of Jean-Jacques* (1772–6), Rousseau will say of himself: "He would be the most virtuous of men if his strength responded to his will"; Rousseau, CWR 1, 184/OC 1, 897.

10 Ibid., p. 159/OC 1, 865.

11 Rousseau's theory that the "natural capacity of being self-sufficient" is the "hard core" of "being good" is explained by Meier, *The Lesson of Carl Schmitt*, p. 98; Meier, *On the Happiness of the Philosophic Life*, pp. 98–134, 206.

12 Cf. Thomä, *Vom Glück in der Moderne*, p. 108.

13 The "Detracteur le plus outré" mentioned by Rousseau is Bernard de Mandeville.

14 Hollis, *The Philosophy of Social Science*, pp. 131–5 (against Hobbes); Hollis, *Trust Within Reason*, pp. 150–3 (on Rousseau). Regarding the critique of *homo oeconomicus*, see, e.g., Sen, "Rational Fools" (unfortunately, Sen misses the opportunity to interpret his discussion of the "fool" – which he uses to skewer the concept of the rational actor – as a critique of Hobbes's irrational "Fool"). The empirical findings that speak against self-interest come primarily from the fields of experimental economics and comparative anthropology; cf., e.g., Fehr and Gächter, "Cooperation and Punishment in Public Good Experiments"; Tomasello, *Why We Cooperate*, pp. 3, 44 (who references Hobbes and Rousseau and gives preference to the latter).

15 Cf., e.g., Gauthier, *Rousseau*.

16 Regarding Rousseau's observation that, in the course of becoming civilized, people begin to "appreciate one another" (DI 166; OC 3, 170), cf. Honneth, *The Struggle for Recognition*, p. 185, note 19. However, the symmetry of social relationships is only hinted at in the *Second Discourse*. Rousseau leaves it open as to whether appreciation

leads to mutual appraisal (and therefore also to competition) or whether it presupposes symmetry (E 233f.; OC 4, 520–2).

17 We find a similar kind of doubling in the definitions of pity formulated by Rousseau's contemporaries. David Hume, Adam Smith, Gotthold Lessing, and others refer to a physical reaction on the one hand, e.g., that people recoil when they see someone else being hit. On the other hand, they discuss the mental power of the "imagination," which allows one to imagine oneself in another's place or to simulate their feelings; cf., e.g., Smith, *The Theory of Moral Sentiments*, p. 35. According to Debes, Smith's writing is dominated by the second version, which he refers to as "simulation theory"; Debes tends to attribute the first version, which he calls "contagion theory," to Hume; cf. Debes, "Adam Smith and the Sympathetic Imagination." Regarding sympathy in the works of Smith, Lessing, and Rousseau, cf. also Thomä, "Leben als Teilnehmen," pp. 19–22, 30f.

18 The debate about the affiliation of the so-called Counter-Enlighteners (such as Rousseau, Herder, etc.) with the Enlightenment was kindled largely by the writings of Isaiah Berlin; cf. Berlin, *Three Critics of the Enlightenment*; regarding this debate, cf. Thomä, "Leben als Teilnehmen," pp. 7–11.

19 Rousseau, "Essay on the Origin of Languages." Rousseau strikes a new tone here. In the *Second Discourse*, the gentleness of the natural man was set as a bulwark against the "lumiéres [sic!] funestes," the "fatal enlightenment" of the civilized man (DI 166; OC 3, 170). Regarding this shift in his theory of pity, which comes down to pity being linked to reflection, cf. Audi, *Rousseau: éthique et passion*, pp. 139–46.

20 Rousseau, CWR 9, 29 ("Letter to Beaumont")/OC 4, 937; cf. Neuhouser, *Rousseau's Theodicy of Self-Love*, p. 5.

21 Cf. Koselleck, *Critique and Crisis*, p. 163.

22 Rousseau, SC 159 ("On the General Society of Mankind")/OC 3, 288.

23 Rousseau, CWR 9, 299 (*Letters Written from the Mountain*)/OC 3, 892.

24 Rousseau, CWR 1, 9, 112 (*Rousseau, Judge of Jean-Jacques*)/OC 1, 669, 806. Regarding the distinction between *amour de soi* and *amour propre*, cf. Thomä, *Erzähle dich selbst*, pp. 192–222 (Chapter IV.2: "Die Selbstliebe und das Gefühl der eigenen Existenz [zu Rousseau]"); Thomä, *Vom Glück in der Moderne*, pp. 270–91 (Chapter 7: "Zur Rehabilitierung der Selbstliebe").

25 Rousseau, CWR 1, 112 (*Rousseau, Judge of Jean-Jacques*)/OC 1, 806.

26 Ibid., p. 113/OC 1, 806.

27 In an impressive study, Frederick Neuhouser has defended *amour-propre* against the preconception that it is fundamentally negative. He emphasizes the ambivalence of *amour-propre* but downplays the fact that it leans toward wickedness in the writings of Rousseau. This becomes clear when he quotes at length the same passage that I have cited, but he leaves out the closing words, namely, that *amour-propre* brings forth "a multitude of bad things and a small number of good things"; cf. Neuhouser, *Rousseau's Theodicy of Self-Love*, pp. 1f.

28 Rousseau, CWR 1, 112f. (*Rousseau, Judge of Jean-Jacques*)/OC 1, 806.

29 Regarding the opposition between "mutual understanding and agreement" on the one hand and "competition and jealousy" on the other, cf. Rousseau, SC 153 ("On the General Society of Mankind")/OC 3, 282.

30 Tarde, *The Laws of Imitation*, pp. 70, 146; Veblen, *The Theory of the Leisure Class*, pp. 27–34; Girard, *Des choses cachées depuis la fondation du monde*, pp. 401–9.

31 Rousseau, CWR 8, 6 (*The reveries of the solitary walker*)/OC 1, 999.

32 Rousseau, CWR 9, 28 ("Letter to Beaumont")/OC 4, 936; cf. Rousseau, SC 154 ("On the General Society of Mankind")/OC 3, 282, as well as E 282; OC 4, 589. Regarding Rousseau's love of order, cf. Audi, *Rousseau, éthique et passion*, pp. 347–86.

33 Cf. Arendt, *Über die Revolution*, pp. 99f.: "Compassion for others, which certainly runs counter to one's own interests, is the emotional sentiment, as it were, in which this rebellion against oneself and engagement with the general will is most easily and naturally realized."

34 "Agency is empathy's blind spot"; Slaby, "Empathy's Blind Spot," p. 249; for a critique of pity as mere sentiment, cf. Neuhouser, *Rousseau's Theodicy of Self-Love*, p. 222.
35 Rousseau, SC 154 ("On the General Society of Mankind")/OC 3, 283.
36 Ibid., p. 157/OC 3, 286; regarding this important passage, see Neuhouser, *Rousseau's Theodicy of Self-Love*, p. 195.
37 Rousseau, SC 157f. ("On the General Society of Mankind")/OC 3, 286f.
38 Ibid., p. 155/OC 3, 284.
39 Cf. Thomä, "Synergie und Sympathie."
40 Pateman, *The Sexual Contract*, pp. 97f.
41 Cf. Todorov, *Frêle bonheur*.
42 Rousseau, CWR 1, 112 (*Rousseau, Judge of Jean-Jacques*)/OC 1, 806.
43 Rousseau, CWR 9, 261 (*Letters Written from the Mountain*)/OC 3, 841f. In the *Social Contract*, Rousseau goes so far as to say that when "one believes himself the others' master" one is "more a slave than they" (SC 41; OC 3, 351). While the identity of the master hinges on the fact that he can wield power over others, the slave is only passively affected by his relation to his master. For this reason, he can separate himself from it more easily. Rousseau's observation anticipates Hegel's thoughts on lordship and bondage (PS 111–18), but it unfortunately plays no role in the annotations to the *Phenomenology of Spirit*.
44 For a refutation of Rousseau's critique of represenation, see Ankersmit, *Aesthetic Politics*, pp. 28f.
45 Rousseau, CWR 10, 344 (*Letter to d'Alembert on the Theater*)/OC 5, 115.
46 Starobinski, *Jean-Jacques Rousseau*, p. 109. Esposito (*Communitas*, pp. 51f.) follows Starobinski when he writes that Rousseau dreams the dream of "the absoluteness of the individual closed in on his own existence." Regarding the "tautology of sovereignty" in Hobbes and Rousseau, cf. Rancière, *Disagreement*, p. 78. The interpretation of Rousseau was pre-formed by Schmitt, *Political Romanticism*, p. 67: "The romantic, who began as an individualistic rebel, appears as a collectivist."
47 Whether this self-sufficiency has something repellent, antisocial, or wicked about it is the subject of a famous dispute between Rousseau and Diderot; cf. Meier, *On the Happiness of the Philosophic Life*, p. 37: "Diderot's sentence from *Le Fils naturel*, which concentrated his criticism of Jean-Jacques and carried it to the public as a poisoned arrow, *Il n'y a que le méchant qui soit seul*, Rousseau answers with the maxim: *Quiconque se suffit à lui-même ne veut nuire à qui que ce soit.*"
48 In the original version of the *Social Contract*, Rousseau writes: "*que ton frère te soit comme toi-même*" (OC 3, 330).
49 Regarding collective narcissism in a different context, see Adorno, *Gesammelte Schriften*, Vol. 8, p. 114 ("Theorie der Halbbildung" [1959]).
50 Cf., e.g., Balibar, *Les frontières de la démocratie*, pp. 124–50; Honig, *Democracy and the Foreigner*, p. 40: "Democracy's energies and origins always point beyond the (national) borders and commonalities that have heretofore presented themselves as democracy's necessary conditions."
51 This is clear in his sharp criticism of Diderot in the first version of the *Social Contract*; cf. Rousseau, SC 153–62 ("On the General Society of Mankind")/OC 3, 283–7.
52 Cf. Neuhouser, *Rousseau's Theodicy of Self-Love*, pp. 235, 253.
53 Cf., e.g., Honig, *Democracy and the Foreigner*, pp. 41–72.
54 Rancière, *Disagreement*, pp. 27, 78.
55 The *locus classicus* for the accusation of illiberalism is Constant, "The liberty of the ancients compared with that of the moderns," p. 318: "Rousseau [...] this sublime genius, animated by the purest love of liberty, has nevertheless furnished deadly pretexts for more than one kind of tyranny" with his model of "collective sovereignty." The accusation of totalitarianism was established by Talmon, *The Origins of Totalitarian Democracy*, and Crocker, *Nature and Culture*.
56 Regarding praise for the "homogeneity" of Rousseau's concept of the people, cf.

Schmitt, *The Crisis of Parliamentary Democracy*, pp. 13f. Regarding Esposito's criticism of the "individual closed in on his own existence" in a transparent society, see note 46 above.

57 Cf. Rousseau, CWR 4, 24 ("Political Fragments")/OC 3, 485.

58 Arendt, *On Revolution*, p. 67.

59 Regarding criticism of the "power of binding [. . .] posterity to the '*end of time*'" as a complaint against the powers of a government or generation, cf. Paine, *Collected Writings*, p. 438; regarding the theory "that no society can make a perpetual constitution, or even a perpetual law," cf. Jefferson, *Writings*, p. 963; regarding the controversy surrounding Rousseau, Paine, Jefferson, etc., cf. Preuss, *Revolution, Fortschritt und Verfassung*, pp. 19–33; Honig, *Emergency Politics*, p. 28; Rubenfeld, *Freedom and Time*, pp. 18–26. Regarding the generation as the "daughter of democracy," cf. Pierre Nora, "Generation." Regarding the dramatization of the shift in generations as the possibility of change, cf. the classic essay by Mannheim, "The Problem of Generations," p. 293f.

60 Tönnies, according to the account by Schmitt, *The Leviathan*, p. 68; regarding criticism of the "*revolution as a permanent occurrence*," see Schelsky, "Das Freiheitswollen der Völker und die Idee des Planstaates," p. 27; regarding the critique of Rousseau's "permanent revolution," see Koselleck, *Critique and Crisis*, p. 163; in his defense, see Hirsch, *Recht auf Gewalt?*, p. 165.

61 Rousseau, CWR 4, pp. 8–10 ("Discourse on the Virtue Most Necessary for a Hero")/ OC 2, 1271–3.

62 Cf. Davies, *The Heart of Europe*, p. 292; Smith, "Nationalism, Virtue, and the Spirit of Liberty in Rousseau's *Government of Poland*," p. 434.

63 This is Kendall's thesis, "Introduction: How to Read Rousseau's *Government of Poland*," pp. xxiv f.

64 Cf. Benjamin, *Selected Writings*, Vol. 1, pp. 251f. ("Critique of Violence"); Menke, *Law and Violence*, pp. 33–61.

65 Thoreau, *Collected Essays and Poems*, p. 224, cf. p. 346: "My thoughts are murder to the State."

66 Cf., e.g., Arendt, *Crises of the Republic*, pp. 49–102 ("Civil Disobedience"); Rawls, *A Theory of Justice*, pp. 293–343; Balibar, *Equaliberty*, pp. 277–94 ("Conclusion: Resistance, Insurrection, Insubordination"); Ogien and Laugier, *Pourquoi désobéir en démocratie?*; cf. also the wealth of material at thedisobedienceproject.wordpress.com, accessed on September 29, 2017.

67 Serres, *The Parasite*, p. 118.

68 Ibid., pp. 118f.

69 Arendt, *The Origins of Totalitarianism*, p. 139.

Chapter III. Rameau's nephew as a *puer robustus*: Denis Diderot

1 DOC 15, pp. 94–124. A short excerpt from this article can be found in English in Diderot, *Political Writings*, pp. 27–9.

2 Brucker, *Historia critica philosophiae a tempore resuscitatarum in occidente literarum ad nostra tempora* [1742–44], Tomi IV, pars altera, pp. 145–99 (Caput sextum: De Thoma Hobbesio); regarding Diderot's handling of Brucker's work and all instances in which Diderot refers to the *puer robustus*, cf. Thielemann, "Diderot and Hobbes," pp. 228–36; Charles Dédéyan, *Diderot et la pensée anglaise*, pp. 241–74, esp. pp. 272f.

3 Diderot, *Political Writings*, pp. 27f./DOC 15, 122.

4 Ibid., p. 28/DOC 15, 122f.

5 Turgot, "A Philosophical Review of the Successive Advances of the Human Mind," p. 41/"Tableau philosophique des progrès successifs de l'esprit humain," pp. 215f.

6 Diderot, *Political Writings*, p. 28/DOC 15, 123.

7 Diderot and D'Alembert, *Encyclopédie*, Vol. 14, p. 311. This article is not reprinted in Diderot's *Œuvres complètes*, but the ARTFL Encyclopédie Project of the University of Chicago unambiguously attributes it to Diderot.

8 This sentence is constructed in a strange way in the original French: "La définition d'Hobbes est fausse, ou l'homme devient bon à mesure qu'il s'instruit." I do not read this as a critique but rather as a description of two different interpretations of Hobbes. Therefore, I would paraphrase the sentence as follows: "One either says that Hobbes's definition is false, or one says (with Hobbes!) that man is good to the extent that he educates himself." The alternative paraphrase would be: "Hobbes's definition is false, which is clear in that man becomes good to the extent that he educates himself." This second version makes no sense, however, because Hobbes bets precisely on moralization and rationalization as a package deal. Unfortunately, the English translation in the *Cambridge Texts in the History of Political Thought* opts for this second, incorrect option: "As man becomes good with the acquisition of knowledge, so is the definition of Hobbes false" (Diderot, *Political Writings*, p. 29).

9 Helvétius, *Treatise on Man*, Vol. 1, p. 135/*De l'Homme*, Vol. 1, p. 112 (II.8).

10 Ibid., Vol. 2, pp. 20f./ibid., Vol. 2, p. 31 (V.4).

11 Ibid., p. 11/ibid., p. 16 (V.3).

12 Ibid., Vol. 1, pp. 124, 96/ibid., Vol. 1, pp. 102, 79 (II.7, II.1).

13 Ibid., pp. 279, 289/ibid., pp. 230, 238 (IV.1, IV.4).

14 Helvétius, *Essays on the Mind*, p. 248/*De l'Esprit*, p. 321 (III.9).

15 Helvétius, *Treatise on Man*, Vol. 2, p. 453 ("Recapitulation, Section 1")/*De l'Homme*, Vol. 2, p. 692 ("Récapitulation 1").

16 Ibid., Vol. 1, p. 289/*De l'Homme*, Vol. 1, p. 238 (IV.4).

17 Robespierre, *Oeuvres, Tome X*, p. 452; cf. Habermas, *Theory and Practice*, p. 106.

18 Regarding Helvétius as one of the "great physicians of the mind," cf., e.g., Bentham, *A Fragment on Government*, p. 123 ("From a draft preface"); regarding the ability to condition and control human behavior, with a reference to Helvétius, cf. Bentham, *Works*, Vol. IV, p. 65 ("Panopticon; or, the Inspection-House" [1791]).

19 Cf. Helvétius, *Essays on the Mind*, p. 57/*De l'Esprit*, p. 73 (II.5).

20 Durkheim, *The Division of Labor in Society*, pp. 304, 309, 399. For good measure, it should be said that Durkheim himself does not want to combat anomie by abolishing autonomy (as others do).

21 The spectrum ranges from Auguste Comte's sociological positivism to Edward Bellamy's socialist utopia of regulation on the one side and to Ernst Forsthoff's theory of the state as the provider of public services on the other side ("*Daseinsvorsorge*").

22 Helvétius, *Treatise on Man*, Vol. 2, pp. 18f./*De l'Homme*, Vol. 2, p. 28 (V.3).

23 Helvétius, *Treatise on Man*, Vol. 1, pp. 119f./*De l'Homme*, Vol. 1, pp. 98f. (II.6).

24 Diderot and d'Alembert (eds.), *Encyclopédie*, Vol. 17, p. 460. The article quoted here describing the word "voluptueux" is attributed to Diderot according to the ARTFL Encyclopédie Project of the University of Chicago.

25 Barthes, *Sade, Fourier, Loyola*, p. 126. This decoupling of sensuality and self-preservation remains a topos in more recent times; cf., e.g., Bataille, "General Economy," p. 184: "I will begin with a basic fact: the living organism [. . .] ordinarily receives more energy than is necessary for maintaining life."

26 Diderot's critique of Hobbism can be found in both his early work *Apologie de M. l'abbé de Prades* (DOC 1, 467) and his later critique of Bougainville's colonialism in Tahiti (DOC 2, 203). Cf. Naville, *Thomas Hobbes*, p. 207; Klausen, "Of Hobbes and Hospitality in Diderot's *Supplement to the Voyage of Bougainville*," pp. 171f.

27 Baudelaire, *Œuvres complètes*, Vol. 2, p. 247 ("le plus hasardeux et le plus aventureux").

28 Diderot, *Political Writings*, pp. 28f./DOC 15, 123.

29 In Diderot's original, the list of negative traits reads: "misérable, abject, vil, abomina-ble." In *De cive*, Hobbes talks of a "statu misero & odioso" (C[l] 81); this was ren-dered in French by Hobbes's secretary, Samuel Sorbière, as "odieux & misérable état"; Hobbes, *Œuvres philosophiques et politiques, Tome premier, contenant les Élémens du Citoyen*, p. xxxii. Diderot, whose knowledge of Hobbes was mostly second-hand, was doubtless familiar with this translation; cf. Thielemann, "Diderot and Hobbes," p. 266. Of course, all of these formulations recall the famous turn of phrase from *Leviathan*, that life in a state of nature is "solitary, poor, nasty, brutish, and short."

30 "O stercus pretiosum" means "O precious turd."

31 Trilling, *Sincerity and Authenticity*, p. 28.

32 Cf. Bryson, *The Chastised Stage*, p. 80.

33 Cf. Trilling, *Sincerity and Authenticity*, p. 31; Gearhart, "The Dialectic and Its Aesthetic Other," p. 1064.

34 Keats, *Complete Poems and Selected Letters*, p. 500 (letter to Richard Woodhouse dated October 27, 1818).

35 Gide, *The Counterfeiters*, p. 68. The successor to these (and many other) authors is Foucault, *The Archaeology of Knowledge*, p. 19: "Do not ask who I am and do not ask me to remain the same."

36 Mornet, "La véritable signification du *Neveu de Rameau*," p. 883.

37 Various arguments have been put forward. It has been said that Diderot ultimately comes down on the side of the "Me" or, conversely, on the side of the nephew, or that he overcomes and overrides these two extreme positions, etc. For an overview of the range of interpretations, cf., e.g., Jauss, *The Dialogical and the Dialectical Neveu de Rameau*; Gearhart, "The Dialectic and its Aesthetic Other," p. 1054. The superiority of the "Me" is argued by, e.g., Mornet, "La véritable signification du *Neveu de Rameau*," pp. 907f. For an argument in favor of the nephew's superiority, cf. Laufer, "Structure et signification du 'Neveu de Rameau' de Diderot," p. 413. For an integrative solution, cf. Spitzer, *Linguistics and Literary History*, pp. 154, 157; Curtius, *European Literature and the Latin Middle Ages*, pp. 573ff.; Crocker, "'Le Neveu de Rameau,' une expéri-ence morale," p. 150.

38 Regarding this aporetic reading, cf., e.g., Jauss, *The Dialogical and the Dialectical Neveu de Rameau*, pp. 1ff.

39 Jauss, *The Dialogical and the Dialectical Neveu de Rameau*, p. 17.

40 Rex, "Music and the Unity of *Le Neveu de Rameau*," p. 97.

41 Dieckmann, "Diderots *Le Neveu de Rameau* und Hegels Interpretation des Werkes," p. 184.

42 Gearhart, "The Dialectic and Its Aesthetic Other," p. 1051.

43 Jauss, *The Dialogical and the Dialectical Neveu de Rameau*, pp. 2ff. Like Socrates, the nephew is referred to as an "accoucheur," for example (RN 80; CR 653; cf. Plato, *Theaetetus* 149b–151d). Another of Socrates's nicknames, the "torpedo fish," would also suit the nephew well; cf. Plato, *Meno* 80a.

44 Regarding Diderot, cf. Bakhtin, *Problems of Dostoevsky's Poetics*, p. 143; regarding Menippean satire, ibid., pp. 112–78. Regarding Diderot and Menippus, cf. Kristeva, *Strangers to Ourselves*, pp. 138, 142. Jauss contents himself with calling Menippean satire the link between Plato and Diderot (*The Dialogical and the Dialectical Neveu de Rameau*, pp. 2f.). It breaks this link open, however.

45 Bakhtin, *Problems of Dostoevsky's Poetics*, p. 178; regarding the context and impact of this genre, cf. Morson and Emerson, *Mikhail Bakhtin*, pp. 461–91.

46 Bakhtin, *Problems of Dostoevsky's Poetics*, pp. 115f.

47 Bakhtin, *The Dialogic Imagination*, p. 126 ("Forms of Time and Chronotope in the Novel"). Cf. Turner, *The Ritual Process*, p. 110f.: "All these [. . .] types are structurally inferior or 'marginal,' yet they represent what Henri Bergson would have called 'open' as against 'closed morality' [. . .]. In closed or structured societies, it is the marginal or 'inferior' person or the 'outsider' who often comes to symbolize what David Hume

has called 'the sentiment for humanity' [. . .]." Turner is referring to David Hume when he uses the term "sentiment for humanity," but he could just as easily have referred to Rousseau.

48 "Rameau est un *hybride*," writes Starobinski, "Le dîner chez Bertin," p. 195. He neglects to mention that the "Me" is also a hybrid. Long before Starobinski, Kenneth Burke remarked on "the divisiveness [. . .] within Lui himself"; see Burke, *A Rhetoric of Motives*, p. 142.

49 Regarding Diderot's experimentalism, cf. Suckling, "Diderot's Politics," p. 282. The "Me" supports at least three different positions that do not fit together. First, he defends the "man of genius" who runs riot. Second, he admires Diogenes (RN 86f.; CR 659), who cultivates a frugal love of wisdom. Third, the "Me" recommends working for the common good. Diderot's image of the nephew is just as much a hybrid; at times the nephew places himself in the service of the "beauties of musical art" (RN 73; CR 646), at other times in the service of generous benefactors. Artist, servant, self-made man, and animal are all part of his repertoire.

50 Cf. Diderot's *Encyclopédie* article on "Génie" in PhS 1, 235–41; DOC 15, 35–41.

51 Cf. Turner, *The Ritual Process*, p. 95: "Liminal entities are neither here nor there; they are betwixt and between the positions assigned and arrayed by law, custom, convention, and ceremonial."

52 Cf. Smoliarova, "Distortion and Theatricality," pp. 10–12.

53 A similar conclusion is reached (in a different way) by Agamben, *Infancy and History*, pp. 50f.

54 Beiser, *The Early Political Writings of the German Romantics*, p. 18 ("Pollen," No. 50).

55 Emerson, *Essays & Lectures*, p. 412.

56 Baudelaire, *The Painter of Modern Life and Other Essays*, p. 8/*Œuvres complètes*, Vol. 2, p. 690. In "An Opium-Eater" he comes back to the idea "that genius is but childhood clearly expressed"; cf. Baudelaire, *Artificial Paradises*, p. 139/*Œuvres complètes*, Vol. 1, p. 498. Whether Baudelaire's – and thus Diderot's – commendation of childhood should be criticized or celebrated is the subject of a debate between Sartre and Bataille; cf. Sartre, *Baudelaire*, pp. 52–6; Bataille, *Literature and Evil*, p. 27f. I'm on Bataille's side.

57 Humboldt, *On Language*, pp. 62, 148, 49, 62.

58 Diderot writes: "And for the obvious reason that no two of us are exactly alike, we never understand exactly and are never exactly understood. [. . .] We realize how much variety there is [*bien de la diversité*] in people's opinions, and there is a thousand times more that we don't notice and fortunately cannot notice [*il y en a mille fois davantage qu'on n'aperçoit pas, et qu'heureusement on ne saurait apercevoir*]" (*Rameau's Nephew/D'Alembert's Dream*, p. 222; DOC 2, 180f.). This passage has been cited as evidence for the aporia theory; cf. Gearhart, "The Dialectic and its Aesthetic Other," p. 1064. But Gearhart can only uphold this interpretation by simply *leaving out* Diderot's fortunate neglect of the diversity in opinions, which then leads to understanding and agreement.

59 Humboldt, *On Language*, p. 63; cf. Thomä, "Leben als Teilnehmen," p. 31.

60 Wittgenstein, *On Certainty*, p. 28 (§§96f.).

61 Hegel, PR 219 (§181); Tocqueville, DIA 3, p. 887; O 2, 616; Marx, MECW 3, 77, 162f.; Foucault, *Power*, p. 325; Rancière, *Disagreement*, p. 66. Cf. also Fox, "The Virgin and the Godfather," p. 110.

62 Diderot does not go so far as to leave power in the hands of the genius. The genius, he says rather coolly, is "more suited to overthrowing or founding states than to maintaining them, and to restoring order rather than following it" (PhS 1, 240; DOC 15, 40).

63 Regarding Rameau's nephew as "one of those eccentrics," cf. Kristeva, *Strangers to Ourselves*, p. 134.

64 Cf. Citton, "Political Agency and the Ambivalence of the Sensible," pp. 133f.

65 Goethe cited in *Rameau's Nephew and First Satire*, pp. 108f. ("Notes on Persons and Matters That Are Mentioned in the Dialogue *Rameau's Nephew*").

66 Foucault, *History of Madness*, p. 345/*Histoire de la folie à l'âge classique*, p. 434.

67 Regarding Hegel's reluctance to mention Diderot in the *Phenomenology of Spirit*, cf. Hulbert, "Diderot in the Text of Hegel," p. 272; Schmidt, "The Fool's Truth: Diderot, Goethe, and Hegel," p. 632. In general, cf. Thomä, "Hegel – Diderot – Hobbes."

68 Trilling, *Sincerity and Authenticity*, pp. 33f.

69 Only partial templates for this paraphrase can be found in Diderot; cf. RN 23; CR 600 ("I was dumbfounded by how insightful and at once how sordid what he said was, by how right and then how wrong his ideas were, by how totally perverse his sentiments were, by the spectacle of such utter depravity, and by how uncommonly open about it he was"); RN 69; CR 643 ("these feelings were tinged with ridicule, and it transformed their nature"). Regarding the differences between Hegel's paraphrase and Diderot's template, cf. Hulbert, "Diderot in the Text of Hegel," pp. 279f.

70 However, I agree with Herbert Dieckmann's complaint that Hegel is "undoubtedly unjust" in his criticism of the "Me." The "Me" has a large repertoire of behaviors, including criticizing rules; cf. Dieckmann, "Diderots Le Neveu de Rameau und Hegels Interpretation des Werkes," pp. 167, 184.

71 Unfortunately, researchers have sorely neglected the leading role played by Diderot in the introduction of the alienation concept. He is never even mentioned by scholars such as Jaeggi, *Alienation*. Diderot's leading role becomes even more significant when we consider that while Hegel had already encountered the concept of *aliénation* through Rousseau, he translated it as *Entäußerung* ("externalization"). He obviously first encountered *Entfremdung* ("alienation") through Goethe's translation of Diderot. Regarding *Entäußerung*/externalization, cf. Hegel, *Hegel and the Human Spirit*, p. 124; regarding the difference bewteen *Entäußerung* and *Entfremdung* in Hegel, cf. Dupré, *Marx's Social Critique of Culture*, pp. 19–21.

72 In the original: "Je sais aussi m'aliéner; talent sans lequel on ne fait rien qui vaille." Regarding this important passage from Diderot's letter to Madame Riccoboni from November 18, 1758, and "aliénation délibérée et volontaire" in Diderot, cf. Lacoue-Labarthe, *L'imitation des modernes*, pp. 34f.

73 Regarding Hegel's procedural concept of liberation, cf. Pippin, *Hegel on Self-Consciousness*, pp. 15–18, 57, 60, 87.

74 Cf. Gehlen, *Gesamtausgabe*, Vol. 4, pp. 366–79 ("Über die Geburt der Freiheit aus dem Geist der Entfremdung").

75 "The destructive character sees no image hovering before him. He has few needs, and the least of them is to know what will replace what has been destroyed." – "The étui-man looks for comfort, and the case is its quintessence. The inside of the case is the velvet-lined trace that he has imprinted on the world." Benjamin, *Selected Writings*, Vol. 2, Part 2, pp. 541f. ("The Destructive Character").

76 In his *Elements of the Philosophy of Right*, Hegel characterizes Diogenes as the "unprepossessing product" of a divided society (PR 231 [§195]). Analogous to this, he speaks of being forced to "flee from [. . .] an internally divided reality" in his *Lectures on the Philosophy of World History*, p. 143.

77 Here I am following Speight, *Hegel, Literature and the Problem of Agency*, p. 83.

78 Hegel, *Hegel and the Human Spirit*, p. 120.

79 Regarding Hegel's interpretation of *Rameau's Nephew* as a prerevolutionary document that is just as important as his thoughts on "Lordship and Bondage," cf. Agamben, *The Man Without Content*, pp. 22–6.

80 Bernard Williams disagrees with the interpretation of the nephew as a transitional figure, but he ultimately describes him in much the same way as Hegel; Williams, *Truth and Truthfulness*, pp. 185–91.

81 Cf., on the other hand, Trilling, *Sincerity and Authenticity*, p. 46, who believes the nephew is absolutely capable of "admiration and love"; "Contrary to Hegel's

view, there is really not much malice in Rameau; he is by no means identical with Dostoevsky's Underground Man."

82 Critics of the conclusiveness of Hegel's synthesis, in which system and history, spirit and life, are expected to be unified without loss, range from Kierkegaard and Adorno to Foucault and Derrida – and beyond. I follow their thinking, but it is beyond my scope to reconstruct their arguments here.

83 Hulbert, "Diderot in the Text of Hegel," p. 269; cf. Gearhart, "The Dialectic and its Aesthetic Other," p. 1065.

84 Foucault, *Language, Madness, and Desire*, p. 16.

85 Foucault, *History of Madness*, pp. 344, 346/*Histoire de la folie à l'âge classique*, pp. 432, 434f.

86 Cf., e.g., Foucault, *History of Madness*, pp. 46, 348, 372, 376, 481, 533/*Histoire de la folie à l'âge classique*, pp. 69, 437, 440, 465, 471, 597, 642f.; regarding Foucault's fight against the "protracted Hegelianism" of his early years, cf. Thomä, Kaufmann, and Schmid, *Der Einfall des Lebens*, p. 256. Regarding the relationship between Hegel's and Foucault's interpreations of Diderot, cf. Pillen, *Hegel in Frankreich*, pp. 219–46; Kelm, *Hegel und Foucault*, p. 349.

87 Foucault, *Language, Madness, and Desire*, pp. 16ff.

88 Foucault quotes a passage from §408 of Hegel's *Encyclopaedia* of 1830 (*Hegel's Philosophy of Mind*, pp. 36ff.) and, in the original French version of his book, uses ellipses to gloss over Hegel's aside, in which Hegel praises Pinel; *Histoire de la folie à l'âge classique*, p. 597 (the aside has been reinserted in the English translation; Foucault, *History of Madness*, p. 481). Regarding criticism of Foucault's omission, cf. Derrida, *Signature Derrida*, p. 296 ("The History of Madness in the Age of Psychoanalysis").

89 Foucault, *History of Madness*, pp. 346, 349f./*Histoire de la folie à l'âge classique*, p. 435, 438f.

90 Ibid., pp. 46f./ibid., pp. 69f.

91 Ibid., pp. 373, 393, 516/ibid., pp. 454, 467, 637.

92 Ibid., p. 518/ibid., p. 639.

93 Foucault, *Language, Madness, and Desire*, p. 20.

94 Foucault, *History of Madness*, pp. 348, 517/*Histoire de la folie à l'âge classique*, pp. 437, 638.

95 Ibid., pp. 378, 365ff., 378, 374/ibid., pp. 474, 458ff., 472, 468.

96 Cf. the chapter "Michel Foucault (1926–1984): Das Schwellenwesen" in Thomä, Kaufmann, and Schmid, *Der Einfall des Lebens*, pp. 250–66.

97 Foucault, *History of Madness*, pp. 519, 521/*Histoire de la folie à l'âge classique*, pp. 639, 641.

98 Rilke, *The Notebooks of Malte Laurids Brigge*, p. 34.

99 Foucault, *History of Madness*, p. 373/*Histoire de la folie à l'âge classique*, p. 467.

100 Ibid., p. 345/ibid., p. 433.

101 Foucault, *Language, Madness, and Desire*, p. 25.

102 Foucault, *History of Madness*, p. 46/*Histoire de la folie à l'âge classique*, p. 69.

103 Foucault, *History of Madness*, p. 543 ("Madness, the absence of an œuvre: Appendix I of 1972 edition").

104 Ibid., p. 549; Foucault, "A Preface to Transgression," p. 36.

105 Foucault, *The Government of Self and Others*, p. 27.

106 Foucault, *History of Madness*, p. 532; ibid., *Histoire de la folie à l'âge classique*, pp. 656f.

107 Michelet, *The Sea*, p. 166; ibid., *History of the French Revolution*, p. 33; cf. Chase, "Jules Michelet and the Nineteenth-Century Concept of Insanity," pp. 743, 746.

108 Carlyle, *The Works*, Vol. 12, p. 196 ("Sartor Resartus").

109 Carlyle, *The French Revolution*, Vol. 1, p. 38; ibid., *The Works*, Vol. 10, p. 38f.; cf. Tambling, "Carlyle through Nietzsche: Reading 'Sartor Resartus,'" p. 330.

Chapter IV. Unloving child, wicked son, strong savior: Friedrich Schiller

1 Herder, *On World History,* p. 128.
2 Cf. Thomä, *Väter,* pp. 28–35.
3 Regarding the Karlsschule, cf. Müller-Seidel, *Friedrich Schiller und die Politik,* p. 50. The young Schiller knew Hobbes and Rousseau only through secondary sources; cf. Liepe, "Der junge Schiller und Rousseau," p. 33; Williams, "The Ambivalences in the Plays of the Young Schiller," p. 28; Fisher, "Familial Politics and Political Families," pp. 78, 95. Jacob Friedrich Abel – Schiller's most important teacher at the Karlsschule – based his lectures largely on Ferguson and also referenced Helvétius; cf. Riedel (ed.), *Jacob Friedrich Abel.* Schiller also had this teacher to thank for the idea of fraternal strife, as it was from Abel that he heard the story passed down by Henry Home of "Francis, Duke of Brittany," who threw his "brother Gilles in prison" and "let him starve" (ibid., p. 163 [*Dissertatio de origine characteris animi*]). Cf. also Masson, "Un ancêtre de Franz Moor," pp. 3f. Going beyond *The Robbers,* we find various references to Hobbes in Schiller's later works. Peter-André Alt describes the monarch in *Don Carlos* as being "well-versed in *Leviathan*" and believes Schiller's knowledge of Hobbes comes primarily from Rousseau's critique of Hobbes in the *Social Contract*; cf. Alt, *Schiller,* p. 448; regarding the traces of Hobbes's in *Fiesco,* cf. ibid., pp. 338–44.
4 Even though the history of the reception of Hobbes does not confirm this, it seems as if "Franz [Moor] had read Hobbes" (Michelsen, *Der Bruch mit der Vater-Welt,* p. 78). In fact, however, Schiller draws on Helvétius's description of self-interest, which he was familiar with through Abel's teaching. Franz Moor is therefore Helvétius's "pupil"; cf. Riedel, *Die Anthropologie des jungen Schiller,* pp. 178f.
5 Quoted in Barron, "Warnings from a Student Turned Killer," p. A12.
6 The young Schiller's indirect knowledge of Rousseau stems primarily from Jacobi's tribute to Rousseau from 1778; cf. Liepe, "Der junge Schiller und Rousseau," pp. 40–5.
7 Regarding "the death of Christ as the perfect and definitive sacrifice, which makes all other sacrifices outmoded," see Girard, *The Scapegoat,* p. 200.
8 A path can be traced from the internalization of legal norms as found in Schiller to criticism of the rational choice approach; cf. Halberstam, "Of Grace and Dignity in Law: A Tribute to Friedrich Schiller," pp. 214–16.
9 Schiller, "The Criminal of Lost Honor," pp. 42, 44.
10 Walzer, *Spheres of Justice,* pp. 105f.
11 Schiller, "The Criminal of Lost Honor," p. 52.
12 Tocqueville, *Tocqueville on America After 1840,* p. 354/O 2, 635.
13 Regarding the "isolation of the eponymous hero," cf. Koschorke, "Brüderbund und Bann," p. 115. Schiller himself said of Tell: "His concern is a private matter, and it remains so until the end, when it becomes enmeshed with the public matter." Regarding this quote from a letter to Iffland and its interpretation, cf. Müller-Seidel, *Friedrich Schiller und die Politik,* p. 198.
14 Regarding Schiller's intensive reception of the philosophy of sympathy and its use in the *Tell* play, cf. Riedel, *Die Anthropologie des jungen Schiller,* pp. 100–51; Kaiser, "Idylle und Revolution," pp. 97f.
15 Smith, *The Theory of Moral Sentiments,* p. 223.
16 Hegel, *Early Theological Writings,* pp. 233f.; cf. Habermas, *Theory and Practice,* p. 132f.
17 Erhard, *Über das Recht des Volks zu einer Revolution und andere Schriften,* p. 54; cf. Müller-Seidel, *Friedrich Schiller und die Politik,* pp. 28f.
18 Kaiser, "Idylle und Revolution," p. 99.
19 Bellah et al., *Habits of the Heart,* p. 145.
20 Schiller, *Poet of Freedom,* p. 311/SW 1, 133, 872.
21 Ibid., p. 309/SW 1, 133.
22 Sartre, *Critique of Dialectical Reason,* p. 437.

23 Müller-Seidel, *Friedrich Schiller und die Politik*, p. 29.
24 Cf. Borchmeyer, "Die Tragödie vom verlorenen Vater," pp. 161f.
25 Cf. Thomä, *Väter*, pp. 55–60, 70–5, 343.
26 Quoted in Ozouf, *L'homme régénéré*, p. 162.
27 Cf., e.g., Hunt, *The Family Romance of the French Revolution*, pp. 53–88 ("The Band of Brothers"); David, *Fraternité et Révolution française 1789–1799*; Ozouf, *L'homme régénéré*, pp. 158–82 ("La Révolution française et l'idée de fraternité").
28 Cf. the still-apt Durkheim, *The Division of Labor in Society*, p. 150: "This is because for such a contract to be feasible, at any given time all individual wills should be in agreement regarding the common foundations of the social organisation."
29 For the following quotes from Hume, cf. "Of the Original Contract," p. 476. Cf. Thomä, *Väter*, pp. 37f.
30 In doing so, Schiller raises doubts in advance about Hegel's idea from *Elements of the Philosophy of Right* to bring the universal to life or to "lead a universal life." He also anticipates Kierkegaard's critique of Hegel, according to which the "concept of existence" is not a "paragraph in the system," it is "an absolute protest against the system"; cf. Kierkegaard, *Concluding Unscientific Postscript*, Vol. 1, pp. 122f.
31 This internal split has been analyzed by Freud, Elias, Horkheimer, Adorno, and others. Regarding Kant, Schiller, and Freud, see p. 238. For a more recent interpretation of the "divided subject" that forces individuals into a state of "*heroic humiliation*," cf. Balibar, "What Makes a People a People?", pp. 114f.

Chapter V. The *puer robustus* as victim and hero: Victor Hugo

1 Jacques Du Breul, *Le théâtre des antiquitez*, p. 52. Hugo based his novel on Du Breul's historical account (ND[f] 831f.).
2 Hugo, *Notre-Dame de Paris, 1482 – Les Travailleurs de la Mer*, p. 543. Hugo's source for the phrase *homo homini monstrum* is not Hobbes, however, but rather an earlier inscription from the sixteenth century on the tower of the "manoir de Tourville" in Crozet, which Hugo discovered on a trip in August 1825; cf. the commentary in ND[f] 859, 878.
3 Hugo, *Œuvres complètes*, Vol. 3, p. 1177 ("Feuilles paginées," p. 1827). Hugo returns to the motif of man as a wolf in a later novel; cf. Hugo, *L'Homme qui rit*, pp. 55–77. In the "Journal des idées, des opinions et des lectures d'un jeune Jacobite" (1819), written by the 17-year-old Hugo, there are references to both Hobbes and Rousseau, indicating that he perhaps also could have encountered the *puer robustus* in Rousseau; cf. Hugo, *Œuvres complètes*, Vol. 5, pp. 54, 57f., 98. Regarding the description of the social contract that Hugo took directly from Rousseau, see p. 143.
4 Hugo, *The Works of Victor Hugo*, Vol. 3, p. 44 ("Preface" to *Cromwell*)/*Œuvres complètes*, Vol. 3, pp. 56, 78 ("Préface" [à *Cromwell*], 1827).
5 Hugo, *Hans of Iceland*, pp. 478f./*Han d'Islande*, pp. 465f.
6 Shelley, *Frankenstein*, p. 68. Regarding Hugo's reception of Shelley, cf. Roman, *Victor Hugo et le roman philosophique*, pp. 243, 327.
7 Moretti, "The Dialectic of Fear," pp. 68f.
8 Hugo, *Œuvres complètes*, Vol. 5, p. 197; here I am following Mehlman, *Revolution and Repetition*, p. 88.
9 Cf. Hirschman, *The Passions and the Interests*, pp. 7–66.
10 Cf. the pointers in Mehlman, *Revolution and Repetition*, pp. 87f.
11 Michelet, *The People*, p. 93. Michelet's thoughts on the "child" and the "people" serve as a motto in Badiou et al., *What is a People?*, p. vii. Regarding Michelet's connection between people and childhood, cf. also Chase, "Jules Michelet and the Nineteenth-Century Concept of Insanity: A Romantic's Reinterpretation."
12 The "cesspool" out of which the gamin rises represents more than just squalidness for Hugo, who also sees in it the remainder of the real, natural life as conceived of by

Rousseau; regarding Hugo's fascination with the "sincerity of muck" (M[e] 1034; M[f] II, 652), cf. Stallybrass and White, *The Politics and Poetics of Transgression*, p. 140.

13 Kojève, *Introduction à la lecture de Hegel*, p. 435: "La fin du Temps humain ou de l'Histoire [. . .] signifie tout simplement la cessation de l'Action au sens fort du terme." Regarding Fukuyama's reception of Kojève, see p. 333.

14 Cf. Chevalier, *Classes laborieuses et classes dangeureuses*, p. 518.

15 Hugo writes in 1841: "À tous les étages de la société [. . .], tout ce qui fait le mal sciemment, c'est la populace. En haut: égoïsme et oisiveté; en bas: envie et fainéantise; voilà les vices de ce qui est populace" (*Correspondance 1835–1882*, pp. 43f. [Letter to Pierre Vinçard from July 2, 1841]). Cf. also Chevalier, *Classes laborieuses et classes dangeureuses*, p. 92; Michel, *Les Barbares, 1789–1848*, p. 458.

16 Ibid., p. 270: "De l'enfant trouvé au monstre, de Gavroche à Quasimodo, il n'y a qu'un pas."

17 Regarding Hugo and Delacroix, cf. the comment in M[f] 1, 937. Thanks go to Jakob Thomä for the reference to the special significance of Gavroche.

18 Hugo calls Gavroche a "fairy larrikin" (see above), but he also refers to the rebels on the barricades as "specters" who demonstrate the "heroism of monsters" (M[e] 1024; M[f] II, 637). Hugo's characterization served as the inspiration for Derrida's discussion of the "specter" of the revolution in *Specters of Marx*, p. 134.

19 Regarding the education of the people and the sense of unease about this, cf. Rancière, *The Ignorant Schoolmaster*, pp. 130–4.

20 Hugo, *Choses vues 1830–1848*, p. 687.

21 Balzac, *Père Goriot*, pp. 12f., 48, 89, 97f., 152f./*La Comédie humaine*, Vol. III, pp. 60, 93, 132, 141, 151, 189, 191.

22 Balzac, *A Harlot High and Low*, pp. 434, 542/*La Comédie humaine*, Vol. VI, pp. 821, 924.

23 Ibid., p. 460f./ibid., p. 847; regarding one part of this quote, cf. Chevalier, *Classes laborieuses et classes dangeureuses*, p. 495.

24 Balzac, *Père Goriot*, pp. 92f./*La Comédie humaine*, Vol. III, p. 135.

25 Ibid., pp. 96f./ibid., p. 139.

26 Balzac, *A Harlot High and Low*, p. 425/*La Comédie humaine*, Vol. VI, p. 813.

27 Ibid., pp. 543, 552/ibid., pp. 933, 935.

28 Curtius, *Balzac*, pp. 184–6. The first quote is from Balzac, *Père Goriot*, p. 94/*La Comédie humaine*, Vol. III, p. 136. The closing quote is also from Balzac, *Lost Illusions*, p. 650/*La Comédie humaine*, Vol. V, p. 703: "I myself love power for power's sake!"

29 Balzac, *A Harlot High and Low*, pp. 443, 460/*La Comédie humaine*, Vol. VI, pp. 830 ("l'état naturel" italicized in original), 846.

30 Regarding Balzac's "sympathy for the rebel" who opposes the "rule of bourgeois mediocrity," cf. Curtius, *Balzac*, p. 180. Regarding "high society's constantly growing admiration for the underworld" and its "taste for the anarchical cynicism of its offspring" which was "classically expressed in Balzac's novels," cf. Arendt, *The Origins of Totalitarianism*, p. 155. The attraction of the criminal has an even more direct effect on other classes; cf. Benjamin, *Selected Writings*, Vol. 1, p. 239 ("Critique of Violence"): "The figure of the 'great' criminal [. . .] has aroused the secret admiration of the public."

31 This is how one observer characterized Baudelaire's appearance on June 26, 1848. Even as early as February he was out and about with his gun; cf. the brief excerpts from eyewitness accounts in Sahlberg (ed.), *Baudelaire 1848*, pp. 22–4. Regarding Baudelaire's complicated relationship with Hugo and his role in the February and June rebellions in Paris in 1848, cf. Oehler, *Ein Höllensturz der Alten Welt*; Sahlberg, *Baudelaire und seine Muse auf dem Weg zur Revolution*, pp. 72–82, 162.

32 Baudelaire, *Paris Spleen and Le Fanfarlo*, pp. 28f./*Œuvres complètes*, Vol. 1, pp. 297–9; regarding the "little savage" in Baudelaire, cf. Oehler, *Ein Höllensturz der alten Welt*, pp. 301, 305.

33 Arendt, *Elemente und Ursprünge totalitärer Herrschaft*, p. 247.

34 Baudelaire, *Paris Spleen and Le Fanfarlo*, pp. 98f./*Œuvres complètes*, Vol. 1, pp. 357–9.
35 Clark, *The Absolute Bourgeois*, p. 177; see ibid., p. 174: "But what he wanted to fix in his mind – what he repeated over and over in his notes and diaries – was the fact that revolution was evil, and the fact of *his own assent to that evil.*"
36 Baudelaire, *Baudelaire as a Literary Critic*, p. 289 (*"Les Misérables"*), *Selected Writings on Art and Literature*, p. 121 ("The Universal Exihibition of 1855")/*Œuvres complètes*, Vol. 2, p. 224 (*"Les Misérables* par Victor Hugo"), p. 588 ("Exposition universelle 1855"). Baudelaire is credited with having introduced the word "américaniser" to the French language. Nietzsche eagerly seized upon it in his late reading of Baudelaire and griped about the "American lust for gold" in *The Gay Science*, p. 258.
37 Baudelaire, *Paris Spleen and Le Fanfarlo*, p. 98/*Œuvres complètes*, Vol. 1, p. 357.
38 Baudelaire, *The Flowers of Evil*, p. 149/*Œuvres complètes*, Vol. 1, p. 75.
39 Baudelaire, *My Heart Laid Bare*, p. 178/*Œuvres complètes*, Vol. 1, p. 679 ("Mon cœur mis à nu"). The talk of "Christ" on the barricades comes from an article probably written by Baudelaire in *Le Salut Public* dated March 1, 1848: *Œuvres complètes*, Vol. 2, p. 1035. Regarding the "dual aspect of Satan" in Baudelaire, cf. Benjamin, *Selected Writings*, Vol. 4, p. 11 ("The Paris of the Second Empire in Baudelaire"); regarding the "love of God" and "love of Satan," cf. Sahlberg, *Baudelaire und seine Muse auf dem Weg zur Revolution*, p. 125, cf. pp. 68–82; regarding the "good hatred of the people" and "Baudelairian Satanism," cf. Oehler, *Pariser Bilder 1*, pp. 155–68; Oehler, *Ein Höllensturz der Alten Welt*, pp. 291f.
40 Baudelaire, *Baudelaire as a Literary Critic*, pp. 242 ("Victor Hugo"), 289 (*"Les Misérables"*)/*Œuvres complètes*, Vol. 2, pp. 136, 224.
41 Baudelaire, *Œuvres complètes*, Vol. 2, pp. 1040f. The relevant article from the *Tribune nationale* of April 1848 has not been published in English.
42 Baudelaire, *Baudelaire as a Literary Critic*, p. 243/*Œuvres complètes*, Vol. 2, pp. 136f.
43 Baudelaire, *Baudelaire as a Literary Critic*, p. 286; cf. *Artificial Paradises*, p. 68/*Œuvres complètes*, Vol. 2, p. 128 ("Théophile Gautier"); cf. Vol. 1, p. 435 ("Le poème du hachisch"). Regarding the contradiction between the role of father and brother, see p. 126.
44 Baudelaire, *Baudelaire as a Literary Critic*, p. 243/*Œuvres complètes*, Vol. 2, p. 136.

Chapter VI. Siegfried, foolish boy: Richard Wagner

1 Regarding Hobbes and Wagner as well as the contradiction between artificial politics and "untouched nature," cf. Bermbach, *Der Wahn des Gesamtkunstwerks*, p. 281; cf. pp. 191, 195f., 198f., 202.
2 This dual strategy relates to the complicated development of Wagner's worldview, which led him from an early enthusiasm for Feuerbach's Materialism, through Arthur Schopenhauer's denial of the world, to Christianization. The salvation concepts that Wagner develops in the Ring Cycle fluctuate between these reference points. I cannot address this in detail here; cf. Thomä, *Totalität und Mitleid*, pp. 80–2, 112–19. Cf. also Nietzsche, *The Works of Friedrich Nietzsche*, Vol. 3, pp. 13f. (*The Case of Wagner*), p. 82 (*Nietzsche contra Wagner*).
3 Wagner, *Sämtliche Schriften und Dichtungen*, Vol. 12, p. 221.
4 Cosima Wagner, *Cosima Wagner's Diaries*, Vol. 1, p. 965 (entry dated May 25, 1877).
5 Regarding Wagner's attacks on Jews, whom he calls the "speculators" who "can starve Germany to death," cf., e.g., Cosima Wagner, *Cosima Wagner's Diaries*, Vol. 2, p. 413 (entry dated December 19, 1879); cf. also the essays "Judaism in Music" (WPW 3, 75–122) and "Modern" (WPW 6, 41–9). This also includes Wagner's critique of Heine's art of "lies" (WPW 3, 99f.).
6 Wieland Wagner, quoted in Borchmeyer, "'Faust' und der 'Ring des Nibelungen,'" p. 137.

7 Schumpeter, *Capitalism, Socialism and Democracy*, p. 137.
8 Regarding the practical ambition of the Ring, cf. Dahlhaus, *Gesammelte Schriften*, Vol. 7, p. 222.
9 Wagner, *Selected Letters of Richard Wagner*, p. 301.
10 Regarding Brünnhilde's pity as the starting point for Sergei Eisenstein's reception of Wagner, cf. Thomä, *Totalität und Mitleid*, pp. 185–91, 200–25.
11 Wagner, *Wagner's Prose Works*, Vol. 8, p. 236.
12 Freud was looking to Otto Rank here, who also uses Siegfried as an example of this "lie"; see Rank, *The Myth of the Birth of the Hero*, pp. 53–5, 61, 68, 72, 89–93.
13 Williams, "Wagner and Politics," p. 39.
14 Eisler, "Einiges über das Verhalten der Arbeitersänger und -musiker in Deutschland," p. 246.
15 Wagner, *My Life*, p. 385. Regarding Bakunin as a "naive berserker," cf. also Schmitt, *Roman Catholicism and Political Form*, p. 36. Regarding Siegfried's "inexperienced" freedom and the "complete liberation from ties to the past" that actually make him a relative of Don Juan, cf. Köpnick, *Nothungs Modernität*, pp. 73, 235.
16 Ozouf, *L'homme régénéré*, pp. 134, 145f.
17 Incidentally, not long before this, Engels wrote a short play entitled "Horned Siegfried." Thanks go to Schneider, *Die kranke schöne Seele der Revolution*, pp. 246f., for pointing me to this infrequently mentioned text.
18 Sontag, *Under the Sign of Saturn*, p. 132.
19 Wagner, *Selected Letters of Richard Wagner*, p. 269.
20 Ibid., p. 308.
21 John Oliver Hobbes (pseudonym for Pearl Craigie) in 1899, quoted in Peretti, "Democratic Leitmotivs," p. 36.
22 Fontane, quoted in Gregor-Dellin, *Richard Wagner*, p. 360.
23 Adorno, *In Search of Wagner*, p. 120.
24 Kitcher and Schacht, *Finding an Ending*, p. 187.
25 Levin, *Richard Wagner, Fritz Lang, and the Nibelungen*, pp. 124, 129 (it is not Wagner's Siegfried whom Levin characterizes in this way, however, but the Siegfried from Fritz Lang's *Nibelungen*).
26 Regarding the "marionettes" in Wagner, cf. Bloch, *Spirit of Utopia*, p. 90.
27 Cf. Thomä, *Totalität und Mitleid*, pp. 185–91.

Chapter VII. The *puer robustus* between Europe and America: Alexis de Tocqueville

1 Regarding Tocqueville's theory that the Americans were ahead of the Europeans in a positive sense here, cf. Offe, *Reflections on America*, pp. 8f., 66f., 81.
2 Salvandy, *Seize Mois ou La Révolution et les Révolutionnaires*, p. 300. Michel, who pointed me in the direction of Salvandy, refers to a later edition of this work and incorrectly states that Salvandy was replying to Tocqueville; cf. Michel, *Les Barbares*, p. 572.
3 Regarding the "ouvrier" as an "enfant robuste" or "homme robuste," cf. Frégier, *Des classes dangeureuses de la population*, Vol. 1, p. 194, and Vol. 2, p. 35; Sandelin, *Répertoire général d'Économie politique ancienne et moderne*, Vol. 5, p. 56.
4 Machiavelli, *Discourses on Livy*, p. 44; cf. Brown, *Manhood and Politics*, p. 74.
5 Tocqueville, *Writings on Empire and Slavery*, p. 111 ("Essay on Algeria")/O 2, 752.
6 Weber rejects the idea that democracy is "a mass fragmented into atoms" and praises the Americans' "ability to form social groups"; see Weber, "'Churches' and 'Sects' in North America," pp. 10f.
7 For a critique of Tocqueville's "deceptively 'pure'" image of democracy in the "American laboratory," cf. Gauchet, "Tocqueville, America, and Us," pp. 192, 155.
8 Hamilton, Jay, and Madison, *The Federalist*, Vol. II, pp. 191ff. (No. 63).

9 Jefferson, *Writings*, pp. 255, 245, 253 (*Notes on the State of Virginia* [1787]).

10 Jefferson, *Writings*, p. 274, cf. the letter dated June 18, 1799, in Jefferson, *Writings*, pp. 1064f.

11 Tocqueville, *Memoir on Pauperism*, p. 22/O 2, 1161.

12 Mill, *Collected Works*, Vol. 3: *Principles of Political Economy* [1848], pp. 758, 769.

13 Like Smith and Hegel before him and Marx after him, Tocqueville uses the example of a pin factory here (DIA 3, 982–5; O 2, 672–5); cf. Smith, *The Wealth of Nations*, pp. 4f.; Hegel, *System of Ethical Life and First Philosophy of Spirit*, p. 248; Marx, MECW 6, 189f.; 35, 463.

14 Pendleton's comment can be found in Niles (ed.), *Principles and Acts of the Revolution in America*, p. 404; cf. Arendt, *On Revolution*, pp. 137f.

15 Pinker, *The Better Angels of Our Nature*, p. 103.

16 In an anonymous article in *The New York Times* from April 6, 1852, the Californian is described as a "young wild man" (which recalls Diderot's "little savage") – not critically, however, but with unabashed enthusiasm: "California is a wonderful land; a social anomaly. It is a child in years, but a giant in vital energy. The tight-fitting and constricting dresses, in which matured societies are arrayed, are unsuited to the young wild man."; Anon., "Land Titles in California," p. 2. Thomas de Quincey, against whom this *New York Times* article was directed, had complained that "some myriads of energetic and enterprising men" had nothing better to do than "[crowd] all sail towards the same object of private gain and public confusion" (Quincey, "California," pp. 199, 201).

17 Schmitt, *The* Nomos *of the Earth in the International Law of the* Jus Publicum Europaeum, pp. 95f.

18 Thoreau, *Collected Essays and Poems*, p. 357.

19 Tocqueville, *Toqueville on America After 1840*, p. 63/*Œuvres complètes*, Vol. 7, p. 89: "I have lately broken somewhat the chain of my relations with the United States. I regret this and would like to renew them" (letter dated June 15, 1843).

20 Tocqueville, *Recollections*, p. 240/O 1, 1146.

21 Tocqueville, *Recollections*, p. 226/*Œuvres complètes*, III/3, p. 44.

22 Tocqueville, *Democracy in America*, edited by J. P. Mayer, p. 755/O 1, 1133 (Speech in the Chamber of Deputies, January 1848).

23 Tocqueville, *Toqueville on America After 1840*, p. 136/*Œuvres complètes*, Vol. VII, pp. 146f. It is worth remembering that robbery and conquest were central to Rousseau's and Hobbes's characterization of the state of nature; cf. Rousseau, DI 218; OC 3, 219; see p. 48; Hobbes, L[e] 88.

24 Tocqueville, *Toqueville on America After 1840*, pp. 139, 165/*Œuvres complètes*, Vol. VII, pp. 148, 152.

25 Ibid., pp. 188f/*Œuvres complètes*, Vol. VII, pp. 182f.

26 Abensour overlooks this point and discusses Tocqueville's political theory only as an intervention against "savage instincts"; cf. Abensour, *Democracy Against the State*, p. 1.

27 Arendt, *On Revolution*, p. 139.

28 Tocqueville, *Recollections*, p. 236/O 1, 1142.

29 Tocqueville, *Toqueville on America After 1840*, p. 183/*Œuvres complètes*, Vol. VII, p. 177. Regarding Tocqueville's later commentary on the USA in his correspondence, cf. Wolin, *Tocqueville Between Two Worlds*, p. 556; regarding Tocqueville's growing disappointment with the USA, cf. Craiutu and Jennings, "Interpretive Essay: The Third *Democracy*: Tocqueville's Views of America after 1840" in *Toqueville on America After 1840*, pp. 26–33. One of the few interpretations to mention (if only fleetingly) the *puer robustus* in Tocqueville is Janara, *Democracy Growing Up*, pp. 109, 219.

30 Tocqueville, *Toqueville on America After 1840*, p. 184/*Œuvres complètes*, Vol. VII, p. 179.

31 Ibid., p. 336/Vol. VI/2, p. 190.

32 Ibid., p. 186.

33 Regarding Durkheim, see above, p. 382, n. 20.

34 Hardin, "The Tragedy of the Commons."
35 Shakespeare, *Complete Works*, p. 943 (*Othello*, I.1).
36 Regarding Nietzsche and Tocqueville, cf. Fukuyama, *The End of History*, pp. 308–10. Regarding Kojève as a link between Nietzsche and Fukuyama, see p. 333.
37 For the following, cf. Royce, *California*; Royce, *The Philosophy of Loyalty*; Wilson, *The New Freedom*, p. 222, cf. ibid., pp. 163–91; Dewey, *The Later Works*, Vol. 11, pp. 289–95 ("The Future of Liberalism" [1934]); Arendt, *On Revolution*, pp. 138ff.; Walzer, *Spheres of Justice*; Hirschman, *Shifting Involvements*.
38 Hegel, *Lectures on the Philosophy of History*, p. 168.
39 Heine, *Ludwig Börne: A Memorial*, pp. 29f.
40 Tocqueville, *Lettres choisis – Souvenirs*, p. 649 (letter to Stöffels dated March 9, 1849). Regarding the uprising of June 1848, cf. O 3, 842f.: "Cette insurrection de Juin [...] ne fut pas, à vrai dire, une lutte politique [...] mais un combat de classe, une sorte de guerre servile [...], le soulèvement de toute une population contre une autre."
41 Regarding his description of himself as a conservative, see Tocqueville, *Œuvres complètes*, Vol. III/2, p. 87.
42 Cf. Cavell, *Conditions Handsome and Unhandsome*, p. 16.
43 My critique follows that of Gauchet, "Tocqueville, America, and Us," pp. 172–4.
44 Jefferson, *Writings*, pp. 882, 890, 963.
45 Whitman, *Poetry and Prose*, pp. 334–6. Following on from Thoreau and Emerson, we find in Ogien and Laugier, *Pourquoi désobéir en démocratie?*, p. 28: "C'est ici et maintenant, chaque jour, que se règle mon consentement à ma société; je ne l'ai pas donné, en quelque sorte, une fois pour toutes. Non que mon consentement soit mesuré ou conditionnel: mais il est, constamment, en discussion, ou en *conversation*. C'est cela qui définit la possibilité du dissentiment."
46 Cf. Foucault, *The History of Sexuality*, Vol. 2, p. 200.
47 Nietzsche's copies of Mill's *Gesammelte Werke* [*Collected Works*] can be viewed online through the catalog of the Klassik Stiftung Weimar.
48 Mill, *Collected Works*, Vol. 18, p. 188. He also warns elsewhere that Europe could become "another China"; cf. Mill, *Collected Works*, Vol. 18, pp. 271, 274 ("On Liberty").
49 Mill, *Collected Works*, Vol. 18, p. 264.
50 Mill, *Collected Works*, Vol. 26, p. 188 ("Traité de Logique"): "Hobbes a appelé le méchant, *un enfant robuste*."
51 Mill, *Collected Works*, Vol. 18, p. 129 ("Civilization").
52 Mill, *Collected Works*, Vol. 18, pp. 262f., 265 ("On Liberty"). Mill had private reasons for such criticism: it distanced him from his youth, when he had been considered "a 'made' or manufactured man," i.e., a puppet controlled by his rigid father. He wrote that he lacked "spontaneity" and an "energetic character"; cf. Mill, *Collected Works*, Vol. 1, pp. 163, 613, 39; cf. Ball, "The Formation of Character," pp. 34f.
53 Mill, *Collected Works*, Vol. 18, pp. 269, 267f., 261 ("On Liberty").
54 Mill, *Collected Works*, Vol. 10, pp. 258, 242 ("Utilitarianism").
55 Mill, *Collected Works*, Vol. 18, pp. 219, 272, 274 ("On Liberty"). It is clear from his review of Tocqueville's *Democracy* book that Mill took the phrase "tyranny of the majority" from Tocqueville (DIA 2, 410ff.; O 2, 287ff.); cf. Mill, *Collected Works*, Vol. 18, p. 177.
56 Mill, *Collected Works*, Vol. 18, p. 268 ("On Liberty").
57 Ibid., p. 269.
58 Ibid., p. 267. Regarding criticism of the "prospect of social acceptance," cf. Mikics, *The Romance of Individualism in Emerson and Nietzsche*, p. 11.
59 In one passage not highlighted by Nietzsche, Mill says "it is important to give the freest scope possible to uncustomary things, in order that it may in time appear which of these are fit to be converted into customs"; Mill, *Collected Works*, Vol. 18, p. 269.
60 Cf., e.g., Mikics, *The Romance of Individualism in Emerson and Nietzsche*, pp. 7–15;

Mabille, *Nietzsche and the Anglo-Saxon Tradition*, pp. 106–27; Thomä, *Vom Glück in der Moderne*, p. 169.

61 Mill, *Collected Works*, Vol. 18, p. 275 ("On Liberty"). Nietzsche also highlighted this passage.
62 Sorel, *Reflections on Violence*, p. 232f.
63 Cf. Brown, *Politics Out of History*, p. 133: "What if instead of defending politics and democracy against Nietzsche's critiques, [. . .] we [. . .] attempted to discern how they might enrich democratic political projects?"
64 Foucault, *Society Must Be Defended*, pp. 39, 111.
65 Foucault, *History of Sexuality*, Vol. 1, p. 92; Foucault, *Power/Knowledge*, pp. 187–90 ("The History of Sexuality").
66 This unsubstantiated Jaurès quote is cited without a source by Bourdeau, *Les maîtres de la pensée contemporaine*, p. 139. The lectures given by Jaurès in Geneva, to which Bourdeau refers, are documented only in newspaper articles; cf. Rebérioux, "La philosophie de Nietzsche et le socialisme, trois conférences de Jaurès," p. 14. Georges Sorel picked up Jaurès' theory of the proletariat and publicized it, leading Bataille to categorize him as a representative of the "Nietzschean left"; cf. Sorel, *Reflections on Violence*, p. 233; Bataille, "Nietzsche and the Fascists" in *Visions of Excess*, pp. 184f.

Chapter VIII. The *puer robustus* as a revolutionary: Karl Marx and Friedrich Engels

1 Mehring, *Geschichte der Deutschen Sozialdemokratie*, Vol. 3, p. 123. Some interpreters of Marx mention Marx's *puer robustus* quote but do not analyze it in any detail; cf. Elster, *Making Sense of Marx*, p. 429; Freund, "Karl Marx, un admirateur discret de Thomas Hobbes," p. 353; Löwy, "Karl Marx et Friedrich Engels comme sociologues de la religion," p. 47.
2 Regarding England, cf. Bicheno, *An Inquiry into The Nature of Benevolence*, p. 25; regarding France, cf. Farge, *Fragile Lives*, pp. 131f. The "sturdy beggars" appear in the USA, too; cf. Stanley, "Beggars Can't Be Choosers."
3 Raynal, *Histoire philosophique et politique des établissemens et du commerce des Européens dans les Deux Indes* [1770], Vol. 6, p. 425. This first edition was published anonymously; in later editions, the cited passage was changed slightly; cf., e.g., Raynal, *Histoire philosophique et politique des établissemens et du commerce des Européens dans les Deux Indes* [1783], Vol. 9, p. 19.
4 Raynal, *Histoire philosophique et politique* [1783], Vol. 9, p. 22; Vol. 8, p. 278.
5 Raynal, *Histoire philosophique et politique* [1770], Vol. 6, pp. 421f. I will refrain from explaining the difference between Raynal's bourgeois revolution and Marx's proletarian one here.
6 Regarding Trotsky, cf. Merleau-Ponty, *Adventures of the Dialectic*, p. 208/*Les Aventures de la Dialectique*, p. 279.
7 Regarding the discussion of Marx's attitude toward industry and technology, cf., e.g., Marcuse, *Eros and Civilization*, pp. 100f.; Castoriadis, *Crossroads in the Labyrinth*, pp. 235–54.
8 Stirner, *The Ego and Its Own*, p. 229.
9 This is the classic liberal description according to Turgot, "Fondation, (Politique & Droit naturel)," p. 75. Regarding Marx's critique of "abstract individualism," cf. Lukes, *Individualism*, p. 77.
10 Carlyle, *The Works*, Vol. 6, pp. 418, 357 ("Past and Present"); cf. Engels' review of Carlyle, MECW 3, 454, 451.
11 Even Hegel noted that, on account of being "tangled" in the "whole," the "individual's skill" was no longer a guarantee for "sustaining his existence"; see Hegel, *Hegel and the Human Spirit*, p. 139. He describes the "immense power" of civil society, which

"draws people to itself and requires them to work for it, to owe everything to it, and to do everything by its means" (PR 263, [§238 *Addition*]).

12 Regarding the differentiation of the concept of rights in agreement with and in opposition to Marx, cf. Menke, *Kritik der Rechte*, pp. 269–71, 296–300.

13 Quoted in Arendt, *The Jewish Writings*, p. 140. Cf. Merleau-Ponty, *Humanism and Terror*, pp. xiv–xv: "Principles [. . .] are alibis the moment they cease to animate external and everyday life. A regime which is nominally liberal can be oppressive in reality."

14 Cf. Lassalle, *Gesammelte Reden und Schriften*, Vol. 5, pp. 275f.; regarding the critique of this passage, cf. Lukács, *History and Class Consciousness*, p. 195.

15 Ludwig Feuerbach's critique of the state, in his analysis of Hobbes, fails as dramatically as that of Marx and of Sigmund Freud later on: "The state [. . .] only inhibits and limits individuals so that they [. . .] relate only to themselves and their sensory Self and remain just as bestial and brutal as they were in statu naturali"; Feuerbach, *Gesammelte Werke*, Vol. 2: *Geschichte der neuern Philosophie von Bacon von Verulam bis Benedikt Spinoza* [1833], p. 127.

16 Lefort, *The Political Forms of Modern Society*, p. 250 ("Politics and Human Rights")/ *L'invention démocratique*, p. 58. Habermas had previously demonstrated that Marx's critique of "the central presupposition underlying the Anglo-Saxon tradition of Natural Law" goes hand in hand with his disregard for the French "idea of a political society"; see Habermas, *Theory and Practice*, pp. 111f.

17 Cf. Rancière, *Disagreement*, pp. 17f.

18 Regarding "polarization," cf. Avineri, *Hegel's Theory of the Modern State*, pp. 147f.

19 Foucault, *The Birth of Biopolitics*.

20 Lefort, *The Political Forms of Modern Society*, p. 180.

21 Even conservative thinkers at the time said "it is the awareness of this helplessness that brings forth the proletarian spirit" (Riehl, *Die bürgerliche Gesellschaft*, p. 453).

22 Cf. with references to Plato and Ballanche: Rancière, *Disagreement*, pp. 21ff.; regarding the topos of the poor as "animals," cf. also White, *Tropics of Discourse*, pp. 193f.

23 Hegel, *Hegel and the Human Spirit*, p. 164.

24 Carlyle, *The Works*, Vol. 10, pp. 36f. (*The French Revolution*). More references to workers as "animals" can be found in the works of Saint-Marc Girardin, Lamartine, Musset, Mérimée, Berlioz, George Sand, Balzac, Eugène Sue, Proudhon, and others. Cf. Michel, *Les Barbares, 1789–1848*, p. 210; Oehler, *Pariser Bilder I*, p. 123; Oehler, *Ein Höllensturz der alten Welt*, pp. 27–36; Chevalier, *Classes laborieuses et classes dangeureuses*, pp. 495, 511f., 518.

25 Hastings, "Years of liberal dogma have spawned a generation of amoral, uneducated, welfare dependent, brutalised youngsters."

26 Bauer, *Der Streit der Kritik mit Kirche und Staat*, p. 278. Bauer's phrase "the naked savages are among us" is probably a veiled quote from a novel that had recently been published by Eugène Sue, *Les Mystères de Paris*, Vol. 1, p. 3: "Les barbares [. . .] sont au milieu de nous." Regarding Sue, cf. Chevalier, *Classes laborieuses et classes dangeureuses*, p. 511; regarding Marx's reading of Sue, see MECW 4, 55–77, 162–209.

27 Scholars have curiously overlooked the most important predecessor to Hegel's theory of the double mob. Even Rousseau contrasts citizens interested in "the good of all" with "the other party" composed of "people who swim in opulence and the most abject people" (Rousseau, CWR 9, 300/OC 3, 890). In the period after Hegel and Marx, too, there is talk of a double mob. Nietzsche writes: "Mob above and mob below!" (PN 383; cf. Ruda, *Hegel's Rabble*, p. 49). Cf. also the chapter "The Alliance Between Mob and Capital" in Arendt, *The Origins of Totalitarianism*, pp. 147ff.

28 Hegel, *Die Philosophie des Rechts: Vorlesung von 1821/22*, pp. 222f.

29 Regarding the "*Lazzaroni*" who "all want to be masters," cf. Kant, *Anthropology from a Pragmatic Point of View*, p. 218. For a sympathetic characterization of the "lazzarone," on the other hand, cf. Goethe, *Italian Journey*, p. 321. Regarding Marx's interpretation of the "Lazzaroni" and the "lazarus-layers of the working class," cf. MECW

11, 149; MECW 35, 638. Regarding the history of the "Lazzaroni," cf. Hobsbawm, *Primitive Rebels*, pp. 113–17.

30 Hegel, *Die Philosophie des Rechts: Vorlesung von 1821/22*, p. 222; cf. Ruda, *Hegel's Rabble*, pp. 37, 149.

31 Hegel, *Hegel's Philosophy of Mind*, p. 142.

32 Hegel, *Die Philosophie des Rechts: Vorlesung von 1821/22*, pp. 223f.

33 Ruda, *Hegel's Rabble*, p. 47, cf. pp. 43, 51f.

34 Regarding Marx's dual rabble, cf. Rancière, *The Philosopher and His Poor*, pp. 95–8.

35 Regarding the critique of Marx's description of the lumpenproletariat, cf. Bussard, "The 'Dangerous Class' of Marx and Engels," p. 687; Bovenkerk, "The Rehabilitation of the Rabble," pp. 22–34.

36 Gramsci, *Gefängnishefte*, Vol. 9, pp. 2185–200; Gramsci, *Selections from the Prison Notebooks*, pp. 206f.

37 Regarding the "disorderly classes," cf. Jones, *Outcast London*, pp. 285–96, 343f. Regarding "ragpickers" (*Lumpensammler*) and the "*lumpenproletariat*," cf. Benjamin, *Selected Writings*, Vol. 4, pp. 8, 43 ("The Paris of the Second Empire in Baudelaire"). Regarding the "lowest strata of society" as "heterogeneous elements," cf. Bataille, "The Psychological Structure of Fascism," pp. 128f. Regarding the "*third* element which in its heterogeneity, asymmetry, and unexpectedness, breaks the unity of two specular terms, and rots away their *closure*," cf. Mehlman, *Revolution and Repetition*, p. 19, cf. also ibid., pp. 13–17, 30f., 38.

38 Regarding the relationship between Marx and Bakunin, cf. Huard, "Marx et Engels devant la marginalité," p. 14; Stallybrass, "Marx and Heterogeneity," p. 89; Draper, "The Concept of the 'Lumpenproletariat' in Marx and Engels," pp. 2299f., 2308f.

39 Bakounine, "Fragment, formant une suite de *L'Empire Knouto-Germanique*" [1872], p. 414. Regarding Bakunin's praise for the lumpenproletariat, cf. Bovenkerk, "The Rehabilitation of the Rabble," p. 35, as well as the earlier Schmitt, *Roman Catholicism and Political Form*, p. 37.

40 Rancière, *The Philosopher and His Poor*, p. 96.

41 Sorel, *Reflections on Violence*, pp. 123f.

42 In 1930, Max Horkheimer wrote: "Even today, the realization of a socialist order would be better for all proletarians than is capitalism but the difference between the present circumstances of the regularly employed and their personal life under socialism seems less certain, hazier, than the danger of dismissal, misery, penitentiary and death which he can look forward to, were he to participate in a revolutionary uprising or possibly just a strike"; Horkheimer, *Dawn and Decline*, p. 62.

43 Stirner, *The Ego and Its Own*, p. 230.

44 Ibid., pp. 17f.

45 Machiavelli, *The Prince*, p. 71; Nietzsche, *The Will to Power*, p. 461.

46 Regarding Flaubert, cf. Derrida, *Rogues*, pp. 64f.; regarding Carlyle, cf. Engels' letter to Marx from September 23, 1851, in MECW 38, 461; cf. also Rancière, *The Philosopher and His Poor*, p. 107.

47 Dumont, *From Mandeville to Marx*, p. 133; cf. ibid., pp. 126–45, 216. Regarding the discussion of the "species-being" and "community" among Marx's contemporaries, especially Feuerbach and Stirner, cf. Balibar, "Philosophical Anthropology or Ontology of Relations? Exploring the Sixth Thesis on Feuerbach."

48 Dumont, *From Mandeville to Marx*, pp. 128, 137; cf. ibid., p. 167. Regarding criticism of Dumont's "holism," cf. Balibar, "Marx, the joker in the pack (or the included middle)", pp. 22f.

49 Dumont, *From Mandeville to Marx*, p. 141.

50 Hardt and Negri, *Empire*, p. 157.

51 Hegel, *Werke I*, p. 459.

52 Balibar, "'Klassenkampf' als Begriff des Politischen," p. 451.

53 Merleau-Ponty, *Adventures of the Dialectic*, p. 231/*Les Aventures de la Dialectique*,

p. 311 ("l'universel en acte"); cf. Merleau-Ponty, *Humanism and Terror*, p. 116: "The proletariat is universal *de facto*, or manifestly in its very condition of life."

54 Cf., by contrast, the brilliant critique in Rancière, *Disagreement*, pp. 87f.

55 Merleau-Ponty, *Adventures of the Dialectic*, p. 46/*Les Aventures de la Dialectique*, p. 65.

56 Lukács, *History and Class Consciousness*, pp. 46, 183.

57 Rancière, *The Philosopher and His Poor*, p. 80/*Le philosophe et ses pauvres*, pp. 121f.

58 This thesis was inspired by Derrida's remark that "on both sides, between revolution and counter-revolution" only "specters and conjurations" are summoned up (*Specters of Marx*, p. 147).

59 In Marx's later works there are still a few allusions to the immiseration thesis (MECW 20, 148f.; MECW 35, 20, 639f., 750f.).

60 Herwegh, *Neue Gedichte*, pp. 132f.

61 Rousseau, SC 155 ("On the General Society of Mankind")/OC 3, 283f. Regarding this passage, cf. also Esposito, *Communitas*, pp. 57f.

62 Marx is following Hegel here, who writes in 1801: "The community of a person with others must not be regarded as a limitation of the true freedom of the individual but essentially as its enlargement" (*The Difference Between Fichte's and Schelling's System of Philosophy*, p. 145).

63 Cf. Abensour, *Democracy Against the State*, p. 87.

64 Cf. Rancière, *The Philosopher and His Poor*, pp. 82–7.

65 Regarding Marx's and Engels' ambivalent attitude toward brotherhood, cf. David, *Le printemps de la fraternité*, pp. 161–3.

66 Cf. Jones, *Outcast London*, p. 347.

67 Cf. Merleau-Ponty, *Adventures of the Dialectic*, p. 46/*Les Aventures de la Dialectique*, p. 65: "But then, even if Marxism and its philosophy of history are nothing else than the 'secret of the proletariat's existence,' it is not a secret that the proletariat itself possesses but one that the theoretician deciphers."

68 For a critique, cf. Lukes, *Liberals & Cannibals*, pp. 160f.

69 Rancière, *Disagreement*, pp. 83, 85, 90. For a critique of metapolitics that is less precise than that of Rancière, cf. Žižek, *The Ticklish Subject*, pp. 187–97.

70 Lefort, *Le temps présent*, p. 359; Lefort, *The Political Forms of Modern Society*, p. 254 ("Politics and Human Rights")/*L'invention démocratique*, p. 63. Regarding criticism of the "primacy of economics," see the earlier Adorno, *Negative Dialectics*, pp. 321f.

71 Rancière, *Disagreement*, p. 14.

72 Balibar, "Marx, the joker in the pack (or the included middle)," pp. 14ff.

73 Abensour, *Democracy Against the State*, pp. xxxiii, xl, xli, 69, cf. ibid., pp. 98, 105–10. Lefort himself writes: "Il est vrai que la démocratie [...] est plus profondément elle-même en étant démocratie sauvage" (Lefort, *Le temps présent*, p. 389). Whether Lefort's "savage democracy" is actually compatible with Marx, as Abensour claims, seems doubtful to me.

74 Merleau-Ponty, *Adventures of the Dialectic*, p. 52/*Les Aventures de la Dialectique*, p. 72: "Revolutionary politics cannot bypass this moment when it dares to step into the unknown."

75 Herzen, "From the Other Shore," p. 379. Georges Sorel turns Herzen's skeptical speech into a celebration of spontaneity; Sorel, *La Décomposition du Marxisme*, p. 62.

76 Stoppard, *The Coast of Utopia*, p. 335. Stoppard's motto "and still to go on" is undoubtedly an allusion to Beckett, i.e., an optimistic variation on *Waiting for Godot*, in which Vladimir says: "Let us do something, while we have the chance! It is not every day that we are needed. [...] But at this place, at this moment of time, all mankind is us, whether we like it or not. Let us make the most of it, before it is too late!" (Beckett, *Waiting for Godot*, p. 90).

Chapter IX. The *puer robustus* as Oedipus: Sigmund Freud

1 Rank, *The Incest Theme in Literature and Legend*, pp. 21, 67.
2 Anna Freud followed in her father's footsteps; she also quotes the Diderot passage and uses the phrase "little savages" in her description of childish behavior; cf. Freud, "Psychoanalyse des Kindes," p. 12, and Freud, *Introduction to Psychoanalysis: Lectures for Child Analysts and Teachers*, p. 113.
3 Freud, *The Complete Letters of Sigmund Freud to Wilhelm Fliess*, p. 272.
4 Cf. Bollack, "Der Menschensohn: Freuds Ödipusmythos," pp. 669, 672, 683.
5 Bergmann, "The Oedipus Complex and Psychoanalytic Technique," p. 536.
6 Regarding Hobbes and Freud, cf., e.g., Weinstein and Weinstein, "Freud on the Problem of Order: The Revival of Hobbes," p. 41.
7 For an interpretation of Freud based on contract theory, cf. Rieff, *Freud*, p. VII; Pateman, *The Sexual Contract*, p. 103; Esposito, *Communitas*, pp. 35–45; Manow, *Politische Ursprungsphantasien*, pp. 35–41.
8 For an explication of Freud's argument, cf. Cavell, *Becoming a Subject*, pp. 83–94.
9 Aichhorn, *Wayward Youth*; Bernfeld, *Vom dichterischen Schaffen der Jugend*.
10 Malinowski, *Sex and Repression in Savage Society*, p. 65.
11 Cf. Hessing, *Der Fluch des Propheten*, p. 321; Zaretsky, *Secrets of the Soul*, p. 105.
12 Horkheimer, "The Authoritarian State," p. 99.
13 I will briefly address these effects later on in connection with Federn, see pp. 248f. Cf. Thomä, *Väter*, pp. 44–7, 178–89.
14 Schmitt, *The Crisis of Parliamentary Democracy*, p. 52; Schmitt, *Roman Catholicism and Political Form*, p. 33; Mann, *Diktatur der Vernunft*; Roth, *Werke 2: Das journalistische Werk 1924–1928*, pp. 59f.; Kelsen, *Verteidigung der Demokratie*, p. 98 ("Allgemeine Staatslehre").
15 In his smart profile of Schmitt from 1924, Hugo Ball cited various classical references for the "dictatorship of reason," including Thomas Aquinas, Locke, and Kant; cf. Ball, "Carl Schmitt's Political Theology," p. 80.
16 Kelsen, *The Essence and Value of Democracy*, p. 28.
17 Kant, *Political Writings*, p. 46 ("Idea for a Universal History with a Cosmopolitan Purpose").
18 Kant, *Political Writings*, p. 112 ("Perpetual Peace").
19 Schiller, "Briefe an den Prinzen Friedrich Christian von Schleswig-Holstein-Sonderburg-Augustenburg," p. 41.
20 CWS 8, 204 ("On Grace and Dignity"); "Kallias or Concerning Beauty," p. 159; CWS 8, 42 ("Letters on the Aesthetical Education of Man"). Regarding the similarities between Freud and Schiller as well as the "tyranny of reason," cf. Marcuse, *Eros and Civilization*, pp. 197, cf. ibid. 187–90.
21 Ogien and Laugier, *Le principe démocratie*, p. 77. Regarding the "transversal dimension" of democratic politics, cf. the earlier Lefort, *The Political Forms of Modern Society*, p. 257 ("Politics and Human Rights")/*L'invention démocratique*, p. 66.
22 Regarding the potential of "identification," cf. Ricœur, *Freud and Philosophy*, pp. 477–83.
23 Cf. Thomä, "Synergie und Sympathie."
24 Smith, *The Theory of Moral Sentiments*, pp. 12f.; cf. Thomä, "Leben als Teilnehmen," pp. 17–26.
25 Tarde, *The Laws of Imitation*, p. 79.
26 Freud and Andreas-Salomé, *Letters*, p. 9; cf. Andreas-Salomé, "Zum Typus Weib," p. 9.
27 Smith, *The Theory of Moral Sentiments*, p. 15.
28 Rank, *The Trauma of Birth*, p. 94; cf. Marcuse, *Eros and Civilization*, p. 68.
29 Cf. Honneth, *The I in We*, pp. 201–16.
30 Cf. David, *Fraternité et Révolution française 1789–1799*; David, *Le Printemps de la Fraternité*; Bayertz (ed.), *Solidarity*. From a gender theory perspective, it is interesting

NOTES TO PP. 242–9

that Jules Michelet makes a connection between maternal and fraternal sociality; cf. Chase, "Jules Michelet and the Nineteenth-Century Concept of Insanity," pp. 730, 733; Barthes, *Michelet*, p. 156 ("Matria").

31 Cf. Brunner, "Oedipus politicus."

32 Cf. Honneth, *The I in We*, pp. 193–200.

33 Regarding Freud's characterization of the USA as an "anti-Paradise" and a "gigantic mistake," cf. Gay, "Freud's America," p. 306.

34 Gorer, *The American People*, pp. 29, 32.

35 Lasch, *The Culture of Narcissism*; for a precise critique of Lasch, cf. Benjamin, *The Bonds of Love*, p. 139.

36 In an interesting debate with Otto Rank, Freud rails against his father role, saying he prefers to be viewed as David taking on Goliath – even though this role is reserved for Rank; cf. Kramer, "Insight and Blindness: Visions of Rank," pp. 15f.; Lieberman, *Acts of Will: The Life and Work of Otto Rank*, pp. 203–7.

37 Reinhoudt and Audier, *The Walter Lippmann Colloquium*, pp. 93–188; cf. Foucault, *The Birth of Biopolitics*, pp. 132ff., 160f.

38 Sennett, *The Corrosion of Character*, pp. 119–22. The neoliberalism that Sennett attacks, however, is different from that discussed by Lippmann and others in the 1930s.

39 Jones, "A Preface to Politics: Von Walter Lippmann," p. 456.

40 Lippmann, *A Preface to Politics*, pp. 37, 45.

41 Ibid., pp. 147, 269.

42 Lippmann, *Drift and Mastery*, p. 103.

43 Lippmann, *A Preface to Politics*, p. 51.

44 Regarding this Lippmann quote from 1912, cf. Leuchtenburg, "Walter Lippmann's *Drift and Mastery*," p. 4.

45 Lippmann, *A Preface to Politics*, pp. 46–9.

46 Lippmann, *Drift and Mastery*, pp. 123–34; Lippmann, *A Preface to Morals*, p. 91.

47 Lippmann, *A Preface to Politics*, pp. 13–15.

48 Ibid., pp. 46, 50.

49 Ibid., pp. 51, 316f.

50 Lippmann, *Drift and Mastery*, pp. 108f.

51 Lippmann, *A Preface to Morals*, p. 183.

52 Cf. Barber, *Strong Democracy*; Sandel, *Democracy's Discontent*.

53 Federn, *Zur Psychologie der Revolution*, p. 20.

54 Ibid., pp. 4, 6, 13.

55 Ibid., pp. 13, 15, 8.

56 Ibid., pp. 5, 23. This recalls Lippmann's criticism of "terrorists."

57 Ibid., pp. 15, 22.

58 Ibid., pp. 29, 22, 24, cf. also ibid., pp. 16–18. He makes repeated positive reference to the fraternity of the French Revolution, see ibid., pp. 11, 14, 24.

59 Ibid., pp. 5, 18, 16.

60 Ibid., pp. 22, 18, 27. One should not view Federn as a prophet of the downfall of democracy and rise of a new dictator; in this vein, however, see Loewenberg, "The Psychohistorical Origins of the Nazi Youth Cohort," p. 268.

61 Federn, *Zur Psychologie der Revolution*, p. 29.

62 Regarding Blüher, cf., e.g., Reulecke, "Männerbund versus Familie"; Brunotte, *Zwischen Eros und Krieg*, pp. 70–117; Bruns, *Politik des Eros*.

63 Lorenz, "Dr. Paul Federn: Zur Psychologie der Revolution: Die vaterlose Gesellschaft"; Lorenz, "Hans Blüher: Die Rolle der Erotik in der männlichen Gesellschaft." Both reviews were published in 1920.

64 Blüher, *Wandervogel: Geschichte einer Jugendbewegung. 1. Teil*, pp. 75, 78.

65 The *Imago* essay "Über Gattenwahl und Ehe" ("On Spouse Selection and Marriage") was reprinted in: Blüher, *Die Rolle der Erotik in der männlichen Gesellschaft*, Vol. II, pp. 13f., 19.

66 Ibid., pp. 94, 120f.
67 Blüher, *Wandervogel: Geschichte einer Jugendbewegung. 1. Teil*, p. 81.
68 Blüher, *Philosophie auf Posten*, pp. 97–124, 169–202.
69 Blüher, *Die Rolle der Erotik in der männlichen Gesellschaft*, Vol. II, p. 221, cf. ibid., p. 91; Blüher, *Die drei Grundformen der sexuellen Inversion (Homosexualität)*, p. 29.
70 Cf. Neubauer, "Sigmund Freud und Hans Blüher in bisher unveröffentlichten Briefen."
71 Blüher, *Die Rolle der Erotik in der männlichen Gesellschaft*, Vol. I, p. 223.
72 Blüher, *Die deutsche Wandervogelbewegung als erotisches Phänomen*, p. 12; Blüher, *Die Rolle der Erotik in der männlichen Gesellschaft*, Vol. II, p. 91.
73 Blüher, *Familie und Männerbund*, p. 22; cf. Bruns, *Politik des Eros*, pp. 107f.
74 Blüher, *Die Rolle der Erotik in der männlichen Gesellschaft*, Vol. II, p. 95. Blüher is paraphrasing passages from Schurtz, *Altersklassen und Männerbünde*, pp. 206, 224, 261.
75 Blüher, *Führer und Volk in der Jugendbewegung*, p. 10; Blüher, *Die Rolle der Erotik in der männlichen Gesellschaft*, Vol. II, pp. 217f., 220.
76 Talk of a "better kind of father," which threatens his own concept, can be found in Blüher, *Wandervogel: Geschichte einer Jugendbewegung. 2. Teil*, p. 21.
77 Blüher, *Die Rolle der Erotik in der männlichen Gesellschaft*, Vol. II, pp. 102, 171; Blüher, *Führer und Volk in der Jugendbewegung*, pp. 3, 14. This fits with Carl Schmitt's claim from 1933 that "between leader and following" there is a kind of "ethnic identity [*Artgleichheit*]."
78 Adorno, *Gesammelte Schriften*, Vol. 8, pp. 418, 425 ("Freudian Theory and the Pattern of Fascist Propaganda" [1951]); cf. Benjamin, *Bonds of Love*, p. 145.
79 Regarding the "*male association deficiency*" among Jews, cf. Blüher, *Die Rolle der Erotik in der männlichen Gesellschaft*, Vol. II, p. 170.
80 Cf., e.g., Völger and Welck (eds.), *Männerbande – Männerbünde*; Savage, *Teenage: The Creation of Youth 1875–1945*.
81 Scholars disagree on just how much the Nazis could draw on Blüher's thinking; regarding the continuity thesis, cf. Laqueur, *Young Germany*, pp. 42–4; regarding the differences, cf. Reulecke, "Männerbund versus Familie," p. 204; for a summary, cf. Roseman, "Generationen als 'Imagined Communities,'" pp. 195f.
82 Mann, "On the German Republic," p. 130. Regarding Mann and Blüher, cf., e.g., Wisskirchen, "Republikanischer Eros"; Bruns, *Politik des Eros*, pp. 108, 387, 390f.
83 Mann, "Freud's Position in the History of Modern Thought," p. 195. Regarding Freud's reserved reaction to Mann's romantic interpretation, cf. Freud and Andreas-Salomé, *Letters*, pp. 181f. (letter dated July 28, 1929).
84 Mann, *Reflections of a Nonpolitical Man*, pp. 341, 223.
85 Ibid., pp. 190, 201f.
86 Ibid., p. 341. It is impossible to overlook the reference to Sombart, *Händler und Helden [Merchants and Heroes]*. Regarding the popular contrast between "feminine" democrats and masculine "warriors," cf. also Jünger, "Krieg und Krieger," p. 65.
87 Mann, *Diaries 1918–1939*, p. 66 (entry dated September 17, 1919).
88 Cf. Wisskirchen, "Republikanischer Eros."
89 Mann, "On the German Republic," p. 130.
90 Ibid., p. 121, cf. 128.
91 Novalis, *Notes for a Romantic Encyclopaedia*, p. 148 (No. 797); Whitman, *Poetry and Prose*, p. 258 ("I Sing the Body Electric"); cf. Mann, "On the German Republic," pp. 128f.
92 Schurtz, *Altersklassen und Männerbünde*, p. 52.
93 Beiser, *The Early Political Writings of the German Romantics*, p. 45 ("Faith and Love," No. 36); cf. Mann, "On the German Republic," p. 124.
94 Beiser, *The Early Political Writings of the German Romantics*, p. 77 ("Christianity or Europe"); cf. Mann, "On the German Republic," p. 120. The fact that Novalis himself

pleads for a balance between republican freedom and monarchical ties cannot be concealed.

95 Mann, "On the German Republic," pp. 125, 128, 122.

96 Ibid., p. 129.

97 Whitman, *Poetry and Prose*, p. 253 ("I Sing the Body Electric"), p. 268 ("In Paths Untrodden"), p. 272 ("For You O Democracy"); cf. Mann, "Of the German Republic," pp. 128, 130.

98 Lubich, "Thomas Mann's Sexual Politics," pp. 110f.

99 Baeumler, "Metaphysik und Geschichte," pp. 1117, 1126.

100 Baeumler, *Männerbund und Wissenschaft*, p. 39.

101 Ibid., p. 38.

102 Baeumler, "Einleitung," pp. ccvii, cclxxii, ccxciii.

103 Baeumler, *Männerbund und Wissenschaft*, pp. 41, 34, 39. Like Blüher and even Freud, Baeumler references Heinrich Schurtz; cf. Baeumler, *Männerbund und Wissenschaft*, p. 167, and "Einleitung," pp. cciv, cclxxx. For an early critique of Schurtz, see Weber, *Economy and Society*, p. 906; cf. Brown, *Manhood and Politics*, pp. 131–6, 149.

104 Baeumler, *Politik und Erziehung*, p. 75 (with a critique of Hans Blüher and Gustav Wyneken).

105 Rathkolb, "Hans Kelsens Perzeptionen Freudscher Psychoanalyse," p. 88; Potacs, "Hans Kelsen und der Marxismus," p. 185.

106 However, cf. Balibar, "The Invention of the Superego: Freud and Kelsen, 1922"; Herrera, "Communauté sans substance, inéluctable contrainte: Le Freud de Kelsen"; Honneth, *Freedom's Right*, pp. 315–17. Balibar and Honneth view Kelsen primarily as a corrective to Freud and do not make full use of the potential of his arguments.

107 Kelsen, "The Conception of the State and Social Psychology," pp. 11, 15f., 20f.

108 The minutes of the meeting are published in Fallend, *Sonderlinge, Träumer, Sensitive*, p. 217.

109 Kelsen, *Der soziologische und der juristische Staatsbegriff*, p. 30.

110 Kelsen, *Essays in Legal and Moral Philosophy*, p. 61 ("God and the State").

111 Kelsen, *The Essence and Value of Democracy*, p. 92.

112 Regarding the "totem," with references to Freud and Durkheim, cf. Kelsen, *Essays in Legal and Moral Philosophy*, pp. 64, 66f. ("God and the State"); regarding "idea" or "ideology," cf. id., "The Conception of the State and Social Psychology," p. 23.

113 Kelsen, *The Essence and Value of Democracy*, p. 92; cf. id., *Verteidigung der Demokratie*, pp. 134, 143 ("Demokratie [1926]").

114 Kelsen, *The Essence and Value of Democracy*, p. 33.

115 Kelsen, *Der Staat als Integration*, pp. 33f. (regarding Smend); id., *Essays in Legal and Moral Philosophy*, p. 108 ("State-form and World-outlook"; regarding the "state-self").

116 Kelsen, *Essays in Legal and Moral Philosophy*, p. 108 ("State-form and World-outlook"); cf. Dreier, "Kelsens Demokratietheorie," pp. 81f., 85f.

117 Kelsen, *Essays in Legal and Moral Philosophy*, pp. 105f. ("State-form and World-outlook"); cf. Herrera, "Communauté sans substance, inéluctable contrainte: Le Freud de Kelsen," p. 80. Regarding the "idea of democracy" as "the absence of leadership," cf. also Kelsen, *The Essence and Value of Democracy*, p. 88.

118 Kelsen, *Essays in Legal and Moral Philosophy*, p. 105 ("State-form and World-outlook").

119 Kelsen, *The Essence and Value of Democracy*, p. 91.

120 Balibar therefore falls short with his thesis that Kelsen the legal scholar, with his "supraindividual" state, provided a model for the "super-ego" of Freud the psychologist; cf. Balibar, "The Invention of the Superego: Freud and Kelsen, 1922."

121 Kelsen, "The Conception of the State and Social Psychology," p. 15; id., *Der soziologische und der juristische Staatsbegriff*, p. 23.

122 Kelsen, *Essays in Legal and Moral Philosophy*, p. 100 ("State-form and World-outlook").

123 Ibid., p. 99.
124 Kelsen, "Platonic Love," p. 4. Regarding the "excess of authority," "pitiless suppression of every opposition" and the "tyrannical character [. . .] whom Plato had always felt as the devil in his own heart," cf. ibid., p. 105.
125 Ibid., pp. 8f.
126 Ibid.
127 Ibid., pp. 40f. His talk of "inversion" is a play on the "Typus inversus" of the male association; cf. Blüher, Die Rolle der Erotik in der männlichen Gesellschaft, Vol. I, pp. 119–43.
128 Kelsen, The Essence and Value of Democracy, p. 31.
129 Kelsen, Der Staat als Integration, p. 50 (the quote within the quote is Kelsen quoting himself). Regarding "the dynamic of law" in Kelsen's work, cf. the convincing interpretation of Colliot-Thélène, "Pour une politique des droits subjectifs," pp. 247f.
130 Heller, "Staatslehre," p. 362. Regarding the contrast between Kelsen and Schmitt, cf. Dreier, "Kelsens Demokratietheorie," pp. 89–93.
131 Kelsen, Der Staat als Integration, p. 48.
132 Kelsen, The Essence and Value of Democracy, p. 37. Kelsen sharply criticized the Soviet Union later on, but as a professor in America he was also targeted by the Communist-hunting McCarthy, who subjected him to a meticulous investigation; cf. the interesting research by Rathkolb, "Hans Kelsen und das FBI."
133 Kelsen, Society and Nature, p. 21; cf. Levy-Bruhl, Primitive Mentality, pp. 384–409.
134 Lepsius, "Kelsens Demokratietheorie," p. 85.
135 Dewey, The Middle Works, Vol. 14, pp. 211f. (Human Nature and Conduct).
136 Dewey, The Later Works, Vol. 14, pp. 224–230 ("Creative Democracy – The Task Before Us"), ibid., Vol. 11, p. 131 ("Authority and Social Change"). Cf. Bernstein, "John Dewey on Democracy: The Task Before Us."
137 Honig, Emergency Politics, p. XV.

Chapter X. Anarchists, adventurers, young rowdies, and little savages: Carl Schmitt, Leo Strauss, Helmut Schelsky, and Max Horkheimer

1 Vialatoux, La cité totalitaire de Hobbes; Capitant, "Hobbes et l'État totalitaire"; Taylor, "The Ethical Doctrine of Hobbes"; cf. Tarlton, "Rehabilitating Hobbes: Obligation, Anti-Fascism and the Myth of a 'Taylor Thesis'"; Collingwood, The New Leviathan.
2 Borkenau, Der Übergang vom feudalen zum bürgerlichen Weltbild, pp. 439–82.
3 Parsons, The Structure of Social Action, pp. 89–94.
4 Neumann, Behemoth, p. 5.
5 Arendt, "Expansion and Philosophy of Power"; id., The Origins of Totalitarianism, pp. 125–47; regarding Arendt, cf. Keedus, "Liberalism and the Question of 'The Proud': Hannah Arendt and Leo Strauss as Readers of Hobbes," p. 326.
6 Elias, The Civilizing Process, pp. 372, 370.
7 Tönnies, Thomas Hobbes; Oakeshott, "Introduction." Regarding Oakeshott, cf. Müller, "Re-imagining Leviathan: Schmitt and Oakeshott on Hobbes and the Problem of Political Order."
8 A rather incomplete overview can be found in the book by Foisneau, Merle, and Sorell (eds.), "Leviathan" Between the Wars.
9 Mannheim, "The Problem of Generations"; following Mannheim, cf. the internationally influential survey by Murdock and McCron, "Consciousness of class and consciousness of generation."
10 Balibar, "Le Hobbes de Schmitt, le Schmitt de Hobbes," p. 29; the puer robustus is also mentioned in Balibar, Spinoza and Politics, p. 105. (The original French text is missing the relevant chapter on "Politics and Communication.")

11 Tönnies, "Hobbes and the *Zoon Politikon*," p. 55; cf. Borkenau, *Der Übergang*, p. 459; Arendt, *The Origins of Totalitarianism*, pp. 139f.
12 Schmitt, *Der Wert des Staates und die Bedeutung des Einzelnen*, p. 9; id., *Glossarium*, p. 244; cf. Däubler, *Das Nordlicht*, Vol. 2, p. 556.
13 Schmitt, *The Crisis of Parliamentary Democracy*, p. 15.
14 Schmitt, *Staat, Grossraum, Nomos*, p. 45; id., *The Concept of the Political*, p. 70; id., *State, Movement, People*, p. 17.
15 Schmitt, *The Concept of the Political*, p. 70; id., *State, Movement, People*, p. 41.
16 Schmitt, *The Crisis of Parliamentary Democracy*, p. 50; id., *State, Movement, People*, p. 27.
17 Schmitt, *Positionen und Begriffe*, p. 111; id., *State, Movement, People*, p. 39.
18 Schmitt, *The Crisis of Parliamentary Democracy*, p. 35.
19 Schmitt, *The Concept of the Political*, pp. 61, 72, 35.
20 Schmitt, *Political Theology*, p. 65.
21 Schmitt, *The Concept of the Political*, pp. 60, 84.
22 Schmitt, *Der Wert des Staates und die Bedeutung des Einzelnen*, pp. 84, 90; cf. Däubler, *Das Nordlicht*, Vol. 1, p. 481 ("They always seek, full of haste, to preserve their individual happiness, / Because they are weak, the shallow end of the storm of life"). Regarding Schmitt's "devotion" on the border between eroticism and politics, cf. Mehring, *Carl Schmitt: A Biography*, pp. 44f.
23 Schmitt, *State, Movement, People*, pp. 25, 13.
24 Regarding the "total state," see Schmitt, *Der Hüter der Verfassung*, p. 79; regarding the "total leader-state," see id., *State, Movement, People*, p. 52; regarding the reinterpretation of democracy and the *demos*, see id., *The Crisis of Parliamentary Democracy*, pp. 9f., 25–9, and Schmitt, *Staat, Grossraum, Nomos*, pp. 48f.
25 Schmitt, *Roman Catholicism and Political Form*, p. 27.
26 Schmitt, *Political Theology*, p. 65; cf. id., *The Concept of the Political*, p. 94, and id., *The Leviathan in the State Theory of Thomas Hobbes*, p. 37.
27 Schmitt, *Roman Catholicism and Political Form*, pp. 8, 19, 18, 25f.
28 Schmitt, *State, Movement, People*, pp. 47f.
29 Hitler, *Reden, Schriften, Anordnungen*, Vol. II/1, pp. 106f.; regarding Hitler and Christ, cf. Ley, "Apokalyptische Bewegungen in der Moderne," p. 25.
30 Hitler, *Mein Kampf*, p. 65; Schmitt, *Das Judentum in der Rechtswissenschaft*, pp. 14, 16 ("Eröffnung der wissenschaftlichen Vorträge"); ibid., p. 34 ("Schlusswort"); regarding the conference on "Judaism in Legal Studies," cf. Gross, *Carl Schmitt and the Jews*, pp. 68–78; Meier, *The Lesson of Carl Schmitt*, p. 154f.
31 This sentence can be found in Schmitt's essay on Hobbes entitled "Die vollendete Reformation" ("The Completed Reformation") from 1965, reprinted in Schmitt, *Der Leviathan*, p. 139, cf. id., *Glossarium*, p. 184: "Thomas Hobbes's most important sentence remains: Jesus is the Christ." For an analysis and critique, cf. Meier, *The Lesson of Carl Schmitt*, pp. 117–21. There is also a connection here to Schmitt's critique of Dostoevsky's famous legend of the Grand Inquisitor, which, in Schmitt's view, presents the image of an anarchistically distorted Christ (Schmitt, *Roman Catholicism in Political Form*, p. 32).
32 Schmitt, *Glossarium*, p. 119.
33 Schmitt, *The Leviathan*, p. 32; regarding the relationship between God and representation, cf. ibid., pp. 93f. ("The State as Mechanism in Hobbes and Descartes" [1936/37]); Schmitt, *Roman Catholicism in Political Form*, p. 19.
34 Schmitt, *The Leviathan*, pp. 35–7; cf. ibid., pp. 91–103 ("The State as Mechanism in Hobbes and Descartes").
35 Hitler, *Mein Kampf*, p. 398.
36 Schmitt, *Ex Captivitate Salus*, p. 52. Schmitt referes to both Bodin and Hobbes as brothers, but it is immediately apparent that Hobbes is his favorite brother.
37 Regarding the changes in Schmitt's opinion of Hobbes, cf. Mehring, "Carl Schmitt,

NOTES TO PP. 270–5

Leo Strauss, Thomas Hobbes und die Philosophie," pp. 380–6; Altini, "Hobbes in der Weimarer Republik," pp. 9–19.

38 Schmitt, *The Leviathan*, p. 97 ("The State as Mechanism in Hobbes and Descartes").

39 Schmitt occasionally weakens the link between power and morality; see *The Concept of the Political*, p. 58. For instance, he changed the phrase "moral disjunction" to "political disjunction" in his personal copy of *The Crisis of Parliamentary Democracy*, p. 57; regarding this change, see Schickel, *Gespräche mit Carl Schmitt*, p. 74.

40 Schmitt, *Political Theology*, pp. 65, 56; regarding the "good" or "evil" nature of man, cf., e.g., Schmitt, *Political Romanticism*, p. 26; id., *Roman Catholicism and Political Form*, p. 32; id., *Glossarium*, pp. 63, 105; id., *Der Begriff des Politischen*, p. 121 (from the notes to the 1963 edition); id., *Der Leviathan*, p. 176 (from the Hobbes essay of 1965).

41 Schmitt, *Political Theology*, p. 56.

42 Schmitt, *The Crisis of Parliamentary Democracy*, p. 56; cf. id., *The Concept of the Political*, p. 58, and *Glossarium*, p. 63.

43 Schmitt, *Der Wert des Staates und die Bedeutung des Einzelnen*, pp. 84f., 108; id., *The Leviathan*, pp. 21f.

44 Schmitt, *The Concept of the Political*, pp. 60f.

45 Schmitt, *Political Theology*, p. 66, cf. ibid., p. 55.

46 Ibid., p. 64; regarding Schmitt and Bakunin, cf. Meier, *The Lesson of Carl Schmitt*, pp. 7–9.

47 Schmitt, *The Crisis of Parliamentary Democracy*, p. 73; cf. id., *The Concept of the Political*, p. 74.

48 Cf. Schmitt, *Roman Catholicism and Political Form*, pp. 17, 36. In 1929 he wrote: "Only a weak state is a capitalistic servant to private property" (*Positionen und Begriffe*, p. 113). In keeping with Schmitt, Ball writes: "The capitalist industrial state of today, as well as the socialist state of tomorrow, [...] are founded on vacuous and non-existent needs; their fatalistic objective is a self-governing and self-regulating flow of economic processes" ("Carl Schmitt's Political Theology," p. 92).

49 Cf. Bakunin, "Brief an die Pariser Zeitung *Le Réveil* (1869)," p. 127.

50 Lévinas, *Otherwise Than Being or Beyond Essence*, p. 194, note 3; cf. Abensour, *Democracy Against the State*, pp. 101, 124; Lefort, *Writing*, pp. 207–35.

51 Schmitt, *The Leviathan*, p. 36.

52 Schmitt, *Political Theology*, p. 56.

53 Schmitt, *Der Wert des Staates und die Bedeutung des Einzelnen*, p. 93.

54 Schmitt, *Roman Catholicism and Political Form*, pp. 26f.; regarding the fascist state as a *"higher* third party," id., *Positionen und Begriffe*, p. 109.

55 Schmitt, *The Leviathan*, pp. 97, 100 ("The State as Mechanism in Hobbes and Descartes"); cf. ibid., pp. 35, 47. Regarding "egoists," cf., e.g., Schmitt, *Der Wert des Staates und die Bedeutung des Einzelnen*, pp. 85, 93.

56 Schmitt, *Political Theology*, pp. 63f.; cf. Baudelaire, *My Heart Laid Bare and other prose writings*, pp. 200f./*Œuvres complètes*, Vol. 1, p. 703 ("My Heart Laid Bare"): "Commerce is essentially *satanic.*" Regarding the satanic in Baudelaire, see p. 150.

57 Schmitt, *Der Wert des Staates und die Bedeutung des Einzelnen*, p. 94.

58 Schmitt, *State, Movement, People*, pp. 49, 52.

59 Ibid., p. 51.

60 Ibid., pp. 48, 51. For a critique, cf. Marcuse, "The struggle against liberalism in the totalitarian view of the state," pp. 21f.

61 Schmitt, *On the Three Types of Juristic Thought*, p. 95.

62 Schmitt, *State, Movement, People*, p. 48.

63 Schmitt, *The Concept of the Political*, p. 46; id., *State, Movement, People*, pp. 50f.

64 Koselleck, *Critique and Crisis*, pp. 37f.

65 Schmitt, *The Leviathan*, pp. 55f., 57, 65.

66 Ibid., pp. 10, 59; for his critique of other "Jewish philosopher[s]" and scholars, such as

404

Mendelssohn and Stahl-Jolson, ibid., pp. 60f., 69f.; for his attack against "Jews" and Spinoza after 1945, cf. id., *Glossarium*, p. 290; regarding Schmitt's antisemitism in his *Leviathan* book, cf. Gross, *Carl Schmitt and the Jews*, pp. 155–71, as well as Meier, *The Lesson of Carl Schmitt*, p. 96.

67 Schmitt, *Der Begriff des Politischen*, p. 10.
68 Cf., e.g., Schmitt, *The Nomos of the Earth*, pp. 242–58, 300–4.
69 Ibid., pp. 305, 308; regarding *cujus regio, ejus oeconomia*, cf. id., *The Concept of the Political*, pp. 87f.
70 Regarding the thesis that a partisan is different from an indignant lone fighter such as Kleist's "Michael Kohlhaas" or "from the noble or ignoble robber baron," see Schmitt, *Theory of the Partisan*, p. 91; for context, cf. Müller, *A Dangerous Mind*, pp. 144–55.
71 Schickel, *Gespräche mit Carl Schmitt*, pp. 25f.
72 Ibid., p. 24, cf. ibid., pp. 87, 183f.; Schmitt, *Theory of the Partisan*, pp. 59, 92.
73 Schickel, *Gespräche mit Carl Schmitt*, p. 85.
74 Schmitt, *Theory of the Partisan*, p. 94. Regarding the distinction between pirate and partisan, see ibid., pp. 70f., and regarding their relationship, cf. Heller-Roazen, *The Enemy of All*, pp. 169f.
75 Schmitt, *Die Tyrannei der Werte*, p. 40.
76 Ibid., pp. 39, 51.
77 Strauss, *Natural Right and History*, p. 166.
78 Strauss, "German Nihilism," pp. 357, 360f.; cf. Altman, "Leo Strauss on 'German Nihilism'"; Steiner, *Weimar in Amerika*, pp. 115–28. The text of Strauss's lecture was published in 1999 but has received little attention from scholars to date.
79 Strauss, "German Nihilism," p. 360.
80 Regarding the "last man," cf. ibid., p. 360; id., *On Tyranny*, pp. 208, 239, 291; id., *Introduction to Political Philosophy*, p. 97; regarding the "new despotism," cf. id., "Notes on Tocqueville."
81 "Correspondence between Karl Löwith and Leo Strauss," p. 183.
82 Strauss, "German Nihilism," p. 358.
83 Bergson, *The Two Sources of Morality and Religion*, pp. 229–34; Popper, *The Open Society and Its Enemies*, Vol. 1, p. 178; Turner, *The Ritual Process*, pp. 109ff. Strauss would return later to his critique of the "open society"; cf. Strauss, *An Introduction to Political Philosophy*, p. 149.
84 Strauss, "German Nihilism," p. 358.
85 Ibid.
86 Carlyle, *Works*, Vol. 13, pp. 266f. (*Latter-Day Pamphlets* [1850]); cf. Schmitt, *The Leviathan*, p. 22.
87 Strauss, "The Living Issues of German Postwar Philosophy," p. 125; Strauss is quoting Yorck von Wartenburg here; cf. Dilthey and Yorck von Wartenburg, *Briefwechsel 1877–1897*, p. 83.
88 Strauss, "German Nihilism," pp. 361f. Here Strauss is alluding to an extremely popular book from the time, *The Century of the Child* by the Swedish educator Ellen Key.
89 Strauss, *Natural Right and History*, pp. 318–23; cf. id., "The Living Issues of German Postwar Philosophy," pp. 123f.; id., *An Introduction to Political Philosophy*, pp. 249–310 ("Progress or Return? The Contemporary Crisis in Western Civilization").
90 Cf., e.g., Strauss, *What Is Political Philosophy?*, pp. 56–77 ("Political Philosophy and History"); id., *An Introduction to Political Philosophy*, pp. 99–124 ("Natural Right and the Historical Approach").
91 Strauss, "German Nihilism," p. 357. Cf. the later comments in id., *On Tyranny*, p. 209; id., *Natural Right and History*, p. 5.
92 Strauss, *The Rebirth of Classical Political Rationalism*, p. 26.
93 Pippin, *Idealism as Modernism*, p. 220.
94 Strauss, "German Nihilism," pp. 358, 371.

NOTES TO PP. 281–5

95 Ibid., pp. 358, 360, 369.
96 "Notes on Carl Schmitt, *The Concept of the Political*," p. 122. Cf. Strauss, *Natural Right and History*, pp. 181f.; regarding Strauss's position on liberalism, cf. Meier, *Carl Schmitt and Leo Strauss: The Hidden Dialogue*, pp. 84ff.
97 Cf. Gauthier, *Morals by Agreement*, pp. 157–70; id., *The Logic of Leviathan*; Hampton, *Hobbes and the Social Contract Tradition*; for context, cf. Vallentyne (ed.), *Contractarianism and Rational Choice*; Gauthier and Sugden (eds.), *Rationality, Justice and the Social Contract*; for a critique, cf. Kraus, *The Limits of Hobbesian Contractarianism*; Hollis, *Trust Within Reason*, pp. 95–8.
98 Regarding the argument against the supremacy of "self-preservation," see Strauss, *An Introduction to Political Philosophy*, p. 93; id., *Natural Right and History*, p. 292.
99 Strauss, *What Is Political Philosophy?*, p. 194; regarding "charity," cf. PPH 116. Regarding Strauss's moral-philosophical interpretation of Hobbes, cf. Altini, "Hobbes in der Weimarer Republik," pp. 26–30.
100 Strauss, *What Is Political Philosophy?*, p. 194.
101 Cf. McCormick, "Fear, Technology, and the State," p. 629.
102 Cf. Strauss, "Notes on Carl Schmitt, *The Concept of the Political*," pp. 118f.
103 Strauss, *Natural Right and History*, pp. 286f. Cf. Pippin, *Idealism as Modernism*, pp. 215f.: "He [...] asserts that such a reconcilation [among all citizens] based on enlightened self-interest founders on the gang-of-robbers problem, or that the position must recommend non-cooperation and active defection when the risk of detection is low."
104 Strauss, *Spinoza's Critique of Religion*, p. 96.
105 Strauss, *The City and Man*, p. 6.
106 Strauss, *Thoughts on Machiavelli*, p. 279.
107 Hobbes, *Man and Citizen: De Homine and De Cive*, p. 40 (*De homine*, X.3)/*Opera*, Vol. II, p. 91; cf. Strauss, PPH 9.
108 Regarding Strauss's letter to Löwith, cf., e.g., Altman, "The Alpine Limits of Jewish Thought," p. 17.
109 Strauss, *An Introduction to Political Philosophy*, p. 344, cf. ibid., p. 98.
110 Strauss, "Notes on Carl Schmitt, *The Concept of the Political*," pp. 108–15. Schmitt himself alternates between "evil" and "dangerous"; see Schmitt, *The Concept of the Political*, p. 58.
111 Strauss, "Notes on Carl Schmitt, *The Concept of the Political*," p. 122.
112 Strauss, *An Introduction to Political Philosophy*, p. 327.
113 Strauss, *Thoughts on Machiavelli*, p. 283. The state itself becomes evil when it ceases to gear itself toward "truth" and instead delivers itself up to the selective "love" of a ruler for his subjects, a "subpolitical" lobby, or the interests of a single class, for example; Strauss, *On Tyranny*, p. 199; id., *An Introduction to Political Philosophy*, p. 149; regarding Marx's reduction of the state to class interests, cf. HCR 139.
114 Strauss, *An Introduction to Political Philosophy*, p. 325.
115 Strauss, *What is Political Philosophy?*, pp. 280f.
116 Strauss, "German Nihilism," p. 358.
117 Strauss, *The City and Man*, pp. 5, 7; cf. id., *Persecution and the Art of Writing*, p. 34; id., *What Is Political Philosophy?*, p. 23.
118 Strauss, *An Introduction to Political Philosophy*, p. 344.
119 Strauss, *On Tyranny*, pp. 209, 200.
120 Strauss, *An Introduction to Political Philosophy*, p. 345; id., *On Tyranny*, p. 206.
121 Strauss, *On Tyranny*, pp. 201, 196.
122 Ibid., p. 196; id., *An Introduction to Political Philosophy*, pp. 316, 318; regarding Strauss's "skepticism," cf. Smith, "Leo Strauss's Platonic Liberalism," p. 800; on the other hand, the fact that Strauss cannot be reduced solely to this defensive interpretation is demonstrated by Wallach, "Smith, Strauss, and Platonic Liberalism," p. 428.
123 Strauss, *The Rebirth of Classical Political Rationalism*, pp. 13–18.

124 Strauss, *An Introduction to Political Philosophy*, pp. 91f.
125 Dewey, *The Middle Works*, Vol. 14, p. 193 (*Human Nature and Conduct*); cf. Rorty, *Truth and Progress*, p. 207.
126 Strauss, *What Is Political Philosophy?*, p. 38.
127 Emerson, *Essays & Lectures*, p. 261.
128 Schelsky, "Das Freiheitswollen der Völker und die Idee des Planstaates," p. 14.
129 Strauss, *What Is Political Philosophy?*, p. 38.
130 Strauss, *An Introduction to Political Philosophy*, pp. 323–9.
131 Schelsky, *Sozialistische Lebenshaltung*, pp. 10f., 47f.
132 Regarding the early revolutionary interpretation of National Socialism, cf. Hans Freyer, *Revolution von rechts*; regarding the late praise for restoration, cf. Schelsky, *Auf der Suche nach Wirklichkeit*, pp. 405–14 ("Über das Restaurative in unserer Zeit").
133 Schelsky's interpretation of Hobbes is, at best, treated as an afterthought to the Schmitt and Strauss discussion; cf. Palaver, "Carl Schmitt, mythologue politique," pp. 202–6; Meier, *The Lesson of Carl Schmitt*, pp. 111–15; Rottleuthner, "Leviathan oder Behemoth?", pp. 259–65.
134 Schelsky, *Sozialistische Lebenshaltung*, pp. 10f., 22.
135 Ibid., p. 41; cf. Hitler, *Mein Kampf*, p. 423.
136 Schelsky, *Sozialistische Lebenshaltung*, pp. 30–2. Regarding the state as a "means to an end," cf. Hitler, *Mein Kampf*, p. 393; cf. also ibid., p. 383. Regarding other references to Hitler and Goebbels, cf. Schelsky, *Sozialistische Lebenshaltung*, pp. 14, 20, 24, 25, 28, 30, 35, 41.
137 Regarding this fusion, cf. Thomä, "Heidegger und der Nationalsozialismus," p. 116.
138 Schelsky, *Sozialistische Lebenshaltung*, p. 27.
139 Schelsky, *Rückblicke eines "Anti-Soziologen,"* pp. 23, 147.
140 Regarding the "violence of *action*" in German idealism and in the case of Hitler, see Gehlen, *Gesamtausgabe*, Vol. 2, pp. 356f.; cf. Thomä, "The Difficulty of Democracy," pp. 79–84.
141 Regarding the "will to power" and Nietzsche: TH 31, 33, 88, 93, 119, 121, 127–9. Regarding the pragmatism of John Dewey and William James, see TH 35f., 142, 158f., 161, 163, 167f., 182, 189, 429, 422, 433, 441.
142 For an argument against the assumption that man's nature is weak, cf. TH 117; for an argument against the assumption that man's nature is evil or "bad," cf. TH 26, as well as Schelsky, "Die Totalität des Staates bei Hobbes," p. 185. For an argument against the premise of a "positive communal drive," cf. TH 111.
143 Schelsky, "Die Totalität des Staates bei Hobbes," p. 186.
144 "The Jewish scholar Leo Strauss" is repeatedly criticized by Schelsky, but he is also praised for his "important insights" (TH 217f., 263, 281, 316, 323). Carl Schmitt is Schelsky's most important point of reference, but he is often mentioned with critical intent (TH 117, 354, 393, 398, 400, 402ff., 417, 426, 434). After Schmitt published his essay on "The State as Mechanism in Hobbes and Descartes" in 1936–7, Schelsky responded with his essay on "The Totality of the State in Hobbes" in 1937–8, to which Schmitt responded in turn with his *Leviathan* book.
145 Schmitt, *Der Wert des Staates und die Bedeutung des Einzelnen*, p. 93.
146 Cf. Hobbes, *Man and Citizen: De Homine and De Cive*, p. 60 (*De homine*, XII.9)/ *Opera*, Vol. II, p. 109.
147 Smend, "Constitution and Constitutional Law," p. 215.
148 Schelsky is referring here to Dewey, *The Middle Works*, Vol. 14, p. 136 (*Human Nature and Conduct*): "A passionate activity learns to work itself up."
149 This is why the defenders of negative liberty latch on to Hobbes, and its critics turn against him; cf. Berlin, *Liberty*, pp. 73, 173; by contrast, cf. Taylor, "What's wrong with negative liberty," pp. 211ff.
150 For a similar view, cf. Rottleuthner, "Leviathan oder Behemoth?", pp. 260f.

151 Schelsky, "Das Freiheitswollen der Völker und die Idee des Planstaates," p. 79; regarding the state and individual, cf. ibid., pp. 21f., 29, 40, 42, 46, 56, 73.

152 Schelsky, "Das Freiheitswollen der Völker und die Idee des Planstaates," pp. 15f., 84; he quotes Dewey, *The Middle Works*, Vol. 14, p. 194 (*Human Nature and Conduct*): "All moral judgment is experimental and subject to revision."

153 Schelsky, "Das Freiheitswollen der Völker und die Idee des Planstaates," p. 26. Cf. ibid., pp. 40, 48, 51–5.

154 Ibid., p. 53, cf. ibid., pp. 16f.

155 Ibid., pp. 64, 88. Regarding *Daseinsfürsorge* ("public welfare") and *Daseinsvorsorge* ("public services"), cf. ibid., pp. 43, 64; Schelsky, *Die skeptische Generation*, p. 460. The model for the shift from the "total state" to "social provisions" is Forsthoff, *Der totale Staat*; id., "Einleitung: Die Daseinsvorsorge in heutiger Sicht." Regarding the "integration responsibility" of the state as the fulfillment of the "vital and cultural needs" of citizens, cf. Schelsky, *Auf der Suche nach Wirklichkeit*, pp. 43f.; Smend, "Constitution and Constitutional Law," pp. 217f.

156 Regarding the influence of Smend and Schmitt after 1945, see Günther, *Denken vom Staat her*, and Müller, *A Dangerous Mind*, pp. 63–75; regarding Kelsen's marginalization, see Möllers, *Der vermisste Leviathan*, p. 32.

157 It was Schelsky's depoliticization strategy that Schmitt opposed after 1945; see *Der Leviathan*, p. 174 ("Die vollendete Reformation" [1965]).

158 Schelsky, *Die skeptische Generation*, p. 74; cf. his later sneering critique of Ernst Bloch as a "moved youth" who proclaimed "immaturity" to be a "life principle," Schelsky, *Die Hoffnung Blochs*, p. 110.

159 Mannheim, *Diagnosis of Our Time*, pp. 36, 46, 48, partially quoted in Schelsky, *Die skeptische Generation*, p. 28.

160 Schelsky, *Die skeptische Generation*, p. 60, cf. ibid., p. 48.

161 Freyer, *Revolution von rechts*, p. 16.

162 Schelsky, *Die skeptische Generation*, pp. 83, 92f., 164, 458, cf. ibid., p. 451.

163 Ibid., pp. 451–5, cf. p. 463. Schelsky bases his argument on the analysis of "passive consumership" in Riesman, *The Lonely Crowd*, p. 190.

164 Schelsky, *Auf der Suche nach Wirklichkeit*, p. 410.

165 Schelsky, *Die skeptische Generation*, p. 164.

166 Ibid., p. 455, with a reference to Riesman, *The Lonely Crowd*, p. 171.

167 Gehlen, *Moral und Hypermoral*, p. 110. In Gehlen's work, this is intended to be an explicit objection to Schelsky.

168 Cf. Poiger, *Jazz, Rock, and Rebels*, pp. 71–105.

169 MacInnes, *Absolute Beginners*; regarding this book, cf. the impressive early essays by Stuart Hall, "Absolute Beginnings: Reflections on the Secondary Modern Generation" and "Politics of Adolescence?".

170 Regarding the statistical and historical facts, cf. Kaiser, *Randalierende Jugend*, pp. 24–7, 102–4; Bondy et al., *Jugendliche stören die Ordnung*.

171 This characterization, which dates back to the early twentieth century, is found in Schultz, *Die Halbstarken*, p. 7, cf. ibid., p. 33: "These *Halbstarken* [. . .] form a mob, they are a dreadful, terrifying power, especially in metropolitan life; a sludge that sinks more and more to the bottom."

172 Weisenborn, *Die Barbaren*, pp. 66, 178. The "barbarian of the present day" is, of course, an allusion to Nietzsche's "new barbarians" (*The Will to Power*, 478); regarding earlier discussion of barbarians, see p. 205. Regarding various Hobbes motifs, including the "war of all against all," cf. Weisenborn, *Die Barbaren*, pp. 8, 33f., 231f.

173 Muchow, "Zur Psychologie und Pädagogik der 'Halbstarken,'" p. 446; Muchow's strong influence can be seen in Schelsky, *Die skeptische Generation*, pp. 493–508. Regarding Muchow, cf. Peukert, "Die 'Halbstarken,'" p. 544; Poiger, *Jazz, Rock, and Rebels*, pp. 96f. With the "reversion to a wild type," Muchow is doing what few other people did at the time and making explicit reference to Elias, *The Civilizing Process*.

174 Muchow, "Zur Psychologie und Pädagogik der Halbstarken," p. 445.
175 Schelsky, *Die skeptische Generation*, p. 495.
176 Ibid., p. 497.
177 Kluth, "Die 'Halbstarken' – Legende oder Wirklichkeit?", p. 496.
178 Quoted in Kaiser, *Randalierende Jugend*, pp. 113f.
179 Krüger, "Sprachlose Rebellen?"
180 Cf. Schelsky, *Auf der Suche nach Wirklichkeit*, pp. 347f.
181 Bondy et al., *Jugendliche stören die Ordnung*, p. 71; Kaiser, *Randalierende Jugend*, p. 198.
182 Schelsky, *Die skeptische Generation*, p. 455.
183 Regarding "uselessness" (*Nutzlosigkeit*), cf. Kaiser, *Randalierende Jugend*, p. 39; regarding the "unproductive coexistence" of the *Halbstarken*, cf. Bondy et al., *Jugendliche stören die Ordnung*, p. 85. This unproductive activism can be linked to Bataille's theory of anti-economic "expenditure," see Bataille, "General Economy," p. 167.
184 Schelsky, *Die skeptische Generation*, pp. 488f., 497.
185 Cf. Fischer-Kowalski, *1958-Hooligans and 1968-Students*. Rudi Dutschke, Rainer Langhans, and Benno Ohnesorg, for example, were all born in 1940.
186 Horn and Mitscherlich, "Vom 'halbstarken' zum starken Protest."
187 Arendt, *Crises of the Republic*, p. 203 ("Thoughts on Politics and Revolution").
188 Schelsky, *Auf der Suche nach Wirklichkeit*, p. 411. He allows for a single exception to his general tranquilization thesis – namely, heroic characters who use their "creative capabilities" in the sense of "a vitality situated above institutions" (ibid., pp. 263, 267, 413). These characters recall Strauss's unorthodox "gentleman" and Arnold Gehlen's "meta-routinier"; Gehlen, *Gesamtausgabe*, Vol. 6, p. 253 ("Das Ende der Persönlichkeit" [1956]). What comes to mind here are the "excursions in consciousness" of the artist (Gehlen, *Zeit-Bilder*, p. 205) and the "creative destruction" of the "entrepreneur" (Schumpeter, *Capitalism, Socialism and Democracy*, p. 83).
189 Regarding the relationship between Schelsky and the Frankfurt School, cf. Albrecht et al., *Die intellektuelle Gründung der Bundesrepublik*, pp. 132–88.
190 Adorno's memorandum is reprinted in Kuhr, "Schule und Jugend in einer ausgebombten Stadt," pp. 30f.; cf. the long quote in Schelsky, *Die skeptische Generation*, pp. 307f.
191 Schelsky, *Die skeptische Generation*, pp. 89f. Interestingly, Schelsky refrains from quoting the end of Adorno's text, where Adorno writes that "the phenomenon of political apathy seen so often today is extremely closely related to the social psychology of concretism."
192 Ibid., p. 90; cf. Schelsky, *Auf der Suche nach der Wirklichkeit*, p. 412.
193 Horkheimer, *Critique of Instrumental Reason*, p. 81.
194 Horkheimer, *Critical Theory*, p. 98.
195 Horkheimer, "The Authoritarian State," pp. 96ff., 101ff.
196 Horkheimer, "Postscript" in *Critical Theory*, p. 249.
197 Baeumler, "Einleitung," p. cxviii.
198 Horkheimer, "The Authoritarian State," p. 106.
199 Ibid., p. 103.
200 Horkheimer and Adorno, *Dialectic of Enlightenment*, p. 71.
201 Ibid., pp. 87f.; cf. HGS 12, 274.
202 Horkheimer himself is strangely unaware of the novelty of his troublemaker; in his analysis of fascism, he describes and identifies him with the "ragged mob [Lumpenmob]" criticized by Engels. See BPS 102f., which quotes a letter from September 4, 1870; MECW 44, 63.
203 Regarding "abnégation individuelle," cf. Maistre, *Œuvres complètes*, Vol. 1, pp. 376f.
204 Bellstedt, *Deutsche Weltanschauung*, p. 23.
205 Adorno, *Minima Moralia*, p. 193 (§123).
206 Reich, *The Mass Psychology of Fascism*, p. 63. Horkheimer does not quote this phrase, but Adorno would later speak of a "collective narcissism."

207 Horkheimer, BPS 98; Horkheimer and Adorno, *Dialectic of Enlightenment*, p. 123.

208 A profile of the "chavs" who were primarily held responsible for the protests in England in 2011 can be found in Jones, *Chavs*. Incidentally, one possible etymology of this word has been traced back to the Roma language, in which it is used to describe a wild child. Once again, the *puer robustus* is never far away.

209 Žižek, "Ein Karneval der Underdogs."

210 Horkheimer, "The Authoritarian State," pp. 105, 112.

211 Horkheimer, *Critical Theory*, p. 114 ("Authority and the Family").

212 Letter reprinted in Claussen, *Theodor W. Adorno: One Last Genius*, p. 349.

213 Ibid.; original quote in Habermas, *Theorie und Praxis*, p. 401.

Chapter XI. Good spirits and poisonous weeds: The *puer robustus* in Italy in 1949 and China in 1957

1 Togliatti, "Saluto di Capodanno," p. 1.

2 Regarding this and the following, cf. the contemporary account by Gorresio, *I carissimi nemici*, pp. 332f.

3 Togliatti, "La crisi morale dei giovani italiani," p. 291. He quotes Croce almost verbatim, "Conversazione coi giovani," p. 59. Regarding Croce and the context, cf. La Rovere, *L'eredità del fascismo*, pp. 146–8.

4 Togliatti, "La crisi morale dei giovani italiani," pp. 291f., 302, 293.

5 Ibid., p. 296.

6 Sartre, "Palmiro Togliatti."

7 Goebbels, "Der Faschismus und seine praktischen Ergebnisse," p. 319, cf. 315, 318.

8 Togliatti, "La crisi morale dei giovani italiani," p. 295. Regarding Togliatti's problems in turning fascist youth into communist youth, cf. La Rovere, *L'eredità del fascismo*, p. 236.

9 Pasolini, *Heretical Empiricism*, pp. 150–8.

10 Togliatti, "La crisi morale dei giovani italiani," p. 297.

11 Kierkegaard, *Either/Or*, p. 214; cf. Hegel, PS 119.

12 Togliatti, "La crisi morale dei giovani italiani," p. 306.

13 Heine, *Poetry and Prose*, pp. 244f. (*Germany: A Winter's Tale* [1844], translated by Aaron Kramer).

14 Togliatti, "La crisi morale dei giovani italiani," p. 306.

15 Heine, *Poetry and Prose*, p. 244.

16 Mao explained the "hundred flowers" slogan on various occasions, particularly in speeches from April and May 1956, as well as in January, February, and March 1957; cf. Mao Zedong, *The Writings, 1949–1976*, pp. 66–75 (speech from April 25[?], 1956), pp. 225–45 (speech from January 18, 1957), pp. 308–51 (revised version of speech from February 27, 1957), pp. 351–63 (speech from March 1, 1957), pp. 375–91 (speech from March 12, 1957). Cf. also the important, unedited version of the speech from February 1957 in: MacFarquhar et al. (eds.), *The Secret Speeches of Chairman Mao*, pp. 131–89 ("On the Correct Handling of Contradictions Among the People [Speaking Notes], 27 February 1957"). The content of Mao's speech from May 2, 1956, can only be indirectly reconstructed based on the report by Lu Ting-i (Lu Dingyi), "Let a Hundred Flowers Bloom, Let a Hundred Schools of Thought Contend!" in: Nieh (ed.), *Literature of the Hundred Flowers*, Vol. 1, pp. 19–33, and (in a different translation) in Bowie and Fairbank (eds.), *Communist China 1955–1959*, pp. 151–63. The fact that Lu provides a "very liberal interpretation of Mao's views" is demonstrated by Solomon, *Mao's Revolution and the Chinese Political Culture*, pp. 277–82.

17 MacFarquhar, *The Origins of the Cultural Revolution 1*, pp. 189–99.

18 Mao, *The Writings, 1949–1976*, pp. 386f.

19 Ibid, pp. 417, 312, cf. ibid., pp. 54, 316.

20 Cf. Schwarcz, *The Chinese Enlightenment*, pp. 276–82; MacFarquhar (ed.), *The Hundred Flowers*, pp. 130, 133, 169.
21 Hua Sheng, "Big Character Posters in China," p. 237.
22 MacFarquhar (ed.), *The Hundred Flowers*, p. 134. Copious materials and commentary can be found in: ibid., pp. 3–32, 132–41; id., *The Origins of the Cultural Revolution 1*, pp. 51–6; René Goldman, *The Rectification Campaign of May–June 1957 and the Student Movement at Peking University*; id., "The Rectification Campaign at Peking University: May–June 1957"; Merle Goldman, "Mao's Obsession with the Political Role of Literature and the Intellectuals," pp. 39–58; Spence, *The Search for Modern China*, pp. 568–72; Arkush, "Introduction," pp. xx–xxvi; Solomon, *Mao's Revolution and the Chinese Political Culture*, pp. 277–329; Schwarcz, *The Chinese Enlightenment*, pp. 276–82; Kraus, "Let a Hundred Flowers Blossom, Let a Hundred Schools of Thought Contend."
23 Regarding the dating of the student protests, cf. Goldman, "The Rectification Campaign," p. 141; MacFarquhar, *The Origins of the Cultural Revolution 1*, p. 218; Spence, *The Search for Modern China*, p. 570. An article in *Renmin Ribao* from June 8, 1957, marks the end of the movement; see Yen-lin, "The Witch-Hunting Vanguard," p. 400.
24 Quoted in Rong Di, ["The days of the campaigns for rectification and against rightists at Peking University"]; translated from Chinese into German by Giorgio Strafella and Fu Manli.
25 Regarding the number of victims, cf. MacFarquahar, *The Origins of the Cultural Revolution 1*, p. 314; Teiwes, *Politics and Purges in China*, p. 291.
26 I have used the internationally established pinyin system to romanize Tan Tianrong and other Chinese names. Different spellings are sometimes found in earlier publications, such as T'an T'ien-yung, Tan Tien-jung, etc. In the bibliographical list of authors, however, I have used the spellings found in the original publication.
27 MacFarquhar (ed.), *The Hundred Flowers*, pp. 38f.
28 Mao, *The Writings, 1949–1976*, p. 70.
29 Ibid., p. 727. Regarding "disorder," cf. also ibid., p. 404.
30 The idea that the hundred schools of thought should form a "symphony" with a single "melody" was put forth by Kuo Mo-jo (Guo Moruo) on July 1, 1956. By contrast, an anonymous commentator remarked on July 21, 1956, that "all the various schools ought to create their own music, and not just play according to the music indicated by the conductor"; cf. Solomon, *Mao's Revolution and the Chinese Political Culture*, pp. 283f., and Teiwes, *Politics and Purges in China*, pp. 222f. In April 1957, Ch'u An-p'ing opposed the idea of the party bringing about "a one-family empire"; Goldman, *Literary Dissent in Communist China*, p. 192.
31 Cf. Mao, *The Writings, 1949–1976*, p. 238, note 38.
32 Makarenko, *A Book for Parents*, pp. 21f.; id., *Werke*, Vol. 1, p. 592.
33 Baudelaire chose a different order for the poems in the 1861 edition of *Les Fleurs du Mal* than in the first edition from 1857. He gave up the earlier sequence, which led through Hell to God. Regarding Satan and God in Baudelaire, cf. Bataille, *Literature and Evil*, pp. 35ff.
34 Cf. Yen-lin, "The Witch-Hunting Vanguard," p. 397.
35 Mao, *The Writings, 1949–1976*, p. 594, cf. ibid., p. 626.
36 Regarding this concern, cf. the article in *Renmin Ribao* dated April 21, 1957, by Chien Potsan, quoted in MacFarquhar (ed.), *The Hundred Flowers*, p. 28; for similar opinions from Shen Chih-yuan, cf. ibid., p. 30, and Goldman, *The Rectification Campaign of May–June 1957*, p. 25. Kraus argues that the criminalization strategy was only implemented in the later struggle against so-called rightists, cf. Kraus, "Let a Hundred Flowers Blossom, Let a Hundred Schools of Thought Contend," p. 256; for a similar argument, cf. Goldman, *The Rectification Campaign of May–June 1957*, pp. 72–85 ("Trap or Mistake?").

411

37 Mao, *The Writings, 1949–1976*, pp. 353, 428.
38 Ibid., p. 263.
39 Regarding Stalin and the lack of openness to "contradictions" in the Soviet Union, cf. Mao, *The Writings, 1949–1976*, pp. 253, 440, 465. Regarding Hungary, cf. ibid., pp. 263, 336, 640.
40 Ibid., p. 387.
41 Ibid., p. 243.
42 Ibid., p. 279, cf. ibid., pp. 253, 261.
43 Ibid., p. 404.
44 Ibid., pp. 234, 243, 304, 594.
45 Ibid., p. 332, cf. ibid., p. 356.
46 Schickel, *Gespräche mit Carl Schmitt*, p. 18.
47 MacFarquhar et al. (eds.), *The Secret Speeches of Chairman Mao*, p. 122 (speech in Yinian Tang, January 16, 1957). On May 13, 1957, Mao said: "While disturbances have their bad aspect, they also have a good side" (Mao, *The Writings, 1949–1976*, p. 544). In the version of the speech from February 27, 1957, published on June 19, after the start of the anti-rightist campaign, Mao toned down this call for openness: "We do not approve of disturbances [. . .]. But this is not to say that there is no more possibility for the masses to create disturbances in our country"; Mao, *The Writings, 1949–1976*, pp. 335f.
48 MacFarquhar et al. (eds.), *The Secret Speeches of Chairman Mao*, p. 165 ("On the Correct Handling of Contradictions Among the People [Speaking Notes], 27 February 1957").
49 Mao's praise for "unrest" is quoted in Badiou, *Metapolitics*, p. 132.
50 Mao, *The Writings, 1949–1976*, pp. 330, 333.
51 Ibid., p. 330; for the original version, cf. MacFarquhar et al. (eds.), *The Secret Speeches of Chairman Mao*, p. 166.
52 Mao, *The Writings, 1949–1976*, p. 330.
53 Ibid., p. 311.
54 Ibid., p. 332.
55 This talk of the elimination of enemies can be found in a variant on his speech from January 27, 1957; Mao, *The Writings, 1949–1976*, p. 287.
56 Deng Xiaoping, Mao's eventual successor who, in 1957, was responsible for the "rectification campaign" in his role as General Secretary of the Party's Central Committee, mentioned a long list of various internal enemies in his "Report" of September 1957; see Bowie and Fairbank (eds.), *Communist China 1955–1959*, p. 343. Part of this report is taken verbatim from Mao's text "The Situation in the Summer of 1957"; cf. Mao, *The Writings, 1949–1976*, pp. 653, 657.
57 Quoted in Doolin (ed.), *Communist China: The Politics of Student Opposition*, pp. 14f.
58 Merleau-Ponty, *Adventures of the Dialectic*, pp. 206f./*Les Aventures de la Dialectique*, pp. 278f.
59 Mao, *The Writings, 1949–1976*, p. 603, cf. ibid., p. 622.
60 Regarding "bloody and in no way limited social expenditure," cf. Bataille, "General Economy," p. 172.
61 Schmitt, *The Concept of the Political*, p. 46.
62 The following quotes are taken from Yu Hua, *Brothers*, pp. 67, 89, 111, 161, 125.
63 I am indebted to Giorgio Strafella and Fu Manli for their German translation of Tan's wall newspaper. The text of the wall newspaper has been published in Chinese in Anon. (ed.), [*A collection of articles criticizing Tan Tianrong and other rightists*], pp. 71–3. The location and circumstances of the publication of Tan's newspaper have been described by contemporary witness Rong Di, ["The days of the campaigns for rectification and against rightists at Peking University"] (translated into German by Fu Manli and Giorgio Strafella). Accounts have come down to us from two other

eyewitnesses as well: Goldman, "The Rectification Campaign," p. 142; id., *The Rectification Campaign of May–June 1957 and the Student Movement at Peking University*, pp. 23f.; Tang Chu-kuo, *The Student Anti-communist Movement in Peiping: A Participant's Report on the Movement in May, 1957*, pp. 12f.

64 Tan found the Heraclitus quote in Hegel's *Lectures on the History of Philosophy*; see *Lectures on the History of Philosophy*, Vol. 1, p. 279. The first volume of these lectures was published in Chinese in 1956, cf. Müller, *Die chinesischsprachige Hegel-Rezeption von 1902 bis 2000*, p. 46. Tan reverses the meaning of the lines from Heraclitus; while Heraclitus views the seizure of power by the young as a punishment, it is an act of liberation from the perspective of the students in Beijing.

65 In his text ["The theory that there are two aspects to everything"], Tan dates "revisionism" to the period after Engels' death and "dogmatism" to the period after Lenin's death; cf. Anon. (ed.), [*A collection of reactionary statements among rightists at Peking University*], p. 34 (translated into German by Wei-Hsin Lin and Giorgio Strafella).

66 Tan is referring here to a comment directed at Stalin in a newspaper article from December 1956; cf. Editorial Department of *Renmin Ribao*, "More on the Historical Experience of the Dictatorship of the Proletariat," p. 37.

67 Wei Wei was a Chinese writer who published an essay in 1954 on "Spring," to which Tan is probably referring here.

68 Xu Jin was a Chinese librettist who was criticized for individualistic tendencies. Tan refers to this controversy in his text "What are we fighting for?"; see Anon. (ed.), [*A collection of reactionary statements among rightists at Peking University*], p. 43 (translated into German by Wei-Hsin Lin, Giorgio Strafella and Fu Manli).

69 Li Zhengdao and Yang Zhenning, two Chinese-born physicists working in the USA, conducted experiments with cobalt, to which Tan is alluding when he mentions metal layers and cylinders. They were awarded the Nobel Prize in 1957.

70 The "three virtues" to which Tan refers are the three criteria according to which students at Peking University were evaluated: ideological attitude, diligence, and physical health. I would like to thank Giorgio Strafella for this explanation.

71 Rong Di, ["The days of the campaigns for rectification and against rightists at Peking University"]. Regarding Engels, see p. 197.

72 Regarding Lin Xiling, Liu Jisheng, and his own wall newspaper, cf. ibid. The statement by a "liberal" quoted by Lin Xiling is frequently attributed to Voltaire, but the words were probably put into Voltaire's mouth by his biographer, Evelyn Beatrice Hall. Regarding Lin Xiling, cf. Pan, *Out of Mao's Shadow*, p. 59. Two speeches by Lin Xiling from May 23 and 30, 1957, are reprinted in Doolin (ed.), *Communist China: The Politics of Student Opposition*, pp. 23–42. The following sentences stand out: "Genuine socialism should be very democratic, but ours is undemocratic" (ibid., p. 27); "To feel dissatisfied with reality, I believe, is a good thing. [...] Society is progressive. If we are satisfied with the existing society, there will be no further development" (pp. 36f.).

73 Tan Tianrong, ["Save your souls"] in: Anon. (ed.), [*A collection of reactionary statements among rightists at Peking University*], pp. 38f. (translated into German by Wei-Hsin Lin and Giorgio Strafella).

74 Tan Tianrong, ["What are we fighting for? Another letter to Shen Zenyi"] in: Anon. (ed.), [*A collection of reactionary statements among rightists at Peking University*], p. 45.

75 Regarding "democracy and freedom," ibid. p. 45. It is false to call Tan Tianrong "the first Red Guard," as Granqvist does, cf. *The Red Guard*, p. 39.

76 The following quotes are found in Tan Tianrong, ["Fragmentary thoughts on May Fourth"] in: Anon. (ed.), [*A collection of reactionary statements among rightists at Peking University*], p. 52 (translated into German by Giorgio Strafella). A partial English translation of this text can be found in Schwarcz, *Chinese Enlightenment*, p. 281.

77 MacFarquhar (ed.), *The Hundred Flowers*, pp. 168–70.

78 Ibid., p. 12.
79 After the Hundred Flowers movement, Lin Zhao was imprisoned all the years leading up to her death. In 2004, Tan Tianrong gave a speech at her grave, in which he said: "The blood of a fragile woman is raising the consciousness of a nation" (quoted in Jin Zhong, "In Search of the Soul of Lin Zhao," pp. 90f.). Regarding Lin's tragic story, cf. Pan, *Out of Mao's Shadow*, pp. 49–79, esp. p. 53, with a testimony from Tan Tianrong: "She said to me, 'I was laughing in my heart the whole time, laughing at the party's insanity' [. . .]. Back then, I only felt suffering. I wasn't like her. It never occurred to me the party had gone insane."
80 Mao, *The Writings 1949–1976*, pp. 602, 605.
81 MacFarquahar (ed.), *The Hundred Flowers*, p. 171.
82 Cf. the various documents in Anon. (ed.), [*A collection of articles criticizing Tan Tianrong and other rightists*], pp. 42, 44f., 51 (translated into German by Giorgio Strafella). Excerpts from three inflammatory articles attacking Tan are also reprinted in MacFarquahar (ed.), *The Hundred Flowers*, pp. 135–40.
83 Quoted in Schwarcz, *Chinese Enlightenment*, p. 281.
84 Wang, "Discovering Xingkaihu," pp. 272f., 275, 280f., 290; id., *The Great Northern Wilderness*, pp. 93–100, 133–5.
85 Ai Ch'ing [Ai Qing], "The Gardener's Dream" in: Nieh (ed.), *Literature of the Hundred Flowers*, Vol. II, pp. 276f. Regarding his role during the Hundred Flowers movement, cf. Goldman, *Literary Dissent in Communist China*, pp. 174–6.
86 Regarding these camps and their locations, cf. Wang, *The Great Northern Wilderness*, pp. 66–92.
87 Schwiedrzik, *Literaturfrühling in China?*, p. 115.
88 Regarding Deng's role after Mao's death in the rehabilitation of the victims of the Hundred Flowers movement, cf. Kraus, "Let a Hundred Flowers Blossom, Let a Hundred Schools of Thought Contend," pp. 259–61. Ideas from the Hundred Flowers movement began to be put into action again around 1978, such as the "wall of democracy," cf. Benton, "China Spring," pp. 6–10.
89 Schwiedrzik, *Literaturfrühling in China?*, p. 122.
90 Barrett, "Ai Weiwei: Sunflower Seeds," p. 343.
91 I cannot address the relationship between the Cultural Revolution and the Hundred Flowers movement in detail here; regarding the differences, cf. Solomon, *Mao's Revolution and the Chinese Political Culture*, p. 328.
92 For a polemic retrospective, cf. Wolin, *The Wind from the East*. For a more sympathetic description of Badiou's Maoism, cf. Hallward, *Badiou*, pp. 29–48.
93 The weakness of the Hundred Flowers movement is criticized in Badiou, *The Rebirth of History*, p. 79; cf. id., *The Communist Hypothesis*, p. 157.
94 Badiou, *The Century*, p. 110.
95 Badiou, *Metapolitics*, p. 19.
96 Rancière describes this situation by contrasting "politics" and "police" (*Disagreement*, pp. 21ff.). Regarding the different versions of this thesis, cf. Marchart, *Post-Foundational Political Thought*.
97 Lenin, "On the Question of Dialectics," p. 358; Mao, *The Writings, 1949–1976*, pp. 253, 317, 465.
98 Cf. Badiou, *Metapolitics*, p. 24.
99 Badiou, *The Rebirth of History*, pp. 111f.
100 Regarding the "popular event," cf. ibid., p. 94; regarding the critique of representation with reference to Rousseau, cf. id., *Circonstances 1*, pp. 41–3; cf. id., *The Communist Hypothesis*, pp. 29f., 152f.
101 Badiou, *The Communist Hypothesis*, p. 113.
102 Badiou, *The Century*, p. 60.
103 Regarding a "state in the process of withering away," cf. Badiou, *The Rebirth of History*, pp. 65f., 82; id., *Metapolitics*, p. 79. Also see id., *Being and Event*, pp. 110f.

104 Badiou, *The Century*, p. 62. Regarding the "popular mass uprisings," the "hundreds of new organizations, thousands of newspapers, giant posters, constant meetings and countless clashes" as signs of "freedom," cf. Badiou, "Letter from Alain Badiou to Slavoj Žižek," pp. 275f. Badiou's talk of freedom here is simply cynical.
105 Badiou is occasionally critical of the Cultural Revolution and concedes that it ended in "failure" (ibid., p. 276). But he attributes this failure to the fact that the control of the "party-state" impeded "the positive creation of the new" that he entrusts to "revolutionary shock groups" (Badiou, *The Communist Hypothesis*, pp. 130f., 154).
106 Badiou, *The Rebirth of History*, p. 66.
107 Badiou, *The Communist Hypothesis*, p. 122.
108 Badiou, "Letter from Alain Badiou to Slavoj Žižek," pp. 272f.
109 Badiou, *The Century*, p. 63.
110 Regarding the "enthusiasm" of those who witness revolution, cf. Kant, *Political Writings*, p. 182. ("The Contest of Faculties"); regarding the "enthusiasm" of the revolutionaries themselves, cf. Badiou, *The Communist Hypothesis*, pp. 3, 46.
111 Badiou, *The Rebirth of History*, p. 62.
112 Quoted in Dotzauer, "Ich glaube an radikale Akte."
113 Žižek, "Introduction: Mao Tse-tung, the Marxist Lord of Misrule," p. 25.
114 Ibid., p. 20.
115 Spence, *Mao Zedong*, pp. xii–xiv.
116 Regarding the role of the "Lord of Misrule" during carnival, the short-lived counterworld to the existing order, see Bakhtin, *Rabelais and His World*, pp. 196–9; cf. also Bergeron, "'Richard II' and Carnival Politics"; Bristol, *Carnival and Theater*, pp. 66f.; Burke, *Popular Culture in Early Modern Europe*, pp. 97, 154, 268; Davis, "The Reasons of Misrule: Youth Groups and Charivaris in Sixteenth-Century France," p. 57. Regarding the topicality of this character, cf. Keller, "The Lord of Misrule: Eminem and the Rabelaisian Carnival."
117 Žižek, "Introduction," p. 26. Far removed from Žižek, Jonathan Noble traces the history of the *liumang* (most often translated as "hooligans") to make a connection between the Red Guards of the Cultural Revolution and the power-hungry lone wolves of China today; see Noble, "Wang Shuo and the Commercialization of Literature," p. 599.
118 Yi Shuihan, quoted in Barmé, *In the Red*, pp. 65f.
119 He Xin, quoted in Barmé, *In the Red*, pp. 265f.

Chapter XII. The *puer robustus* today

1 Schumpeter, *Capitalism, Socialism and Democracy*, pp. 81–6; Nietzsche, NCW 8, 34, 127 (*Beyond Good and Evil*). Regarding the connection between the two authors, cf. Reinert and Reinert, "Creative Destruction in Economics."
2 Fukuyama, "The End of History?", p. 8; regarding the "victory of the VCR," cf. id., *The End of History*, pp. 98–108.
3 This thesis was formulated by Paul Wolfowitz, US Deputy Secretary of Defense at the time, in a speech in Singapore in 2002; Wolfowitz, "The Gathering Storm," p. 678.
4 Samuel Johnson said in 1775: "There are few ways in which a man can be more innocently employed than in getting money." Regarding this and the context for it, cf. Hirschman, *The Passions and the Interests*, p. 58.
5 Florida, *The Rise of the Creative Class*; Boltanski and Chiapello, *The New Spirit of Capitalism*.
6 In a hearing before the US Congress in 2010, Senator Carl Levin asked: "Is there not a conflict when you sell something to somebody, and then are determined to bet against that same security; and you don't disclose that to the person you're selling to?" Blankfein responded: "In the context of market-making, that is not a conflict." Cf. Ferguson, *Inside Job*, p. 40.

7 Swiss Financial Market Supervisory Authority FINMA, *Foreign exchange trading at UBS AG*, p. 19. The criminal practices described in this report took place between 2008 and 2013, i.e., even after the eruption of the financial crisis. This makes the quoted statements all the more depressing.

8 Ferguson, *Inside Job*, p. 32.

9 Quoted in Sorkin, *Too Big to Fail*, pp. 547f.

10 Nicodemus, "Arschlöcher gibt es immer" (interview with Larry Hagman), p. 53.

11 Reuter and Tuma, "Mitgefangen, mitgehangen" (interview with Alexander Dibelius), p. 70.

12 Wiedeking, "Schluss mit dem Götzendienst," p. 8.

13 Thatcher, "Interview for *Woman's Own*."

14 Frank, *Luxury Fever*, pp. 1–13.

15 Mayer, *The Fed*, p. 139. I would like to thank Jakob Thomä for directing me to this quote.

16 Moore, "I'm starting to think that the Left might actually be right."

17 Moore, "Our leaders have lost faith in the powers of their people."

18 Robertson, "Glocalisation," p. 40.

19 Invisible Committee, *The Coming Insurrection*, p. 29.

20 Magnus, "Crisis Convergence."

21 Thumann and Assheuer, "Demokratie stiftet keine Identität" (interview with Francis Fukuyama), p. 50.

22 For an argument against the fixation on democratic institutions, cf. the critique by Ogien and Laugier, *Le principe démocratie*, pp. 69, 78.

23 Regarding the "democratic crisis" which "permit[s] a new re-engagement," cf. Crouch, *Postdemocracy*, p. 12; regarding "self-critical democracies," cf. Rosanvallon, *Counter-Democracy*, pp. 150ff.

24 Songwe, "Food, Financial Crises, and Complex Derivatives," p. 3.

25 Hoyng and Schmitz, "Wo bleibt der Aufstand von links?" (interview with Francis Fukuyama), p. 86; Piketty, *Capital in the Twenty-First Century*, p. 26.

26 Cf. Crouch, *Postdemocracy*, p. 4.

27 Streeck, *Buying Time*, pp. 79f.

28 Benhabib, *The Rights of Others*, pp. 183–98.

29 Invisible Committee, *The Coming Insurrection*, p. 36; cf. Tiqqun, *Preliminary Materials for a Theory of the Young-Girl*, p. 13.

30 *Association pour la Taxation des Transactions financière et l'Aide aux Citoyens* (Association for the Taxation of Financial Transactions and Aid to Citizens), an international activist organization established in France in 1998 which supports financial market regulation and fair trade.

31 Invisible Committee, *The Coming Insurrection*, pp. 24f.

32 Balibar, *Equaliberty*, pp. 251ff./"Uprisings in the *banlieues*," pp. 62, 64.

33 Žižek, *Against the Double Blackmail*, p. 39.

34 Economist Intelligence Unit, *Rebels Without a Cause*, p. 6; Žižek, "The Violent Silence of a New Beginning"; Agamben, *The Coming Community*, p. 85. (Agamben means this as a compliment, however.)

35 Tiqqun, *Preliminary Materials for a Theory of the Young-Girl*, p. 114.

36 Žižek, "Use Your Illusions."

37 Hirschman, *Shifting Involvements*, pp. 89f.; regarding "exit" and "voice," cf. ibid., pp. 62ff.

38 Obama did not come up with this line himself, by the way; he probably took it from a poem written in 1978: Jordan, "Poem for South African Women" in *Directed by Desire*, p. 279.

39 Cf. Connolly, *A World of Becoming*.

40 Thoreau, "Walden; or, Life in the Woods," p. 459; cf. Cavell, *This New Yet Unapproachable America*, p. 36.

41 Honig, *Emergency Politics*, p. 15.
42 Graeber, "Occupy's liberation from liberalism."
43 Graeber, "Occupy and anarchism's gift of democracy."
44 Ibid.
45 Quoted in Graeber, "Occupy's liberation from liberalism."
46 Ibid. An absurd exaggeration of this vision can be found in The Invisible Committee, *The Coming Insurrection*, p. 101: "Why shouldn't communes proliferate everywhere?".
47 Žižek, "The Violent Silence of a New Beginning"; ibid., "Occupy Wall Street, Or, The Violent Silence of a New Beginning." The Žižek quotes in the following which are not individually cited, as well as the Applebaum quotes, have been taken from the latter publication.
48 Regarding the "democratic fiction," cf. also Žižek, *Living in the End Times*, p. 444.
49 Žižek is referring to Badiou, *Metapolitics*, p. xxviii.
50 Žižek, *Living in the End Times*, pp. 416, 452, cf. also ibid., pp. 438, 481, as well as id., "Occupy Wall Street," p. 88.
51 Laclau, "Structure, History and the Political," p. 206.
52 Žižek, *Against the Double Blackmail*, pp. 18f.
53 Quoted in McKee, *Strike Art*, p. 85.
54 Butler, *Notes Toward a Performative Theory of Assembly*, p. 2.
55 Ibid., p. 170.
56 Rosanvallon, *Le peuple introuvable*.
57 Butler, *Notes Toward a Performative Theory of Assembly*, p. 20. Her analysis of *We, the people* has naturally been influenced by Derrida, "Declarations of Independence."
58 Butler, *Notes Toward a Performative Theory of Assembly*, pp. 134f.
59 Ibid, p. 3.
60 Regarding "identity in progress" as a fluctuation between subversion and institution, cf. Colliot-Thélène, "Pour une politique des droits subjectifs," pp. 250f. Regarding the productive tension between the "juridico-political form" of democracy and the "power of the people," cf. Rancière, *Hatred of Democracy*, p. 54. Regarding the conflict between "insurrection" and "constitution," cf. Balibar, *Equaliberty*, p. 53.
61 Butler, *Notes Toward a Performative Theory of Assembly*, p. 20.
62 Ibid., p. 105.
63 Arendt, *The Human Condition*, p. 198; id., *Origins of Totalitarianism*, pp. 272, 296; cf. Butler, *Notes Toward a Performative Theory of Assembly*, pp. 73, 80. Regarding the genesis of the entanglement of human and civil rights in the French Revolution, cf. Colliot-Thélène, *Democracy and Subjective Rights*, p. 61.
64 Cf. Mouffe, *The Democratic Paradox*, pp. 4f.; Benhabib, *The Rights of Others*, pp. 43–8; Balibar, *Equaliberty*, p. 284, cf. ibid. pp. 1f., 9–12; Honig, *Emergency Politics*, pp. 15–39; Colliot-Thélène, *Democracy and Subjective Rights*, p. 87; Brown, *Walled States, Waning Sovereignty*, p. 51.
65 Regarding "plasticité," see Colliot-Thélène, "Pour une politique des droits subjectifs," p. 250; regarding the "'fluid' conception of the identity of the *demos*," see id., *Democracy and Subjective Rights*, p. 85; regarding "democratic iteration," see Benhabib, *The Rights of Others*, pp. 179ff.
66 Park, "Human Migration and the Marginal Man," pp. 888, 885f., 892f.
67 Cf. Brague, *Eccentric Culture*, p. 133; Balibar, "Quelles frontières de l'Europe?", p. 97 ("l'Europe est partout hors d'elle-même").
68 The well-known intellectuals Rüdiger Safranski and Peter Sloterdijk have been especially aggressive in their commentary; regarding Safranski, cf. the interview by Rico Bandle, "Deutsche Flüchtlingspolitik: 'Politischer Kitsch'"; regarding Sloterdijk, cf. the interview by Kissler and Schwennicke, "Das kann nicht gut gehen." A report written by the jurist and former constitutional judge Udo Di Fabio on behalf of the Bavarian state government is also enlightening; cf. Di Fabio, *Migrationskrise als föderales Verfassungsproblem*, pp. 45, 49f., 52, 90, 92, 103, 118.

69 Streeck, *Gekaufte Zeit*, pp. 154, 168, 297. For a critique of Streeck's short-circuit between the nation state and democracy, cf. Habermas, "Demokratie oder Kapitalismus?".

70 Safranski, for example, says that Germany is turning into a "failed state"; quoted in Bandle, "Deutsche Flüchtlingspolitik." Streeck explicitly alludes to Hobbes's famous phrase about life in a state of nature when he refers to "post-nationalism" as a "mess" – that is, "nasty, brutish and unfortunately far from short"; see Streeck, "Scenario for a Wonderful Tomorrow."

71 Cf., e.g., Bohman, *Democracy Across Borders*; Habermas, *The Postnational Constellation*.

72 Butler, *Notes Toward a Performative Theory of Assembly*, pp. 20, 124.

73 Holston, *Insurgent Citizenship*, p. 9.

74 Ibid., p. 34.

75 Lagasnerie, *The Art of Revolt*, pp. 46–9, 58, 63, 67f., 72ff.

76 Ibid., pp. 85, 87.

77 Invisible Committee, *The Coming Insurrection*, p. 114.

78 Lagasnerie, *The Art of Revolt*, p. 85.

79 Ibid., pp. 94, 96.

80 Domscheit-Berg, *Inside WikiLeaks*.

81 Breivik, *2083 – A European Declaration of Independence*, pp. 631, 676, 1145.

82 Heidegger, *Being and Time*, p. 167.

83 Even fundamentalism outside of Europe and the USA defines itself at least in part as a reaction to Western influences or so-called "westoxification" or "occidentosis"; cf. Al-i Ahmad, *Occidentosis*; regarding the critique of this, see Buruma and Margalit, *Occidentalism*, p. 54.

84 Zimmermann, "Wenn man die Leute zu Opfern macht, werden sie zu Schlächtern."

85 Cf. Marlière, *Jeunes en cité*, pp. 215, 243, 252f.

86 For findings from qualitative social research and the neurosciences, see Atran, "ISIS is a Revolution"; id., "Response to a Request for Recommendations to the UN Security Council Committee on Counter Terrorism," p. 4.

87 Wieviorka, *Violence*, p. 163.

88 For the following details and quotes, cf. Loch, "Moi, Khaled Kelkal."

89 Marty, "Fundamentalism as a Social Phenomenon," p. 20; cf. Castells, *The Power of Identity*, pp. 13, 67.

90 Regarding the ISIS pamphlet "The Extinction of the Grayzone" from 2015, cf. Atran, "ISIS is a Revolution."

91 Cf. Roy, *Globalized Islam*, pp. 25, 328ff. Regarding the accompanying reinterpretation of *jihad* as a "permanent and individual duty," see ibid., p. 41.

92 Ibid., p. 13.

93 Regarding "identity fusion" with a reference to works by William Swann, cf. Atran, "ISIS is a Revolution."

94 Wieviorka, *Violence*, p. 152f.

95 Khosrokhavar, "Le quasi-individu: de la néo-communauté à la nécro-communauté"; cf. Castells, *The Power of Identity*, p. 22.

96 *The Portable Nietzsche*, p. 129 ("Thus Spoke Zarathustra").

97 Brown, *Walled States, Waning Sovereignty*, p. 7.

98 Colvin, "Is Trump a Bumbling Incompetent or a Canny Disrupter?"

99 Radosh, "Steve Bannon, Trump's Top Guy."

100 Cillizza, "The leaks coming out of the Trump White House cast the president as a clueless child."

101 Richter, "Trump Vs. Kelly: Just Who's the 'Bimbo'?"; id., "Donald Trump Outs Himself as 'Bimbo.'"

102 Martin Nolan, quoted in Martin, "Donald Trump's Anything-Goes Campaign."

103 Wohlfert-Wihlborg, "In the Manhattan Real Estate Game, Billionaire Donald Trump Holds the Winning Cards."

104 Trump and Bohner, *The Art of the Comeback*, p. 233.
105 Reicher and Haslam, "The Politics of Hope: Donald Trump as an Entrepreneur of Identity."
106 Ibid.
107 Kagan, "This is how fascism comes to America"; Kinsley, "Donald Trump is actually a fascist."
108 Müller, *What is Populism?*, p. 20.
109 Todd and Rivera, "McCain Defends a Free Press."
110 Burgo, "The Populist Appeal of Trump's Narcissism"; cf. Krauthammer, "Donald Trump and the fitness threshold": "He lives in a cocoon of solipsism where the world outside himself has value – indeed exists – only insofar as it sustains and inflates him. Most politicians seek approval. But Trump *lives* for the adoration."
111 Eggers, *The Circle*, p. 405.
112 Stirner, *The Ego and Its Own*, p. 282.
113 Moretti, *The Bourgeois*, p. 181. This scene also happens to be a favorite example of Stanley Cavell, cf. *Conditions Handsome and Unhandsome*, pp. 108–15.
114 Ibsen, *Four Major Plays*, pp. 82f. (*A Doll's House*).
115 Ibsen, *Speeches and Letters*, p. 54 ("To the Workingmen of Trondhjem, June 14, 1885").

LIST OF ABBREVIATIONS

AFT	Horkheimer, *Authoritarianism and the Family Today*
BPS	Horkheimer, *Between Philosophy and Social Science*
C[e]	Hobbes, *De Cive: The English Version*
C[l]	Hobbes, *De Cive: The Latin Version*
CR	Diderot, *Contes et Romans*
CWR 1–11	Rousseau, *Collected Writings of Rousseau*
CWS 3–8	Schiller, *Complete Works of Friedrich Schiller*
DA 2	Diderot, *Diderot on Art, Volume 2*
DI	Rousseau, *The* Discourses
DIA 1–4	Tocqueville, *Democracy in America* (ed. Eduardo Nolla)
DOC 1–16	Diderot, *Œuvres complètes*
E	Rousseau, *Emile: Or On Education*
GS	Nietzsche, *The Gay Science*
HA	Hegel, *Aesthetics*
HCR	Strauss, *Hobbes' Critique of Religion*
HGS 5–12	Horkheimer, *Gesammelte Schriften*
KSA 9–13	Nietzsche, *Sämtliche Werke: Kritische Studienausgabe*
L[e]	Hobbes, *Leviathan* (ed. Richard Tuck)
L[l]	Hobbes, *Leviathan: The English and Latin Texts*
M[e]	Hugo, *Les Misérables* (English translation)
M[f]	Hugo, *Les Misérables* (French original)
MECW 2–43	Marx/Engels, *Collected Works*
NCW 2–8	Nietzsche, *The Complete Works of Friedrich Nietzsche*
ND[e]	Hugo, *Notre-Dame de Paris* (English translation)
ND[f]	Hugo, *Notre-Dame de Paris, 1482* (French original)
O 1–3	Tocqueville, *Œuvres*
OC 1–5	Rousseau, *Œuvres complètes*
PhS 1–2	Diderot, *Philosophische Schriften*
PN	Nietzsche, *The Portable Nietzsche*
PPH	Strauss, *The Political Philosophy of Hobbes*
PR	Hegel, *Elements of the Philosophy of Right*
PS	Hegel, *Phenomenology of Spirit*
PW	Hegel, *Political Writings*
RN	Diderot, *Rameau's Nephew*
SC	Rousseau, *The Social Contract*
SE 4–23	Freud, *The Standard Edition*

LIST OF ABBREVIATIONS

SGS 1–3   Strauss, *Gesammelte Schriften*
SW 1, 5   Schiller, *Sämtliche Werke*
TH   Schelsky, *Thomas Hobbes: Eine politische Lehre*
WPW 1–7   Wagner, *Richard Wagner's Prose Works*

REFERENCES

Abensour, Miguel (2011): *Democracy Against the State: Marx and the Machiavellian Moment*. Translated by Max Blechman and Martin Breaugh. Cambridge: Polity. [*La démocratie contre l'État*, 1997]

Adorno, Theodor W. (1970–80): *Gesammelte Schriften*. Edited by Rolf Tiedemann et al. Frankfurt: Suhrkamp.

— (2004 [1973]): *Negative Dialectics*. Translated by E. B. Ashton. London: Routledge. [*Negative Dialektik*, 1966]

— (2005 [1981]): *In Search of Wagner*. Translated by Rodney Livingstone. London: Verso. [*Versuch über Wagner*, 1952]

— (2005 [1974]): *Minima Moralia: Reflections on a Damaged Life*. Translated by E. F. N. Jephcott. London: Verso. [*Minima moralia*, 1951]

Agamben, Giorgio (1993): *The Coming Community*. Translated by Michael Hardt. Minneapolis: University of Minnesota Press. [*La comunità che viene*, 1990]

— (1993): *Infancy and History: The Destruction of Experience*. Translated by Liz Heron. London: Verso. [*Infanzia e storia*, 1978]

— (1998): *Homo Sacer: Sovereign Power and Bare Life*. Translated by Daniel Heller-Roazen. Stanford, CA: Standford University Press. [*Homo sacer: Il potere sovrano e la nuda vita*, 1995]

— (1998): *Means Without End: Notes on Politics*. Translated by Vincenzo Binetti and Cesare Casarino. Minneapolis: University of Minnesota Press. [*Mezzi senza fine – Note sulla politica*, 1996]

— (1999): *The Man Without Content*. Translated by Georgia Albert. Stanford, CA: Stanford University Press. [*L'uomo senza contenuto*, 1994]

Agnew, Jean-Christophe (1986): *Worlds Apart: The Market and the Theater in Anglo-American Thought, 1550–1750*. Cambridge: Cambridge University Press.

Aichhorn, August (1935): *Wayward Youth*. New York: Viking Press. [*Verwahrloste Jugend*, 1925]

Albrecht, Clemens, Günter C. Behrmann, Michael Bock, Harald Homann, and Friedrich H. Tenbruck (2000 [1999]): *Die intellektuelle Gründung der Bundesrepublik: Eine Wirkungsgeschichte der Frankfurter Schule*. Frankfurt: Campus.

Al-i Ahmad, Jalal (1984): *Occidentosis: A Plague from the West*. Translated by R. Campbell. Berkeley, CA: Mizan Press.

Alt, Peter-André (2000–4): *Schiller: Leben – Werk – Zeit. Eine Biographie*. Munich: C. H. Beck.

Altini, Carlo (2006): Hobbes in der Weimarer Republik: Carl Schmitt, Leo Strauss und die Krise der modernen Welt. *Hobbes Studies* 29, pp. 3–30.

Altman, William H. F. (2007): Leo Strauss on "German Nihilism": Learning the Art of Writing. *Journal of the History of Ideas* 68/4, pp. 587–612.
— (2009): The Alpine Limits of Jewish Thought: Leo Strauss, National Socialism, and *Judentum ohne Gott*. *Journal of Jewish Thought and Philosophy* 17/1, pp. 1–46.
Andreas-Salomé, Lou (1914): Zum Typus Weib. *Imago* II, pp. 1–14.
Ankersmit, F. R. (1996): *Aesthetic Politics: Political Philosophy Beyond Fact and Value*. Stanford, CA: Stanford University Press.
Anon. (1852): Land Titles in California. *The New York Times*, April 6, p. 2.
Anon. (ed.) (1957): *Beijing Daxue youpai fenzi fandong yanlun huiji* [*A collection of reactionary statements among rightists at Peking University*]. Beijing.
Anon. (ed.) (1957): *Pipan youpai fenzi Tan Tianrong deng lunwen ji* [*A collection of articles criticizing Tan Tianrong and other rightists*]. Beijing.
Appiah, Kwame Anthony (2009): *Experiments in Ethics*. Cambridge, MA: Harvard University Press.
Arendt, Hannah (1946): Expansion and the Philosophy of Power. *Sewanee Review* 54/4, pp. 601–16.
— (1972): *Crises of the Republic*. San Diego, CA: Harcourt Brace & Company.
— (1974 [1963]): *Über die Revolution*. Munich: Piper.
— (1979 [1951]): *The Origins of Totalitarianism: New Edition with Added Prefaces*. San Diego, CA: Harcourt Brace & Company.
— (1986 [1951]): *Elemente und Ursprünge totalitärer Herrschaft*. Munich: Piper.
— (1990 [1963]): *On Revolution*. London: Penguin Books.
— (1998 [1958]): *The Human Condition*. Chicago, IL: University of Chicago Press.
— (2007): *The Jewish Writings*. Edited by Jerome Kohn and Ron H. Feldman. New York: Schocken Books.
Arkush, David (1981): Introduction. In: *Literature of the Hundred Flowers*, Vol. 1. Edited by Hualing Nieh. New York: Columbia University Press, pp. xiii–xxxviii.
Atran, Scott (2015): ISIS is a Revolution. Available at: aeon.co/essays/why-isis-has-the-potential-to-be-a-world-altering-revolution (accessed on March 21, 2018).
— (2015): Response to a Request for Recommendations to the UN Security Council Committee on Counter Terrorism (November–December 2015). Available at: http://artis international.org/wp-content/uploads/2011/02/Atran-Brief-to-UN-Security-Council-CT. pdf (accessed on August 28, 2018).
Audi, Paul (1997): *Rousseau: éthique et passion*. Paris: Presses Universitaires de France.
Avineri, Shlomo (1972): *Hegel's Theory of the Modern State*. Cambridge: Cambridge University Press.
Badiou, Alain (2003): *Circonstances 1: Kosovo, 11 Septembre, Chirac/Le Pen*. Paris: Léo Scheer.
— (2005): *Metapolitics*. Translated by Jason Barker. London: Verso. [*Abrégé de métapolitique*, 1998]
— (2006): *Being and Event*. Translated by Oliver Feltham. London: Continuum. [*L'etre et venement*, 1988]
— (2007): *The Century*. Translated by Alberto Toscano. Cambridge: Polity. [*Le Siècle*, 2005]
— (2010): *The Communist Hypothesis*. Translated by David Macey and Steve Corcoran. London: Verso. [*L'hypothèse communiste*, 2008]
— (2010): Letter from Alain Badiou to Slavoj Žižek: On the Work of Mao Zedong [2008]. In: *The Communist Hypothesis*. London: Verso, pp. 261–79.
— (2012): *The Rebirth of History: Times of Riots and Uprisings*. Translated by Gregory Elliott. London: Verso. [*Le Réveil de l'histoire*, 2011]
—, Pierre Bourdieu, Judith Butler, Georges Didi-Huberman, Sadri Khiari, and Jacques Rancière (2016): *What is a People?* Translated by Jody Gladding. New York: Columbia University Press. [*Qu'est-ce qu'un peuple?*, 2013]
Baeumler, Alfred (1920): Metaphysik und Geschichte: Brief an Thomas Mann. *Neue Rundschau* 31, pp. 1113–29.

— (1926): Einleitung: Bachofen der Mythologe der Romantik. In: Johann Jacob Bachofen, *Der Mythus von Orient und Occident: Eine Metaphysik der alten Welt*. Edited by Manfred Schroeter. Munich: C. H. Beck, pp. xxiii–ccxciv.

— (1934): *Männerbund und Wissenschaft*. Berlin: Junker und Dünnhaupt.

— (1937): *Politik und Erziehung: Reden und Aufsätze*. Berlin: Junker und Dünnhaupt.

Bakhtin, Mikhail M. (1981): *The Dialogic Imagination: Four Essays*. Translated by Caryl Emerson and Michael Holquist. Austin: University of Texas Press. [*Voprosy literatury i estetiki*, 1975]

— (1984): *Rabelais and His World*. Translated by Hélène Iswolsky. Bloomington: Indiana University Press. [*Tvorchestvo Fransua Rable*, 1965]

— (1999): *Problems of Dostoevsky's Poetics: Theory and History of Literature, Volume 8*. Translated by Caryl Emerson. Minneapolis: University of Minnesota Press. [*Problemy poetiki Dostoevskogo*, 1963]

Bakounine, Michel [Mikhail Bakunin] (1910): Fragment, formant une suite de *L'Empire Knouto-Germanique* [1872]. In: *Œuvres*, Vol. 4. Paris: P. V. Stock, pp. 397–510.

Bakunin, Michael [Mikhail Bakunin] (1975): Brief an die Pariser Zeitung *Le Réveil* (1869). In: *Gesammelte Werke*, Vol. 3. Berlin: Karin Kramer, pp. 126–63.

Balibar, Étienne (1985): Marx, the joker in the pack (or the included middle). Translated by David Watson. *Economy and Society* 14/1, pp. 1–27. ["Marx, le joker ou le tiers inclus," 1981]

— (1992): *Les frontières de la démocratie*. Paris: Le Decouvert.

— (1993): Quelles frontières de l'Europe? In: *Penser l'Europe à ses frontières: Geophilosophie de l'Europe*. Multiple authors. La Tour d'Aigues: Editions de l'Aube, pp. 90–100.

— (2000): What Makes a People a People? Rousseau and Kant. Translated by Erin Post. In: Mike Hill and Warren Montag (eds.), *Masses, Classes, and the Public Sphere*. London: Verso, pp. 105–31.

— (2002): Le Hobbes de Schmitt, le Schmitt de Hobbes. In: Carl Schmitt, *Le Léviathan dans la doctrine de l'État de Thomas Hobbes: Sens et échec d'un symbole politique*. Paris: Seuil, pp. 7–65.

— (2007): Uprisings in the *banlieues*. *Constellations* 14, pp. 47–71.

— (2008): *Spinoza and Politics*. Translated by Peter Snowdon. London: Verso. [*Spinoza et la politique*, 1984]

— (2013): "Klassenkampf" als Begriff des Politischen. In: Rahel Jaeggi and Daniel Loick (eds.), *Nach Marx: Philosophie, Kritik, Praxis*. Berlin: Suhrkamp, pp. 445–62.

— (2014): *Equaliberty: Political Essays*. Translated by James Ingram. Durham, NC: Duke University Press. [*La Proposition de l'Égaliberté*, 2010]

— (2017): Afterword: Philosophical Anthropology or Ontology of Relations? Exploring the Sixth Thesis on Feuerbach. In: *The Philosophy of Marx: Updated New Edition*. Translated by Gregory Elliott and Chris Turner. London: Verso, pp. 123–58 [*La philosophie du Marx*, 1993]

— (2017): The Invention of the Superego: Freud and Kelsen, 1922. In: *Citizen Subject: Foundations for Philosophical Anthropology*. Translated by Stephen Miller. New York: Fordham University Press, pp. 227–55. ["Freud et Kelsen, 1922: L'invention du Surmoi," 2007]

Balke, Friedrich (2009): *Figuren der Souveränität*. Munich: Wilhelm Fink.

Ball, Hugo (2013): Carl Schmitt's Political Theology. Translated by Matthew Vollgraff. *October* 146, pp. 65–92. [Carl Schmitts politische Theologie, 1924]

Ball, Terence (2000): The Formation of Character: Mill's "Ethology" Reconsidered. *Polity* 33/1, pp. 25–48.

Balzac, Honoré de (1976–1981): *La Comédie humaine*. Twelve volumes. Edited by Pierre-George Castex. Paris: Gallimard.

— (2009 [1991]): *Père Goriot*. Translated by A. J. Krailsheimer. Oxford: Oxford University Press. [*Le Père Goriot*, 1835]

— (2014 [1970]): *A Harlot High and Low*. Translated by Rayner Heppenstall. London: Penguin. [*Splendeurs et misères des courtisanes*, 1839–47]

Bandle, Rico (2015): Deutsche Flüchtlingspolitik: "Politischer Kitsch." Interview with Rüdiger Safranski. Available at: https://www.weltwoche.ch/ausgaben/2015-52/arti kel/deutsche-fluechtlingspolitik-politischer-kitsch-die-weltwoche-ausgabe-522015.html (accessed on March 20, 2018).

Barber, Benjamin R. (1984): *Strong Democracy: Participatory Politics for a New Age*. Berkeley: University of California Press.

Barker, William (1994): Introduction. In: Richard Mulcaster, *Positions Concerning the Training Up of Children*. Toronto: University of Toronto Press, pp. xi–lxxviii.

Barmé, Geremie R. (1999): *In the Red: On Contemporary Chinese Culture*. New York: Columbia University Press.

Barrett, David (2010): Ai Weiwei: Sunflower Seeds. *Art Monthly* 11/2, pp. 343–4.

Barron, James (1999): Warnings from a Student Turned Killer. *The New York Times*, May 1, p. A12.

Barthes, Roland (1987): *Michelet*. Translated by Richard Howard. Berkeley: University of California Press. [*Michelet*, 1954]

— (1989 [1976]): *Sade, Fourier, Loyola*. Translated by Richard Miller. Berkeley: University of California Press. [*Sade, Fourier, Loyola*, 1971]

Bataille, Georges (1973): *Literature and Evil*. Translated by Alastair Hamilton. London: Calder and Boyars. [*La littérature et le mal*, 1957]

— (1985): *Visions of Excess: Selected Writings, 1927–1939*. Edited and translated by Allan Stoekl, with Carl R. Lovitt and Donald M. Leslie, Jr. Minneapolis: University of Minnesota Press.

— (1997 [1946]): General Economy. In: Fred Botting and Scott Wilson (eds.), *The Bataille Reader*. Oxford: Blackwell Publishing, pp. 165–209.

— (1997 [1933]): The Psychological Structure of Fascism. In: Fred Botting and Scott Wilson (eds.), *The Bataille Reader*. Oxford: Blackwell Publishing, pp. 122–46.

Baudelaire, Charles (1950): *My Heart Laid Bare and Other Prose Writings*. Edited by Peter Quennell, translated by Norman Cameron. London: George Weidenfeld & Nicholson.

— (1964): *Baudelaire as a Literary Critic*. Translated by Lois Boe Hyslop and Francis E. Hyslop, Jr. University Park, PA: Pennsylvania State University Press.

— (1975–6): *Œuvres complètes*. Two volumes. Edited by Claude Pichois. Paris: Gallimard.

— (1995 [1965]): *The Painter of Modern Life and Other Essays*. Translated and edited by Jonathan Mayne. London: Phaidon Press. ["Le Peintre de la vie moderne," 1863]

— (1996): *Artificial Paradises*. Translated by Stacy Diamond. New York: Citadel Press. [*Les paradis artificiels*, 1860]

— (2006 [1972]): *Selected Writings on Art and Literature*. Translated by P. E. Charvet. London: Penguin Books.

— (2008): *Paris Spleen and Le Fanfarlo*. Translated by Raymond N. MacKenzie. Indianapolis, IN: Hackett Publishing. [*Le Spleen de Paris*, 1869; *Le Fanfarlo*, 1847]

— (2016): *The Flowers of Evil*. Translated by Anthony Mortimer. Richmond: Alma Classics. [*Les Fleurs du mal*, 1857]

Bauer, Edgar (1844 [1843]): *Der Streit der Kritik mit Kirche und Staat*. Bern: Jennt.

Bayertz, Kurt (ed.) (1999): *Solidarity*. Dordrecht: Kluwer Academic.

Beckett, Samuel (1954): *Waiting for Godot: A Tragicomedy in Two Acts*. Translated by Samuel Beckett. New York: Grove Press. [*En attendant Godot*, 1952]

Beier, A. Lee (1985): *Masterless Men: The Vagrancy Problem in England, 1560–1640*. London: Methuen.

Beiser, Frederick C. (ed.) (1996): *The Early Political Writings of the German Romantics*. Translated by Frederick C. Beiser. Cambridge: Cambridge University Press.

Bellah, Robert, Richard Madsen, William M. Sullivan, Ann Swidler, and Steven M. Tipton (1996 [1985]): *Habits of the Heart: Individualism and Commitment in American Life*. Berkeley: University of California Press.

425

Bellstedt, Max (1934): *Deutsche Weltanschauung*. Eisenach: Röth.

Belpoliti, Marco (2009): *Il corpo del capo: Con una nuova postfazione dell'autore*. Parma: Guanda.

Benhabib, Seyla (2004): *The Rights of Others: Aliens, Residents and Citizens*. Cambridge: Cambridge University Press.

Benjamin, Jessica (1988): *The Bonds of Love: Psychoanalysis, Feminism, and the Problem of Domination*. New York: Random House.

Benjamin, Walter (2002 [1996]): *Selected Writings, Volume 1: 1913–1926*. Edited by Marcus Bullock and Michael W. Jennings, translated by Edmund Jephcott et al. Cambridge, MA: Belknap Press.

— (2005 [1999]): *Selected Writings, Volume 2, Part 2: 1931–1934*. Edited by Michael W. Jennings, Howard Eiland, and Gary Smith, translated by Rodney Livingstone et al. Cambridge, MA: Belknap Press.

— (2006 [2003]): *Selected Writings, Volume 4: 1938–1940*. Edited by Michael W. Jennings, Howard Eiland, and Gary Smith, translated by Edmund Jephcott et al. Cambridge, MA: Belknap Press.

Bentham, Jeremy (1838–43): *The Works of Jeremy Bentham*. Edited by John Bowring. Edinburgh: William Tait.

— (1988 [1776]): *A Fragment on Government*. Edited by J. H. Burns and H. L. A. Hart. Cambridge: Cambridge University Press.

Benton, Gregor (1982): China Spring: The Interrupted Rise of the Democratic Movement in People's China. In: Gregor Benton (ed.), *Wild Lilies, Poisonous Weeds: Dissident Voices from People's China*. London: Pluto Press, pp. 1–15.

Bergeron, David M. (1991): "Richard II" and Carnival Politics. *Shakespeare Quarterly* 42/1, pp. 33–43.

Bergmann, Martin S. (2010): The Oedipus Complex and Psychoanalytic Technique. *Psychoanalytic Inquiry* 30, pp. 535–40.

Bergson, Henri (1935): *The Two Sources of Morality and Religion*. Translated by R. Ashley Audra and Cloudesley Brereton. London: Macmillan. [*Les deux sources de la morale et la religion*, 1932]

Berlin, Isaiah (2000): *Three Critics of the Enlightenment: Vico, Hamann, Herder*. Princeton, NJ: Princeton University Press.

— (2002 [1969]): *Liberty: Incorporating Four Essays on Liberty*. Edited by Henry Hardy. Oxford: Oxford University Press.

Bermbach, Udo (1994): *Der Wahn des Gesamtkunstwerks: Richard Wagners politisch-ästhetische Utopie*. Frankfurt: Fischer.

— (2001): Wotan: Der Gott als Politiker. In: *"Alles ist nach seiner Art": Figuren in Richard Wagners "Der Ring des Nibelungen."* Stuttgart: Metzler, pp. 27–48.

Bernfeld, Siegfried (1924): *Vom dichterischen Schaffen der Jugend: Neue Beiträge zur Jugendforschung*. Leipzig: Internationaler Psychoanalytischer Verlag.

Bernstein, Richard (1986): John Dewey on Democracy: The Task Before Us. In: *Philosophical Profiles: Essays in a Pragmatic Mode*. Cambridge: Polity, pp. 260–72.

Bicheno, James Ebenezer (1817): *An Inquiry into The Nature of Benevolence, chiefly with a View to Elucidate the Principles of the Poor Laws, and to Show Their Immoral Tendency*. London: Rowland Hunter.

Blake, William (1988): *The Complete Poetry & Prose*. Edited by David Erdman. New York: Anchor Books.

Bloch, Ernst (2000): *The Spirit of Utopia*. Translated by Anthony A. Nassar. Stanford, CA: Stanford University Press. [*Geist der Utopie*, 1918/1923]

Blüher, Hans (1913): *Die drei Grundformen der sexuellen Inversion (Homosexualität): Eine sexuologische Studie*. Leipzig: Max Spohr.

— (1914 [1912]): *Die deutsche Wandervogelbewegung als erotisches Phänomen: Ein Beitrag zur Erkenntnis der sexuellen Inversion*. Berlin: Weise.

— (1917): *Die Rolle der Erotik in der männlichen Gesellschaft*, Vol. I. Jena: Eugen Diederichs.

426

REFERENCES

— (1917): *Führer und Volk in der Jugendbewegung*. Jena: Eugen Diederichs.
— (1918): *Familie und Männerbund*. Leipzig: Der neue Geist Verlag.
— (1919): *Die Rolle der Erotik in der männlichen Gesellschaft*, Vol. II. Jena: Eugen Diederichs.
— (1919 [1912]): *Wandervogel: Geschichte einer Jugendbewegung. 1. Teil: Heimat und Aufgang. 2. Teil: Blüte und Niedergang*. Berlin: Hans Blüher Verlag.
— (1928): *Philosophie auf Posten: Gesammelte Schriften 1916–1921*. Heidelberg: Kampmann.
Bohman, James (2007): *Democracy across Borders: From Dêmos to Dêmoi*. Cambridge, MA: MIT Press.
Bollack, Jean (1993): Der Menschensohn: Freuds Ödipusmythos. *Psyche* 47, pp. 647–83.
Boltanski, Luc and Ève Chiapello (2007): *The New Spirit of Capitalism*. Translated by Gregory Elliott. London: Verso. [*Le nouvel esprit du capitalisme*, 1999]
Bondy, Curt et al. (1957): *Jugendliche stören die Ordnung: Bericht und Stellungnahme zu den Halbstarkenkrawallen*. Munich: Juventa.
Booth, William (1890): *In Darkest England and the Way Out*. New York: Funk and Wagnalis.
Borchmeyer, Dieter (1987): Die Tragödie vom verlorenen Vater: Der Dramatiker Schiller und die Aufklärung – das Beispiel der "Räuber." In: Helmut Brandt (ed.), *Friedrich Schiller: Angebot und Diskurs*. Berlin: Aufbau, pp. 160–84.
— (1987): "Faust" und der "Ring des Nibelungen": Der Mythos des 19. Jahrhunderts in zwiefacher Gestalt. In: *Wege des Mythos in der Moderne. Richard Wagner: "Der Ring des Nibelungen."* Munich: dtv, pp. 133–58.
Borkenau, Franz (1976 [1934]): *Der Übergang vom feudalen zum bürgerlichen Weltbild: Studien zur Geschichte der Philosophie der Manufakturperiode*. Darmstadt: Wissenschaftliche Buchgesellschaft.
Bourdeau, Jean (1904): *Les maîtres de la pensée contemporaine*. Paris: Félix Alcan.
Bovenkerk, Frank (1984): The Rehabilitation of the Rabble: How and Why Marx and Engels Wrongly Depicted the Lumpenproletariat as a Reactionary Force. *Netherlands Journal of Sociology* 20, pp. 13–41.
Bowie, Robert R. and John K. Fairbank (eds.) (1971 [1962]): *Communist China 1955–1959: Policy Documents with Analysis*. Cambridge, MA: Harvard University Press.
Brague, Rémi (2002): *Eccentric Culture: A Theory of Western Civilization*. Translated by Samuel Lester. South Bend, IN: St. Augustine's Press. [*Europe, la voie romaine*, 1992]
Bredekamp, Horst (2007): Thomas Hobbes's Visual Strategies. In: Patricia Springborg (ed.), *The Cambridge Companion to Hobbes's* Leviathan. Cambridge: Cambridge University Press, pp. 29–60.
Breivik, Anders Behring (2011): *2083 – A European Declaration of Independence*. Available at: www.deism.com/images/breivik-manifesto-2011.pdf (accessed on March 21, 2018).
Bristol, Michael D. (1985): *Carnival and Theater: Plebeian Culture and the Structure of Authority in Renaissance England*. London: Methuen.
Brown, Wendy (1988): *Manhood and Politics: A Feminist Reading in Political Theory*. Totowa, NJ: Rowman & Littlefield.
— (2001): *Politics Out of History*. Princeton, NJ: Princeton University Press.
— (2010): *Walled States, Waning Sovereignty*. New York: Zone Books.
Brucker, Jakob (1766 [1742–44]): *Historia critica philosophiae a tempore resuscitatarum in occidente literarum ad nostra tempora*. Tomi IV, pars altera. Leipzig: Bernhard Christopher Breitkopf.
Brunner, José (1998): Oedipus politicus: Freud's Paradigm of Social Relations. In: Michael S. Roth (ed.), *Freud: Conflict and Culture*. New York: Alfred A. Knopf, pp. 80–93.
Brunotte, Ulrike (2004): *Zwischen Eros und Krieg*. Berlin: Wagenbach.
Bruns, Claudia (2008): *Politik des Eros: Der Männerbund in Wissenschaft, Politik und Jugendkultur (1880–1934)*. Cologne: Böhlau.

427

Bryson, Scott S. (1991): *The Chastised Stage: Bourgeois Drama and the Exercise of Power.* Saratoga, CA: Anma Libri.

Buck-Morss, Susan (2009): *Hegel, Haiti, and Universal History.* Pittsburgh, PA: University of Pittsburgh Press.

Burgo, Joseph (2015): The Populist Appeal of Trump's Narcissism. Psychology Today, August 14. Available at: www.psychologytoday.com/blog/shame/201508/the-populist-appeal-trumps-narcissism (accessed on March 26, 2018).

Burke, Kenneth (1950): *A Rhetoric of Motives.* New York: Prentice-Hall.

Burke, Peter (2009 [1978]): *Popular Culture in Early Modern Europe.* Farnham: Ashgate.

Buruma, Ian and Avishai Margalit (2004): *Occidentalism: The West in the Eyes of Its Enemies.* New York: Penguin.

Bussard, Robert L. (1987): The "Dangerous Class" of Marx and Engels: The Rise of the Idea of the *Lumpenproletariat. History of European Ideas* 8, pp. 675–92.

Butler, Judith (2015): *Notes Toward a Performative Theory of Assembly.* Cambridge, MA: Harvard University Press.

Calderón de la Barca, Pedro (1990 [1655]): *The Great Theatre of the World.* Adapted by Adrian Mitchell. Woodstock, IL: Dramatic Publishing. [*El gran teatro del mundo,* 1655]

Capitant, René (1936): Hobbes et l'État totalitaire. *Archives de Philosophie du droit et de Sociologie juridique* 6/1–2, pp. 46–75.

Carlyle, Thomas (1896): *The French Revolution: A History.* Three volumes. New York: Charles Scribner's Sons.

— (1897): *The Works of Thomas Carlyle (Complete).* New York: Peter Fenelon Collier.

Castells, Manuel (2010 [1997]): *The Power of Identity.* Oxford: Blackwell.

Castoriadis, Cornelius (1984): *Crossroads in the Labyrinth.* Translated by Kate Soper and Martin Ryle. Cambridge, MA: MIT Press. [*Les carrefours du labyrinthe,* 1978]

— (2005): *The Imaginary Institution of Society.* Translated by Kathleen Blamey. Cambridge: Polity. [*L'institution imaginaire de la société,* 1975]

Cavell, Marcia (2006): *Becoming a Subject: Reflections in Philosophy and Psychoanalysis.* Oxford: Oxford University Press.

Cavell, Stanley (1989): *This New Yet Unapproachable America: Lectures after Emerson after Wittgenstein.* Albuquerque, NM: Living Batch Press.

— (1990): *Conditions Handsome and Unhandsome: The Constitution of Emersonian Perfectionism.* Chicago, IL: University of Chicago Press.

Chase, Richard R. (1992): Jules Michelet and the Nineteenth-Century Concept of Insanity: A Romantic's Reinterpretation. *French Historical Studies* 17, pp. 725–46.

Chevalier, Louis (2007 [1958]): *Classes laborieuses et classes dangeureuses à Paris pendant la première moitié du XIXᵉ siècle.* Paris: Tempus Perrin.

Cillizza, Chris (2017): The leaks coming out of the Trump White House cast the president as a clueless child. *The Washington Post,* January 26. Available at: www.washingtonpost.com/news/the-fix/wp/2017/01/26/the-leaks-coming-out-the-trump-white-house-cast-the-boss-as-a-clueless-child/?utm_term=.7f46f44803a7 (accessed on March 25, 2018).

Citton, Yves (2009): Political Agency and the Ambivalence of the Sensible. In: Gabriel Rockhill and Philip Watts (eds.), *Jacques Rancière: History, Politics, Aesthetics.* Durham, NC: Duke University Press, pp. 120–39.

Clark, Timothy J. (1999 [1973]): *The Absolute Bourgeois: Artists and Politics in France 1848–1851.* Berkeley: University of California Press.

Claussen, Detlev (2008): *Theodor W. Adorno: One Last Genius.* Translated by Rodney Livingstone. Cambridge, MA: Harvard University Press. [*Theodor W. Adorno: Ein letztes Genie,* 2003]

Collingwood, Robin George (1999 [1942]): *The New Leviathan or Man, Society, Civilization and Barbarism.* Oxford: Oxford University Press.

Colliot-Thélène, Catherine (2009): Pour une politique des droits subjectifs: la lutte pour les droits comme lutte politique. *L'Année sociologique* 59, pp. 231–58.

— (2018): *Democracy and Subjective Rights: Democracy Without* Demos. Translated by Arianne Dorval. London: Rowman & Littlefield. [*Demokratie ohne Volk*, 2011]

Colvin, Geoff (2016): Is Trump a Bumbling Incompetent or a Canny Disrupter? Available at: fortune.com/2016/07/11/donald-trump-bumbling-incompetent-canny-disrupter (accessed on March 25, 2018).

Connolly, William E. (2011): *A World of Becoming*. Durham, NC: Duke University Press.

Constant, Benjamin (2003 [1988]): The Liberty of the Ancients Compared with that of the Moderns. In: *Political Writings*. Translated and edited by Biancamaria Fontana. Cambridge: Cambridge University Press, pp. 307–28. [De la liberté des Anciens comparée à celle des Modernes, 1819]

Croce, Benedetto (1914): *Historical Materialism and the Economics of Karl Marx*. Translated by C. M. Meredith. New York: The Macmillan Company. [*Materialismo Storico ed Economia Marxistica*, 1900]

— (1993 [1944]): Conversazione coi giovani. In: *Scritti e discorsi politici (1943–1947)*, Vol. 2. Edited by Angela Carella. Naples: Bibliopolis, pp. 58–63.

Crocker, Lester G. (1961): "Le Neveu de Rameau," une expérience morale. *Cahiers de l'Association Internationale des Études Françaises* 13, pp. 133–55.

— (1963): *Nature and Culture: Ethical Thought in the French Enlightenment*. Baltimore, MD: Johns Hopkins University Press.

Crouch, Colin (2004): *Postdemocracy*. Cambridge: Polity.

Curtius, Ernst Robert (1923): *Balzac*. Bonn: Cohen.

— (2013 [1953]): *European Literature and the Latin Middle Ages*. Translated by Willard R. Trask. Princeton, NJ: Princeton University Press. [*Europäische Literatur und lateinisches Mittelalter*, 1948]

Dahlhaus, Carl (2004): *Gesammelte Schriften in 10 Bänden. Band 7: 19. Jahrhundert IV. Richard Wagner – Texte zum Musiktheater*. Edited by Hermann Danuser. Laaber: Laaber-Verlag.

Däubler, Theodor (1921–2 [1910]): *Das Nordlicht*. Two volumes. Leipzig: Insel.

David, Marcel (1987): *Fraternité et Révolution française 1789–1799*. Paris: Aubier.

— (1992): *Le printemps de la fraternité: Genèse et vicissitudes 1830–1851*. Paris: Aubier.

Davies, Norman (2001): *Heart of Europe: The Past in Poland's Present*. Oxford: Oxford University Press.

Davis, Nathalie Zemon (1971): The Reasons of Misrule: Youth Groups and Charivaris in Sixteenth-Century France. *Past & Present* 50, pp. 41–75.

Debes, Remy (2016): Adam Smith and the Sympathetic Imagination. In: Ryan Patrick Hanley (ed.), *Adam Smith: His Life, Thought, and Legacy*. Princeton, NJ: Princeton University Press, pp. 192–207.

Dédéyan, Charles (1987): *Diderot et la pensée anglaise*. Florence: Leo S. Olschki.

Del Lucchese, Filippo (2010): *Tumultes et indignation: Conflit, droit et multitude chez Machiavel et Spinoza*. Paris: Editions Amsterdam.

Derrida, Jacques (2002): Declarations of Independence. In: Elizabeth Rottenberg (ed.), *Negotiations: Interventions and Interviews, 1971–2001*, essay translated by Tom Keenan and Tom Pepper. Stanford, CA: Stanford University Press, pp. 46–54. ["Déclarations d'Indépendence," 1984]

— (2005): *Rogues: Two Essays on Reason*. Translated by Pascale-Anne Brault and Michael Naas. Stanford, CA: Stanford University Press. [*Voyous: Deux essais sur la raison*, 2003]

— (2006 [1994]): *Specters of Marx: The State of the Debt, the Work of Mourning and the New International*. Translated by Peggy Kamuf. New York: Routledge. [*Spectres de Marx*, 1993]

— (2013): *Signature Derrida*. Edited by Jay Williams. Chicago, IL: University of Chicago Press.

Dewey, John (2008 [1969]): *The Early Works, 1882–1898. Volume 1: 1882–1888*. Edited by Jo Ann Boydston. Carbondale, IL: Southern Illinois University Press.

— (2008 [1983]): *The Middle Works, 1899–1924. Volume 14: 1922.* Edited by Jo Ann Boydston. Carbondale, IL: Southern Illinois University Press.

— (2008 [1987]): *The Later Works, 1925–1953. Volume 11: 1935–1937.* Edited by Jo Ann Boydston. Carbondale, IL: Southern Illinois University Press.

Diderot, Denis (1875–77): *Œuvres complètes.* Edited by J. Assézat and M. Tourneux: Paris: Garnier.

— (1961): *Philosophische Schriften.* Two volumes. Edited and translated by Theodor Lücke. Berlin: Aufbau.

— (1966): *Rameau's Nephew/D'Alembert's Dream.* Translated by Leonard Tancock. London: Penguin.

— (1992): *Political Writings.* Translated and edited by John Hope Mason and Robert Wokler. Cambridge: Cambridge University Press.

— (1995): *Diderot on Art, Volume 2: The Salon of 1767.* Translated by John Goodman. New Haven, CT: Yale University Press.

— (2004): *Contes et Romans.* Edited by Michel Delon. Paris: Gallimard.

— (2006): *Rameau's Nephew and First Satire.* Translated by Margret Mauldon. Oxford: Oxford University Press.

— (2014): *Denis Diderot's Rameau's Nephew: A Multi-Media Edition.* Translated by Kate E. Tunstall and Caroline Warman. Cambridge, UK: Open Book Publishers.

— and Jean Le Rond D'Alembert (eds.) (1751–65): *Encyclopédie ou Dictionnaire raisonné des sciences, des art et des métiers, par une société des gens de lettres,* Paris: André Le Breton et al.

Dieckmann, Herbert (1980): Diderots *Le Neveu de Rameau* und Hegels Interpretation dieses Werkes. In: *Diderot und die Aufklärung.* Munich: Kraus International, pp. 161–94.

Di Fabio, Udo (2016): *Migrationskrise als föderales Verfassungsproblem.* Available at: www.bayern.de/wp-content/uploads/2016/01/Gutachten_Bay_DiFabio_formatiert.pdf (accessed on March 20, 2018).

Dilthey, Wilhelm and Paul Yorck von Wartenburg (1923): *Briefwechsel 1877–1897.* Halle: Niemeyer.

Domscheit-Berg, Daniel (2011): *Inside WikiLeaks: My Time with Julian Assange at the World's Most Dangerous Website.* Translated by Jefferson Chase. London: Jonathan Cape. [*Inside WikiLeaks: Meine Zeit bei der gefährlichsten Website der Welt,* 2011]

Doolin, Dennis J. (ed.) (1964): *Communist China: The Politics of Student Opposition.* Stanford, CA: Stanford University Press.

Dotzauer, Gregor (2013): "Ich glaube an radikale Akte." Interview mit Olivier Assayas. *Tagesspiegel,* May 29. Available at: www.tagesspiegel.de/kultur/interview-ich-glaube-an-radikale-akte/8273510.html (accessed on January 10, 2016).

Draper, Hal (1972): The Concept of the "Lumpenproletariat" in Marx and Engels. *Économie et Sociétés* 6/12, pp. 2285–312.

Dreier, Horst (1997): Kelsens Demokratietheorie: Grundlegung, Strukturelemente, Probleme. In: Robert Walter and Clemens Jabloner (eds.), *Hans Kelsens Wege sozial-philosophischer Forschung.* Vienna: Manz, pp. 79–102.

— (2009): *Gilt das Grundgesetz ewig? Fünf Kapitel zum modernen Verfassungsstaat.* Munich: Carl Friedrich von Siemens Stiftung.

Du Breul, Jacques (1612): *Le theatre des antiquitez de Paris.* Paris: Claude de la Tour.

Dumont, Louis (1977): *From Mandeville to Marx: The Genesis and Triumph of Economic Ideology.* Chicago, IL: University of Chicago Press. [*Homo aequalis I: Genèse et épanouissement de l'idéologie économique,* 1977]

Dupré, Louis (1983): *Marx's Social Critique of Culture.* New Haven, CT: Yale University Press.

Durkheim, Émile (1997): *The Division of Labor in Society.* Translated by W. D. Halls. Houndmills: Macmillan. [*De la division du travail social,* 1893]

Economist Intelligence Unit (2013): *Rebels Without a Cause: What the Upsurge of Protest Movements Means for Global Politics.* London: The Economist Intelligence Unit.

Editorial Department of *Renmin Ribao* (1959): "More on the Historical Experience of the Dictatorship of the Proletariat." In: Anonymous (ed.), *The Historical Experience of the Dictatorship of the Proletariat*. Peking: Foreign Languages Press, pp. 21–64.

Eggers, Dave (2013): *The Circle*. London: Penguin.

Eisler, Hanns (1973 [1935]): Einiges über das Verhalten der Arbeitersänger und -musiker in Deutschland. In: *Musik und Politik: Schriften 1924–1948*. Leipzig: VEB Deutscher Verlag für Musik, pp. 242–65.

Elias, Norbert (2000 [1994]): *The Civilizing Process: Sociogenetic and Psychogenetic Investigations*. Translated by Edmund Jephcott. Oxford: Blackwell. [*Über den Prozess der Zivilisation*, 1939]

Elster, Jon (1985): *Making Sense of Marx*. Cambridge: Cambridge University Press.

Emerson, Ralph Waldo (1983): *Essays & Lectures*. Edited by Joel Porte. New York: Library of America.

Erhard, Johann Benjamin (1976): *Über das Recht des Volks zu einer Revolution* [1795] *und andere Schriften*. Edited by Hellmut G. Haasis. Frankfurt: Syndikat.

Esposito, Roberto (2010): *Communitas: The Origin and Destiny of Community*. Translated by Timothy C. Campbell. Stanford, CA: Stanford University Press. [*Communitas: Origine e destino della comunità*, 1998]

Eyben, Emiel (1993): *Restless Youth in Ancient Rome*. Translated by Patrick Daly. London: Routledge. [*De jonge Romein volgens de literair bronnen der periode ca. 200 v. Chr. tot ca. 500 n. Chr.*, 1977]

Ezrahi, Yaron (1995): The Theatrics and Mechanics of Action: The Theater and the Machine as Political Metaphors. *Social Research* 62, pp. 299–322.

Fallend, Karl (1995): *Sonderlinge, Träumer, Sensitive: Psychoanalyse auf dem Weg zur Institution und Profession. Protokolle der Wiener Psychoanalytischen Vereinigung und biographische Studien*. Vienna: Jugend & Volk.

Farge, Arlette (1993): *Fragile Lives: Violence, Power and Solidarity in Eighteenth-Century Paris*. Translated by Carol Shelton. Cambridge, MA: Harvard University Press. [*La vie fragile*, 1986]

Federn, Paul (1919): *Zur Psychologie der Revolution: Die vaterlose Gesellschaft*. Leipzig: Anzengruber.

Fehr, Ernst and Simon Gächter (2000): Cooperation and Punishment in Public Goods Experiments. *American Economic Review* 90/4, pp. 980–94.

Ferguson, Charles (2010): *Inside Job* [transcript]. Available at: www.sonyclassics.com/awards-information/insidejob_screenplay.pdf (accessed on March 7, 2018).

Feuerbach, Ludwig (1969–2004): *Gesammelte Werke*. Edited by Werner Schuffenhauer. Berlin: De Gruyter.

Filmer, Robert (1991 [1680]): *Patriarcha and Other Writings*. Cambridge: Cambridge University Press.

Fischer-Kowalski, Marina (1982): *1958-Hooligans and 1968-Students: One Generation, Two Rebellions*. Vienna: Institute für Höhere Studien.

Fisher, Jamey (2005): Familial Politics and Political Families: Consent, Critique, and the Fraternal Social Contract in Schillers *Die Räuber*. *Goethe Yearbook* 13, pp. 75–103.

Fleisser, Marieluise (1972): *Gesammelte Werke*. Edited by Günther Rühle. Frankfurt: Suhrkamp.

Florida, Richard (2002): *The Rise of the Creative Class*. New York: Basic Books.

Foisneau, Luc, Jean-Christophe Merle, and Tom Sorell (eds.) (2005): *"Leviathan" Between the Wars: Hobbes's Impact on Early Twentieth Century Political Philosophy*. Frankfurt: Peter Lang.

Forsthoff, Ernst (1933): *Der totale Staat*. Hamburg: Hanseatische Verlagsanstalt.

— (1959): Einleitung: Die Daseinsvorsorge in heutiger Sicht. In: *Rechtsfragen der leistenden Verwaltung*. Stuttgart: Kohlhammer, pp. 9–22.

Foucault, Michel (1972 [1961]): *Histoire de la folie à l'âge classique*. Paris: Gallimard.

— (1977): A Preface to Transgression. In: *Language, Counter-Memory, Practice: Selected*

Essays and Interviews. Edited by Donald F. Bouchard, translated by Donald F. Bouchard and Sherry Simon. Ithaca, NY: Cornell University Press, pp. 29–52.

— (1978–86): *The History of Sexuality*. Three volumes. Translated by Robert Hurley. New York: Vintage Books. [*L'Histoire de la sexualité*, 1976–84]

— (1980 [1972]): *Power/Knowledge: Selected Interviews and Other Writings, 1972–1977*. Edited and translated by Colin Gordon et al. New York: Pantheon Books.

— (1997): *Ethics: Subjectivity and Truth: The Essential Works of Michel Foucault 1954–1984, Volume 1*. Edited by Paul Rabinow, translated by Robert Hurley et al. New York: New Press.

— (2001): *Power: The Essential Works of Michel Foucault 1954–1984, Volume 3*. Translated by Robert Hurley et al. New York: New Press.

— (2002 [1989]): *The Archaeology of Knowledge*. Translated by A. M. Sheridan Smith. London: Routledge. [*L'Archéologie du savoir*, 1969]

— (2003): *Abnormal: Lectures at the Collège de France 1974–75*. Translated by Graham Burchell. London: Verso. [*Les Anormaux*, 1999]

— (2003): *Society Must Be Defended: Lectures at the Collège de France 1975–76*. Edited by Mauro Bertani and Alessandro Fontant, translated by David Macey. New York: Picador Books. [*Il faut défendre la société*, 1997]

— (2008): *The Birth of Biopolitics: Lectures at the Collège de France 1978–79*. Translated by Graham Burchell. Houndmills: Palgrave Macmillan. [*Naissance de La Biopolitique: Cours au College de France, 1978–1979*, 2004]

— (2009): *History of Madness*. Translated by Jonathan Murphy and Jean Khalfa. London: Routledge. [*Folie et Déraison: Histoire de la Folie à l'âge classique*, 1961]

— (2010): *The Government of Self and Others: Lectures at the Collège de France 1982–1983*. Edited by Frédéric Gros, translated by Graham Burchell. Houndmills: Palgrave Macmillan. [*Gouvernement de soi et des autres: Cours au Collège de France, 1982–1983*, 2008]

— (2015): *Language, Madness, and Desire: On Literature*. Edited by Philippe Artières et al., translated by Robert Bononno. Minneapolis: University of Minnesota Press. [*La grande étrangère: À propos de littérature*, 2013]

Fox, Robin (1993): The Virgin and the Godfather: Kinship Versus the State in Greek Tragedy and After. In: Paul Benson (ed.), *Anthropology and Literature*. Urbana: University of Illinois Press, pp. 107–50.

Frank, Robert (1999): *Luxury Fever: Money and Happiness in an Era of Excess*. Princeton, NJ: Princeton University Press.

Frégier, Honoré Antoine (1840): *Des classes dangeureuses de la population dans les grandes villes et des moyens de les rendre meilleures*. Vol. 1/2. Paris: J. B. Baillière.

Freud, Anna, (1932): Psychoanalyse des Kindes, *Zeitschrift für psychoanalytische Pädagogik* VI/1, pp. 5–20.

— (1974): *The Writings of Anna Freud, Volume I: Introduction to Psychoanalysis: Lectures for Child Analysts and Teachers, 1922–1935*. New York: International Universities Press. [*Einführung in die Psychoanalyse für Pädagogen*, 1930]

Freud, Sigmund (1955–74): *The Standard Edition of the Complete Psychological Works of Sigmund Freud*. Twenty-four volumes. Translated and edited by James Strachey. London: Vintage.

— (1985): *The Complete Letters of Sigmund Freud to Wilhelm Fliess, 1887–1904*. Translated and edited by Jeffrey Moussaieff Masson. Cambridge, MA: Belknap Press.

— (2001 [1961]): *The Future of Illusion, Civilization and its Discontents* and *Other Works*. Translated by James Strachey. London: Vintage. [*Das Unbehagen in der Kultur*, 1929]

— and Lou Andreas-Salomé (1985 [1972]): *Letters*. Edited by Ernst Pfeiffer, translated by William and Elaine Robson Scott. New York: W.W. Norton & Company. [*Briefwechsel*, 1966]

Freund, Julien (1981): Karl Marx, un admirateur discret de Thomas Hobbes. *Revue européenne des sciences sociales* 20, pp. 349–59.

REFERENCES

Freyer, Hans (1931): *Revolution von rechts*. Jena: Eugen Diedrichs.
Frost, Samantha (2001): Faking it: Hobbes's Thinking-Bodies and the Ethics of Dissimulation. *Political Theory* 29, pp. 30–57.
— (2008): *Lessons from a Materialist Thinker: Hobbesian Reflections on Ethics and Politics*. Stanford, CA: Stanford University Press.
Fukuyama, Francis (1989): The End of History? *National Interest* 16, pp. 3–18.
— (1992): *The End of History and the Last Man*. New York: Free Press.
Fumerton, Patricia (2006): *Unsettled: The Culture of Mobility and the Working Poor in Early Modern England*. Chicago, IL: University of Chicago Press.
Gauchet, Marcel, (2016): Tocqueville, America, and Us: On the Genesis of Democratic Societies. Translated by Jacob Hamburger. *The Tocqueville Review/La Revue Tocqueville*, 37/2, pp. 163–231. ["Alexis de Tocqueville, l'Amérique et nous," 1980]
Gauthier, David P. (1979): *The Logic of Leviathan: The Moral and Political Theory of Thomas Hobbes*. Oxford: Clarendon Press.
— (1982): Three against Justice: The Foole, the Sensible Knave, and the Lydian Shepherd. *Midwest Studies in Philosophy* 7, pp. 11–29.
— (1987): *Morals by Agreement*. Oxford: Oxford University Press.
— (2006): *Rousseau: The Sentiment of Existence*. Cambridge: Cambridge University Press.
— and Robert Sugden (eds.) (1993): *Rationality, Justice and the Social Contract: Themes from Morals by Agreement*. New York: Harvester Wheatsheaf.
Gay, Peter (1985): Freud's America. In: Frank Trommler and Joseph McVeigh (eds.), *America and the Germans: An Assessment of a Three-Hundred-Year History. Volume 2: The Relationship in the Twentieth Century*. Philadelphia: University of Pennsylvania Press, pp. 303–14.
Gearhart, Suzanne (1986): The Dialectic and its Aesthetic Other: Hegel and Diderot. *Modern Language Notes* 101/5, pp. 1042–66.
Gehlen, Arnold (1960): *Zeit-Bilder: Zur Soziologie und Ästhetik moderner Malerei*. Frankfurt: Athenäum.
— (1969): *Moral und Hypermoral: Eine pluralistische Ethik*. Frankfurt: Vittorio Klostermann.
— (1980–): *Gesamtausgabe*. Edited by Karl-Siegbert Rehberg. Frankfurt: Vittorio Klostermann.
Gide, André (1966 [1931]): *The Counterfeiters*. Translated by Dorothy Bussy. Harmondsworth: Penguin. [*Les Faux-Monnayeu*, 1925]
Girard, René (1978): *Des choses cachées depuis la fondation du monde*. Paris: Grasset.
— (1986): *The Scapegoat*. Translated by Yvonne Freccero. Baltimore, MD: Johns Hopkins University Press. [*Le Bouc émissaire*, 1982]
Goebbels, Joseph (1967 [1934]): Der Faschismus und seine praktischen Ergebnisse. In: Ernst Nolte (ed.), *Theorien über den Faschismus*. Cologne: Kiepenheuer und Witsch, pp. 314–19.
Goethe, Johann Wolfgang von (1970 [1962]): *Italian Journey*. Translated by W. H. Auden and Elizabeth Mayer. London: Penguin Books. [*Italienische Reise*, 1816–17]
— (2016): *The Essential Goethe*. Edited by Matthew Bell. Princeton, NJ: Princeton University Press.
Goldman, Merle (1967): *Literary Dissent in Communist China*. Cambridge, MA: Harvard University Press.
— (1989): Mao's Obsession with the Political Role of Literature and the Intellectuals. In: Roderick MacFarquhar, Eugene Wu, and Timothy Cheek (eds.), *The Secret Speeches of Chairman Mao*. Cambridge, MA: Harvard University Press, pp. 39–58.
Goldman, René (1962): The Rectification Campaign at Peking University: May–June 1957. *China Quarterly* 12, pp. 138–53.
— (1962): *The Rectification Campaign of May–June 1957 and the Student Movement at Peking University*. Master's thesis (typescript). New York: Columbia University.

433

Goldsmith, Maurice M. (1981): Picturing Hobbes's Politics? The Illustrations to Philosophical Rudiments. *Journal of the Warburg and Courtauld Institutes* 44, pp. 232–7.

Gorer, Geoffrey (1948): *The American People: A Study in National Character*. New York: W.W. Norton & Company.

Gorresio, Vittorio (1949): *I carissimi nemici*. Milan: Longanesi.

Graeber, David (2011): Occupy and Anarchism's Gift of Democracy. *The Guardian*, November 15. Available at: www.theguardian.com/commentisfree/cifamerica/2011/nov/15/occupy-anarchism-gift-democracy (accessed on March 13, 2018).

— (2012): Occupy's Liberation from Liberalism: The Real Meaning of May Day. *The Guardian*, May 7. Available at: www.theguardian.com/commentisfree/cifamerica/2012/may/07/occupy-liberation-from-liberalism (accessed on March 13, 2018).

Gramsci, Antonio (1971): *Selections from the Prison Notebooks*. Edited and translated by Quentin Hoare and Geoffrey Nowell Smith. London: Lawrence & Wishart.

— (1999): *Gefängnishefte*, Vol. 9. Hamburg: Argument. [*Quaderni del carcere*, 1975]

Granqvist, Hans (1967): *The Red Guard: A Report on Mao's Revolution*. London: Pall Mall.

Gregor-Dellin, Martin (1980): *Richard Wagner: Sein Leben – sein Werk – sein Jahrhundert*. Munich: Piper.

Gross, Raphael (2007): *Carl Schmitt and the Jews: The "Jewish Question," the Holocaust, and German Legal Theory*. Translated by Joel Golb. Madison: University of Wisconsin Press. [*Carl Schmitt und die Juden: Eine deutsche Rechtslehre*, 2000]

Günther, Frieder (2004): *Denken vom Staat her: Die bundesdeutsche Staatsrechtslehre zwischen Dezision und Integration 1949–1970*. Munich: Oldenbourg.

Guillemin, Henri (1962): Jean-Jacques Rousseau, trouble-fête. *Livres de France* 10, pp. 7–9.

Habermas, Jürgen (1978 [1963]): *Theorie und Praxis: Sozialphilosophische Studien*. Frankfurt: Suhrkamp.

— (2001): *The Postnational Constellation: Political Essays*. Translated and edited by Max Pensky. Cambridge: Polity. [*Die postnationale Konstellation: Politische Essays*, 1998]

— (2007 [1973]): *Theory and Practice*. Translated by John Viertel. Cambridge: Polity.

— (2013): Demokratie oder Kapitalismus? Vom Elend der nationalstaatlichen Fragmentierung in einer kapitalistisch integrierten Weltgesellschaft. *Blätter für deutsche und internationale Politik* 58/5, pp. 59–70.

Halberstam, Daniel (2006): Of Grace and Dignity in Law: A Tribute to Friedrich Schiller. In: Walter Hinderer (ed.), *Friedrich Schiller und der Weg in die Moderne*. Würzburg: Königshausen & Neumann, pp. 205–19.

Hall, Stuart (1959): Absolute Beginnings: Reflections on The Secondary Modern Generation. *Universities & Left Review* 7, pp. 17–25.

— (1959): Politics of Adolescence? *Universities & Left Review* 6, pp. 2–4.

— (1990) The Emergence of Cultural Studies and the Crisis of the Humanities. *October* 53, pp. 11–23.

Hallward, Peter (2003): *Badiou: A Subject to Truth*. Minneapolis: University of Minnesota Press.

Hamilton, Alexander, John Jay, and James Madison (1788): *The Federalist: A Collection of Essays, Written in Favour of the New Constitution, As Agreed Upon by the Federal Convention, September 17, 1787, in Two Volumes*. New York: J. and A. McLean.

Hampton, Jean (1986): *Hobbes and the Social Contract Tradition*. Cambridge: Cambridge University Press.

Hardin, Garrett (1968): The Tragedy of the Commons. *Science* 162, pp. 1243–8.

Hardt, Michael and Antonio Negri (2000): *Empire*. Cambridge, MA: Harvard University Press.

Hastings, Max (2011): Years of Liberal Dogma Have Spawned a Generation of Amoral, Uneducated, Welfare Dependent, Brutalised Youngsters. *Daily Mail*, August 10. Available at: www.dailymail.co.uk/debate/article-2024284/UK-riots-2011-Liberal-dogma-spawned-generation-brutalised-youths.html (accessed on January 10, 2018).

REFERENCES

Hegel, Georg Wilhelm Friedrich (1892): *Lectures on the History of Philosophy*, Vol. 1. Translated by E. S. Haldane. London: Kegan Paul, Trench, Trübner & Co. [*Vorlesungen über die Geschichte der Philosophie*, 1840]
— (1894): *Hegel's Philosophy of Mind, Translated from the Encyclopaedia of the Philosophical Sciences*. Translated by William Wallace. Oxford: Clarendon Press. [*Enzyklopädie der philosophischen Wissenschaften im Grundrisse*, 1830]
— (1977): *The Difference Between Fichte's and Schelling's System of Philosophy*. Translated by H. S. Harris and Walter Cerf. Albany, NY: State University of New York Press. [*Differenz des Fichte'schen und Schelling'schen Systems der Philosophie*, 1801]
— (1977): *Phenomenology of Spirit*. Translated by A. V. Miller. Oxford: Oxford University Press. [*Phänomenologie des Geistes*, 1807]
— (1979): *System of Ethical Life and First Philosophy of Spirit*. Edited and translated by H. S. Harris and T. M. Knox. Albany, NY: State University of New York Press. [*System der Sittlichkeit*, 1802–3; *Enzyklopädie der philosophischen Wissenschaften, Dritter Teil: Philosophie des Geistes*, 1817]
— (1983): *Hegel and the Human Spirit*. Translated by Leo Rauch. Detroit, MI: Wayne State University Press. [*Jenaer Systementwürfe III*, 1976]
— (1984 [1975]): *Lectures on the Philosophy of World History*. Translated by H. B. Nisbet. Cambridge: Cambridge University Press. [*Vorlesungen über die Philosophie der Geschichte*, 1837]
— (1986): *Werke 1: Frühe Schriften*. Edited by Eva Moldenhauer and Karl Markus Michel. Frankfurt: Suhrkamp.
— (1988): *Aesthetics: Lectures on Fine Art, Volume I*. Translated by T. M. Knox. Oxford: Clarendon Press. [*Vorlesungen über die Ästhetik*, 1835]
— (1996 [1948]): *Early Theological Writings*. Translated by T. M. Knox and Richard Kroner. Philadelphia: University of Pennsylvania Press.
— (1999): *Political Writings*. Edited by Lawrence Dickety and H. B. Nisbet, translated by H. B. Nisbet. Cambridge: Cambridge University Press.
— (2003 [1991]): *Elements of the Philosophy of Right*. Edited by Allen W. Wood, translated by H. B. Nisbet. Cambridge: Cambridge University Press. [*Grundlinien der Philosophie des Rechts*, 1821]
— (2005): *Die Philosophie des Rechts: Vorlesung von 1821/22*. Edited by Hansgeorg Hoppe. Frankfurt: Suhrkamp.
— (2015): *The Science of Logic*. Edited and translated by George di Giovanni. Cambridge: Cambridge University Press. [*Wissenschaft der Logik*, 1812–16]
Heidegger, Martin (1962): *Being and Time*. Translated by John Macquarrie and Edward Robinson. Oxford: Blackwell. [*Sein und Zeit*, 1927]
Heine, Heinrich (2006): *Ludwig Börne: A Memorial*. Translated by Jeffrey L. Sammons. Rochester, NY: Camden House. [*Ludwig Börne: Eine Denkschrift*, 1840]
— (2006 [1982]): *Poetry and Prose*. Edited by Jost Hermand and Robert C. Holub. New York: Continuum.
Heller, Hermann (1971 [1934]): Staatslehre. In: *Gesammelte Schriften*, Vol. 3. Leiden: Sijthoff, pp. 79–395.
Heller-Roazen, Daniel (2009): *The Enemy of All: Piracy and the Law of Nations*. Brooklyn, NY: Zone Books.
[Helvétius, Claude Adrien] (1758): *De l'Esprit*. Paris: Durand. [first edition published anonymously]
Helvétius, Claude Adrien (1773): *De l'Homme, de ses facultés intellectuelles et de son éducation*. London: Typographical Society.
— (1810 [1807]): *A Treatise on Man, His Intellectual Faculties and His Education. In two volumes*. Translated by William Hooper. London: Albion Press.
— (1810): *De l'Esprit; or, Essays on the Mind, and its Several Faculties*. Translated by William Mudford. London: Albion Press.
Herder, Johann Gottfried (2015 [1997]): *On World History: An Anthology*. Edited by Hans

Adler and Ernst A. Menze, translated by Ernst A. Menze with Michael Palma. London: Routledge.

Herrera, Carlos Miguel (2007): Communauté sans substance, inéluctable contrainte: Le Freud de Kelsen. *Incidence* 3, pp. 73–86.

Herwegh, Georg (1877): *Neue Gedichte*. Zurich: Verlagsmagazin.

Herzen, Alexander (1956): From the Other Shore. In: *Selected Philosophical Works*. Translated by L. Navrozov. Moscow: Foreign Languages Publishing House, pp. 336–469.

Hessing, Jakob (1993): *Der Fluch des Propheten: Drei Abhandlungen zu Sigmund Freud*. Frankfurt: Jüdischer Verlag im Suhrkamp Verlag.

Hill, Christopher (1958): *Puritanism and Revolution: Studies in Interpretation of the English Revolution of the Seventeenth Century*. London: Martin Secker & Warburg.

— (1997 [1965]): *Intellectual Origins of the English Revolution Revisited*. Oxford: Clarendon Press.

Hirsch, Alfred (2004): *Recht auf Gewalt? Spuren philosophischer Gewaltrechtfertigung nach Hobbes*. Munich: Wilhelm Fink.

Hirschman, Albert O. (1982): *Shifting Involvements: Private Interest and Public Action*. Princeton, NJ: Princeton University Press.

— (2013 [1977]): *The Passions and the Interests: Political Arguments for Capitalism Before its Triumph*. Princeton, NJ: Princeton University Press.

Hitler, Adolf (1943 [1925/27]): *Mein Kampf*. Translated by Ralph Mannheim. Boston, MA: Houghton Mifflin.

— (1992): *Reden, Schriften, Anordnungen*, Vol. II.1. Edited by Bärbel Dusik. Munich: Saur.

Hobbes, Thomas (1787): *Œuvres philosophiques et politiques, Tome premier, contenant les Élémens du Citoyen*. Neufchatel: De l'Imprimerie de la Société Typographique.

— (1839): *The English Works of Thomas Hobbes*. Eleven volumes. Edited by William Molesworth. London: John Bohn.

— (1839 [1658]): *Opera Philosophica quae Latina Scripsit*, Vol. 2. Edited by William Molesworth. London: John Bohn.

— (1983 [1642]): *De Cive: The English Version. The Philosophical Works, Vol. III*. Edited by Howard Warrender. Oxford: Clarendon Press.

— (1983 [1642]): *De Cive: The Latin Version. The Philosophical Works, Vol. II*. Edited by Howard Warrender. Oxford: Clarendon Press.

— (1996 [1651]): *Leviathan*. Edited by Richard Tuck. Cambridge: Cambridge University Press.

— (1998 [1972]): *Man and Citizen: De Homine and De Cive*. Translated by Charles T. Wood, T. S. K. Scott-Craig and Bernard Gert. Indianapolis, IN: Hackett Publishing.

— (1998 [1642]): *On the Citizen*. Edited and translated by Richard Tuck and Michael Silverthorne. Cambridge: Cambridge University Press.

— (2012 [1652/1668]): *Leviathan: The English and Latin Texts. The Philosophical Works, Vol. IV/V*. Edited by Noel Malcolm. Oxford: Clarendon Press.

— (2013 [1889]): *The Elements of Law Natural and Politic*. Edited by Ferdinand Tönnies. London: Routledge.

Hobsbawm, Eric J. (1965 [1959]): *Primitive Rebels: Studies in Archaic Forms of Social Movement in the 19th and 20th Centuries*. New York: W.W. Norton & Company.

Hoekstra, Kinch (1997): Hobbes and the Foole. *Political Theory* 25/5, pp. 620–54.

Hollis, Martin (1998): *Trust Within Reason*. Cambridge: Cambridge University Press.

— (2002 [1994]): *The Philosophy of Social Science: An Introduction*. Cambridge: Cambridge University Press.

Holston, James (2007): *Insurgent Citizenship*. Princeton, NJ: Princeton University Press.

Honig, Bonnie (1993): *Political Theory and the Displacement of Politics*. Ithaca, NY: Cornell University Press.

— (2001): *Democracy and the Foreigner*. Princeton, NJ: Princeton University Press.

— (2009): *Emergency Politics: Paradox, Law, Democracy*. Princeton, NJ: Princeton University Press.

Honneth, Axel (2005 [1995]): *The Struggle for Recognition: The Moral Grammar of Social Conflicts*. Translated by Joel Anderson. Cambridge: Polity. [*Kampf um Anerkennung: Zur moralischen Grammatik sozialer Konflikte*, 1992]
— (2012): *The I in We: Studies in the Theory of Recognition*. Translated by Joseph Ganahl. Cambridge: Polity. [*Das Ich im Wir: Studien zur Anerkennungstheorie*, 2010]
— (2014): *Freedom's Right: The Social Foundations of Democratic Life*. Translated by Joseph Ganahl. Cambridge: Polity. [*Das Recht der Freiheit: Grundriss einer demokratischen Sittlichkeit*, 2011]
Horace (2000): *The Complete Odes and Epodes*. Translated by David West. Oxford: Oxford University Press.
— (2001): *The Epistles of Horace*. Translated by David Ferry. New York: Farrar, Straus and Giroux.
— (2002): *The Odes: New Translations by Contemporary Poets*. Princeton, NJ: Princeton University Press.
Horkheimer, Max (1949): Authoritarianism and the Family Today. In: Ruth Nanda Anshen (ed.), *The Family: Its Function and Destiny*. New York: Harper and Brothers, pp. 359–69. ["Autorität und Familie in der Gegenwart," 1947]
— (1978): *Dawn and Decline: Notes 1926–1931 and 1950–1969*. Translated by Michael Shaw. New York: The Seabury Press. [*Notizen und Dämmerung*, 1974]
— (1985 [1978]): The Authoritarian State. In: Andrew Arato and Eike Gebhardt (eds.), *The Essential Frankfurt School Reader*. New York: Continuum, pp. 95–117. ["Autoritärer Staat," 1940]
— (1988–96): *Gesammelte Schriften*. Nineteen volumes. Edited by A. Schmidt and G. Schmid Noerr. Frankfurt: Fischer.
— (1995): *Between Philosophy and Social Science: Selected Early Writings*. Edited and translated by G. Frederick Hunter, Matthew S. Kramer, and John Torpey. Cambridge, MA: MIT Press.
— (2002 [1972]): *Critical Theory: Selected Essays*. Translated by Matthew J. O'Connell et al. New York: Continuum. [*Kritische Theorie*, 1968]
— (2012 [1974]): *Critique of Instrumental Reason: Lectures and Essays Since the End of World War II*. Translated by Matthew J. O'Connell et al. London: Verso.
Horkheimer, Max and Theodor W. Adorno (2002 [1944]): *Dialectic of Englightenment: Philosophical Fragments*. Edited by Gunzelin Schmid Noerr, translated by Edmund Jephcott. Stanford, CA: Stanford University Press. [*Dialektik der Aufklärung und Schriften 1940–1950*, 1987]
Horn, Klaus and Alexander Mitscherlich (1982 [1968]): Vom "halbstarken" zum starken Protest. *Psyche* 36, pp. 1120–43.
Hoyng, Hans and Gregor Peter Schmitz (2012): Wo bleibt der Aufstand von links? Interview with Francis Fukuyama. *Spiegel* 5, pp. 86–8.
Hua Sheng (1990): Big Character Posters in China: A Historical Survey. *Journal of Chinese Law* 4, pp. 234–56.
Huard, Raymond (1988): Marx et Engels devant la marginalité: La découverte du lumpen-proletariat. *Romantisme* 59, pp. 5–17.
Hugo, Victor (1894): *Hans of Iceland*. Translated by George Burnham Ives. Boston, MA: Little, Brown and Company.
— (1898): *Correspondance 1836–1882*. Paris: Calmann Lévy.
— (1909): *The Works of Victor Hugo, Volume 3: Dramas*. Translated by George Burnham Ives. Boston, MA: Little, Brown and Company.
— (1967–70): *Œuvres complètes*. Edited by Jean Massin. Paris: Le Club Français du Livre.
— (1972): *Choses vues: Souvenirs, journaux, cahiers 1830–1848*. Edited by Hubert Juin. Paris: Gallimard.
— (1975): *Notre-Dame de Paris, 1482 – Les Travailleurs de la Mer*. Edited by Jacques Seebacher and Yves Gohin. Paris: Gallimard.
— (1981 [1823]): *Han d'Islande*. Edited by Bernard Leuilliot. Paris: Gallimard.

437

— (1995 [1862]): *Les Misérables*, Volumes 1 and 2. Edited by Yves Gohin. Paris: Gallimard.

— (1999 [1993]): *Notre-Dame de Paris*. Translated by Alban Krailsheimer. Oxford: Oxford University Press.

— (2002 [1869]): *L'Homme qui rit*. Edited by Roger Borderie. Paris: Gallimard.

— (2008): *Les Misérables*. Translated by Julie Rose. New York: Random House.

— (2009 [1831]): *Notre-Dame de Paris, 1482*. Edited by Benedikte Andersson. Paris: Gallimard.

Hulbert, James (1983): Diderot in the Text of Hegel: A Question of Intertextuality. *Studies in Romanticism* 22/2, pp. 267–91.

Humboldt, Wilhelm von (1999): *On Language: On the Diversity of Human Language Construction and its Influence on the Mental Development of the Human Species*. Edited by Michael Losonsky, translated by Peter Heath. Cambridge: Cambridge University Press. [*Ueber die Verschiedenheit des menschlichen Sprachbaus und ihren Einfluss auf die geistige Entwicklung des Menschengeschlechts*, 1836]

Hume, David (1985 [1748]): Of the Original Contract. In: *Essays Moral, Political, and Literary*. Indianapolis, IN: Liberty Fund, pp. 465–87.

Hunt, Lynn (1992): *The Family Romance of the French Revolution*. Berkeley: University of California Press.

Ibsen, Henrik (1910): *Speeches and New Letters*. Translated by Arne Kidal. Boston, MA: The Gorham Press.

— (2008): *Four Major Plays: A Doll's House, Ghosts, Hedda Gabler, The Master Builder*. Translated by James McFarlane and Jens Arup. Oxford: Oxford University Press.

Invisible Committee (2009): *The Coming Insurrection*. Los Angeles, CA: Semiotext(e). [*L'insurrection qui vient*, 2007]

Jaeggi, Rahel (2014): *Alienation*. Translated by Frederick Neuhouser and Alan E. Smith. New York: Columbia University Press. [*Entfremdung*, 2005]

Jameson, Virginia B. (1984): *Virtus* Re-Formed: An "Aesthetic Response" Reading of Horace, *Odes* III 2. *Transactions of the American Philological Association* 114, pp. 219–40.

Janara, Laura (2002): *Democracy Growing Up: Authority, Autonomy, and Passion in Tocqueville's Democracy in America*. Albany, NY: State University of New York Press.

Jauss, Hans Robert (1983): *The Dialogical and the Dialectical Neveu de Rameau: How Diderot Adopted Socrates and Hegel Adopted Diderot. Protocol of the Forty-fifth Colloquy*. Berkeley, CA: Center for Hermeneutical Studies in Hellenistic and Modern Culture, pp. 1–29. ["Der dialogische und der dialektische, Neveu de Rameau" in *Ästhetische Erfahrung und Literarische Hermeneutik*, 1977]

Jefferson, Thomas (1984): *Writings*. Edited by Merrill D. Peterson. New York: Library of America.

Jensen, Michael C. and William H. Meckling (1976): Theory of the Firm: Managerial Behavior, Agency Costs and Ownership Structure. *Journal of Financial Economics* 3, pp. 305–60.

Jin Zhong (2004): In Search of the Soul of Lin Zhao. *China Rights Forum* 3, pp. 90–1.

Jones, Ernest (1913): A Preface to Politics: Von Walter Lippmann. *Imago* II, pp. 452–6.

Jones, Gareth Stedman (1976): *Outcast London: A Study in the Relationship Between Classes in Victorian Society*. Harmondsworth: Peregrine.

Jones, Owen (2011): *Chavs: The Demonization of the Working Class*. London: Verso.

Jordan, June (2007 [1978]): Poem for South African Women. In: Jan Heller Levi and Sara Miles (eds.), *Directed by Desire: The Collected Poems of June Jordan*. Port Townsend, WA: Copper Canyon Press.

Jünger, Friedrich Georg (1930): Krieg und Krieger. In: Ernst Jünger (ed.), *Krieg und Krieger*. Berlin: Junker und Dünnhaupt, pp. 51–67.

Jütte, Robert (1994): *Poverty and Deviance in Early Modern Europe*. Cambridge: Cambridge University Press.

Kagan, Robert (2016): This is how fascism comes to America. *Washington Post*, May 18. Available at: www.washingtonpost.com/opinions/this-is-how-fascism-comes-to-america/2016/05/17/c4e32c58-1c47-11e6-8c7b-6931e66333e7_story.html?utm_term=. f8298572b9fe (accessed on March 26, 2018).

Kahn, Victoria (2001): Hamlet or Hecuba: Carl Schmitt's Decision. *Representations* 83, pp. 67–96.

— (2004): *Wayward Contracts: The Crisis of Political Obligation in England, 1640–1674.* Princeton, NJ: Princeton University Press.

Kaiser, Gerhard (1974): Idylle und Revolution: Schillers "Wilhelm Tell." In: Richard Brinkmann et al., *Deutsche Literatur und Französische Revolution: Sieben Studien.* Göttingen: Vandenhoeck & Ruprecht, pp. 87–128.

Kaiser, Günther (1959): *Randalierende Jugend: Eine soziologische und kriminologische Studie über die sogenannten "Halbstarken."* Heidelberg: Quelle & Meyer.

Kant, Immanuel (1999): An Answer to the Question: What Is Enlightenment? In: *Practical Philosophy.* Translated and edited by Mary J. Gregor. Cambridge: Cambridge University Press, pp. 11–22. ["Beantwortung der Frage: Was ist Aufklärung?", 1784]

— (2001): *Lectures on Ethics.* Edited and translated by Peter Heath. Cambridge: Cambridge University Press.

— (2006): *Anthropology from a Pragmatic Point of View.* Edited and translated by Robert B. Louden. Cambridge: Cambridge University Press. [*Anthropologie in pragmatischer Hinsicht,* 1798]

— (2016 [1970]): *Political Writings.* Edited by Hans Reiss, translated by H. B. Nisbet. Cambridge: Cambridge University Press.

Kantorowicz, Ernst H. (1951): *Pro patria mori* in Medieval Political Thought. *American Historical Review* 56/3, pp. 472–92.

Kavka, Gregory S. (1995): The Rationality of Rule-Following: Hobbes's Dispute with the Foole. *Law and Philosophy* 14/1, pp. 5–34.

Keats, John (2001): *Complete Poems and Selected Letters.* New York: Random House.

Keedus, Liisi (2012): Liberalism and the Question of "The Proud": Hannah Arendt and Leo Strauss as Readers of Hobbes. *Journal of the History of Ideas* 73/2, pp. 319–41.

Keller, James R. (2007): The Lord of Misrule: Eminem and the Rabelaisian Carnival. *Americanist* 24, pp. 101–16.

Kelm, Holden (2015): *Hegel und Foucault: Die Geschichtlichkeit des Wissens als Entwicklung und Transformation.* Berlin: Walter de Gruyter.

Kelsen, Hans (1922): *Der soziologische und der juristische Staatsbegriff.* Tübingen: Mohr.

— (1923): *Hauptprobleme der Staatsrechtslehre.* Tübingen: Mohr.

— (1924): The Conception of the State and Social Psychology with Special Reference to Freud's Group Theory. *International Journal of Psycho-Analysis* 5, pp. 1–38. ["Der Begriff des Staates und die Sozialpsychologie: Mit besonderer Berücksichtigung von Freuds Theorie der Masse," 1922]

— (1930): *Der Staat als Integration: Eine prinzipielle Auseinandersetzung.* Vienna: Springer.

— (1942): Platonic Love, translated by George B. Wilbur. *American Imago* 3/1–2, pp. 3–110. ["Die platonische Liebe," 1933]

— (1943): *Society and Nature: A Sociological Inquiry.* Chicago, IL: University of Chicago Press.

— (1973): *Essays in Legal and Moral Philosophy.* Selected by Ota Weinberger, translated by Peter Heath. Dordrecht: D. Reidel.

— (2006): *Verteidigung der Demokratie: Abhandlungen zur Demokratietheorie.* Edited by Matthias Jestaedt and Oliver Lepsius: Tübingen: Mohr Siebeck.

— (2013): *The Essence and Value of Democracy.* Edited by Nadia Urbinati and Carlo Invernizzi Accetti, translated by Brian Graf. Lanham, MD: Rowman & Littlefield [*Vom Wesen und Wert der Demokratie,* 1920]

Kendall, Willmoore (1985): Introduction: How to Read Rousseau's *Government of Poland.* In: Jean-Jacques Rousseau, *The Government of Poland.* Indianapolis, IN: Hackett, pp. ix–xxxix.

Khosrokhavar, Farhad (1995): Le quasi-individu: de la néo-communauté à la nécro-communauté. In: François Dubet and Michel Wieviorka (eds.), *Penser le sujet: Autour d'Alain Touraine*. Paris: Fayard, pp. 235–56.

Kierkegaard, Sören (1992): *Concluding Unscientific Postscript to* Philosophical Fragments, *Volume 1*. Edited and translated by Howard V. Hong and Edna H. Hong. Princeton, NJ: Princeton University Press. [*Afsluttende uvidenskabelig Efterskrift til de philosophiske Smuler*, 1846]

— (1992): *Either/Or: A Fragment of Life*. Translated by Alastair Hannay. London: Penguin. [*Enten – Eller*, 1843]

Kinsley, Michael (2016): Donald Trump is actually a fascist. *Washington Post*, December 9. Available at: www.washingtonpost.com/opinions/donald-trump-is-actually-a-fascist/2016/12/09/e193a2b6-bd77-11e6-94ac-3d324840106c_story.html?utm_term=.9a28e1614102 (accessed on March 26, 2018).

Kissler, Alexander and Christoph Schwennicke (2016): Das kann nicht gut gehen [interview with Peter Sloterdijk]. *Cicero* 2, pp. 14–23.

Kitcher, Philip and Richard Schacht (2004): *Finding an Ending: Reflections on Wagner's Ring*. Oxford: Oxford University Press.

Klausen, Jimmy Casas (2005): Of Hobbes and Hospitality in Diderot's Supplement to the "Voyage of Bougainville." *Polity* 37, pp. 167–92.

Kluth, Heinz (1956): Die "Halbstarken" – Legende oder Wirklichkeit? *deutsche jugend* 4, pp. 495–502.

Kojève, Alexandre (1968): *Introduction à la lecture de Hegel: Leçons sur la* Phénoménologie de l'Ésprit *professées de 1933 à 1939 à l'École des Hautes Études*. Edited by Raymond Queneau. Paris: Gallimard.

Köpnick, Lutz (1994): *Nothungs Modernität: Wagners "Ring" und die Poesie der Macht*. Munich: Wilhelm Fink.

Koschorke, Albrecht (2003): Brüderbund und Bann: Das Drama der politischen Inklusion in Schillers *Tell*. In: Uwe Hebekus, Ethel Matala de Mazza and Albrecht Koschorke (eds.), *Das Politische: Figurenlehre des sozialen Körpers nach der Romantik*. Munich: Wilhelm Fink, pp. 106–22.

Koselleck, Reinhart (1988): *Critique and Crisis: Enlightenment and the Pathogenesis of Modern Society*. Translated by Thomas McCarthy. Cambridge, MA: MIT Press. [*Kritik und Krise: Eine Studie zur Pathogenese der bürgerlichen Welt*, 1959]

— (2006): *Begriffsgeschichten: Studien zur Semantik und Pragmatik der politischen und sozialen Sprache*. Frankfurt: Suhrkamp.

Kramer, Robert (1996): Insight and Blindness: Visions of Rank. In: Otto Rank, *A Psychology of Difference: The American Lectures*. Edited by Robert Kramer. Princeton, NJ: Princeton University Press, pp. 3–47.

Kraus, Jody S. (1993): *The Limits of Hobbesian Contractarianism*. Cambridge: Cambridge University Press.

Kraus, Richard (2011): Let a Hundred Flowers Blossom, Let a Hundred Schools of Thought Contend. In: Ban Wang (ed.), *Words and Their Stories: Essays on the Language of the Chinese Revolution*. Leiden: Brill, pp. 249–62.

Krauthammer, Charles (2016): Donald Trump and the fitness threshold. *Washington Post*, August 4. Available at: www.washingtonpost.com/opinions/donald-trump-and-the-fitness-threshold/2016/08/04/b06bae34-5a69-11e6-831d-0324760ca856_story.html?utm_term=.d9ed13a36040 (accessed on March 26, 2018).

Kristeva, Julia (1991): *Strangers to Ourselves*. Translated by Leon S. Roudiez. New York: Columbia University Press. [*Étrangers à nous-mêmes*, 1988]

Krüger, Heinz-Hermann (1983): Sprachlose Rebellen? Zur Subkultur der "Halbstarken" in den Fünfziger Jahren. In: Wilfried Breyvogel (ed.), *Autonomie und Widerstand: Zur Theorie und Geschichte des Jugendprotestes*. Essen: Rigodon, pp. 78–82.

Kuhr, Irma (1952): Schule und Jugend in einer ausgebombten Stadt. In: Irma Kuhr and Giselheid Koepnick, *Schule und Jugend in einer ausgebombten Stadt – Mädchen einer Oberprima*. Darmstadt: Roether, pp. 1–206.

La Rovere, Luca (2008): *L'eredità del fascismo: Gli intellectuali, i giovani e la transizione al postfascismo 1943–1948*. Turin: Bollati Boringhieri.

Laclau, Ernesto (2000): Structure, History and the Political. In: Judith Butler, Ernesto Laclau, and Slavoj Žižek (eds.), *Contingency, Hegemony, Universality: Contemporary Dialogues on the Left*. London: Verso, pp. 182–212.

Lacoue-Labarthe, Philippe (1986): *L'imitation des modernes (Typographies 2)*. Paris: Galilée.

Lagasnerie, Geoffroy de (2017): *The Art of Revolt: Snowden, Assange, Manning*. Translated by Erik Butler. Stanford, CA: Stanford University Press. [*L'art de la révolte: Snowden, Assange, Manning*, 2015]

Laqueur, Walter Z. (1984 [1962]): *Young Germany: A History of the German Youth Movement*. New Brunswick, NJ: Transaction Books.

Larmore, Charles (2008): *The Autonomy of Morality*. Cambridge: Cambridge University Press.

Lasch, Christopher (1979): *The Culture of Narcissism: American Life in an Age of Diminishing Expectations*. New York: W.W. Norton & Company.

Lassalle, Ferdinand (1919–20): *Gesammelte Reden und Schriften*. Berlin: Paul Cassirer.

Laufer, Roger (1960): Structure et signification du "Neveu de Rameau" de Diderot. *Revue des Sciences humaines* 100, pp. 399–413.

Lefort, Claude (1981): *L'invention démocratique: Les limites de la domination totalitaire*. Paris: Librairie Arthème Fayard.

— (1986): *The Political Forms of Modern Society: Bureaucracy, Democracy, Totalitarianism*. Edited by John B. Thompson. Cambridge: Polity.

— (2000): *Writing: The Political Test*. Translated by David Ames Curtis. Durham, NC: Duke University Press. [*Écrire: À l'épreuve du politique*, 1992]

— (2007): *Le temps présent: Essais 1945–2005*. Paris: Belin.

Lenin, Vladimir Ilyich (1976 [1915]): On the Question of Dialectics. In: *Collected Works*, Vol. 38. Translated by Clemence Dutt. Moscow: Progress Publishers, pp. 357–61.

Lepsius, Oliver (2009): Kelsens Demokratietheorie. In: Tamara Ehs (ed.), *Hans Kelsen: Eine politikwissenschaftliche Einführung*. Vienna: Nomos, pp. 67–89.

Leuchtenburg, William E. (2015 [1961]): Walter Lippmann's *Drift and Mastery*. In: Walter Lippmann, *Drift and Mastery: An Attempt to Diagnose the Current Unrest* [1914]. Madison: The University of Wisconsin Press, pp. 1–14.

Levin, David J. (1998): *Richard Wagner, Fritz Lang, and the Nibelungen: The Dramaturgy of Disavowal*. Princeton, NJ: Princeton University Press.

Lévinas, Emmanuel (1991): *Otherwise Than Being or Beyond Essence*. Translated by Alphonso Lingis. Dordrecht: Kluwer Academic. [*Autrement qu'être ou au-delà de l'essence*, 1974]

Levy-Bruhl, Lucien (1923): *Primitive Mentality*. Translated by Lilian A. Clare. London: George Allen & Unwin. [*La mentalité primitive*, 1922]

Ley, Michael (1997): Apokalyptische Bewegungen in der Moderne. In: Michael Lay and Julius H. Schoeps (eds.), *Der Nationalsozialismus als politische Religion*. Bodenheim: Philo, pp. 12–29.

Lieberman, E. James (1985): *Acts of Will: The Life and Work of Otto Rank*. New York: Free Press.

Liepe, Wolfgang (1963 [1926]): Der junge Schiller und Rousseau: Eine Nachprüfung der Rousseaulegende um den "Räuber"-Dichter. In: *Beiträge zur Literatur- und Geistesgeschichte*. Neumünster: Wachholtz, pp. 29–64.

Linebaugh, Peter and Marcus Rediker (2000): *The Many-Headed Hydra: Sailors, Slaves, Commoners, and the Hidden History of the Revolutionary Atlantic*. Boston, MA: Beacon Press.

Lippmann, Walter (1913): *A Preface to Politics*. New York: Mitchell Kennerley.

— (1929): *A Preface to Morals*. New York: The Macmillan Company.

— (2015 [1914]): *Drift and Mastery: An Attempt to Diagnose the Current Unrest*. Madison: The University of Wisconsin Press.

441

Lloyd, Sharon A. (2009): *Morality in the Philosophy of Thomas Hobbes: Cases in the Law of Nature*. Cambridge: Cambridge University Press.

Loch, Dietmar (1995): Moi, Khaled Kelkal. Available at: upvericsoriano.files.wordpress.com/2009/06/dossier-khaled-kelkal.pdf (accessed on March 21, 2018).

Locke, John (1824 [1691]): *The Works of John Locke, Volume 4*. London: Rivington.

Loewenberg, Peter (1983): The Psychohistorical Origins of the Nazi Youth Cohort. In: *Decoding the Past: The Psychohistorical Approach*. New York: Alfred A. Knopf, pp. 240–83.

Lohmann, Dieter (1989): "Dulce et decorum est pro patria mori." Zu Horaz c. III 2. In: *Schola Anatolica: Freundesgabe für Hermann Steinthal*, Tübingen: Kollegium und Verein der Freunde des Uhland-Gymnasiums Tübingen, pp. 336–72.

Lorenz, Emil (1920): Dr. Paul Federn: Zur Psychologie der Revolution: Die vaterlose Gesellschaft. *Imago* VI, pp. 91–2.

— (1920): Hans Blüher: Die Rolle der Erotik in der männlichen Gesellschaft. *Imago* VI, pp. 92–4.

Löwy, Michael (1995): Karl Marx et Friedrich Engels comme sociologues de la religion. *Archives des sciences sociales des religions* 89, pp. 41–52.

Lubich, Frederick A. (1994): Thomas Mann's Sexual Politics: Lost in Translation. *Comparative Literature Studies* 31/2, pp. 107–27.

Lukács, Georg (1971): *History and Class Consciousness: Studies in Marxist Dialectics*. Translated by Rodney Livingstone. Cambridge, MA: MIT Press. [*Geschichte und Klassenbewußtsein*, 1923]

Lukes, Steven (1973): *Individualism*. Oxford: Blackwell.

— (2003): *Liberals & Cannibals: The Implications of Diversity*. London: Verso.

Mabille, Louise (2009): *Nietzsche and the Anglo-Saxon Tradition*. London: Continuum.

MacFarquhar, Roderick (1974): *The Origins of the Cultural Revolution 1: Contradictions Among the People 1956–1957*. London: Oxford University Press.

— (ed.) (1960): *The Hundred Flowers*. London: Stevens and Sons.

—, Timothy Cheek, and Eugene Wu (eds.) (1989): *The Secret Speeches of Chairman Mao: From the Hundred Flowers to the Great Leap Forward*. Cambridge, MA: Harvard University Press.

Machiavelli, Niccolò (1996): *Discourses on Livy*. Translated by Harvey C. Mansfield and Nathan Tarcov. Chicago, IL: University of Chicago Press. [*Discorsi sopra la prima deca di Tito Livio*, 1531]

— (2009): *The Prince*. Translated by Tim Parks. London: Penguin. [*De Principatibus/Il Principei*, 1513/1532]

MacInnes, Colin (1986 [1959]): *Absolute Beginners*. London: Penguin.

Macpherson, C. B. (2011 [1962]): *The Political Theory of Possessive Individualism: Hobbes to Locke*. Oxford: Oxford University Press.

Magnus, George (2011): Crisis Convergence. *Foreign Policy*, August 31. Available at: foreignpolicy.com/2011/08/31/crisis-convergence (accessed on March 8, 2018).

Maistre, Joseph de (1884): *Œuvres complètes*, Vol. 1. Lyon: Vitte et Perrussel.

Makarenko, Anton S. (1954): *A Book for Parents*. Tranlsated by Robert Daglish. Moscow: Foreign Languages Publishing House. [*Kniga dlya roditeley*, 1937]

— (1970): *Werke*, Vol. 1. Berlin: Volk und Wissen.

Maleuvre, Jean-Yves (1995): Les Odes Romaines d'Horace, ou un chef-d'œuvre ignoré de la cacozélie (presque) invisible. *Revue belge de philologie et d'histoire* 73/1, pp. 53–72.

Malinowski, Bronislaw (2001 [1927]): *Sex and Repression in Savage Society*. London: Routledge. [*Mutterrechtliche Familie und Ödipuskomplex*, 1924]

Mann, Heinrich (1923): *Diktatur der Vernunft*. Berlin: Die Schmiede.

Mann, Thomas (1933): Freud's Position in the History of Modern Thought. In: *Past Masters and Other Papers*. Translated by H. T. Lowe-Porter. New York: Alfred A. Knopf, pp. 165–98. ["Die Stellung Freuds in der modernen Geistesgeschichte," 1929]

442

— (1982): *Diaries 1918–1939: 1918–1921, 1933–1939*. Translated by Richard and Clara Winston. New York: Harry N. Abrams.

— (1987 [1983]): *Reflections of a Nonpolitical Man*. Translated by Walter D. Morris. New York: Ungar. [*Betrachtungen eines Unpolitischen*, 1918]

— (2007): On the German Republic. *Modernism/modernity* 14/1, pp. 109–32. ["Von deutscher Republik," 1922]

Mannheim, Karl (1943): *Diagnosis of Our Time: Wartime Essays of a Sociologist*. London: Routledge & Kegan Paul.

— (2000 [1936]): The Problem of Generations. In: Paul Kecskemeti (ed.), *Essays on the Sociology of Knowledge: Collected Works of Karl Mannheim, Volume 5*. New York: Routledge, pp. 276–322. ["Das Problem der Generationen," 1923]

Manow, Philip (2011): *Politische Ursprungsphantasien: Der Leviathan und sein Erbe*. Constance: Konstanz University Press.

Mao Zedong (1992): *The Writings 1949–1976, Vol. II: January 1956–December 1957*. Edited by John K. Leung and Michael Y. M. Kau. Armonk, NY: M.E. Sharpe.

Marchart, Oliver (2007): *Post-Foundational Political Thought: Political Difference in Nancy, Lefort, Badiou and Laclau*. Edinburgh: Edinburgh University Press.

Marcuse, Herbert (1974 [1955]): *Eros and Civilization: A Philosophical Inquiry into Freud*. Boston, MA: Beacon Press.

— (2009 [1968]): The Struggle against Liberalism in the Totalitarian View of the State. In: *Negations: Essays in Critical Theory*. Translated by Jeremy J. Shapiro. London: MayFlyBooks, pp. 1–30. ["Der Kampf gegen den Liberalismus in der totalitären Staatsauffassung," 1934]

Marlière, Éric (2005): *Jeunes en cités: Diversité des trajectoires ou destin commun?* Paris: L'Harmattan.

Martin, Jonathan (2016): Donald Trump's Anything-Goes Campaign Sets an Alarming Political Precedent. *The New York Times*, September 17. Available at: www.nytimes.com/2016/09/18/us/politics/donald-trump-presidential-race.html (accessed on March 25, 2018).

Marty, Martin E. (1988): Fundamentalism as a Social Phenomenon. *Bulletin of the American Academy of Arts and Sciences* 42/2, pp. 15–29.

Marx, Karl (1973): *Grundrisse: Introduction to the Critique of Political Economy*. Translated by Martin Nicolaus. New York: Random House. [*Grundrisse der Kritik der Politischen Ökonomie*, 1939]

Marx, Karl and Friedrich Engels (1975–2004): *Collected Works*. Fifty volumes. Translated by Richard Dixon et al. London: Lawrence & Wishart.

Masson, David (1877): *The Life of John Milton*, Vol. V. London: Macmillan and Co.

Masson, Raoul (1970): Un ancêtre de Franz Moor. *Études Germaniques* 25/1, pp. 1–6.

Mayer, Martin (2001): *The Fed: The Inside Story of How the World's Most Powerful Financial Institution Drives Markets*. New York: Free Press.

McClay, Wilfred M. (1994): *The Masterless: Self and Society in Modern America*. Chapel Hill: University of North Carolina Press.

McCormick, John P. (1994): Fear, Technology, and the State: Carl Schmitt, Leo Strauss, and the Revival of Hobbes in Weimar and National Socialist Germany. *Political Theory* 22/4, pp. 619–52.

McKee, Yates (2016): *Strike Art: Contemporary Art and the Post-Occupy Condition*. London: Verso.

Mehlman, Jeffrey (1977): *Revolution and Repetition: Marx/Hugo/Balzac*. Berkeley: University of California Press.

Mehring, Franz (1913 [1877]): *Geschichte der Deutschen Sozialdemokratie*, Vol. 3. Stuttgart: Dietz.

Mehring, Reinhard (2005): Carl Schmitt, Leo Strauss, Thomas Hobbes und die Philosophie. *Philosophisches Jahrbuch* 112, pp. 380–94.

— (2014): *Carl Schmitt: A Biography*. Translated by Daniel Steuer. Cambridge: Polity. [*Carl Schmitt: Aufstieg und Fall*, 2009]

Meier, Heinrich (1995): *Carl Schmitt and Leo Strauss: The Hidden Dialogue*. Translated by J. Harvey Lomax. Chicago, IL: University of Chicago Press. [*Carl Schmitt, Leo Strauss und "Der Begriff des Politischen": Zu einem Dialog unter Abwesenden*, 1988]

— (2011 [1998]): *The Lesson of Carl Schmitt: Four Chapters on the Distinction Between Political Theology and Political Philosophy*. Translated by Marcus Brainard. Chicago, IL: University of Chicago Press. [*Die Lehre Carl Schmitts: Vier Kapitel zur Unterscheidung Politischer Theologie und Politischer Philosophie*, 1994]

— (2016): *On the Happiness of the Philosophic Life: Reflections on Rousseau's* Rêveries *in Two Books*. Translated by Robert Berman. Chicago, IL: University of Chicago Press. [*Über das Glück des philosophischen Lebens. Reflexionen zu Rousseaus* Rêveries *in zwei Büchern*, 2011]

Menke, Christoph (2009): *Tragic Play: Irony and Theater from Sophocles to Beckett*. Translated by James Phillips. New York: Columbia University Press. [*Die Gegenwart der Tragödie: Versuch über Urteil und Spiel*, 2005]

— (2015): *Kritik der Rechte*. Berlin: Suhrkamp.

— (2018): *Law and Violence: Christophe Menke in Dialogue*. Manchester: Manchester University Press. [*Recht und Gewalt*, 2011]

Mercier, Louis Sébastien (1784): *Le Tableau de Paris: Nouvelle édition, corrigée et augmentée*, Vol. 3. Amsterdam: s.n.

Merleau-Ponty, Maurice (1955): *Les Aventures de la Dialectique*. Paris: Gallimard.

— (1973): *Adventures of the Dialectic*. Translated by Joseph Bien. Evanston, IL: Northwestern University Press.

— (1998 [1969]): *Humanism and Terror: An Essay on the Communist Problem*. Translated by John O'Neill. Boston, MA: Beacon Press. [*Humanisme et Terreur: Essai sur la Problème Communiste*, 1947]

Michel, Pierre (1981): *Les Barbares, 1789–1848: Un mythe romantique*. Lyon: Presses universitaires de Lyon.

Michelet, Jules (1846): *The People*. Translated by C. Cocks. London: Longman, Brown, Green, and Longmans. [*Le Peuple*, 1846]

— (1847): *History of the French Revolution*. Translated by C. Cocks. London: H.G. Bohn. [*Histoire de la Révolution française*, 1847–53]

— (1861): *The Sea*. Translated by J. W. Palmer. New York: Rudd & Carleton. [*La Mer*, 1861]

Michelsen, Peter (1979): *Der Bruch mit der Vater-Welt: Studien zu Schillers "Räubern."* Heidelberg: Carl Winter.

Mikics, David (2003): *The Romance of Individualism in Emerson and Nietzsche*: Athens: Ohio University Press.

Mill, John Stuart (1869–86): *Gesammelte Werke*. Edited by Theodor Gomperz. Leipzig: Fues.

— (1963–91): *Collected Works of John Stuart Mill*. Thirty-three volumes. Edited by J. M. Robson. Toronto: University of Toronto Press.

Möllers, Christoph (2008): *Der vermisste Leviathan: Staatstheorie in der Bundesrepublik Deutschland*. Frankfurt: Surhkamp.

Mommsen, Theodor (1894): *The History of Rome*, Vol. 3. Translated by William Purdie Dickson. London: Richard Bentley & Son. [*Römische Geschichte*, 1854]

Moore, Charles (2011): I'm starting to think that the Left might actually be right. *The Telegraph*, July 22. Available at: www.telegraph.co.uk/news/politics/8655106/Im-starting-to-think-that-the-Left-might-actually-be-right.html (accessed on March 8, 2018).

— (2011): Our leaders have lost faith in the powers of their people. *The Telegraph*, July 29. Available at: www.telegraph.co.uk/news/politics/8671359/Our-leaders-have-lost-faith-in-the-powers-of-their-people.html (accessed on March 8, 2018).

Moretti, Franco (1982): The Dialectic of Fear. *New Left Review* 136, pp. 67–85.

— (2013): *The Bourgeois: Between History and Literature*. London: Verso.

444

Mornet, Daniel (1927): La véritable signification du *Neveu de Rameau*. *Revue des Deux Mondes* 40, pp. 881–908.

Morson, Gary Saul and Caryl Emerson (1990): *Mikhail Bakhtin: Creation of a Prosaics*. Stanford, CA: Stanford University Press.

Mouffe, Chantal (2000): *The Democratic Paradox*. London: Verso.

Muchow, Hans Heinrich (1956): Zur Psychologie und Pädagogik der "Halbstarken." *Unsere Jugend* 8.9./8.10./8.11, pp. 388–94, 442–9, 486–91.

Mullaney, Steven (1988): *The Place of the Stage: License, Play, and Power in Renaissance England*. Chicago, IL: University of Chicago Press.

Müller, Jan-Werner (2003): *A Dangerous Mind: Carl Schmitt in Post-War European Thought*. New Haven, CT: Yale University Press.

— (2010): Re-imagining Leviathan: Schmitt and Oakeshott on Hobbes and the Problem of Political Order. *Critical Review of International Social and Political Philosophy* 13/2–3, pp. 317–36.

— (2016): *What is Populism?* Philadelphia: University of Pennsylvania Press. [*Was ist Populismus? Ein Essay*, 2016]

Müller, Martin (2002): *Die chinesischsprachige Hegel-Rezeption von 1902 bis 2000: Eine Bibliographie*. Frankfurt: Peter Lang.

Müller-Seidel, Walter (2009): *Friedrich Schiller und die Politik: "Nicht das Grosse, nur das Menschliche geschehe."* Munich: C.H. Beck.

Murdock, Graham and Robin McCron (2006 [1975]): Consciousness of Class and Consciousness of Generation. In: Stuart Hall and Tony Jefferson (eds.), *Resistance Through Rituals: Youth Subcultures in Post-war Britain*. Abingdon: Routledge, pp. 162–76.

Naville, Pierre (1988): *Thomas Hobbes*. Paris: Plon.

Neubauer, John (1996): Sigmund Freud und Hans Blüher in bisher unveröffentlichten Briefen. *Psyche* 50, pp. 123–48.

Neuhouser, Frederick (2008): *Rousseau's Theodicy of Self-Love: Evil, Rationality, and the Drive for Recognition*. Oxford: Oxford University Press.

Neumann, Franz (1942): *Behemoth: The Structure and Practice of National Socialism*. London: Victor Gollancz.

Nicodemus, Katja (2011): Arschlöcher gibt es immer [interview with Larry Hagman]. *Die Zeit*, November 3, pp. 53–4.

Nieh, Hualing (ed.) (1981): *Literature of the Hundred Flowers*. Vols. 1/2. New York: Columbia University Press.

Nietzsche, Friedrich (1899): *The Works of Friedrich Nietzsche, Vol. 3: The Case of Wagner, Nietzsche Contra Wagner, The Twilight of the Idols, The Antichrist*. Translated by Thomas Common. London: T. Fisher Unwin.

— (1968): *The Will to Power*. Translated by Walter Kaufmann and R. J. Hollingdale. New York: Random House. [*Der Wille zur Macht*, 1906]

— (1974): *The Gay Science: With a Prelude in Rhymes and an Appendix of Songs*. Translated by Walter Kaufmann. New York: Vintage Books. [*Fröhliche Wissenschaft*, 1882]

— (1980 [1967]): *Sämtliche Werke: Kritische Studienausgabe in 15 Bänden*. Edited by Giorgio Colli and Mazzino Montinari. Munich: dtv.

— (1982 [1954]): *The Portable Nietzsche*. Edited and translated by Walter Kaufmann. New York: Penguin.

— (1995–): *The Complete Works of Friedrich Nietzsche*. Nineteen volumes. Edited by Alan D. Schrift and Duncan Large. Translated by Richard T. Gray, Brittain Smith et al. Stanford, CA: Stanford University Press. [*Sämtliche Werke, Kritische Studienausgabe in 15 Bänden*, 1980]

— (1996): *Human, All Too Human: A Book for Free Spirits*. Translated by R. J. Hollingdale. Cambridge: Cambridge University Press. [*Menschliches, Allzumenschliches*, 1878]

— (2007): *Ecce Homo: How to Become What You Are*. Translated by Duncan Large. Oxford: Oxford University Press. [*Ecce Homo*, 1908]

REFERENCES

— (2007 [1997]): The Greek State. In: *On the Genealogy of Morality and Other Writings.* Edited by Keith Ansell-Pearson, translated by Carol Diethe. Cambridge: Cambridge University Press, pp. 164–73. ["Der griechische Staat," 1872]

Niles, Hezekiah (ed.) (1822): *Principles and Acts of the Revolution in America.* Baltimore, MD: William Ogden Niles.

Noble, Jonathan (2003): Wang Shuo and the Commercialization of Literature. In: Joshua Mostow (ed.), *The Cambridge Companion to Modern East Asian Literature.* New York: Columbia University Press, pp. 598–603.

Nora, Pierre (1996): Generation. In: *Realms of Memory: The Construction of the French Past, Vol. I: Conflicts and Divisions.* Translated by Arthur Goldhammer. New York: Columbia University Press, pp. 499–612. [*Les lieux de mémoire*, 1992]

Novalis (2007): *Notes for a Romantic Encyclopaedia: Das Allgemeine Brouillon.* Translated and edited by David W. Wood. Albany, NY: State University of New York Press.

Oakeshott, Michael (1975 [1946]): Introduction to *Leviathan.* In: *Hobbes on Civil Association.* Indianapolis, IN: Liberty Fund, pp. 1–79.

Oehler, Dolf (1979): *Pariser Bilder I (1830–1848): Antibourgeoise Ästhetik bei Baudelaire, Daumier und Heine.* Frankfurt: Suhrkamp.

— (1988): *Ein Höllensturz der Alten Welt: Zur Selbsterforschung der Moderne nach dem Juni 1848.* Frankfurt: Suhrkamp.

Offe, Claus (2005): *Reflections on America: Tocqueville, Weber and Adorno in the United States.* Translated by Patrick Camiller. Cambridge: Polity. [*Selbstbetrachtung aus der Ferne: Tocqueville, Weber und Adorno in den Vereinigten Staaten*, 2004]

Ogien, Albert and Sandra Laugier (2010): *Pourquoi désobéir en démocratie?* Paris: La Découverte.

— and — (2014): *Le principe démocratie: Enquête sur les nouvelles formes du politique.* Paris: La Découverte.

Ozouf, Mona (1989): *L'homme régénéré: Essais sur la Révolution française.* Paris: Gallimard.

Paine, Thomas (1995): *Collected Writings.* Edited by Eric Foner. New York: Library of America.

Palaver, Wolfgang (2002): Carl Schmitt, mythologue politique. In: Carl Schmitt, *Le Léviathan dans la doctrine de l'État de Thomas Hobbes: Sens et échec d'un symbole politique.* Paris: Seuil, pp. 191–242.

Pan, Philip P. (2008): *Out of Mao's Shadow: The Struggle for the Soul of a New China.* New York: Simon & Schuster.

Park, Robert E. (1928): Migration and the Marginal Man. *American Journal of Sociology* 33/6, pp. 881–93.

Parsons, Talcott (1949): *The Structure of Social Action: A Study of Social Theory with Special Reference to a Group of Recent European Writers.* Glencoe, IL: Free Press.

Pasolini, Pier Paolo (2005 [1988]): *Heretical Empiricism.* Translated by Ben Lawton and Loise K. Barnett. Washington, DC: New Academia Publishing. [*Empirismo eretico*, 1972]

Pateman, Carol (1988): *The Sexual Contract.* Stanford, CA: Stanford University Press.

Peretti, Burton W. (1989): Democratic Leitmotivs in the American Reception of Wagner. *19th-Century Music* 13/1, pp. 28–38.

Pettit, Philip (2008): *Made With Words: Hobbes on Language, Mind, and Politics.* Princeton, NJ: Princeton University Press.

Peukert, Detlev (1984): Die "Halbstarken": Protestverhalten von Arbeiterjugendlichen zwischen Wilhelminischem Kaiserreich und Ära Adenauer. *Zeitschrift für Pädagogik* 30, pp. 533–48.

Piketty, Thomas (2014): *Capital in the Twenty-First Century.* Translated by Arthur Goldhammer. Cambridge, MA: Harvard University Press. [*Le capital au XXI siècle*, 2013]

Pillen, Angelika (2003): *Hegel in Frankreich: Vom unglücklichen Bewusstsein zur Unvernunft.* Freiburg: Karl Alber.

446

Pinker, Steven (2011): *The Better Angels of Our Nature: Why Violence Has Declined.* New York: Viking.

Pippin, Robert B. (1997): *Idealism as Modernism: Hegelian Variations.* Cambridge: Cambridge University Press.

— (2011): *Hegel on Self-Consciousness: Desire and Death in the* Phenomenology of the Spirit. Princeton, NJ: Princeton University Press.

Pitkin, Hanna F. (1967): *The Concept of Representation.* Berkeley: University of California Press.

Plato (1997): *Complete Works.* Edited by John M. Cooper. Indianapolis, IN: Hackett Publishing.

Plessner, Helmuth (1982 [1948]): Zur Anthropologie des Schauspielers. In: *Gesammelte Schriften,* Vol. 7. Frankfurt: Suhrkamp, pp. 399–418.

Poiger, Uta G. (2000): *Jazz, Rock, and Rebels: Cold War Politics and American Culture in a Divided Germany.* Berkeley: University of California Press.

Popper, Karl R. (1945): *The Open Society and Its Enemies,* Vol. I/II. London: George Routledge and Sons.

Potacs, Michael (2009): Hans Kelsen und der Marxismus. In: Robert Walter, Werner Ogris, and Thomas Olechowski (eds.), *Hans Kelsen: Leben – Werk – Wirksamkeit.* Vienna: Manz, pp. 183–93.

Power, Henry (1664): *Experimental Philosophy, in Three Books.* London: T. Roycroft.

Preuss, Ulrich K. (1990): *Revolution, Fortschritt, Verfassung: Zu einem neuen Verfassungsverständnis.* Berlin: Wagenbach.

Pugliatti, Paola (2003): *Beggary and Theatre in Early Modern England.* Aldershot: Ashgate.

Pye, Christopher (1984): The Sovereign, the Theatre, and the Kingdome of Darknesse: Hobbes and the Spectacle of Power. *Representations* 8, pp. 84–106.

Quincey, Thomas de (1856 [1852]): California and the Gold Mania. In: *Letters to a Young Man and Other Papers.* Boston, MA: Ticknor and Fields, pp. 199–246.

Radosh, Ronald (2016): Steve Bannon, Trump's Top Guy, Told Me He Was "A Leninist" Who Wants To "Destroy the State." Daily Beast, August 22. Available at: www.thedailybeast.com/articles/2016/08/22/steve-bannon-trump-s-top-guy-told-me-he-was-a-leninist.html (accessed on March 25, 2018).

Rancière, Jacques (1994): *The Names of History: On the Poetics of Knowledge.* Translated by Hassan Melehy. Minneapolis: University of Minnesota Press. [*Les noms de l'histoire,* 1992]

— (1999): *Disagreement: Politics and Philosophy.* Translated by Julie Rose. Minneapolis: University of Minnesota Press. [*La Mésentente: Politique et Philosophie,* 1995]

— (2003): *The Philosopher and His Poor.* Edited by Andrew Parker, translated by John Drury, Corinne Oster, and Andrew Parker. Durham, NC: Duke University Press. [*Le philosophe et les pauvres,* 1983]

— (2006): *Hatred of Democracy.* Translated by Steve Corcoran. London: Verso. [*La haine de la démocratie,* 2005]

— (2007 [1991]): *The Ignorant Schoolmaster: Five Lessons in Intellectual Emancipation.* Translated by Kristin Ross. Stanford, CA: Stanford University Press. [*Maître ignorant,* 1987]

— (2009): *The Emancipated Spectator.* Translated by Gregory Elliott. London: Verso. [*Le spectateur émancipé,* 2008]

— (2015 [2004]): Who is the Subject of the Rights of Man? In: *Dissensus: On Politics and Aesthetics.* Edited and translated by Steven Corcoran. London: Bloomsbury, pp. 70–83.

Rank, Otto (1914): *The Myth of the Birth of the Hero: A Psychological Interpretation of Mythology.* Translated by F. Robbins and Smith Ely Jelliffe. New York: The Journal of Nervous and Mental Disease Publishing Company. [*Der Mythus von der Geburt des Helden. Versuch einer psychologischen Mythendeutung,* 1909]

— (1929): *The Trauma of Birth.* London: Kegan Paul, Trench, Trubner & Co. [*Das Trauma der Geburt und seine Bedeutung für die Psychoanalyse,* 1924]

— (1992): *The Incest Theme in Literature and Legend: Fundamentals of a Psychology of*

447

Literary Creation. Translated by Gregory C. Richter. Baltimore, MD: Johns Hopkins University Press. [*Das Inzest-Motiv in Dichtung und Sage*, 1912]

Rathkolb, Oliver (2000): Hans Kelsens Perzeptionen Freudscher Psychoanalyse (unter Berücksichtigung rechtstheoretischer Auseinandersetzungen). In: Eveline List (ed.), *Psychoanalyse und Recht*. Vienna: LexisNexis ARD ORAC, pp. 85–91.

— (2009): Hans Kelsen und das FBI während des McCarthysmus in den USA. In: Robert Walter, Werner Ogris, and Thomas Olechowski (eds.), *Hans Kelsen: Leben – Werk – Wirksamkeit*. Vienna: Manz, pp. 339–48.

Rawls, John (1999 [1971]): *A Theory of Justice*. Cambridge, MA: Belknap Press.

[Raynal, Guillaume Thomas] (1770): *Histoire philosophique et politique des établissements et du commerce des Européens dans les Deux Indes*. Amsterdam: s.n. [first edition published anonymously]

Raynal, Guillaume Thomas (1783): *Histoire philosophique et politique des établissements et du commerce des Européens dans les Deux Indes*. Geneva: Pellet.

Rebérioux, Madeleine (1961): La philosophie de Nietzsche et le socialisme, trois conférences de Jaurès. *Bulletin de la Société d'études jaurésiennes* 2/3, pp. 6–14.

Reich, Wilhelm (1970): *The Mass Psychology of Fascism*. Edited by Mary Higgins and Chester M. Raphael, translated by Vincent R. Carfagno. New York: Farrar, Straus and Giroux. [*Massenpsychologie des Faschismus*, 1933]

Reicher, Stephen and S. Alexander Haslam (2016): The Politics of Hope: Donald Trump as an Entrepreneur of Identity. *Scientific American*, November 19. Available at: www.scientificamerican.com/article/the-politics-of-hope-donald-trump-as-an-entrepreneur-of-identity (accessed on March 25, 2018).

Reinert, Hugo and Erik S. Reinert (2006): Creative Destruction in Economics: Nietzsche, Sombart, Schumpeter. In: Jürgen G. Backhaus and Wolfgang Drechsler (eds.), *Friedrich Nietzsche (1844–1900): Economy and Society*. New York: Springer Science+Business Media, pp. 55–85.

Reinhoudt, Jurgen and Serge Audier (2018): *The Walter Lippmann Colloquium: The Birth of Neo-Liberalism*. Cham, Switzerland: Palgrave Macmillan.

Reulecke, Jürgen (1985): Männerbund versus Familie: Bürgerliche Jugendbewegung und Familie in Deutschland im ersten Drittel des 20. Jahrhunderts. In: Thomas Koebner, Rolf-Peter Janz, and Frank Trommler (eds.), *"Mit uns zieht die neue Zeit." Der Mythos Jugend*. Frankfurt: Suhrkamp, pp. 199–223.

Reuter, Wolfgang and Thomas Tuma (2009): Mitgefangen, mitgehangen [interview with Alexander Dibelius]. *Spiegel* 19, pp. 70–2.

Rex, Walter E. (2003): Music and the Unity of *Le Neveu de Rameau*. *Diderot Studies* 29, pp. 83–99.

Richter, Stephan (2015): Trump Vs. Kelly: Just Who's the "Bimbo"? *The Globalist*, August 11. Available at: www.theglobalist.com/trump-kelly-bimbo-politics-elections (accessed on March 25, 2017).

— (2016): Donald Trump Outs Himself as "Bimbo." *The Globalist*, April 4. Available at: https://www.theglobalist.com/donald-trump-outs-himself-as-bimbo (accessed on March 25, 2018).

Ricœur, Paul (1970): *Freud and Philosophy: An Essay on Interpretation*. Translated by Denis Savage. New Haven, CT: Yale University Press. [*De l'interprétation: Essai sur Sigmund Freud*, 1965]

Riedel, Volker (1996): Zwischen Ideologie und Kunst: Bertolt Brecht, Heiner Müller und Fragen der modernen Horaz-Forschung. In: Helmut Krasser and Ernst A. Schmidt (eds.), *Zeitgenosse Horaz: Der Dichter und seine Leser seit zwei Jahrtausenden*. Tübingen: Gunter Narr, pp. 392–423.

Riedel, Wolfgang (1985): *Die Anthropologie des jungen Schiller*. Würzburg: Königshausen & Neumann.

— (ed.) (1995): *Jacob Friedrich Abel: Eine Quellenedition zum Philosophieunterricht an der Stuttgarter Karlsschule (1773–1782)*. Würzburg: Königshausen & Neumann.

448

Rieff, Philip (1965 [1959]): *Freud: The Mind of the Moralist.* London: University Paperbacks.

Riehl, Wilhelm Heinrich (1861 [1851]): *Die bürgerliche Gesellschaft.* Stuttgart: Cotta.

Riesman, David (2001 [1950]): *The Lonely Crowd.* New Haven, CT: Yale University Press.

Rilke, Rainer Maria (2009): *The Notebooks of Malte Laurids Brigge.* Translated and edited by Michael Hulse. London: Penguin. [*Die Aufzeichnungen des Malte Laurids Brigge*, 1910]

Robertson, Roland (1995): Glocalization: Time-Space and Homogeneity-Heterogeneity. In: Mike Featherstone, Scott Lash, and Roland Robertson (eds.), *Global Modernities.* London: Sage Publications, pp. 25–44.

Robespierre, Maximilien (1967): *Oeuvres de Maximilien Robespierre, Tome X: Discours.* Paris: Presses Universitaires de France.

Roman, Myriam (1999): *Victor Hugo et le roman philosophique.* Paris: Honoré Champion.

Rong Di, Bei Da zhengfeng yundong fan-you de rizi [The days of the campaigns for rectification and against rightists at Peking University]. Available at: www.21ccom.net/articles/lsjd/lccz/article_2010112925462.html (accessed on June 18, 2015; translated by Giorgio Strafella).

Rorty, Richard (1998): *Truth and Progress: Philosophical Papers, Vol. 3.* Cambridge: Cambridge University Press.

Rosanvallon, Pierre (1998): *Le peuple introuvable: Histoire de la représentation démocratique en France.* Paris: Gallimard.

— (2008): *Counter-Democracy: Politics in an Age of Distrust.* Translated by Arthur Goldhammer. Cambridge: Cambridge University Press. [*La contre-démocratie: La politique à l'âge de la défiance*, 2006]

Roseman, Mark (2005): Generationen als "Imagined Communities": Mythen, generationelle Identitäten und Generationenkonflikte in Deutschland vom 18. bis zum 20. Jahrhundert. In: Ulrike Jureit and Michael Wildt (eds.), *Generationen: Zur Relevanz eines wissenschaftlichen Grundbegriffs.* Hamburg: Hamburger Edition, pp. 180–99.

Roth, Joseph (1990): *Werke 2: Das journalistische Werk 1924–1928.* Cologne: Kiepenheuer & Witsch.

Rottleuthner, Hubert (1983): Leviathan oder Behemoth? Zur Hobbes-Rezeption im Nationalsozialismus – und ihrer Neuauflage. *Archiv für Rechts- und Sozialphilosophie* 69/2, pp. 247–65.

Rousseau, Jean-Jacques (1959–95): *Œuvres complètes.* Volumes 1–5. Edited by Bernard Gagnebin and Marcel Raymond. Paris: Gallimard.

— (1965–89): *Correspondance complète.* Edited by R. A. Leigh. Geneva: Institut et Musée Voltaire.

— (1979): *Emile: Or On Education.* Translated by Allan Bloom. New York: Basic Books. [*Émile, ou De l'éducation*, 1762]

— (1990–): *The Collected Writings of Rousseau.* Fourteen volumes. Edited by Roger D. Masters and Christopher Kelly, translated by Judith R. Bush, Christopher Kelly, and Roger D. Masters. Hanover, NH: University Press of New England.

— (2001) *Diskurs über die Ungleichheit.* Edited and translated by Heinrich Meier. Paderborn: Schöningh.

— (2003) *The Discourses and Other Early Political Writings.* Edited and translated by Victor Gourevitch. Cambridge: Cambridge University Press.

— (2012): *The Social Contract and Other Later Political Writings.* Edited and translated by Victor Gourevitch. Cambridge: Cambridge University Press.

Roy, Olivier (2004): *Globalized Islam: The Search for a New Ummah.* New York: Columbia University Press.

Royce, Josiah (1948 [1886]): *California: From the Conquest in 1846 to the Second Vigilance Committee in San Francisco. A Study of American Character.* New York: A.A. Knopf.

— (1995 [1908]): *The Philosophy of Loyalty.* Nashville, TN: Vanderbildt University Press.

449

REFERENCES

Rubenfeld, Jed (2001): *Freedom and Time: A Theory of Constitutional Self-Government.* New Haven, CT: Yale University Press.

Ruda, Frank (2011): *Hegel's Rabble: An Investigation into Hegel's Philosophy of Right.* London: Continuum.

Sade, Donatien-Alphonse-François de (2012): *Justine, or the Misfortunes of Virtue.* Translated by John Phillips. Oxford: Oxford University Press. [*Justine ou Les Malheurs de la vertu*, 1791]

Sahlberg, Oskar (1977): *Baudelaire 1848: Gedichte der Revolution.* Berlin: Wagenbach.

— (1980): *Baudelaire und seine Muse auf dem Weg zur Revolution.* Frankfurt: Suhrkamp.

Salvandy, Narcisse-Achille (1831): *Seize Mois ou La Révolution et les Révolutionnaires.* Paris: Ladvocat.

Sandel, Michael (1996): *Democracy's Discontent: America in Search of a Public Philosophy.* Cambridge, MA: Harvard University Press.

Sandelin, Alexander (1850): *Répertoire général d'Économie politique ancienne et moderne.* La Haye: P.H. Noordendorp.

Sartre, Jean-Paul (1964): Palmiro Togliatti. *Les Temps Modernes* 221/October, pp. 577–87.

— (1967 [1950]): *Baudelaire.* Translated by Martin Turnell. New York: New Directions. [*Baudelaire*, 1947]

— (2004 [1976]): *Critique of Dialectical Reason, Volume 1: Theory of Practical Ensembles.* Translated by Alan Sheridan-Smith. London: Verso. [*Critique de la Raison Dialectique*, 1960]

Savage, Jon (2008 [2007]): *Teenage: The Creation of Youth 1875–1945.* London: Pimlico.

Schelsky, Helmut (1934): *Sozialistische Lebenshaltung.* Leipzig: Eichblatt.

— (1937/38): Die Totalität des Staates bei Hobbes. *Archiv für Rechtsphilosophie* 31, pp. 176–93.

— (1946): Das Freiheitswollen der Völker und die Idee des Planstaates. In: *Das Freiheitswollen der Völker und die Idee des Planstaates – Freiheitsgedanke und Pflichtgedanke.* Karlsruhe: Volk und Zeit, pp. 7–89.

— (1957): *Die skeptische Generation: Eine Soziologie der deutschen Jugend.* Düsseldorf: Eugen Diedrichs.

— (1965): *Auf der Suche nach Wirklichkeit: Gesammelte Aufsätze.* Düsseldorf: Eugen Diedrichs.

— (1979): *Die Hoffnung Blochs: Kritik der marxistischen Existenzphilosophie eines Jugendbewegten.* Stuttgart: Klett-Cotta.

— (1981): *Rückblicke eines "Anti-Soziologen."* Opladen: VS Verlag für Sozialwissenschaften.

— (1981 [1940]): *Thomas Hobbes: Eine politische Lehre.* Berlin: Duncker & Humblot.

Schenker, David J. (1992): Poetic Voices in Horace's Roman Odes. *Classical Journal* 88/2, pp. 147–66.

Schickel, Joachim (1993): *Gespräche mit Carl Schmitt.* Berlin: Merve.

Schiller, Friedrich (1902): *Complete Works of Friedrich Schiller.* Eight volumes. New York: P.F. Collier and Son.

— (1979) *The Robbers and Wallenstein.* Translated by F. J. Lamport. London: Penguin Books. [*Die Räuber*, 1781; *Wallenstein*, 1800]

— (1984 [1793]): Briefe an den Prinzen Friedrich Christian von Schleswig-Holstein-Sonderburg-Augustenburg ("Augustenburger Briefe"). In: Jürgen Bolten (ed.), *Schillers Briefe über die ästhetische Erziehung.* Frankfurt: Suhrkamp, pp. 31–87.

— (1985): *Poet of Freedom.* Volume 1. Translated by William F. Wertz. New York: New Benjamin Franklin House.

— (2003): Kallias or Concerning Beauty. In: J. M. Bernstein (ed.), *Classic and Romantic German Aesthetics.* Translated by Stefan Bird-Pollan. Cambridge: Cambridge University Press, pp. 145–83. ["Kallias oder Über die Schönheit," 1793]

— (2008): The Criminal of Lost Honor: A True Story. In: Jeffrey L. High (ed. and trans.), *Schiller's Literary Prose Works: New Translations and Critical Essays.* Rochester, NY: Camden House, pp. 39–55. ["Der Verbrecher aus verlorener Ehre," 1786]

Schmidt, James (1996): The Fool's Truth: Diderot, Goethe, and Hegel. *Journal of the History of Ideas* 57, pp. 625–44.

Schmitt, Carl (1936): *Das Judentum in der Rechtswissenschaft. Ansprachen, Vorträge und Ergebnisse der Reichsgruppe Hochschullehrer des NSRB am 3. und 4. Oktober 1936. 1. Die deutsche Rechtswissenschaft im Kampf gegen den jüdischen Geist*. Berlin: Deutscher Rechts-Verlag.

— (1940): *Positionen und Begriffe im Kampf mit Weimar – Genf – Versailles 1923–1939*. Hamburg: Hanseatische Verlagsanstalt.

— (1982 [1938]): *Der Leviathan in der Staatslehre des Thomas Hobbes: Sinn und Fehlschlag eines politischen Symbols*. Cologne: Hohenheim.

— (1988 [1985]): *The Crisis of Parliamentary Democracy*. Translated by Ellen Kennedy. Cambridge, MA: MIT Press. [*Die geistesgeschichtliche Lage des heutigen Parlamentarismus*, 1923]

— (1995) *Staat, Grossraum, Nomos: Arbeiten aus den Jahren 1916–1969*. Berlin: Duncker & Humblot.

— (1996 [1931]): *Der Hüter der Verfassung*. Berlin: Duncker & Humblot.

— (1996): *Roman Catholicism and Political Form*. Translated by G. L. Ulmen. Westport, CT: Greenwood Press. [*Römischer Katholizismus und politische Form*, 1923]

— (2001): *State, Movement, People: The Triadic Structure of Political Unity (1933)/The Question of Legality (1950)*. Edited and translated by Simona Draghici. Corvallis, OR: Plutarch Press. [*Staat, Bewegung, Volk*, 1933; *Das Problem der Legalität*, 1950]

— (2002 [1963]): *Der Begriff des Politischen: Text von 1932 mit einem Vorwort und drei Korollarien*. Berlin: Duncker & Humblot.

— (2004 [1914]): *Der Wert des Staates und die Bedeutung des Einzelnen*. Berlin: Duncker & Humblot.

— (2004): *On the Three Types of Juristic Thought*. Translated by Joseph W. Bendersky. Westport, CT: Praeger. [*Über die drei Arten des rechtswissenschaftlichen Denkens*, 1934]

— (2005 [1985]): *Political Theology: Four Chapters on the Concept of Sovereignty*. Translated by George Schwab. Chicago, IL: University of Chicago Press. [*Politische Theologie. Vier Kapitel zur Lehre von der Souveränität*, 1922/1934]

— (2006): *Hamlet or Hecuba: The Irruption of Time into Play*. Edited and translated by Simona Draghici. Corvallis, OR: Plutarch Press. [*Hamlet oder Hekuba: Der Einbruch der Zeit in das Spiel*, 1956]

— (2006): *The Nomos of the Earth in the International Law of the* Jus Publicum Europaeum. Translated by G. L. Ulmen. New York: Telos Press. [*Der Nomos der Erde im Völkerrecht des Jus Publicum Europaeum*, 1950]

— (2007 [1996]): *The Concept of the Political*. Translated by George Schwab. Chicago, IL: University of Chicago Press. [*Der Begriff des Politischen*, 1932]

— (2007): *Theory of the Partisan: Intermediate Commentary on the Concept of the Political*. Translated by G. L. Ulmen. New York: Telos Press. [*Theorie des Partisanen: Zwischenbemerkung zum Begriff des Politischen*, 1963]

— (2008): *The Leviathan in the State Theory of Thomas Hobbes: Meaning and Failure of a Political Symbol*. Translated by George Schwab and Erna Hilfstein. Chicago, IL: University of Chicago Press. [*Der Leviathan in der Staatslehre des Thomas Hobbes. Sinn und Fehlschlag eines politischen Symbols*, 1938]

— (2011 [1967]): *Die Tyrannei der Werte*. Berlin: Duncker & Humblot.

— (2015): *Glossarium: Aufzeichnungen aus den Jahren 1947 bis 1958*. Edited by Gerd Giesler and Martin Tielke. Berlin: Duncker & Humblot.

— (2017): *Ex Captivitate Salus: Experiences, 1945–47*. Edited by Andreas Kalyvas and Federico Finchelstein, translated by Matthew Hannah. Cambridge: Polity. [*Ex Captivitate Salus*, 1950]

— (2017): *Political Romanticism*. Translated by Guy Oakes. London: Routledge. [*Politische Romantik*, 1919]

Schneider, Manfred (1980): *Die kranke schöne Seele der Revolution: Heine, Börne, das "Junge Deutschland," Marx und Engels.* Frankfurt: Syndikat.

Schultz, Clemens (1912): *Die Halbstarken.* Leipzig: Paul Eger.

Schumpeter, Joseph Alois (2010 [1942]): *Capitalism, Socialism and Democracy.* London: Routledge.

Schurtz, Heinrich (1902): *Altersklassen und Männerbünde: Eine Darstellung der Grundformen der Gesellschaft.* Berlin: Georg Reimer.

Schwarcz, Vera (1986): *The Chinese Enlightenment: Intellectuals and the Legacy of the May Fourth Movement of 1919.* Berkeley: University of California Press.

Schwiedrzik, Wolfgang M. (1980): *Literaturfrühling in China? Gespräche mit chinesischen Schriftstellern.* Cologne: Prometh.

Sen, Amartya (1997 [1982]): Rational Fools: A Critique of the Behavioural Foundations of Economic Theory. In: *Choice, Welfare and Measurement.* Cambridge, MA: Harvard University Press, pp. 84–106.

Sennett, Richard (1998): *The Corrosion of Character: The Personal Consequences of Work in the New Capitalism.* New York: W.W. Norton & Company.

Serres, Michel (1982): *The Parasite.* Translated by Lawrence R. Schehr. Baltimore, MD: Johns Hopkins University Press. [*Der Parasit*, 1981]

Shakespeare, William (2002 [1998]): *The Arden Shakespeare Complete Works, Revised Edition.* Edited by Richard Proudfoot, Ann Thompson, and David Scott Kastan. London: Cengage Learning.

Shapin, Steven and Simon Schaffer (1985): *Leviathan and the Air-Pump: Hobbes, Boyle, and the Experimental Life.* Princeton, NJ: Princeton University Press.

Shell, Susan Meld (2012): Stalking *Puer Robustus*: Hobbes and Rousseau on the Origin of Human Malice. In: Eve Grace and Christopher Kelly (eds.), *The Challenge of Rousseau.* Cambridge: Cambridge University Press, pp. 271–91.

Shelley, Mary W. (2012): *Frankenstein: The 1818 Text – Contexts – Criticism.* Edited by J. Paul Hunter. New York: W.W. Norton and Company.

Simmel, Georg (1971): The Adventurer. Translated by David Kettler. In: Donald N. Levine (ed.), *On Individuality and Social Forms: Selected Writings.* Chicago, IL: University of Chicago Press, pp. 187–98. [*Philosophische Kultur*, 1911]

Skinner, Quentin (2002): *Visions of Politics, Vol. 3: Hobbes and Civil Science.* Cambridge: Cambridge University Press.

— (2005): Hobbes on Representation. *European Journal of Philosophy* 13, pp. 155–84.

— (2008): *Hobbes and Republican Liberty.* Cambridge: Cambridge University Press.

Slaby, Jan (2014): Empathy's Blind Spot. *Medicine, Health Care and Philosophy* 17/2, pp. 249–58.

Smend, Rudolf (2000): Constitution and Constitutional Law. In: Arthur Jacobson and Bernhard Schlink (eds.), *Weimar: A Jurisprudence of Crisis.* Translated by Belinda Cooper. Berkeley: University of California Press, pp. 213–48. ["Verfassung und Verfassungsrecht," 1928]

Smith, Adam (2000 [1776]): *The Wealth of Nations.* Edited by Edwin Cannan. New York: Modern Library.

— (2002 [1759]): *The Theory of Moral Sentiments.* Edited by Knud Haakonssen. Cambridge: Cambridge University Press.

Smith, Jeffrey A. (2003): Nationalism, Virtue, and the Spirit of Liberty in Rousseau's *Government of Poland. Review of Politics* 65, pp. 409–37.

Smith, Steven B. (2000): Leo Strauss's Platonic Liberalism. *Political Theory* 28/6, pp. 787–809.

Smoliarova, Tatiana (2006): Distortion and Theatricality: Estrangement in Diderot and Shklovsky. *Poetics Today* 27, pp. 3–33.

Solomon, Richard H. (1971): *Mao's Revolution and the Chinese Political Culture.* Berkeley: University of California Press.

Sombart, Werner (1915): *Händler und Helden: Patriotische Besinnungen.* Munich: Duncker & Humblot.

Songwe, Vera (2011): Food, Financial Crises, and Complex Derivatives: A Tale of High Stakes Innovation and Diversification. *Economic Premise* 69, pp. 1–9.

Sontag, Susan (1980): *Under the Sign of Saturn*. New York: Vintage Books.

Sophocles (1984): *The Three Theban Plays: Antigone, Oedipus the King, Oedipus at Colonus*. Translated by Robert Fagles. New York: Penguin.

Sorel, Georges (1908): *La Décomposition du Marxisme*. Paris: Rivière.

— (2004): *Reflections on Violence*. Edited by Jeremy Jennings. Cambridge: Cambridge University Press. [*Réflexions sur la violence*, 1908]

Sorkin, Andrew Ross (2010 [2009]): *Too Big to Fail: Inside the Battle to Save Wall Street*. London: Penguin.

Speight, Allen (2001): *Hegel, Literature and the Problem of Agency*. Cambridge: Cambridge University Press.

Spence, Jonathan (1990): *The Search for Modern China*. New York: W.W. Norton & Company.

— (1999): *Mao Zedong: A Life*. London: Penguin.

Spinoza, Benedict de (2012): *Theological-Political Treatise*. Edited by Jonathan Israel, translated by Michael Silverthorne and Jonathan Israel. Cambridge: Cambridge University Press. [*Tractatus theologico-politicus*, 1670]

Spitzer, Leo (1948): *Linguistics and Literary History: Essays in Stylistics*. Princeton, NJ: Princeton University Press.

Springborg, Patricia (2011): Hobbes's Fool the *Insipiens*, and the Tyrant-King. *Political Theory* 39, pp. 85–111.

Sreedhar, Susanne (2010): *Hobbes on Resistance: Defying the Leviathan*. Cambridge: Cambridge University Press.

Stallybrass, Peter (1990): Marx and Heterogeneity: Thinking the Lumpenproletariat. *Representations* 31, pp. 69–95.

— and Allon White (1986): *The Politics and Poetics of Transgression*. Ithaca, NY: Cornell University Press.

Stanley, Amy Dru (1992): Beggars Can't Be Choosers: Compulsion and Contract in Postbellum America. *Journal of American History* 78, pp. 1265–93.

Starobinski, Jean (1976): Le dîner chez Bertin. In: Wolfgang Preisendanz and Rainer Warning (eds.), *Das Komische: Poetik und Hermeneutik VII*. Munich: Wilhelm Fink, pp. 191–204.

— (1988): *Jean-Jacques Rousseau: Transparency and Obstruction*. Translated by Arthur Goldhammer. Chicago, IL: University of Chicago Press. [*Jean-Jacques Rousseau: la transparence et l'obstacle*, 1971]

Steiner, Stephan (2013): *Weimar in Amerika: Leo Strauss' politische Philosophie*. Tübingen: Mohr.

Stirner, Max (1995): *The Ego and Its Own*. Translated by Steven Tracy Byington. Cambridge: Cambridge University Press. [*Der Einzige und sein Eigentum*, 1845]

Stoppard, Tom (2008 [2002]): *The Coast of Utopia: Voyage – Shipwreck – Salvage*. London: Faber and Faber.

Strauss, Leo (1952): *Persecution and the Art of Writing*. Glencoe, IL: Free Press.

— (1958): *Thoughts on Machiavelli*. Glencoe, IL: Free Press.

— (1962): Notes on Tocqueville. Transcript of a lecture on *Natural Right* in autumn 1962. [previously available at archive.org/details/LeoStraussOnAlexisDeTocqueville, last accessed on June 20, 2013].

— (1963): *The City and Man*. Chicago, IL: University of Chicago Press.

— (1965 [1953]): *Natural Right and History*. Chicago, IL: University of Chicago Press.

— (1982 [1965]): *Spinoza's Critique of Religion*. Translated by E. M. Sinclair. New York: Schocken Books. [*Die Religionskritik Spinozas als Grundlage seiner Bibelwissenschaft*, 1930]

— (1988): Correspondence between Karl Löwith and Leo Strauss. *The Independent Journal of Philosophy* 5/6, pp. 177–91.

453

— (1988 (1959]): *What Is Political Philosophy? And Other Studies*. Chicago, IL: University of Chicago Press.

— (1989 [1975]: *An Introduction to Political Philosophy: Ten Essays*. Edited by Hilail Gildin. Detroit, MI: Wayne State University Press.

— (1989): *The Rebirth of Classical Political Rationalism: An Introduction to the Thought of Leo Strauss*. Chicago, IL: Chicago University Press.

— (1995 [1932]): Notes on Carl Schmitt, *The Concept of the Political*. Translated by J. Harvey Lomax. In: (2007) Carl Schmitt, *The Concept of the Political*. Chicago, IL: University of Chicago Press, pp. 97–122.

— (1996 [1936]): *The Political Philosophy of Hobbes: Its Basis and Its Genesis*. Translated by Elsa M. Sinclair. Chicago, IL: University of Chicago Press. [*Hobbes' politische Wissenschaft in ihrer Genesis*, 1935]

— (1999 [1941]): German Nihilism. *Interpretation* 26/3, pp. 353–78.

— (2001 [1948]): *On Tyranny: Revised and Expanded Edition Including the Strauss-Kojève Correspondence*. Edited by Victor Gourevitch and Michal S. Roth. Chicago, IL: University of Chicago Press.

— (2006 [1940]): The Living Issues of German Postwar Philosophy. In: Heinrich Meier, *Leo Strauss and the Theologico-Political Problem*. Translated by Marcus Brainard. Cambridge: Cambridge University Press, pp. 115–39. [*Das theologisch-politische Problem*, 2006]

— (2008–13): *Gesammelte Schriften*, Vol. 1–3. Edited by Heinrich Meier. Stuttgart: J.B. Metzler.

— (2011): *Hobbes's Critique of Religion and Related Writings*. Translated and edited by Gabriel Bartlett and Svetozar Minkov. Chicago, IL: University of Chicago Press. [*Gesammelte Schriften, Band 3: Hobbes' politische Wissenschaft und zugehörige Schriften – Briefe*, 2008]

Streeck, Wolfgang (2014): *Buying Time: The Delayed Crisis of Democratic Capitalism*. Translated by Patrick Camiller. London: Verso. [*Gekaufte Zeit: Die vertagte Krise des demokratischen Kapitalismus*, 2013]

— (2016): Scenario for a Wonderful Tomorrow. *London Review of Books* 38/7, March 31. Available at: www.lrb.co.uk/v38/n07/wolfgang-streeck/scenario-for-a-wonderful-tomorrow (accessed on March 20, 2018).

Suckling, Norman (1973): Diderot's Politics. *Diderot Studies* 16, pp. 275–93.

Sue, Eugène (1842): *Les Mystères de Paris*, Vol. 1. Paris: Charles Gosselin.

Swiss Financial Market Supervisory Authority FINMA (2014): *Foreign Exchange Trading at UBS AG: Investigation conducted by FINMA. Report*. Bern: FINMA.

Talmon, Jacob (1952): *The Origins of Totalitarian Democracy*. London: Secker & Warburg.

Tambling, Jeremy (2007): Carlyle through Nietzsche: Reading "Sartor Resartus." *Modern Language Review* 102/2, pp. 326–40.

Tang Chu-kuo (1960): *The Student Anti-communist Movement in Peiping: A Participant's Report on the Movement in May, 1957*. Taipei: Asian Peoples' Anti-Communist League Republic of China.

Tarde, Gabriel de (1903): *The Laws of Imitation*. Translated by Elsie Clews Parsons. New York: Henry Holt and Company. [*Les lois de l'imitation*, 1890]

Tarlton, Charles D. (1998): Rehabilitating Hobbes: Obligation, Anti-Fascism and the Myth of a "Taylor Thesis." *History of Political Thought* 19/3, pp. 407–38.

Taylor, Alfred E. (1938): The Ethical Doctrine of Hobbes. *Philosophy* 13, pp. 406–24.

Taylor, Charles (1985): What's Wrong with Negative Liberty. In: *Philosophy and the Human Sciences: Philosophical Papers 2*. Cambridge: Cambridge University Press, pp. 211–29.

— (2004): *Modern Social Imaginaries*. Durham, NC: Duke University Press.

Teiwes, Frederick C. (1979): *Politics and Purges in China: Rectification and the Decline of Party Norms, 1950–1965*. New York: M.E. Sharpe.

Thatcher, Margaret (1987): Interview for *Woman's Own*. Available at: http://www.mar

REFERENCES

garetthatcher.org/speeches/displaydocument.asp?docid=106689 (accessed on March 7, 2018).

Thielemann, Leland (1952): Diderot and Hobbes. *Diderot Studies* 2, pp. 221–78.

Thomä, Dieter (2003): *Vom Glück in der Moderne*. Frankfurt: Suhrkamp.

— (2004): Der "Herrenlose": Gegenfigur zu Agambens "homo sacer" – Hauptfigur einer anderen Theorie der Moderne. *Deutsche Zeitschrift für Philosophie* 52, pp. 965–84.

— (2006): *Totalität und Mitleid: Richard Wagner, Sergej Eisenstein und unsere ethisch-ästhetische Moderne*. Frankfurt: Suhrkamp.

— (2007): The Difficulty of Democracy: Rethinking the Political in the Philosophy of the Thirties (Gehlen, Schmitt, Heidegger). In: Anson Rabinbach and Wolfgang Bialas (eds.), *Nazi Germany and the Humanities: How German Academics Embraced Nazism*. London: Oneworld Publications, pp. 75–100.

— (2007 [1998]): *Erzähle dich selbst: Lebensgeschichte als philosophisches Problem*. Frankfurt: Suhrkamp.

— (2008): *Väter: Eine moderne Heldengeschichte*. Munich: Carl Hanser.

— (2011): Leben als Teilnehmen: Überlegungen im Anschluss an Johann Gottfried Herder. *Deutsche Zeitschrift für Philosophie* 59, pp. 5–32.

— (2013): Hegel – Diderot – Hobbes: Überschneidungen zwischen Politik, Ästhetik und Ökonomie. In: Axel Honneth and Gunnar Hindrichs (eds.): *Freiheit: Stuttgarter Hegel-Kongress 2011*. Frankfurt: Vittorio Klostermann, pp. 167–94.

— (2013): Heidegger und der Nationalsozialismus: In der Dunkelkammer der Seinsgeschichte. In: Dieter Thomä (ed.), *Heidegger-Handbuch: Leben – Wirk – Wirkung. 2., überarbeitete und erweiterte Auflage*. Stuttgart: J.B. Metzler, pp. 108–33.

— (2016): Synergie und Sympathie: Eine sozialphilosophische Skizze. In: Tatjana Petzer and Stephan Steiner (eds): *Synergie: Kultur- und Wissensgeschichte einer Denkfigur*. Munich: Wilhelm Fink, pp. 111–27.

—, Vincent Kaufmann, and Ulrich Schmid (2015): *Der Einfall des Lebens: Theorie als geheime Autobiographie*. Munich: Carl Hanser.

Thoreau, Henry David (1985 [1854]): Walden; or, Life in the Woods. In: Robert F. Sayre (ed.), *A Week on the Concord and Merrimack Rivers – Walden; or, Life in the Woods – The Maine Woods – Cape Cod*. New York: Literary Classics of the United States, pp. 321–587.

— (2001): *Collected Essays and Poems*. Edited by Elizabeth Hall Witherell. New York: Library of America.

Thumann, Michael and Thomas Assheuer (2016): "Demokratie stiftet keine Identität." Ist das Modell des Westens am Ende? Ein Gespräch mit dem amerikanischen Politikwissenschaftler Francis Fukuyama. *Die Zeit* 13, pp. 49–50.

Tiqqun (2012): *Preliminary Materials for a Theory of the Young-Girl*. Translated by Ariana Reines. Los Angeles, CA: Semiotext(e). [*Premiers Matériaux pour une Théorie de la Jeune-Fille*, 2001]

Tocqueville, Alexis de (1951–): *Œuvres complètes*. Paris: Gallimard.

— (1991–2004): *Œuvres* Vol. 1–3. Edited by André Jardin. Paris: La Pléiade.

— (1997 [1968]): *Memoir on Pauperism*. Translated by Seymour Drescher. London: Civitas. [*Mémoire sur le paupérisme*, 1835]

— (2000 [1966]): *Democracy in America*. Edited by J. P. Mayer, translated by George Lawrence. New York: Perennial Classics.

— (2001): *Writings on Empire and Slavery*. Edited and translated by Jennifer Pitts. Baltimore, MD: Johns Hopkins University Press.

— (2003): *Lettres choisis: Souvenirs 1814–1859*. Edited by Françoise Mélonio and Laurence Guellec. Paris: Gallimard.

— (2009): *Toqueville on America After 1840: Letters and Other Writings*. Edited and translated by Aurelian Craiutu and Jeremy Jennings. Cambridge: Cambridge University Press.

— (2010): *Democracy in America*. Four Volumes. Edited by Eduardo Nolla, translated by James T. Schleifer. Indianapolis, IN: Liberty Fund.

REFERENCES

— (2016): *Recollections: The French Revolution of 1848 and Its Aftermath.* Edited by Olivier Zunz, translated by Arthur Goldhammer. Charlottesville: University of Virginia Press. [*Souvenirs*, 1893]

Todd, Chuck and Matt Rivera (2017): McCain Defends a Free Press: "That's How Dictators Get Started." Available at: www.nbcnews.com/politics/donald-trump/sen-mccain-meet-press-defends-free-press-after-trump-tweet-n722831 (accessed on March 26, 2018).

Todorov, Tzvetan (1985): *Frêle bonheur: Essai sur Rousseau.* Paris: Hachette.

Togliatti, Palmiro (1949): Saluto di Capodanno. *L'Unità*, January 1, p. 1.

— (1984 [1947]): La crisi morale dei giovani italiani. In: L. Gruppi (ed.), *Opere*, Vol. 5. Rome: Editori Riuniti, pp. 287–307.

Tomasello, Michael (2009): *Why We Cooperate.* Cambridge, MA: MIT Press.

Tönnies, Ferdinand (1971): Hobbes and the *Zoon Politikon*. In: Werner J. Cahnman and Rudolf Heberle (eds.), *On Sociology: Pure, Applied, and Empirical.* Chicago, IL: University of Chicago Press, pp. 48–61. ["Hobbes und das Zoon politikon," 1923]

— (1971 [1896/1925]): *Thomas Hobbes: Leben und Lehre.* Edited by Karl-Heinz Ilting. Stuttgart: Frommann.

Travill, A. A. (1987): Juan Luis Vives: The *De Subventione Pauperum. Canadian Bulletin of Medical History* 4, pp. 165–81.

Trilling, Lionel (1972): *Sincerity and Authenticity: The Charles Eliot Norton Lectures, 1969–1979.* Cambridge, MA: Harvard University Press.

Trump, Donald J. and Kate Bohner (1997): *Trump: The Art of the Comeback.* New York: Times Books.

Trüstedt, Katrin (2011): *Die Komödie der Tragödie: Shakespeares "Sturm" am Umschlagplatz von Mythos und Moderne, Rache und Recht, Tragik und Spiel.* Constance: Konstanz University Press.

Turgot, Anne Robert Jacques (1757): Fondation, (Politique & Droit naturel). In: Denis Diderot and Jean Le Rond D'Alembert (eds.), *Encyclopédie*, Vol. 7. Paris: André Le Breton et al., pp. 72–5.

— (1913 [1750]): Tableau philosophique des progrès successifs de l'esprit humain. In: *Œuvres* Vol. 1. Paris: Félix Alcan, pp. 214–35.

— (2010 [1973]): A Philosophical Review of the Successive Advances of the Human Mind. In: Ronald L. Meek (ed. and trans.), *Turgot on Progress, Sociology and Economics.* Cambridge: Cambridge University Press, pp. 41–60.

Turner, Victor (1969): *The Ritual Process: Structure and Anti-Structure.* New York: Aldine De Gruyter.

Vallentyne, Peter (ed.) (1991): *Contractarianism and Rational Choice: Essays on David Gauthier's* Morals by Agreement. Cambridge: Cambridge University Press.

Veblen, Thorstein (1994 [1899]): *The Theory of the Leisure Class.* New York: Penguin.

Vialatoux, Joseph (1952 [1935]): *La cité totalitaire de Hobbes: Théorie naturaliste de la civilisation.* Lyon: Chronique sociale de France.

Vieira, Mónica Brito (2009): *The Elements of Representation in Hobbes: Aesthetics, Theatre, Law, and Theology in the Construction of Hobbes's Theatre of the State.* Leiden: Brill.

Vives, Juan Luis (1917): *Concerning the Relief of the Poor.* In: Margaret M. Sherwood (ed.), *Studies in Social Work*, No. 11. New York, pp. 1–47. [*De subventione pauperum*, 1526]

Völger, Gisela and Karin von Welck (eds.) (1990): *Männerbande, Männerbünde: Zur Rolle des Mannes im Kulturvergleich.* Cologne: Rautenstrauch-Joest-Museum.

Wagner, Cosima (1978/80): *Cosima Wagner's Diaries.* Two Volumes. Edited by Martin Gregor-Dellin and Dietrich Mack, translated by Geoffrey Skelton. London: Collins. [*Die Tagebücher*, 1976–1977]

Wagner, Richard (1871–1883): *Gesammelte Schriften und Dichtungen.* Ten volumes. Leipzig: E.W. Fritzsch.

— (1895–1912): *Richard Wagner's Prose Works.* Eight volumes. Translated by William Ashton Ellis. London: Kegan Paul, Trench, Trübner & Co.

REFERENCES

— (1911): *Sämtliche Schriften und Dichtungen*, Vol. 11/12. Leipzig: Breitkopf & Härtel.
— (1977): *The Ring of the Nibelung*. Translated by Andrew Porter. New York: W.W. Norton & Company. [*Der Ring des Nibelungen*, 1863]
— (1983): *My Life*. Translated by Andrew Gray, edited by Mary Whittall. Cambridge: Cambridge University Press. [*Mein Leben*, 1870–80]
— (1987): *Selected Letters of Richard Wagner*. Translated and edited by Stewart Spencer and Barry Millington. London: Dent.
— (2011 [1993]): *Lohengrin*. Translated by Andrew Porter. Richmond, UK: Overture Publishing.
— (2011): *Parsifal*. Translated by Lionel Salter. Richmond, UK: Overture Publishing.
Wallach, John R. (2001): Smith, Strauss, and Platonic Liberalism. *Political Theory* 29/3, pp. 424–9.
Walzer, Michael (1983): *Spheres of Justice: A Defense of Plurality and Equality*. New York: Basic Books.
Wang, Ning (2005): *The Great Northern Wilderness: Political Exiles in the People's Republic of China*. Ph.D. Thesis (typescript). University of British Columbia.
Wang, Willie [Ning] (2008): Discovering Xingkaihu: Political Inmates in a PRC Labor Camp. *East Asia* 25, pp. 267–92.
Weber, Max (1978): *Economy and Society: An Outline of Interpretive Sociology*. Edited by Guenther Roth and Claus Wittich. Berkeley: University of California Press. [*Wirtschaft und Gesellschaft: Grundriss der verstehenden Soziologie*, 1921–2]
— (1985): "Churches" and "Sects" in North America: An Ecclesiastical Socio-Political Sketch. Translated by Colin Loader. *Sociological Theory* 3/1, pp. 7–13. ["Kirchen" und "Sekten," 1906]
Weinstein, Michael and Deena Weinstein (1979): Freud on the Problem of Order: The Revival of Hobbes. *Diogenes* 27, pp. 39–56.
Weisenborn, Günter (1931): *Barbaren: Roman einer studentischen Tafelrunde*. Berlin: Sieben-Stäbe-Verlag.
Welwei, Karl-Wilhelm and Mischa Meier (1997): Der Topos des ruhmvollen Todes in der zweiten Römerode des Horaz. *Klio* 79/1, pp. 107–16.
White, Hayden (1978): *Tropics of Discourse: Essays in Cultural Criticism*. Baltimore, MD: Johns Hopkins University Press.
Whitman, Walt (1982): *Poetry and Prose*. Edited by Justin Kaplan. New York: Library of America.
Wiedeking, Wendelin (2009): Schluss mit dem Götzendienst. *Financial Times Deutschland*, March 30, p. 8.
Wieland, Christoph Martin (1879): Patriotischer Beitrag zu Deutschlands höchstem Flor, veranlasst durch einen unter diesem Titel im Jahr 1780 in Druck erschienenen Vorschlag eines Ungenannten. In: *Werke*, Vol. 33. Berlin: Gustav Hempel, pp. 153–67.
Wieviorka, Michel (2009): *Violence: A New Approach*. Translated by David Macey. London: Sage Publications. [*La violence*, 2004]
Williams, Anthony (1974): The Ambivalences in the Plays of the Young Schiller about Contemporary Germany. In: Bernd Lutz (ed.), *Deutsches Bürgertum und literarische Intelligenz 1750–1800: Literaturwissenschaft und Sozialwissenschaften*, Vol. 3. Stuttgart: Metzler, pp. 1–112.
Williams, Bernard (2000): Wagner and Politics. *The New York Review of Books* 47/17, pp. 36–43.
— (2002): *Truth and Truthfulness: An Essay in Genealogy*. Princeton, NJ: Princeton University Press.
Wilson, Woodrow (1913): *The New Freedom: A Call for the Emancipation of the Generous Energies of a People*. New York: Doubleday, Page & Company.
Wisskirchen, Hans (1992): Republikanischer Eros: Zu Walt Whitmans und Hans Blühers Rolle in der politischen Publizistik Thomas Manns. In: Gerhard Härle (ed.),

"Heimsuchung und süßes Gift": Erotik und Poetik bei Thomas Mann. Frankfurt: Fischer Taschenbuch Verlag, pp. 17–40.

Wittgenstein, Ludwig (1972): *On Certainty.* Translated by Denis Paul and G. E. M. Anscombe. New York: Harper and Row. [*Über Gewissheit*, 1969]

— (1998): *Culture and Value.* Translated by Peter Winch. Malden, MA: Blackwell. [*Vermischte Bemerkungen*, 1977]

— (2009): *Philosophical Investigations.* Translated by G. E. M. Anscombe, P. M. S. Hacker and Joachim Schulte. Chichester: Wiley-Blackwell. [*Philosophische Untersuchungen*, 1953]

Wohlfert-Wihlborg, Lee (1981): In the Manhattan Real Estate Game, Billionaire Donald Trump Holds the Winning Cards. *People*, November 16. Available at: people.com/archive/in-the-manhattan-real-estate-game-billionaire-donald-trump-holds-the-winning-cards-vol-16-no-20 (accessed on March 25, 2018).

Wolfowitz, Paul (2002): The Gathering Storm: The Threat of Global Terror and Asia/Pacific Security. *Vital Speeches of the Day* 68/21, pp. 674–9.

Wolin, Richard (2010): *The Wind from the East: French Intellectuals, the Cultural Revolution, and the Legacy of the 1960s.* Princeton, NJ: Princeton University Press.

Wolin, Sheldon S. (2001): *Tocqueville Between Two Worlds: The Making of a Political and Theoretical Life.* Princeton, NJ: Princeton University Press.

Yen-lin Chung (2011): The Witch-Hunting Vanguard: The Central Secretariat's Roles and Activities in the Anti-Rightist Campaign. *China Quarterly* 206, pp. 391–411.

Yu Hua (2009): *Brothers: A Novel.* Translated by Eileen Cheng-yin Chow and Carlos Rojas. London: Picador.

Zaitchik, Alan (1982): Hobbes's Reply to the Fool: The Problem of Consent and Obligation. *Political Theory* 10, pp. 245–66.

Zaretsky, Eli (2005 [2004]): *Secrets of the Soul: A Social and Cultural History of Psychoanalysis.* New York: Vintage Books.

Zimmermann, Martina (2015): Wenn man die Leute zu Opfern macht, werden sie zu Schlächtern [interview with Jo Dalton, February 27, 2015]. Available at: www.deutschlandfunk.de/rapper-jo-dalton-wenn-man-die-leute-zu-opfern-macht-werden.807.de.html?dram:article_id=312846 (accessed on March 21, 2018).

Žižek, Slavoj (1999): *The Ticklish Subject: The Absent Centre of Political Ontology.* London: Verso.

— (2007): Introduction: Mao Tse-tung, the Marxist Lord of Misrule. In: Mao Tse-tung, *On Practice and Contradiction.* London: Verso, pp. 1–28.

— (2008): Use Your Illusions. *London Review of Books*, November 14. Available at: https://www.lrb.co.uk/2008/11/14/slavoj-zizek/use-your-illusions (accessed March 13, 2018).

— (2011 [2010]): *Living in the End Times.* London: Verso.

— (2011): The Violent Silence of a New Beginning. *In These Times*, October 26. Available at: http://inthesetimes.com/article/12188/the_violent_silence_of_a_new_beginning (accessed on March 12, 2018).

— (2012): Occupy Wall Street, Or, The Violent Silence of a New Beginning. In: *The Year of Dreaming Dangerously.* London: Verso, pp. 77–89.

— (2016): *Against the Double Blackmail: Refugees, Terror and Other Troubles with the Neighbours.* London: Allen Lane.

— (2016): Ein Karneval der Underdogs. *Spiegel* 3, pp. 128–30.

INDEX

Brazil, 353
Brecht, Bertolt, 43
Bristol, Michael, 33
Brito Viera, Mónica, 33
Brown, Wendy, 360n97
Brucker, Jakob, 79
Buchholz, Horst, 294
Buffett, Warren, 335
Burgo, Joseph, 368n110
Burke, Edmund, 280
Butler, Judith, 348, 350–2, 353n72

Calderón de la Barca, Pedro, 12
Caliban, 29, 134
Capitant, René, 264
Carlos the Jackal (film), 329
Carlyle, Thomas, 110–11, 201, 204, 212, 280
Catholic Church, 267, 268
Charlie Hebdo attacks (2015), 357
Chen Yi, 317
China
    1919 protests, 311, 321
    Badiou on, 327
    Communist Party, 310, 316, 328
    Cultural Revolution, 276, 318, 321, 325, 327–31
    Hundred Flowers period, 2, 311–24, 325
    May Fourth movement, 311, 321, 322
    poisonous weeds, 312–20, 325
    puer robustus, 306, 307, 320–4
    Tan Tianrong, 2, 312, 317, 318–23, 325, 327
    Tiananmen Square protests (1989), 312
    Tocqueville on, 187
    see also Mao Zedong
Churchill, Winston, 281
Cillizza, Chris, 363n100
civil disobedience, 76, 347, 354
Clark, Timothy, 152
Clinton, Hillary, 364
closed society, 279–86, 360
Cole, Nigel, 354
Collingwood, Robin George, 264
Colvin, Geoff, 362n98
communism, 306–31
concretism, 298
Copernicus, Nicolaus, 316
Corneille, Pierre, 82
cosmopolitanism, 69, 77
Counter-Enlightenment, 55
Croce, Benedetto, 183, 307

Cromwell, Oliver, 132, 135
Curtius, Ernst Robert, 149

Dallas (TV), 335
Dalton, Jo, 357
Darwin, Charles, 316
Däubler, Theodor, 266, 267
Dean, James, 294, 344
Delacroix, Eugène, 146
democracy
    Badiou and, 349, 351
    Butler on, 350–2
    capitalism and, 337, 348, 349
    conditions, 360–1
    creative democracy, 9
    democratic paradox, 69, 339, 352–5
    Dewey, 9, 261–2, 279, 292, 346
    financial crisis and, 336, 340
    Freud, 231–45
    inequality and, 341
    insurgent democracy, 9, 224
    Kelsen, 256–61, 279, 292, 370
    Mann, 252–5
    plasticity, 352
    populism and, 369–70
    savage democracy, 224
    Schelsky and, 293, 367
    Schmitt on, 266, 267, 268
    Strauss and, 279, 285
    Tocqueville, 186
    transnational democracy, 353
    troublemakers and, 9, 345
    Trump and, 367, 369
    wild democracy, 9
    Žižek and, 348–50
Deng Xiaoping, 324
depoliticization, 178, 211–13, 279, 293, 297, 300, 370
Derrida, Jacques, 310
Descartes, René, 108, 109
Dewey, John, 9, 30, 181, 261–2, 279, 286, 291, 292, 346
Dibelius, Alexander, 336
Diderot, Denis
    alienation, 104, 185
    ambivalent *puer robustus*, 81–8, 106
    Baudelaire and, 152
    childhood, 166
    D'Alembert's Dream, 99
    Discourse on Dramatic Poetry, 96–7, 99
    eccentric troublemakers, 8, 101–2, 165
    Enlightenment, 79, 80
    Father of the Family, 114
    Foucault and, 102, 107–10